# LANDSCAPE PLANTS

## Their Identification, Culture and Use

# LANDSCAPE PLANTS

## Their Identification, Culture and Use

By

Ferrell M. Bridwell

Delmar Publishers Inc.™

## NOTICE TO THE READER

Cover photo of Doug Dorough's Yard in Georgia courtesy of Ferrell M. Bridwell
Cover design: Judi Orozco and Wendy Troeger

For information, address Delmar Publishers Inc.
3 Columbia Circle, Box 15-015
Albany, New York 12212

Delmar Staff
Publisher: Tim O'Leary
Associate Editor: Cathy L. Carter
Project Editor: Wendy Troeger

COPYRIGHT © 1994
BY DELMAR PUBLISHERS INC.
The trademark ITP is used under license.

Printed in the United States of America
published simultaneously in Canada
by Nelson Canada
a division of The Thomson Corportion

2 3 4 5 6 7 8 9 10 XXX 00 99 98 97 96 95

**Library of Congress Cataloging-in-Publication Data**

Bridwell, Ferrell M.
    Landscape plants : their identification, culture & use / Ferrell
M. Bridwell.
      p.     cm.
    Includes bibliographical references (p. 527) and index.
    ISBN 0-8273-6017-7
    1. Landscape plants.   2. Landscape plants—Identification.
I. Title.
SB435.B72 1994
712—dc20                       93-28665
                                     CIP

# PREFACE

The purpose of this text is to assist students, nurserymen, landscape architects, educators, homeowners, and others in accurately identifying landscape plants. The landscape notes suggest some possible uses for each plant, but the notes are not intended to be all-inclusive. Individual creativity regarding usage is encouraged.

The color photos in this text enhance the learning of plant materials. Color is indispensable in the accurate presentation of plants, and it adds a dimension that is not possible with line drawings or black and white pictures. The many subtle shades and hues in the plant world are often hard to describe, and must be seen to be fully appreciated. I hope that this added dimension will prove beneficial in your work.

Another feature, designed to make learning easier, is consistency in placement of descriptive data. The gridlike location of data is intended to provide "at-a-glance" location of essential information. This "user-friendly" approach insures that similar data will appear in the same location on each page. This was accomplished by avoiding unnecessary wordiness that gives the appearance of more, but often isn't.

The plants are presented according to size groups. This approach allows one to select plants more quickly for a particular purpose. With the trend toward smaller gardens, especially in residential communities, size is often more important than any one plant species. Those educators preferring to utilize a different approach will find the indices "user-friendly" and adaptable to most any approach.

The related species, hybrids, varieties, and cultivars presented are not intended to represent complete listings. While some prefer the hardiness and reliability of original species, others are more excited about new cultivars. I have chosen to present cultivars that are readily available in the nursery trade or that are worthy of wide-spread usage. In many cases, cultivars have proven superior to the species in one or more traits. Some ornamental grasses and herbaceous materials are included due to wide-spread use and availability through nurseries that specialize primarily in woody ornamentals.

The Publisher and I welcome your comments and suggestions. This text incorporates the ideas and suggestions of many individuals, and your input is invited as we seek to educate, motivate, and inspire. We hope that you find our approach refreshingly useful. We haven't re-invented the wheel, but we hope to give you a more enjoyable ride!

Ferrell M. Bridwell

# ABOUT THE AUTHOR

**F**errell Bridwell has been an instructor in the public school system for over 25 years. He has taught Agriscience and Horticulture Technology in four different schools, and served as Curator of Horticulture at the Roper Mountain Science Center in Greenville, South Carolina for five years. He has taught numerous organized classes for adults in Landscape Design, Plant Materials, and Greenhouse Growing. In addition, he has conducted summer inservice training programs for classroom teachers in Environmental Science. While serving as Curator of Horticulture, Bridwell designed and supervised the development of a memorial arboretum.

Mr. Bridwell has been very active in professional organizations and has served on numerous committees and advisory councils on the secondary and post-secondary levels. In 1981–82, Mr. Bridwell was recognized by AVA as the Outstanding Vocational Educator for the Southeastern states. In 1983, he was recognized as Conservation Teacher of the Year for the Southeastern states by the National Association of Conservation Districts. Mr. Bridwell has been listed in *Who's Who in American Vocational Education.*

Mr. Bridwell has also served as a textbook reviewer. In addition, he served as contributing author for the text, *Metrics in Vocational Education,* while serving on the National Metrics Council, Vocational Education Sector Committee.

Mr. Bridwell has traveled extensively and photographed plants for over 20 years. Except for a few borrowed slides, he photographed the plants in this text, including the cover. In addition, he did the pen and ink sketches in the book.

# ACKNOWLEDGEMENTS

Evolution of this book is the result of the encouragement and support of many individuals. I wish to thank the hundreds of former students, both youths and adults, who encouraged me to organize my slides into book form. I hope that this text will serve as an appropriate reference as they pursue their careers in horticulture.

Appreciation is hereby acknowledged to the following individuals who served as reviewers:

Dr. Barry L. Bequette
Associate Professor of Horticulture
Sam Houston State University
Huntsville, Texas

Dr. D. Kim Black
Professor of Horticulture
Rick's College
Rexburg, Idaho

Robert Dockery
Western Piedmont Community College
Morgantown, North Carolina

Mark Schusler
Tarrant County Junior College
Fort Worth, Texas

William Boon
Iowa State University
Ames, Iowa

Barbara A. Ryder
Assistant Professor of Horticulture and Landscape Architecture
Washington State University
Pullman, Washington 99164-6414

The following individuals assisted in locating plants to research and photograph: Dr. Ross Clark, Curator of Adult Education, The Morton Arboretum; Dr. J. C. Raulston, Director, North Carolina State University Arboretum; Dr. David Bradshaw, Professor of Horticulture, Clemson University; and David and Debra

## ACKOWLEDGEMENTS

Lichtenfelt of Lichtenfelt Nurseries, Inc., Greer, S.C. In addition, Mr. Rodger Duer, Director of Marketing, Monrovia Nursery Company, provided some of the pictures for the text.

Acknowledgement is in order for the individuals of Delmar Publishers most responsible for the publishing of the text. I wish to thank Mr. Mark Huth, Senior Editor, for his perception of the need for such a text, and his leadership in supplying the budget and staff necessary to get the job done. I wish to express thanks in a very special way to Cathy Carter, Associate Editor, and Wendy Troeger, Production Editor. I would like to thank Cathy for her patience, support, and understanding. Her friendly, yet firm motivation, provided the "spark" when things got tough. I would like to thank Wendy for her creative insight, perseverance, and vision. To have worked with such true professionals is part of my reward.

# DEDICATION

This book is dedicated to the love of my life and best friend, my wife Jo Ann, who very ably handled domestic matters while I disappeared for hours, even days at a time, to photograph, study, or do research. Without her dedicated assistance, interest, and support, there would be no book.

# SECTION 1:  DATA AND NOMENCLATURE

## Chapter 1: Plant Identification

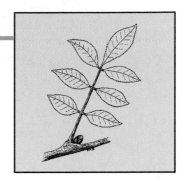

## Chapter 2: Interpretation of Data

## Chapter 3: Functional and Aesthetic Uses of Plants

# SECTION 2:   LANDSCAPE PLANTS

# TABLE OF CONTENTS

## Chapter 10: Medium Trees

## Chapter 11: Large Trees

## Chapter 12: Grasses, Palms, and Bamboo

# Data and Nomenclature

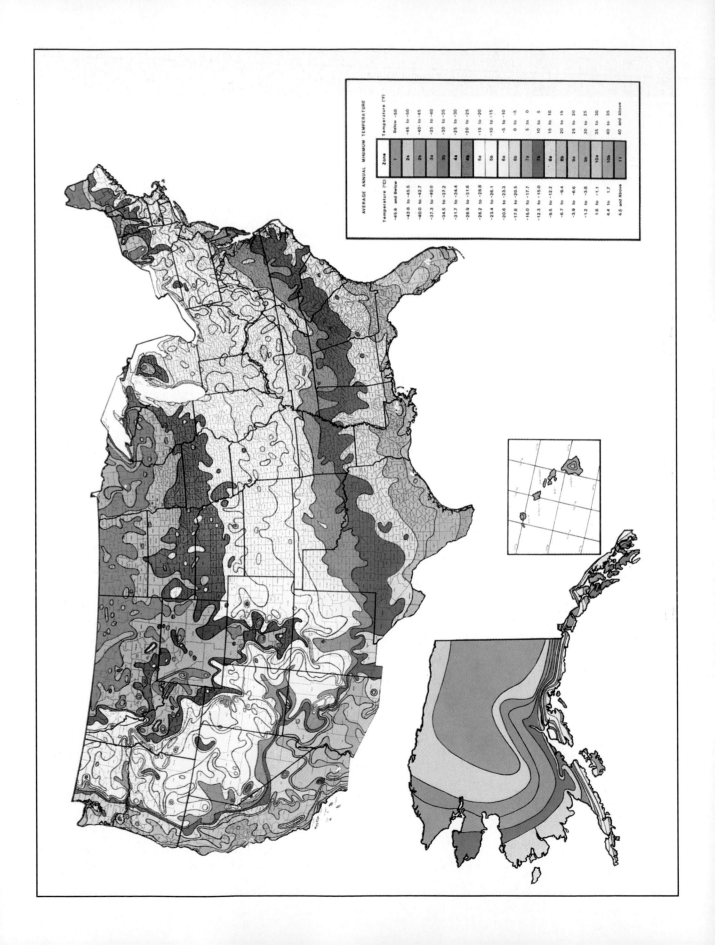

AVERAGE ANNUAL MINIMUM TEMPERATURE

| Zone | Temperature (°F) |
|------|------------------|
| 1 | Below -50 |
| 2a | -45 to -50 |
| 2b | -40 to -45 |
| 3a | -35 to -40 |
| 3b | -30 to -35 |
| 4a | -25 to -30 |
| 4b | -20 to -25 |
| 5a | -15 to -20 |
| 5b | -10 to -15 |
| 6a | -5 to -10 |
| 6b | 0 to -5 |
| 7a | 5 to 0 |
| 7b | 10 to 5 |
| 8a | 15 to 10 |
| 8b | 20 to 15 |
| 9a | 25 to 20 |
| 9b | 30 to 25 |
| 10a | 35 to 30 |
| 10b | 40 to 35 |
| 11 | 40 and Above |

| Temperature (°C) |
|------------------|
| -45.6 and Below |
| -42.8 to -45.5 |
| -40.0 to -42.7 |
| -37.3 to -40.0 |
| -34.5 to -37.2 |
| -31.7 to -34.4 |
| -28.9 to -31.6 |
| -26.2 to -28.8 |
| -23.4 to -26.1 |
| -20.6 to -23.3 |
| -17.8 to -20.5 |
| -15.0 to -17.7 |
| -12.3 to -15.0 |
| -9.5 to -12.2 |
| -6.7 to -9.4 |
| -3.9 to -6.6 |
| -1.2 to -3.8 |
| 1.6 to -1.1 |
| 4.4 to 1.7 |
| 4.5 and Above |

# Chapter 1

# PLANT IDENTIFICATION

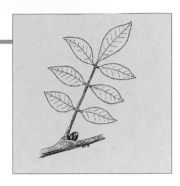

## PLANT NAMES

A plant may be identified in many ways. Most often a plant is identified by characteristics of its leaves, but it is also possible to identify a plant by its flowers, fruit, bark, twigs, buds, or habit of growth. The process of identification can range from very simple to complex. For example, the identification of most familiar Oak trees is simple during the warm season when the leaves are present; however, identification becomes very complex during the winter season when the leaves are gone. At that time, one must rely on minute details of buds or leaf scars, minor bark characteristics, and other clues. This text will not address every detail, but, rather, it will emphasize the major characteristics used in identification, as well as those features that make a plant a good choice for landscaping purposes.

When one learns a new plant, one must associate a name with the plant in order to file the plant into memory and be able to communicate effectively with others about the particular plant. Plant names may be grouped into two categories—**common names** and **botanical names**.

### COMMON NAMES

Common names are those names people of an area give to a plant. Common names of plants can evolve in different ways, just as the names of towns, rivers, roads, and other landmarks evolve over a period of time. Our first experiences with plant names are common names. One advantage to such names is that they are usually easy to remember. Names such as Sugar Maple, White Oak, and Sweetgum are common names with which many people are familiar. The major disadvantage is that common names often vary from one location to another. For example, the names Liriope, Lirio, Lilyturf, and Monkeygrass can all refer to the same plant. This can be confusing and frustrating when communicating with others, since there are no world-wide standards that govern common names. In fact, you could develop your own common names—many people do.

### BOTANICAL NAMES

Botanical names, or scientific names for plants, help to eliminate confusion in the plant kingdom. A disadvantage for the beginning gardener or student of horticulture is that botanical names are written in Latin and are sometimes difficult to remember, especially at first. Latin is the standardized language of scientists worldwide. *Cercis canadensis* is the botanical name for the Eastern Redbud anywhere in the world, regardless of what it is commonly called in a particular location.

The **binomial system** or two-name system developed by Carolus Linnaeus in 1753, is a system that allows botanical names to be written using the genus and species names. Often, a third name is included after the species name to indicate a **variety** or **cultivar** within the species. This system assures that no two plants will have the exact same botanical name. This eliminates much confusion, and it gives all who work with plants a common language.

*Genus.* The first word in a botanical name is the genus. A genus is a group of plants having more common characteristics than with plants of any other group. Sometimes only one major characteristic may determine the genus. For example, all Oaks belong to the genus *Quercus* and have many common characteristics. One major characteristic of Oaks is that they produce nut-like fruits called acorns. A genus name begins with a capital letter, and is either underlined or italicized.

*Species.* The second word of a botanical name is the species. The species is the name given to a group of similar plants within a genus that have common differences with other groups of the same genus. When a new genus is discovered, a species name is assigned that identifies some characteristic of the plant. As different plants are discovered within the genus, new species names are assigned to those groups. Some genera have many species. For instance, the Oaks (*Quercus*) have many species such as *Quercus alba* (White Oak), *Quercus stellata* (Post Oak), *Quercus palustris* (Pin Oak), and so on. Species names are written in lower case and either italicized or underlined.

Very often in landscape plants, a third name appears after the species name. This third name will identify a particular variety, sometimes thought of as a subspecies, or it may identify a cultivar (cultivated variety). The variety or cultivar name is especially important in modern landscape work, since thousands exist. The list grows larger each year. An understanding of the differences between a true variety and a cultivar will help the individual interested in landscaping to understand important characteristics of various plants.

*Variety.* A true variety is a form of a certain species that varies from the established species in one or more characteristics. The characteristics are passed on with a high degree of purity or certainty when the plant is reproduced by seed (sexual reproduction). Some varieties produce 80 or 90 percent purity from seed. To assure absolute purity, the variety is usually propagated by cuttings, budding, grafting, or tissue culture (asexual propagation).

The true variety is written in Latin using lower case letters and underlined, or italicized. An example of a true variety is the Red Japanese Barberry. It varies from the species by having red leaves as opposed to the green leaves of the species. The variety name can be written in one of two forms as follows:

*Berberis thunbergii* var. *atropurpurea*
or
*Berberis thunbergii atropurpurea*

*Cultivar.*   A cultivar, or cultivated variety, is a variety that will not reproduce purely from seed over several generations. A cultivar originates as a "sport" (mutation), or as a result of crossbreeding or cross-pollination. It is usually produced by asexual means such as cutting, budding, grafting, or tissue culture. Often, a cultivar is discovered by an individual who secures a plant patent for exclusive rights to reproduce and sell the plant. There are many patented plants available in the nursery industry. A patented plant that proves very popular can result in much profit to the individual holding the patent. A cultivar may be written in Latin, or it may be named in any language at the option of the person who first discovers it. The name of a cultivar that originates as a mutation is enclosed in single quotes, but it is not underlined or italicized. An example of a cultivar of this type is the October Glory Maple. It is written as:

*Acer rubrum* 'October Glory'

or

*Acer rubrum* cv. October Glory

Varieties and cultivars that are the result of crossbreeding are written somewhat differently. A cross or hybrid between two species is given a Latin name if it is a new species, or a proper name if it is a cultivar. In either case, an x is substituted for the species name. Latin names are italicized or underlined. Proper names of hybrid cultivars are enclosed in single quotes and capitalized.

Glossy Abelia was developed as a cross between *Abelia chinensis* and *Abelia uniflora.* It is written as:

*Abelia* x *grandiflora*

Emily Brunner Holly is a result of a cross between *Ilex latifolia* and *Ilex cornuta.* It is written as:

*Ilex* x 'Emily Brunner'

As one works with botanical names, they become easier to remember, and new names are learned at a faster rate. In addition, common names of some plants are identical to the genus name. No one knows all botanical names. The beginner should acquire lists, references, and other materials that contain both common and botanical names. When writing plant names, always include the appropriate botanical name as a second name. Over a period of years, beginners will find that they can associate many botanical names with common names. Eventually, they can take great pride in using botanical names.

## PLANT PARTS

The orderly classification of plants based on relationships and differences is called **taxonomy**. Taxonomy takes into account the various parts of a plant as well as its color and shape. It is possible to identify almost all plants from above-ground parts, although roots and below-ground parts vary. For instance, a Sweetgum tree has a taproot system, but it is easily identified by its leaves and stem characteristics.

It is important to have access to reference material on the terminology used by taxonomists in describing plant characteristics. The drawings and explanations contained in this text should prove helpful; however, the usefulness of the material as a reference is more important than any attempt at memorization.

## LEAVES

The leaves of a plant are used extensively in the identification of plants as they are present for a longer period of time than the flowers or fruit. Usually, the plant genus can be determined from the leaves. The species and any varieties or cultivars are often linked to color of flowers, fruit characteristics, or other minute feature and are therefore sometimes impossible to determine from leaves.

Plants are grouped into the categories **deciduous** and **evergreen**. A deciduous plant loses its leaves during the dormant season (winter) and grows a new crop of leaves in the spring. An evergreen retains foliage throughout the entire year, although it sheds older leaves from time to time.

*Broadleaf and Narrowleaf.*  The foliage of a plant is either **broad** or **narrow**. Narrowleaf plants have leaves that are needle-like, scale-like, awl-like, or linear. These plants include the Pine, Cedar, Juniper, Fir, Spruce, Larch, Cypress, Arborvitae, and Hemlock. Narrowleaf plants are usually referred to as **Conifers** (cone-bearing) and are, with a few exceptions, evergreen plants. Their foliage fulfills the purpose of food manufacturing in much the same way as broadleaf plants.

Broadleaf plants have a flattened portion called the **blade**. They make up the majority of the plants in our environment and may be either deciduous or evergreen. Most trees and shrubs marketed in the nursery industry are broadleaf. Generally speaking, most horticulturalists refer to broadleaf plants as **hardwoods**, whereas conifers are referred to as **softwoods**.

*Simple and Compound Leaves.*  A close examination of leaves reveals that they are either **simple** or **compound**. Simple leaves have one flattened blade, while compound leaves are composed of two or more **leaflets**. Sometimes a leaflet may be larger in size than many simple leaves, therefore one must learn to look for the **axillary bud** to determine if the leaf is simple or compound. The axillary bud is a bud in the axil, or angle, of the stem and leaf **petiole**. Its function is to produce a new leaf or stem. LEAFLETS DO NOT HAVE AXILLARY BUDS. Once the axillary bud is located, one need only observe what is attached to the petiole. In addition, there is an **abscission layer** of corky material at the point where petiole and stem meet. This allows for easy removal of the petiole from the stem, but it is not noticeable to the eye. (see Figure 1–1)

Most plants have simple leaves; however, many common native plants and cultivated landscape plants have compound leaves. Hickory, Ash, Locust, Pecan, Bald Cypress, Walnut, and Wisteria all have compound leaves, to name just a few.

*Types of Compound Leaves.*  Compound leaves are either **palmately compound**, **pinnately compound**, or **bipinnately compound**. A palmately compound leaf has each leaflet attached to a common point, and the leaflets appear in a whorled pattern (Buckeye). Usually there are either 5 or 7 leaflets. Pinnately compound leaves have leaflets proportionately spaced throughout the petiole, as with the Ash or Hickory. Bipinnately compound leaves are often called **twice-divided**,

because the **petiolules** contain several leaflets, and there are usually several petiolules per leaf. Honeylocust and Mimosa leaves are excellent examples of bipinnation.
(see Figure 1–2)

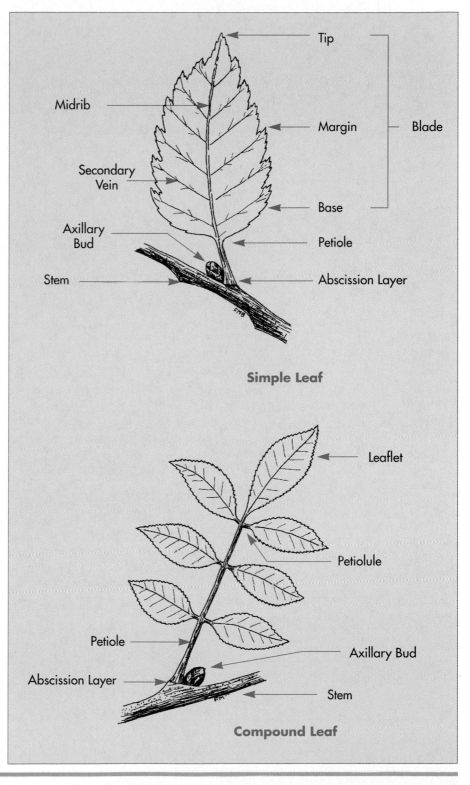

**Simple Leaf**

**Compound Leaf**

**Figure 1–1.**

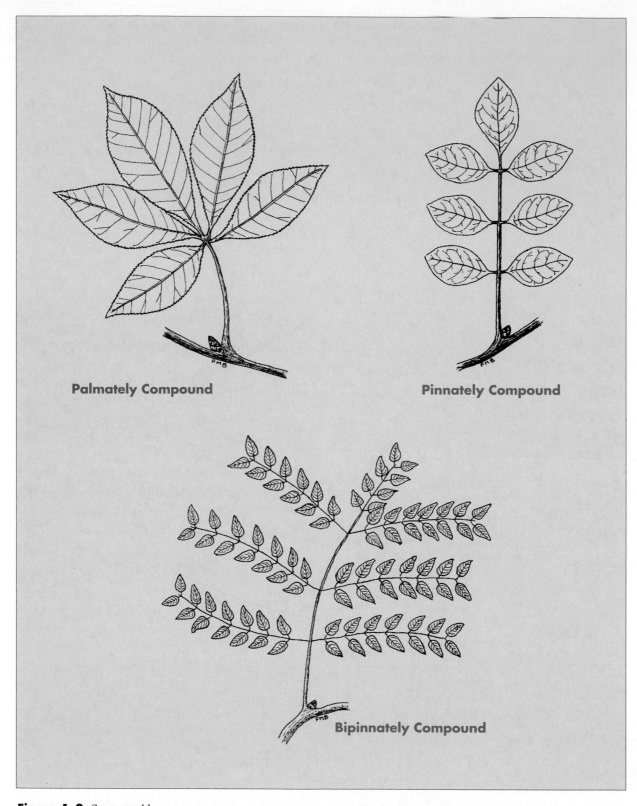

**Palmately Compound**

**Pinnately Compound**

**Bipinnately Compound**

**Figure 1–2.** Compound leaves.

## LEAF ARRANGEMENT

Both compound and simple leaves vary in their pattern of arrangement along the stem. Depending upon the species, leaves may be arranged in **alternate**, **opposite**, or **whorled** patterns. In alternate arrangement, the leaves are alternated or staggered along the stem. This is a common pattern, and is characteristic of many plants, such as Oak trees. In an opposite arrangement, the leaves appear in opposite pairs along the stem. The petiole of each leaf in a pair is attached at the same point along the stem. This arrangement exists in many familiar plants, including Maple trees. Whorled arrangement involves the arrangement of leaves in a spiral-like pattern, with several leaf petioles attached at the same point along a stem. Many ground covers, ornamental grasses, and other landscape plants have leaves that arise from a whorled pattern at the base of the stem. Examples are Pampas Grass and the Cast Iron Plant. (see Figure 1–3)

The arrangement of leaves is extremely important in the proper identification of plants. The novice gardener or beginning student should pay close attention to

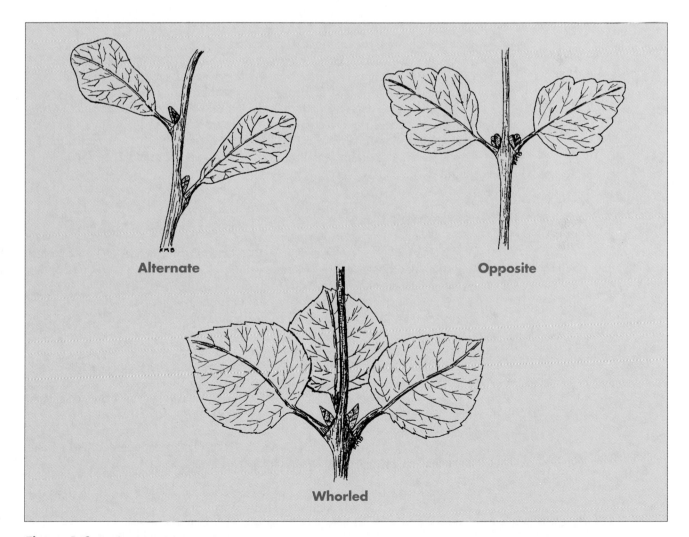

**Figure 1–3.** Leaf arrangement.

this feature from the very start. In many cases, leaf arrangement is the primary consideration. For example, Tea Olives (*Osmanthus*) have very Holly-like leaves, complete with sharp spines or "stickers" along the margins of the leaf. All Hollies, however, have alternate arrangement, while Tea Olives have opposite arrangement. No matter how it appears, if it has opposite arrangement, it is not a Holly!

Emphasis must be placed upon arrangement in compound leaves. Compound leaves, like simple leaves, may be arranged differently along the stem. Beginners sometimes mistake Ash for Hickory. Both have pinnately compound leaves, but the pinnately compound leaves of the Hickory are arranged alternately along the stem, while the compound leaves of the Ash are opposite. Always use reference books and other materials that give the leaf arrangement as part of the description.

## LEAF VENATION

Leaf venation refers to the pattern of the primary or largest veins in a leaf. There are three main patterns of leaf venation - **pinnate**, **palmate**, and **parallel**. Pinnately-veined leaves have one primary vein or **midrib** that extends from the petiole to the leaf tip in the center of the leaf. It has noticeable secondary veins that branch off of the midrib at regular intervals, giving a "fishbone" effect. Oaks, Birches, and Beeches are familiar examples having this type of venation. The veins of palmately-veined leaves have several main veins that originate at the same place along the base of the leaves at the junction of the petiole. These main veins radiate in a fan-type pattern and extend to the various lobes (divisions) of the leaves. Maples and Sweetgum varieties serve as the classic examples. Parallel-veined plants have many veins that run parallel to each other and to the margin of the leaf. This pattern is typical of most grasses and grass-related plants. (see Figure 1–4)

## LEAF SHAPES

The shapes of leaves vary greatly in nature, and most references are quite confusing when describing leaves. The descriptions, along with the illustrations, should prove to be valuable reference material when identifying plants.

The overal shape of the leaf is probably the one most common feature in identifying plants. It is the feature which we notice first, and it is the most variable. The following is a brief description of each illustrated shape. (see Figure 1–5)

*Needle-like.* These are long, slender leaves typical of the Pines and some other conifers. The needles are arranged in bundles called **fascicles** and are held together at the base by a sheath. Needles appear in fasicles of 2, 3, or 5, depending upon the species.

*Awl-like.* This foliage is a type of needle that is small and pointed like a woodworker's awl. Many Juniper species have awl-like foliage.

*Scale-like.* Scale-like foliage is tiny and overlaps along the stem in a tight pattern. Scales are not sharp pointed as with awl-like foliage.

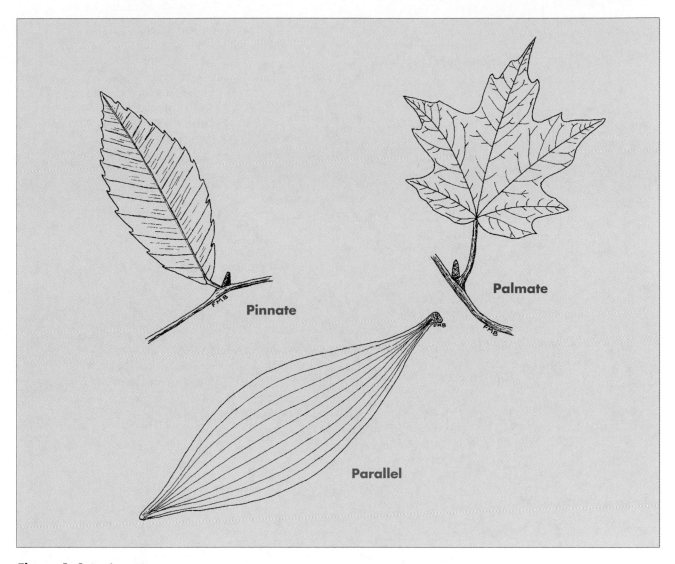

**Figure 1–4.** Leaf venation.

*Oblong.* This is a leaf type that is four times (or more) as long as it is broad, with a rounded base and tip.

*Linear.* A linear leaf is a flat leaf several times as long as broad, and is pointed at the tip.

*Lanceolate.* This is a pointed leaf that is broad at the base, giving it a lance or spear-head shape.

*Oblanceolate.* This type is an inverted lance with the pointed part at the base and the rounded part at the tip.

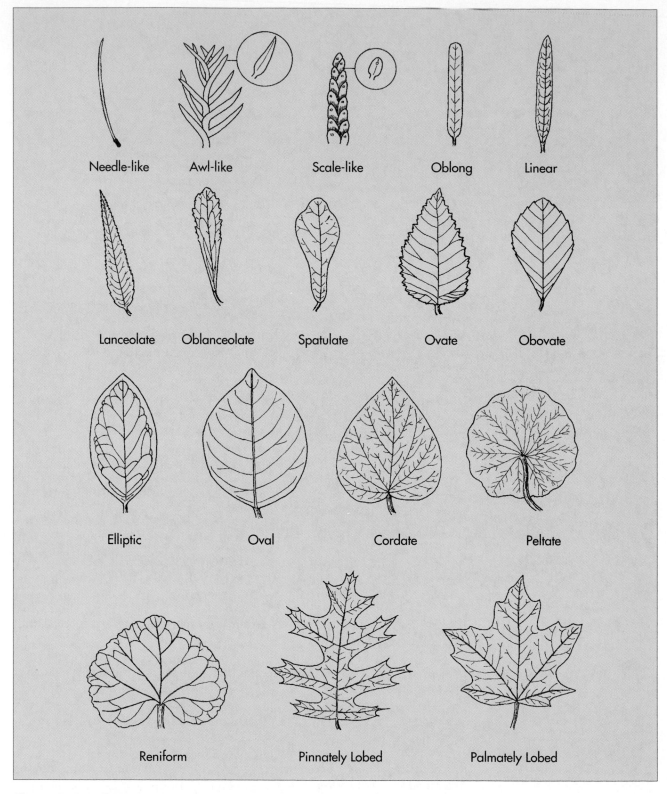

**Figure 1–5.** Leaf shapes.

*Spatulate.* This shape resembles a spatula and is broad at the tip and more narrow at the base.

*Ovate.* An ovate leaf is two to three times as long as broad, having a pointed tip and rounded base.

*Obovate.* This leaf is the inverse of an ovate leaf, with the pointed part at the base.

*Elliptic.* This is a leaf shaped like an ellipse or circular cone. It is broader in the middle, tapering to the tip and base.

*Oval.* This shape is similar to ovate but much broader. The width is almost equal to the length.

*Cordate.* This is a heart-shaped leaf with the length slightly greater than the width.

*Peltate.* This is a rounded leaf with the petiole attached at the center of the leaf blade.

*Reniform.* This leaf type is broadly heart-shaped with the width being greater than the length.

*Pinnately lobed.* This shape has several deeply cut lobes, with primary veins branching off the midrib to each lobe; this is characteristic of the Oaks.

*Palmately lobed.* Palmately lobed leaves have 3 to 7 lobes with primary veins originating at the junction of the petiole and base; an example is the Maples.

## LEAF MARGINS, TIPS, AND BASES

Upon close examination of a few plants, one begins to realize the great detail of differences in leaf composition. Not only is there variation in overall shapes, but even the **margins**, **tips** (apices), and **bases** (petiole end) vary considerably. The following explanations and illustrations will provide a valuable reference in describing plants. Get some practical experience. Get a few leaf samples, and compare them to the drawings. You will begin to pay more attention to detail in plant leaves. (see Figure 1–6)

*Leaf Margins.* Leaf margins refers to the outer edge of the leaf blade. There are many plants that have similar overall shape only to vary in the margin. The following are explanations of the margins illustrated in Figure 1–6.

- *Entire:* the margins are smooth.
- *Serrate:* the margins have large, saw-like teeth that are angled forward toward the tip.
- *Double Serrate:* this is similar to serrate, but there are two points on each serrated lobe.

# PLANT PARTS

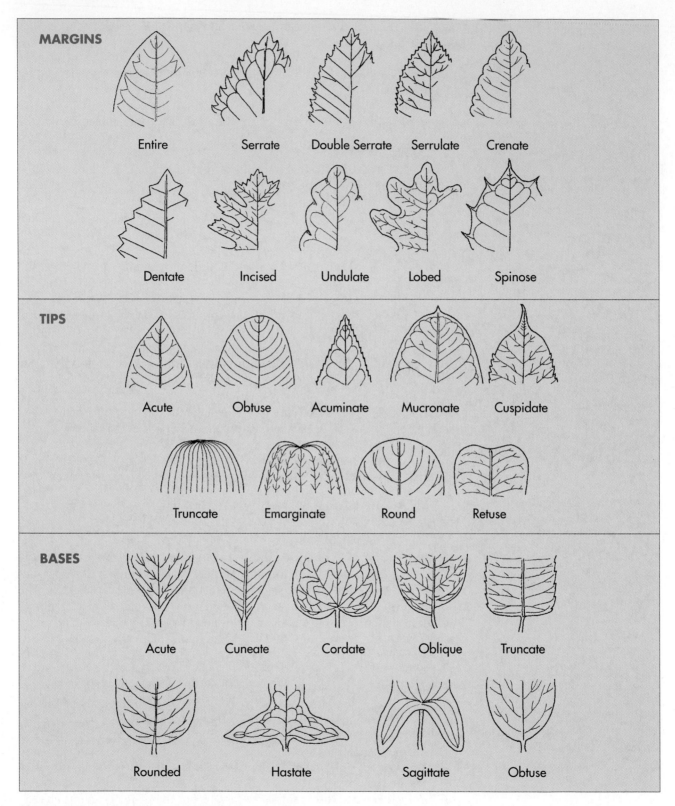

**Figure 1–6.** Leaf margins, tips, and bases.

- *Serrulate:* the margins have small, saw-like teeth, and are much smaller than serrate.
- *Crenate:* crenate has large, rounded teeth on the margins.
- *Dentate:* this is similar to serrate, except that the saw-like teeth point outward instead of forward toward the tip.
- *Incised:* this margin has pointed lobes that are deeply cut toward the midrib; appearing toothed and lobed.
- *Undulate:* the margins are wavy.
- *Lobed:* this margin has deeply cut lobes that are rounded and smooth at the ends.
- *Spinose:* the margins contain sharp pointed spines such as for some Hollies.

*Leaf Tips.* The tips or apices (singular, apex) refers to the leaf end opposite the petiole. The following are illustrated in Figure 1–6.

- *Acute:* the tip curves broadly to a point.
- *Obtuse:* the tip is narrowly rounded.
- *Acuminate:* the tip is triangular, tapering to a long point.
- *Mucronate:* similar to obtuse, except that there is a point in the center of the tip.
- *Cuspidate:* this tip is similar to mucronate, but the point is much longer.
- *Truncate:* the tip is blunt and forms a 90 degree angle to the midrib.
- *Emarginate:* the tip is indented toward the midrib.
- *Round:* the tip is broadly rounded.
- *Retuse:* retuse has a smooth-flowing, shallow indentation at the tip.

*Leaf Bases.* Leaf bases, like tips, are also very diverse. The following are descriptions of the illustrations in Figure 1–6.

- *Acute:* the base curves broadly to a point at the petiole.
- *Cuneate:* the base is triangular, coming to a point at the petiole.
- *Cordate:* cordate has a broad heart shape.
- *Oblique:* one half of the blade ends at a higher point on the petiole than the other half.
- *Truncate:* the base is flat and forms a 90 degree angle to the midrib.
- *Rounded:* self explanatory.
- *Hastate:* each half of the blade contains a pointed lobe that projects outward.
- *Sagittate:* each half of the blade contains a pointed lobe that projects downward almost parallel to the petiole.
- *Obtuse:* this base is narrowly rounded at the petiole.

## FLOWERS

During the warm season, flowers become an important feature in correctly identifying plants. The arrangement pattern is generally characteristic for the plant's genus. Individual species and varieties or cultivars are more dependent upon size and color characteristics, which one learns through direct and practical experience with plants. The following are flower types commonly found in landscape plants. (see Figures 1–7 and 1–8)

*Solitary.* This indicates a single flower attached to the stem. Many ornamental plants fall into this category.

*Spike.* The **peduncle** (main flower stalk) contains tightly attached flowers. The spike projects upward from the foliage.

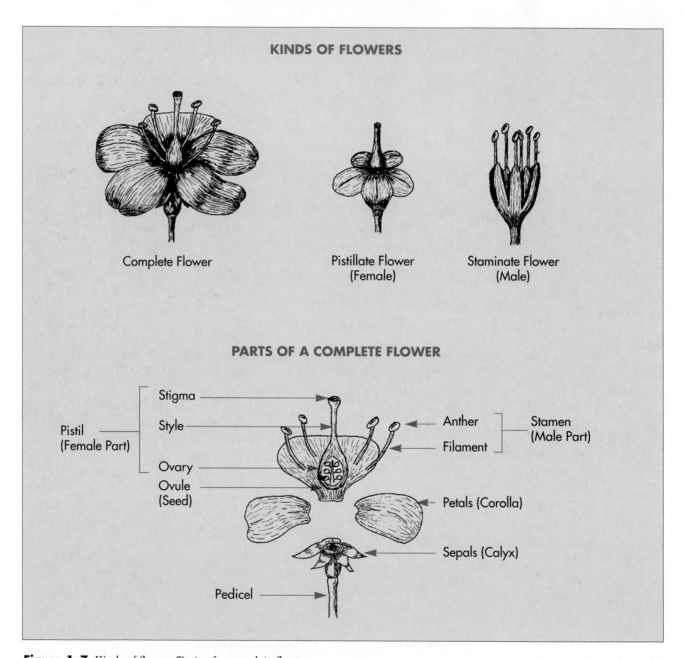

**KINDS OF FLOWERS**

Complete Flower

Pistillate Flower
(Female)

Staminate Flower
(Male)

**PARTS OF A COMPLETE FLOWER**

Stigma

Style

Ovary

Ovule
(Seed)

Pistil
(Female Part)

Anther

Filament

Stamen
(Male Part)

Petals (Corolla)

Sepals (Calyx)

Pedicel

**Figure 1–7.** Kinds of flowers/Parts of a complete flower.

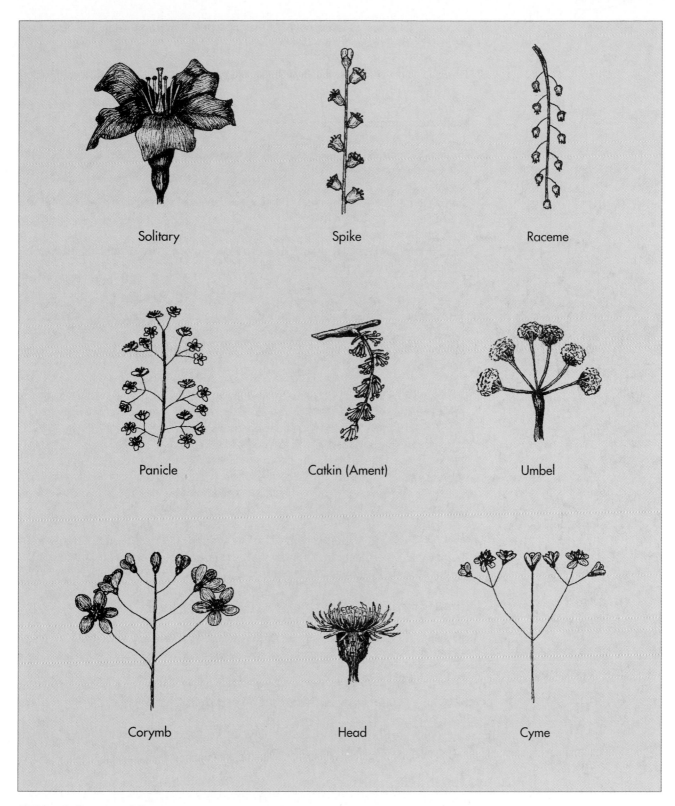

**Figure 1–8.** Types of flowers.

*Raceme.* The raceme is a drooping cluster having flowers attached to the peduncle by a **pedicel** or secondary flower stalk.

*Panicle.* This flower type has multiflowered pedicels attached along the peduncle.

*Catkins.* Many clusters of male (staminate) flowers are attached to a drooping peduncle.

*Umbel.* The umbel has flowers in which the pedicles originate at the same point along the peduncle.

*Corymb.* Flowers have pedicels that are attached at alternating points along the peduncle.

*Head.* The head is a composite of miniature flowers that appears to be one flower; Chrysanthemums are an example.

*Cyme.* Multiflowered pedicels attach themselves at the same point on the peduncle. The overall appearance is flattened, with the center flowers opening first.

## FRUITS

The purpose of a typical flower is to produce a fruit that contains seed. As a carrier for the all-important seed, a fruit is really a ripened flower ovary. When the petals of the flower have fallen, the plant channels its energy into the ovary, which increases in size and maturity before falling in late season.

Fruits are just as variable as leaf or flower types, therefore providing yet another means of plant identification. Unfortunately, fruit is present only for a relatively short period, and is usually most abundant during late summer and fall. Several fruit types are illustrated. (see Figure 1–9)

*Samara.* The samaras are "winged" fruits containing a seed with a transparent membrane. The membrane literally serves as a wing to propel the seed for distribution by wind; Ash, Maple, and Elm are examples.

*Acorn (Nut).* This is a hard fruit that contains one seed; all Oaks produce acorns.

*Strobile.* The strobile is a small, soft, and cone-like fruit that contains many "winged" seeds; Birch is typical.

*Clusters (of Small Drupes).* Cluster fruits (multiple fruits) are composed of many tiny fruits developed from many flowers; Raspberry is typical.

*Capsules.* Capsules are hard fruits that split into two or more parts at maturity to expose the seed; the Willows have capsule fruits.

*Nutlet.* The nutlet is a kind of "glorified" samara but is larger; American Hornbeam is an example. Some nutlets have more than one "wing."

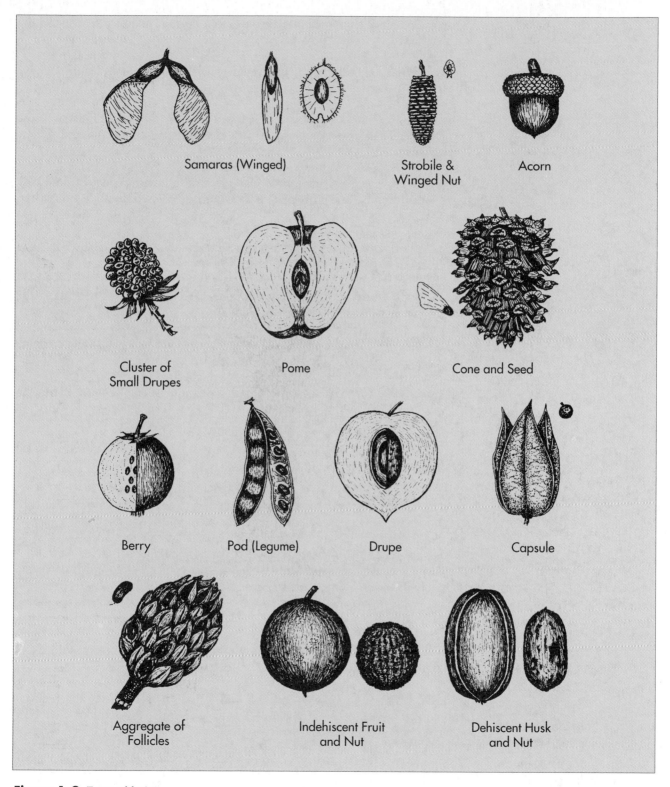

**Figure 1–9.** Types of fruits.

*Cones.* Cones are composed of many burs that open at maturity to disperse the "winged" seed.

*Berry.* Berries are fleshy fruits that contain seed randomly dispersed throughout the flesh; Blueberries are representative.

*Aggregate of Samaras.* This is a fruit that develops from several pistils in the same flower. Each pistil develops a samara-like fruit that contains a seed; Yellow Poplar is typical.

*Aggregate of Follicles.* This fruit is composed of follicles produced from many pistils. Each follicle is a fruit that splits to release many seeds; Magnolia is an example.

*Drupe.* Flesh surrounds a stony **endocarp** or stone that encloses the seed; Peach and Holly are examples.

*Pome.* Pome fruits are fleshy fruits that encircle a center "core" containing the seed; Apples are the best example.

*Pod (Legumes).* The fruit is a pod that separates into two halves and contains several seeds; Eastern Redbud and Locust trees are good examples.

*Husk and Nut.* The husk is a capsule fruit that splits along two or more lines to release a hard-shelled nut; typical plants are Pecan and Hickory.

## STEMS

Stems and stem parts are too varied and complex to adequately cover in this text. It is desirable that one be able to identify the plant without researching twigs and stems. However, there are keys that describe stem detail, and such keys can be used as reference materials to identify plants when the need arises.

It would be advisable for the plant enthusiast to learn the various parts of a stem, along with the functions of the parts. Figure 1–10 illustrates the parts of a typical stem. An explanation of the functions of stem parts follows. (see Figure 1–10)

*Terminal Bud.* This is the bud at the tip of the stem that will provide for growth in length of the stem.

*Lenticel.* Lenticels are small, corky growths along the stem. They allow for gas exchanges between the atmosphere and plant cells. Some plants, such as Cherries, have very noticeable lenticels.

*Lateral Buds.* These are buds along the length of the stem that will form a new leaf or lateral branch.

*Node.* A node is any area along a stem where leaves or side branches are found.

*Bud Scale.* Bud scales are tiny scales that cover a bud before it opens and begins to grow.

*Leaf Scar.* This is a scar that is left when a leaf drops from the stem. Leaf scars vary among plants and are useful in identification.

*Vascular Bundle Scars.* These are small round holes that serve as connecting veins between the stem and leaf. They vary in number, arrangement, and pattern from plant to plant.

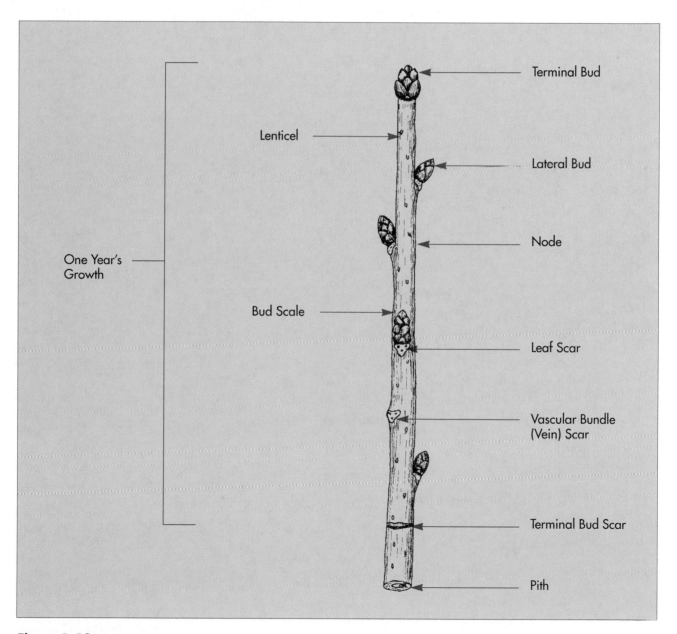

**Figure 1-10.** Parts of a stem.

*Terminal Bud Scar.* This is a ring-like scar that encircles the stem. It is left when the terminal bud begins to grow and increase in length. The stem adds one bud scar per year, so it is possible to determine the age of a stem by counting the bud scars on a branch or stem.

*Pith.* Pith is soft tissue in the center of the stem. Its color, size, texture, and other characterics vary from plant to plant.

# Chapter 2

# INTERPRETATION OF DATA

This chapter explains some of the data given for plants throughout the text. It would be advisable for beginning gardeners or horticulturalists to read the information provided under each category of this chapter. It is impossible to describe each plant exactly. Two plants of the same origin and species may perform differently in two different locations within a landscape. Therefore, an attempt is made to describe the average or typical plant. Hopefully, variations that you encounter will vary only slightly from the expected performance. Always leave some allowance for variation, especially in the size of the plant.

**ZONES**   Zones are geographic areas based on climate. Zones are more accurately described as **hardiness zones**, for they are based on the average coldest days of the year that can be expected for a particular area. As one would expect, severe winters, with record low temperatures, sometimes injure or kill some of the less hardy plants in an area. On the other hand, plants that are less hardy often thrive out of the recommended zone during consecutive years of milder winters. Global warming may also have an impact on the future.

The zone numbers used in the text are based on a map of hardiness zones prepared by the United States Department of Agriculture (USDA) (see page 2). You should learn the zone(s) for your area, as well as bordering zones. If you are located near the boundary of two zones, you can often grow plants for both zones. In addition, it is very common to see someone successfully cultivate a plant on their property that is not recommended for that zone. This usually involves a working knowledge of the establishment or selection of **microclimates** within the yard that are colder or warmer than the rest of the yard.

The zone numbers given for the plants in this text are based on personal experience, as well as the experience of many others in the nursery trade. The zones listed are ADVISORY ONLY, but an attempt has been made to be as accurate as possible. If in doubt, consult a local nursery or the Extension Service.

In listing zones, the lowest number represents the northern limit recommended, while the highest number represents the southern limit for the plant.

## SIZE

Size is based on overall height and width at maturity. The size of a plant is used to group it into one of several groups such as Dwarf Shrubs, Medium Trees, and so on. The sizes listed in this text represent averages. You will find variations from the average due to climate, soil conditions, and other factors.

The size of a plant should not limit its use entirely. Other desirable features, such as leaf characteristics, flower detail, or overall plant shape may determine the desirability for a specific location in the landscape. The mature size of plants can often be controlled by proper pruning techniques, such as heading-back or by limiting fertilizer or water. If you desire a low-maintenance or no-maintenance landscape, proper size selection will be one of your primary considerations.

## GROWTH HABIT

The habit of growth, or shape of a plant, is one of the most important considerations in landscape plant selection. Plants vary greatly in habit. The habit of a plant can be used to great advantage in the landscape, so long as variety is not the sole objective. While variety is very desirable, too much variety can look confusing and detract from the beauty of a landscape. Study the landscapes in your area to determine the impact of variety on each. (see Figure 2–1)

## TEXTURE

Texture is associated with the size and type of leaf. **Fine-textured** plants usually have smaller leaves and few, if any, coarse features such as spines, twists, and other features that "standout" in leaf characteristics. **Medium-textured** plants are usually larger and have more coarse features. **Coarse-textured** plants have the largest leaves of all plants and are very noticeable, especially when planted near finer-textured plants. In addition, stem and growth characteristics may have a bearing on texture. For example, some deciduous plants are neat and refined when the leaves are present, but they may be coarse, stiff, or extremely noticeable when the leaves are gone.

Using texture to enhance a landscape is more evident among gardeners or horticulturalists who have studied plants and have begun to notice detailed differences among plants. As one acquires more practical experience in identification of plants, attention to texture will become more useful.

## LEAVES, FLOWERS, AND FRUIT

### LEAVES

The size, color, and shape of leaves determines their usefulness in the landscape. An attempt has been made to give an average size, since great variations can occur. Shape is sometimes a very noticeable feature. For example, the Royal Paulownia is easily recognized by its large, heart-shaped leaves.

The color of leaves varies considerably. Plant leaves vary from very light green to dark green, with many shades in between. Some leaves are red while others are yellow; many other colors can show up in leaves as well. **Variegated** plants have leaves with two or more distinct colors per leaf. Fall is especially interesting, since numerous plants show a foliage color change when cooler weather arrives. For many plants, fall foliage color determines their use or usefulness in the land-

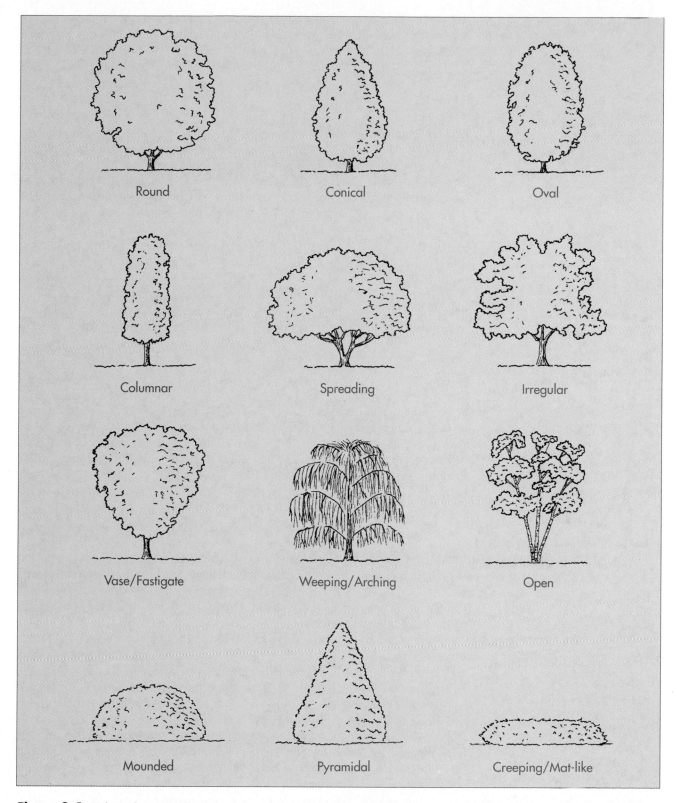

**Figure 2–1.** Habits of growth (Plant shapes).

scape. For example, the Ginkgo or Maidenhair Tree is quite commonplace during the summer but, when fall arrives, it is unequalled in beauty with its bold, bright yellow leaves. Fall color changes are noted in the plant data charts.

## FLOWERS

Flowers are a very popular feature in plant identification and selection. Though flowers persist on the average for a relatively short period, one has only to observe a Yoshino Cherry in its peak of flowering to appreciate its importance in landscaping. Many plants are spectacular in flower. In addition, every month of the calendar finds some plant in bloom. Many gardens are beautiful in April, but lack color for the remainder of the year. It is possible to plan a landscape for year-round color.

The text gives the average flowering period for plants having noticeable flowers. Wherever the flower is not noticeable or lacks attractiveness, the text reads INCONSPICUOUS, NOT ORNAMENTAL, or NOT SHOWY. The average flowering period will be delayed a few weeks in the northernmost states, while flowering in the deep south is usually several weeks earlier. In addition, mild winters cause early flowering, whereas cold springs might delay flowering.

## FRUIT

The importance of fruit is often overlooked. Fruits usually occur in late summer or fall, and can persist for many months. The berries of Pyracantha, pomes of Hybrid Crabapples, and cones of Eastern White Pine are examples of fruit that give added interest to various plants. Wherever the fruit is not noticeable or insignificant, the text will state that the fruit is NOT NOTICEABLE or NOT ORNAMENTAL.

## EXPOSURE/ CULTURE

In addition, plants vary as to their need for water, fertility level, pH, soil type and organic matter, and the time or recommendations for pruning. Wherever possible, plants should be located where these conditions are favorable or where necessary modifications have been made. The local extension service is a helpful source of additional information.

Sunlight conditions, however, are a major factor in plant selection. Plants usually perform best in either full sun, full shade, or part shade, but many plants are not particular as to light requirements. It is necessary to place plants in the light conditions best suited for them, so the light requirements are emphasized in this text. For example, a flowering plant that is recommended for full sun will not flower as profusely in shade, hence its usefulness to the landscape is diminished. When planning a landscape, check the light conditions of the site and double check the recommended light requirements for the plant. I have seen many fine landscapes diminished because of failure to match plants to the light conditions.

## PESTS

Pests, such as insects and diseases, are a complex area of study. Most can be controlled; some cannot. Dutch Elm Disease was devastating to the Elm in the Eastern United States because it could not be controlled. Aphids, on the other hand, are insects that deform new growth on some plants, but are easily controlled with an appropriate spray program. Seldom do aphids kill the plant.

Many insects and diseases attack plants. To list and describe all would take many volumes of text. Almost all plants are attacked by pests; some plants are bothered by dozens of pests. Fortunately, most pests are not completely destructive, as with the Dutch Elm Disease or Mimosa Wilt. On the other hand, many plants must be chemically treated to insure their survival. For example, plants in the *Euonymus* genus must be treated regularly for Euonymus Scale, which can be destructive. Since the *Euonymus* genus has many fine landscape species, the cost and trouble are certainly worth the effort.

The text does not list all pests for all plants. Rather, the major pests are included in the data. Wherever a plant is free of pests or only mildly bothered, the text states NONE or NO SERIOUS PESTS. Again, local nurseries or the extension service can be very helpful in identifying pests and the recommended treatment. When you purchase plants, inquire as to any pest problems to be aware of for each plant. Preventive measures, such as regular spraying, usually go a long way in avoiding pest problems.

## VARIETIES AND CULTIVARS

The number of varieties and cultivars in the nursery trade is almost endless. Such plants as Daylily, Crabapple, and Rhododendron (Azaleas included) offer hundreds, even thousands, of named varieties. The text lists those varieties the author is familiar with, or that have wide-range acceptance. There are many varieties that vary only in minute, almost microscopic, features.

The text will identify important varieties and cultivars as SELECTED CULTIVARS, and closely related species as RELATED SPECIES. Whenever you are introduced to a new variety, inquire as to the exact differences or advantages over the more familiar varieties. Sometimes the difference is significant; sometimes it is trivial.

## GROWTH RATE

Growth rate is an important consideration in landscaping. It varies from very rapid to extremely slow. Rate of growth sometimes affects price, as the slower-growing varieties usually cost much more, while the faster-growing plants are often less expensive. In addition, one can justify starting with a much smaller plant at initial planting when using a faster-growing plant. Sometimes the savings in dollars and labor can be quite substantial.

Growth rate is often considered when choosing trees for shade, plants for hedges (screens), and plants that will serve as ground cover. In most of these cases, faster-growing species are more popular. However, faster-growing plants sometimes require more maintenance, so this is not always an advantage.

As with other factors, growth rates listed are considered average. A fast-growing plant may grow less rapidly when soil and other environmental factors are not adequate. This is especially true when soils lack sufficient moisture or nitrogen.

## LANDSCAPE NOTES

The landscape notes that accompany each plant in the text represent the usefulness of each in a landscape setting. Most plants have both desirable and undesirable features. Some of the generalizations are widely acknowledged in the nursery trade, whereas some are highly judgemental and opinionated. It would be impossible to deal with plants on a regular basis and avoid forming opinions. Indeed, you will form many of your own. Always consider the usefulness of a particular plant to the landscape. Good landscapes are both attractive and useful, and the overall design of a landscape is more important than any one feature or species of plants.

The text does not mention every possible use of a particular plant. As you begin to observe plants more closely, you will find that one species is often used for a wide variety of purposes. Observe those uses! Visualize a particular plant being used for some new purpose that you have not observed. One should be influenced by, but not limited to, the opinions of others.

Terms used to describe the possible uses of plants are defined in Chapter 3.

# FUNCTIONAL AND AESTHETIC USES OF PLANTS

The great variety of plants that are available in the modern landscape industry makes it possible to find an appropriate plant for almost any conceivable landscape need. Fortunately, this great variety means there are usually several different plants from which to choose in satisfying the need. The purpose of this chapter is to explain some of the terminology used throughout the landscape industry in describing plant usage. Much of this terminology is used in describing the plants included in this book.

As you expand your knowledge and understanding of plants, you will begin to notice the conditions under which familiar plants are used. You will find that a particular plant is attractive in one landscape setting but unbecoming in another. Some plants are more attractive with certain styles of architecture, while some look best in a certain type of environment. The landscape notes will serve as a beginning, but you will develop your own style and techniques as you become more familiar with the plants in your area.

## ACCENT OR SPECIMEN PLANTS

An accent or specimen plant is a plant that has features or characteristics that make it more noticeable than the average plant. Some specimen plants have features that are more pronounced than others. In addition, some may serve as accents during a particular season and blend in with other plants during another season. Seasonal considerations that provide accent are flowers, fruit, and fall color. Year-round considerations are leaf shape and color, stem color, plant shape or growth habit, and bark characteristics.

It is possible to have several specimen plants in a landscape; however, caution must be exercised to avoid confusion in the landscape, as plants and areas of the yard compete for attention. Probably the greatest use of a specimen is to draw attention to a particular area in the landscape. For example, you may wish to enhance the front entrance area to cause visitors to use it, to make it seem friendly and inviting, or to draw attention to a feature such as a handcarved door or flagstone surface. (see Figure 3–1)

**Figure 3–1.** A plant used to accent an entry.

## FOCAL POINTS

A focal point is an area of the landscape that attracts attention based on its beauty, interest, or function. A specimen plant or grouping of specimen plants may constitute a focal point. For example, a bed of flowering plants such as Lilac or some annual plants may provide a focal point as seen from a patio or viewed through a family room window. Focal points may be located for family viewing or to enhance the beauty of the residence as seen by the viewing public.

Often, a focal point is a natural feature or a man-made structure that may utilize specimen plants. Examples are streams and ponds, waterfalls, statuary, reflection pools, gazebos, berms, swimming pools, garden seats, and others. Features are more attractive as a focal point when carefully selected plants are used to add interest. Electrical lighting can be used to extend the usefulness or impact of a focal point beyond daylight hours. Many focal points take on a different character at night. (see Figure 3–2)

## FOUNDATION AND CORNER PLANTS

Foundation plants are any plants used on, against, or near the foundation or walls of a home or other structure. Such plantings are used to "tie" the residence to the rest of the yard and to eliminate the abrupt angle where the foundation joins the ground. These are probably the most important plants in a landscape, since they are intended to enhance the beauty of the residence while helping to blend the structure into the garden or surroundings. A home without plants looks incomplete.

Most often, foundation plants should be evergreen. Deciduous plants, when used, should be carefully located to avoid a disturbing look during the winter months. One technique is to use evergreen background plants and deciduous plants as foreground plants. When this technique is used, it is important that foreground plants be species that are shorter in height at maturity. One exception is when a single tree or tree-form plant is used as an accent plant.

**Figure 3–2.** Statuary can serve as a focal point.

The most important plants in the foundation are the corner plants. The front of any building has two or more distinct corners that form an abrupt 90 degree angle to the side walls. These harsh corners compete for attention with the rest of the structure. It is advisable to "soften" the corners first. This serves as an excellent starting point in the design. A good rule-of-thumb is to select plants that will be ONE-HALF TO TWO-THIRDS THE HEIGHT OF THE CORNER AT MATURITY. Obviously, larger structures can handle larger plants, whereas one-story dwellings necessitate plants that are dwarf or medium in height at maturity. Select corner plants very carefully as they will receive much attention. (see Figure 3–3)

The second most important plants are those that will be used under windows. These plants are usually dwarf or medium in size. The primary consideration is to choose plants that will mature at SIX INCHES OR MORE BELOW THE WINDOW CASING. This will allow the plants to grow to their natural shape without the necessity of frequent pruning. Taller growing plants may be used where bare wall space is available. Other plant species should be used to complete the foundation.

There are two recommendations that will add interest to the planting:

1. Repeat some plants from one side of the residence to the other. This will give an organized look.
2. Use variety in height, texture, or color in order to avoid monotony.

**Figure 3–3.** An appropriate corner planting.

Symmetrical structures will require each side of the foundation planting to be identical. A symmetrical structure has the door centered, and each side of the structure is a mirror image of the other.

Asymmetrical structures are not exact on either side of the front door, so the plantings will not be exact. However, BALANCE must be maintained by avoiding excessive plantings on one side with few plantings on the other. The best indication of balance is if it LOOKS balanced when viewed from a distance of 100 feet or more.

## TREE-FORM PLANTS

Tree-form plants are shrubs and selected trees that normally branch to the ground, but have had the lower limbs removed to resemble a tree. The trend toward tree-form plants has greatly expanded the use of selected plants. For example, many large Hollies, which were thought of as corner plants or hedges, are now tree-formed and used as accent or specimen plants. The trend is toward tree-forming many species of plants to achieve various effects. Often, shrubs used for tree-form are multi-stem plants, and they add interesting form to the landscape. (see Figure 3–4)

Many plants are sold as **standards**. Standards are usually shrubs that have been trained to one single, straight stem with the lower branches removed. Often, standards are grafted plants.

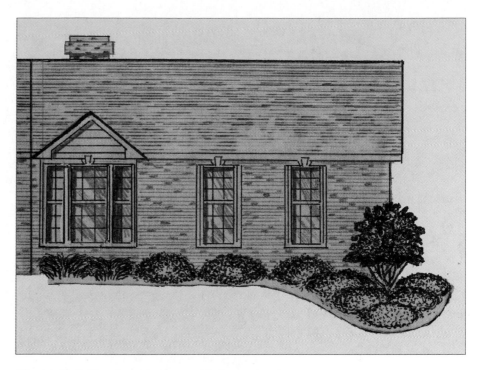

**Figure 3–4.** Tree-form shrubs provide interesting form.

## NATURALIZING

Naturalizing can be described as a design process or landscaping technique whereby the man-made landscape "fits" into the native surroundings. The two primary considerations in naturalizing are the natural terrain (land features) and native plants.

One type of landscape that lends itself to naturalizing is the woodland landscape. Such a landscape looks best if the plants selected are native plants or cultivars of native plants. Native plants such as Rhododendron, Mountain Laurel, and Virginia Sweetspire fit very well into a natural setting and normally look attractive without being sheared.

There are many native trees, shrubs, vines, and ground covers in North America. In selecting and using plants for naturalizing, please note that seldom does one find perfectly round globes or plants growing in straight lines. Select plants that look good in their natural state, and use an offset or random pattern in locating plants.

There are many conditions where naturalizing is appropriate. Consider the location and its surroundings. Attempt to enhance the natural beauty without drastically changing the mood of the habitat. A hillside garden with stone outcrops is a great place to develop a rock garden effect utilizing interesting native shrubs and flowers. Desert-like areas, swampy areas, and beach locations provide additional opportunities for naturalizing.

Many non-native plants can be used in naturalizing. As you study and learn different plants, consider whether a particular plant looks natural in its outline or habit of growth. If it appears too symmetrical or refined, it might not be the best choice for naturalizing.

## FORMAL PLANTINGS

Formal plantings are usually associated with architecture, garden design, and plants selected. American Colonial Architecture is quite formal, and is often symmetrical, especially the front entry. Formal gardens, with their geometric shapes, serve as the ultimate in formal design. Usually, we associate straight lines, clipped hedges, symmetrically sheared plants, and topiary with more formal landscapes. Other man-made features, such as fencing material or paving, can be more or less formal depending upon the choice of materials.

Some landscape plants are more formal than others. For instance, Old English Boxwood has fine, tightly-held foliage on a globular shaped plant. It is much easier to shape and maintain than Bush St. John's Wort; hence, Old English Boxwood lends itself more easily to formal landscapes.

As you learn more individual plants, you will begin to recognize those that appear more formal. (see Figure 3–5)

## LOW-MAINTENANCE PLANTS

Low-maintenance plants are those that require little care to maintain their shape, so they require less pruning. Such plants usually require a minimal amount of fertilizers, pesticides, or supplemental moisture. In addition, ground covers enjoy increased popularity, because they require far less care than lawn grasses. Dwarf shrubs are more popular than ever in foundation plantings because they are easily maintained below window levels or within established borders.

**Figure 3–5.** A formal garden with geometric lines.

## EASY-TO-GROW PLANTS

Easy-to-grow plants are those that thrive in a wide variety of soil conditions. These plants have a high rate of survival when transplanted, and are usually not bothered by destructive pests. One of the reasons for the popularity of Junipers is that they are very easy to grow and survive almost anywhere except in wet soils or shade. Red-tip Photinia or Fraser Photinia was once an easy-to-grow plant of enormous popularity. Unfortunately, a leaf spot fungus has destroyed large numbers of plants, and it is no longer a reliable survivor in the landscape.

## CONTRAST AND TEXTURE

Contrast refers to the differences in appearance of plants, and is usually associated with color or texture. Texture has to do with the degree of refinement in bark, leaves, branches, and twigs. The overall effect may vary from very fine to very coarse. Most often the size and appearance of the leaves will dictate texture; however, a plant that is less coarse in leaf may appear stiff, scraggly, or harsh during winter when it is bare. Seasonal consideration must be taken into account, especially with deciduous material.

Architectural features also have texture. Rustic materials and stone tend to be coarse whereas some brick or smooth, painted boards may appear very refined. Many designers suggest that coarse architectural features look best with some coarse-textured plants, and refined features are enhanced with fine to moderate plant textures. The more contrasting the textures used, the more noticeable the area becomes. Sometimes it is desirable to use contrasting plants to add interest, variety, or some special effect. Coarse-textured plants can be effectively used with a background of large, fine-textured plants. Be especially cautious when using contrasting colors. Simply stated, some color combinations do not work well together.

Pay more attention to contrast in plant combinations. As you become more observant, you will form your own opinions of those that work and those that don't!

## MASSING OR GROUPING

The concept of massing has two primary considerations. First, it means that plants in a group are spaced close enough to look like a mass without overcrowding. The spacing should allow plants to touch, or almost touch, when mature. This will increase the visual impact of the planting, especially with flowering plants. Do not align the plants in a straight line with equal gaps between the plants. This makes the planting look like a formation of little "toy soldiers," while lacking any semblance of creativity.

Second, massing gives an uninterrupted flow to well-chosen plant material. For example, suppose you desired a combination of red Azaleas and white Azaleas in a planting. The concept of massing suggests that a grouping of all white Azaleas and another grouping of red Azaleas would be more pleasing to the eye than alternating red, white, red, white, and so on.

There are many instances when a single plant may be used to give a variation in the scheme. This is especially true of trees, corner plants, and entrance plants. However, the majority of the plants in a design will be used in groups of three or more of the same species.

## SCREENING

Screening is the use of plants as a substitute for fencing or walls. Most often, plants are used as a hedge to provide privacy or to screen an undesirable view. Whether the planting is to be clipped or left natural, plants should be selected that mature at the height desired for the screen. This will enable one to enjoy the desired effect with a minimum of maintenance and care.

Sometimes it is desirable to screen a particular area in a landscape without screening your property from all humanity. For example, you might grow a vine on a trellis or arbor to make a patio or terrace more private. Plants may also be used effectively to soften noise pollution or control speed of wind. Under very harsh conditions, a combination of both fencing and plants may prove more effective.

## GROUND COVER PLANTS

One of the more popular trends in modern landscaping is the use of ground cover plants to cover larger areas of land. In other words, it is the use of low-growing plants as a substitute for lawn grasses. Such an approach enables one to add great interest and variety to the landscape, while reducing the surface area in need of regular mowing. In addition, many ground cover type plantings will grow in locations not suitable for lawn grasses, such as densely shaded areas, steep banks, or under low-branching trees.

Many spreading or creeping ground cover plants are featured in this text. In addition, some shrubs and vines have ground-covering potential. The notes for individual plants will reflect this usage wherever appropriate.

# Landscape Plants

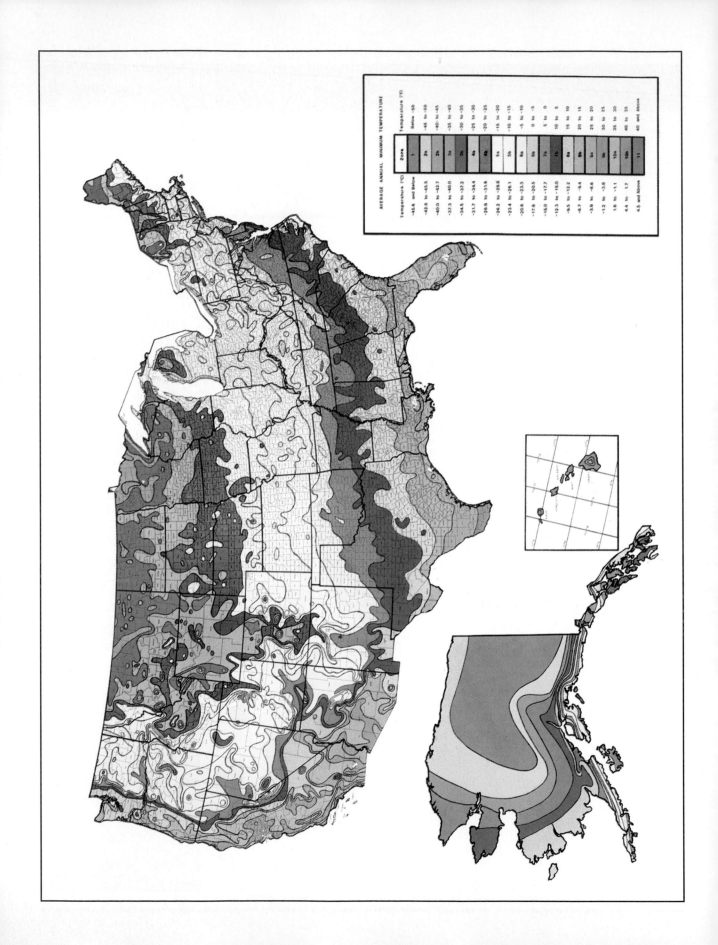

AVERAGE ANNUAL MINIMUM TEMPERATURE

| Zone | Temperature (°F) | Temperature (°C) |
|---|---|---|
| 1 | Below -50 | -45.6 and Below |
| 2a | -45 to -50 | -42.8 to -45.5 |
| 2b | -40 to -45 | -40.0 to -42.7 |
| 3a | -35 to -40 | -37.3 to -40.0 |
| 3b | -30 to -35 | -34.5 to -37.2 |
| 4a | -25 to -30 | -31.7 to -34.4 |
| 4b | -20 to -25 | -28.9 to -31.6 |
| 5a | -15 to -20 | -26.2 to -28.8 |
| 5b | -10 to -15 | -23.4 to -26.1 |
| 6a | -5 to -10 | -20.6 to -23.3 |
| 6b | 0 to -5 | -17.8 to -20.5 |
| 7a | 5 to 0 | -15.0 to -17.7 |
| 7b | 10 to 5 | -12.3 to -15.0 |
| 8a | 15 to 10 | -9.5 to -12.2 |
| 8b | 20 to 15 | -6.7 to -9.4 |
| 9a | 25 to 20 | -3.9 to -6.6 |
| 9b | 30 to 25 | -1.2 to -3.8 |
| 10a | 35 to 30 | 1.6 to -1.1 |
| 10b | 40 to 35 | 4.4 to 1.7 |
| 11 | 40 and Above | 4.5 and Above |

## Chapter 4

# GROUND COVERS

**G**round covers are low-growing, perennial plants that take the place of turf in a landscape. The ground cover plants in this text are mostly woody, but a few important herbaceous plants are included.

Ground covers may be deciduous or evergreen, and the classification includes both broadleaf and narrowleaf types. In addition, many vines and some shrubs can be used for covering ground. Most true ground covers, however, spread to form a solid mass over a period of time. This necessitates some regular maintenance during the warm season to confine the plant to the desired boundaries.

Some major uses of ground covers are as follows:

▼ Covering ground in areas that are inconvenient to mow, such as steep banks, under low-branched trees, and in raised planters.
▼ Covering ground where turf grass does poorly, such as heavy shade and poor or wet soils.
▼ Adding variety or interest to the landscape while reducing the total area in need of routine mowing or watering.

# *Ajuga reptans*

**Ajuga, Bugleflower, Bugleweed**

▲ 'Burgundy Glow'

▲ 'Catlin's Giant'

**ZONES:**
4, 5, 6, 7, 8, 9

**HEIGHT:**
4″ to 6″

**WIDTH:**
Indefinite

**FRUIT:**
Tiny seed; NOT ORNAMEN-TAL.

**TEXTURE:**
Coarse

**GROWTH RATE:**
Very RAPID in moist soil.

**HABIT:**
Spreads by stolons into dense mat, similar to strawberry.

**FAMILY:**
Labiatae

**LEAF COLOR:** Species is dark green. Cultivars vary considerably.

**LEAF DESCRIPTION:** SIMPLE, 4″ to 5″ long and 1″ to 2″ wide, obovate with an obtuse tip, slightly wavy margin that is smoother or entire near the base and tip, WHORLED arrangement.

**FLOWER DESCRIPTION:** Tiny blue, white, or rose-pink flowers on 4″ to 8″ pyramidal spikes, depending on the clutivar. Blooms in mid-spring.

**EXPOSURE/CULTURE:** The plant should be located in areas of part shade or in areas that receive no more than 4 hours of sunlight daily. Prefers well-drained loamy or heavy soil, but needs a location where it will receive high moisture.

**PEST PROBLEMS:** Crown rot is often a problem in the hot and humid southeastern states. Aphids, nematodes, and spider mites pose less of a problem.

**SELECTED CULTIVARS:** 'Alba' - Has white flowers. 'Atropurpurea' - Has attractive bronze-purple foliage. 'Burgundy Glow' - New foliage is burgundy, while mature foliage is variegated with cream, pink, and rose-pink. 'Catlin's Giant' - Much taller blue flower spikes rise above bronze-green foliage. Outstanding. 'Giant Green' - Large, metallic-bronze foliage. 'Rubra' - Has rosey-red flower spikes. 'Variegata' - Leaves variegated with light green, pink, and cream colors.

**RELATED SPECIES:** *Ajuga genevensis* - This species is non-stoloniferous; hence, it is more easily contained in the garden. Leaves are slightly to densely hairy. *Ajuga pyramidalis* - This species is non-stoloniferous, but spreads by rhizomes.

**LANDSCAPE NOTES:** Ajuga is an excellent ground cover for moist, shady areas. Flowering is excellent, and foliage texture adds interest. Containment is a factor to consider with most Ajugas.

## *Arctostaphylos uva-ursi*

**Bearberry, Kinnikinick**

**ZONES:**
2, 3, 4, 5, 6

**HEIGHT:**
8" to 12"

**WIDTH:**
Indefinite

**FRUIT:**
1/4" brilliant red drupes in fall.

**TEXTURE:**
Fine

**GROWTH RATE:**
Moderate to slow.

**HABIT:**
Low-growing and broad-spreading with arching branches.

**FAMILY:**
Ericaceae

**LEAF COLOR:** Dark green during the growing season, taking on a reddish tint during winter.

**LEAF DESCRIPTION:** SIMPLE leaves 1/4" to 3/4" long and 1/4" to 1/2" wide, obovate, margins entire or slightly toothed, ALTERNATE arrangement.

**FLOWER DESCRIPTION:** Tiny pinkish-white flowers, 1/4", urn-shaped, borne in racemes. Not bold, but quite attractive on close inspection.

**EXPOSURE/CULTURE:** Full sun or part shade. Prefers sandy soils that lack high fertility. Can be grown on sand dunes, where it exhibits tolerance for salt. Can be grown in other soils, but should not be fertilized. Requires very little pruning or care.

**PEST PROBLEMS:** Black mildew, leaf gall, leaf spots.

**SELECTED CULTIVARS:** 'Massachusetts' - Produces a heavier flower and berry crop, while showing resistance to leaf spot and gall. 'Wood's Red' - A more compact form with smaller leaves and larger berries.

**RELATED SPECIES:** There are many species, but *A. uva-ursi* is the primary species in cultivation.

**LANDSCAPE NOTES:** This is an outstanding ground cover for the northern zones and western regions. It gives an effect that is similar to that of the dwarf Cotoneasters in the southern zones.

## *Aspidistra elatior*

**Cast-iron Plant, Aspidistra**

**ZONES:**
6, 7, 8, 9, 10

**HEIGHT:**
1 1/2' to 2'

**WIDTH:**
2' to 3'

**FRUIT:**
Small berry; NOT NOTICE-ABLE.

**TEXTURE:**
Very coarse.

**GROWTH RATE:**
Slow

**HABIT:**
Upright whorled clumps, developing from rhizomes.

**FAMILY:**
Liliaceae

**LEAF COLOR:** Dark green, sometimes displaying a blackish tint.

**LEAF DESCRIPTION:** SIMPLE, 15″ to 20″ long, 3″ to 5″ wide, long ovate shape, acuminate tip, stiff petiole that is 1/4 to 1/2 the length of the blade, linear parallel venation, entire margins, WHORLED arrangement.

**FLOWER DESCRIPTION:** Small and brown-purple, appearing at ground level, bell-shaped, NOT NOTICEABLE.

**EXPOSURE/CULTURE:** Shade plant. Can tolerate full shade or partial shade, burning badly in the presence of too much direct sunlight. Tolerates drought conditions; can be grown under overhangs and stairways, in containers, and in other areas not suitable for most plants. Protect from wind.

**PEST PROBLEMS:** Occasionally attacked by scale insects, especially when grown in containers or planters indoors.

**SELECTED CULTIVARS:** 'Variegata' - This cultivar has alternating stripes of green and white. When grown in highly fertile conditions, many of the stripes fade.

**LANDSCAPE NOTES:** Cast-iron plant is valued by designers for its strong textural effect. It can add interest to dull areas of the landscape not suitable for many other plants. It is especially useful in gardens where a large number of fine-textured plants are used. The effect is more dramatic when used in mass, rather than single lines.

## *Cotoneaster dammeri*

**Bearberry Cotoneaster**

**ZONES:**
6, 7, 8

**HEIGHT:**
12″ to 15″

**WIDTH:**
3′ to 6′

**FRUIT:**
Bright red berries in fall.

**TEXTURE:**
Fine

**GROWTH RATE:**
Moderately fast.

**HABIT:**
Prostrate and spreading. Pendulous branches.

**FAMILY:**
Rosaceae

**LEAF COLOR:** Dark green, developing a purplish tinge in fall and winter.

**LEAF DESCRIPTION:** SIMPLE leaves, 3/4″ to 1 1/4″ long and half as wide, elliptic, margins entire, ALTERNATE arrangement. Leaves become deciduous in northern zones.

**FLOWER DESCRIPTION:** White flowers, 1/2″, appearing in spring or early summer.

**EXPOSURE/CULTURE:** Full sun to light shade. Will grow in a wide variety of well-drained soils. Requires a minimal amount of light pruning.

**PEST PROBLEMS:** Fire blight, aphids, lace bugs, and spider mites. Fire blight and spider mites can be quite destructive if preventive measures are not taken.

**SELECTED CULTIVARS:** 'Coral Beauty' - Lower growing form with a heavier berry crop. One of the most popular cultivars. 'Eichholz' - Fruit is a showy carmine red. Large leaves change from bright green to gold or orange-red in autumn. 'Major' - Has larger leaves than the species and is more hardy. 'Mooncreeper' - Very low-growing form that has glossy dark green leaves and larger flowers. 'Skogholm' - A more vigorous form for covering large areas; fewer berries.

**LANDSCAPE NOTES:** Bearberry Cotoneaster is most effective when used in mass plantings or located near plants with contrasting foliage.

# *Cotoneaster salicifolius* 'Repens'    Dwarf Willowleaf Cotoneaster

**ZONES:**
5, 6, 7, 8, 9

**HEIGHT:**
2' to 3'

**WIDTH:**
5' to 8'

**FRUIT:**
1/4" bright red berries in fall and winter.

**TEXTURE:**
Fine

**GROWTH RATE:**
Usually rapid.

**HABIT:**
Spreading and irregular; arched branches.

**FAMILY:**
Rosaceae

**LEAF COLOR:** Dark green and very lustrous; purple tinged in fall.

**LEAF DESCRIPTION:** SIMPLE, 1" to 1 1/2" long and 1/4" to 1/2" wide, ovate-lance-olate, entire margins, ALTERNATE arrangement. Becomes deciduous in northernmost zones.

**FLOWER DESCRIPTION:** White, 1/4" in 1" flat corymbs, not especially noticeable. Blooms in spring.

**EXPOSURE/CULTURE:** Best in full sun, but will tolerate partial shade. It is easy to grow in most soil types, but it prefers well-drained soil that is slightly acid.

**PEST PROBLEMS:** Lace bugs, scale, spider mites. The species and cultivars are not nearly as prone to fire blight as many of the other Cotoneasters.

**SELECTED CULTIVARS:** None. This is a cultivar of *C. salicifolius,* a large evergreen to semi-evergreen shrub.

**RELATED CULTIVARS:** 'Emerald Carpet' - Larger leaves than 'Repens'. 'Gnome' - Low-growing (1') with smaller leaves. Outstanding form. 'Repandens' - Another name for 'Repens'. 'Scarlet Leader' - Wide-spreading form with reddish-purple leaves in winter.

**LANDSCAPE NOTES:** This is truly one of the outstanding dwarf Cotoneasters. Foliage is especially attractive, is extremely vigorous for ground covering, and is bothered less by pests.

## *Cyrtomium falcatum*                                      **Holly Fern**

**ZONES:**
8, 9

**HEIGHT:**
1' to 2'

**WIDTH:**
2' to 3'

**FRUIT:**
NONE. Sori (spore clusters).

**TEXTURE:**
Moderately coarse.

**GROWTH RATE:**
Moderate

**HABIT:**
Upright with arching fronds.

**FAMILY:**
Polypodiaceae

**LEAF COLOR:** Dark glossy green.

**LEAF DESCRIPTION:** COMPOUND leaves (fronds), 1' to 2' long, leaflets (pinnae) 1" to 2" long with serrated margins and ovate shape, petioles (rachises) form WHORLED clumps from the ground.

**FLOWER DESCRIPTION:** NONE, THIS IS A TRUE FERN.

**EXPOSURE/CULTURE:** Must be grown in full shade or partial shade. It requires a fertile soil that is high in organic matter. Pruning should be limited to the removal of dead or damaged fronds.

**PEST PROBLEMS:** None of a serious nature. Occasionally bothered by mealybugs or scale.

**SELECTED CULTIVARS:** 'Compactum' - A more compact form. 'Rochfordianum' - This cultivar has superior foliage to the species, and is the most popular.

**LANDSCAPE NOTES:** Holly Fern is a strikingly beautiful plant with holly-like leaflets (pinnae) forming fronds that take on the characteristic growth habit of ferns. This is a plant to feature, and is especially attractive in groupings.

## *Euonymus fortunei var. coloratus* — Red Wintercreeper

▲ Fall color

**ZONES:**
4, 5, 6, 7, 8, 9

**HEIGHT:**
12″ to 14″

**WIDTH:**
Indefinite

**FRUIT:**
Pinkish capsule; RARE.

**TEXTURE:**
Fine to medium.

**GROWTH RATE:**
Rapid

**HABIT:**
Vine-like and pendulous.

**FAMILY:**
Celastraceae

**LEAF COLOR:** Dark green, turning plum-purple during fall and winter.

**LEAF DESCRIPTION:** SIMPLE, 1 1/2″ to 2″ long and 1″ wide, ovate shape with serrulate margins, OPPOSITE arrangement.

**FLOWER DESCRIPTION:** Tiny, greenish or purplish, in cymes. RARELY FLOWERING.

**EXPOSURE/CULTURE:** Grows in sun or shade. Adaptable to a wide range of soil types and conditions. Avoid very wet conditions. May need occasional pruning to prevent climbing on walls or to confine to an area, especially when bordered by a solid surface.

**PEST PROBLEMS:** EUONYMUS SCALE, anthracnose, aphids, leaf spots, mildews.

**SELECTED CULTIVARS:** None. This is a cultivar of *E. fortunei,* a large evergreen shrub.

**RELATED CULTIVARS:** 'Kewensis' - Lower-growing form with tiny, 1/4″ leaves. Ideal for small areas. 'Minimus' - Low-growing with 1/2″ leaves. var. *radicans* - Leaves to 2″. Thicker leaves and larger stems. Will climb. 'Variegata' has leaves marked with white, pink, or yellow.

**LANDSCAPE NOTES:** Red Wintercreeper is a low-maintenance ground cover that takes on a totally different appearance during the winter months with its plum-colored foliage. It is appropriate for both small and large areas.

# *Hedera canariensis*

**Algerian Ivy**

**ZONES:**
7, 8, 9, 10

**HEIGHT:**
1′ as a ground cover.

**WIDTH:**
Indefinite

**FRUIT:**
Tiny blue-black; NOT ORNA-MENTAL.

**TEXTURE:**
Coarse

**GROWTH RATE:**
Moderate

**HABIT:**
Trailing and vine-like. Will climb on vertical surfaces.

**FAMILY:**
Araliaceae

**LEAF COLOR:** Lustrous dark green.

**LEAF DESCRIPTION:** SIMPLE, 6″ to 8″ long and 4″ to 6″ wide, 3 to 7 lobed and smooth, cordate base, acute tip (usually), overall shape is heart-shaped except for lobes, ALTERNATE arrangement.

**FLOWER DESCRIPTION:** Tiny greenish flowers in umbels on mature stems, NOT ORNAMENTAL.

**EXPOSURE/CULTURE:** Should be located in partial shade to dense shade. Tolerant of a wide range of soil types from sandy soils to heavy soils. Does best when moisture is higher and fertility is at medium or higher levels. Needs moderate pruning to control.

**PEST PROBLEMS:** Bacterial leaf spots, scale insects, snails, spider mites.

**SELECTED CULTIVARS:** 'Canary Cream' - Green leaves with creamy white margins. 'Gloire de Marengo' - Leaves variegated with green and snow white. 'Green' - Bright green leaves that darken with maturity. 'Variegata' - Leaves variegated with green, gray, and creamy white.

**LANDSCAPE NOTES:** Algerian Ivy is an aggressive plant that makes a bold statement in the landscape. It is limited in range and not as hardy as English Ivy. It can be used as a ground cover or vine, since it climbs on solid surfaces.

## *Hedera colchica* — Colchis Ivy, Persian Ivy

**ZONES:**
6, 7, 8, 9

**HEIGHT:**
1' as ground cover.

**WIDTH:**
Indefinite

**FRUIT:**
1/4" black drupe; NOT ORNA-MENTAL.

**TEXTURE:**
Coarse due to size and stiffness.

**GROWTH RATE:**
Moderate

**HABIT:**
Vine-like and stiff. Will climb on vertical surfaces.

**FAMILY:**
Araliaceae

**LEAF COLOR:** Dull dark green.

**LEAF DESCRIPTION:** SIMPLE, 3" to 5" long and wide, leathery and stiff, heart-shaped (cordate) with entire margins, fragrant when crushed, ALTERNATE arrangement.

**FLOWER DESCRIPTION:** Tiny greenish flowers in loose umbels, not commonly flowering, NOT ORNAMENTAL.

**EXPOSURE/CULTURE:** Recommended for shade, but often does well in full sun. It is adaptable to a wide variety of soils. Prefers medium or higher levels of fertility and moisture. Needs moderate pruning to control. Should not be allowed to climb on painted surfaces.

**PEST PROBLEMS:** Bacterial leaf spot, mildews, mealybugs, scale, slugs, spider mites.

**SELECTED CULTIVARS:** 'Dentata Variegata' - Leaves variegated with green, gray, and pale yellow. 'Sulphur Heart' - Leaves have a yellow blotch near the center.

**LANDSCAPE NOTES:** This is one of the best Ivies for hardiness, and is tolerant of many conditions. However, it does appear stiff at times, giving it a rugged character. Colchis Ivy can be grown as a ground cover or vine.

# *Hedera helix*

**Common English Ivy**

**ZONES:**
5, 6, 7, 8, 9

**HEIGHT:**
1′ as a ground cover.

**WIDTH:**
Indefinite

**FRUIT:**
1/4″ black drupes; NOT ORNA-MENTAL.

**TEXTURE:**
Medium or coarse, depending on cultivar.

**GROWTH RATE:**
Moderate to rapid.

**HABIT:**
Trailing and vine-like. Will climb.

**FAMILY:**
Araliaceae

**LEAF COLOR:** Dark green.

**LEAF DESCRIPTION:** SIMPLE, 3″ to 4″ long and wide, 3 to 5 lobed and smooth, cordate base on young leaves to acute base on adult leaves, acute tip, leaf veins lighter in color than blade, ALTERNATE arrangement.

**FLOWER DESCRIPTION:** Tiny greenish white flowers in loose, open umbels, NOT ORNAMENTAL.

**EXPOSURE/CULTURE:** Should be planted in part shade to shade. Will tolerate some direct light if moisture is provided. Does best in organic soil, with medium to high moisture and fertility. Needs moderate pruning to control. Should not be allowed to climb on painted surfaces.

**PEST PROBLEMS:** Bacterial leaf spot, fungal leaf spots, mildews, mealybugs, scale insects, snails, slugs, spider mites.

**SELECTED CULTIVARS:** 'Baltica' - Smaller leaves than the species but similar in shape and color. 'Chester' - Leaves variegated with green and yellow. Less hardy than the species. 'Gold Dust' - Green leaves with yellow specks. Not as hardy. 'Hahn's' - Lighter green. Prominent center lobe. Tolerates more sun. 'Needlepoint' - Narrow, sharp-pointed center lobe. 'Thorndale' - Veins creamy white and showy. More cold hardy than species. 'Wilson' - Foliage is dark green with curly edges.

**LANDSCAPE NOTES:** English Ivy has long been used as a ground cover, especially in the south. It has been used effectively as a climbing plant on brick surfaces. A moderate amount of care is needed to maintain as a ground cover. It is very appropriate for covering large areas.

## *Helleborus orientalis*        **Lenten Rose**

**ZONES:**
3, 4, 5, 6, 7, 8

**HEIGHT:**
12" to 18"

**WIDTH:**
1 1/2' to 2'

**FRUIT:**
Black capsule; NOT ORNA-MENTAL.

**TEXTURE:**
Coarse

**GROWTH RATE:**
Slow at first, then moderate.

**HABIT:**
Forms spreading, erect mounds; reseeds freely.

**FAMILY:**
Ranunculaceae

**LEAF COLOR:** Dark green.

**LEAF DESCRIPTION:** PALMATELY COMPOUND, 8" to 12" wide, leaflets 4" long and 2" wide, leaflets elliptic with serrulate margins, leaves arranged in WHORLED pattern and arising from the crown.

**FLOWER DESCRIPTION:** White, mauve, or purple, fading to green, 1 1/2" to 2" wide. Blooms in JANUARY. Very ornamental.

**EXPOSURE/CULTURE:** Must be planted in partial shade or shade. Tends to do better when planted in organic soil with moderate moisture. Responds to fertilization. Does not require pruning to maintain, although seeds will scatter and germinate outside of defined areas, necessitating removal of unwanted plants.

**PEST PROBLEMS:** NONE SERIOUS. Chewing insects occasionally feed on foliage.

**SELECTED CULTIVARS:** 'White Magic' - White flowers, fading to pink. Actually a hybrid of *H. orientalis* and *H. niger*.

**RELATED SPECIES:** *H. niger* - Christmas Rose. White flowers fading to pale pink. Grows 10" to 12" with smaller leaves than *H. orientalis*.

**LANDSCAPE NOTES:** Lenten Rose begins flowering in winter when most gardens are at the peak of dullness. The flowers continue into early spring. An ideal plant to provide color in shaded areas.

# *Hypericum calycinum*

**Aaron's Beard St. John's Wort**

**ZONES:**
5, 6, 7, 8

**HEIGHT:**
12″ to 18″

**WIDTH:**
Indefinite

**FRUIT:**
1/2″ red-brown capsule; NOT ATTRACTIVE.

**TEXTURE:**
Medium in summer, less refined in winter.

**GROWTH RATE:**
Rapid, once established.

**HABIT:**
Low and arching, spreading indefinitely from stolons.

**FAMILY:**
Hypericaceae

**LEAF COLOR:** Blue-green during growing season, turning purplish-green in fall.

**LEAF DESCRIPTION:** SIMPLE, 1 1/2″ to 2″ long and 1″ wide, ovate shape with entire margins, OPPOSITE arrangement.

**FLOWER DESCRIPTION:** Bright yellow, to 3″ wide, born singly or in clusters of 2 or 3, stamens forming a thick "brush". Blooms in mid-spring to late spring.

**EXPOSURE/CULTURE:** Best if located in full sun or partial shade. Tolerates a wide range of soils, including sandy soils. Moderate or less water requirements. Foliage often looks bad after winter exposure, so it is best to mow the plants to ground level in early spring.

**PEST PROBLEMS:** Scale

**SELECTED CULTIVARS:** None

**RELATED SPECIES:** Several shrub-like species exist. See Chapter 6—Dwarf Shrubs.

**LANDSCAPE NOTES:** Aaron's Beard is often used for erosion control, especially in naturalized sections of the garden. It is appropriate as a feature plant in small or large areas.

## *Iberis sempervirens*

**Evergreen Candytuft**

**ZONES:**
4, 5, 6, 7, 8, 9

**HEIGHT:**
8" to 12"

**WIDTH:**
1 1/2' to 2'

**FRUIT:**
1/4" silicle; NOT NOTICE-ABLE.

**TEXTURE:**
Fine in summer, more rugged in winter.

**GROWTH RATE:**
Moderate

**HABIT:**
Spreading into a rounded, thick mound.

**FAMILY:**
Cruciferae

**LEAF COLOR:** Dark green.

**LEAF DESCRIPTION:** SIMPLE, 1/2" to 2" long and 1/8" to 1/4" wide, linear or narrow oblong in shape with entire margins, ALTERNATE arrangement.

**FLOWER DESCRIPTION:** Tiny white flowers in very showy 1" diameter racemes, arising from lateral axils. Flowers in early spring and continues into summer.

**EXPOSURE/CULTURE:** Full sun or part shade. Should be planted in well-drained soil, as it will rot under wet conditions. Prefers medium fertility. Shape and compactness can be maintained with a minimum of shearing. Prune after flowering every two or three years.

**PEST PROBLEMS:** None

**SELECTED CULTIVARS:** 'Christmas Snow' - Blooms in both spring and fall. 'Little Gem' - Very low form, maturing at 6". 'October Glory' - Compact. Blooms in spring and fall. 'Snowflake' - Has stiffer stems than the species, making it more erect in habit.

**LANDSCAPE NOTES:** The compactness and mounded shape make this plant effective as a border plant in the garden. It does well in rock garden areas, and it has attractive foliage when it is not flowering. It provides good contrast when planted in mass with coarse-textured plants in the background.

# *Juniperus chinensis var. sargentii*

**Sargent Juniper**

**ZONES:**
4, 5, 6, 7, 8, 9

**HEIGHT:**
1′ to 1 1/2′

**WIDTH:**
7 1/2′ to 8′

**FRUIT:**
1/4″ cones; blue maturing to brown.

**TEXTURE:**
Fine

**GROWTH RATE:**
Moderate

**HABIT:**
Wide-spreading with long, whip-like branches that arch.

**FAMILY:**
Cupressaceae

**LEAF COLOR:** Blue-green

**LEAF DESCRIPTION:** 1/4″ SCALE-LIKE leaves, appearing in WHORLS of 3 on many branchlets, grooved on the underside.

**FLOWER DESCRIPTION:** Tiny yellowish flowers in spring. NOT ORNAMENTAL and NOT NOTICEABLE.

**EXPOSURE/CULTURE:** Prefers full sunlight. Adaptable to a wide range of conditions and soil types. Does remarkably well in dry, sandy soils. Grows best with moderate moisture, but survives better in dry soil than any other Juniper. Avoid wet soils. Prune to maintain shape.

**PEST PROBLEMS:** Bagworms, Juniper twig blight, scale insects, spider mites.

**SELECTED CULTIVARS:** 'Aureo-variegata' - Yellow variegation at tips of branchlets. 'Glauca' - Lower growing form with thinner leaves; more refined. 'Viridis' - Green Sargent Juniper. Has rich green foliage all year long.

**SPECIAL NOTE:** There are many cultivars of *J. chinensis*. Several appear in Chapters 7, 8, and 9.

**LANDSCAPE NOTES:** Sargent Juniper is a beautiful ground cover that is famous for its ability to thrive under extreme conditions. It is the gardener's answer to low-maintenance.

## *Juniperus conferta*

**Shore Juniper**

**ZONES:**
5, 6, 7, 8, 9

**HEIGHT:**
1 1/2' to 2'

**WIDTH:**
4' to 6'

**FRUIT:**
1/2" blue cones, maturing to blue-black.

**TEXTURE:**
Fine

**GROWTH RATE:**
Rapid, once established.

**HABIT:**
Spreading and bushy with upright branchlets.

**FAMILY:**
Cupressaceae

**LEAF COLOR:** Bright bluish-green all year round.

**LEAF DESCRIPTION:** 1/4" to 1/2" NEEDLE-LIKE leaves, awl-shaped and pointed. White groove on top surface.

**FLOWER DESCRIPTION:** INCONSPICUOUS

**EXPOSURE/CULTURE:** Best in full sun, but tolerates light shade. Grows in a wide range of soil types, including sand. Will not tolerate wet conditions. Pruning is not necessary except to confine to edge of border.

**PEST PROBLEMS:** Bagworms, canker, spider mites.

**SELECTED CULTIVARS:** 'Blue Pacific' - More compact. (Featured on the next page.) 'Compacta' - Very compact form with light green needles. 'Emerald Sea' - USDA introduction. Dense mat of erect stems and emerald green needles.

**LANDSCAPE NOTES:** Shore Juniper is a worthy plant for covering larger areas of ground. It roots along horizontal stems and forms a dense mat. It performs well in raised planters or pots. It drapes over walls - sometimes several feet, making a gorgeous display of foliage.

## *Juniperus conferta 'Blue Pacific'*     **Blue Pacific Juniper**

**ZONES:**
5, 6, 7, 8, 9

**HEIGHT:**
To 1′

**WIDTH:**
4′ to 5′

**FRUIT:**
1/2″ blue cone, maturing to blue-black.

**TEXTURE:**
Fine

**GROWTH RATE:**
Moderate

**HABIT:**
Low and spreading.

**FAMILY:**
Cupressaceae

**LEAF COLOR:** Blue-green, holding its color better than the species during winter.

**LEAF DESCRIPTION:** 1/4″ NEEDLE-LIKE leaves, awl-shaped and pointed, arranged in BUNDLES of 3.

**FLOWER DESCRIPTION:** INCONSPICUOUS

**EXPOSURE/CULTURE:** Best in full sun, but is tolerant of some shade. Grows in a wide range of soil types as long as it is well-drained. Requires less pruning than the species and is more hardy.

**PEST PROBLEMS:** Bagworms, canker, spider mites.

**SELECTED CULTIVARS:** None. This is a cultivar of *J. conferta,* worthy of emphasis.

**LANDSCAPE NOTES:** 'Blue Pacific' has become more popular than the species due to better color and greater hardiness. However, it is slower-growing than the species and this might be a primary consideration in selection.

# *Juniperus horizontalis 'Bar Harbor'*     **Bar Harbor Juniper**

**ZONES:**
3, 4, 5, 6, 7, 8, 9

**HEIGHT:**
8″ to 10″

**WIDTH:**
5′ to 6′

**FRUIT:**
1/4″ glaucous blue cones;
RARE.

**TEXTURE:**
Fine

**GROWTH RATE:**
Moderate

**HABIT:**
Low, spreading, procumbent,
and very dense.

**FAMILY:**
Cupressaceae

**LEAF COLOR:** Blue-green in summer, turning purplish in fall and winter.

**LEAF DESCRIPTION:** 1/6″ SCALE-LIKE leaves in OPPOSITE PAIRS on young shoots. 1/4″ AWL-LIKE needles in opposite pairs on older growth.

**FLOWER DESCRIPTION:** INCONSPICUOUS

**EXPOSURE/CULTURE:** Needs full sunlight. Grows well in many soil types and conditions, except wet or poorly drained soils. Grows well in alkaline soils, and requires a minimal level of fertility. Requires little, if any, pruning.

**PEST PROBLEMS:** Bagworms, Juniper twig blight, spider mites.

**RELATED CULTIVARS:** 'Blue Chip' - Slightly lower growing. Blue foliage has purple-tinged tips in winter. 'Blue Mat' - Grows to 6″ tall with dark purplish foliage in winter. 'Hughes' - Same size as 'Bar Harbor', but foliage has less purple tint in winter. 'Huntington Blue' - Intense blue-gray foliage that turns silvery-plum in winter.

**SPECIAL NOTE:** More *J. horizontalis* cultivars on the following pages.

**LANDSCAPE NOTES:** Bar Harbor Juniper is an excellent ground cover for sunny locations. It is preferred by many designers over 'Blue Rug' because it has more height and is more noticeable on flat ground.

## *Juniperus horizontalis 'Douglasii'* — Waukegan Juniper

**ZONES:**
3, 4, 5, 6, 7, 8, 9

**HEIGHT:**
12″ to 15″

**WIDTH:**
7′ to 8′

**FRUIT:**
NONE, usually.

**TEXTURE:**
Fine

**GROWTH RATE:**
Moderate

**HABIT:**
Trailing and wide-spreading.

**FAMILY:**
Cupressaceae

**LEAF COLOR:** Steel blue in summer; tinged purple in winter.

**LEAF DESCRIPTION:** 1/8″ to 1/5″ SCALES arranged in OPPOSITE PAIRS on new growth. Foliage appears more flattened than 'Plumosa'.

**FLOWER DESCRIPTION:** INCONSPICUOUS

**EXPOSURE/CULTURE:** Needs full sunlight. Can be grown in a wide range of soils and conditions. 'Douglasii' is especially useful in sandy soils. Pruning is sometimes necessary to contain or confine to planting borders.

**PEST PROBLEMS:** Bagworms, Juniper twig blight, spider mites.

**SELECTED CULTIVARS:** None. This is a cultivar. Has more in common with 'Plumosa' than the others.

**SPECIAL NOTE:** More *J. horizontalis* cultivars under the following section.

**LANDSCAPE NOTES:** Waukegan Juniper is one of the older cultivars. It has proven its usefulness for over a century, and it still outperforms many cultivars in sandy soils. Great for xeriscaping.

# *Juniperus horizontalis 'Plumosa'* — Andorra Juniper

▲ 'Plumosa Compacta'

**ZONES:**
3, 4, 5, 6, 7, 8

**HEIGHT:**
Around 2'

**WIDTH:**
7' to 8'

**FRUIT:**
NONE

**TEXTURE:**
Fine

**GROWTH RATE:**
Moderately rapid.

**HABIT:**
Wide-spreading and dense.

**FAMILY:**
Cupressaceae

**LEAF COLOR:** Grayish-green in summer; plum-purple in winter.

**LEAF DESCRIPTION:** 1/6" SCALES arranged in OPPOSITE PAIRS on younger shoots; 1/4" awl-like needles on older growth.

**FLOWER DESCRIPTION:** INCONSPICUOUS

**EXPOSURE/CULTURE:** Needs full sunlight. Grows well in any soil, except poorly drained soils. Will thrive with little, if any, chemical fertilizer. The plant sometimes needs pruning to control long, horizontal branches.

**PEST PROBLEMS:** Bagworms, Juniper twig blight, spider mites.

**RELATED CULTIVARS:** 'Plumosa Compacta' - More compact form, 12" to 18" tall and very dense. 'Youngstown' - Compact habit with bright green foliage that assumes a slight bronze-purple tinge in winter. 'Winter Blue' - Foliage is lighter green and becomes a vivid blue in winter.

**SPECIAL NOTE:** More *J. horizontalis* cultivars follow this listing.

**LANDSCAPE NOTES:** Andorra Juniper is a widely used ground cover that is a proven performer under a variety of conditions. The winter color is very noticeable, but may not combine well with red structures in the landscape.

## *Juniperus horizontalis 'Prince of Wales'*

**Prince Of Wales Juniper**

**ZONES:**
3, 4, 5, 6, 7, 8

**HEIGHT:**
5" to 6"

**WIDTH:**
3' to 4'

**FRUIT:**
NONE

**TEXTURE:**
Fine

**GROWTH RATE:**
Moderately rapid.

**HABIT:**
Low and spreading with uniform "starburst" pattern.

**FAMILY:**
Cupressaceae

**LEAF COLOR:** Bright green and glaucous; assumes a slight purple tinge in winter.

**LEAF DESCRIPTION:** 1/6" SCALES arranged in OPPOSITE PAIRS on new growth, becoming more needle-like with age.

**FLOWER DESCRIPTION:** INCONSPICUOUS

**EXPOSURE/CULTURE:** Needs full sunlight. Adapts very well to a wide range of conditions, similar to most Junipers. Responds to moderate fertilization. Requires almost no pruning due to superior radial symmetry.

**PEST PROBLEMS:** Bagworms, Juniper twig blight, spider mites.

**RELATED CULTIVARS:** 'Alberta' - Very similar to 'Prince of Wales'.

**LANDSCAPE NOTES:** Prince of Wales Juniper is one of the hardiest Juniper cultivars. The plant is noted for its consistently radial pattern of growth. A truly outstanding cultivar.

## *Juniperus horizontalis 'Wiltonii'*      **Blue Rug Juniper**

**ZONES:**
3, 4, 5, 6, 7, 8, 9

**HEIGHT:**
3″ to 6″

**WIDTH:**
4′ to 6′

**FRUIT:**
1/4″ to 1/3″ blue cone; NOT COMMON.

**TEXTURE:**
Fine

**GROWTH RATE:**
Moderate

**HABIT:**
Prostrate and dense; branches occasionally root.

**FAMILY:**
Cupressaceae

**LEAF COLOR:** Silvery-blue foliage that assumes a slight purplish tinge in winter.

**LEAF DESCRIPTION:** 1/8″ to 1/6″ SCALE-LIKE leaves arranged in OPPOSITE PAIRS. Scales are closely pressed to the stem, especially on younger shoots.

**FLOWER DESCRIPTION:** INCONSPICUOUS

**EXPOSURE/CULTURE:** Must have full sun. The plant is adaptable to a wide range of well-drained soil types. Requires little, if any, pruning. Because of its low habit, weeds may be a problem until a solid mat is achieved.

**PEST PROBLEMS:** Bagworms, Juniper twig blight, spider mites.

**RELATED CULTIVARS:** None. This is a cultivar of *J. horizontalis*.

**LANDSCAPE NOTES:** Blue Rug certainly lives up to its name, as it gives the appearance of a carpet in the landscape. It is especially useful for erosion control on slopes, banks, and berms. Its popularity is enhanced by good year-round foliage and low-maintenance qualities, once established. Rocks and boulders look nice in Blue Rug plantings.

# *Juniperus procumbens*

## Japanese Garden Juniper

**ZONES:**
4, 5, 6, 7, 8, 9

**HEIGHT:**
1 1/2' to 2'

**WIDTH:**
8' to 10'

**FRUIT:**
1/4" cone; NOT COMMON.

**TEXTURE:**
Fine

**GROWTH RATE:**
Moderate

**HABIT:**
Low-spreading with ascending tips.

**FAMILY:**
Cupressaceae

**LEAF COLOR:** Light, blue-green all year.

**LEAF DESCRIPTION:** 1/4" to 1/3" NEEDLE-LIKE leaves arranged in IRREGULAR CLUSTERS of 3. Each needle has a visible midrib near the tip. Upper surface of needle is concave, while the lower surface is convex.

**FLOWER DESCRIPTION:** Tiny, green; NOT NOTICEABLE.

**EXPOSURE/CULTURE:** Needs full sunlight. The plant will thrive under a wide range of conditions and soil types. Does not thrive well in poorly drained or wet soils. Pruning is minimal.

**PEST PROBLEMS:** Juniper twig blight, two-spotted mites.

**SELECTED CULTIVARS:** 'Nana' - Much shorter and more compact. (Featured on the next page.) 'Variegata' - Same growth habit as species. Branches alternate with blue-green and lemon yellow foliage.

**LANDSCAPE NOTES:** Japanese Garden Juniper grows more densely than most Juniper species. It has diverse possibilities in the landscape, and it responds well to shearing. Often overlooked by designers because of the seemingly endless development of *J. horizontalis* cultivars.

## *Juniperus procumbens 'Nana'*     Dwarf Japgarden Juniper

**ZONES:**
4, 5, 6, 7, 8, 9

**HEIGHT:**
4″ to 6″

**WIDTH:**
8′ to 10′

**FRUIT:**
NONE, usually.

**TEXTURE:**
Fine

**GROWTH RATE:**
Slow

**HABIT:**
Spreading dense mat; mounding in center of plant.

**FAMILY:**
Cupressaceae

**LEAF COLOR:** Bluish-green during all seasons.

**LEAF DESCRIPTION:** 1/8″ to 1/4″ AWL-SHAPED NEEDLES that are both shorter and thicker than the species. Upper surface is concave, while the lower surface is convex. Midrib is visible.

**FLOWER DESCRIPTION:** INCONSPICUOUS

**EXPOSURE/CULTURE:** Needs full sun. Tolerates most well-drained soils and will grow in slightly acid to alkaline soils. Responds well to pruning.

**PEST PROBLEMS:** Juniper twig blight, two-spotted mites.

**SELECTED CULTIVARS:** None. This is a cultivar, worthy of emphasis.

**LANDSCAPE NOTES:** Dwarf Japgarden Juniper forms a spectacular mass of light blue-green foliage. Little mounds interrupt the flat nature of the plant, giving it a very different and noticeable effect in the landscape. Its beauty is enhanced when used on rolling terrain, especially berms. Absolutely one of the best low-growing Junipers.

## *Juniperus squamata 'Blue Star'*  **Blue Star Juniper**

**ZONES:**
4, 5, 6, 7, 8

**HEIGHT:**
2 1/2' to 3'

**WIDTH:**
4' to 5'

**FRUIT:**
1/4" black cone; NOT COMMON.

**TEXTURE:**
Fine

**GROWTH RATE:**
Somewhat slow.

**HABIT:**
Forms a spreading mound.

**FAMILY:**
Cupressaceae

**LEAF COLOR:** Rich steel-blue during all seasons.

**LEAF DESCRIPTION:** 1/8" to 1/6" AWL-SHAPED SCALES, arranged in irregular CLUSTERS of 3. Pointed tips.

**FLOWER DESCRIPTION:** Greenish, INCONSPICUOUS.

**EXPOSURE/CULTURE:** Full sun. Adaptable to a wide range of well-drained soils. Can tolerate hot, dry conditions, but cannot take high humidity. Not especially good for the southeast. Requires very little pruning.

**PEST PROBLEMS:** Juniper twig blight, spider mites.

**RELATED CULTIVARS:** 'Blue Carpet' - Lower-growing form to 1'. Silvery-blue foliage.

**LANDSCAPE NOTES:** Blue Star Juniper is a specimen plant with striking foliage when grown under favorable conditions. The steel-blue needles at the tips give the impression of twinkling stars. It is a plant to feature and probably inappropriate for covering large expanses, where other Juniper species might prove superior.

## *Liriope muscari* — Lilyturf, Lirio, Liriope

▲ 'Monroe's White'

▲ 'Majestic'

**ZONES:**
6, 7, 8, 9

**HEIGHT:**
12″ to 15″

**WIDTH:**
12″ to 18″

**FRUIT:**
1/8″ black berries in fall.

**TEXTURE:**
Fine to medium.

**GROWTH RATE:**
Moderate

**HABIT:**
Clump-forming, grass-like, and pendulous.

**FAMILY:**
Liliaceae

**LEAF COLOR:** Dark green; developing brown tinge in winter.

**LEAF DESCRIPTION:** SIMPLE, 12″ to 18″ long and 1/2″ wide, arranged in WHORLS arising from the crown. Grass-like with parallel veins.

**FLOWER DESCRIPTION:** Lilac, lavender, purple, or white blooms, depending on cultivar, clustered on 4″ or taller spikes that rise slightly above the foliage. Flowers in August and September.

**EXPOSURE/CULTURE:** Sun or shade. Adaptable to a wide range of conditions. Mow to ground in late winter to remove older leaves. Produces abundant new foliage in early spring.

**PEST PROBLEMS:** No serious pests.

**SELECTED CULTIVARS:** 'Big Blue' - Lavender-blue spikes. One of the most popular cultivars. 'Majestic' - Deep, large, lavender coxcomb spikes. Requires more shade than the species. 'Monroe's White' - White flower spikes. Must be grown in shade. 'Royal Purple' - Deep purple flower spikes. 'Webster Wideleaf' - Leaves to 1″ wide. Lavender spikes; not as profuse as other cultivars.

**LANDSCAPE NOTES:** This is a carefree plant that is quite handsome during flowering and fruiting. Clumps may be divided and planted elsewhere in the garden. It has been used extensively along walks and in shrub borders, but is being used more in massed plantings.

## *Liriope muscari 'Variegata'*  Variegated Lilyturf, Variegated Liriope

**ZONES:**
6, 7, 8, 9

**HEIGHT:**
12″ to 15″

**WIDTH:**
12″ to 18″

**FRUIT:**
1/8″ black berries in fall.

**TEXTURE:**
Fine to medium.

**GROWTH RATE:**
Slow to moderate.

**HABIT:**
Grass-like and pendulous.

**FAMILY:**
Liliaceae

**LEAF COLOR:** Green with yellow stripes. Yellow less brilliant in winter.

**LEAF DESCRIPTION:** SIMPLE, 12″ to 18″ long and 1/2″ wide, arranged in WHORLS, arising from base. Grass-like, having parallel veins.

**FLOWER DESCRIPTION:** Tall spikes of lavender-purple flowers in August and September.

**EXPOSURE/CULTURE:** Best in shade; however, it can be grown in sun. It is tolerant of a wide range of conditions. Mow to ground in late winter; new growth will show more vivid color.

**PEST PROBLEMS:** No serious pests.

**SIMILAR CULTIVARS:** 'Gold Banded' - Leaves green with gold margins. Large lavender spikes. 'John Burch' - Leaves green with yellow margins. Large lavender spikes. 'Sunproof' - More adaptable to harsh conditions, such as parking lots. The most sun tolerant Lilyturf.

**SPECIAL NOTE:** This plant is often confused with *Ophiopogon jaburan* 'Vittata', which has much shorter, almost hidden, flower spikes.

**LANDSCAPE NOTES:** As with any variegated plant, location of the plant should be carefully planned. Variegated Lilyturf makes a bold statement in the landscape. Be careful not to overuse this one.

# *Liriope spicata*

**Creeping Lilyturf**

▲ 'Silver Dragon'

**ZONES:**
6, 7, 8, 9

**HEIGHT:**
10″ to 12″

**WIDTH:**
Indefinite

**FRUIT:**
1/8″ black berries on spikes in fall.

**TEXTURE:**
Fine

**GROWTH RATE:**
Usually rapid.

**HABIT:**
Non-clumping, pendulous; spreads by underground suckers.

**FAMILY:**
Liliaceae

**LEAF COLOR:** Medium to dark green; brownish tinge in winter.

**LEAF DESCRIPTION:** SIMPLE, 14″ to 16″ long and 1/4″ to 1/3″ wide, WHORLED at base of clump, grass-like with parallel veins.

**FLOWER DESCRIPTION:** Tiny, light lilac flowers on 2″ to 3″ spikes that rise slightly above the foliage. Flowers in August and September. Not as spectacular in flower as *Liriope muscari*.

**EXPOSURE/CULTURE:** Does best in part shade, but tolerates sun if not too intense. Grows well in any good soil and is tolerant of either moist or dry soils. Will sucker faster under moist conditions. Can be confined by steel, concrete, brick, or other edging which is at least 12″ to 18″ deep.

**PEST PROBLEMS:** No serious pests. Scale has been reported in the southeast.

**SELECTED CULTIVARS:** 'Silver Dragon' - Silver-white striping on leaves. Whitish-green berries in fall. Outstanding.

**LANDSCAPE NOTES:** This non-clump-forming species is especially appropriate for covering large areas in the landscape. It is ideal for erosion control on sloping areas. It is a finer textured plant than *Liriope muscari,* and gives a more uniform appearance since it doesn't form clumps. However, the blooms are not as noticeable. It must be confined as described above. This is an excellent ground cover that effectively controls weeds, once established.

## *Mahonia repens*

**Creeping Mahonia**

**ZONES:**
5, 6, 7, 8

**HEIGHT:**
10″ to 12″

**WIDTH:**
Indefinite

**FRUIT:**
1/4″ black berries in clusters in fall.

**TEXTURE:**
Coarse

**GROWTH RATE:**
Somewhat slow.

**HABIT:**
Stiff, spreading by underground stolons.

**FAMILY:**
Berberidaceae

**LEAF COLOR:** Dull blue-green in summer, turning purple in winter.

**LEAF DESCRIPTION:** COMPOUND leaves with 3 to 7 leaflets. Leaflets are 1 1/2″ to 3″ long and 1″ to 2″ long. Leaflets have long ovate shape with holly-like spinose margins. Compound leaves are ALTERNATE in arrangement.

**FLOWER DESCRIPTION:** Tiny, six-petaled, deep yellow flowers, clustered on 2″ to 3″ racemes during spring, usually April through June.

**EXPOSURE/CULTURE:** Needs partial shade to prevent sunburn in winter. Will grow in well-drained soil, preferably moist and organic. Tends to do better in acid soils. Pruning is minimal to remove unsightly foliage in spring.

**PEST PROBLEMS:** No serious pests.

**SELECTED CULTIVARS:** None

**RELATED SPECIES:** *M. nervosa* - Cascades Mahonia. This is more shrub-like, to a height of 2′. More prone to burning than is *M. repens.*

**LANDSCAPE NOTES:** Creeping Mahonia is well-suited for naturalizing or as a rock garden plant.

## *Microbiota decussata*        Siberian Carpet Cypress

Courtesy Monrovia Nursery Co.

**ZONES:**
2, 3, 4, 5, 6, 7, 8

**HEIGHT:**
10″ to 14″

**WIDTH:**
6′ to 12′

**FRUIT:**
Small naked seed; NOT COMMON.

**TEXTURE:**
Fine

**GROWTH RATE:**
Slow to moderate.

**HABIT:**
Low and wide-spreading with pendulous branches.

**FAMILY:**
Cupressaceae

**LEAF COLOR:** Rich green in summer, turning copper to bronze in winter.

**LEAF DESCRIPTION:** Tiny, AWL-SHAPED needles held tightly on branchlets; branchlets are flattened and lacy, forming sprays that are very ornamental.

**FLOWER DESCRIPTION:** NOT NOTICEABLE.

**EXPOSURE/CULTURE:** Full sun or partial shade. Unlike most conifers, it actually performs exceptionally in shade. Survives well in most well-drained soils. Virtually maintenance-free.

**PEST PROBLEMS:** None

**SELECTED CULTIVARS:** None

**LANDSCAPE NOTES:** The plant gives a Juniper-like appearance in the garden. The plant was discovered in Soviet Siberia, and it is one of the hardiest of all landscape plants. The foliage reminds one of the coniferous sprays used in floral arrangements. Although it is low-growing like the dwarf Junipers, its foliage is more similar to that of Arborvitae.

## *Ophiopogon japonicus*

**Mondo Grass, Monkey Grass**

**ZONES:**
7, 8, 9

**HEIGHT:**
6″ to 10″

**WIDTH:**
Indefinite

**FRUIT:**
1/8″ blue-black berries in fall.

**TEXTURE:**
Fine

**GROWTH RATE:**
Moderate to rapid.

**HABIT:**
Spreading, pendulous, and grass-like. Forms a very dense mat.

**FAMILY:**
Liliaceae

**LEAF COLOR:** Deep green, taking on a slight brown tint in winter.

**LEAF DESCRIPTION:** SIMPLE, 10″ to 12″ long and 1/8″ to 1/6″ wide; arranged in WHORLS arising from grass-like clumps. Parallel veins. Spreads by stolons.

**FLOWER DESCRIPTION:** Pale lilac flowers on 1″ to 2″ spikes in late summer. Spikes are mostly hidden by the foliage.

**EXPOSURE/CULTURE:** Grows in sun or shade, but best in shade. Does well in most well-drained soils. Tends to prefer organic soil where average moisture is maintained. Provide a 12″ deep steel, concrete, or brick edging to prevent suckering into lawn areas. Mow in late winter to eliminate old growth.

**PEST PROBLEMS:** No serious pests. Rabbits have been known to nibble the foliage.

**SELECTED CULTIVARS:** 'Nanus' - Dwarf Mondo. Very low-growing with leaves only 3″ to 5″ long. 'Variegatus' - Foliage has green and white stripes. White flowers.

**LANDSCAPE NOTES:** Mondo Grass provides excellent erosion control, once established. The plant is much more refined in appearance than Lilyturf. It grows extremely densely and loses the clump-like characteristics when mature. It is often used as a border for planting beds, but is very attractive in mass, especially under trees or in well-defined planting beds.

## *Pachysandra procumbens*     **Alleghany Pachysandra**

**ZONES:**
4, 5, 6, 7, 8, 9

**HEIGHT:**
10″ to 12″

**WIDTH:**
Indefinite

**FRUIT:**
Small capsule; NOT ORNA-
MENTAL.

**TEXTURE:**
Medium

**GROWTH RATE:**
Slow to moderate.

**HABIT:**
Low-growing and dense;
spreads by rhizomes.

**FAMILY:**
Buxaceae

**LEAF COLOR:** Grayish-green

**LEAF DESCRIPTION:** SIMPLE, 3″ long and 2″ wide, obovate shape with coarsely toothed margins (dentate) toward the tip and smooth (entire) near the base. ALTERNATE arrangement.

**FLOWER DESCRIPTION:** White or purplish flowers on 3″ spikes that arise from the base of the stem. Flowers in early spring.

**EXPOSURE/CULTURE:** Grows in full shade or part shade. Adaptable to a wide range of soil types, but prefers organic soil that is well-drained. Needs protection in northernmost zones to remain evergreen. May need containment, since it spreads by underground stems.

**PEST PROBLEMS:** No serious pests.

**SELECTED CULTIVARS:** None

**LANDSCAPE NOTES:** Alleghany Pachysandra is an excellent ground cover for shaded areas. It is not as refined as *P. terminalis,* but combines nice foliage with coarse texture to add variety in the landscape.

# *Pachysandra terminalis*

**Japanese Spurge**

▲ 'Silver Edge'

**ZONES:**
4, 5, 6, 7, 8

**HEIGHT:**
6″ to 10″

**WIDTH:**
Indefinite

**FRUIT:**
1/3″ white drupe; NOT ORNA-MENTAL.

**TEXTURE:**
Fine to medium.

**GROWTH RATE:**
Somewhat slow.

**HABIT:**
Erect stems, low-growing, spreading by rhizomes into a dense mat.

**FAMILY:**
Buxaceae

**LEAF COLOR:** Olive-green

**LEAF DESCRIPTION:** SIMPLE, 1 1/2″ to 2 1/2″ long and 1″ wide, obovate shape with dentate margins from middle to tip, entire at base. ALTERNATE arrangement.

**FLOWER DESCRIPTION:** Small, creamy white on 1 1/2″ to 2″ terminal spikes; not especially showy. Flowers in early spring.

**EXPOSURE/CULTURE:** Needs shade. Prefers well-drained organic soils. Needs a moderate amount of moisture to perform well. Looks sickly yellow when allowed too much sun. Easier to contain than most suckering ground covers.

**PEST PROBLEMS:** Stem rot, scale, mites, nematodes.

**SELECTED CULTIVARS:** 'Green Carpet' - Wider leaves that are deeper green in color. Flowers more profusely. 'Variegata' - Sometimes listed as 'Silver Edge'. Green leaf with white margins.

**LANDSCAPE NOTES:** Japanese Spurge is one of the more attractive ground covers when conditions are optimal. I have seen large areas suffering from too much sun. The fleshy stems are easily crushed, so the plants should not be located adjacent to foot traffic. Outdoor pets, especially dogs, can hinder the plant. This is a gourmet plant for the avid gardener.

## *Phlox subulata*

**Moss Pink, Thrift**

**ZONES:**
3, 4, 5, 6, 7, 8, 9

**HEIGHT:**
4″ to 6″

**WIDTH:**
Indefinite

**FRUIT:**
3-valved capsule; NOT ORNA-MENTAL.

**TEXTURE:**
Fine

**GROWTH RATE:**
Moderate

**HABIT:**
Low, spreading mounds, rooting along the stems.

**FAMILY:**
Polemoniaceae

**LEAF COLOR:** Light to yellowish-green.

**LEAF DESCRIPTION:** Leaves to 1″ long and 1/4″ wide, AWL-SHAPED and needle-like, pointed, crowded along the stems, OPPOSITE arrangement. Leaves near the tip may be alternate.

**FLOWER DESCRIPTION:** White, pink, red, blue, or purple, depending on the cultivar. Flowers are 3/4″ wide and have 5 petals, sepal lobes, and stamens. Flowers profusely in early spring.

**EXPOSURE/CULTURE:** Needs full sun. Grows well in any well-drained soil, but does best in sandy soils. Will thrive in hot, dry locations. Not demanding as to fertility, but avoid high rates wherever possible. Weeds may present a problem. Divide (thin) every 3 to 5 years.

**PEST PROBLEMS:** Red spider mite has been reported.

**SELECTED CULTIVARS:** 'Alba' - White flowers. 'Alexander's Pink' - Pink flowers. 'Blue Emerald' - Blue flowers. Blooms over a longer period. 'Blue Hills' - Sky blue flowers. 'Millstream Daphne' - Pink flowers with a yellow "eye". 'Red Wings' - Crimson red flowers with dark red centers. 'Scarlet Flame' - Bright scarlet flowers. 'White Delight' - Abundant, pure white flowers.

**RELATED VARIETIES:** var. *atropurpurea* - Purple flowers.

**LANDSCAPE NOTES:** This is an outstanding ground cover for rock gardens, draping over walls, low borders, and massing.

## *Rosa pimpinellifolia 'Petite Pink'*  Petite Pink Rose

**ZONES:**
5, 6, 7, 8

**HEIGHT:**
2' to 3'

**WIDTH:**
3' to 5'

**FRUIT:**
Black hip with hairy achenes.

**TEXTURE:**
Fine, lacy foliage.

**GROWTH RATE:**
Moderate to rapid.

**HABIT:**
Dense and mounded; tips may root.

**FAMILY:**
Rosaceae

**LEAF COLOR:** Bright green.

**LEAF DESCRIPTION:** COMPOUND, 5 to 9 leaflets, 1/2″ to 3/4″ long and 1/3″ to 1/2″ wide, leaflets ovate with serrated margins, ALTERNATE arrangement. Stems or canes may have spines.

**FLOWER DESCRIPTION:** Pink, 1/2″ to 1″, double, fading to white. Flowers in spring for approximately 3 weeks.

**EXPOSURE/CULTURE:** Full sun or light shade. Adaptable to a wide range of soils from clay to sand. Drought-resistant and salt-resistant. Pruning should be done after flowering. It may be sheared heavily to keep compact.

**PEST PROBLEMS:** No serious pests.

**SELECTED CULTIVARS:** None

**SPECIAL NOTE:** At this writing, authorities disagree as to the species for this plant. Some attribute the plant to *R. pimpinellifolia,* while others place it in *R. wichuraiana.*

**LANDSCAPE NOTES:** 'Petite Pink' is an outstanding ground cover for adverse conditions in sunny exposures. It is especially effective on sloping banks, and can be used to stabilize sand dunes in coastal areas. Evergreen to around 15 degrees. This plant should be more widely used in both commercial and residential landscapes. Great for xeriscaping!

## *Santolina chamaecyparissus*    Lavender Cotton, Silver Santolina

**ZONES:**
7, 8, 9

**HEIGHT:**
1′ to 1 1/2′

**WIDTH:**
3 1/2′ to 4′

**FRUIT:**
1/2″ brown pod; NOT ATTRACTIVE.

**TEXTURE:**
Fine

**GROWTH RATE:**
Moderate

**HABIT:**
Thick, spreading mound.

**FAMILY:**
Compositae

**LEAF COLOR:** Silver-green to gray-green.

**LEAF DESCRIPTION:** Leaves 1/2″ to 1″ long and 1/8″ wide, PINNATELY COMPOUND with tiny leaflets, ALTERNATE arrangement. Highly aromatic foliage when crushed.

**FLOWER DESCRIPTION:** 1/2″ button-like flowers, bright yellow and very showy, rising several inches above the foliage. Quite attractive before flowers die. Flowers in June.

**EXPOSURE/CULTURE:** Plant in full sun. Tolerant of any well-drained soil, but prefers loamy to sandy soils. Will not stand frequent waterings as the plant will rot and become loose in habit. Flower heads should be removed after they fade. Great plant for shearing.

**PEST PROBLEMS:** Can develop fungus problems where moisture is high or during damp, humid weather.

**SELECTED CULTIVARS:** 'Nana' - Similar to species, but slower growing. Matures at 10″ to 12″.

**LANDSCAPE NOTES:** Lavender Cotton should be considered for its silvery foliage effect, as well as its attractive blooms. It does especially well in rock garden settings and in raised planters. It can be used in foundation plantings so long as it does not receive frequent waterings. Provides great foliage effect against dark backgrounds.

## *Santolina virens*

**Green Santolina**

**ZONES:**
7, 8, 9

**HEIGHT:**
1' to 1 1/2'

**WIDTH:**
3 1/2' to 4'

**FRUIT:**
1/2" brown pod; NOT ORNA-MENTAL.

**TEXTURE:**
Fine.

**GROWTH RATE:**
Moderate

**HABIT:**
Thick, spreading mound.

**FAMILY:**
Compositae

**LEAF COLOR:** Deep emerald green, sometimes turning brownish in winter.

**LEAF DESCRIPTION:** 1 1/2" to 2" long and 1/16" to 1/8" wide, PINNATELY COMPOUND with tiny leaflets, ALTERNATE arrangement. Highly aromatic foliage when crushed.

**FLOWER DESCRIPTION:** 1/2" button-like flowers, bright yellow, rising several inches above the foliage. Starts flowering in June.

**EXPOSURE/CULTURE:** Plant in full sun. Tolerant of any well-drained soil, but prefers loamy to sandy soils. Will not stand frequent waterings as the plant will rot and become loose in habit. Flower heads should be removed after flowering when they begin to turn brown. Responds well to shearing.

**PEST PROBLEMS:** Fungus rot when moisture is high or during long periods of rain or high humidity.

**SELECTED CULTIVARS:** None

**LANDSCAPE NOTES:** This plant is similar in many ways to Lavender Cotton, but has larger leaves and a radically different color. It does well in rock gardens, raised planters, and foundation plantings. It is often used as a border plant or a low hedge. Like Lavender Cotton, it cannot be watered with the same frequency as many other plants. This is an old "standby" that Grandma will remember.

## *Sarcococca hookerana var. humilis*     Himalayan Sweet Box

**ZONES:**
6, 7, 8, 9

**HEIGHT:**
12″ to 15″

**WIDTH:**
Around 2′

**FRUIT:**
1/4″ black drupe; NOT ORNA-MENTAL.

**TEXTURE:**
Medium

**GROWTH RATE:**
Slow

**HABIT:**
Loose, informal mound. Spreads slowly by stolons.

**FAMILY:**
Buxaceae

**LEAF COLOR:** Dark green and glossy.

**LEAF DESCRIPTION:** SIMPLE, 1 1/2″ to 2″ long and 3/4″ wide; narrow elliptic shape with entire margins. ALTERNATE arrangement.

**FLOWER DESCRIPTION:** 1/4″ white flowers, fragrant, arising from the axils of leaves. Mostly inconspicuous, except for fragrance.

**EXPOSURE/CULTURE:** Needs part shade to full shade. Will not prosper in full sun. Prefers organic, moist, well-drained soil. Partial to acid soil. May need light annual pruning to remove dead wood or to shape.

**PEST PROBLEMS:** None

**SELECTED CULTIVARS:** None

**RELATED SPECIES:** *S. ruscifolia* - Fragrant Sarcococca. Grows 2′ to 3′ tall and is less cold hardy than Himalayan Sweet Box (zones 6, 7). Noticeable red drupes.

**LANDSCAPE NOTES:** Himalayan Sweet Box is noted for its fragrance and informal appearance. It deserves a prominent, well-chosen location. Not a good choice for maintenance-free landscapes.

# Vinca major

**Big Periwinkle**

▲ 'Variegata'

**ZONES:**
4, 5, 6, 7, 8, 9

**HEIGHT:**
12" to 18"

**WIDTH:**
Indefinite

**FRUIT:**
None

**TEXTURE:**
Medium

**GROWTH RATE:**
Rapid

**HABIT:**
Upright, spreading stems that root along the ground.

**FAMILY:**
Apocynaceae

**LEAF COLOR:** Dark green.

**LEAF DESCRIPTION:** SIMPLE, 2" to 3" long and 1" to 1 1/2" wide, ovate shape with entire margins, OPPOSITE arrangement. Sometimes cordate (heart-shaped).

**FLOWER DESCRIPTION:** 1 1/2" to 2", light blue, five-petaled. Flowers in early spring. Abundant and attractive.

**EXPOSURE/CULTURE:** Grows in sun or shade. Will thrive in almost any soil type, but is partial to moist, organic soils. Usually requires moderate pruning to confine to bed areas. Does not like hot, dry conditions.

**PEST PROBLEMS:** Leaf blight, leaf gall, dieback.

**SELECTED CULTIVARS:** 'Variegata' - Green leaves with creamy markings. Sometimes reverts to solid green.

**LANDSCAPE NOTES:** Big Periwinkle has larger leaves and flowers than *V. minor*, and tolerates more sun. It is probably more suitable for covering large areas or for erosion control. This plant grows too fast to use in small areas of the landscape.

## *Vinca minor*

**Common Periwinkle, Cemetary Vine**

▲ 'Alba'

**ZONES:**
4, 5, 6, 7, 8, 9

**HEIGHT:**
4″ to 6″

**WIDTH:**
Indefinite

**FRUIT:**
Follicle; NOT COMMON.

**TEXTURE:**
Fine

**GROWTH RATE:**
Moderate to rapid.

**HABIT:**
Low and spreading; stems rooting along the ground.

**FAMILY:**
Apocynaceae

**LEAF COLOR:** Glossy dark green.

**LEAF DESCRIPTION:** SIMPLE, 1″ to 1 1/4″ long and 1/2″ wide, ovate shape with entire margins. OPPOSITE arrangement.

**FLOWER DESCRIPTION:** 1″ lilac-blue, 5-petaled, funnel-shaped with spreading petals. Flowers in early spring. Flower color varies among the cultivars.

**EXPOSURE/CULTURE:** Grows best in shade or part shade. Tolerant of many soil types, but prefers moist organic soils of medium fertility. Does not require as much pruning as *V. major*.

**PEST PROBLEMS:** Blight, leaf gall, stem canker, dieback.

**SELECTED CULTIVARS:** 'Alba' - Similar to above, but with pure white flowers. 'Atropurpurea' - Deep purple flowers. Very showy. 'Bowles' - Clumping habit and less spreading; lavender-blue flowers. 'Jekyll's White' - White flowers. 'Sterling Silver' - Green leaves with cream colored margins.

**LANDSCAPE NOTES:** Common Periwinkle is suitable for large areas, and is more suitable for smaller areas than Big Periwinkle. Looks good under trees, especially Dogwood and other small trees. Great for naturalizing.

## *Epimedium x versicolor* 'Sulphureum' — **Yellow Barrenwort**

**ZONES:**
4, 5, 6, 7, 8

**HEIGHT:**
10″ to 12″

**WIDTH:**
Indefinite

**FRUIT:**
NONE

**TEXTURE:**
Somewhat coarse.

**GROWTH RATE:**
Moderate to slow.

**HABIT:**
Dense and upright.

**FAMILY:**
Berberidaceae

**LEAF COLOR:** Green in summer; brown and ragged during winter.

**LEAF DESCRIPTION:** COMPOUND leaf, biternate with 3 divisions, each division having 3 leaflets. Leaflets 2″ to 3″ long, cordate in shape with serrated margins, WHORLED arrangement from the base.

**FLOWER DESCRIPTION:** Bright yellow, 3/4″ to 1″ long, 4 spur-like petals surrounded by 4 pale yellow inner sepals that serve as petals. Flowers in spring on new growth.

**EXPOSURE/CULTURE:** Needs part shade to deep shade. Soil should be well-drained, moist, and highly organic. Will not tolerate dry soils. Annual fertilization is recommended when grown under trees. May require some maintenace to confine. Prune in late winter to remove dead growth.

**PEST PROBLEMS:** None, except occasional attack by chewing insects.

**SELECTED CULTIVARS:** None. This is a cultivar of *E.* x *versicolor,* which has red-mottled leaves and flowers.

**RELATED SPECIES:** *E. pinnatum* - Has green foliage, 1/2″ to 1/4″ flowers are red-brown with bright yellow inner sepals. A parent of *E.* x *versicolor. E. grandiflorum* - Foliage is red in spring and bronze in fall. Flowers are violet with red inner sepals, 1″ to 2″ long. A parent of *E.* x *versicolor.*

**LANDSCAPE NOTES:** Barrenwort is an outstanding ground cover for naturalizing under woodland trees and for rock gardens. HERBACEOUS PERENNIAL.

## *Epimedium x youngianum*

**Young's Barrenwort**

**ZONES:**
5, 6, 7, 8

**HEIGHT:**
10" to 12"

**WIDTH:**
Indefinite

**FRUIT:**
NONE

**TEXTURE:**
Somewhat coarse.

**GROWTH RATE:**
Moderate to slow.

**HABIT:**
Dense and upright; spreading by rhizomes.

**FAMILY:**
Berberidaceae

**LEAF COLOR:** Green in season, bronze in spring, and reddish in fall.

**LEAF DESCRIPTION:** COMPOUND leaf, biternate with 3 divisions, each having 3 leaflets. Leaflets 2" to 3" long, cordate shape with serrated margins, WHORLED arrangement arising from the base of the plant.

**FLOWER DESCRIPTION:** White or rose, 1/2" to 3/4" long; pendulous. Flowers in spring on new growth.

**EXPOSURE/CULTURE:** Needs light shade to deep shade. Soil should be well-drained, moist, and highly organic. Will not tolerate dry soils. Fertilization is important when grown under trees. Plants may require some maintenance to confine. Prune in late winter to remove ragged growth.

**PEST PROBLEMS:** No serious pests. Sometimes bothered by chewing insects.

**SELECTED CULTIVARS:** 'Niveum' - Flowers pure white. 'Roseum' - Flowers rose-lilac in color.

**LANDSCAPE NOTES:** Barrenwort is an ideal ground cover for use under trees in shaded gardens, and it makes a nice plant for use in rock gardens and hillside gardens. HERBACEOUS PERENNIAL.

## *Hemerocallis hybrida*

**Hybrid Daylily**

**ZONES:**
4, 5, 6, 7, 8, 9

**HEIGHT:**
1′ to 4′ depending on cultivar.

**WIDTH:**
3′ to 4′ or more.

**FRUIT:**
Dehiscent capsule; NOT ORNAMENTAL.

**TEXTURE:**
Medium to coarse.

**GROWTH RATE:**
Somewhat rapid.

**HABIT:**
Clump-forming, arched leaves; spreading by rhizomes. Very vigorous.

**FAMILY:**
Ranunculaceae

**LEAF COLOR:** Varies from green to gray-green to blue-green depending on the cultivar.

**LEAF DESCRIPTION:** SIMPLE, 1′ to 4′ long and 1/2″ to 1 1/2″ wide (depending on cultivar), long linear shape with entire margins, WHORLED, two-ranked, arising from base.

**FLOWER DESCRIPTION:** (Depends on cultivar.) 3″ to 6″ wide, 6-parted perianth giving appearance of 6 petals, colors ranging through orange, pink, purple, red, white, yellow, to bicolored. Flowers in summer.

**EXPOSURE/CULTURE:** Needs full sun to light shade. Too much shade will reduce flowering. Tolerant of a wide range of soils, but prefers well-drained, organic soil. Minimal fertilization needed. Remove dead flowers after flowering. Rake dead foliage in early spring. May be divided and transplanted.

**PEST PROBLEMS:** Thrips, slugs and snails, spider mites, nematodes, leaf blight.

**SELECTED CULTIVARS:** 'Aztec Gold' - Low growing and rapid spreading with yellow-gold flowers. 'Baggette' - Variegated (bi-tone) blooms of rose-lavender and yellow. 'Eenie Weenie' - Light yellow flowers on 12″ plants. 'Hyperion' - One of the best. Heavy blooming with citron-yellow flowers. Grows 3 1/2′ tall. 'Ming Toy' - Orange-red with golden throat. Blooms early. Grows 1 1/2′ tall. 'Royal Red' - Red flowers with golden yellow throat. Grows 2′ tall. 'Stella De Ora' - Yellow flowers. 1′ to 2′ tall plants. Blooms May through September. Very popular.

**LANDSCAPE NOTES:** Daylilies make excellent plants for massing, especially in borders. There are literally thousands of varieties. Recent development is with tetraploids for even greater variety. Dwarf cultivars are in high demand.

## *Hosta lancifolia* — Narrow-leaved Plantain Lily

**ZONES:**
3, 4, 5, 6, 7, 8, 9

**HEIGHT:**
1 1/2' to 2'

**WIDTH:**
2' to 2 1/2'

**FRUIT:**
3-valved capsule; NOT COMMON.

**TEXTURE:**
Coarse

**GROWTH RATE:**
Moderate to slow.

**HABIT:**
Rounded clump; spreads by rhizomes.

**FAMILY:**
Liliaceae

**LEAF COLOR:** Dark green (depending on cultivar), turning brown in winter.

**LEAF DESCRIPTION:** SIMPLE, 6″ to 8″ long and 3″ to 3 1/2″ wide, ovate-lanceolate in shape with entire margins, slightly wavy, parallel leaf veins, WHORLED arrangement, arising from basal clumps.

**FLOWER DESCRIPTION:** Violet with faint white streaks, 1 1/2″ long, bell-shaped, appearing in loose racemes of 5 to 30 flowers. Flower stalks 1 1/2' to 3'. Flowers in summer.

**EXPOSURE/CULTURE:** Light shade to dense shade. Prefers well-drained, organic soil with adequate moisture. Annual fertilization is recommended, as well as supplemental water during drought. Remove flower stalks to base after flowers die.

**PEST PROBLEMS:** Slugs, snails, and chewing insects sometimes attack foliage.

**SELECTED CULTIVARS:** 'Albo-marginata' - Has white leaf margins. 'Tardiflora' - Flowers in fall instead of summer.

**RELATED SPECIES:** *H. sieboldii* - Seersucker Plantain Lily. Similar to 'Albo-marginata', except that the variegated bands are smaller. Fruit/seed production is heavier.

**LANDSCAPE NOTES:** All Hostas make excellent ground covers for shady locations. Unlike many plants, flower production is generous in shade. Hostas can be used as single specimens, in massed plantings, in raised planters, or as border plants. The plant is valued for its bold foliage effect and its dense, symmetrical habit. HERBACEOUS PERENNIAL.

## *Hosta plantaginea*

**Fragrant Plantain Lily**

**ZONES:**
3, 4, 5, 6, 7, 8, 9

**HEIGHT:**
1 1/2' to 2'

**WIDTH:**
2' to 3'

**FRUIT:**
3-valved capsule; NOT COMMON

**TEXTURE:**
Coarse

**GROWTH RATE:**
Moderate

**HABIT:**
Rounded clump; spreading by rhizomes.

**FAMILY:**
Liliaceae

**LEAF COLOR:** Yellowish-green to dark green and glossy.

**LEAF DESCRIPTION:** SIMPLE, 8″ to 10″ long and 5″ to 6″ wide, ovate shape with cordate base and entire margins, parallel veins, WHORLED arrangement, arising from basal clump.

**FLOWER DESCRIPTION:** White, 5″ long and 2″ wide, funnel-shaped, rising well above foliage on multi-flowered racemes. Very fragrant. Flowers in late summer.

**EXPOSURE/CULTURE:** Light shade to dense shade. Does best in well-drained, organic soil. Should be fertilized annually, and supplemental water should be supplied during dry periods. Remove flower stalks to base after flowers die.

**PEST PROBLEMS:** Slugs, snails, and chewing insects sometimes attack foliage.

**RELATED SPECIES:** *H. sieboldiana* - Has thick, gray-green leaves and 1 1/2″ pale lilac flowers. Cordate leaves.

**LANDSCAPE NOTES:** Fragrant Plantain Lily is the only Plantain Lily with fragrant flowers. The plant is very coarse and quite spectacular in flower. Can be used in mass or as a border in front of taller plantings. It is large enough for specimen status. A good plant for naturalizing.

## *Hosta sieboldiana* — Siebold Plantain Lily

**ZONES:**
3, 4, 5, 6, 7, 8, 9

**HEIGHT:**
2' to 3'

**WIDTH:**
2 1/2' to 3 1/2'

**FRUIT:**
3-valved capsule; NOT ORNA-MENTAL.

**TEXTURE:**
Coarse

**GROWTH RATE:**
Slow to moderate.

**HABIT:**
Rounded clump; spreading by rhizomes.

**LEAF COLOR:** Bluish-green (depending on cultivar); turning brownish in winter.

**LEAF DESCRIPTION:** SIMPLE, 10″ to 15″ long and 8″ to 12″ wide, broad cordate shape with entire margins, parallel veins deeply cut, giving ribbed or puckered effect, WHORLED, arising from basal clumps.

**FLOWER DESCRIPTION:** Pale lilac, 1 1/2″ long, funnel-shaped in racemes of 6-10 flowers, often hidden by foliage. Flowers in summer.

**EXPOSURE/CULTURE:** Light shade to dense shade. Prefers well-drained, organic soil. Needs additional water during droughts. Any fertilizer application should be light.

**PEST PROBLEMS:** Occasional attack by slugs, snails, or chewing insects.

**SELECTED CULTIVARS:** 'Elegans' - Blue-green leaves with lavender cast to flowers. 'Frances Williams' - Blue-green leaves with gold margins. PICTURED. 'Great Expectations' - Cream colored leaves with blue-green margins.

**LANDSCAPE NOTES:** Siebold Plantain Lily is a very noticeable specimen plant in the garden. Many of the best Hostas appear in this group. 'Frances Williams' is the most highly prized.

# Chapter 5

# VINES

**V**ines are climbing plants that can add much interest to the landscape when carefully selected and located in the garden. Vines climb in many ways, including aerial roots, adhesive discs, twining stems, tendrils, and leaf petioles. Some will climb on solid surfaces, while others require either support or attachment. Fruiting varieties can serve as screens, while providing fruit to the family. Evergreen vines give a year-round effect, while deciduous vines often die completely to the ground in winter. Other common uses of vines are as follows:

▼ Specimen plants on bare wall space, posts, or poles.
▼ Screens or privacy plants when grown on fences or other supports.
▼ Overhead shade for patios or decks when used on trellises or arbors.
▼ Ground covers (some species) to take the place of turf.

## *Akebia quinata*

**Fiveleaf Akebia**

**ZONES:**
5, 6, 7, 8

**HEIGHT:**
20′ to 30′

**WIDTH:**
20′ to 30′

**FRUIT:**
2″ to 3″ fleshy pods; somewhat attractive.

**TEXTURE:**
Medium

**GROWTH RATE:**
Rapid

**HABIT:**
Broad-spreading; climbs by twining.

**FAMILY:**
Lardizabalaceae

**LEAF COLOR:** Blue-green in summer; tinged purplish in fall.

**LEAF DESCRIPTION:** PALMATELY COMPOUND, leaflets 2″ to 3″ long and 1″ to 1 1/2″ wide, leaflets elliptic in shape with entire margins, ALTERNATE arrangement of compound leaves.

**FLOWER DESCRIPTION:** Brownish purple, 1″ long in loose racemes (female). Male flowers in center of raceme are smaller and lighter in color. Fragrant; somewhat showy. Flowers in early spring.

**EXPOSURE/CULTURE:** Grows best in sun or part shade. Adaptable to any well-drained soil; not demanding as to fertility or moisture. Some pruning might be necessary to control growth, especially in smaller gardens. Very agressive; capable of attaining huge size.

**PEST PROBLEMS:** None

**SELECTED CULTIVARS:** 'Alba' - Has white flowers and white fruit.

**RELATED SPECIES:** *A. trifoliata* - Compound leaf has 3 leaflets.

**LANDSCAPE NOTES:** Akebia makes an excellent vine for fences and arbors, and it should be more widely used by designers. It should be noted that this plant is SEMI-EVERGREEN or DECIDUOUS in the NORTHERNMOST ZONES.

## *Bignonia capreolata*

**Crossvine**

**ZONES:**
6, 7, 8, 9

**HEIGHT:**
Indefinite (50′)

**WIDTH:**
Indefinite

**FRUIT:**
6″ flat, pod-like brown capsule.

**TEXTURE:**
Medium

**GROWTH RATE:**
Rapid

**HABIT:**
Climbing by means of tendrils.

**FAMILY:**
Bignoniaceae

**LEAF COLOR:** Dark green in summer; purplish to reddish in winter.

**LEAF DESCRIPTION:** SIMPLE, 3″ to 5″ long and one-third as wide, oblong-elliptic shape with entire or slightly undulating margins. OPPOSITE arrangement.

**FLOWER DESCRIPTION:** Yellow-red with paler throat, funnel-shaped with 5-parted corolla, appearing in small axillary cymes. Flowers in spring.

**EXPOSURE/CULTURE:** Full sun to shade. Prefers well-drained organic soil, but will tolerate moisture. Pruning is usually necessary to control or confine. Prune after flowering.

**PEST PROBLEMS:** No serious pests.

**SELECTED CULTIVARS:** None

**LANDSCAPE NOTES:** Crossvine, so named due to cross shape of stem in horizontal cross-section, is a hardy and easy-to-grow vine. It can be used anywhere a vine is desirable in the landscape. This includes screening when a surface or support is provided. Great plant for naturalizing! Some authorities now classify this under the genus *Anisostichus*.

## X *Fatshedera lizei*     **Bushivy**

**ZONES:**
7, 8, 9

**HEIGHT:**
6' to 8'

**WIDTH:**
Variable

**FRUIT:**
1" bluish berry; NOT ORNA-MENTAL.

**TEXTURE:**
Coarse

**GROWTH RATE:**
Moderate

**HABIT:**
A vine-like shrub, needing support when used as a vine.

**FAMILY:**
Araliaceae

**LEAF COLOR:** Lustrous green.

**LEAF DESCRIPTION:** SIMPLE, 5" to 10" long and wide, petiole 5" or longer, palmately lobed with five deep-cut lobes, somewhat star-shaped, ALTERNATE arrangement.

**FLOWER DESCRIPTION:** Light green, tiny in 1" spherical umbels. Umbels form a panicle that is 3" to 5" wide. Not fragrant. Flowers in fall (October).

**EXPOSURE/CULTURE:** Full shade or part shade. Thrives in any well-drained soil of average moisture and fertility. Will climb, but often needs support. Pruning is restricted to shaping or training, as desired.

**PEST PROBLEMS:** No serious pests.

**SELECTED CULTIVARS:** 'Variegata' - Green leaves with white margins. Not as hardy as the species.

**RELATED SPECIES:** X *F. undulata* - Ruffled Leaf Wonder. This species has a more leathery texture and wavy, undulating leaves.

**LANDSCAPE NOTES:** Bushivy is often used to fill bare wall space that has a narrow planting strip. It may be trained to a trellis or espaliered to the wall. Great accent plant, especially near an entry. This plant is an INTERGENERIC cross between *Fatsia japonica* and *Hedera helix*.

# Ficus pumila

**ZONES:**
8, 9, sometimes 7

**HEIGHT:**
Indefinite

**WIDTH:**
Indefinite

**FRUIT:**
Yellow-green, pear-shaped;
VERY RARE.

**TEXTURE:**
Fine

**GROWTH RATE:**
Rapid, once established.

**HABIT:**
Very flat, dense vine. Climbs by aerial roots.

**FAMILY:**
Moraceae

**LEAF COLOR:** Dull medium green.

**LEAF DESCRIPTION:** SIMPLE, 1″ to 1 1/2″ long and 1/2″ to 3/4″ wide, heart-shaped (cordate) with entire margins, ALTERNATE arrangement. Older leaves can grow to 3″ or longer.

**FLOWER DESCRIPTION:** Tiny and inconspicuous. RARELY FOUND.

**EXPOSURE/CULTURE:** Needs full shade or part shade. It is tolerant of any well-drained soil, but prefers moderately high moisture. When located properly, it is a rapid grower that needs regular pruning to maintain its refined character and to control or confine.

**PEST PROBLEMS:** Scale

**SELECTED CULTIVARS:** 'Minima' - Tiny leaves to 1/2″ or smaller. Very refined character. Good indoor plant. 'Variegata' - Green and white leaves. Less cold hardy than the species.

**LANDSCAPE NOTES:** Climbing Fig is a beautiful foliage plant, having a more refined, formal appearance than most vines. It is a great choice for covering brick walls or stonework, but should never be used on painted surfaces. The plant can survive in Zone 7, if grown against heated wall space and protected from wind. This plant is often used in formal gardens of the south, and it makes an outstanding background for statuary.

# *Gelsemium sempervirens*

## Carolina Jessamine

**ZONES:**
7, 8, 9

**HEIGHT:**
15′ to 20′

**WIDTH:**
20′ to 30′

**FRUIT:**
1″ to 2″ 2-valved capsule; NOT ORNAMENTAL.

**TEXTURE:**
Fine

**GROWTH RATE:**
Moderate to rapid.

**HABIT:**
Twining, bushy vine. Needs support for climbing.

**FAMILY:**
Loganiaceae

**LEAF COLOR:** Dark green.

**LEAF DESCRIPTION:** SIMPLE, 1″ to 3″ long and 1/2″ to1 1/4″ wide, ovate-lanceolate shape with entire margins, glossy, OPPOSITE arrangement.

**FLOWER DESCRIPTION:** Bright yellow, 1″ long and fragrant. Bugle-shaped (funnel-shaped) appearing as a single flower or in small cymes. Flowers in late winter or early spring.

**EXPOSURE/CULTURE:** Grows in sun or shade. Tolerant of different soil types, but prefers moist, well-drained, organic soil. Should be sheared after flowering to control or maintain shape. Will climb or drape over walls. Can be used for erosion control as a ground cover on sloping ground.

**PEST PROBLEMS:** No serious pests.

**SELECTED CULTIVARS:** 'Plena' - Produces double flowers. Also listed as 'Pride of Augusta'.

**LANDSCAPE NOTES:** Carolina Jessamine can be used as a vine on fences, arbors, trellises, lamp posts, and other structures that allow twining. It is noted for its fragrant yellow flowers in early spring, but has equally attractive foliage.

# Lonicera x heckrottii

**Goldflame Honeysuckle**

**ZONES:**
4, 5, 6, 7, 8, 9

**HEIGHT:**
10' to 15'

**WIDTH:**
Variable

**FRUIT:**
Red berry; VERY, VERY RARE.

**TEXTURE:**
Medium

**GROWTH RATE:**
Moderate to rapid.

**HABIT:**
Twining; needs support.

**FAMILY:**
Caprifoliaceae

**LEAF COLOR:** Bluish-green

**LEAF DESCRIPTION:** SIMPLE, 1 1/2" to 3" long and 1" to 2" wide, oval or elliptic shape with entire margins, OPPOSITE arrangement. Leaves near the tip are fused. Stems of plant are purplish.

**FLOWER DESCRIPTION:** Coral-pink outside and yellow inside, 2" long and funnel-shaped in spikes. Begins flowering in spring and continues for several weeks. Fragrant.

**EXPOSURE/CULTURE:** Needs full sun or part shade. Should be planted in well-drained soil with moderate moisture. Prune to control or maintain shape. Easy to grow.

**PEST PROBLEMS:** No serious pests.

**SELECTED CULTIVARS:** None

**RELATED SPECIES:** *L. periclymenum* - (Woodbine). This species has creamy-white flowers with purplish tint; has red berries in fall.

**LANDSCAPE NOTES:** Goldflame Honeysuckle is one of the most popular climbing Honeysuckles. It should be featured in a well-chosen spot in the garden. It is SEMI-EVERGREEN to DECIDUOUS in the NORTHERNMOST zones.

## *Lonicera sempervirens*  Trumpet Honeysuckle, Coral Honeysuckle

**ZONES:**
4, 5, 6, 7, 8, 9

**HEIGHT:**
15′ to 20′

**WIDTH:**
Indeterminate

**FRUIT:**
1/4″ red berry; not spectacular.

**TEXTURE:**
Medium-fine

**GROWTH RATE:**
Rapid

**HABIT:**
Twining; needs support.

**FAMILY:**
Caprifoliaceae

**LEAF COLOR:** Blue-green in summer; new growth reddish.

**LEAF DESCRIPTION:** SIMPLE, 1 1/2″ to 2 1/2″ long and 1″ to 2″ wide, oblong or ovate shape with entire margins, OPPOSITE arrangement, leaves near tip are perfoliate or connate (fused).

**FLOWER DESCRIPTION:** 1 1/2″ to 2″, reddish-orange with yellow throat, funnel-shaped, whorled in spikes at the ends of shoots. Flowers in spring and summer. Very fragrant.

**EXPOSURE/CULTURE:** Needs full sun or part shade. Should be planted in well-drained soil that receives reasonable moisture. Prune after flowering to control or shape. Considered easy to grow and worth the effort.

**PEST PROBLEMS:** None

**SELECTED CULTIVARS:** 'Magnifica' - Scarlet-red flowers with yellow throats. Later flowering. 'Sulphurea' - Has solid yellow flowers.

**LANDSCAPE NOTES:** Unusual foliage and flowers make this a plant to feature. Can be trained to climb on trellises or fences.

# *Rosa banksiae*

**Lady Bank's Rose**

**ZONES:**
7, 8, 9

**HEIGHT:**
12′ to 18′

**WIDTH:**
Indeterminate

**FRUIT:**
NONE

**TEXTURE:**
Fine to medium.

**GROWTH RATE:**
Rapid

**HABIT:**
Irregular vine; needs support or attachment.

**FAMILY:**
Rosaceae

**LEAF COLOR:** Dark green.

**LEAF DESCRIPTION:** COMPOUND, leaflets 1 1/4″ to 3″ long and 1/2″ to 1 1/4″ wide, leaflets broad lanceolate shape with serrulate margins. ALTERNATE arrangement to the compound leaves.

**FLOWER DESCRIPTION:** 1″ flowers, white or light yellow, in multi-flower umbels, single or double. Flowers in April, May, and June. Very attractive.

**EXPOSURE/CULTURE:** Needs full sun or light shade. Thrives in most well-drained soil types. Needs pruning to control. Requires less care than many rose species. Reliable.

**PEST PROBLEMS:** No serious pests.

**SELECTED CULTIVARS:** 'Alba-plena' - Has miniature, white double flowers. 'Lutea' - Has canary yellow double flowers.

**LANDSCAPE NOTES:** Lady Bank's Rose is an excellent climber, but must be espaliered or supported. It is a great choice for arbors since it grows rapidly and produces dense shade. It is often used on fences as a focal point or screen. It is mostly thornless. It is SEMI-EVERGREEN or DECIDUOUS in the NORTHERN-MOST zone.

## *Smilax lanceolata*

**Smilax, Jackson Brier**

**ZONES:**
6, 7, 8, 9

**HEIGHT:**
to 20′+

**WIDTH:**
Indeterminate

**FRUIT:**
3/8″ reddish-brown berry;
NOT ORNAMENTAL.

**TEXTURE:**
Medium

**GROWTH RATE:**
Moderate to rapid.

**HABIT:**
Climbs by tendril pairs; roots
spread by rhizomes.

**FAMILY:**
Liliaceae

**LEAF COLOR:** Bright green and lustrous.

**LEAF DESCRIPTION:** SIMPLE, 2″ to 3 1/2″ long and 1″ to 2″ wide, lanceolate-ovate to ovate shape with entire, often undulating margins. ALTERNATE arrangement.

**FLOWER DESCRIPTION:** Greenish-white to yellowish, tiny in axillary umbels. Not abundant and not showy.

**EXPOSURE/CULTURE:** Sun or shade. The plant prefers moist, well-drained, organic soils. pH adaptable. Prune during any season to control growth. NOT LOW-MAINTENANCE.

**PEST PROBLEMS:** No serious pests.

**SELECTED CULTIVARS:** None

**LANDSCAPE NOTES:** Smilax is a handsome woody vine that can be used effectively on arbors, trellises, fences, or walls. Its outstanding attribute is the lustrous green foliage that is used in floral arrangements and other decorations. This is an often-overlooked vine of outstanding ornamental potential.

# *Trachelospermum asiaticum*

**Asiatic Jasmine**

**ZONES:**
7, 8, 9

**HEIGHT:**
12′ to 15′

**WIDTH:**
12′ to 15′

**FRUIT:**
Pod; RARE; NOT ORNAMENTAL.

**TEXTURE:**
Fine to medium.

**GROWTH RATE:**
Moderate

**HABIT:**
Spreading, rooting along stem. Twining stems.

**FAMILY:**
Apocynaceae

**LEAF COLOR:** Dark green; new growth reddish.

**LEAF DESCRIPTION:** SIMPLE, 1″ to 2″ long and 1/2″ wide, veins lighter in color than the blade, ovate shape with entire margins, OPPOSITE arrangement.

**FLOWER DESCRIPTION:** 1/2″ to 3/4″, pale yellow, star-shaped, fragrant. Flowers in May and June.

**EXPOSURE/CULTURE:** Plant in part shade. Prefers soil that is fertile, moist, and organic. May need pruning to confine. Will not climb on solid surfaces, but twines on posts and trees.

**PEST PROBLEMS:** Scale

**SELECTED CULTIVARS:** 'Nortex' - Has lance-shaped foliage. 'Solo' - Slower growing and not as tall. Narrow, pointed foliage. 'Variegatum' - Variegated creamy white. Develops burgundy tinge in fall.

**LANDSCAPE NOTES:** Asiatic Jasmine is an interesting dual-purpose plant that can be used as a ground cover or vine. It is not a true climber, and is probably used more often as a ground cover.

# *Trachelospermum jasminoides*   Confederate Jasmine, Star Jasmine

**ZONES:**
8, 9

**HEIGHT:**
10′ to 20′

**WIDTH:**
Indeterminate

**FRUIT:**
2 1/2″ pod; NOT ORNAMENTAL.

**TEXTURE:**
Fine to medium.

**GROWTH RATE**
Moderately rapid.

**HABIT:**
Twining; needs support for climbing on solid surfaces.

**FAMILY:**
Apocynaceae

**LEAF COLOR:** Dark green leaves having darker veins.

**LEAF DESCRIPTION:** SIMPLE, 1″ to 3″ long and 1/2″ to1 1/2″ wide, ovate shape with entire margins, OPPOSITE arrangement.

**FLOWER DESCRIPTION:** 1″ wide, white, fragrant flowers. Star-shaped (five-petaled), appearing in loose clusters in May and June.

**EXPOSURE/CULTURE:** Needs part shade or full shade. This plant is tolerant of a wide range of soils and moisture conditions. Will flower even in dense shade. Prune after flowering to control, as needed.

**PEST PROBLEMS:** No serious pests.

**SELECTED CULTIVARS:** 'Madison' - More hardy form that will grow in Zone 7. 'Variegatum' - Leaves are green and white.

**LANDSCAPE NOTES:** This plant grows well on fences, trellises, arbors, posts, and trees. Especially noted for its fragrance and attractive foliage. Can be used as a VINE or GROUND COVER.

# *Campsis grandiflora*                    **Chinese Trumpetcreeper**

▲ *c. radicans*

▲ *c. radicans*

**ZONES:**
7, 8, 9

**HEIGHT:**
20′ to 25′

**WIDTH:**
Indeterminate

**FRUIT:**
3″ to 4″ capsule; NOT ORNA-MENTAL.

**TEXTURE:**
Medium

**GROWTH RATE:**
Rapid

**HABIT:**
Dense, irregular climber; climbing by aerial roots.

**FAMILY:**
Bignoniaceae

**LEAF COLOR:** Dark green in summer; turning yellowish in fall before dropping.

**LEAF DESCRIPTION:** COMPOUND, leaflets 2″ to 3″ long and 1″ to 1 1/2″ wide, ovate shape with coarsely serrated margins and acuminate tip, 7 to 9 leaflets, leaves having OPPOSITE arrangement.

**FLOWER DESCRIPTION:** 1 1/2″ to 3″ long, orange-red with 5 lobes. Several flowers bunched into drooping panicles during summer and continuing through September.

**EXPOSURE/CULTURE:** Grows in sun or part shade. This plant is adaptable and will grow almost anywhere. Very easy to grow, but sometimes difficult to control. Should be planted in a location that allows freedom (space) to accomodate frequent pruning.

**PEST PROBLEMS:** Leaf spots, scale, chewing insects. None serious.

**SELECTED CULTIVARS:** None

**RELATED SPECIES:** *C. radicans* - Trumpetvine. Very similar to above, but has smaller flowers. Zone 5. *C.* x *tagliabuana* - Cross between *C. grandiflora* and *C. radicans*. Salmon red flowers. Zone 5.

**LANDSCAPE NOTES:** All of the trumpetcreepers make excellent accent plants for the garden, as long as they are controlled. This is an excellent plant for naturalizing.

## *Clematis hybrida* — Hybrid Clematis, Large-flowered Clematis

**ZONES:**
4, 5, 6, 7, 8

**HEIGHT:**
5′ to 25′; cultivars vary.

**WIDTH:**
Indeterminate

**FRUIT:**
Small, one-seeded; NOT ORNAMENTAL.

**TEXTURE:**
Medium

**GROWTH RATE:**
Moderate

**HABIT:**
Twining; needs support for climbing.

**FAMILY:**
Ranunculaceae

**LEAF COLOR:** Most often green, but sometimes blue-green.

**LEAF DESCRIPTION:** COMPOUND, sometimes simple at stem tips, leaflets 1″ to 4″ long and 1/2″ wide, leaflets ovate with entire margins. OPPOSITE arrangement.

**FLOWER DESCRIPTION:** 2″ to 8″ wide, borne solitary or in cymes of 2 or 3, many shades of white, pink, red, blue, lavender, or violet. Flowers spring through summer. Flowers vary by cultivar.

**EXPOSURE/CULTURE:** Part shade is best. Top needs warmth, roots need cooler environment; it is essential to provide mulch. Prefers well-drained, organic soil that receives regular moisture. Provide supplemental water during dry periods. Occasional pruning desired.

**PEST PROBLEMS:** Leaf spots, stem rot, scale.

**SELECTED CULTIVARS:** 'Comtesse de Bouchard' - Silvery-rose 6″ flowers. 'Elsa Spath' - Blue flowers in late summer. 'Henryi'- 7″ white flowers, June to September. 'Mrs. N. Thompson' - Violet with scarlet bar. 'Marie Boisselot' - Pale pink, becoming white. 'Nelly Moser' - 7″ pale pink flowers with red bar. 'Niobe' - Deep ruby-red with gold stamens. 'Pink Champagne' - 6″ to 7″ rosey-red flowers. 'William Kennett' - 7″ lavender-blue flowers.

**RELATED SPECIES:** *C.* x *jackmanii* - One of the best! Very large, velvety purple flowers.

**LANDSCAPE NOTES:** Hybrid Clematis cultivars are some of the most noticeable specimen plants in landscaping. They are most often used on lamp posts, mail boxes, and trellises, but can be adapted to a number of areas. The biggest problem is choosing between the hundreds of fine cultivars that are available.

# *Clematis maximowicziana*

**Sweetautumn Clematis**

**ZONES:**
5, 6, 7, 8

**HEIGHT:**
20′ to 30′

**WIDTH:**
Indeterminate

**FRUIT:**
Gray, one-seeded, plume-like;
ATTRACTIVE.

**TEXTURE:**
Medium

**GROWTH RATE:**
Rapid

**HABIT:**
Twining stem and petioles;
needs support in order to
climb.

**FAMILY:**
Ranunculaceae

**LEAF COLOR:** Bright green to blue-green.

**LEAF DESCRIPTION:** COMPOUND, leaflets 2 1/2″ to 4″ long and 1″ to 2″ wide, leaflets ovate shape with cordate base and entire margins, 3 to 5 leaflets. OPPOSITE arrangement.

**FLOWER DESCRIPTION:** 1″ white flowers in panicles arising from leaf axils. Abundant, giving a lacy effect. Attractive. Flowers in August and continues into October.

**EXPOSURE/CULTURE:** Sun or part shade. Prefers well-drained, organic soil that receives regular moisture. Prune in early spring to remove unwanted wood and to encourage heavy flowering. This plant is considered easy to grow and is reliable.

**PEST PROBLEMS:** Spider mites.

**SELECTED CULTIVARS:** None

**LANDSCAPE NOTES:** Sweetautumn Clematis is very easy to grow, and it provides fragrant, delicate flowers late in the season. It can be trained on posts, fences, trellises, and arbors for screening or focalization. A favorite of many home gardeners.

## *Clematis virginiana* — Virginsbower

**ZONES:**
4, 5, 6, 7, 8, 9

**HEIGHT:**
15′ to 18′

**WIDTH:**
Indeterminate

**FRUIT:**
Small, gray, one-seeded achene.

**TEXTURE:**
Medium

**GROWTH RATE:**
Moderate

**HABIT:**
Twining stems and petioles; needs support for climbing.

**FAMILY:**
Ranunculaceae

**LEAF COLOR:** Bright green in summer; purple-tinged in fall.

**LEAF DESCRIPTION:** COMPOUND, 3 leaflets, each leaflet 2 1/2″ to 3 1/2″ long and 1″ to 2″ wide, leaflets ovate shape with both entire and coarsely serrated margins. OPPOSITE arrangement.

**FLOWER DESCRIPTION:** 1″ off-white flowers in 4″ to 5″ panicles that arise from the leaf axils. Very abundant. Flowers in mid-summer through early fall.

**EXPOSURE/CULTURE:** Sun or part shade. Prefers well-drained, organic soil. Needs plenty of moisture for best appearance. Prune as desired to control spread or to train. Easier to control than *C. maximowicziana*.

**PEST PROBLEMS:** Mites, scale, whiteflies. None serious.

**SELECTED CULTIVARS:** None

**RELATED SPECIES:** *C. montana* - Anemone Clematis. Has white, 4-petaled flowers. Various colored cultivars available. *C. tangutica* - Golden Clematis. Has large yellow flowers in June and July. *C. viticella* - Italian Clematis. Has funnel-like 2″ flowers in summer. Cultivars of red, purple, or violet.

**LANDSCAPE NOTES:** Virginsbower, while not spectacular, is attractive and reliable. Good plant for naturalizing.

## *Hydrangea anomala subsp. petiolaris* — **Climbing Hydrangea**

**ZONES:**
4, 5, 6, 7, 8

**HEIGHT:**
50′ to 60′

**WIDTH:**
Indeterminate

**FRUIT:**
Brown capsule; NOT ORNA-MENTAL.

**TEXTURE:**
Coarse

**GROWTH RATE:**
Slow when first established.

**HABIT:**
Climbing, without support, by aerial roots.

**FAMILY:**
Saxifragaceae

**LEAF COLOR:** Dark green.

**LEAF DESCRIPTION:** SIMPLE, 2″ to 3 1/2″ long and 2″ to 3″ wide, wide ovate in shape with serrated margins. Petioles almost as long as leaves. OPPOSITE arrangement.

**FLOWER DESCRIPTION:** White, 1″ to 1 1/2″ across, borne in several-branched, flat-topped corymbs that are 6″ or broader, the outer flowers being sterile. Fragrant. Flowers in early summer.

**EXPOSURE/CULTURE:** Needs sun or part shade. Will not bloom as well in deeper shade. Does best in porous soil that is high in organic matter and somewhat moist. Responds favorably to moderate fertilization. Easier to control than most vines.

**PEST PROBLEMS:** No serious pests.

**SELECTED CULTIVARS:** None

**LANDSCAPE NOTES:** Climbing Hydrangea is excellent for naturalizing. It was taken from the wild, and it looks best in a less formal setting. Great for climbing on stonework, rustic boards, poles, and garden trees.

## *Parthenocissus quinquefolia* — **Virginia Creeper**

**ZONES:**
3, 4, 5, 6, 7, 8, 9

**HEIGHT:**
25′ to 40′

**WIDTH:**
Varies with the structure.

**FRUIT:**
Blue-black berries in fall.

**TEXTURE:**
Coarse

**GROWTH RATE:**
Moderate to rapid.

**HABIT:**
Climbing by tendrils, having adhesive discs that literally "glue" themselves to any surface.

**FAMILY:**
Vitaceae

**LEAF COLOR:** Green in summer; turning reddish in fall.

**LEAF DESCRIPTION:** PALMATELY COMPOUND having 5 whorled leaflets, 4″ to 5″ long and half as wide, leaflets ovate to elliptic with acuminate tips, serrated margins. ALTERNATE arrangement.

**FLOWER DESCRIPTION:** Greenish-white, INCONSPICUOUS, in cymes under the foliage. Flowers in summer.

**EXPOSURE/CULTURE:** Will grow in full sun to shade. Easy to grow in almost any conditions, including poor, stony soils and sand. Will act as ground cover when it has nothing to climb on. Commonly found in the wild due to bird attraction to the berries.

**PEST PROBLEMS:** Mildews, beetles. None serious.

**SELECTED CULTIVARS:** 'Engelmannii' - Has smaller leaflets. 'Saint-paulii' - Has smaller leaflets and clings better to surfaces.

**LANDSCAPE NOTES:** Virginia Creeper is a beautiful climbing vine often mistaken for Poison Ivy, which has only 3 leaflets. Fall color is brilliant, and it is great for naturalizing. Can be used as a VINE or GROUND COVER.

# *Parthenocissus tricuspidata*

**Boston Ivy**

**ZONES:**
4, 5, 6, 7, 8

**HEIGHT:**
25' to 35'

**WIDTH:**
Indeterminate

**FRUIT:**
1/4" blue-black berries.

**TEXTURE:**
Coarse

**GROWTH RATE:**
Rapid

**HABIT:**
Climbing by tendrils with disc-like adhesions.

**FAMILY:**
Vitaceae

**LEAF COLOR:** Dark green and shiny in summer; red in fall.

**LEAF DESCRIPTION:** SIMPLE, 5" to 8" long and wide, 3-lobed margins that are coarsely serrated. ALTERNATE arrangement.

**FLOWER DESCRIPTION:** Greenish in cymes, NOT COMMON and NOT NOTICEABLE.

**EXPOSURE/CULTURE:** Sun or shade. Grows in almost any soil except waterlogged, and will withstand drought. Very easy to grow and hard to get rid of when renovating. Pruning is necessary in order to control. Grow on large structures that are easily accessible.

**PEST PROBLEMS:** Aphids on new growth, mites, scale.

**SELECTED CULTIVARS:** 'Green Showers' - Larger rich green leaves. Burgundy in fall. Ice-blue fruits. 'Lowii' - Small-leaved Boston Ivy. Much smaller leaves and easier to control. 'Purpurea' - Has red-purple leaves throughout the growing season. 'Veitchii' - Very dense, bright green, maple-like leaves. Turns orange or scarlet in fall.

**LANDSCAPE NOTES:** Boston Ivy is an excellent climbing plant for large walls and structures. It is especially attractive on brick walls and fences. The effect is quite dramatic, and one should plan its use carefully with a degree of commitment. Used often in estate-type landscapes. It is not a good choice for the small home garden. Outstanding vine that will climb on anything.

# *Polygonum aubertii*

**Silver Lace Vine**

**ZONES:**
4, 5, 6, 7, 8, 9

**HEIGHT:**
25' to 30'

**WIDTH:**
30' to 35'

**FRUIT:**
Small achenes; NOT ORNA-MENTAL.

**TEXTURE:**
Medium

**GROWTH RATE:**
Rapid

**HABIT:**
Twining; requires support. Multiplies by rhizomes.

**FAMILY:**
Polygonaceae

**LEAF COLOR:** Lustrous green.

**LEAF DESCRIPTION:** SIMPLE, 1 1/2" to 3" long and 1" to 1 1/2" wide, ovate shape with hastate base, margins entire or undulating, OPPOSITE arrangement.

**FLOWER DESCRIPTION:** White, infrequently pinkish, 1/4", appearing in panicles near branch ends in mid-summer. Fragrant and attractive.

**EXPOSURE/CULTURE:** Sun or shade. Grows in almost any soil that is not water-logged. Can be trained on fences, arbors, trellises, and other non-solid structures. Requires pruning to control. Considered very easy to grow.

**PEST PROBLEMS:** Japanese beetles and other chewing insects.

**SELECTED CULTIVARS:** None

**LANDSCAPE NOTES:** Silver Lace Vine covers itself in mid-summer with panicles of lace-like whitish flowers. It performs especially well on wooden fences, and should be located on borders of the yard or other areas where space is generous. This vine will succeed where other vines fail. Will grow to 15' in one season. An excellent vine that has proven itself over the years.

## *Wisteria floribunda*        **Japanese Wisteria**

▲ 'Texas Purple'

▲ 'Issai Perfect', both photos courtesy of Monrovia Nursery Co.

**ZONES:**
5, 6, 7, 8, 9

**HEIGHT:**
25' to 30'

**WIDTH:**
Indeterminate

**FRUIT:**
6" brown pod; bean-like and pubescent.

**TEXTURE:**
Medium

**GROWTH RATE:**
Rapid

**HABIT:**
Climbs by twining stems on poles, arbors, or trees.

**FAMILY:**
Fabaceae

**LEAF COLOR:** Green in summer; green to yellowish in fall.

**LEAF DESCRIPTION:** ODD PINNATELY COMPOUND, 13 to 19 leaflets, leaflets 2" to 3" long, ovate-elliptic shape with entire margins. ALTERNATE arrangement.

**FLOWER DESCRIPTION:** Violet to violet-blue (red, pink, or white cultivars), 3/4" long in dense, pendulous, terminal racemes to 18". Flowers in spring with the leaves. Fragrant and very showy.

**EXPOSURE/CULTURE:** Full sun or light shade. Prefers moist, well-drained soil, but is tolerant of a wide range of soil pH values. Prune after flowering to shape or control growth. NOT LOW MAINTENANCE.

**PEST PROBLEMS:** Mildew, webworms, scale.

**SELECTED CULTIVARS:** 'Alba' - Has dense, white flower racemes. 'Issai Perfect' - Has white flower racemes, even on very young plants. 'Ivory Tower' - Produces abundant white flowers that are more fragrant than the species. 'Rosea' - Has fragrant, rose-pink racemes to 18". 'Royal Purple' - Has bright, violet-purple racemes. 'Texas Purple' - Has violet-purple racemes at an earlier age.

**RELATED SPECIES:** *W. sinensis* - Chinese Wisteria (see next page).

**LANDSCAPE NOTES:** Japanese Wisteria is a vigorous twining vine that can be used as an arbor plant, espalier, or as a shrub in lawn areas. This is an attractive, showy plant while in bloom, but should be grown with the understanding that regular maintenance is required to control growth.

## *Wisteria sinensis*       Chinese Wisteria

**ZONES:**
5, 6, 7, 8, 9

**HEIGHT:**
Around 35′

**WIDTH:**
Indeterminate

**FRUIT:**
A stiff, velvety pod to 6″ long; NOT ORNAMENTAL.

**TEXTURE:**
Medium

**GROWTH RATE:**
Rapid, once established.

**HABIT:**
Spreading and mounded, with arching branches; twines on posts and trees.

**FAMILY:**
Fabaceae

**LEAF COLOR:** Medium green.

**LEAF DESCRIPTION:** COMPOUND, usually 11 leaflets, leaflets 2″ to 3″ long and 1″ to 2″ wide, ovate-lanceolate in shape with entire margins. ALTERNATE arrangement to compound leaves.

**FLOWER DESCRIPTION:** Bluish-violet, 1″ long in racemes that are approximately 1′ in length. Flowers before the leaves appear in early spring.

**EXPOSURE/CULTURE:** Needs full sunlight for best flowering. Will grow in a wide range of soil types and pH conditions. Needs pruning to restrain. If not restrained, can take over areas of the yard, especially trees. Not a low-maintenance plant under most conditions.

**PEST PROBLEMS:** No serious pests.

**RELATED CULTIVARS:** 'Alba' - Has white flowers. 'Black Dragon' - Flowers are double, dark purple. 'Jako' - White, fragrant flowers. 'Purpurea' - Flowers purplish-violet.

**LANDSCAPE NOTES:** Wisteria is an excellent landscape plant, valued for its spectacular floral display in spring. The plant, with a little attention, can be controlled. Its best use is as a vine for arbors and trellises, or as a shrub in the lawn area, away from other trees. An "old timey" plant that has proven itself.

# Chapter 6

## DWARF SHRUBS

**D**warf shrubs that grow less than 4′ in height have become increasingly popular in recent years. People have increased their knowledge of landscape plants, and they have learned that, in most cases, dwarf plants are much easier to maintain in the landscape. In addition, home gardens have become smaller as a result of suburban living.

The nursery industry continues to develop dwarf forms of larger landscape plants, and this trend will most certainly continue for many years. Some of the popular uses of dwarf shrubs are as follows:

▼ Plantings under low windows in the foundation.
▼ "Bed" areas or groupings in the landscape.
▼ Plantings in raised beds and berms.
▼ Garden borders or low-growing hedges.
▼ Massed plantings on banks and other sloping areas for erosion control or ground cover effect.

## *Abelia x grandiflora 'Sherwood'*  Dwarf Abelia, Sherwood Abelia

**ZONES:**
6, 7, 8, 9

**HEIGHT:**
2 1/2' to 3'

**WIDTH:**
3 1/2' to 4'

**FRUIT:**
One-seeded achene; NOT ORNAMENTAL.

**TEXTURE:**
Fine

**GROWTH RATE:**
Moderately rapid.

**HABIT:**
Spreading and mounded, with arching branches.

**FAMILY:**
Caprifoliaceae

**LEAF COLOR:** Green with slight purple tinge in summer; bronze or red tint in winter.

**LEAF DESCRIPTION:** SIMPLE, 1/2" to 1" long and 3/8" to 5/8" wide, ovate shape with serrated margins (widely spaced), short petiole, OPPOSITE arrangement.

**FLOWER DESCRIPTION:** 1/2" to 3/4" long, white, bell-shaped in small terminal panicles. Flowers from June until the first killing frost.

**EXPOSURE/CULTURE:** Full sun to light shade. Blooms less in shade. Prefers well-drained, organic soil but is adaptable to a wide range of conditions. Will not bloom as well during drought unless supplemental water is provided. Prune to maintain shape and remove irregular growth.

**PEST PROBLEMS:** Aphids, along with ants, are seen frequently on new growth. Easily controlled.

**RELATED CULTIVARS:** 'Francis Mason' - Variegated Dwarf Abelia. Green and yellow leaves with soft pink flowers. 'Prostrata' - Very low-growing ground cover type. Has a tendency toward irregular growth, not covering as uniformly as many ground covers.

**LANDSCAPE NOTES:** Dwarf Abelia is a compact, dense-growing form of Glossy Abelia (medium shrub) which has interesting form. It combines well with other evergreens, and it can be used effectively as a foundation plant or in massed planting beds. The plant has a very long bloom period as compared to most flowering shrubs. Stems are smooth and reddish. TENDS TO BE SEMI-EVERGREEN, having less foliage in winter.

# *Azalea obtusum (Rhododendron obtusum)*     **Kurume Azalea**

▲ 'Sherwood Red'

▲ 'Coral Bells'

▲ 'Pink Pearl'

**ZONES:**
6, 7, 8, 9

**HEIGHT:**
3' to 4'

**WIDTH:**
3' to 6'

**FRUIT:**
Capsule; NOT ORNAMENTAL.

**TEXTURE:**
Fine to medium.

**GROWTH RATE:**
Moderate

**HABIT:**
Dense and spreading.

**FAMILY:**
Ericaceae

**LEAF COLOR:** Green in summer; green to red in winter.

**LEAF DESCRIPTION:** SIMPLE, 1" to 1 1/2" long and 1/2" to 1" wide, ovate to oval in shape with entire margins, hairy (downy) surface, ALTERNATE arrangement. Stems of plant hairy.

**FLOWER DESCRIPTION:** 1" to 1 1/2", pink, red, white, violet, scarlet, or salmon color, depending on the cultivar. Flowers in April or May.

**EXPOSURE/CULTURE:** Light (filtered) shade. Prefers well-drained, organic soil, with acidic reaction. Very sensitive to deep planting. Should be planted slightly higher than surrounding soil. Also, very sensitive to drought. Should be mulched heavily and fertilized with organic fertilizers. Pruning should be minimal.

**PEST PROBLEMS:** Spider mites, lace bugs, leaf gall, leaf spot.

**SELECTED CULTIVARS:** 'Appleblossom' - Flowers are pink with a white throat. 'Coral Bells' - Pink flowers. One of the hardiest and most popular cultivars. 'Hershey's Red' - Bright red. Very popular. 'Hinodegiri' - Compact with red flowers. Very hardy and reliable. 'Sherwood Red' - Has orange-red flowers. 'Snow' - Most popular white azalea. Heavy bloomer.

**LANDSCAPE NOTES:** Kurume Azaleas offer a breathtaking display of color in spring. They cover themselves with flowers and are most effective when planted in groups or masses of the same color. Some cultivars make nice foundation plants.

## *Azalea x satsuki (Rhododendron x satsuki)*     Satsuki Hybrid Azalea

▲ 'Gumpo Pink'

▲ 'Heawa'

**ZONES:**
6, 7, 8, 9

**HEIGHT:**
2' to 3'

**WIDTH:**
3' to 4'

**FRUIT:**
Capsule; NOT ORNAMENTAL.

**TEXTURE:**
Fine

**GROWTH RATE:**
Moderate.

**HABIT:**
Wide, spreading, compact mounds.

**FAMILY:**
Ericaceae

**LEAF COLOR:** Green

**LEAF DESCRIPTION:** SIMPLE, 1" to 1 1/2" long and 1/2" to 3/4" wide, ovate shape with entire margins, downy surface. ALTERNATE arrangement.

**FLOWER DESCRIPTION:** 2" to 4 1/2", white, pink, rose, orange, purple, or variegated, depending on cultivar. Flowers late, May and June. Often has more than one color of flowers on the same plant. This is characteristic of Satsuki hybrids.

**EXPOSURE/CULTURE:** Sun to part shade. Prefers well-drained, organic soil of acidic reaction. Subject to drowning if planted deep. Needs supplemental water during drought. Fertilize with organic fertilizers only. Prune lightly after flowering to maintain shape.

**PEST PROBLEMS:** Spider mites, lace bugs.

**SELECTED CULTIVARS:** 'Beni-Kirishima' - Has orange-red flowers. 'Gumpo Pink' - Very compact with rose-pink flowers. 'Gumpo White' - Very compact. White flowers. 'Gunrei' - White flowers with occasional pink flowers on same plant. 'Heawa' - White with sports of pink and rose. 'Higasa' - Deep rose-pink. 4 1/2" flowers.

**LANDSCAPE NOTES:** Satsuki Azaleas add color when other Azaleas are out of bloom. These plants are valuable for outstanding foliage all year long. Can be used in beds or as foundation plants. Very popular form for low-maintenace landscaping. There are many cultivars.

# *Berberis verruculosa*

**Warty Barberry**

**ZONES:**
6, 7, 8

**HEIGHT:**
3 1/2' to 4'

**WIDTH:**
3' to 5'

**FRUIT:**
1/4" black berries.

**TEXTURE:**
Fine

**GROWTH RATE:**
Somewhat slow.

**HABIT:**
Rounded and spreading; pendulous branches.

**FAMILY:**
Berberidaceae

**LEAF COLOR:** Lustrous green in summer; mahogany-bronze in winter.

**LEAF DESCRIPTION:** SIMPLE, 3/4" to 1 1/4" long and 3/8" to 5/8" wide, ovate to long ovate shape with spinose margins, margins curving under, ALTERNATE arrangement, appearing somewhat clustered.

**FLOWER DESCRIPTION:** 1/4" to 1/2" yellow flowers, showy but not dominant. Flowers in spring.

**EXPOSURE/CULTURE:** Sun or light shade. Prefers well-drained loamy soil, but is tolerant of most soils, except wet. Some light pruning might be necessary to maintain habit of growth. Leaves are spiny but not considered greatly hazardous.

**PEST PROBLEMS:** No serious pests.

**SELECTED CULTIVARS:** None

**LANDSCAPE NOTES:** Warty Barberry gets its name from the wart-like growths covering the stems. It has an informal habit that makes it adaptable for a wide range of functions. The foliage is quite handsome, and changes with the seasons. Flowers and berries, though not abundant, add interest to the plant. Should be more widely used.

## *Buxus sempervirens 'Suffruticosa'* — Dwarf Boxwood, Dwarf Old English Boxwood

**ZONES:**
5, 6, 7, 8

**HEIGHT:**
1' to 3'

**WIDTH:**
1' to 3'

**FRUIT:**
Capsule; INCONSPICUOUS.

**TEXTURE:**
Fine

**GROWTH RATE:**
EXTREMELY slow.

**HABIT:**
Very dense with globular shape.

**FAMILY:**
Buxaceae

**LEAF COLOR:** Dark green. New growth in spring is medium green.

**LEAF DESCRIPTION:** SIMPLE, 1/2" to 3/4" long and to 1/2" wide, ovate to obovate shape with entire margins, OPPOSITE arrangement.

**FLOWER DESCRIPTION:** INCONSPICUOUS

**EXPOSURE/CULTURE:** Full sun or light shade. Prefers well-drained, organic soil but appears quite adaptable. Should be mulched for best growth. Very low-maintenance, except for occasional light pruning to keep plants similar in size and shape.

**PEST PROBLEMS:** Leaf spots, leaf miner, nematodes, spider mites, root rot.

**SELECTED CULTIVARS:** None. This is a cultivar of *B. sempervirens,* a large shrub.

**LANDSCAPE NOTES:** Dwarf Boxwood can be used in mass or as an edging or border plant. It is useful for bordering flower beds, planting beds, lawn borders, walks and drives, and makes a nice dwarf hedge. It is generally associated with more formal architecture, but it is adaptable. It is especially appropriate for use with colonial architecture. EXPENSIVE.

# *Chamaecyparis obtusa 'Nana Gracilis'* Dwarf Hinoki False Cypress

**ZONES:**
4, 5, 6, 7, 8

**HEIGHT:**
4' to 5'

**WIDTH:**
3' to 4'

**FRUIT:**
1/4" round cones (8-10 scales);
RARE.

**TEXTURE:**
Medium fine.

**GROWTH RATE:**
Slow

**HABIT:**
Forms an irregular pyramid
with drooping, frondlike
branches.

**FAMILY:**
Cupressaceae

**LEAF COLOR:** Lustrous green with white markings underneath.

**LEAF DESCRIPTION:** Tiny scale-like leaves that are closely pressed to the stem.
OPPOSITE arrangement.

**FLOWER DESCRIPTION:** NOT NOTICEABLE.

**EXPOSURE/CULTURE:** Full sun or light shade. Prefers well-drained soil in locations that are humid. The roots prefer to be cool, but one must avoid excessive mulching, as the plant is not tolerant of high moisture. Highly individualized character, so avoid pruning.

**PEST PROBLEMS:** Juniper twig blight, root rot, mites. None serious.

**SELECTED CULTIVARS:** None. This is a cultivar of *C. obtusa,* a medium to large evergreen tree.

**LANDSCAPE NOTES:** Dwarf Hinoki False Cypress is a plant to feature in the landscape. Individual plants have their own character, often leaning or twisting. Especially useful for an oriental effect. EXPENSIVE.

# *Chamaecyparis pisifera 'Filifera Aurea Nana'*\*

**ZONES:**
4, 5, 6, 7, 8

**HEIGHT:**
2′ to 3′

**WIDTH:**
3′ to 4′

**FRUIT:**
1/4″ round cone. NOT COMMON.

**TEXTURE:**
Fine

**GROWTH RATE:**
Moderate

**HABIT:**
Rounded with stringy, drooping branches. Dense.

**FAMILY:**
Cupressaceae

**LEAF COLOR:** Bright yellow when exposed to full sun.

**LEAF DESCRIPTION:** Two-ranked, long pointed, needle-like foliage on flattened branchlets.

**FLOWER DESCRIPTION:** Monoecious; NOT NOTICEABLE.

**EXPOSURE/CULTURE:** Best in full sun, but tolerant of light shade. Prefers well-drained, loamy soils, in humid locations. Avoid addition of lime. Requires little, if any, pruning.

**PEST PROBLEMS:** No serious pests.

**SELECTED CULTIVARS:** None. This is a cultivar of *C. pisifera,* a large evergreen tree.

**LANDSCAPE NOTES:** Dwarf Gold Thread-branch Cypress is a bold accent plant with noticeable color and habit of growth. It is well suited to both residential and commericial landscapes, and requires a minimum of maintenance activities. It looks good in combination with broadleaf plantings, and it performs well in rock garden settings. Color of buildings and structures should be considered prior to using.

**\*COMMON NAME:** Dwarf Gold Thread-branch Cypress

# *Cotoneaster glaucophyllus*

**Gray Cotoneaster**

**ZONES:**
6, 7, 8

**HEIGHT:**
3' to 4'

**WIDTH:**
3' to 5'

**FRUIT:**
1/4" orange-red drupe.

**TEXTURE:**
Fine

**GROWTH RATE:**
Moderately rapid.

**HABIT:**
Spreading with arching branches.

**FAMILY:**
Rosaceae

**LEAF COLOR:** Greenish-gray during all seasons.

**LEAF DESCRIPTION:** SIMPLE, 1/2" to 5/8" long and half as wide, ovate shape with acute base and entire margins, ALTERNATE arrangement.

**FLOWER DESCRIPTION:** White, 1/4" to 1/2", in clusters of 6 to 20. Flowers in mid-spring.

**EXPOSURE/CULTURE:** Full sun. Prefers well-drained soil and moderate moisture; however, it is tolerant of dry conditions and will thrive in poor soils. Selective pruning of limbs to maintain its natural shape is all that is needed.

**PEST PROBLEMS:** No serious pests. Occasionally bothered by lacebugs, mites, fire blight.

**SELECTED CULTIVARS:** None

**LANDSCAPE NOTES:** Gray Cotoneaster is valued for its dramatic foliage color, flowers, and fruits. It is an ideal plant to feature in the landscape. It is useful for foundation plantings, borders, and low screens. It is especially useful for ground covering on steep banks. This plant should be more widely used in the recommended zones.

## *Cotoneaster microphyllus*

**Little-leaf Cotoneaster**

**ZONES:**
5, 6, 7, 8

**HEIGHT:**
1′ to 3′

**WIDTH:**
4′ to 6′

**FRUIT:**
1/4″ scarlet red pomes in fall.

**TEXTURE:**
Fine

**GROWTH RATE:**
Moderate to rapid.

**HABIT:**
Low spreading mound with arching branches.

**FAMILY:**
Rosaceae

**LEAF COLOR:** Lustrous dark green with gray underside.

**LEAF DESCRIPTION:** SIMPLE, 1/4″ to 1/2″ long and half as wide, obovate shape with obtuse tip, entire margins. ALTERNATE arrangement.

**FLOWER DESCRIPTION:** 1/4″ to 1/2″ white flowers, noticeable but not all that showy. Flowers in spring.

**EXPOSURE/CULTURE:** Sun or light shade. This plant is adaptable to a wide range of soils, except wet soils. Adapts well to almost any pH, and is tolerant of salt. Occasional pruning might be necessary to maintain shape. Responds well to moderate fertilization.

**PEST PROBLEMS:** Fire blight, spider mites.

**SELECTED CULTIVARS:** 'Emerald Spray' - Emerald green leaves with a very dense growth habit. var. *thymifolius* - Thyme Rockspray Cotoneaster. Leaves are narrow and curl under. This is a very tight-branched variety with numerous branches. Very nice variety.

**LANDSCAPE NOTES:** Little-leaf Cotoneaster is really a semi-deciduous shrub that is often used as a ground cover. It is the finest textured Cotoneaster, and provides good contrast in combination with coarse-textured plantings.

## *Danae racemosa*

**Alexandrian Laurel**

**ZONES:**
8, 9

**HEIGHT:**
2′ to 3′

**WIDTH:**
3′ to 4′

**FRUIT:**
1/4″ to 1/2″ orange-red berry in fall.

**TEXTURE:**
Medium

**GROWTH RATE:**
Slow

**HABIT:**
Irregularly rounded with arching branches.

**FAMILY:**
Liliaceae

**LEAF COLOR:** Dark green and glossy.

**LEAF DESCRIPTION:** SIMPLE, 2″ to 4″ long and one-third as wide, broad lanceolate shape with entire margins, ALTERNATE arrangement. NOTE: Leaves of this plant are really flattened stems.

**FLOWER DESCRIPTION:** Tiny whitish flowers in terminal racemes in spring. Not especially noticeable.

**EXPOSURE/CULTURE:** Must be grown in shade; burns in the presence of too much direct light. Prefers well-drained, organic soil. Responds favorably to supplemental watering and moderate fertilization. Requires very little maintenance pruning.

**PEST PROBLEMS:** No serious pests.

**SELECTED CULTIVARS:** None

**LANDSCAPE NOTES:** Alexandrian Laurel is a very graceful plant with a growth habit that reminds one of Dwarf Bamboo. Both the leaves and fruit are very attractive. The leaves are often used in floral arrangements because of the flattened and glossy appearance. Unfortunately, its range is limited, but it can be grown in Zone 7, with protection. This plant makes a good indoor container plant.

## *Daphne odora*    Winter Daphne

▲ 'Variegata'

**ZONES:**
7, 8, 9

**HEIGHT:**
To 4'

**WIDTH:**
3' to 4'

**FRUIT:**
Brown drupe; NOT COMMON.

**TEXTURE:**
Medium

**GROWTH RATE:**
Slow

**HABIT:**
Dense and mounded under ideal conditions.

**FAMILY:**
Thymelaeaceae

**LEAF COLOR:** Dark green. Cultivars vary in leaf colorings.

**LEAF DESCRIPTION:** SIMPLE, 2 1/2" to 3 1/2" long and one-third as wide, narrow elliptical shape with entire margins, ALTERNATE arrangement.

**FLOWER DESCRIPTION:** Rose-purple in 1" to 1 1/2" terminal clusters. Very fragrant. Flowers in January and February. Showy, but noted more for its fragrance.

**EXPOSURE/CULTURE:** Light shade to shade. Prefers well-drained, organic soil. Does not take kindly to fertilization, and is considered by many as hard to grow. Pruning is minimal, but necessary, to thicken wherever dense plants are desired.

**PEST PROBLEMS:** Fungus diseases, viruses, mealybugs.

**SELECTED CULTIVARS:** 'Alba' - Has pale white flowers. 'Aureo-marginata' - Has pale yellow leaf margins. Flowers rose-purple with white centers. 'Variegata' - Bright yellow leaf margins with pink flowers.

**LANDSCAPE NOTES:** Winter Daphne adds color and fragrance to the garden during the "dead" of winter when many plants are dull. Variegated forms add color and accent to the garden throughout the year. Considered temperamental by many, it is not a choice for mass plantings or extensive use in commericial landscapes.

# *Gardenia jasminoides 'Radicans'*

**Dwarf Gardenia**

**ZONES:**
7, 8, 9, 10

**HEIGHT:**
1 1/2' to 2'

**WIDTH:**
2 1/2' to 3'

**FRUIT:**
Small berry; NOT COMMON.

**TEXTURE:**
Fine to medium.

**GROWTH RATE:**
Moderate

**HABIT:**
Spreading, free-flowing mound.

**FAMILY:**
Rubiaceae

**LEAF COLOR:** Dark glossy green.

**LEAF DESCRIPTION:** SIMPLE, 1" to 2" long and half as wide, elliptical to lanceolate shape with entire margins, OPPOSITE pairs, but sometimes WHORLED in threes.

**FLOWER DESCRIPTION:** White, 1 1/2" to 2" across. Very fragrant. Flowers in June.

**EXPOSURE/CULTURE:** Full sun or part shade. Prefers well-drained, organic soil that is acidic in reaction. Responds favorably to supplemental moisture, especially when blooming. Pruning is very minimal.

**PEST PROBLEMS:** White flies, aphids, scale, mites, nematodes.

**SELECTED CULTIVARS:** None. This is a cultivar of *G. jasminoides,* a medium to large shrub.

**LANDSCAPE NOTES:** Dwarf Gardenia is a beautiful dwarf shrub under ideal conditions, and is somewhat hardier than the species. It has many uses in the garden, but is especially useful in mass where it provides a ground cover effect. It is prized for its fragrant and delicate flowers. It is best below Zone 7, but will thrive in Zone 7 with limited protection. Can be grown indoors.

## Hypericum patulum

**Goldencup St. Johnswort**

**ZONES:**
5, 6, 7, 8

**HEIGHT:**
3' to 3 1/2'

**WIDTH:**
3' to 4'

**FRUIT:**
Brown capsule; NOT ORNA-MENTAL.

**TEXTURE:**
Medium

**GROWTH RATE:**
Moderate to rapid.

**HABIT:**
Spreading with arched branches.

**FAMILY:**
Hypericaceae

**LEAF COLOR:** Dark green.

**LEAF DESCRIPTION:** SIMPLE, 2″ to 2 1/2″ long and half as wide, ovate shape with entire margins, OPPOSITE arrangement.

**FLOWER DESCRIPTION:** Golden yellow, approximately 2″ wide, borne solitary or occasionally in cymes, five-petaled with long stamens that give a "brush" effect. Flowers throughout summer.

**EXPOSURE/CULTURE:** Full sun or light shade. Prefers well-drained soil of any pH. Does not flourish as well in extremes of high heat and humidity. Prune in early spring to produce lush growth and abundant flowers in summer.

**PEST PROBLEMS:** No serious pests.

**SELECTED CULTIVARS:** 'Sungold' - Hardy cultivar with 2 1/2″ flowers. var. *grandiflorum* - Has the largest flowers; 3″ and greater. var. *henryi* - The most vigorous form with larger flowers.

**LANDSCAPE NOTES:** Goldencup St. Johnswort is an excellent plant for naturalizing in the shrub border in sun or light shade. It offers an accent of yellow that is noticeable, but not overdone. It is a SEMI-EVERGREEN plant in the NORTHERNMOST of the recommended zones.

# Ilex cornuta 'Carissa'

**Carissa Holly**

**ZONES:**
6, 7, 8, 9

**HEIGHT:**
3' to 4'

**WIDTH:**
4' to 5'

**FRUIT:**
NONE

**TEXTURE:**
Medium to coarse.

**GROWTH RATE:**
Moderate to slow.

**HABIT:**
Compact, densely branching mound.

**FAMILY:**
Aquifoliaceae

**LEAF COLOR:** Dark green and waxy.

**LEAF DESCRIPTION:** SIMPLE, 2″ to 3″ long and half as wide, ovate to elliptical shape, entire margins, except for one spine at the tip. Leaf appears "raised" between veins (bullate), ALTERNATE arrangement.

**FLOWER DESCRIPTION:** Tiny, yellowish; VERY RARE.

**EXPOSURE/CULTURE:** Full sun or part shade. Tolerates a wide range of conditions and soil types, except wet soils. Very heat- and drought-resistant. Requires a minimum of pruning to shape.

**PEST PROBLEMS:** Scale insects.

**SELECTED CULTIVARS:** None. This is a sport (mutation) of *I. cornuta* 'Rotunda'.

**LANDSCAPE NOTES:** Carissa Holly has become widely used in the recommended zones, primarily as a substitute for the over-planted 'Rotunda'. It has the same culture and growth habit as 'Rotunda', but is less hazardous to plant and maintain. Dense growth and superior foliage make this an ideal foundation plant or low hedge.

# *Ilex cornuta* 'Rotunda'

**Dwarf Horned Holly, Rotunda Holly**

**ZONES:**
6, 7, 8, 9

**HEIGHT:**
3' to 3 1/2'

**WIDTH:**
4' to 4 1/2'

**FRUIT:**
1/4" red berries; NOT ABUNDANT.

**TEXTURE:**
Coarse

**GROWTH RATE:**
Moderate to slow.

**HABIT:**
Extremely dense and mounded.

**FAMILY:**
Aquifoliaceae

**LEAF COLOR:** Lustrous dark green.

**LEAF DESCRIPTION:** SIMPLE, 2" to 3" and half as wide, general shape is oblong with prominent spinose margins, very stiff, ALTERNATE arrangement. Leaves somewhat hazardous.

**FLOWER DESCRIPTION:** Tiny, yellowish in axils of leaves, NOT CONSPICUOUS.

**EXPOSURE/CULTURE:** Full sun or part shade. Adaptable to a wide range of soil types and conditions, except wet soils. Handles heat and drought very well, and is often used in the harsh extremes of commercial landscapes. Requires very little pruning.

**PEST PROBLEMS:** Scale is the major problem.

**SELECTED CULTIVARS:** None. This is a cultivar of *I. cornuta,* a large shrub.

**LANDSCAPE NOTES:** Dwarf Horned Holly is an extremely dense shrub that is rugged enough for a wide range of landscape conditions. It is excellent as a foundation shrub or as a low hedge. Equally ideal for residential or commercial usage.

# Ilex crenata 'Green Lustre'

**Green Luster Holly**

**ZONES:**
5, 6, 7, 8

**HEIGHT:**
3' to 4'

**WIDTH:**
4' to 6'

**FRUIT:**
1/4" black drupe.

**TEXTURE:**
Fine

**GROWTH RATE:**
Moderate

**HABIT:**
Low and broad-spreading; broader than tall.

**FAMILY:**
Aquifoliaceae

**LEAF COLOR:** Dark green.

**LEAF DESCRIPTION:** SIMPLE, 1" to 1 1/4" long and half as wide, elliptic or oval shape, crenate to serrulate margins, ALTERNATE arrangement.

**FLOWER DESCRIPTION:** Tiny, greenish-white on tiny cymes, NOT NOTICEABLE.

**EXPOSURE/CULTURE:** Sun or part shade. Does best in slightly acid, heavy soils. Not suited for sandy soil or dry conditions. Responds favorably to supplemental fertilizer and water. Prune to shape.

**PEST PROBLEMS:** Spider mites, nematodes.

**SELECTED CULTIVARS:** None. This is a cultivar of *I. crenata,* a large shrub.

**LANDSCAPE NOTES:** Green Luster Holly is yet another of the ever-popular Japanese Hollies. It provides interesting form, being somewhat flat in habit, yet attaining good size. The leaves are larger than 'Helleri', and remind one of 'Rotundifolia'. The plant is more cold hardy than 'Rotundifolia'.

## Ilex crenata 'Helleri'

**Helleri Holly**

**ZONES:**
6, 7, 8

**HEIGHT:**
2' to 3'

**WIDTH:**
4' to 5'

**FRUIT:**
NONE, usually.

**TEXTURE:**
Fine

**GROWTH RATE:**
Moderate

**HABIT:**
Dense mound; broader than tall.

**FAMILY:**
Aquifoliaceae

**LEAF COLOR:** Dark green.

**LEAF DESCRIPTION:** SIMPLE, 1/2" long and 1/4" wide, elliptic or oval shape, crenate to serrulate margins, ALTERNATE arrangement.

**FLOWER DESCRIPTION:** NOT NOTICEABLE.

**EXPOSURE/CULTURE:** Sun or shade. Prefers slightly acid, heavy soils. Not as drought-tolerant as some Hollies. Does not perform well in sandy soils or soils that are alkaline. Responds well to pruning. Supplemental water and moderate fertilization are favorable.

**PEST PROBLEMS:** Scale, spider mites. Nematodes in sandy soils.

**SELECTED CULTIVARS:** None. This is a cultivar of *I. crenata,* a large shrub having many cultivars of various sizes.

**RELATED CULTIVARS:** 'Green Island' - More open in growth habit than 'Helleri'. Similar in size. 'Green Luster' - More open growth. Leaves larger than 'Helleri'. (SEE PREVIOUS PLANT.) 'Kingsville Green Cushion' - Low-growing to 1'. 'Repandens' - Similar to 'Helleri', but noticeably spreading in habit. 'Stokes' - Not as prostrate as 'Helleri', but with superior glossy foliage. 'Tiny Tim' - More open in habit and having superior cold hardiness.

**LANDSCAPE NOTES:** Helleri Holly is a proven selection for the recommended zones. Overplanted, but still superior.

# *Ilex vomitoria* 'Nana'

**Dwarf Yaupon Holly**

▲ 'Schelling's Dwarf'

**ZONES:**
7, 8, 9, 10

**HEIGHT:**
3' to 4'

**WIDTH:**
4' to 5'

**FRUIT:**
1/4" red drupe; usually not seen.

**TEXTURE:**
Fine

**GROWTH RATE:**
Moderate

**HABIT:**
Dense and mounded; broader than tall.

**FAMILY:**
Aquifoliaceae

**LEAF COLOR:** Dark green; new foliage in spring much lighter.

**LEAF DESCRIPTION:** SIMPLE, 1/2" to 1" long and half as wide, elliptic to oval in shape, margin has a few widely-spaced teeth (serrated), ALTERNATE arrangement. DISTINCT GRAY STEMS SEPARATE IT FROM HELLERI HOLLY.

**FLOWER DESCRIPTION:** NOT NOTICEABLE.

**EXPOSURE/CULTURE:** Full sun to part shade. Adaptable to a wide range of soil types and conditions. Will grow in clay or sand. Very drought-tolerant, but will withstand moderately wet, humid conditions. Superior to Helleri Holly for hot or sandy conditions. Very little pruning needed.

**PEST PROBLEMS:** No serious pests.

**SELECTED CULTIVARS:** None. This is a cultivar of *I. vomitoria,* a large shrub.

**RELATED CULTIVARS:** 'Schelling's Dwarf' - Stokes Dwarf. Leaves smaller, giving it a similarity to Helleri Holly. More compact than 'Nana'. 'Straughn's' - Leaves smaller than 'Nana' and listed as stronger or more resistant to breakage.

**LANDSCAPE NOTES:** Dwarf Yaupon makes an outstanding foundation plant or low hedge. It performs better than Helleri Holly under adverse conditions. ALL YAUPONS HAVE BEAUTIFUL SMOOTH, GRAY-WHITE BARK.

# *Jasminum floridum*

**Florida Jasmine, Showy Jasmine**

**ZONES:**
7, 8, 9

**HEIGHT:**
3′ to 4′

**WIDTH:**
5′ to 6′

**FRUIT:**
Tiny black berry; VERY RARE.

**TEXTURE:**
Fine

**GROWTH RATE:**
Moderate

**HABIT:**
Open mound with pendulous branches.

**FAMILY:**
Oleaceae

**LEAF COLOR:** Medium to dark green.

**LEAF DESCRIPTION:** COMPOUND, 3 leaflets (sometimes 5), each leaflet 1″ long and half as wide, leaflets ovate in shape with entire margins, ALTERNATE arrangement of the compound leaves.

**FLOWER DESCRIPTION:** Yellow, approximately 3/4″ long, 5-petaled. Flowers April through June.

**EXPOSURE/CULTURE:** Full sun or part shade. Prefers well-drained soil, but is adaptable to a wide range of soil types and moisture conditions. It is a graceful plant when left unpruned; however, it is easily pruned to a variety of shapes.

**PEST PROBLEMS:** No serious pests.

**SELECTED CULTIVARS:** None

**RELATED SPECIES:** *J. multipartitum* - African Jasmine. Dark shiny leaves. White, fragrant flowers, opening from pink buds. Zone 9. *J. nitidum* - Angel Wing Jasmine. Large leaves with fragrant, white pinwheel flowers.

**LANDSCAPE NOTES:** Florida Jasmine is showy, but not boldly so. It adds sparkle to dull areas of the garden and is sometimes used in foundation plantings. It can be used as a low hedge or ground cover.

# *Juniperus chinensis 'Armstrongii'*

**Armstrong Juniper**

**ZONES:**
4, 5, 6, 7, 8, 9

**HEIGHT:**
3' to 4'

**WIDTH:**
3' to 5'

**FRUIT:**
1/3" blue cone; maturing to brown.

**TEXTURE:**
Fine

**GROWTH RATE:**
Moderate to rapid.

**HABIT:**
Upright with spreading horizontal branches. Graceful.

**FAMILY:**
Cupressaceae

**LEAF COLOR:** Light green to yellowish-green.

**LEAF DESCRIPTION:** SCALE-LIKE, 1/16", soft and lacy except for very old growth. Arranged in OPPOSITE pairs or WHORLED in threes.

**FLOWER DESCRIPTION:** Dioecious; NOT NOTICEABLE.

**EXPOSURE/CULTURE:** Full sun, not tolerant of shade. Adaptable to any soil type or pH level. Will withstand drought, but does not thrive in wet soils. Grouped plants display uniformity of growth, so pruning is not normally needed. VERY, VERY easy to grow.

**PEST PROBLEMS:** Juniper twig blight, spider mites, bagworms. None severe.

**SELECTED CULTIVARS:** None. This is a cultivar of *J. chinensis* 'Pfitzeriana', a large evergreen shrub.

**RELATED CULTIVARS:** 'Fruitlandii' - Very dense, vigorous growing form with bright green foliage. 'Nick's Compacta' - Very compact form to 3' with gray-green foliage. 'Pfitzeriana Compacta' - Similar to 'Nick's Compacta', but growing only 1' to 2' high.

**LANDSCAPE NOTES:** Armstrong Juniper is superior in form and foliage. It combines well with broadleaf evergreens.

# *Juniperus chinensis 'Gold Coast'*

**Gold Coast Juniper**

▲ Courtesy of Monrovia Nursery Co.

**ZONES:**
4, 5, 6, 7, 8, 9

**HEIGHT:**
2 1/2' to 3'

**WIDTH:**
4' to 5'

**FRUIT:**
1/3" bluish cone; maturing to brown.

**TEXTURE:**
Fine

**GROWTH RATE:**
Moderate

**HABIT:**
Compact and spreading.

**FAMILY:**
Cupressaceae

**LEAF COLOR:** Golden yellow new growth; older growth, yellow-green.

**LEAF DESCRIPTION:** NEEDLE-LIKE juvenile growth to SCALE-LIKE mature growth, 1/16", soft and lacy. Arranged in OPPOSITE pairs or WHORLED in groups of three.

**FLOWER DESCRIPTION:** Dioecious; NOT NOTICEABLE.

**EXPOSURE/CULTURE:** Needs full sun, not tolerant of shade. Chinese Junipers are adaptable to many soil types and pH levels. One of the best plants for drought tolerance, but cannot handle wet conditions. Pruning is not usually necessary.

**PEST PROBLEMS:** Twig blight, spider mites, bagworms.

**SELECTED CULTIVARS:** None. This is a cultivar.

**RELATED CULTIVARS:** 'Gold Sovereign' - Bright yellow foliage all year. Slow growing to around 2'. 'Old Gold' - Foliage is bronze-gold all year. Moderate grower to about 3'. 'Saybrook Gold' - Bright yellow-gold in summer; bronze-gold in winter. To about 3'.

**LANDSCAPE NOTES:** Gold Coast Juniper is a refined plant with colorful foliage all year. It looks best as a foreground plant in combination with dark green broadleaf plants. An accent or specimen plant.

# *Juniperus communis 'Repanda'*     **Dwarf Common Juniper**

**ZONES:**
2, 3, 4, 5, 6, 7

**HEIGHT:**
1′ to 1 1/2′

**WIDTH:**
3′ to 4′

**FRUIT:**
1/4″ to 1/2″ blue or black cone.

**TEXTURE:**
Fine

**GROWTH RATE:**
Slow to moderate.

**HABIT:**
Dense, semi-prostrate with ascending branches; very symmetrical.

**FAMILY:**
Cupressaceae

**LEAF COLOR:** Medium green in season; develops slight bronze cast in winter.

**LEAF DESCRIPTION:** AWL-LIKE to NEEDLE-LIKE, sharply pointed, 1/4″ to 1/2″ long, WHORLED in groups of three. Top surface concave with a white, linear band (stripe).

**FLOWER DESCRIPTION:** Dioecious; NOT NOTICEABLE.

**EXPOSURE/CULTURE:** Full sun or very light shade. Tolerates any soil except extremely wet soils. Thrives under dry, sandy conditions. Requires little, if any, pruning.

**PEST PROBLEMS:** Twig blight, spider mites, bagworms.

**SELECTED CULTIVARS:** None. This is a cultivar of *J. communis,* a small evergreen tree. However, the following is a related variety: var. *depressa* - Grows 3′ to 4′ tall with branchlets growing at 45 degrees to 60 degrees to the ground.

**LANDSCAPE NOTES:** Dwarf Common Juniper is one of the hardiest shrubs for harsh conditions. It is suitable for clay or sandy coastal conditions. This plant is most effective in mass for a ground cover effect.

## *Juniperus davurica* 'Expansa'

**Parson's Juniper**

**ZONES:**
4, 5, 6, 7, 8, 9

**HEIGHT:**
1' to 2'

**WIDTH:**
3' to 5'

**FRUIT:**
1/2" blue-green "berries" (cones).

**TEXTURE:**
Fine

**GROWTH RATE:**
Moderate

**HABIT:**
Stiff and spreading; branches raised above ground.

**FAMILY:**
Cupressaceae

**LEAF COLOR:** Gray-green during all seasons.

**LEAF DESCRIPTION:** SCALE-LIKE or NEEDLE-LIKE, 1/16" to 1/4", arranged in OPPOSITE groups of three.

**FLOWER DESCRIPTION:** NOT NOTICEABLE.

**EXPOSURE/CULTURE:** Full sun or very light shade. Grows in almost any soil type or condition except wet soils. Withstands drought and grows well in coastal sands. Grows epecially well in the southeast, and is bothered less by twig blight than other Junipers. Requires very little pruning.

**PEST PROBLEMS:** Twig blight, spider mites, bagworms.

**SELECTED CULTIVARS:** None. This is a cultivar.

**RELATED CULTIVARS:** 'Expansa Aureospicata' - Dark green with bright yellow variegation. 'Expansa Variegata' - Dark green with creamy white variegation.

**LANDSCAPE NOTES:** Parson's Juniper is sometimes listed as a ground cover and is often used for that purpose. It is a superior Juniper with rugged character, and is widely used in commercial landscapes. It is equally suited for home gardens, and best used in mass.

# *Juniperus sabina* 'Broadmoor'

**Broadmoor Savin Juniper**

▲ 'Moor-Dense' Courtesy of Monrovia Nursery Co.

**ZONES:**
3, 4, 5, 6, 7

**HEIGHT:**
2' to 2 1/2'

**WIDTH:**
6' to 8'

**FRUIT:**
None (male cultivar).

**TEXTURE:**
Fine

**GROWTH RATE:**
Moderate

**HABIT:**
Spreading with ascending branchlets; may mound in center.

**FAMILY:**
Cupressaceae

**LEAF COLOR:** Grayish-green

**LEAF DESCRIPTION:** SCALE-LIKE or NEEDLE-LIKE, 1/16" to 1/5", arranged in OPPOSITE pairs (4-ranked). Leaves give off a foul odor when crushed.

**FLOWER DESCRIPTION:** Dioecious or monoecious; NOT NOTICEABLE.

**EXPOSURE/CULTURE:** Full sun. Adaptable to a wide range of well-drained soils. Tolerates dry conditions, but is not suited for humid regions of the southeast. Little, if any, pruning is necessary.

**PEST PROBLEMS:** Bagworms, spider mites. Resistant to Juniper blight.

**SELECTED CULTIVARS:** None. This is a cultivar of *J. sabina,* a large evergreen shrub.

**RELATED CULTIVARS:** 'Arcadia' - Grows to 1 1/2' and has grass-green foliage. 'Moor-Dense' - A flatter growing version of 'Broadmoor'. Monrovia introduction. 'Skandia' - Very dwarf to about 1' with grayish-green foliage. var. *tamariscifolia* - Tamarix Juniper. Mounded to 4' with blue-green foliage. Commonly used but very susceptible to Juniper blight.

**LANDSCAPE NOTES:** Broadmoor Savin Juniper thrives in poor soil in sunny exposures, and is suitable as a ground cover or as a foundation plant. It is an outstanding choice for northern or western regions of the U.S.

## *Juniperus virginiana* 'Grey Owl'                 Grey Owl Juniper

**ZONES:**
2, 3, 4, 5, 6, 7, 8, 9

**HEIGHT:**
2 1/2' to 3'

**WIDTH:**
4' to 5'

**FRUIT:**
1/4" purplish-blue "berries" (cones).

**TEXTURE:**
Fine

**GROWTH RATE:**
Moderate

**HABIT:**
Wide spreading and compact; somewhat open in center.

**FAMILY:**
Cupressaceae

**LEAF COLOR:** Silvery-gray, taking on a distinct gray cast.

**LEAF DESCRIPTION:** SCALE-LIKE 1/16" leaves on older growth, NEEDLE-LIKE 1/4" leaves on juvenile growth. OPPOSITE pairs (4-ranked).

**FLOWER DESCRIPTION:** Mostly dioecious; NOT NOTICEABLE.

**EXPOSURE/CULTURE:** Full sun. Adaptable to a wide range of well-drained soil types. Will grow under adverse conditions. Pruning is usually not needed.

**PEST PROBLEMS:** Bagworms, cedar-apple rust, Juniper blight.

**SELECTED CULTIVARS:** None. This is a cultivar of *J. virginiana,* a large evergreen tree.

**RELATED CULTIVARS:** 'Blue Cloud' - Taller growing (4') with gray-green foliage. 'Silver Spreader' - Has distinct silver-gray foliage that is more silver than 'Grey Owl'. Monrovia introduction.

**LANDSCAPE NOTES:** Grey Owl Juniper has many possibilities in the landscape. It is an excellent choice for foundations, low borders, massing, ground covering, and as an accent plant. Foliage color is quite dramatic, and has interesting form. With a little imagination, one can visualize an owl with out-stretched wings.

# *Leucothoe fontanesiana*

**Drooping Leucothoe, Doghobble**

▲ 'Girard's Rainbow'

**ZONES:**
5, 6, 7, 8, 9

**HEIGHT:**
3' to 4'

**WIDTH:**
4' to 5'

**FRUIT:**
5-lobed brown capsule; NOT ORNAMENTAL.

**TEXTURE:**
Coarse

**GROWTH RATE:**
Moderately slow.

**HABIT:**
Gracefully arching branches on spreading plant.

**FAMILY:**
Ericaceae

**LEAF COLOR:** Lustrous dark green; bronze-purple in winter.

**LEAF DESCRIPTION:** SIMPLE, 3" to 5" long and 1" to 1 1/2" wide, ovate-lanceolate to lanceolate in shape with serrulate-spinose margins. ALTERNATE arrangement.

**FLOWER DESCRIPTION:** White, 1/4", urn-shaped, in drooping 3" axillary racemes. Fragrant. Flowers in April to May.

**EXPOSURE/CULTURE:** Light shade to dense shade. Very particular as to soil and conditions. Does best in low pH soils similar to that for *Rhododendron*. Needs well-drained soil with high organic matter. Will not tolerate drought. Selectively prune older "canes" each year to rejuvenate.

**PEST PROBLEMS:** Leaf spot diseases. Can be serious at times.

**SELECTED CULTIVARS:** 'Nana' - Dwarf form to 2' high with a spread of 5'. Very dense. 'Girard's Rainbow' - Variegated. New growth green with white, pink, or copper markings. 'Scarletta' - New growth red, maturing to green; rich burgundy in fall.

**LANDSCAPE NOTES:** Drooping Leucothoe is a loose, informal plant that is nice for naturalizing in shaded gardens. The shiny leaves contrast well with the dull foliage of many woodland plants. Makes a nice speciment plant, and is great for massing and screening in garden borders.

## *Ligustrum japonicum* 'Rotundifolium'     **Curlyleaf Ligustrum**

**ZONES:**
7, 8, 9, 10

**HEIGHT:**
3' to 4'

**WIDTH:**
2' to 3'

**FRUIT:**
1/4" black berry (drupe).

**TEXTURE:**
Medium

**GROWTH RATE:**
Slow

**HABIT:**
Upright, stiff, and dense; taller than broad.

**FAMILY:**
Oleaceae

**LEAF COLOR:** Dark green.

**LEAF DESCRIPTION:** SIMPLE, 1" to 2" long and 3/4" to 1 1/4" wide, broad ovate shape with entire margins that are very thick and often twisted. OPPOSITE arrangement.

**FLOWER DESCRIPTION:** White, tiny in 2" to 4" pyramid-shaped panicles. Not spectacular. Flowers in May.

**EXPOSURE/CULTURE:** Sun or shade. Adaptable to a wide range of soils and conditions. Prefers well-drained soils. Prune as desired for shaping.

**PEST PROBLEMS:** None

**SELECTED CULTIVARS:** None. This is a cultivar of *L. japonicum,* a large evergreen shrub.

**LANDSCAPE NOTES:** Twisted foliage makes Curlyleaf Ligustrum a plant to feature. It is too unusual to use in quantity, but it certainly has use as a foundation plant to accent an area of the house or garden. Makes a nice corner plant, and performs well in rock gardens. Use with moderation.

## *Lonicera pileata*

**Privet Honeysuckle**

**ZONES:**
6, 7, 8, 9

**HEIGHT:**
2' to 3'

**WIDTH:**
3' to 4'

**FRUIT:**
1/4" translucent purple berry;
RARE.

**TEXTURE:**
Fine

**GROWTH RATE:**
Moderate

**HABIT:**
Spreading with arched
branches; densely layered.

**FAMILY:**
Caprifoliaceae

**LEAF COLOR:** Lustrous green.

**LEAF DESCRIPTION:** SIMPLE, 3/4" to 1 1/2" long and 1/4" to 5/8" wide, ovate to oblong-lanceolate shape with entire margins. OPPOSITE arrangement.

**FLOWER DESCRIPTION:** Whitish, 1/4" to 1/2" long, occuring in pairs. Not showy. Flowers in May.

**EXPOSURE/CULTURE:** Shade or part shade. Adaptable to any well-drained soil. Requires moisture and moderate fertilization for best appearance. Pruning is minimal.

**PEST PROBLEMS:** No serious pests.

**SELECTED CULTIVARS:** None

**RELATED SPECIES:** *L. nitida* 'Yunnan' - Yunnan Honeysuckle. This plant has smaller, more refined leaves, but is less cold hardy.

**LANDSCAPE NOTES:** Privet Honeysuckle is a shrub that is probably best used as a ground cover. It makes a great "facer" shrub for more leggy shrubs, and is interesting in rock gardens and hillside gardens.

# *Mahonia aquifolium*

## Oregon Hollygrape

▲ 'Compacta'

**ZONES:**
5, 6, 7, 8

**HEIGHT:**
3' to 4'

**WIDTH:**
3' to 4'

**FRUIT:**
1/3" to 1/2" blue-black berries; abundant.

**TEXTURE:**
Coarse

**GROWTH RATE:**
Slow

**HABIT:**
Upright and stiff; stems cane-like and unbranched.

**FAMILY:**
Berberidaceae

**LEAF COLOR:** Dark green in season; purplish-bronze in winter.

**LEAF DESCRIPTION:** COMPOUND, pinnate, 5 to 9 leaflets, leaflets 2" to 3" long and half as wide, ovate shape with spinose margins, appearing holly-like. ALTERNATE arrangement.

**FLOWER DESCRIPTION:** Yellow, appearing in 2" to 3" fascicled racemes at the tips of branches. Attractive. Flowers in spring.

**EXPOSURE/CULTURE:** Light shade to heavy shade. Tolerates a wide range of soils as long as it is neither excessively wet nor excessively dry. Does not like hot, dry conditions. Must be protected from harsh winds. Remove older "canes" to ground level to rejuvenate.

**PEST PROBLEMS:** Barberry aphid, leaf spots, leaf rusts, scale, whitefly.

**SELECTED CULTIVARS:** 'Atropurpureum' - Leaves become dark reddish-purple in winter. 'Compacta' - A round and compact form that matures at 2'. Expensive. 'Mayhan Strain' - Dwarf, 2' or less, with more tightly arranged leaves and leaflets.

**LANDSCAPE NOTES:** Oregon Hollygrape is a bold accent plant to contrast with finer textured plants. It is most effective in groupings of three or more. Bright yellow flowers are followed by bunches of blue-black berries before the foliage matures to bronze in winter. An interesting plant during all seasons.

# *Nandina domestica* 'Harbour Dwarf'

**Harbour Dwarf Nandina**

**ZONES:**
6, 7, 8, 9, 10

**HEIGHT:**
2' to 3'

**WIDTH:**
3' to 3 1/2'

**FRUIT:**
1/4" to 1/3" bright red berries.

**TEXTURE:**
Fine to medium.

**GROWTH RATE:**
Moderate

**HABIT:**
Mounded with vertical branching from the ground.

**FAMILY:**
Berberidaceae

**LEAF COLOR:** Dark green in season; reddish-purple tinged in winter.

**LEAF DESCRIPTION:** COMPOUND, bipinnate or tripinnate (thrice divided), three leaflets per division. Leaflets 1" to 2" long and half as wide, ovate shape with entire margins. ALTERNATE arrangement.

**FLOWER DESCRIPTION:** White, to 1/4", appearing on 4" panicles. Not showy. Flowers in May.

**EXPOSURE/CULTURE:** Sun or shade. Nandinas prefer moist, organic soils, but will adapt to almost any conditions. Thin older "canes" to ground every two or three years. Considered very low-maintenance.

**PEST PROBLEMS:** None

**SELECTED CULTIVARS:** None. This is a cultivar of *N. domestica,* a medium-sized shrub.

**LANDSCAPE NOTES:** Harbour Dwarf Nandina has excellent form and foliage color, as well as good berry production. It is used for edgings and borders, raised planters, and as "facer" shrubs. Many authorities consider Harbour Dwarf to be the superior cultivar of Dwarf Nandinas.

## *Nandina domestica* 'Nana Purpurea' — Dwarf Sacred Bamboo

▼ 'Fire Power'

**ZONES:**
6, 7, 8, 9, 10

**HEIGHT:**
1′ to 2′

**WIDTH:**
1′ to 2′

**FRUIT:**
NONE

**TEXTURE:**
Medium

**GROWTH RATE:**
Moderate

**HABIT:**
Rounded and compact; canes not usually branching.

**FAMILY:**
Berberidaceae

**LEAF COLOR:** Light green in season; reddish-purple in winter.

**LEAF DESCRIPTION:** COMPOUND, bipinnate or tripinnate, usually three leaflets per division. Leaflets 1″ to 2″ long and half as wide, ovate shape with entire margins. Foliage "cupped" (convex). ALTERNATE arrangement.

**FLOWER DESCRIPTION:** None

**EXPOSURE/CULTURE:** Sun or shade. Nandinas adapt to a wide range of conditions. Very hardy in the recommended zones. Can be sheared to maintain the global habit of growth. Selected "canes" should be thinned to ground level every two or three years.

**PEST PROBLEMS:** None

**SELECTED CULTIVARS:** None. This is a cultivar.

**RELATED CULTIVARS:** 'Fire Power' - Blaze-red winter color. Leaves not "cupped" as with 'Nana Purpurea'. 'Gulf Stream' - Branches freely from base. New leaves copper, maturing to green. Fall color is orange-red. 'Moon Bay' - Smaller leaves on a broad mound. Bright red in winter. 'San Gabriel' - Has lacy, almost fern-like foliage. Apricot color in winter. 'Wood's Dwarf' - Similar to 'Nana Purpurea', but without "cupped" leaves.

**LANDSCAPE NOTES:** Dwarf Sacred Bamboo is a much sought after plant for both residential and commercial landscapes. Very dwarf plants display striking light green foliage in spring and bold red or purplish leaves in fall. Best used for borders or small groupings of three or more. Use in moderation.

# *Picea abies* 'Nidiformis'

**Bird's Nest Spruce**

**ZONES:**
2, 3, 4, 5, 6, 7

**HEIGHT:**
1' to 2'

**WIDTH:**
3' to 5'

**FRUIT:**
Usually not present.

**TEXTURE:**
Fine

**GROWTH RATE:**
Slow

**HABIT:**
Broad and dense; slightly depressed in the center.

**FAMILY:**
Pinaceae

**LEAF COLOR:** Greenish-gray

**LEAF DESCRIPTION:** SIMPLE, 1/4" to 1/3", NEEDLE-LIKE leaves with linear shape, slightly curved and ending in a blunt point, appearing spirally around the branchlets. Sometimes pectinate on the undersides.

**FLOWER DESCRIPTION:** Monoecious; NOT NOTICEABLE.

**EXPOSURE/CULTURE:** Full sun. Prefers moist, sandy loam that is well-drained, but it adapts to clay soil. Provide supplemental water during dry periods. Pruning is usually not necessary.

**PEST PROBLEMS:** Borers, budworm, two-spotted mites.

**SELECTED CULTIVARS:** None. This is a cultivar of *P. abies,* Norway Spruce, a large evergreen tree.

**RELATED CULTIVARS:** 'Clanbrassiliana' - Dense and flat-topped form growing to 4'. 'Pumila' - A dense form to 4' that has horizontal lower branches, while upper branches are nearly vertical.

**LANDSCAPE NOTES:** Bird's Nest Spruce makes a nice, lush specimen to feature in the foundation planting. It combines well with broadleaf shrubs, and is especially attractive in rock gardens.

# Picea glauca 'Conica'

## Dwarf Alberta Spruce

**ZONES:**
2, 3, 4, 5, 6, 7

**HEIGHT:**
3' to 4', after many years.

**WIDTH:**
2' to 3', after many years.

**FRUIT:**
Not usually present.

**TEXTURE:**
Fine

**GROWTH RATE:**
Extremely slow.

**HABIT:**
Cone-shaped and very dense.

**FAMILY:**
Pinaceae

**LEAF COLOR:** Grass green in season; gray tinged in winter.

**LEAF DESCRIPTION:** SIMPLE, NEEDLE-LIKE, 1/2″ long, four-sided, tapering to a blunt point. ALTERNATE arrangement and crowded.

**FLOWER DESCRIPTION:** Monoecious; NOT NOTICEABLE.

**EXPOSURE/CULTURE:** Sun or very light shade. Grows best in moist, sandy loam, but is adaptable. Protect from harsh winds. Can be sheared to maintain the pyramid shape. Basically low-maintenance.

**PEST PROBLEMS:** Mites, spruce bagworms.

**SELECTED CULTIVARS:** None. This is a cultivar of *P. glauca,* White Spruce, a large evergreen tree.

**LANDSCAPE NOTES:** Dwarf Alberta Spruce is a magnificent rock garden plant or foundation plant that makes a bold accent in the landscape. It requires very little shearing to maintain shape. It is often used as a container plant for porches, decks, and other areas.

# *Picea pungens* 'Glauca Globosa'

## Dwarf Globe Blue Spruce

**ZONES:**
2, 3, 4, 5, 6, 7

**HEIGHT:**
2 1/2' to 3'

**WIDTH:**
3 1/2' to 4 1/2'

**FRUIT:**
2" cone; pendulous and rare.

**TEXTURE:**
Medium

**GROWTH RATE:**
Slow

**HABIT:**
Dense and globular; somewhat flat-topped.

**FAMILY:**
Pinaceae

**LEAF COLOR:** Bluish-green to bluish-white.

**LEAF DESCRIPTION:** NEEDLE-LIKE, 1/2" long and 1/16" wide, sickle-shaped or incurved, pointed; mostly radial arrangement, four-sided with 3 to 4 stomatal lines on each surface.

**FLOWER DESCRIPTION:** Monoecious. Male yellowish and axillary; female greenish to purplish and terminal.

**EXPOSURE/CULTURE:** Full sun. Prefers rich, moist soils, but is adaptable to most well-drained soils. Drought-tolerant. Pruning is not usually necessary.

**PEST PROBLEMS:** Spruce budworms; spider mites in southern part of recommended zones.

**SELECTED CULTIVARS:** None. This is a cultivar of *P. pungens,* a large evergreen tree.

**LANDSCAPE NOTES:** Dwarf Globe Blue Spruce is a fine specimen plant that can be used in foundations, rock gardens, borders, or containers. This is an outstanding plant that is easy to maintain.

## *Pinus mugo 'Compacta'*

**Dwarf Mugo Pine**

**ZONES:**
2, 3, 4, 5, 6, 7

**HEIGHT:**
2' to 4'

**WIDTH:**
3' to 5'

**FRUIT:**
1" black cones; NOT ABUN-DANT.

**TEXTURE:**
Fine to medium.

**GROWTH RATE:**
Extremely slow.

**HABIT:**
Extremely dense, rounded shrub.

**FAMILY:**
Pinaceae

**LEAF COLOR:** Green

**LEAF DESCRIPTION:** SIMPLE, NEEDLE-LIKE, 1" to 2" long, stomates in lines on both top and bottom surfaces. ALTERNATE, fascicled clusters of 2. Very crowded and curved forward toward tip.

**FLOWER DESCRIPTION:** Monoecious; NOT NOTICEABLE.

**EXPOSURE/CULTURE:** Full sun to light shade. Prefers a deep, moist, sandy loam, but is adaptable. Plant can be sheared to make it even more dense.

**PEST PROBLEMS:** Borers, pine shoot moth, scale.

**SELECTED CULTIVARS:** None. This is cultivar of *P. mugo*, Swiss Mountain Pine, a small evergreen tree.

**LANDSCAPE NOTES:** This expensive and slow-growing shrub is virtually maintenance-free. Plants are stiff and almost indestructible. It is a great foundation plant, rock garden plant, or raised planter shrub. Outstanding.

# *Pinus sylvestris 'Albyns'*

**Dwarf Scotch Pine**

**ZONES:**
2, 3, 4, 5, 6, 7

**HEIGHT:**
1' to 2'

**WIDTH:**
5' to 8'

**FRUIT:**
Small oval cone; usually not present.

**TEXTURE:**
Medium

**GROWTH RATE:**
Slow

**HABIT:**
Flat to slightly mounded; branches ascending.

**FAMILY:**
Pinaceae

**LEAF COLOR:** Gray-green

**LEAF DESCRIPTION:** NEEDLE-LIKE, 1" to 2" long, appearing in bundles of 2; radially arranged, margins serrate; upper surface convex with stomatal lines.

**FLOWER DESCRIPTION:** Monoecious, greenish; usually not present.

**EXPOSURE/CULTURE:** Full sun. The plant prefers well-drained, loamy soil, but adapts to poor, droughty sites. Pruning is usually not necessary.

**PEST PROBLEMS:** Many boring-type insects and moths afflict the *Pinus* genus. Check with the Extension Service in your area.

**SELECTED CULTIVARS:** None. This is a cultivar of *P. sylvestris,* Scotch Pine, a large evergreen tree.

**RELATED CULTIVARS:** 'Globosa Viridis' - Globular dwarf form that grows 3' to 4' tall. Dense. 'Nana' - Dwarf form to 2' with more globular shape than 'Albyns'.

**LANDSCAPE NOTES:** Dwarf Scotch Pine may be used in foundation plantings, rock gardens, or containers. It is also an excellent plant for berms and raised planters where the soil is usually drier.

# *Pittosporum tobira* 'Wheeler's Dwarf'

**Wheeler's Dwarf Pittosporum**

▲ 'White Spot'

▲ 'Variegated Hines Hardy'

**ZONES:**
8, 9

**HEIGHT:**
4'

**WIDTH:**
4' to 5'

**FRUIT:**
1/2" brown capsules, NOT ORNAMENTAL.

**TEXTURE:**
Medium

**GROWTH RATE:**
Moderate

**HABIT:**
Upright growth on dense, broad-spreading plant.

**FAMILY:**
Pittosporaceae

**LEAF COLOR:** Dark green.

**LEAF DESCRIPTION:** SIMPLE, 2" to 3" long and half as wide, obovate shape with entire margins, slightly "cupped," ALTERNATE arrangement, appearing whorled at the tips.

**FLOWER DESCRIPTION:** White, 1" long, appearing in clusters, 5-petaled, fragrant— similar to orange blossom. Flowers in April.

**EXPOSURE/CULTURE:** Sun or shade. Tolerant of any well-drained soil in the recommended zones. Does well in sand. Great for beach plantings. Needs minimal pruning to maintain shape.

**PEST PROBLEMS:** Leaf spots, mealy bugs.

**SELECTED CULTIVARS:** None. This is a cultivar of *P. tobira,* a large evergreen shrub.

**RELATED CULTIVARS:** 'Hines Hardy' - More hardy, possibly to Zone 7. A Hines Nurseries introduction. 'Variegated Hines Hardy' - Similar to 'White Spot', but reportedly more hardy. A Hines Nurseries introduction. 'White Spot' - ('Variegata'?) - Gray-green leaves with white margins. Zone 9.

**LANDSCAPE NOTES:** Dwarf Pittosporum is an attractive plant that has limited range outdoors. It is a good selection for indoor landscapes further north.

# Prunus laurocerasus 'Otto Luyken'

**Otto Luyken Laurel**

**ZONES:**
6, 7, 8, 9

**HEIGHT:**
3'

**WIDTH:**
5'

**FRUIT:**
1/2" purplish-black drupe.

**TEXTURE:**
Coarse

**GROWTH RATE:**
Moderate

**HABIT:**
Open and spreading; ascending branches.

**FAMILY:**
Rosaceae

**LEAF COLOR:** Glossy dark green.

**LEAF DESCRIPTION:** SIMPLE, 3 1/2" to 4 1/2" long or longer, 1" to 1 1/2" wide, narrow elliptic shape, mostly entire, ALTERNATE arrangement.

**FLOWER DESCRIPTION:** White, 1/4" in 3" to 4" upright racemes. Very showy. Flowers in mid-spring.

**EXPOSURE/CULTURE:** Sun or shade. Adaptable to any well-drained soil. Rootrot more common in clay. Responds well to regular pruning.

**PEST PROBLEMS:** Shothole fungus, rootrot.

**SELECTED CULTIVARS:** None. This is a cultivar of *P. laurocerasus*, English Laurel, a large evergreen shrub.

**LANDSCAPE NOTES:** Otto Luyken Laurel is valuable for its flower spikes and coarse texture in a dwarf plant. Makes a good foundation plant, but is bothered by fungi when watered from overhead.

## *Raphiolepis indica*

### Indian Hawthorn

**ZONES:**
7, 8, 9, 10

**HEIGHT:**
3' to 4'

**WIDTH:**
4' to 5'

**FRUIT:**
1/4" to 1/2" black berries.

**TEXTURE:**
Medium

**GROWTH RATE:**
Moderately slow.

**HABIT:**
Open, mounded shrub; ascending branches.

**FAMILY:**
Rosaceae

**LEAF COLOR:** Dark green.

**LEAF DESCRIPTION:** SIMPLE, 2" to 3" long and 1" to 2" wide, elliptic to broad elliptic shape with serrated margins. ALTERNATE arrangement.

**FLOWER DESCRIPTION:** White, pink, or rose-pink, 1/2" in upright terminal panicles. Very attractive. Flowers in April.

**EXPOSURE/CULTURE:** Sun or light shade. Needs well-drained soils with a pH of 6.0 to 8.0. Somewhat salt-tolerant; can be used in beach plantings. Little, if any, pruning is needed.

**PEST PROBLEMS:** Leaf spots.

**SELECTED CULTIVARS:** 'Charisma' - Double, soft pink flowers. A Monrovia introduction. 'Enchantress - Rich rose-pink flowers. A Monrovia introduction. 'Indian Princess' - Compact and broad. Large, bright green leaves. Pink flowers, fading to white. A Monrovia introduction. 'Jack Evans' - Broad-spreading with double pink flowers. 'Snow White' - White flowers. 'Spring Rapture' - Prolific rose-red flowers. A Monrovia introduction. 'Springtime' - Leathery, bronzy-green foliage and rich pink flowers. A Monrovia introduction. 'White Enchantress' - Similar to 'Enchantress', except for white flowers. A Monrovia introduction.

**LANDSCAPE NOTES:** Indian Hawthorn is a good substitute for Azaleas, but has a strong character of its own. Once established, it is a heavy blooming plant that is very showy. This makes a nice foundation plant, and it is often used in mass in borders and accent beds.

# Taxus cuspidata 'Intermedia'

**Dwarf Japanese Yew**

**ZONES:**
4, 5, 6, 7

**HEIGHT:**
2' to 3'

**WIDTH:**
4' to 5'

**FRUIT:**
1/4" red seed.

**TEXTURE:**
Medium-fine

**GROWTH RATE:**
Slow

**HABIT:**
Upright with spreading branches.

**FAMILY:**
Taxaceae

**LEAF COLOR:** Medium to dark green.

**LEAF DESCRIPTION:** SIMPLE, 1/2" NEEDLE-LIKE, linear with entire margins, two yellowish bands on lower surface, 2-ranked and SPIRALLY arranged.

**FLOWER DESCRIPTION:** Dioecious; NOT NOTICEABLE.

**EXPOSURE/CULTURE:** Sun or shade. Tolerant of most soils, except wet soils. Needs moist, well-drained soil for best performance. Great plant for polluted areas. Can be sheared into almost any shape.

**PEST PROBLEMS:** Twig blight, spider mites.

**SELECTED CULTIVARS:** None. This is a cultivar of *T. cuspidata,* a small to medium evergreen tree.

**RELATED CULTIVARS:** 'Densa' - Lower, spreading form.

**LANDSCAPE NOTES:** An extensively used plant because of its beautiful foliage and compact habit. Should be used as a foundation plant or low hedge. Shearing will result in super thick plants that resemble Mugo Pine.

# *Tsuga canadensis* 'Jeddeloh'

## Jeddeloh Canadian Hemlock

**ZONES:**
5, 6, 7, 8

**HEIGHT:**
2'

**WIDTH:**
3'

**FRUIT:**
3/4" brown, oval cone.

**TEXTURE:**
Fine

**GROWTH RATE:**
Very slow.

**HABIT:**
Mounded and weeping; depressed in center.

**FAMILY:**
Pinaceae

**LEAF COLOR:** Lime green.

**LEAF DESCRIPTION:** SIMPLE, 1/4" NEEDLES, linear with tiny teeth (spines), two gray-white bands on lower surface, 2-ranked arrangement.

**FLOWER DESCRIPTION:** Monoecious; NOT NOTICEABLE.

**EXPOSURE/CULTURE:** Sun or shade. Needs well-drained, organic soil. Does not handle drought or excessively wet soils. Protect from wind. Pruning is minimal.

**PEST PROBLEMS:** No serious pests. Subject to sunscorch and drought injury.

**SELECTED CULTIVARS:** None. This is a cultivar of *T. canadensis,* a large evergreen tree.

**LANDSCAPE NOTES:** Jeddeloh Canadian Hemlock is an outstanding dwarf conifer. Unlike Junipers, it tolerates much more shade, but requires a regular supply of moisture. It is slow growing for ease in maintenance. Great for massing, foundations, and rock gardens.

# *Yucca filamentosa*

**Adam's Needle Yucca**

▲ 'Starburst' Courtesy of Monrovia Nursery Co.

▲ Courtesy of Monrovia Nursery Co.

**ZONES:**
4, 5, 6, 7, 8, 9

**HEIGHT:**
1′ to 2′

**WIDTH:**
2′ to 3′

**FRUIT:**
1″ brown capsule; NOT ORNAMENTAL.

**TEXTURE:**
Coarse

**GROWTH RATE:**
Moderate

**HABIT:**
Upright with stiff, dagger-like leaves.

**FAMILY:**
Agavaceae

**LEAF COLOR:** Medium green

**LEAF DESCRIPTION:** SIMPLE, 1′ to 2′ long and 1″ to 2″ wide, long linear shape with sharp, stiff, hazardous tips, infolded with sharp margins that have thread-like filaments, WHORLED around short stem.

**FLOWER DESCRIPTION:** White, 2″ to 2 1/2″ wide, appearing on 4′ to 6′ panicles in late spring. Very showy.

**EXPOSURE/CULTURE:** Sun. The plant prefers light, well-drained soil, but is adaptable to all but wet soils. Prune to remove flower stalk after flowers die. Easy to grow and low-maintenance.

**PEST PROBLEMS:** None

**SELECTED CULTIVARS:** 'Ivory Tower' - Plant grows to 3′ high and has ivory-white flower panicles. A Monrovia introduction. 'Starburst' - Has dark green leaves with yellow margins. Yellow margins become pinkish during cold weather. A Monrovia introduction.

**RELATED SPECIES:** *Y. flaccida* - (See next page.) *Y. smalliana* - This species has more narrow leaves and smaller flowers.

**LANDSCAPE NOTES:** Adam's Needle Yucca is a hardy plant (Zone 4) that will grow in any well-drained soil, from clay to sand. It is an accent plant that can be used in foundations, borders, rock gardens, and accent beds. This is a rugged, yet attractive plant, that is ideal for xeriscaping. NOTE: Hazardous spines. Avoid planting where children are present.

## Yucca flaccida

**Floppy Yucca, Weakleaf Yucca**

▲ 'Bright Edge'

**ZONES:**
5, 6, 7, 8, 9

**HEIGHT:**
1' to 2'

**WIDTH:**
2' to 3'

**FRUIT:**
1" brown capsule; NOT ORNA-MENTAL.

**TEXTURE:**
Coarse

**GROWTH RATE:**
Moderate

**HABIT:**
Upright; lower branches pendulous.

**FAMILY:**
Agavaceae

**LEAF COLOR:** Pale medium green.

**LEAF DESCRIPTION:** SIMPLE, 1 1/2' to 2' long and 1" to 2" wide, long linear shape with pointed tips, WHORLED from the crown.

**FLOWER DESCRIPTION:** White to greenish-white, 2" bell-shaped flowers on 3' to 4' stalks. Flowers in June.

**EXPOSURE/CULTURE:** Sun or light shade. Will thrive in hot, dry locations in sand or clay. Great for beach plantings. Pruning is minimal. Prune dead flower stalks each year.

**PEST PROBLEMS:** No serious pests.

**SELECTED CULTIVARS:** 'Golden Sword' - Has yellow center stripes on leaves.

**LANDSCAPE NOTES:** Weakleaf Yucca is a hardy plant with tall spikes of flowers in summer. Not as dangerous as *Y. filamentosa,* since the leaves are flexible. Quite spectacular in bloom. Great plant for beach plantings and rock gardens.

# *Berberis thunbergii var. atropurpurea 'Crimson Pygmy'*\*

**ZONES:**
4, 5, 6, 7, 8

**HEIGHT:**
1′ to 2′

**WIDTH:**
3′ to 4′

**FRUIT:**
Red berry.

**TEXTURE:**
Fine

**GROWTH RATE:**
Moderate

**HABIT:**
Spreading mound; similar to Helleri Holly.

**FAMILY:**
Berberidaceae

**LEAF COLOR:** Reddish-purple

**LEAF DESCRIPTION:** SIMPLE, 1/2″ to 1″ long and 1/4″ to 1/2″ wide, obovate shape with entire margins, ALTERNATE arrangement.

**FLOWER DESCRIPTION:** Yellow, tinged with purple, 1/4″, noticeable, but not spectacular. Flowers in spring.

**EXPOSURE/CULTURE:** Sun for best foliage color. Does best in well-drained, moist soil, but will thrive in dry sites. Pruning is minimal.

**PEST PROBLEMS:** No serious pests.

**SELECTED CULTIVARS:** None. This is a cultivar of *B. thunbergii* var. *atropurpurea,* a medium deciduous shrub.

**RELATED CULTIVARS:** 'Baggatelle'  More compact with smaller leaves.

**LANDSCAPE NOTES:** This is an intense accent plant that makes a great "facer" plant for use with evergreens. It can be used as a border plant when planted in the foreground. The foliage is rich and very noticeable. Good selection for urban conditions.

**\*COMMON NAME:** Crimson Pygmy Barberry

## *Caryopteris incana* 'Longwood Blue'  Blue Spirea, Bluebeard

**ZONES:**
7, 8, 9

**HEIGHT:**
4′

**WIDTH:**
4′ to 5′

**FRUIT:**
Brown, 4-valved; NOT ORNAMENTAL.

**TEXTURE:**
Medium

**GROWTH RATE:**
Moderately rapid.

**HABIT:**
Mounded and open.

**FAMILY:**
Verbenaceae

**LEAF COLOR:** Green; lower surface is gray and hairy (tomentose).

**LEAF DESCRIPTION:** SIMPLE, 2″ to 3″ long and half as wide, ovate to oblong-ovate shape with coarsely serrated margins. OPPOSITE arrangement.

**FLOWER DESCRIPTION:** Blue to lavender-blue, 1/4″ in dense cymes. Flowers in fall.

**EXPOSURE/CULTURE:** Full sun. Prefers well-drained, organic soil. Prune severely in early spring, since it flowers on new growth. Considered easy to grow. Can be grown as a herbaceous perennial further north.

**PEST PROBLEMS:** No serious pests.

**SELECTED CULTIVARS:** None. This a cultivar of *c. incana*.

**RELATED SPECIES:** *C.* x *clandonenis* - This is a hybrid of *C. incana* x *C. mongholica*. It grows to 3′ with blue flowers. 'Blue Mist' has silver-gray foliage and powder-blue flowers. 'Dark Knight' has dark green leaves and deep blue flowers.

**LANDSCAPE NOTES:** Blue Spirea is an excellent plant for low hedges or perennial gardens. The flowers attract butterflies to the garden. This is a great low-maintenance plant.

## *Chaenomeles japonica*

**Japanese Flowering Quince**

**ZONES:**
4, 5, 6, 7, 8

**HEIGHT:**
2 1/2' to 3 1/2'

**WIDTH:**
2 1/2' to 4'

**FRUIT:**
1 1/2", apple-like; edible.

**TEXTURE:**
Medium

**GROWTH RATE:**
Moderate

**HABIT:**
Loosely spreading; many stems.

**FAMILY:**
Rosaceae

**LEAF COLOR:** Dark glossy green.

**LEAF DESCRIPTION:** SIMPLE, 1 1/2" long and half as wide, obovate shape with coarse crenate margins. ALTERNATE arrangement.

**FLOWER DESCRIPTION:** Red or orange, 1 1/2" long, solitary. Flowers in early spring.

**EXPOSURE/CULTURE:** Sun or light shade. Adapts well to most well-drained soils. Prune to thin older shoots after flowering.

**PEST PROBLEMS:** Leaf spot, scale, fireblight.

**SELECTED CULTIVARS:** 'Cameo' - Compact and low with apricot-pink flowers. 'Low and White' - Low with soft white flowers. A Monrovia introduction. 'Minerva' - Large cherry red flowers. 'Orange Delight' - Low with orange-red flowers. 'Pink Beauty' - Upright with rose-pink flowers. 'Super Red' - Upright with bright red flowers. A Monrovia introduction. 'Texas Scarlet' - Low with fire-red flowers.

**LANDSCAPE NOTES:** Japanese Flowering Quince is valuable for its showy flowers during early spring. It should be used in the borders of the property or in mass plantings. Very dependable and hardy. The fruit is edible.

## *Deutzia gracilis*

**Slender Deutzia**

**ZONES:**
5, 6, 7, 8

**HEIGHT:**
2' to 3'

**WIDTH:**
3' to 4'

**FRUIT:**
Brown capsule; NOT ORNA-MENTAL.

**TEXTURE:**
Medium

**GROWTH RATE:**
Moderate

**HABIT:**
Broad, compact mound with arching branches.

**FAMILY:**
Saxifragaceae

**LEAF COLOR:** Light green.

**LEAF DESCRIPTION:** SIMPLE, 1 1/2" to 2 1/2" long and 1" to 1 1/4" wide, ovate-lanceolate shape with serrated margins. OPPOSITE arrangement.

**FLOWER DESCRIPTION:** White, tiny in 2 1/2" to 3" long erect panicles. Blooms in May.

**EXPOSURE/CULTURE:** Sun or light shade. Thrives in any well-drained soil. Prune to thin out older stems after flowering. Do not shear; maintain natural shape.

**PEST PROBLEMS:** No serious pests.

**SELECTED CULTIVARS:** 'Nikko' - White blooms on arching branches. Leaves are burgundy in fall. 'Pink' - Has pink flowers.

**LANDSCAPE NOTES:** Slender Deutzia is a carefree flowering shrub that is best used where color is desired but winter foliage is not important. Grows under a wide range of garden conditions.

## *Hydrangea arborescens*

**Hills-of-Snow Hydrangea**

**ZONES:**
4, 5, 6, 7, 8, 9

**HEIGHT:**
3' to 4'

**WIDTH:**
4' to 5'

**FRUIT:**
Dehiscent capsule; NOT ORNAMENTAL.

**TEXTURE:**
Coarse

**GROWTH RATE:**
Rapid

**HABIT:**
Upright and rounded; somewhat open and loose.

**FAMILY:**
Saxifragaceae

**LEAF COLOR:** Medium green.

**LEAF DESCRIPTION:** SIMPLE, 5" to 6" long and 4" to 5" wide, broad ovate shape with serrated margins. OPPOSITE arrangement.

**FLOWER DESCRIPTION:** White to greenish, appearing in multi-branched 5" to 6" round clusters, outer florets sterile, inner florets fertile. Flowers in summer.

**EXPOSURE/CULTURE:** Full sun for best bloom. Plants need well-drained, somewhat moist and rich soil. Can be pruned heavily in early spring. Do not shear in summer.

**PEST PROBLEMS:** No serious pests.

**SELECTED CULTIVARS:** 'Grandiflora' - Flowers more numerous; non-fruiting. 'Annabelle' - Huge flower clusters to 12" diameter. Outstanding.

**LANDSCAPE NOTES:** Hills-of-Snow Hydrangea is grown for its very noticeable summer blooms. It is considered extremely easy to grow, and looks great in dull areas of the garden border. This is an outstanding plant for naturalizing.

## Hydrangea macrophylla    Florist's Hydrangea, Bigleaf Hydrangea

**ZONES:**
7, 8, 9

**HEIGHT:**
3′ to 4′

**WIDTH:**
5′ to 6′

**FRUIT:**
Capsule; NOT ORNAMENTAL.

**TEXTURE:**
Coarse

**GROWTH RATE:**
Rapid

**HABIT:**
Almost round; broader than tall.

**FAMILY:**
Saxifragaceae

**LEAF COLOR:** Medium green.

**LEAF DESCRIPTION:** SIMPLE, 5″ to 8″ long and 3″ to 6″ wide, ovate shape with serrated margins. OPPOSITE arrangement.

**FLOWER DESCRIPTION:** Pink or blue, 1″ florets in 6″ clusters, outer florets sterile, inner florets fertile. Flowers in summer.

**EXPOSURE/CULTURE:** Sun or light shade. Needs a rich, moist, well-drained soil. Prune heavily in early spring, if needed. Leave natural, do not shear.

**PEST PROBLEMS:** Mildew, wilt, rust.

**SELECTED CULTIVARS:** 'Mariesii' - Lacecap. Has fertile flowers, ringed by sterile flowers. Pink to mauve-pink. 'Mariesii Variegata' - White to creamy-white leaf margins. Lacecap. Soft blue flowers. 'Merritt's Beauty' - Carmine red flowers. 'Nikko Blue' - Deep blue flowers when planted in acid soil. 'Pink Lacecap' - Bright pink flowers. 'White' - Pure white flowers.

**LANDSCAPE NOTES:** Bigleaf Hydrangea produces abundant flower clusters in summer that can be cut and used in arrangements. This plant is most appropriate in shrub borders, but not as a foundation plant against the wall. The species produces blue flower clusters in acid soil and pink blooms in neutral soil.

## *Hypericum frondosum*

**Golden St. John's Wort**

**ZONES:**
5, 6, 7, 8, 9

**HEIGHT:**
3' to 4'

**WIDTH:**
4' to 5'

**FRUIT:**
Dehiscent capsule; NOT ORNAMENTAL.

**TEXTURE:**
Medium

**GROWTH RATE:**
Moderate

**HABIT:**
Upright and open; lower branches arching.

**FAMILY:**
Hypericaceae

**LEAF COLOR:** Bluish-green

**LEAF DESCRIPTION:** SIMPLE, 1 1/2″ to 2 1/2″ long and one-fourth as wide, oblong-ovate to linear shape with entire margins. OPPOSITE arrangement.

**FLOWER DESCRIPTION:** Bright yellow, 1 1/2″ to 2″ across, solitary or in groups, stamens numerous giving a "brush" effect. Blooms in summer.

**EXPOSURE/CULTURE:** Sun or part shade. Prefers moist, organic soil that is well-drained. Will take heavy pruning in early spring, but should not be sheared. Low-maintenance.

**PEST PROBLEMS:** No serious pests, but attracts many bees.

**SELECTED CULTIVARS:** 'Sunburst' - Low-growing to 3'. Heavy bloomer.

**LANDSCAPE NOTES:** Golden St. John's Wort has many possibilities in the landscape, from rock gardens to massing. This is a great plant for dull areas of the garden, and is especially useful for naturalizing. Outstanding woody landscape plant.

## *Jasminum nudiflorum* — Winter Jasmine

**ZONES:**
6, 7, 8, 9, 10

**HEIGHT:**
2 1/2' to 4'

**WIDTH:**
4' to 6'

**FRUIT:**
Black berry; not common.

**TEXTURE:**
Fine

**GROWTH RATE:**
Moderate

**HABIT:**
Broad mound with weeping branches.

**FAMILY:**
Oleaceae

**LEAF COLOR:** Dark green.

**LEAF DESCRIPTION:** COMPOUND, 3 leaflets, each leaflet 1/2" to 1" long and 1/4" to 1/3" wide, long ovate shape with entire margins. OPPOSITE arrangement.

**FLOWER DESCRIPTION:** Yellow, 1" to 1 1/2" long, solitary. Flowers in February through March, before the leaves.

**EXPOSURE/CULTURE:** Sun or shade. Likes well-drained soil with adequate moisture, but will adapt to poor soil and dry conditions. Pruning is minimal.

**PEST PROBLEMS:** No serious pests.

**SELECTED CULTIVARS:** None

**LANDSCAPE NOTES:** Winter Jasmine flowers in the cold of winter before the foliage appears. It is often used as a low hedge along borders, but can be used as a ground cover since the weeping branches often root. Very noticeable in flower. Looks great during summer because of compact, dense habit.

## *Philadelphus* x *virginalis* 'Dwarf Snowflake'

**Dwarf Mockorange**

**ZONES:**
4, 5, 6, 7, 8, 9

**HEIGHT:**
3' to 4'

**WIDTH:**
3' to 4'

**FRUIT:**
Brown capsule; NOT ORNA-MENTAL.

**TEXTURE:**
Medium

**GROWTH RATE:**
Rapid

**HABIT:**
Upright and open; arching with age.

**FAMILY:**
Saxifragaceae

**LEAF COLOR:** Medium green.

**LEAF DESCRIPTION:** SIMPLE, 2″ to 3″ long and half as wide, ovate shape with serrated margins (teeth widely spaced), leaf puckered between veins. OPPOSITE arrangement.

**FLOWER DESCRIPTION:** White, double, 1/2″ to 2″ wide, fragrant. Blooms in spring.

**EXPOSURE/CULTURE:** Full sun or light shade. The plant is very adaptable, but responds favorably to well-drained, organic soil. Prune after flowering, but not later than mid-summer.

**PEST PROBLEMS:** Aphids, mildew.

**SELECTED CULTIVARS:** None. This is a cultivar of *P.* x *virginalis,* Mockorange, a medium size deciduous shrub.

**LANDSCAPE NOTES:** Dwarf Mockorange is a dainty form of the old-fashioned Mockoranges. It provides great accent during bloom and fits into smaller areas. It is a plant well-suited for garden borders, and fits into natural areas. Should be placed where its fragrance can be appreciated.

## *Potentilla fruticosa*                                   **Bush Cinquefoil**

**ZONES:**
2, 3, 4, 5, 6, 7

**HEIGHT:**
2′ to 3′

**WIDTH:**
2′ to 3′

**FRUIT:**
Brown achene; NOT ORNA-MENTAL.

**TEXTURE:**
Fine

**GROWTH RATE:**
Moderate

**HABIT:**
Irregularly rounded; dense.

**FAMILY:**
Rosaceae

**LEAF COLOR:** Medium green.

**LEAF DESCRIPTION:** COMPOUND, usually 5 leaflets, leaflets 1/2″ to 3/4″ long and 1/4″ to 1/2″ wide, oblong-lanceolate shape with entire margins that fold under. ALTERNATE arrangement.

**FLOWER DESCRIPTION:** Bright yellow, 1″ to 2″ wide, 5-petaled. Single, some cultivars double. Solitary or in small groups. Flowers in summer for several weeks.

**EXPOSURE/CULTURE:** Full sun or light shade. Potentilla is tolerant of most well-drained soils. Responds well to supplemental water during drought. Prune after flowers die to shape and remove fruits.

**PEST PROBLEMS:** No serious pests.

**SELECTED CULTIVARS:** 'Abbotswood' - Has white flowers. 'Coronation Triumph' - Oval, upright shape. Bright yellow flowers. 'Gold Star' - Bright yellow 2″ blooms. 'Goldfinger' - Large, golden yellow flowers. 'Longacre' - Acclaimed as drought-tolerant. Soft yellow flowers. 'Red Ace' - Orange-red flowers with pale yellow undersides. A Monrovia introduction. 'Sunset' - Brick-orange flowers. Often mostly yellow during heat of summer.

**LANDSCAPE NOTES:** Potentilla is an excellent border plant or rock garden plant. This is a good plant for perennial plantings. Although woody, there are over 500 species, most of which are herbaceous. This is NOT A GOOD CHOICE FOR SOUTHERN GARDENS.

# *Prunus glandulosa*

## Dwarf Flowering Almond

▼ 'Rosea'

▲ 'Alboplena'

**ZONES:**
4, 5, 6, 7, 8

**HEIGHT:**
3′ to 5′

**WIDTH:**
3′ to 5′

**FRUIT:**
3/8″ dark red drupe; not common.

**TEXTURE:**
Medium

**GROWTH RATE:**
Rapid

**HABIT:**
Upright and open; multi-stemmed.

**FAMILY:**
Rosaceae

**LEAF COLOR:** Medium green in summer; yellowish in fall.

**LEAF DESCRIPTION:** SIMPLE, 2″ to 4″ long and one-third as wide, oblong-lanceolate to narrow elliptic shape with serrulate margins. ALTERNATE arrangement.

**FLOWER DESCRIPTION:** White or pink, 1/2″ wide, single or double, appearing in spring. Very showy.

**EXPOSURE/CULTURE:** Sun. Grows in almost any well-drained soil of acidic or alkaline reaction. Prune to shape after flowering. Very easy to grow. Will thrive in the southwest.

**PEST PROBLEMS:** Aphids on new growth.

**SELECTED CULTIVARS:** 'Alboplena' - Has double, white flowers. 'Rosea' - Has double, pink flowers.

**LANDSCAPE NOTES:** Dwarf Flowering Almond is a rugged, dependable accent plant that is attractive in flower but quite commonplace during the rest of the season. It should be used in dull areas of garden borders with other plantings. This plant is more attractive than credited. A great plant for xeriscaping.

# *Spiraea japonica* 'Alpina'

## Japanese Alpine Spirea

**ZONES:**
4, 5, 6, 7, 8, 9

**HEIGHT:**
1' to 2'

**WIDTH:**
2' to 2 1/2'

**FRUIT:**
Dehiscent follicle; NOT ORNAMENTAL.

**TEXTURE:**
Fine

**GROWTH RATE:**
Moderate

**HABIT:**
Dense, spreading mound.

**FAMILY:**
Rosaceae

**LEAF COLOR:** Bluish-green

**LEAF DESCRIPTION:** SIMPLE, 1/2″ long and 1/4″ wide, ovate to ovate-lanceolate shape with serrated margins. ALTERNATE arrangement.

**FLOWER DESCRIPTION:** Pink or rose-pink, tiny in 2″ clusters. Flowers in May and June.

**EXPOSURE/CULTURE:** Sun or light shade. Does best in well-drained soil that receives moderate to high moisture. Prune immediately after flowering, if needed.

**PEST PROBLEMS:** No serious pests.

**SELECTED CULTIVARS:** None. This is a cultivar of *S. japonica*.

**LANDSCAPE NOTES:** Alpine Spirea makes a fine addition to the perennial-type garden or border in front of evergreen plantings. It has great potential as a plant for edging bed areas or borders. It may be the smallest of the Spireas.

## *Spiraea japonica 'Shirobana'*    **Shirobana Spirea**

**ZONES:**
4, 5, 6, 7, 8, 9

**HEIGHT:**
2′ to 3′

**WIDTH:**
3′

**FRUIT:**
Dehiscent follicles; NOT ORNAMENTAL.

**TEXTURE:**
Fine

**GROWTH RATE:**
Moderate to rapid.

**HABIT:**
Dense and mounded.

**FAMILY:**
Rosaceae

**LEAF COLOR:** Bright green.

**LEAF DESCRIPTION:** SIMPLE, 1/2″ to 1″ long and half as wide, ovate-lanceolate shape with serrated margins. ALTERNATE arrangement.

**FLOWER DESCRIPTION:** White, pink, and red blooms on the same plant, appearing in 2″ to 4″ clusters (corymbs). Summer flowering.

**EXPOSURE/CULTURE:** Sun or light shade. The plant is adaptable to any well-drained soil, but does best in moist sites. Prune after flowering, if needed, to shape.

**PEST PROBLEMS:** No serious pests.

**SELECTED CULTIVARS:** None. This is a cultivar of *S. japonica*.

**LANDSCAPE NOTES:** Shirobana Spirea has one of the longest bloom periods of the genus. Starts flowering in summer and continues into early fall. In addition, the variations in bloom color makes this a plant to feature in a well-chosen location.

## *Spiraea* x *bumalda* 'Anthony Waterer'

**Anthony Waterer Spirea, Dwarf Pink Bridal Wreath**

**ZONES:**
4, 5, 6, 7, 8, 9

**HEIGHT:**
2 1/2' to 4'

**WIDTH:**
3' to 4'

**FRUIT:**
Dehiscent follicle; NOT ORNAMENTAL.

**TEXTURE:**
Fine

**GROWTH RATE:**
Moderate to rapid.

**HABIT:**
Dense and mounded.

**FAMILY:**
Rosaceae

**LEAF COLOR:** Bluish-green; variable.

**LEAF DESCRIPTION:** SIMPLE, 1″ to 2″ long and half as wide, ovate shape with doubly serrated margins. ALTERNATE arrangement.

**FLOWER DESCRIPTION:** Bright rose-pink, 3″ to 5″ somewhat flat clusters. Flowers all summer.

**EXPOSURE/CULTURE:** Sun or light shade. Prefers moist, well-drained soil. Provide additional water during drought. Prune after flowering to encourage additional flowers.

**PEST PROBLEMS:** No serious pests.

**SELECTED CULTIVARS:** None. This is a cultivar of *S.* x *bumalda,* a cross between *S. albiflora* and *S. japonica.*

**LANDSCAPE NOTES:** Anthony Waterer Spirea is one of the most popular Dwarf Spireas. It is easy to grow and provides attractive blooms over a long period. Blends well into natural plantings.

## *Spiraea* x *bumalda* 'Gold Flame'

**Gold Flame Spirea**

**ZONES:**
4, 5, 6, 7, 8, 9

**HEIGHT:**
2' to 3'

**WIDTH:**
3' to 4'

**FRUIT:**
Dehiscent follicle; NOT ORNAMENTAL.

**TEXTURE:**
Fine

**GROWTH RATE:**
Moderate to rapid.

**HABIT:**
Dense, broad mound.

**FAMILY:**
Rosaceae

**LEAF COLOR:** Bronze-gold in spring, yellow-green in summer, and copper-orange in fall.

**LEAF DESCRIPTION:** SIMPLE, 1" to 2" long and half as wide, ovate shape with doubly serrated margins. ALTERNATE arrangement.

**FLOWER DESCRIPTION:** Crimson, in 3" to 5" clusters. Flowers in summer.

**EXPOSURE/CULTURE:** Sun or light shade. Prefers moist, well-drained soil. Provide water during drought; will not perform well under dry conditions. Prune after flowering.

**PEST PROBLEMS:** No serious pests.

**SELECTED CULTIVARS:** None. This is a cultivar of *S.* x *bumalda*.

**LANDSCAPE NOTES:** Gold Flame Spirea is a very colorful plant that provides interesting color changes in foliage, as well as colorful flowers against yellowish leaves. Choose its use and location carefully.

## *Spiraea* x *bumalda* 'Limemound'

**Limemound Spirea**

**ZONES:**
3, 4, 5, 6, 7, 8, 9

**HEIGHT:**
1 1/2' to 2'

**WIDTH:**
2 1/2' to 4'

**FRUIT:**
Dehiscent follicle; NOT ORNAMENTAL.

**TEXTURE:**
Fine

**GROWTH RATE:**
Moderate

**HABIT:**
Very dense, broad mound. Uniform growth.

**FAMILY:**
Rosaceae

**LEAF COLOR:** Lime green; orange-red on reddish stems in fall.

**LEAF DESCRIPTION:** SIMPLE, 1″ to 2″ long and half as wide, ovate shape with doubly serrated margins. ALTERNATE arrangement.

**FLOWER DESCRIPTION:** Light pink, in 2″ to 4″ clusters. Flowers in summer.

**EXPOSURE/CULTURE:** Sun or light shade. Plant in well-drained, moist soil. Avoid dry conditions for best flowering and leaf color. Prune after flowering, if needed.

**PEST PROBLEMS:** No serious pests.

**SELECTED CULTIVARS:** None. This is a cultivar of *S.* x *bumalda*.

**LANDSCAPE NOTES:** Limemound Spirea has excellent foliage and uniform growth habit. It is a very attractive foliage plant in addition to having nice flowers. This is a bold accent plant. A Monrovia introduction.

# Chapter 7

## MEDIUM SIZE SHRUBS

For the purposes of this text, medium shrubs are those that mature at 4 feet to 6 feet in height under normal landscape conditions. "Medium" is not rigidly defined in this text, and in some cases is purely a judgement call based on a combination of height and width.

There is much need for medium size plants in landscaping. In years past, many property owners planted large shrubs around the foundation, only to have overgrown plants that dominated after a few years. Medium size plants are more appropriate than larger shrubs for most modern properties, especially the smaller properties of today's suburban residence.

Some common uses for medium shrubs are:

▼ Corner plants for one-story structures.
▼ Privacy hedges of lower maintenance.
▼ Foundation plants for higher foundations.
▼ Background plants for dwarf plantings.
▼ "Filler" plants for bare wall space.

## *Abies concolor 'Compacta'*       **Compact White Fir**

**ZONES:**
3, 4, 5, 6, 7

**HEIGHT:**
4′ to 4 1/2′

**WIDTH:**
3′ to 4′

**FRUIT:**
Greenish or purplish cones.

**TEXTURE:**
Medium

**GROWTH RATE:**
Extremely slow.

**HABIT:**
Compact, dense, and irregular.

**FAMILY:**
Pinaceae

**LEAF COLOR:** Grayish-green with blue bloom (pruinose).

**LEAF DESCRIPTION:** NEEDLE-LIKE, 1″ to 1 1/2″ long, erect or curving, flattened and convex with 2 white stomata bands beneath, separated by a green band. 2-ranked.

**FLOWER DESCRIPTION:** Monoecious; NOT NOTICEABLE.

**EXPOSURE/CULTURE:** Sun or light shade. Prefers sandy or stony soils to clay soils. More drought-tolerant than most coniferous evergreens. Practically maintenance-free.

**PEST PROBLEMS:** No serious pests.

**SELECTED CULTIVARS:** None. This is a cultivar of *A. concolor,* a large evergreen tree.

**LANDSCAPE NOTES:** This is a rare plant that is easier to grow than to find. Slow growth is overshadowed by the beauty of this gourmet coniferous evergreen. Outstanding!

# *Abelia x grandiflora*

**Glossy Abelia**

**ZONES:**
6, 7, 8, 9

**HEIGHT:**
5′ to 6′

**WIDTH:**
5′ to 6′

**FRUIT:**
Achene; NOT ORNAMENTAL.

**TEXTURE:**
Fine

**GROWTH RATE:**
Moderate

**HABIT:**
Spreading and dense with somewhat pendulous branches.

**FAMILY:**
Caprifoliaceae

**LEAF COLOR:** Reddish-green; purplish tinged in fall.

**LEAF DESCRIPTION:** SIMPLE, 1″ to 1 1/2″ long and half as wide, ovate shape with dentate margins. OPPOSITE arrangement.

**FLOWER DESCRIPTION:** White, 1/2″ to 1″ long, bugle-shaped, in small clusters. Flowers in summer and continues into late fall.

**EXPOSURE/CULTURE:** Sun or part shade. Adapts to a wide range of well-drained soil. Will bloom better if water is provided during drought. Prune anytime as it blooms on new growth.

**PEST PROBLEMS:** Aphids on new growth.

**SELECTED CULTIVARS:** 'Edward Goucher' - (Featured on next page.)

**LANDSCAPE NOTES:** This is an outstanding, proven plant that makes a nice hedge or foundation plant. It flowers freely for several months and has interesting foliage year round. Often used for hedges. Note: Young stems have red pigmentation also.

## Abelia x 'Edward Goucher'

**Edward Goucher Abelia**

**ZONES:**
6, 7, 8, 9

**HEIGHT:**
5' to 6'

**WIDTH:**
5' to 6'

**FRUIT:**
Achene; NOT ORNAMENTAL.

**TEXTURE:**
Fine

**GROWTH RATE:**
Moderate

**HABIT:**
Spreading and dense; branches pendulous.

**FAMILY:**
Caprifoliaceae

**LEAF COLOR:** Reddish-green; purplish in fall.

**LEAF DESCRIPTION:** SIMPLE, 1″ to 1 1/2″ long and half as wide, ovate shape with dentate margins. OPPOSITE arrangement.

**FLOWER DESCRIPTION:** Purplish-pink, 1/2″ to 1″ long, bugle-shaped, in small clusters. Flowers in summer and continues until late fall.

**EXPOSURE/CULTURE:** Sun or light shade. Does best in well-drained soil. Water during droughts for better flowering. Prune as needed for shaping; blooms on new growth.

**PEST PROBLEMS:** Aphids and ants on new growth.

**SELECTED CULTIVARS:** None. This is a cultivar selection from the cross between *A.* x *grandiflora* and *A. schumannii*.

**LANDSCAPE NOTES:** This plant is similar to *A. grandiflora* but has flowers that are a rich purple-pink throughout summer and fall. Leaves and stems have more red pigmentation.

# Aucuba japonica

**Green Aucuba, Japanese Aucuba**

**ZONES:**
6, 7, 8, 9, 10

**HEIGHT:**
5' to 6'

**WIDTH:**
4' to 5'

**FRUIT:**
1/2" red berries (female plants only, with nearby male plants).

**TEXTURE:**
Coarse

**GROWTH RATE:**
Moderate

**HABIT:**
Upright, irregular mound.

**FAMILY:**
Cornaceae

**LEAF COLOR:** Dark green.

**LEAF DESCRIPTION:** SIMPLE, 3" to 7" long and 1 1/2" to 3" wide, ovate to oblong shape with coarsely serrated margins near tip. OPPOSITE arrangement.

**FLOWER DESCRIPTION:** Off-white in panicles in early spring; NOT NOTICE-ABLE. Dioecious, male and female plants.

**EXPOSURE/CULTURE:** Shade only. Does best in well-drained soil. Cannot tolerate sunny exposures as upper foliage will burn to a black crisp. Prune carefully to maintain natural shape.

**PEST PROBLEMS:** None

**SELECTED CULTIVARS:** *Aucuba japonica* 'Variegata' - Featured on next page.

**LANDSCAPE NOTES:** Aucuba is an outstanding, coarse-textured plant for shady areas of the garden. It can be used as a hedge or foundation plant. Berries are simply beautiful, but, unfortunately, one must plant both male and female plants. Plant has a tropical character.

# *Aucuba japonica* 'Variegata'

### Variegated Aucuba, Gold-dust Tree

▲ 'Sulfur'

**ZONES:**
6, 7, 8, 9, 10

**HEIGHT:**
5' to 6'

**WIDTH:**
5' to 6'

**FRUIT:**
1/2" red berries (female plants only, in the presence of male plants).

**TEXTURE:**
Coarse

**GROWTH RATE:**
Moderate

**HABIT:**
Upright, irregular mound.

**FAMILY:**
Cornaceae

**LEAF COLOR:** Green with yellow blotches.

**LEAF DESCRIPTION:** SIMPLE, 3" to 7" long and 1 1/2" to 3" wide, ovate to oblong-ovate shape with coarsely serrated margins. OPPOSITE arrangement.

**FLOWER DESCRIPTION:** Off-white in panicles in early spring. NOT NOTICEABLE. Dioecious, male and female plants.

**EXPOSURE/CULTURE:** Shade only. Does best in moist, well-drained soil. Cannot tolerate sunny exposures as upper foliage will burn badly. Prune to maintain natural shape.

**PEST PROBLEMS:** No serious pests.

**SELECTED CULTIVARS:** None. This is a cultivar of *A. japonica*.

**RELATED CULTIVARS:** 'Picturata' - Has solid yellow blotch in center of leaf. 'Variegata Nana' - Leaves like 'Variegata' but grows to 2 1/2' to 3'.

# *Azalea* x Glenn Dale *(Rhododendron* x Glenn Dale)

Glenn Dale
Azalea

▲ 'Aphrodite'

**ZONES:**
6, 7, 8, 9

**HEIGHT:**
4' to 5'

**WIDTH:**
4' to 5'

**FRUIT:**
Brown pod, rare; NOT NOTICEABLE.

**TEXTURE:**
Medium

**GROWTH RATE:**
Moderate

**HABIT:**
Variable, but dense and somewhat rounded.

**FAMILY:**
Ericaceae

**LEAF COLOR:** Dark green.

**LEAF DESCRIPTION:** SIMPLE, 1 1/2" to 2" long and half as wide, ovate to oblong-ovate shape with entire margins. ALTERNATE arrangement.

**FLOWER DESCRIPTION:** White, pink, salmon, red, rose, purple, or lavender, depending on cultivar. 2 1/2" to 4 1/2" wide. Usually blooms in late April.

**EXPOSURE/CULTURE:** Light shade. Azaleas do best in well-drained, organic soil with acid pH. Add generous amounts of organic matter when planting. Drowns easily in wet soils. Prune after flowering in spring. Not as low-maintenance as acclaimed.

**PEST PROBLEMS:** Leaf gall, spider mites, lacebug.

**SELECTED CULTIVARS:** There are hundreds. 'Aphrodite' - Upright, with 2" rose-pink flowers. 'Buccaneer' - Orange-red flowers. 'Copperman' - Deep red flowers; red foliage in fall. 'H.H. Hume' - White with pale yellow throat. 'Martha Hitchcock' - White flowers with purple edge. BEAUTIFUL. 'Radiance' - Deep rose-pink flowers. 'Treasure' - White flowers with pinkish edges. 'Vesper' - White with yellow-green throat.

**LANDSCAPE NOTES:** Glenn Dale Azaleas provide an excellent floral display, blooming later in the season than Kurume Azaleas. Blooms are large and come in many different colors and shades.

## *Azalea kaempferi (Rhododendron kaempferi)*    Kaempferi Azalea

**ZONES:**
6, 7, 8, 9

**HEIGHT:**
5' to 6'

**WIDTH:**
4' to 5'

**FRUIT:**
Brown pod, rare; NOT ORNA-MENTAL.

**TEXTURE:**
Medium

**GROWTH RATE:**
Moderate

**HABIT:**
Upright and dense.

**FAMILY:**
Ericaceae

**LEAF COLOR:** Dark green.

**LEAF DESCRIPTION:** SIMPLE, 1 1/2" to 2 1/2" long and half as wide, ovate to oblong-ovate shape with entire margins. ALTERNATE arrangement.

**FLOWER DESCRIPTION:** White, pink, red, orchid, or purple, depending on the cultivar. 1 1/2" to 3"; funnel-shaped, usually. Flowers in April to May.

**EXPOSURE/CULTURE:** Light shade. Azaleas do best in well-drained, organic soil of acid pH. Plant higher than surrounding ground to prevent drowning. Prune after flowering, if needed.

**PEST PROBLEMS:** Leaf gall, spider mites, lacebug.

**SELECTED CULTIVARS:** 'Barbara' - Deep pink flowers. 'Holland' - Deep red flowers. Late season bloomer. 'Silver Sword' - Flowers pink or red. 2" blooms. Green foliage with white margins.

**LANDSCAPE NOTES:** This species tends to grow more upright than most, and blooms later. Kaempferi Azaleas are still blooming when the Kurumes are gone. Makes a good background for Kurume Azaleas.

# *Berberis julianae*

**Wintergreen Barberry**

**ZONES:**
5, 6, 7, 8

**HEIGHT:**
5' to 6'

**WIDTH:**
4' to 5'

**FRUIT:**
1/2" blue-black berries; attractive.

**TEXTURE:**
Medium

**GROWTH RATE:**
Slow

**HABIT:**
Forms a dense, impenetrable mound.

**FAMILY:**
Berberidaceae

**LEAF COLOR:** Lustrous green.

**LEAF DESCRIPTION:** SIMPLE, 1 1/2" to 2 1/2" long and one-fourth as wide, elliptic shape with spinose margins. ALTERNATE, but appearing in whorls. Has 1 1/2" needle-like thorns under each leaf cluster.

**FLOWER DESCRIPTION:** Yellow, 1/4" to 1/2", appearing in clusters. Flowers in April. Attractive.

**EXPOSURE/CULTURE:** Sun or shade. Prefers moist, well-drained soil, but is adaptable and considered easy to grow. HAZARDOUS for small children. Prune after flowering, with caution!

**PEST PROBLEMS:** No serious pests.

**SELECTED CULTIVARS:** 'Nana' - Dwarf form to 3'. Mounded habit.

**LANDSCAPE NOTES:** Wintergreen Barberry is a versatile shrub having many uses. It is especially useful as a barrier hedge because of the sharp, needle-like thorns under each cluster of leaves. Impenetrable for man or beast. Great for traffic control. In addition, leaves, flowers, and fruits are all very attractive. Outstanding plant!

# Buxus microphylla var. japonica

**Japanese Boxwood**

**ZONES:**
5, 6, 7, 8, 9, 10

**HEIGHT:**
4' to 6'

**WIDTH:**
3' to 5'

**FRUIT:**
Black capsule; NOT ORNA-MENTAL.

**TEXTURE:**
Fine

**GROWTH RATE:**
Moderate

**HABIT:**
Compact, dense, and rounded.

**FAMILY:**
Buxaceae

**LEAF COLOR:** Medium green; new leaves yellow-green.

**LEAF DESCRIPTION:** SIMPLE, 1/2" to 1" long and half as wide, mostly obovate shape with obtuse or emarginate tip and cuneate base. Entire margins. OPPO-SITE arrangement.

**FLOWER DESCRIPTION:** Terminal, in clusters; NOT NOTICEABLE.

**EXPOSURE/CULTURE:** Sun or part shade. Will grow in a variety of well-drained soils. Doesn't do as well in sunny, dry exposures. Prune as desired to any shape. May need frequent shearing.

**PEST PROBLEMS:** Leaf miner, rootrot, nematodes, spider mites, scale.

**SELECTED CULTIVARS:** 'Green Beauty' - More upright form with dark green foliage all year round.

**RELATED CULTIVARS:** *B.m.* 'Compacta' - Dark green foliage on very dwarf plants (to 1'). *B.m.* 'Kingsville Dwarf' - Very dwarf and slow-growing (to 1'). *B.m.* var. *koreana* 'Wintergreen' - Yellowish winter foliage on 2' plant. Zone 4. *B.m.* 'National' - Upright grower with dark green foliage all year. U.S.A. National Arboretum introduction. *B.* x 'Green Mountain' - Upright oval with small leaves. (Cross between var. *koreana* and *B. sempervirens*.)

**LANDSCAPE NOTES:** Selections of *Buxus microphylla* are varied and numerous. All are more formal than most plants, as they are symmetrical in habit and have fine texture. The plants can be used for a wide variety of purposes such as foundation plants, clipped hedges, border plants, and topiary.

# *Buxus sempervirens*

**Common Boxwood, American Boxwood**

**ZONES:**
6, 7, 8, 9

**HEIGHT:**
5' to 6'

**WIDTH:**
5' to 6'

**FRUIT:**
Dehiscent capsule; NOT ORNAMENTAL.

**TEXTURE:**
Fine

**GROWTH RATE:**
Moderate

**HABIT:**
Round globe; very dense.

**FAMILY:**
Buxaceae

**LEAF COLOR:** Dark green.

**LEAF DESCRIPTION:** SIMPLE, 1" to 1 1/2" long and half as wide, elliptic to obovate shape with obtuse or emarginate tip. Entire margins. OPPOSITE arrangement.

**FLOWER DESCRIPTION:** Tiny, in axillary clusters; NOT NOTICEABLE.

**EXPOSURE/CULTURE:** Sun or light shade. Does best in well-drained soils with high organic matter content. Does not like hot, dry, and sunny conditions. Prune occasionally to maintain refined, global shape.

**PEST PROBLEMS:** Boxwood leaf miner, blight, nematodes, rootrot.

**SELECTED CULTIVARS:** 'Angustifolia' - Oblong leaves; tree-like growth habit. 'Argentea' - Green leaves with white variegation. 'Bullata' - Large, puckered leaves on large, open shrub. 'Fastigiata' - A columnar growing cultivar. 'Inglis' - Pyramidal shape and dark green foliage. 'Pendula' - Weeping branches on tree-like growth. 'Welleri' - Broader than tall with large green leaves. Holds color year round.

**LANDSCAPE NOTES:** Boxwood is somewhat formal in nature due to its global habit of growth. It is still a popular foundation plant and is especially appropriate with colonial architecture.

## *Camellia sinensis*

**ZONES:**
7, 8, 9

**HEIGHT:**
Variable; 5′ to 6′, usually.

**WIDTH:**
4′ to 5′

**FRUIT:**
Brown capsule; NOT ORNA-MENTAL.

**TEXTURE:**
Medium

**GROWTH RATE:**
Moderate

**HABIT:**
Upright; somewhat irregular.

**FAMILY:**
Theaceae

**LEAF COLOR:** Dark green and lustrous.

**LEAF DESCRIPTION:** SIMPLE, 2 1/2″ to 5″ long and 1″ to 2″ wide, elliptic shape with serrated margins. ALTERNATE arrangement.

**FLOWER DESCRIPTION:** White, with brush-like yellow stamens, 1″ to 1 3/4″ wide. Flowers in fall.

**EXPOSURE/CULTURE:** Part shade to shade. Not particular as to soil, but it does best in organic, well-drained soil. Will grow in sun, but performs best in shade. Pruning is minimal.

**PEST PROBLEMS:** Various scales, rootrot.

**SELECTED CULTIVARS:** None

**LANDSCAPE NOTES:** This is an underrated plant that should be more widely grown. It has interesting form and dainty flowers. This is the commercial tea plant grown on tea plantations.

## Chamaecyparis pisifera 'Boulevard'

**Blue Moss Cypress**

**ZONES:**
4, 5, 6, 7, 8

**HEIGHT:**
5' to 6'

**WIDTH:**
4' to 5'

**FRUIT:**
1/4" round cones.

**TEXTURE:**
Fine

**GROWTH RATE:**
Moderate

**HABIT:**
Broad pyramid; symmetrical.

**FAMILY:**
Cupressaceae

**LEAF COLOR:** Silver-blue

**LEAF DESCRIPTION:** AWL-SHAPED, 1/4" to 1/2" long, pointed and linear, curving inward at tips.

**FLOWER DESCRIPTION:** Monoecious; NOT NOTICEABLE.

**EXPOSURE/CULTURE:** Sun or part shade. Prefers well-drained, loamy soils that are lime-free. Requires minimal pruning, if any. Develops its own character.

**PEST PROBLEMS:** No serious pests.

**SELECTED CULTIVARS:** None. This is a cultivar of *C. pisifera,* a large evergreen tree.

**LANDSCAPE NOTES:** Blue Moss Cypress has many uses in the landscape. It makes a nice foundation plant, rock garden plant, or specimen plant. Soft, plume-like foliage and interesting color combine to make this an outstanding selection for residential or commerical landscapes.

## *Euonymus kiautschovicus* 'Manhattan'    **Manhattan Euonymus**

**ZONES:**
5, 6, 7, 8, 9

**HEIGHT:**
5' to 6'

**WIDTH:**
5' to 6'

**FRUIT:**
Capsule with exposed orange-red seed coat in fall.

**TEXTURE:**
Medium

**GROWTH RATE:**
Rapid

**HABIT:**
Upright and open.

**FAMILY:**
Celastraceae

**LEAF COLOR:** Dark green; glossy.

**LEAF DESCRIPTION:** SIMPLE, 2″ to 2 1/2″ long and half as wide, obovate to oval shape with crenate-serrate margins. OPPOSITE arrangement.

**FLOWER DESCRIPTION:** Greenish-white in loose 4″ to 5″ cymes. Flowers in summer.

**EXPOSURE/CULTURE:** Sun or shade. Adaptable to a wide range of soils. Thrives in dry soil. Very responsive to fertilization. Prune anytime to shape.

**PEST PROBLEMS:** Euonymus scale. Not as susceptible to scale as other species in the genus.

**SELECTED CULTIVARS:** None. This is a cultivar of *E. kiautschovicus,* a large semi-evergreen shrub.

**RELATED CULTIVARS:** 'Newport' - Similar in habit to 'Manhattan'. 'Paulii' - More upright growth. Excellent, dark green foliage.

**LANDSCAPE NOTES:** Manhattan Euonymus is a superior plant in its genus. It performs well as a foundation or border plant, and is superior as a hedge. It is tolerant of urban conditions, and thrives in Central Park, New York.

# *Fatsia japonica*

**Fatsia, Japanese Aralia**

**ZONES:**
7, 8, 9

**HEIGHT:**
3' to 6'

**WIDTH:**
5' to 6'

**FRUIT:**
1/4" to 1/2" black drupes.

**TEXTURE:**
Very coarse.

**GROWTH RATE:**
Moderate

**HABIT:**
Rounded and open.

**FAMILY:**
Araliaceae

**LEAF COLOR:** Lustrous dark green.

**LEAF DESCRIPTION:** SIMPLE, 6" to 12" long and 8" to 12" wide, palmately lobed (7 to 9), each lobe serrated. Long leaf petioles. ALTERNATE arrangement.

**FLOWER DESCRIPTION:** White, tiny, in 1" to 2" umbels that form a large cluster. Flowers in fall.

**EXPOSURE/CULTURE:** Shade. Tolerant of most soils, but prefers organic, loamy soils. Will tolerate more moisture than most plants. Protect from sun and wind. Prune only to remove old or dead stems.

**PEST PROBLEMS:** No serious pests.

**SELECTED CULTIVARS:** 'Moseri' - Smaller, compact plant with larger leaves. 'Variegata' - White variegation on tips of lobes and most of the margins.

**LANDSCAPE NOTES:** Fatsia has foliage with a tropical appearance. It is outstanding for textural contrast in the garden and looks great against walls or fences. Very popular plant for use in swimming pool gardens. It can be used for indoor plantscaping.

## *Gardenia jasminoides*

**Cape Jasmine, Gardenia**

**ZONES:**
8, 9, 10

**HEIGHT:**
5' to 6'

**WIDTH:**
5' to 6'

**FRUIT:**
Orange berry; not common.

**TEXTURE:**
Medium

**GROWTH RATE:**
Moderate

**HABIT:**
Rounded; upright.

**FAMILY:**
Rubiaceae

**LEAF COLOR:** Dark green.

**LEAF DESCRIPTION:** SIMPLE, 3″ to 4″ long and half as wide, elliptic to obovate shape with entire margins. OPPOSITE, sometimes whorled.

**FLOWER DESCRIPTION:** White, to 3″, solitary. Very fragrant. Flowers in May and June.

**EXPOSURE/CULTURE:** Sun or shade. Requires organic soil that is well-drained and acid in reaction. Prune to maintain natural shape.

**PEST PROBLEMS:** Scale, mealy bugs, white flies.

**SELECTED CULTIVARS:** 'August Beauty' - Blooms in May through November. Abundant flowers. 'Mystery' - Compact branching. Creamy-white flowers. 'Radicans' - Super dwarf. (Featured in Dwarf Shrubs.) 'Veitchii' - Grows more upright. Abundant flowers.

**LANDSCAPE NOTES:** Gardenia has attractive foliage and large white, fragrant flowers. Distinctive fragrance is noticeable throughout the garden. Place near an entry or patio for family enjoyment. Prune lightly, and bring branches inside for fragrant arrangements.

# *Ilex cornuta* 'Dwarf Burford'

**Dwarf Burford Holly**

**ZONES:**
6, 7, 8, 9

**HEIGHT:**
6' to 7'

**WIDTH:**
5' to 6'

**FRUIT:**
1/4" deep red berries; not abundant.

**TEXTURE:**
Medium

**GROWTH RATE:**
Moderate

**HABIT:**
Upright; somewhat pyramidal.

**FAMILY:**
Aquifoliaceae

**LEAF COLOR:** Deep, glossy green.

**LEAF DESCRIPTION:** SIMPLE, 1" to 1 1/2" long and half as wide, elliptic shape with entire margins, except for one spine at the leaf tip. Puckered between veins. ALTERNATE arrangement.

**FLOWER DESCRIPTION:** Greenish, tiny 4-petaled in leaf axils; NOT ORNAMENTAL.

**EXPOSURE/CULTURE:** Sun or shade. Very adaptable to any well-drained soil. Very drought-resistant. Almost overused in low-maintenance landscapes. Prune, as needed, to maintain natural shape.

**PEST PROBLEMS:** Scale, nematodes, leaf spot.

**SELECTED CULTIVARS:** None. This is a cultivar of *I. cornuta* 'Burfordii', a large evergreen shrub.

**LANDSCAPE NOTES:** One of the best Hollies, having many uses. It is an outstanding corner plant for foundation plantings and makes a beautiful unclipped hedge. Looks great in tree-form, also. It was developed as a substitute for Burford Holly, which is much larger. Used extensively in both residential and commercial landscapes.

## Ilex crenata 'Convexa'

**Convexa Holly**

**ZONES:**
5, 6, 7, 8

**HEIGHT:**
5' to 6'

**WIDTH:**
5' to 6'

**FRUIT:**
1/4" black berries.

**TEXTURE:**
Fine

**GROWTH RATE:**
Moderate

**HABIT:**
Round and dense.

**FAMILY:**
Aquifoliaceae

**LEAF COLOR:** Medium green.

**LEAF DESCRIPTION:** SIMPLE, 1/2" long and half as wide, oval or elliptic shape with crenate or serrated margins, cupped (convex). ALTERNATE arrangement.

**FLOWER DESCRIPTION:** Greenish-white, tiny, spring; NOT NOTICEABLE.

**EXPOSURE/CULTURE:** Sun or shade. Prefers well-drained heavier soils. Doesn't perform well in sand. An annual application of nitrogen encourages better color. Can be sheared into dense, Boxwood-like habit.

**PEST PROBLEMS:** Spider mites.

**SELECTED CULTIVARS:** None. This is a cultivar of *I. crenata,* a large evergreen shrub.

**LANDSCAPE NOTES:** Convexa Holly is a widely used landscape plant that makes a good foundation plant or sheared hedge. It is sometimes confused with Boxwood, but has many differences. It is an outstanding plant when given a reasonable amount of attention and care.

# *Ilex crenata 'Compacta'*

**Compacta Holly**

**ZONES:**
5, 6, 7, 8

**HEIGHT:**
4' to 5'

**WIDTH:**
6' to 8'

**FRUIT:**
Black berries; not common.

**TEXTURE:**
Fine

**GROWTH RATE:**
Moderate

**HABIT:**
Broadly rounded and dense.

**FAMILY:**
Aquifoliaceae

**LEAF COLOR:** Dark green.

**LEAF DESCRIPTION:** SIMPLE, 1/2" to 3/4" long and half as wide, oval or elliptic shape with crenate or serrulate margins. ALTERNATE arrangement.

**FLOWER DESCRIPTION:** Greenish-white, tiny, spring; NOT NOTICEABLE.

**EXPOSURE/CULTURE:** Sun or shade. Does best in slightly acid, well-drained soil. Easily pruned into compact, dense shape.

**PEST PROBLEMS:** Spider mites, rootrot.

**SELECTED CULTIVARS:** None. This is a cultivar of *I. crenata*.

**LANDSCAPE NOTES:** Compacta Holly is one of the thickest growing Hollies. Contrary to public opinion, it becomes quite large over a period of years. Its dense nature can be obtained with a minimum of care. One of the best, but somewhat overplanted.

## Ilex crenata 'Hetzii'

**Hetzi Holly**

**ZONES:**
5, 6, 7, 8

**HEIGHT:**
5' to 6'

**WIDTH:**
6' to 8'

**FRUIT:**
1/4" black berries.

**TEXTURE:**
Fine

**GROWTH RATE:**
Moderate to rapid.

**HABIT:**
Spreading, round, vigorous shrub.

**FAMILY:**
Aquifoliaceae

**LEAF COLOR:** Dark green.

**LEAF DESCRIPTION:** SIMPLE, 3/4" to 1" long and half as wide, oval or elliptic shape with crenate or serrulate margins, cupped (convex). ALTERNATE arrangement.

**FLOWER DESCRIPTION:** Greenish-white, tiny, spring; NOT NOTICEABLE.

**EXPOSURE/CULTURE:** Sun or shade. Prefers well-drained, moist soil with slightly acid reaction. Very dense. Easily pruned to maintain round shape. Prune anytime.

**PEST PROBLEMS:** Spider mites can be destructive.

**SELECTED CULTIVARS:** None. This is a cultivar of *I. crenata*.

**LANDSCAPE NOTES:** A compact, vigorous form of Convexa Holly that grows extremely dense without shearing. Leaves are darker green and larger than Convexa Holly. It makes a fine foundation plant, but should be given plenty of space.

# *Ilex crenata* 'Petite Point'

**Petite Point Holly**

**ZONES:**
5, 6, 7, 8

**HEIGHT:**
5′ to 6′

**WIDTH:**
4′ to 5′

**FRUIT:**
1/4″ black berries.

**TEXTURE:**
Fine

**GROWTH RATE:**
Moderate

**HABIT:**
Upright and pyramidal.

**FAMILY:**
Aquifoliaceae

**LEAF COLOR:** Green

**LEAF DESCRIPTION:** SIMPLE, 1/2″ long and 1/4″ wide, elliptic shape with crenate or serrated margins. ALTERNATE arrangement.

**FLOWER DESCRIPTION:** Greenish-white, tiny, spring; NOT NOTICEABLE.

**EXPOSURE/CULTURE:** Sun or shade. Grows best in well-drained, heavy soil. Can be easily pruned into pyramidal shape.

**PEST PROBLEMS:** Spider mites can be destructive.

**SELECTED CULTIVARS:** None. This is a cultivar of *I. crenata*.

**LANDSCAPE NOTES:** Petite Point is a handsome foundation or specimen plant that resembles Convexa Holly, except that it has a more pyramidal shape. A good substitute for Boxwood or Convexa Holly.

## *Ilex crenata* 'Rotundifolia'　　　　　Round-leaf Holly

**ZONES:**
6, 7, 8,9

**HEIGHT:**
6' to 7'

**WIDTH:**
6' to 8'

**FRUIT:**
NONE

**TEXTURE:**
Fine

**GROWTH RATE:**
Moderate

**HABIT:**
Round and open.

**FAMILY:**
Aquifoliaceae

**LEAF COLOR:** Dark green.

**LEAF DESCRIPTION:** SIMPLE, 1″ to 1 1/4″ long and half as wide, oval to elliptic shape with serrulate margins. ALTERNATE arrangement.

**FLOWER DESCRIPTION:** Greenish-white, tiny, spring; NOT NOTICEABLE.

**EXPOSURE/CULTURE:** Sun to part shade. Very vigorous. Grows in any well-drained soil. Regular pruning may be necessary to control and maintain dense habit.

**PEST PROBLEMS:** Spider mites.

**SELECTED CULTIVARS:** None. This is a cultivar of *I. crenata*.

**LANDSCAPE NOTES:** Round-leaf Holly is a rugged plant that has been widely planted or overplanted in residential landscapes. It should not be planted under windows where it requires heavy pruning. This cultivar is still in demand, but it has been mostly replaced by 'Compacta'.

# *Juniperus chinensis* 'Hetzii Glauca'

**Blue Hetz Juniper**

**ZONES:**
4, 5, 6, 7, 8, 9

**HEIGHT:**
5' to 6'

**WIDTH:**
5' to 6'

**FRUIT:**
Purplish-brown, 1/4" cones; whitish bloom.

**TEXTURE:**
Fine

**GROWTH RATE:**
Moderate

**HABIT:**
Semi-erect; fountain-like.

**FAMILY:**
Cupressaceae

**LEAF COLOR:** Light frost blue.

**LEAF DESCRIPTION:** SCALE-LIKE, with awl-shaped leaves on juvenile branches. Scale-like leaves OPPOSITE, juvenile leaves mostly ternate.

**FLOWER DESCRIPTION:** Yellowish, dioecious; NOT NOTICEABLE.

**EXPOSURE/CULTURE:** Sun only. Will grow in almost any soil or pH level, except wet soils. Very drought tolerant. Can be sheared, but looks best in natural shape.

**PEST PROBLEMS:** Phomopsis blight, occasionally. Bagworms.

**SELECTED CULTIVARS:** None. This is a cultivar of *J. chinensis,* a large evergreen tree.

**RELATED CULTIVARS:** 'Hetzii Columnaris' - Tightly branched, columnar habit with bright green color. 'Maneyi' - Similar to 'Hetzii Glauca' with bluish-green foliage. 'Mint Julep' - Similar to 'Hetzii Glauca' with mint green foliage. A Monrovia introduction.

**LANDSCAPE NOTES:** Blue Hetz Juniper and the related cultivars are excellent low-maintenance shrubs for sunny exposures. They can be effectively used as foundation plants, groupings, and semi-private hedges.

## *Juniperus chinensis* 'Pfitzeriana' — Pfitzer's Juniper

**ZONES:**
4, 5, 6, 7, 8, 9

**HEIGHT:**
5' to 6'

**WIDTH:**
8' to 10'

**FRUIT:**
1/3" dark brown cones; whitish bloom.

**TEXTURE:**
Fine

**GROWTH RATE:**
Moderately rapid.

**HABIT:**
Wide-spreading; somewhat open.

**FAMILY:**
Cupressaceae

**LEAF COLOR:** Green to gray-green.

**LEAF DESCRIPTION:** SCALE-LIKE on older branches, awl-shaped on juvenile branches, 1/16". Scale-like leaves OPPOSITE; juvenile mostly ternate.

**FLOWER DESCRIPTION:** Yellowish, dioecious; NOT NOTICEABLE.

**EXPOSURE/CULTURE:** Sun only. Adapts to any soil except wet soils. Can be sheared, but should be left natural.

**PEST PROBLEMS:** Twig blight, bagworms.

**SELECTED CULTIVARS:** None. This is a cultivar of *J. chinensis*.

**RELATED CULTIVARS:** 'Blue Vase' - Vase-shaped with steel-blue foliage. 'Pfitzeriana Aurea' - Gold Tip Pfitzer. Gray-green foliage, tipped with yellow. 'Pfitzeriana Compacta' - Dwarf form to less than 4'. 'Pfitzeriana Glauca' - Silvery-blue foliage. Somewhat like 'Hetzii Glauca'. 'Robusta Green' - Irregular habit. Brilliant green and dense.

**LANDSCAPE NOTES:** Pfitzer's Juniper is a large-growing plant that is useful for larger properties or structures. It is a very vigorous shrub. An "old standby" that has proven itself.

## *Juniperus chinensis 'Sea Green'*

**ZONES:**
4, 5, 6, 7, 8

**HEIGHT:**
4' to 6'

**WIDTH:**
4' to 5'

**FRUIT:**
NOT NOTICEABLE.

**TEXTURE:**
Fine

**GROWTH RATE:**
Moderate

**HABIT:**
Somewhat vase-shaped and spreading; taller than broad.

**FAMILY:**
Cupressaceae

**LEAF COLOR:** Deep mint green.

**LEAF DESCRIPTION:** SCALE-LIKE on older branches, awl-shaped on juvenile branches, 1/16". Scale-like leaves OPPOSITE; awl-shaped leaves mostly ternate.

**FLOWER DESCRIPTION:** Yellowish, dioecious; NOT NOTICEABLE.

**EXPOSURE/CULTURE:** Sun only. Adapts to any well-drained soil. Drought tolerant. Prune to maintain natural shape.

**PEST PROBLEMS:** Twig blight, bagworms.

**SELECTED CULTIVARS:** None. This is a cultivar of *J. chinensis*.

**LANDSCAPE NOTES:** Sea Green Juniper has outstanding sea-green foliage throughout the year. This shrub can be used in the foundation plantings or as an unclipped hedge.

# *Kalmia latifolia*

## Mountain Laurel

**ZONES:**
5, 6, 7, 8, 9

**HEIGHT:**
5′ to 7′

**WIDTH:**
5′ to 7′

**FRUIT:**
1/4″ brown capsule; NOT ORNAMENTAL.

**TEXTURE:**
Medium

**GROWTH RATE:**
Slow

**HABIT:**
Rounded and irregular; dense.

**FAMILY:**
Ericaceae

**LEAF COLOR:** Dark green.

**LEAF DESCRIPTION:** SIMPLE, 2″ to 4″ long and 1″ to 1 1/2″ wide, elliptic shape with entire margins. OPPOSITE or whorled in threes.

**FLOWER DESCRIPTION:** White to rose with purple markings inside, 1″ or more in large terminal corymbs. Flowers in May through June.

**EXPOSURE/CULTURE:** Light shade or shade. The plant needs organic, well-drained soil with acid reaction. Heavy mulching is needed to insure consistent moisture. Plant high in shallow hole, then mound with mulch. Requires minimal pruning.

**PEST PROBLEMS:** Leaf spots, lacebug, borers.

**SELECTED CULTIVARS:** 'Alba' - Has white flowers. 'Elf'- Dwarf cultivar. Bluish-white flowers. Heavy bloomer. 'Olympic Fire' - Fire red buds open to pale pink flowers. 'Ostbo Red' - Deep red buds that open to deep pink. 'Pink Star' - Light pink, star-shaped flowers. 'Sarah' - Red flowers maturing to rosey-red.

**LANDSCAPE NOTES:** Mountain Laurel is a native American shrub that is outstanding in bloom. It is useful as a foundation plant, but is great for naturalizing in shady areas of the garden. Looks great in mass groupings.

# Ligustrum sinense 'Variegatum'

**Variegated Privet**

**ZONES:**
7, 8, 9

**HEIGHT:**
5' to 6'

**WIDTH:**
5' to 6'

**FRUIT:**
1/4" black drupes.

**TEXTURE:**
Fine

**GROWTH RATE:**
Rapid

**HABIT:**
Rounded; open and spreading.

**FAMILY:**
Oleaceae

**LEAF COLOR:** Dull green with creamy border.

**LEAF DESCRIPTION:** SIMPLE, 1" to 1 1/2" long and half as wide, elliptic shape with entire margins. OPPOSITE arrangement.

**FLOWER DESCRIPTION:** White, tiny, in 2" to 4" panicles. Blooms in late spring. NOT SPECTACULAR.

**EXPOSURE/CULTURE:** Sun or light shade. Grows well in any well-drained soil. Tolerant of drought. Prune in summer for shaping.

**PEST PROBLEMS:** Leaf spots, scale, rootrot.

**SELECTED CULTIVARS:** None. This is a cultivar of *L. sinense*, Chinese Privet, considered a weed by many horticulturalists.

**LANDSCAPE NOTES:** This variegated plant is more open in growth and less noticeable than most variegated plants. It is a great choice as background material for other plantings, especially dwarf Junipers. It provides great contrast in form and color. NOTE: The plant is really semi-evergreen.

# *Mahonia bealei*

**Leatherleaf Mahonia**

**ZONES:**
5, 6, 7, 8

**HEIGHT:**
5′ to 6′

**WIDTH:**
5′ to 6′

**FRUIT:**
1/2″ blue-black berries in clusters; white bloom. Mature in summer and VERY SHOWY.

**TEXTURE:**
Coarse

**GROWTH RATE:**
Moderately slow.

**HABIT:**
Upright, open, and stiff.

**FAMILY:**
Berberidaceae

**LEAF COLOR:** Dark green.

**LEAF DESCRIPTION:** COMPOUND (pinnate) with 11 to 17 leaflets, leaflets 4″ to 5″ long and half as wide, ovate shape with spinose margins. ALTERNATE arrangement.

**FLOWER DESCRIPTION:** Yellow, showy, in 3″ to 5″ racemes. Flowers in early spring.

**EXPOSURE/CULTURE:** Part shade to shade. Grows in any well-drained soil. Does well in sand or clay. Prune older "canes" to ground in early winter. STEMS ARE GOLDEN-YELLOW INSIDE.

**PEST PROBLEMS:** No serious pests.

**SELECTED CULTIVARS:** None.

**LANDSCAPE NOTES:** Leatherleaf Mahonia is a strong accent plant that is best used in combination with fine-textured plants. In addition, the yellow flowers and blue fruit add interest to the plant. It should be more widely used in foundation plantings.

# Mahonia fortunei

**Chinese Mahonia**

**ZONES:**
8, 9, (7 with protection)

**HEIGHT:**
4' to 6'

**WIDTH:**
4' to 5'

**FRUIT:**
1/4" blue-black berry; NOT SHOWY.

**TEXTURE:**
Coarse

**GROWTH RATE:**
Moderate

**HABIT:**
Upright and mounded.

**FAMILY:**
Berberidaceae

**LEAF COLOR:** Dull, deep green.

**LEAF DESCRIPTION:** COMPOUND (pinnate) with 3 to 9 leaflets, each 4" to 5" long and 1/2" to 3/4" wide, lanceolate shape with cuneate base and spinose-serrate margins. ALTERNATE arrangement.

**FLOWER DESCRIPTION:** Yellow, tiny in 2" to 3" racemes. Flowers in early spring.

**EXPOSURE/CULTURE:** Part shade. Adaptable to most soils, except wet soils. Should be mulched heavily for best performance. Prune older "canes" to ground to stimulate new cane growth from base.

**PEST PROBLEMS:** No serious pests.

**SELECTED CULTIVARS:** None

**LANDSCAPE NOTES:** Chinese Mahonia has a more refined, feathery appearance than *M. bealei*; however, the blooms and fruits are not as spectacular. Unfortunately, limited in range (zones). Very nice plant.

## *Myrica cerifera var. pumila*

**Dwarf Wax Myrtle**

**ZONES:**
7, 8, 9

**HEIGHT:**
5′ to 6′

**WIDTH:**
5′ to 8′

**FRUIT:**
(Female plants) Tiny, grayish white; coated with waxy resin.

**TEXTURE:**
Medium

**GROWTH RATE:**
Moderate

**HABIT:**
Rounded; broad-spreading and open.

**FAMILY:**
Myricaceae

**LEAF COLOR:** Medium green.

**LEAF DESCRIPTION:** SIMPLE, 2″ to 3″ long and 3/4″ to 1″ wide, linear to oblanceolate shape with serrated margins. ALTERNATE arrangement.

**FLOWER DESCRIPTION:** Yellowish. Male and female flowers on separate plants. NOT SHOWY.

**EXPOSURE/CULTURE:** Sun or part shade. Will thrive in almost any soil. Native to eastern wetlands. Does well in sandy soils of coastal areas. No pruning is recommended, except occasional "cleanup."

**PEST PROBLEMS:** No serious pests.

**SELECTED CULTIVARS:** None. This is a cultivar of *M. cerifera,* a large evergreen shrub or small tree.

**LANDSCAPE NOTES:** Dwarf Wax Myrtle makes a nice informal, unclipped screen or hedge. It is a great background plant for dwarf materials. Performs well on dunes or berms in combination with dwarf plants, especially Junipers. This is a great choice for naturalizing.

## *Nandina domestica*

**Nandina, Heavenly Bamboo**

**ZONES:**
6, 7, 8, 9

**HEIGHT:**
5' to 6'

**WIDTH:**
3' to 4'

**FRUIT:**
1/4" bright red berries in large panicles; VERY SHOWY.

**TEXTURE:**
Fine to medium.

**GROWTH RATE:**
Moderate

**HABIT:**
Upright and irregular; non-branching canes.

**FAMILY:**
Berberidaceae

**LEAF COLOR:** Medium green in summer; brilliant red in winter.

**LEAF DESCRIPTION:** COMPOUND (tripinnate; 3 times divided), leaflets 1 1/2" to 2" long and half as wide, ovate shape with cuneate base. Entire margins. ALTERNATE arrangement.

**FLOWER DESCRIPTION:** White, tiny, in 8" to 12" panicles. Showy. Flowers in early spring.

**EXPOSURE/CULTURE:** Sun or light shade. Plant prefers moist, fertile soil, but is adaptable. To prevent "leggy" appearance, prune some older canes to ground and some at different levels.

**PEST PROBLEMS:** No serious pests.

**SELECTED CULTIVARS:** 'Alba' - Has white berries and lighter green foliage. 'San Gabriel' - Upright to 4', with very fine, lacy or "needle-like" foliage.

**LANDSCAPE NOTES:** Nandina is a delicate, lacy green plant that turns red in winter. Brilliant clusters of red berries smother the plant in fall. It is an interesting plant where vertical growth is needed, and looks great in tree-form. This plant has been overshadowed by the obsession with dwarf Nandinas in recent years. This is an outstanding plant that has proven itself over the years.

# *Pieris japonica*

**Japanese Pieris, Japanese Andromeda**

**ZONES:**
6, 7, 8

**HEIGHT:**
5' to 6'

**WIDTH:**
4' to 6'

**FRUIT:**
Brown capsule; NOT ORNA-MENTAL.

**TEXTURE:**
Medium

**GROWTH RATE:**
Moderately slow.

**HABIT:**
Upright; irregular and open.

**FAMILY:**
Ericaceae

**LEAF COLOR:** Dark green; new growth reddish.

**LEAF DESCRIPTION:** SIMPLE, 2" to 3" long and one-third as wide, broad linear to oblanceolate shape with acute tip and cuneate base. Serrulate margins. ALTER-NATE arrangement.

**FLOWER DESCRIPTION:** White, tiny and urn-shaped, appearing in 5" to 6" pen-dulous panicles. SHOWY. Flowers in spring.

**EXPOSURE/CULTURE:** Part shade or shade. Does best in moist, organic, well-drained soil of acidic reaction. Pruning is minimal. Prune after flowering for shaping.

**PEST PROBLEMS:** Lacebugs, rootrot, stem dieback (phytophthora).

**SELECTED CULTIVARS:** 'Dorothy Wycoff' - Deep pink flowers. 'Mountain Fire' - New foliage is fiery-red. White flowers. 'Temple Bells' - New foliage varies from bronze to red and finally, dark green. Dense ivory flower clusters. 'Valley Valentine' - Buds and flowers deep red. 'Variegata' - New leaves narrowly mar-gined with pink, maturing to white. 'White Cascade' - Profuse flowering (white) for a longer period of time.

**RELATED SPECIES:** *P. floribunda* - Mountain Andromeda. Has stiff branches and upright, 4" panicles. More adaptable with less problems. Zone 4 hardy. *P. formosa* - Much larger plant (20') with large, 6" leaves. Erect flower panicles to 6". Zone 7.

**LANDSCAPE NOTES:** Japanese Pieris has graceful, showy flower clusters in spring. The foliage resembles Mountain Laurel when flowers are gone. This is an attractive plant that combines well with other plantings as a foundation or speci-men plant. Flowers are very similar to Lily-of-the-Valley. Great for naturalizing.

# *Pinus strobus 'Nana'*

**Dwarf White Pine**

**ZONES:**
3, 4, 5, 6, 7

**HEIGHT:**
4 1/2′ to 5′

**WIDTH:**
4′ to 5′

**FRUIT:**
4″ brown cones.

**TEXTURE:**
Fine

**GROWTH RATE:**
Slow

**HABIT:**
Compact and globose; branch tips ascending.

**FAMILY:**
Pinaceae

**LEAF COLOR:** Blue-green.

**LEAF DESCRIPTION:** NEEDLE-LIKE, 3″ to 4″ long, appearing in bundles of 5 needles. Finely serrated margins. Bundles ALTERNATELY arranged.

**FLOWER DESCRIPTION:** Greenish, monoecious (male and female cones); NOT ORNAMENTAL.

**EXPOSURE/CULTURE:** Sun or light shade. Best suited for well-drained, organic soil, but is adaptable to extremes. Prune when terminal buds elongate in spring, if desired.

**PEST PROBLEMS:** White pine blister rust.

**SELECTED CULTIVARS:** None. This is a cultivar of *P. strobus,* a large evergreen tree.

**LANDSCAPE NOTES:** The unusual nature of this pine makes it appropriate as a specimen plant in a well-selected location. It is an appropriate choice for rock gardens or stone-mulched areas.

## *Prunus laurocerasus* 'Schipkaensis'      Schip Laurel

**ZONES:**
6, 7, 8, 9

**HEIGHT:**
4′ to 6′

**WIDTH:**
4′ to 6′

**FRUIT:**
1/2″ purplish drupe.

**TEXTURE:**
Coarse

**GROWTH RATE:**
Moderate

**HABIT:**
Irregular, upright, and spreading.

**FAMILY:**
Rosaceae

**LEAF COLOR:** Lustrous dark green.

**LEAF DESCRIPTION:** SIMPLE, 3″ to 6″ long and 1″ to 1 3/4″ wide, narrow elliptic to oblong shape with acute tip. Serrated margins near tip. ALTERNATE arrangement.

**FLOWER DESCRIPTION:** White, tiny, in 2″ to 4″ ascending racemes. Fragrant. Flowers in May.

**EXPOSURE/CULTURE:** Sun or shade. Does best in organic, well-drained soil. Can be used in coastal plantings. Takes shearing, if desired.

**PEST PROBLEMS:** "Shothole" fungus, chewing insects.

**SELECTED CULTIVARS:** None. This is a cultivar of *P. laurocerasus,* English Laurel, a large evergreen shrub or small tree.

**LANDSCAPE NOTES:** Schip Laurel is a versatile plant that makes an excellent natural hedge or foundation plant. It performs well even in shady locations. It is not spectacular in flower, but the foliage provides good textural contrast.

## *Prunus laurocerasus 'Zabeliana'*     **Zabel Laurel**

**ZONES:**
6, 7, 8

**HEIGHT:**
3' to 4'

**WIDTH:**
8' to 10'

**FRUIT:**
Purplish drupe.

**TEXTURE:**
Coarse

**GROWTH RATE:**
Moderate

**HABIT:**
Broadly spreading; irregular.

**FAMILY:**
Rosaceae

**LEAF COLOR:** Lustrous dark green.

**LEAF DESCRIPTION:** SIMPLE, 3" to 5" long and 1" to 1 1/2" wide, narrow elliptic to oblong shape with acute tip. Entire margins. ALTERNATE arrangement.

**FLOWER DESCRIPTION:** White, tiny, in 2" to 4" racemes. Fragrant. Flowers in May.

**EXPOSURE/CULTURE:** Sun or shade. Performs well in moist soils that are well-drained and high in organic matter. Very hardy. Prune or shear as desired.

**PEST PROBLEMS:** "Shothole" fungus, chewing insects.

**SELECTED CULTIVARS:** None. This is a cultivar of *P. laurocerasus.*

**LANDSCAPE NOTES:** Zabel Laurel is a broad plant that can be used as a foundation or border plant. It produces more flowers than Schip Laurel and is broader and shorter. An excellent plant when given adequate space for growth. (Listed here as a medium plant because of the broad spread.)

## *Rhododendron carolinianum* — Carolina Rhododendron

**ZONES:**
6, 7, 8

**HEIGHT:**
4′ to 6′

**WIDTH:**
4′ to 6′

**FRUIT:**
Brownish capsule; NOT ORNAMENTAL.

**TEXTURE:**
Coarse

**GROWTH RATE:**
Slow

**HABIT:**
Rounded and irregular.

**FAMILY:**
Ericaceae

**LEAF COLOR:** Green with faint blue tinge.

**LEAF DESCRIPTION:** SIMPLE, 2″ to 3″ long and 1″ to 1 1/2″ wide, elliptic shape with entire margins. ALTERNATE arrangement.

**FLOWER DESCRIPTION:** White, pink, or rose, 1 1/2″ wide in 4″ racemes. Flowers in spring.

**EXPOSURE/CULTURE:** Sun or part shade. Must be planted in well-drained, organic soil of acidic reaction. Plant in shallow holes, if any, and mound with mulch. Prune carefully; leave in natural shape.

**PEST PROBLEMS:** Dieback, rootrot, leaf gall, leaf spots, lacebugs.

**SELECTED CULTIVARS:** 'Album' - White flowers. var. *album* - Lighter green leaves. Flowers white with a yellow-green throat. var. *luteum* - Has yellow flowers.

**RELATED SPECIES:** *R. catawbiense* - Catawba Rhododendron. (Treated in this text as a Large Evergreen Shrub.)

**LANDSCAPE NOTES:** Carolina Rhododendron is an excellent plant for the more natural landscape. It does well in the filtered light of birch, honeylocust, pines, and other "open" trees.

# *Rhododendron hybrida*

**Hybrid Rhododendron**

▲ 'Anna Rose Whitney'

▲ 'Scintillation'

▲ 'Unique'

▲ 'Jean Marie de Montague'

**ZONES:**
H1, 4–7; H2, 5–8; H3, 6–8

**HEIGHT:**
5' to 7'+

**WIDTH:**
6' to 7'+

**FRUIT:**
Brown capsule; NOT ORNA-MENTAL.

**TEXTURE:**
Coarse

**GROWTH RATE:**
Slow at first, then moderate.

**HABIT:**
Irregularly rounded and dense.

**FAMILY:**
Ericaceae

**LEAF COLOR:** Dark green; may show purple or yellow tinge in winter.

**LEAF DESCRIPTION:** SIMPLE, 4" to 6" long and 1 3/4" to 2" wide, elliptic or oblong with obtuse tip and rounded base. Entire margins. Very firm and thick. ALTERNATE arrangement.

**FLOWER DESCRIPTION:** Many shades of red, pink, white, lilac, purple, or yellow. 2" to 5" in umbel-shaped racemes (trusses) of several flowers. Flowers in spring.

**EXPOSURE/CULTURE:** Sun or shade. Must be planted in well-drained, organic soil of acidic pH. Plant on top of ground or in shallow hole. Mound with good, composted mulch. Prune carefully, after flowering.

**PEST PROBLEMS:** Dieback, rootrot, leaf gall, leaf spots, nematodes, beetles, borers, aphids, leaf miner, cankers, blights, lacebugs, mealybugs, scale. Rhododendrons are bothered by numerous pests. Consult the local extension office for your area. Many hundreds of cultivars exist!

**SELECTED CULTIVARS:** H1 hybrids: 'America' - Bright red in bell-shaped racemes. 'English Roseum' - Lilac-purple blooms with yellow throats. 'Nova Zembla' - Red blooms; vigorous and compact. 'Roseum Elegans' - Rose-lilac trusses. Extremely vigorous. H2 hybrids: 'Gomer Waterer' - Soft white blooms on compact plant. 'Rocket' - Coral-pink blooms with red blotches; stamens white. 'Scintillation' - Pastel-pink with bronze blotches. 'Trilby' - Crimson blooms with black blotches. Red-stemmed plant. H3 hybrids: 'Anna Rose Whitney' - Huge rose-pink trusses. 'Elizabeth' - Solid red trusses. 'Unique' - Yellow blooms with peach tinge.

**LANDSCAPE NOTES:** Hybrid Rhododendrons are some of the showiest specimen plants in landscaping. Flower clusters are large and come in many choices of colors. A gourmet plant for serious gardeners.

## *Rosa chinensis*                              **Chinese Rose**

**ZONES:**
7, 8, 9

**HEIGHT:**
4′ to 5′

**WIDTH:**
4′ to 5′

**FRUIT:**
Small achene; NOT ORNA-
MENTAL.

**TEXTURE:**
Medium

**GROWTH RATE:**
Moderate

**HABIT:**
Upright and open; somewhat
rounded.

**FAMILY:**
Rosaceae

**LEAF COLOR:** Medium to dark green.

**LEAF DESCRIPTION:** COMPOUND (3 to 5 leaflets), leaflets 1″ to 2″ long and half as wide, ovate shape with pointed tip and entire margins. ALTERNATE arrangement.

**FLOWER DESCRIPTION:** Various shades of pink and white on the same plant. 2″ wide small corymbs. Flowers in spring and summer. Very showy.

**EXPOSURE/CULTURE:** Sun to light shade. Prefers well-drained, organic soil, but is reasonably adaptable. Prune after flowering as needed.

**PEST PROBLEMS:** No serious pests.

**SELECTED CULTIVARS:** 'Minima' - Very dwarf (1 1/2′ to 2′). Rosey-red flowers. 'Semperflorens' - Crimson-red, solitary flowers. 'Viridiflora' - Flowers green; double.

**RELATED VARIETIES:** NOTE: There are more than 100 species of roses and thousands of cultivars - too numerous to consider in this text.

**LANDSCAPE NOTES:** Chinese Rose is a very noticeable rose species with its multi-color flowers on the same plant. Give this plant a prominent site in the garden border, and be prepared to answer questions from your guests. A real "eye-catcher."

# *Taxus cuspidata 'Thayerae'*

**Japanese Yew**

**ZONES:**
4, 5, 6, 7

**HEIGHT:**
5' to 6'

**WIDTH:**
6' to 8'

**FRUIT:**
Tiny, red; showy.

**TEXTURE:**
Fine

**GROWTH RATE:**
Slow

**HABIT:**
Broadly spreading.

**FAMILY:**
Taxaceae

**LEAF COLOR:** Dark green.

**LEAF DESCRIPTION:** NEEDLE-LIKE, 1" long, linear, 2-ranked with ranks forming "vees," 2 yellowish bands on underside, SPIRALLY arranged.

**FLOWER DESCRIPTION:** (Dioecious plants); NOT NOTICEABLE.

**EXPOSURE/CULTURE:** Sun or shade. Grows in any well-drained soil. pH adaptable. Does not like windy locations. Prune as desired to thicken or shape. May be sheared.

**PEST PROBLEMS:** No serious pests.

**SELECTED CULTIVARS:** None. This is a cultivar of *T. cuspidata,* a small evergreen tree.

**LANDSCAPE NOTES:** This is a hardy plant with many uses in the home garden or commercial business. Yews respond very well to pruning, and, as a result, make outstanding hedges. They may be sheared into shapes (topiary). Unclipped, they are loose and informal. Attractive bark is reddish-brown and exfoliating.

## *Thuja occidentalis* 'Rheingold' — Rheingold Arborvitae

**ZONES:**
3, 4, 5, 6, 7, 8

**HEIGHT:**
4′ to 5′

**WIDTH:**
3′ to 4′

**FRUIT:**
1/2″ brown cone; 4 or 5 scale pairs; NOT ORNAMENTAL.

**TEXTURE:**
Fine

**GROWTH RATE:**
Very slow.

**HABIT:**
Globe-shaped; dense.

**FAMILY:**
Cupressaceae

**LEAF COLOR:** Golden-yellow in summer; copper-gold in winter.

**LEAF DESCRIPTION:** SCALE-LIKE older leaves; juvenile leaves needle-like, 1/10″. ALTERNATE arrangement.

**FLOWER DESCRIPTION:** NOT NOTICEABLE.

**EXPOSURE/CULTURE:** Sun. Does best in well-drained soil that is moist. Mulch heavily to hold moisture. Pruning is not generally necessary.

**PEST PROBLEMS:** Bagworms, mites.

**SELECTED CULTIVARS:** None. This is a cultivar of *T. occidentalis,* American Arborvitae, a large evergreen tree.

**SIMILAR CULTIVARS:** 'Aurea' - Broad cone shape with yellow foliage. 'Ellwangeriana Aurea' - Very similar to 'Rheingold', which was developed from this cultivar.

**LANDSCAPE NOTES:** This is a cone-shaped or global shrub with very noticeable foliage that makes it a definite specimen plant. Careful site selection and placement are necessary for this very striking accent plant.

# *Yucca gloriosa*

**Spanish Dagger, Moundlily Yucca**

**ZONES:**
6, 7, 8, 9

**HEIGHT:**
4′ to 5′

**WIDTH:**
3′ to 4′

**FRUIT:**
Indehiscent black capsules, numerous on long stalks; NOT ORNAMENTAL. Should be removed.

**TEXTURE:**
Coarse

**GROWTH RATE:**
Moderate

**HABIT:**
Upright; very stiff trunk; older leaves drooping.

**FAMILY:**
Agavaceae

**LEAF COLOR:** Medium green.

**LEAF DESCRIPTION:** SIMPLE, 1 1/2′ to 2 1/2′ long and 2″ to 2 1/2″ wide, long linear shape with pointed tips and entire margins. ALTERNATE in whorled pattern.

**FLOWER DESCRIPTION:** White, tinged reddish, 4″ long on 4′ to 8′ spikes. Flowers July to September. VERY, VERY SHOWY.

**EXPOSURE/CULTURE:** Sun. Does best in well-drained, sandy soils, but can be grown in clay. No pruning except to remove terminal stalk when flower petals die.

**PEST PROBLEMS:** None

**SELECTED CULTIVARS:** None

**LANDSCAPE NOTES:** Yuccas make a bold accent in the landscape and are sometimes mistaken for palms. However, the flower spikes distinguish them easily. All Yuccas thrive in any soil and are native to sandy beaches. Do not plant where small children play - leaves are a definite hazard.

## Azalea x Exbury (Rhododendron x Exbury)     Exbury Hybrid Azalea

**ZONES:**
5, 6, 7, 8

**HEIGHT:**
4′ to 5′

**WIDTH:**
4′ to 5′

**FRUIT:**
Brown capsule; NOT ORNA-MENTAL.

**TEXTURE:**
Medium

**GROWTH RATE:**
Slow

**HABIT:**
Low-spreading, irregular, and open.

**FAMILY:**
Ericaceae

**LEAF COLOR:** Dark green.

**LEAF DESCRIPTION:** SIMPLE, 2″ to 3″ long and 3/4″ to 1″ wide, elliptic shape with entire margins. ALTERNATE arrangement.

**FLOWER DESCRIPTION:** Yellow to orange to red, 2″ to 3″ in large, many-flowered trusses. Flowers in May.

**EXPOSURE/CULTURE:** Sun or shade. Azaleas do best in well-drained, organic soil with consistent moisture and a pH reaction that is acidic. Good drainage is essential; do not plant too deeply. Pruning is minimal.

**PEST PROBLEMS:** Lacebug, spider mites.

**SELECTED CULTIVARS:** 'Cannon's Double' - Double, golden-yellow flowers with orange blotch. 'Firefly' - Red flowers. 'Gibraltar' - Coppery-red flowers with fringed petals. Beautiful. 'Golden Flare' - Yellow with reddish-orange blotch. 'Klondyke' - Orange flowers with yellow-orange blotch. 'Sun Chariot' - Yellow flowers. 'Sunset Pink' - Rose-pink flowers with yellow blotch. 'White Swan' - White flowers with yellowish blotch.

**LANDSCAPE NOTES:** Exbury Azaleas are some of the best deciduous Azaleas. These are among the finest plants for naturalizing in wooded locations and borders of the garden. Much more hardy than the evergreen types.

# *Berberis thunbergii*

**Japanese Barberry**

**ZONES:**
4, 5, 6, 7, 8

**HEIGHT:**
4′ to 6′

**WIDTH:**
4′ to 6′

**FRUIT:**
1/4″ to 1/2″ red berries.

**TEXTURE:**
Fine to medium.

**GROWTH RATE:**
Moderate

**HABIT:**
Dense and rounded with arching branches.

**FAMILY:**
Berberidaceae

**LEAF COLOR:** Bright green in summer; orange or reddish in fall.

**LEAF DESCRIPTION:** SIMPLE, 1/2″ to 1″ long and one-third as wide, narrow obovate in shape with entire margins, sometimes having a single spine at the tip. ALTERNATE arrangement.

**FLOWER DESCRIPTION:** Yellow, 1/2″ in small clusters. Not spectacular. Flowers in spring.

**EXPOSURE/CULTURE:** Sun or light shade. Grows in most soils, except very wet soils. Moderately drought-tolerant. Prune anytime, but retain natural shape.

**PEST PROBLEMS:** No serious pests.

**SELECTED CULTIVARS:** Featured in next section.

**LANDSCAPE NOTES:** Japanese Barberry is an "old standby" that has been used in difficult environments such as schools and parks for years. It still has merit in the residential or commercial landscape, and a little attention will yield quality performance. Stems usually have small spines at leaf nodes, but they are not very hazardous.

## *Berberis thunbergii 'Aurea'* — Golden Japanese Barberry

**ZONES:**
4, 5, 6, 7, 8

**HEIGHT:**
4' to 5'

**WIDTH:**
4' to 5'

**FRUIT:**
1/4" red berries; NOT ABUNDANT.

**TEXTURE:**
Fine to medium.

**GROWTH RATE:**
Moderate

**HABIT:**
Upright and mounded; dense.

**FAMILY:**
Berberidaceae

**LEAF COLOR:** Bright yellow.

**LEAF DESCRIPTION:** SIMPLE, 1/2" to 1" long and one-third as wide, narrow obovate to oblong shape with entire margins, sometimes spine-tipped. ALTERNATE arrangement.

**FLOWER DESCRIPTION:** Yellow, 1/2" in small clusters; NOT ABUNDANT. Flowers in April.

**EXPOSURE/CULTURE:** Sun or light shade. Best color in full sun. Reasonably drought-tolerant and adaptable to soils, except wet soils. Prune to natural shape.

**PEST PROBLEMS:** No serious pests.

**SELECTED CULTIVARS:** None. This is a cultivar of *B. thunbergii*.

**RELATED CULTIVARS:** 'Bonanza Gold' - Dwarf; growing about half as large as 'Aurea'.

**LANDSCAPE NOTES:** This is a bold accent or specimen plant that can be used effectively in well-chosen locations in the garden. It probably should not be used in quantity, except in very large gardens. This plant will not go unnoticed. Very beautiful foliage.

# *Berberis thunbergii var. atropurpurea*     **Red Japanese Barberry**

**ZONES:**
4, 5, 6, 7, 8

**HEIGHT:**
4' to 6'

**WIDTH:**
4' to 6'

**FRUIT:**
1/4" to 1/2" red berries.

**TEXTURE:**
Fine to medium.

**GROWTH RATE:**
Moderate

**HABIT:**
Dense and rounded; some-what arching.

**FAMILY:**
Berberidaceae

**LEAF COLOR:** Red to purplish-red.

**LEAF DESCRIPTION:** SIMPLE, 1/2" to 1" long and one-third as wide, narrow obovate shape with entire margin, sometimes spine-tipped. ALTERNATE arrangement.

**FLOWER DESCRIPTION:** Yellow, 1/2" in small clusters. Flowers in spring. Not spectacular.

**EXPOSURE/CULTURE:** Sun or light shade. Adaptable to any soil, except wet soils. Very drought-tolerant. Can be sheared to any form, but looks best natural.

**PEST PROBLEMS:** No serious pests.

**SELECTED CULTIVARS:** None. This is a variety of *B. thunbergii*.

**LANDSCAPE NOTES:** Red Japanese Barberry provides color to the garden border and is a carefree, easy to grow plant. The stems have the characteristic spines, but are not considered hazardous. Does well in urban landscapes.

## *Berberis thunbergii var. atropurpurea 'Rose Glow'**

**ZONES:**
4, 5, 6, 7, 8

**HEIGHT:**
4' to 5'

**WIDTH:**
4' to 5'

**FRUIT:**
1/4" red berries; NOT ABUN-DANT.

**TEXTURE:**
Fine to medium.

**GROWTH RATE:**
Moderate

**HABIT:**
Upright mound; open and pendulous.

**FAMILY:**
Berberidaceae

**LEAF COLOR:** Reddish-purple; leaves on new growth are mottled with pinkish-red.

**LEAF DESCRIPTION:** SIMPLE, 1/2" to 1" long and one-third as wide, narrow obovate to oblong shape with entire margins, sometimes spine-tipped. ALTERNATE arrangement.

**FLOWER DESCRIPTION:** Yellow, 1/2" in small clusters. Flowers in April. NOT ABUNDANT.

**EXPOSURE/CULTURE:** Sun or light shade. Prefers moist, well-drained soil, but adapts to dry conditions. Can be sheared, but looks best natural.

**PEST PROBLEMS:** No serious pests.

**SELECTED CULTIVARS:** None. This is a cultivar of *B. thunbergii.*

**LANDSCAPE NOTES:** This is a very popular selection. It provides interesting foliage and adapts well to urban conditions. Can be used effectively in both residential and commercial applications.

**\*COMMON NAME:** Rose Glow Barberry

# *Callicarpa americana*

## American Beautyberry

▲ var. *lactea*

**ZONES:**
7, 8, 9, 10

**HEIGHT:**
4' to 5'

**WIDTH:**
5' to 6'

**FRUIT:**
Violet drupes, encircling the leaf axils; shiny. OUTSTANDING AND VERY ORNAMENTAL.

**TEXTURE:**
Coarse

**GROWTH RATE:**
Moderate

**HABIT:**
Irregularly mounded; open and loose.

**FAMILY:**
Verbenaceae

**LEAF COLOR:** Medium green; yellowish in fall.

**LEAF DESCRIPTION:** SIMPLE, 4″ to 6″ long and 2″ to 2 1/2″ wide, elliptic to oblong-ovate with serrated margins. OPPOSITE arrangement.

**FLOWER DESCRIPTION:** Bluish-pink, tiny, in cymes in leaf axils. Flowers on new growth in summer.

**EXPOSURE/CULTURE:** Sun or part shade. Tolerant of most soils, but does best where moisture level is moderate. Mulch to maintain moisture level. Cut to ground every few years to control size or to rejuvenate.

**PEST PROBLEMS:** No serious pests.

**SELECTED CULTIVARS:** var. *lactea* - Has white berries.

**RELATED SPECIES:** *C. bodinieri* - A large shrub with violet fruits in dense cymes, arising from leaf axils. Not as showy as *C. americana*.

**LANDSCAPE NOTES:** This plant looks good as an individual specimen or in groupings. It is a border plant for the garden, and does well in partial shade under border trees. The fruit is spectacular in fall. This is a fine choice for naturalizing.

## *Callicarpa japonica* 'Leucocarpa' — White Japanese Beautyberry

▲ (species)

**ZONES:**
6, 7, 8

**HEIGHT:**
4' to 6'

**WIDTH:**
6' to 8'

**FRUIT:**
White drupes in clusters (NOT ENCIRCLING THE STEM).

**TEXTURE:**
Coarse

**GROWTH RATE:**
Moderate

**HABIT:**
Irregularly mounded; open.

**FAMILY:**
Verbenaceae

**LEAF COLOR:** Medium green in summer; yellowish in fall.

**LEAF DESCRIPTION:** SIMPLE, 2 1/2" to 5" long and half as wide, elliptic shape with serrate or serrulate margins, long acuminate tip with cuneate base. OPPO-SITE arrangement.

**FLOWER DESCRIPTION:** White or pink, arising in multi-flowered cymes from leaf axils on new growth in summer. NOT ORNAMENTAL.

**EXPOSURE/CULTURE:** Sun or part shade. The plant is adaptable to most soils, but is partial to moist soil. Prune to ground every 4 or 5 years to rejuvenate.

**PEST PROBLEMS:** No serious pests.

**SELECTED CULTIVARS:** None. This is a cultivar of *C. japonica,* the species, which has bright violet to purple fruits.

**LANDSCAPE NOTES:** Japanese Beautyberry is best suited for naturalizing in garden borders, as a specimen, or in groupings. It is not especially noticeable until the fruits appear. Under favorable conditions, the plant can be spectacular in fruit.

## *Chaenomeles speciosa*

**Flowering Quince**

**ZONES:**
4, 5, 6, 7, 8

**HEIGHT:**
6' to 7'

**WIDTH:**
6' to 7'

**FRUIT:**
2" to 3" apple-like; edible.

**TEXTURE:**
Medium

**GROWTH RATE:**
Moderate

**HABIT:**
Upright and open.

**FAMILY:**
Rosaceae

**LEAF COLOR:** Dark green.

**LEAF DESCRIPTION:** SIMPLE, 1 1/2" to 3" long and half as wide, ovate to oblong shape with cuneate base. Serrated margins. Stipule pairs at bases of petioles. ALTERNATE arrangement.

**FLOWER DESCRIPTION:** White, pink, red or orange-red, 1 1/4" to 1 3/4" wide. Flowers in March. SHOWY.

**EXPOSURE/CULTURE:** Sun or light shade. Prefers moist, organic, well-drained soils. Does best in acid soils. Prune to thin after flowering.

**PEST PROBLEMS:** Scale, fire blight, mites, leaf spot.

**SELECTED CULTIVARS:** 'Alba' - Single white flowers, tinged with pink. 'Orange Delight' - Very bright salmon-orange flowers. Single. 'Rosea Plena' - Semi-double, pink to coral-pink flowers. 'Rubra Grandiflora' - Single. Deep crimson-red flowers. 'Sanguinea Plena' - Semi-double. Rosey-red flowers. 'Toyo-Nishiki' - Single. White, pink, and red flowers on same plant.

**LANDSCAPE NOTES:** Flowering Quince is a beautiful shrub when in flower. It should be used in combination with other plantings in the border. Quince is prized for its early blooms, which are useful in flower arrangements.

## *Enkianthus campanulatus* — Red-veined Enkianthus

Courtesy of Monrovia Nursery Co.

**ZONES:**
5, 6, 7

**HEIGHT:**
5' to 8'

**WIDTH:**
4' to 6'

**FRUIT:**
1/2" to 2/3" brown, 5-valved capsule; NOT ORNAMENTAL.

**TEXTURE:**
Medium

**GROWTH RATE:**
Slow

**HABIT:**
Upright and layered.

**FAMILY:**
Ericaceae

**LEAF COLOR:** Medium green in summer; orange to red in fall.

**LEAF DESCRIPTION:** SIMPLE, 1 1/2" to 3" long and half as wide, elliptic shape with serrated margins. Sparsely pubescent above and beneath. ALTERNATE arrangement.

**FLOWER DESCRIPTION:** Yellowish to pale orange with red veins, 1/2", bell-shaped corolla with 5 lobes, appearing in pendulous racemes or umbels. Flowers in late spring. Showy.

**EXPOSURE/CULTURE:** Full sun to part shade. The plant prefers moist, organic, well-drained soil of acidic pH. Should be mulched to maintain consistent moisture. Prune after flowering to shape.

**PEST PROBLEMS:** No serious pests.

**SELECTED CULTIVARS:** 'Albiflorus' - Flowers are white to off-white with no red veins. var. *palibinii* - This variety has solid red flower racemes.

**LANDSCAPE NOTES:** Enkianthus makes a nice landscape plant for garden borders as a specimen or screen. It has attractive flowers and excellent fall foliage. This is an ideal plant for naturalizing, and it grows under similar conditions as *Rhododendron* species.

# *Euonymus alatus 'Compactus'*

**Burning Bush, Winged Euonymus**

**ZONES:**
3, 4, 5, 6, 7, 8, 9

**HEIGHT:**
5' to 6'

**WIDTH:**
5' to 6'

**FRUIT:**
Purplish capsule; aril orange.

**TEXTURE:**
Medium

**GROWTH RATE:**
Moderate to slow.

**HABIT:**
Spreading and mounded; dense.

**FAMILY:**
Celastraceae

**LEAF COLOR:** Dark green; turning brilliant glowing red in fall.

**LEAF DESCRIPTION:** SIMPLE, 1" to 2" long and half as wide, elliptic to obovate shape with acute apex. Serrated margins. Usually OPPOSITE; occasionally alternate or whorled.

**FLOWER DESCRIPTION:** Greenish, tiny, in cymes. Late spring. NOT ORNAMENTAL.

**EXPOSURE/CULTURE:** Sun or shade. Adaptable to a wide range of well-drained soils. Plant can be sheared into extremely dense character. Sometimes used as a sheared hedge.

**PEST PROBLEMS:** No serious pests.

**SELCTED CULTIVARS:** None. This is a cultivar of *E. alatus,* a large deciduous shrub.

**SIMILAR CULTIVARS:** 'Rudy Haag' - More compact than 'Compactus'. Lighter fall color.

**LANDSCAPE NOTES:** This is an outstanding selection for the garden border or planting beds. Choose a site that is noticeable and not crowded. Sometimes used as a clipped hedge on larger properties. BOLD! Note: Stems have corky growths, similar to Winged Elm, which add interest in winter.

## *Hydrangea quercifolia*  **Oakleaf Hydrangea**

**ZONES:**
4, 5, 6, 7, 8, 9

**HEIGHT:**
4' to 5'

**WIDTH:**
5' to 8'

**FRUIT:**
Small brown capsule; NOT ORNAMENTAL.

**TEXTURE:**
Coarse

**GROWTH RATE:**
Moderate

**HABIT:**
Open and broad-spreading; colonizing.

**FAMILY:**
Saxifragaceae

**LEAF COLOR:** Dark green in summer; orange to reddish in fall.

**LEAF DESCRIPTION:** SIMPLE, 5″ to 8″ long and almost as wide, nearly circular with 3 to 7 lobes (usually 5), lobes coarsely serrated, sometimes deeply cut. Lower surface whitish and hairy (downy). OPPOSITE arrangement. Young stems reddish-brown and hairy; older bark exfoliating to show brown inner bark.

**FLOWER DESCRIPTION:** White, maturing to pinkish (sterile flowers), inner fertile flowers greenish, 1″ in 6″ to 12″ erect panicles, appearing in May and June. VERY SHOWY.

**EXPOSURE/CULTURE:** Light shade to shade. Does best in moist, well-drained soil. Not prosperous in dry, sunny sites. Prune after flowering to thicken or shape.

**PEST PROBLEMS:** No serious pests.

**SELECTED CULTIVARS:** 'Snowflake' - Large pure white flower panicles to 12″ or larger. 'Snow Queen' - White flowers maturing to pink. Fall color is burgundy and very showy. Outstanding.

**LANDSCAPE NOTES:** Oakleaf Hydrangea is one of the showiest deciduous shrubs for summer flowers and fall foliage color. It prospers in shady areas and should be used as a specimen in garden borders. Coarse foliage provides an interesting contrast as a background plant for fine-textured plants. Outstanding and reasonably low-maintenance.

## *Itea virginica*

### Sweetspire, Virginia Sweetspire

**ZONES:**
5, 6, 7, 8, 9

**HEIGHT:**
5' to 6'

**WIDTH:**
3' to 5'

**FRUIT:**
1/4" to 1/2" capsule; NOT ORNAMENTAL.

**TEXTURE:**
Medium

**GROWTH RATE:**
Moderate

**HABIT:**
Erect and spreading.

**FAMILY:**
Saxifragaceae

**LEAF COLOR:** Medium green in summer; crimson-red in fall.

**LEAF DESCRIPTION:** SIMPLE, 2" to 3" long and one-third as wide, elliptic shape with serrulate margins. ALTERNATE arrangement.

**FLOWER DESCRIPTION:** White, tiny in 4" to 6" racemes, upright and pendulous. Flowers in May and June. Very unusual and showy.

**EXPOSURE/CULTURE:** Sun or shade. Prefers moist, organic soils of any pH. Tolerates wetter conditions than most plants. Requires minimal pruning after flowering.

**PEST PROBLEMS:** No serious pests.

**SELECTED CULTIVARS:** 'Henry's Garnet' - This is a dwarf form (less than 4') with garnet-red foliage in fall. Great cultivar.

**LANDSCAPE NOTES:** Sweetspire makes an excellent addition to the garden border. It is desirable for its racemes of noticeable flowers in spring, as well as good foliage color in fall. This is an outstanding choice for naturalizing.

## *Kerria japonica*

**Japanese Kerria**

**ZONES:**
5, 6, 7, 8, 9

**HEIGHT:**
4' to 6'

**WIDTH:**
4' to 6'

**FRUIT:**
Achene; NOT ORNAMENTAL.

**TEXTURE:**
Medium

**GROWTH RATE:**
Moderate

**HABIT:**
Upright and arching; open and loose.

**FAMILY:**
Rosaceae

**LEAF COLOR:** Bright medium green.

**LEAF DESCRIPTION:** SIMPLE, 1" to 3" long and half as wide, oblong-ovate shape with double serrate margins, awl-shaped stipules. ALTERNATE arrangement.

**FLOWER DESCRIPTION:** Yellow, single or double, to 2" wide. VERY SHOWY. Flowers in spring.

**EXPOSURE/CULTURE:** Sun or part shade. Very adaptable to most soils, but does not like heavy, wet soils. Considered durable and easy to grow. Pruning is minimal.

**PEST PROBLEMS:** Chewing insects. None serious.

**SELECTED CULTIVARS:** 'Picta' - Leaves edged with white. 'Pleniflora' - Double-flowered. The most common cultivar.

**LANDSCAPE NOTES:** Kerria is a very attractive plant that is especially useful for naturalizing. Does well under polluted, urban conditions, and should be used more for public areas. It is a great plant for use in the perennial garden.

## *Lonicera xylosteum* 'Clavey's Dwarf'

**Dwarf European Fly Honeysuckle**

**ZONES:**
4, 5, 6

**HEIGHT:**
4' to 6'

**WIDTH:**
4' to 6'

**FRUIT:**
Dark red berry.

**TEXTURE:**
Medium

**GROWTH RATE:**
Rapid

**HABIT:**
Mounded with arched branches.

**FAMILY:**
Caprifoliaceae

**LEAF COLOR:** Bluish-green

**LEAF DESCRIPTION:** SIMPLE, 1 1/2″ to 2″ long and half as wide, ovate shape with cuneate base and entire margins. OPPOSITE arrangement.

**FLOWER DESCRIPTION:** Yellowish-white, 1/2″ long, appearing in pairs. Fragrant. Flowers in May.

**EXPOSURE/CULTURE:** Sun or part shade. Does well in most well-drained soils. Needs occasional pruning to control or prevent leggy nature.

**PEST PROBLEMS:** No serious pests.

**SELECTED CULTIVARS:** None. This is a cultivar of *L. xylosteum,* a large shrub.

**LANDSCAPE NOTES:** This is a nice plant that can be used in foundation planting, borders, and informal hedges. Considered very easy to grow, and is a good plant for naturalizing.

## *Neviusia alabamensis*

**Alabama Snow Wreath**

**ZONES:**
4, 5, 6, 7, 8

**HEIGHT:**
4' to 6'

**WIDTH:**
4' to 6'

**FRUIT:**
Brown achene; NOT ORNA-MENTAL.

**TEXTURE:**
Medium

**GROWTH RATE:**
Moderate

**HABIT:**
Upright and arching; rhizomatous.

**FAMILY:**
Rosaceae

**LEAF COLOR:** Medium green.

**LEAF DESCRIPTION:** SIMPLE, 2″ to 3″ long and 1″ to 2″ wide, ovate shape with doubly serrated margins. ALTERNATE arrangement.

**FLOWER DESCRIPTION:** White, lacking petals, numerous showy anthers. Appearing in multi-flower cymes. Flowers in spring.

**EXPOSURE/CULTURE:** Sun or shade. Grows in any moist, well-drained soil. Considered easy to grow. Prune after flowering to maintain shape.

**PEST PROBLEMS:** No serious pests.

**SELECTED CULTIVARS:** None

**LANDSCAPE NOTES:** Alabama Snow Wreath is a native plant that can work well in garden borders and planting beds. It is a great choice for naturalizing, and could be used effectively in perennial-type plantings as a background plant.

## *Rhodotypos scandens*

**Black Jetbead**

**ZONES:**
5, 6, 7, 8

**HEIGHT:**
4' to 5'

**WIDTH:**
5' to 6'

**FRUIT:**
Black achene; shiny and pea-like.

**TEXTURE:**
Medium to coarse.

**GROWTH RATE:**
Moderate

**HABIT:**
Irregular and open.

**FAMILY:**
Rosaceae

**LEAF COLOR:** Medium green.

**LEAF DESCRIPTION:** SIMPLE, 2" to 3" long and half as wide, ovate shape with narrow pointed tips, double serrated margins, puckered between veins. OPPOSITE arrangement.

**FLOWER DESCRIPTION:** White, 4-petaled, solitary, 1 1/2" to 2" wide. Showy. Flowers in late spring.

**EXPOSURE/CULTURE:** Sun or shade. The plant will prosper in most soils and locations. Can be pruned after flowering to encourage a more dense habit. Almost care-free.

**PEST PROBLEMS:** No serious pests.

**SELECTED CULTIVARS:** None

**LANDSCAPE NOTES:** Black Jetbead is not a plant in great demand, but has its merits and performs with little attention. It is a good choice for naturalizing.

## *Ribes alpinum* 'Pumilum'       Compact Alpine Currant

**ZONES:**
3, 4, 5, 6, 7, 8

**HEIGHT:**
4' to 5'

**WIDTH:**
4' to 5'

**FRUIT:**
Scarlet berry.

**TEXTURE:**
Medium

**GROWTH RATE:**
Moderate

**HABIT:**
Rounded, upright, and dense.

**FAMILY:**
Saxifragaceae

**LEAF COLOR:** Bright green.

**LEAF DESCRIPTION:** SIMPLE, 1" to 2" long and wide, palmately lobed (usually 3) with serrated margins on lobes. ALTERNATE arrangement.

**FLOWER DESCRIPTION:** Male and female plants. Female flowers greenish-yellow in erect racemes after the leaves. NOT SHOWY. Flowers in early spring.

**EXPOSURE/CULTURE:** Sun or shade. Tolerant of any well-drained soil. pH adaptable. Easily pruned to desired shapes.

**PEST PROBLEMS:** Leaf spot, anthracnose.

**SELECTED CULTIVARS:** None. This is a cultivar of *R. alpinum,* a somewhat larger shrub.

**LANDSCAPE NOTES:** Compact Alpine Currant is a good plant for massing, and is especially well-suited to clipped, semi-private hedges. There are outstanding hedges of Compact Alpine Currant at the Morton Arboretum.

## *Spiraea nipponica 'Snowmound'*

**Snowmound Spirea**

**ZONES:**
4, 5, 6, 7, 8

**HEIGHT:**
4' to 6'

**WIDTH:**
4' to 6'

**FRUIT:**
Dehiscent follicle; NOT ORNAMENTAL.

**TEXTURE:**
Fine

**GROWTH RATE:**
Moderate

**HABIT:**
Rounded and open; somewhat arching.

**FAMILY:**
Rosaceae

**LEAF COLOR:** Dark bluish-green.

**LEAF DESCRIPTION:** SIMPLE, 3/4" to 1 1/2" long and one-third as wide, elliptic to obovate shape and serrated at tips. ALTERNATE arrangement.

**FLOWER DESCRIPTION:** White, 1/4" in multi-flower, rounded corymbs. VERY SHOWY. Flowers in May or June.

**EXPOSURE/CULTURE:** Sun or light shade. Does best in well-drained soil with moderate or higher levels of moisture for best bloom. Prune older stems to ground to thin or to rejuvenate.

**PEST PROBLEMS:** No serious pests.

**SELECTED CULTIVARS:** None. This is a cultivar of *S. nipponica,* a larger deciduous shrub.

**RELATED CULTIVARS:** 'Rotundifolia' - Has larger leaves and appears denser.

**LANDSCAPE NOTES:** Snowmound Spirea provides colorful flowers and foliage in the garden. Although it needs ample water for best performance, it is a rugged plant that tolerates urban conditions. It looks especially good in mass.

## *Spiraea thunbergii* — Thunberg Spirea

**ZONES:**
5, 6, 7, 8

**HEIGHT:**
4′ to 5′

**WIDTH:**
4′ to 5′

**FRUIT:**
Dehiscent follicles; NOT ORNAMENTAL.

**TEXTURE:**
Fine

**GROWTH RATE:**
Rapid

**HABIT:**
Upright and arching.

**FAMILY:**
Rosaceae

**LEAF COLOR:** Light to medium green.

**LEAF DESCRIPTION:** SIMPLE, 1/2″ to 1 1/4″ long and one-fourth as wide, linear-lanceolate shape with serrated margins. ALTERNATE arrangement.

**FLOWER DESCRIPTION:** White, 1/4″ in small, 1″ to 2″ sessile umbels. VERY SHOWY. Flowers in early spring.

**EXPOSURE/CULTURE:** Sun. Does best in moist, well-drained soil, but is adaptable. Needs to be pruned heavily after flowering to promote dense habit.

**PEST PROBLEMS:** No serious pests.

**SELECTED CULTIVARS:** None

**LANDSCAPE NOTES:** Thunberg Spirea is an "old standby" that has proven itself over the years. It is rugged, and with a little care, can be an attractive plant throughout the warm season. It is one of the first plants to bloom in spring.

# *Syringa microphylla*

**ZONES:**
4, 5, 6, 7

**HEIGHT:**
5′ to 6′

**WIDTH:**
6′ to 8′

**FRUIT:**
Brown capsule; NOT ORNA-MENTAL.

**TEXTURE:**
Medium

**GROWTH RATE:**
Moderate

**HABIT:**
Broad and dense.

**FAMILY:**
Oleaceae

**LEAF COLOR:** Medium green.

**LEAF DESCRIPTION:** SIMPLE, 1″ to 1 1/2″ long and half as wide, ovate shape with entire margins. OPPOSITE arrangement.

**FLOWER DESCRIPTION:** Lilac color, 1/4″ in 3″ to 4″ lateral panicles. Fragrant. Flowers in spring.

**EXPOSURE/CULTURE:** Full sun or light shade. Does best in moist, light, deep soils, but is adaptable. Pruning is minimal after flowering.

**PEST PROBLEMS:** No serious pests. Bothered less by blights and mildews than Common Lilac.

**SELECTED CULTIVARS:** None

**LANDSCAPE NOTES:** Littleleaf Lilac is a relatively easy to grow form as compared to other Lilacs. It is not as spectacular in flower as Common Lilac, but is adequately attractive. It is probably best suited for garden borders or in small masses.

## *Vaccinium ashei*

**Rabbiteye Blueberry**

**ZONES:**
7, 8, 9

**HEIGHT:**
4' to 7'

**WIDTH:**
4' to 6'

**FRUIT:**
1/3" glaucous, blue-black berry; edible; July.

**TEXTURE:**
Fine to medium

**GROWTH RATE:**
Moderate

**HABIT:**
Upright and rounded; multi-stemmed and open.

**FAMILY:**
Ericaceae

**LEAF COLOR:** Blue-green and glaucous in summer; yellowish, orange, or red in fall.

**LEAF DESCRIPTION:** SIMPLE, 1 1/2" to 3" long and half as wide, ovate to elliptic shape with entire margins, sparsely pubescent. ALTERNATE arrangement.

**FLOWER DESCRIPTION:** White, often tinged pink, 1/4" to 1/3" long and urn-shaped, borne in racemes arising from leaf axils. Flowers in spring with the leaves. ABUNDANT AND SHOWY.

**EXPOSURE/CULTURE:** Sun or light shade. The plant does best in organic, well-drained soil, and it requires an acidic pH. Prune after fruit drop to thin or head-back canes.

**PEST PROBLEMS:** Spider mites.

**SELECTED CULTIVARS:** 'Brightwell' - Has medium-sized berries that ripen in early season. 'Tifblue' - Has large, light blue berries that ripen in late season. Widely used in commerce. Note: Many others exist. Consult the Extension Service in your area for recommended cultivars.

**RELATED SPECIES:** *V. corymbosum* - Highbush Blueberry. This species is similar to *V. ashei,* but is hardy further north (zone 4). It performs poorly in the Southeast.

**LANDSCAPE NOTES:** Rabbiteye Blueberry is a commercial fruit that makes a dual-purpose plant in the modern landscape. It is a beautiful plant under landscape conditions, while supplying edible fruit in the garden. Bird-lovers will find that the plant attracts many species of birds. This is a great plant for xeriscaping.

## *Viburnum carlesii*

**Korean Spice Viburnum**

**ZONES:**
5, 6, 7

**HEIGHT:**
4' to 6'

**WIDTH:**
5' to 8'

**FRUIT:**
Blue-black drupe; NOT ORNA-MENTAL

**TEXTURE:**
Medium

**GROWTH RATE:**
Moderately slow.

**HABIT:**
Rounded and dense; some-what upright.

**FAMILY:**
Caprifoliaceae

**LEAF COLOR:** Dark green; reddish in fall.

**LEAF DESCRIPTION:** SIMPLE, 2″ to 4″ long and half as wide, ovate shape with serrated margins. OPPOSITE arrangement.

**FLOWER DESCRIPTION:** White, 1/4″ to 1/3″ in 2″ to 4″ cymes. Fragrant. Flowers in spring.

**EXPOSURE/CULTURE:** Sun or light shade. Plant is very adaptable, and grows in most soils except wet soils. Prune after flowering as desired.

**PEST PROBLEMS:** No serious pests.

**SELECTED CULTIVARS:** 'Compactum' - More compact than the species and having more flowers.

**LANDSCAPE NOTES:** Korean Spice Viburnum has deep pink buds that open to white flowers with a sweet, spicy fragrance. It is an interesting plant that can be used to brighten dull garden borders or planting beds. Should be used more in landscaping.

# Chapter 8

# LARGE SHRUBS

The large shrubs described in this text are species which grow over 6 feet in height and branch from ground level to apex. Large shrubs, especially those that have noticeable, ornamental flowers, are among the most beautiful of the woody ornamental plants. Many of these plants were parent plants of dwarf and medium size shrubs that are so popular in modern landscaping.

Some of the large shrubs in this text might be considered trees by some authorities. An attempt is made here to identify those plants that are often used in the landscape industry as shrubs. For example, many of the larger species in the *Ilex* genus (Hollies) are used as shrubs because of their shrub-like characteristics, but many become as large as some trees if not maintained as shrubs.

Large shrubs have many useful possibilities in landscaping, even though their use in small urban and suburban gardens must be limited. Some common uses of large shrubs are:

▼ Corner plants for two-story or larger structures.
▼ Background plants in shrub borders.
▼ Hedges and privacy screens.
▼ Windbreaks and soundbreaks.
▼ Tree-formed specimen plants.

## Azalea indica (Rhododendron indica)

**Southern Indian Azalea**

▼ 'G.G. Gerbin'

▼ 'George L. Tabor'

'Formosa' ▶

**ZONES:**
8, 9

**HEIGHT:**
6' to 10'

**WIDTH:**
6' to 10'

**FRUIT:**
Brown pod; NOT ORNAMENTAL.

**TEXTURE:**
Fine to medium.

**GROWTH RATE:**
Moderate

**HABIT:**
Upright and spreading.

**FAMILY:**
Ericaceae

**LEAF COLOR:** Dark green; hairy on both surfaces.

**LEAF DESCRIPTION:** SIMPLE, 1 1/2″ to 2″ long and 1/2″ to 1″ wide, narrow elliptic to oblong-ovate shape with entire margins. ALTERNATE arrangement.

**FLOWER DESCRIPTION:** White, pink, red, orchid, or lavender, depending on cultivar. 1 1/2″ to 3″ long. Blooms in April.

**EXPOSURE/CULTURE:** Light shade to shade. Does best in well-drained, organic soil of acid reaction. Will drown in wet soils. PLANT HIGH. Prune only after flowering.

**PEST PROBLEMS:** Spider mites, lacebugs, leaf gall.

**SELECTED CULTIVARS:** 'Brilliant' - Watermelon-red flowers. Single. 'Duc de Rohan' - Salmon-pink flowers. Single. 'Fielder's White' - Large, frost-white flowers. Single. 'Formosa' - Purple flowers. Single. 'G. G. Gerbin' - White flowers. Single. 'George L. Tabor' - Orchid and white. Single. 'Nuccio's Carnival' - Rose-red. Single or semi-double. 'Nuccio's Carnival Clown' - Large purple flowers. Single. 'Orange Ruffles' - Orange-red, ruffled flowers. Single. 'Rosea' - Rose-red. Semi-double. 'White Grandeur' - Snow-white, large flowers. Double.

**LANDSCAPE NOTES:** Southern Indian Azaleas are outstanding plants for larger gardens in the South. These are the Azaleas for which Charleston, Savannah, and other historic southern towns are famous. Outstanding.

# *Camellia japonica*

**Japanese Camellia**

▲ 'Silver Waves'

▲ 'Pink Perfection'

▲ 'Jordon's Pride'

**ZONES:**
7, 8, 9

**HEIGHT:**
8' to 12'

**WIDTH:**
7' to 8'

**FRUIT:**
Brown capsule; NOT ORNA-MENTAL.

**TEXTURE:**
Coarse

**GROWTH RATE:**
Moderate

**HABIT:**
Upright; open to pyramidal.

**FAMILY:**
Theaceae

**LEAF COLOR:** Dark green.

**LEAF DESCRIPTION:** SIMPLE, 2 1/2″ to 4 1/2″ long and half as wide, elliptic shape with serrated margins. ALTERNATE arrangement.

**FLOWER DESCRIPTION:** White, pink, red, or variegated, depending on cultivar. 3 1/2″ to 5 1/2″ wide, double or single. Flowers in October through April, depending on cultivar.

**EXPOSURE/CULTURE:** Light shade to part shade. Plants need moist, organic, well-drained soil of acid pH. Mulch to hold moisture level. Prune after flowering or during flowering for table arrangements.

**PEST PROBLEMS:** Leaf gall, tea scale, rootrot, flower blight, thrips, mealy bugs.

**SELECTED CULTIVARS:** 'Colonel Fireye' - Dark red. Large and formal. 'Daikagura Variegated' - Rose-red splotched with white. Large peony type. 'Jordon's Pride' - Variegated; light pink with white and deep pink streaked margin. Semi-double. 'Magnoliaeflora' - Large blush-pink flowers. Semi-double. 'Mrs. Charles Cobb' - Dark red, semi-double flowers. 'Nuccio's Pearl' - White with pearl-pink margins. Fully double. 'Pink Perfection' - Light pink. Formal, double flowers. 'Silver Waves' - White flowers with wavy edges. Semi-double. 'Spellbound' - Coral-rose. Semi-double.

**LANDSCAPE NOTES:** Camellias are among the most beautiful flowering plants. Thousands of cultivars provide an endless supply of different colors and size combinations of flowers. One of the favorites in the South for fresh flower arrangements. Available in single, semi-double, or double blooms.

## *Camellia sasanqua* — Sasanqua Camellia

▲ 'Setsugeka'

▲ 'Sparkling Burgundy'

**ZONES:**
7, 8, 9

**HEIGHT:**
6' to 10'

**WIDTH:**
5' to 8'

**FRUIT:**
Brown capsule; NOT ORNA-MENTAL.

**TEXTURE:**
Medium

**GROWTH RATE:**
Moderate

**HABIT:**
Upright and dense.

**FAMILY:**
Theaceae

**LEAF COLOR:** Deep green.

**LEAF DESCRIPTION:** SIMPLE, 1 1/2" to 2" long and 1/2" to 1" wide, elliptic shape with serrated margins. ALTERNATE arrangement.

**FLOWER DESCRIPTION:** White, pink, or red, depending on cultivar. 1 1/2" to 2" long. Flowers in October and November.

**EXPOSURE/CULTURE:** Sun or shade. Must be grown in moist, well-drained, acid soil. Incorporate organic matter at time of planting. Mulch for consistent moisture retention. Prune after flowering or during flowering for floral arrangements.

**PEST PROBLEMS:** Leaf gall, tea scale, rootrot, thrips, mealy bugs.

**SELECTED CULTIVARS:** 'Apple Blossom' - White flowers with cerise-red edges. Golden-yellow stamens. Single. 'Cleopatra' - Rose-pink. Semi-double. 'Hana Jiman' - White petals, tipped pink. Semi-double. 'Mine-No-Yuki' - White flowers. Semi-double. 'Setsugeka' - Compact upright growth. White ruffled petals with yellow stamens. Semi-double. 'Sparkling Burgundy' - Deep pink. Peony form. 'Yuletide' - Bright red with yellow stamens. Single.

**LANDSCAPE NOTES:** Sasanqua is more refined than Japanese Camellia and provides excellent color during late fall and early winter. The plant is suitable for foundations, borders, and focal areas. It makes a beautiful tree-form plant and can be used as an espaliered specimen. Flowers are single or double.

# *Chamaecyparis obtusa 'Crippsii'*

**Golden Hinoki Cypress**

**ZONES:**
4, 5, 6, 7, 8

**HEIGHT:**
10' to 15'

**WIDTH:**
6' to 10'

**FRUIT:**
Orange-brown cone, 1/4" to 3/8".

**TEXTURE:**
Fine

**GROWTH RATE:**
Moderate

**HABIT:**
Broad and conical; fan-shaped branchlets.

**FAMILY:**
Cupressaceae

**LEAF COLOR:** Golden yellow outer branches; yellowish-green on inside.

**LEAF DESCRIPTION:** SCALE-LIKE, 1/10", pressed to stem, whitish lines beneath. Arranged in OPPOSITE pairs.

**FLOWER DESCRIPTION:** Monoecious; NOT NOTICEABLE.

**EXPOSURE/CULTURE:** Part shade to full sun. The plant prefers well-drained, moist, cool soil. It favors humid conditions, but not excessive heat or windy conditions. Do not prune, leave natural.

**PEST PROBLEMS:** Mites, scale. No serious pests.

**SELECTED CULTIVARS:** None. This is a cultivar of *C. obtusa,* a large evergreen tree.

**RELATED SPECIES:** *C. lawsoniana* - Very large (to 150') evergreen tree with ascending branches that "nod" at the tips. Usually dense and conical with blue-green, scale-like foliage. Hundreds of cultivars exist.

**LANDSCAPE NOTES:** Golden Hinoki Cypress is a noticeable specimen or accent plant. It is one of many lower-growing forms that can be grown in a limited space. Choose a location carefully for this bright and beautiful foliage plant. The plant has nice reddish-brown, exfoliating bark, which is usually hidden by foliage.

## *Chamaecyparis obtusa 'Gracilis'* — Slender Hinoki Cypress

**ZONES:**
4, 5, 6, 7, 8

**HEIGHT:**
12′ to 16′

**WIDTH:**
4′ to 6′

**FRUIT:**
3/8″ orange-brown cone, 8 to 10 scales.

**TEXTURE:**
Fine

**GROWTH RATE:**
Moderate

**HABIT:**
Conical and spreading; branchlets irregularly arranged.

**FAMILY:**
Cupressaceae

**LEAF COLOR:** Lustrous green; new growth is reddish.

**LEAF DESCRIPTION:** SCALE-LIKE, 1/10″, whitish markings beneath. Closely pressed in OPPOSITE pairs.

**FLOWER DESCRIPTION:** Monoecious; NOT NOTICEABLE.

**EXPOSURE/CULTURE:** Full sun to part shade. Does best in moist, well-drained soil, lightly mulched. Prefers humid conditions, but does not like excessive heat or wind. Does well near walls. Pruning is not usually necessary or recommended.

**PEST PROBLEMS:** Mites, scale. No serious pests.

**RELATED CULTIVARS:** 'Filicoides' - Foliage is dense on short, frond-like branchlets and is fern-like. Gives an Oriental effect.

**SELECTED CULTIVARS:** None. This is a cultivar of *C. obtusa,* a large evergreen tree.

**LANDSCAPE NOTES:** Slender Hinoki Cypress makes a nice specimen plant due to its unique and interesting, frond-like branchlets. Can be used effectively as a foundation plant for taller structures, and is sometimes used as a container specimen.

# *Choisya ternata*

**Mexican Orange**

**ZONES:**
7, 8, 9

**HEIGHT:**
5′ to 9′

**WIDTH:**
5′ to 9′

**FRUIT:**
Small dehiscent capsule; NOT ORNAMENTAL.

**TEXTURE:**
Medium

**GROWTH RATE:**
Moderate

**HABIT:**
Globular and dense.

**FAMILY:**
Rosaceae

**LEAF COLOR:** Lustrous green.

**LEAF DESCRIPTION:** PALMATELY COMPOUND, 3 leaflets, leaflets 3″ to 4″ long and half as wide, elliptic to obovate shape with entire margins. OPPOSITE arrangement.

**FLOWER DESCRIPTION:** White, 1″ long, appearing in small terminal corymbs in mid-spring and continuing into summer. Fragrant, abundant, and showy.

**EXPOSURE/CULTURE:** Sun or light shade. Requires a moist, well-drained, organic soil of acid pH. Prune after flowering.

**PEST PROBLEMS:** No serious pests.

**SELECTED CULTIVARS:** None

**LANDSCAPE NOTES:** Mexican Orange is an attractive plant that is especially noticeable in flower. It can be used as a specimen in foundation plantings, garden borders, accent beds, or as screening material. It has nice foliage, and is very fragrant in bloom. This is a nice landscape plant that should be more widely used in the recommended zones.

## *Cotoneaster lacteus f. parneyi*

**Parney's Cotoneaster**

**ZONES:**
6, 7, 8

**HEIGHT:**
8′ to 12′

**WIDTH:**
6′ to 10′

**FRUIT:**
1/4″ red pome; persisting.

**TEXTURE:**
Medium

**GROWTH RATE:**
Moderate

**HABIT:**
Upright and broad; pendulous branches.

**FAMILY:**
Rosaceae

**LEAF COLOR:** Dark green; whitish and hairy beneath.

**LEAF DESCRIPTION:** SIMPLE, 1″ to 3″ long and half as wide, elliptic shape with mucronate tip and entire margins. ALTERNATE arrangement.

**FLOWER DESCRIPTION:** White, tiny, in 2″ to 3″ clusters (corymbs). Flowers in late spring.

**EXPOSURE/CULTURE:** Sun. Prefers well-drained, acid, or slightly acid soil. The plant is reasonably drought-tolerant and hardy. Prune after flowering for shaping or control.

**PEST PROBLEMS:** Fire blight, spider mites, lace bug, scale.

**SELECTED CULTIVARS:** None

**LANDSCAPE NOTES:** Parney's Cotoneaster is a nice plant for sunny exposures in the garden border. It has ornamental flower clusters in spring, followed by clusters of red fruit in fall. This is a nice plant for naturalizing.

## *Cryptomeria japonica* 'Globosa Nana'

**Globe Japanese Cryptomeria**

**ZONES:**
6, 7, 8, 9

**HEIGHT:**
6' to 9'

**WIDTH:**
5' to 10'

**FRUIT:**
Small, brown globose cone.

**TEXTURE:**
Fine

**GROWTH RATE:**
Moderate

**HABIT:**
Broad cone; dense and compact.

**FAMILY:**
Taxodiaceae

**LEAF COLOR:** Yellowish-green in summer; blue-green cast in winter.

**LEAF DESCRIPTION:** AWL-LIKE, curving inward, 1/8" to 1/4" long, appressed (close to stem), spirally arranged; 4-angled with stomata on each surface.

**FLOWER DESCRIPTION:** Monoecious; male flowers axillary, female flowers terminal; NOT SHOWY.

**EXPOSURE/CULTURE:** Sun or light shade. Prefers moist, fertile, well-drained sites. Pruning is minimal, but plant will tolerate shearing. More cold hardy than the species.

**PEST PROBLEMS:** Leaf blight, stem blight.

**BARK/STEMS:** Branchlets ascending; trunk on older stems having reddish, exfoliating bark.

**SELECTED CULTIVARS:** None. This is a cultivar of *C. japonica,* a large evergreen tree.

**LANDSCAPE NOTES:** Globe Japanese Cryptomeria is an excellent plant where dense foliage is desired, such as foundations or screening. It is also used as an accent specimen. This plant is somewhat formal, and is not the best plant for naturalizing. This is a superior plant where soil conditions are favorable.

## *Elaeagnus pungens* 'Fruitlandii'   Fruitland Elaeagnus

**ZONES:**
6, 7, 8, 9, 10

**HEIGHT:**
8' to 10'

**WIDTH:**
8' to 10'

**FRUIT:**
1/2" red drupe; NOT COMMON.

**TEXTURE:**
Medium

**GROWTH RATE:**
Rapid

**HABIT:**
Spreading with arching branches; dense.

**FAMILY:**
Elaeagnaceae

**LEAF COLOR:** Green with silvery scales and undersides.

**LEAF DESCRIPTION:** SIMPLE, 3" to 4" long and one-third as wide, oval to elliptic shape with wavy margins. ALTERNATE arrangement.

**FLOWER DESCRIPTION:** Off-white, 1/4" to 1/2", funnel-shaped in small, axillary clusters. Fragrant. Flowers in fall.

**EXPOSURE/CULTURE:** Sun. The plant is adaptable to a wide range of soils from clay to sand. It is very drought-tolerant and is used in coastal plantings. Needs regular pruning due to rapid growth.

**PEST PROBLEMS:** No serious pests.

**SELECTED CULTIVARS:** None. This is a cultivar of *E. pungens*.

**RELATED CULTIVARS:** 'Aurea' - Bright yellow leaf margins. 'Aurea-variegata' - Yellow blotch in center of leaf.

**LANDSCAPE NOTES:** Fruitland Elaeagnus is the best of the *Elaeagnus* genus. It makes an excellent unclipped hedge or background plant for other plantings. The silver undersides give an overall silver cast to the foliage. It should be pruned to allow its natural arching character. Good for espalier. Very easy to grow.

# *Euonymus japonica*

**Japanese Euonymus**

▼ 'Albo-marginata'

▼ 'Ovatus-Aureus'

▲ Species

**ZONES:**
7, 8, 9, 10

**HEIGHT:**
8' to 12'

**WIDTH:**
4' to 6'

**FRUIT:**
1/4" pink capsule; NOT ORNA-MENTAL.

**TEXTURE:**
Medium

**GROWTH RATE:**
Moderate

**HABIT:**
Erect and oval.

**FAMILY:**
Celastraceae

**LEAF COLOR:** Dark green.

**LEAF DESCRIPTION:** SIMPLE, 1 1/2" to 3" long and half as wide, elliptic to narrow oval shape with serrated margins. OPPOSITE arrangement.

**FLOWER DESCRIPTION:** Greenish-white, tiny, in axillary cymes. Flowers in June; NOT ORNAMENTAL.

**EXPOSURE/CULTURE:** Sun or shade. Very adaptable to soil types from clay to sand. Very drought-resistant. Great for coastal plantings. Grows thickly with little pruning.

**PEST PROBLEMS:** Euonymus scale, crown gall, anthracnose. Note: Scale is highly destructive, and the plant must be sprayed regularly.

**SELECTED CULTIVARS:** 'Albo-marginata' - Has white leaf margins. 'Grandifolia' - Has larger leaves on a tightly branched plant. 'Ovatus-Aureus' - Has yellow margins. 'Silver King' - Featured in next section. 'Sun Spot' - Has thick green leaves with yellow centers. A Wight's Nursery introduction.

**LANDSCAPE NOTES:** Euonymus is one of the most attractive large shrubs if one is persistent in watching for scale. Otherwise, this is a durable, easy to grow, versatile plant in the landscape.

## *Euonymus japonica* 'Silver King'          Silver King Euonymus

**ZONES:**
7, 8, 9, 10

**HEIGHT:**
8' to 12'

**WIDTH:**
4' to 6'

**FRUIT:**
1/4" pink capsule; NOT ORNA-MENTAL.

**TEXTURE:**
Medium

**GROWTH RATE:**
Moderate

**HABIT:**
Upright, dense, and oval.

**FAMILY:**
Celastraceae

**LEAF COLOR:** Leathery green with silver-white margins.

**LEAF DESCRIPTION:** SIMPLE, 1 1/2" to 3" long and half as wide, elliptic shape with serrated margins. OPPOSITE arrangement.

**FLOWER DESCRIPTION:** Greenish-white, tiny, in axillary cymes. Flowers in June; NOT NOTICEABLE.

**EXPOSURE/CULTURE:** Sun or shade. The plant will grow in almost any soil except excessively wet soil. Very drought-tolerant. Needs little pruning to maintain character.

**PEST PROBLEMS:** Euonymus scale, crown gall, anthracnose.

**SELECTED CULTIVARS:** None. This is a cultivar of *E. japonica*.

**LANDSCAPE NOTES:** Silver King Euonymus is a bold accent plant that is more adaptable in the landscape than the many yellow-variegated types. This is an older cultivar that is "easier to digest" and that has proven itself over the years.

# *Feijoa sellowiana*

**Pineapple Guava**

**ZONES:**
8, 9, 10

**HEIGHT:**
8′ to 12′

**WIDTH:**
6′ to 10′

**FRUIT:**
2″ to 3″ reddish-green berry;
edible.

**TEXTURE:**
Medium

**GROWTH RATE:**
Moderate to rapid.

**HABIT:**
Rounded and spreading;
somewhat open.

**FAMILY:**
Myrtaceae

**LEAF COLOR:** Medium green; silvery and tomentose beneath.

**LEAF DESCRIPTION:** SIMPLE, 1 1/2″ to 3″ long and half as wide, elliptic to elliptic-oblong shape with entire margins. OPPOSITE arrangement.

**FLOWER DESCRIPTION:** White petals that are purplish within, having red stamens. 1″ to 2″ long and 4-petaled. Flowers in spring.

**EXPOSURE/CULTURE:** Full sun to light shade. Prefers well-drained, sandy soils. Does not perform in clay. Great for coastal plantings. Pruning is minimal to maintain shape.

**PEST PROBLEMS:** No serious pests.

**SELECTED CULTIVARS:** 'Nazemetz' - Has larger fruits. 'Pineapple Gem' - Supposedly has more abundant fruits.

**LANDSCAPE NOTES:** This is an excellent plant for foundations, screens, or borders. The foliage is very attractive, as are the flowers and fruits. This is a good plant for naturalizing and xeriscaping. Unfortunately, it is for tropical-like climates.

## *Ilex aquifolium* 'Aureo-marginata' — Variegated English Holly

▼ Species

**ZONES:**
6, 7, 8, 9

**HEIGHT:**
Slowly to 40'; usually much smaller.

**WIDTH:**
Slowly to 30'; usually much smaller.

**FRUIT:**
1/4" red berries (drupes). Must have both male and female plants.

**TEXTURE:**
Medium

**GROWTH RATE:**
Slow

**HABIT:**
Pyramidal to broad-spreading.

**FAMILY:**
Aquifoliaceae

**LEAF COLOR:** Green with yellow margins.

**LEAF DESCRIPTION:** SIMPLE, 2" to 3" long and half as wide, ovate to elliptic shape with undulating and spinose margins. Thick, shiny, and leathery. ALTERNATE arrangement.

**FLOWER DESCRIPTION:** Dioecious; small, yellowish; NOT ORNAMENTAL.

**EXPOSURE/CULTURE:** Sun or shade. Prefers well-drained, loamy soils. Does not perform well in deep sands. Prune to maintain natural shape.

**PEST PROBLEMS:** No serious pests.

**SELECTED CULTIVARS:** None. This is a cultivar of *I. aquifolium,* English Holly.

**RELATED CULTIVARS:** 'Argenteo-marginata' - Green leaves with creamy-white margins. 'Ciliata Major' - New growth purple; leaves bronzy-green with larger, curving spines. 'Gold Coast' - Male form (no berries). Small evergreen shrub with small, green leaves, edged golden-yellow. A Monrovia Nurseries introduction. 'Sparkler' - Upright form; vigorous. Produces abundant fruit at an earlier age. A Monrovia Nurseries introduction.

**LANDSCAPE NOTES:** Variegated English Holly is a fine variation of the ever-popular *I. aquifolium.* It makes a nice hedge, foundation plant for larger structures, or lawn specimen. Berry production is heavy when male pollinators are present. Branches are often used in Christmas wreaths and holiday decorations.

# Ilex cornuta

**Chinese Horned Holly**

▼ 'O' Spring

**ZONES:**
6, 7, 8, 9

**HEIGHT:**
8′ to 12′

**WIDTH:**
8′ to 10′

**FRUIT:**
1/4″ bright red berries (drupes), on female plants. Showy.

**TEXTURE:**
Medium

**GROWTH RATE:**
Slow to moderate.

**HABIT:**
Rounded, upright, and stiff.

**FAMILY:**
Aquifoliaceae

**LEAF COLOR:** Dark green and shiny.

**LEAF DESCRIPTION:** SIMPLE, 2″ to 3 1/2″ long and half as wide, oblong to rectangular shape with 5 or more "horned" spines on margins. Very stout and thick. ALTERNATE arrangement.

**FLOWER DESCRIPTION:** Dioecious; tiny, yellowish and 4-petaled; NOT NOTICEABLE.

**EXPOSURE/CULTURE:** Sun or shade. Will grow in a wide range of soils and is very drought-tolerant. Can be sheared, as desired, to maintain shape. Harder to prune than most plants.

**PEST PROBLEMS:** Tea scale.

**SELECTED CULTIVARS:** 'Ancient Delcambre' - Has long, narrow leaves with a single spine at tip. 'Berries Jubilee' - More dwarf, mounded form with heavy crop of large, red berries. A Monrovia Nurseries introduction. 'Burfordii' - (Featured on next page.) 'Cajun Gold' - Green leaves with golden-yellow margins. 'Dazzler' - Heavy fruiting, upright form. 'D' Or' - Has yellow berries. 'Needlepoint' - Very similar to 'Ancient Delcambre'. 'Willowleaf' - Has longer, twisted leaves.

**LANDSCAPE NOTES:** Chinese Horned Holly is noted for its dark green and lustrous foliage as well as its bright berries. It is the "mother plant" for many cultivars and hybrids, and is often overlooked. An outstanding selection that makes a nice foundation plant or hedge. The plant is still worthy of landscape use.

## *Ilex cornuta* 'Burfordii' — Burford Holly

▲ 'D'Or'

**ZONES:**
6, 7, 8, 9

**HEIGHT:**
10' to 20'

**WIDTH:**
8' to 16'

**FRUIT:**
1/4" to 1/3" red drupes (on previous season's growth).

**TEXTURE:**
Medium

**GROWTH RATE:**
Moderate

**HABIT:**
Very dense; somewhat rounded.

**FAMILY:**
Aquifoliaceae

**LEAF COLOR:** Lustrous dark green.

**LEAF DESCRIPTION:** SIMPLE, 2" to 3" long and half as wide, elliptic to obovate shape with a single spine at tip. Thick and stiff. ALTERNATE arrangement.

**FLOWER DESCRIPTION:** Dioecious; yellowish; 4-petaled; NOT ORNAMENTAL.

**EXPOSURE/CULTURE:** Sun or shade. Very drought-tolerant. Adapts well to most soil types. Very difficult to transplant. Will tolerate heavy shearing.

**PEST PROBLEMS:** Scale on new growth.

**SELECTED CULTIVARS:** None. This is a cultivar of *I. cornuta*.

**RELATED CULTIVARS:** 'Dwarf Burford' - (Described in Chapter 7.) The most popular Burford.

**LANDSCAPE NOTES:** Burford Holly is a large, thick shrub that is taller than broad. It is extremely dense, and mature plants produce a heavy crop of berries. Size is a factor in its use, and it is difficult to keep below 10'. Makes a nice hedge or foundation plant. Looks great in tree-form also.

# *Ilex latifolia*

**ZONES:**
7, 8, 9

**HEIGHT:**
8′ to 10′

**WIDTH:**
5′ to 8′

**FRUIT:**
1/4″ to 1/3″ red to orange-red drupes; appearing in clusters at nodes.

**TEXTURE:**
Coarse

**GROWTH RATE:**
Moderate

**HABIT:**
Irregular pyramid; dense.

**FAMILY:**
Aquifoliaceae

**LEAF COLOR:** Lustrous dark green.

**LEAF DESCRIPTION:** SIMPLE, 3 1/2″ to 7″ long and one-third as wide, oblong elliptic shape with sharply serrated margins. Thick and leathery. ALTERNATE arrangement.

**FLOWER DESCRIPTION:** Dioecious; yellowish, tiny, in axillary panicles.

**EXPOSURE/CULTURE:** Sun or shade. Prefers well-drained, moderately moist soil. Not as drought-tolerant as *I. cornuta*. Prune as needed to maintain pyramidal shape.

**PEST PROBLEMS:** No serious pests.

**SELECTED CULTIVARS:** None

**LANDSCAPE NOTES:** Lusterleaf Holly is a good description of the plant. Its coarse yet shiny dark green foliage is especially attractive in the garden. It is an excellent foundation plant for corners or as a speciment plant. Great for tree-forming also.

# *Ilex opaca* 'Croonenburg'

**Croonenburg American Holly**

**ZONES:**
6, 7, 8, 9

**HEIGHT:**
10′ to 20′

**WIDTH:**
5′ to 10′

**FRUIT:**
1/4″ red drupes in fall.

**TEXTURE:**
Medium

**GROWTH RATE:**
Moderate

**HABIT:**
Pyramidal or narrowly cone-shaped.

**FAMILY:**
Aquifoliaceae

**LEAF COLOR:** Dark green in all seasons.

**LEAF DESCRIPTION:** SIMPLE, 2″ to 3″ long and half as wide, elliptic shape with spinose margins (fewer than the species). ALTERNATE arrangement.

**FLOWER DESCRIPTION:** Monoecious and self pollinating; NOT ORNAMENTAL.

**EXPOSURE/CULTURE:** Sun or shade. Prefers moist, well-drained soils of acidic reaction. Pruning is accomplished to maintain natural shape. Should be mulched more heavily in full sun.

**PEST PROBLEMS:** Leaf spots, scale, leaf miner, mildews.

**SELECTED CULTIVARS:** None. This is a cultivar of *I. opaca,* a medium-sized evergreen tree.

**LANDSCAPE NOTES:** Croonenburg American Holly is one of several cultivars that are superior to the species. It can be used anywhere that height is required, such as screening or in taller foundations. It is self-pollinating.

## *Ilex opaca* 'Greenleaf'

**Greenleaf American Holly**

**ZONES:**
6, 7, 8, 9

**HEIGHT:**
10' to 20'

**WIDTH:**
5' to 10'

**FRUIT:**
1/4" red drupes in fall and winter.

**TEXTURE:**
Medium

**GROWTH RATE:**
Moderate

**HABIT:**
Pyramidal or narrowly cone-shaped.

**FAMILY:**
Aquifoliaceae

**LEAF COLOR:** Medium green in all seasons.

**LEAF DESCRIPTION:** SIMPLE, 1" to 2 1/2" long and half as wide, elliptic to ovate shape with spinose margins. ALTERNATE arrangement.

**FLOWER DESCRIPTION:** Dioecious. Not showy.

**EXPOSURE/CULTURE:** Sun or part shade. Prefers moist, well-drained, acid soil. Should be mulched in full sun. Prune to maintain natural shape or to thicken.

**PEST PROBLEMS:** Leaf miners, scales, mildews.

**SELECTED CULTIVARS:** None. This is a cultivar of *I. opaca,* the species, a medium evergreen tree.

**LANDSCAPE NOTES:** Greenleaf American Holly is a popular cultivar of *I. opaca.* It is more compact than the species and sets fruit at a younger age. It is useful as a corner plant for multi-story structures or as screening material. It can be used as a lawn specimen, especially when tree-formed. NOT FOR XERISCAPING.

## *Ilex pernyi*

**Pernyi Holly**

**ZONES:**
6, 7, 8, 9

**HEIGHT:**
9′ to 10′

**WIDTH:**
4′ to 5′

**FRUIT:**
1/4″ red drupes.

**TEXTURE:**
Medium

**GROWTH RATE:**
Slow

**HABIT:**
Upright with drooping twigs.

**FAMILY:**
Aquifoliaceae

**LEAF COLOR:** Dark green.

**LEAF DESCRIPTION:** SIMPLE, 1/2″ to 1 1/2″ long and half as wide, ovate shape with one spine at tip and 2 to 3 spines on each side. Very stiff. ALTERNATE arrangement.

**FLOWER DESCRIPTION:** Dioecious; yellowish, 4-petaled, tiny, in axillary panicles.

**EXPOSURE/CULTURE:** Sun or shade. Adapts well to most well-drained soils. Reasonably drought-tolerant. Prune annually to thicken and shape.

**PEST PROBLEMS:** No serious pests.

**SELECTED CULTIVARS:** 'Compacta' - Grows denser than the species. 'Vetchii' - Has larger leaves and fruits.

**LANDSCAPE NOTES:** Drooping twigs and leaf tips combine to give an overall arching effect to this unusual Holly. It should be used as a specimen plant in the garden. It is often used as a semi-espaliered plant, and is attractive in tree-form.

# *Ilex vomitoria*

**Yaupon Holly**

**ZONES:**
7, 8, 9, 10

**HEIGHT:**
10' to 15'

**WIDTH:**
5' to 8'

**FRUIT:**
1/4" translucent red berries (drupes); OUTSTANDING!

**TEXTURE:**
Fine

**GROWTH RATE:**
Moderate

**HABIT:**
Upright and irregular.

**FAMILY:**
Aquifoliaceae

**LEAF COLOR:** Dark green.

**LEAF DESCRIPTION:** SIMPLE, 1" to 1 1/2" long and half as wide, ovate to elliptic shape with crenate margins, ALTERNATE arrangement.

**FLOWER DESCRIPTION:** Dioecious; yellowish, tiny; NOT NOTICEABLE.

**EXPOSURE/CULTURE:** Sun or shade. Tolerant of a wide range of soils from dry and sandy to wet. Native to swamps of coastal areas. Will tolerate heavy pruning. Very easy to grow.

**PEST PROBLEMS:** No serious pests.

**SELECTED CULTIVARS:** 'Nana' - (Featured in Chapter 6.) 'Pendula' - (Featured on next page.)

**LANDSCAPE NOTES:** Yaupon Holly is a native plant that is less formal than most of the Hollies. It is noted for its shiny, translucent berries that are abundant throughout the plant. It can be used as a foundation plant or specimen plant. Light gray bark is very attractive and very noticeable.

## *Ilex vomitoria* 'Pendula'

**Weeping Yaupon Holly**

**ZONES:**
7, 8, 9, 10

**HEIGHT:**
10' to 15'

**WIDTH:**
5' to 8'

**FRUIT:**
1/4" translucent red drupes; OUTSTANDING!

**TEXTURE:**
Fine

**GROWTH RATE:**
Moderate

**HABIT:**
Upright; weeping branches.

**FAMILY:**
Aquifoliaceae

**LEAF COLOR:** Dark green.

**LEAF DESCRIPTION:** SIMPLE, 1" to 1 1/2" long and half as wide, ovate to elliptic shape with crenate margins, ALTERNATE arrangement.

**FLOWER DESCRIPTION:** Dioecious; yellowish, tiny; NOT ORNAMENTAL.

**EXPOSURE/CULTURE:** Sun or shade. Very adaptable and tolerant of soils from wet to dry. Great in sandy soils. Light pruning ONLY to confine or shape. Do not destroy natural shape.

**PEST PROBLEMS:** No serious pests.

**SELECTED CULTIVARS:** None. This is a cultivar of *I. vomitoria*.

**LANDSCAPE NOTES:** Weeping Yaupon is a plant to feature in the garden. Careful attention should be given to selection of the best location. Can be used as a foundation plant and looks especially nice near an entry or porch.

# *Ilex x attenuata 'Fosteri'*

**Fosteri Holly**

**ZONES:**
6, 7, 8, 9

**HEIGHT:**
15' to 20'

**WIDTH:**
6' to 10'

**FRUIT:**
1/4" to 1/3" deep red drupes
(on current season's growth).

**TEXTURE:**
Fine

**GROWTH RATE:**
Moderate

**HABIT:**
Slender, upright cone.

**FAMILY:**
Aquifoliaceae

**LEAF COLOR:** Lustrous dark green.

**LEAF DESCRIPTION:** SIMPLE, 1 1/2" to 2 1/2" long and half as wide, elliptic to ovate-oblong shape with spinose margins. ALTERNATE arrangement.

**FLOWER DESCRIPTION:** Dioecious; yellowish, tiny; NOT ORNAMENTAL.

**EXPOSURE/CULTURE:** Sun or shade. Prefers well-drained soil with moderate moisture content. Fairly drought-tolerant, but performs better in organic soil that is mulched. Lateral branches can be sheared to thicken. Do not prune top of terminal growth until desired maximum height is attained.

**PEST PROBLEMS:** No serious pests.

**SELECTED CULTIVARS:** None

**RELATED CULTIVARS:** 'East Palatka' - A more open form that has fewer spines on leaves than 'Fosteri'. 'Hume #2' - (Featured on next page.) 'Savannah' - (Featured later in this chapter.)

**LANDSCAPE NOTES:** Fosteri Holly is an excellent large shrub for tall, bare walls of the foundation. It can be used as a specimen or as an unclipped screen. It should be allowed to grow to its natural shape and trimmed accordingly. A cultivar of the cross between *I. cassine* and *I. opaca*. Often used in tree-form.

## *Ilex x attenuata 'Hume #2'*

**Hume Holly**

**ZONES:**
6, 7, 8, 9

**HEIGHT:**
20' to 25'

**WIDTH:**
15' to 20'

**FRUIT:**
1/4" red berries (drupes).

**TEXTURE:**
Medium

**GROWTH RATE:**
Moderate

**HABIT:**
Upright; pyramidal to oval.

**FAMILY:**
Aquifoliaceae

**LEAF COLOR:** Lustrous dark green.

**LEAF DESCRIPTION:** SIMPLE, 1 1/2" to 2 1/2" long and half as wide, elliptic shape with entire margin except for one spine at tip. ALTERNATE arrangement.

**FLOWER DESCRIPTION:** Dioecious; yellowish; NOT ORNAMENTAL.

**EXPOSURE/CULTURE:** Sun or shade. Prefers well-drained, fairly moist soil. Will perform during drought if mulch is provided. Should be pruned selectively to thicken or control size.

**PEST PROBLEMS:** No serious pests.

**SELECTED CULTIVARS:** None. This is a cultivar.

**LANDSCAPE NOTES:** Hume #2 Holly is similar in many ways to Native American Holly, but is smaller and has only one spine per leaf. It is generally considered superior to American Holly. A vigorous grower that should be more widely used.

# *Ilex x attenuata 'Savannah'*

**Savannah Holly**

**ZONES:**
6, 7, 8, 9

**HEIGHT:**
15' to 25'

**WIDTH:**
8' to 12'

**FRUIT:**
1/4" bright red berries (drupes); ABUNDANT.

**TEXTURE:**
Medium

**GROWTH RATE:**
Rapid

**HABIT:**
Pyramidal; loose.

**FAMILY:**
Aquifoliaceae

**LEAF COLOR:** Dull medium green.

**LEAF DESCRIPTION:** SIMPLE, 2" to 4" long and half as wide, elliptic shape with spinose margins. ALTERNATE arrangement.

**FLOWER DESCRIPTION:** Dioecious; yellowish, tiny; NOT ORNAMENTAL.

**EXPOSURE/CULTURE:** Sun or shade. Grows under a wide range of conditions and well-drained soil types. Easy to grow. Will take heavy shearing, but do not top until desired height is achieved.

**PEST PROBLEMS:** No serious pests.

**SELECTED CULTIVARS:** None. This is a cultivar.

**LANDSCAPE NOTES:** Savannah Holly is a fine shrub for two-story or taller foundations. It offers a contrast to plants having darker foliage. Fruiting is extra heavy on this female plant. It is often used as a specimen in tree-form, and can be sheared for thicker foliage.

# *Ilex* x 'Emily Brunner'

**Emily Brunner Holly**

**ZONES:**
7, 8, 9

**HEIGHT:**
15' to 18'

**WIDTH:**
10' to 15'

**FRUIT:**
1/3" bright red drupes, clustered at nodes. Sometimes hidden by foliage.

**TEXTURE:**
Coarse

**GROWTH RATE:**
Moderate

**HABIT:**
Broad pyramid; extremely dense.

**FAMILY:**
Aquifoliaceae

**LEAF COLOR:** Lustrous medium green.

**LEAF DESCRIPTION:** SIMPLE, 3" to 4" long and half as wide, elliptic shape with spinose margins. Stiff and leathery. ALTERNATE arrangement.

**FLOWER DESCRIPTION:** Dioecious; yellowish, tiny.

**EXPOSURE/CULTURE:** Sun or part shade. Adaptable to a wide range of well-drained soils. Will not tolerate wet soils. Very thick; needs very little pruning.

**PEST PROBLEMS:** Scale

**SELECTED CULTIVARS:** None

**LANDSCAPE NOTES:** Emily Brunner Holly is one of the thickest growing Hollies in landscaping. The broad, flat leaves and abundant bright berries add to its interest. It is used for foundation plantings, and makes an excellent hedge or screen. A low-maintenance plant. The plant is a hybrid of *I. cornuta* and *I. latifolia*.

# *Ilex* x *koehneana* 'Wirt L. Winn'

**Koehne Holly**

**ZONES:**
7, 8, 9

**HEIGHT:**
15' to 20'

**WIDTH:**
8' to 15'

**FRUIT:**
1/4" - 1/3" red drupes in fall.

**TEXTURE:**
Medium coarse.

**GROWTH RATE:**
Moderate

**HABIT:**
Broad Pyramid; dense.

**FAMILY:**
Aquifoliaceae

**LEAF COLOR:** Dark green in all seasons.

**LEAF DESCRIPTION:** SIMPLE, 2" to 4" long and half as wide, elliptic shape with spinose margins. ALTERNATE arrangement.

**FLOWER DESCRIPTION:** Dioecious; NOT ORNAMENTAL.

**EXPOSURE/CULTURE:** Sun or part shade. The plant prefers a moist, well-drained soil, but is reasonably drought-tolerant. Pruning is minimal to maintain shape.

**PEST PROBLEMS:** No serious pests.

**SELECTED CULTIVARS:** None. This is a cultivar.

**LANDSCAPE NOTES:** This cross between *I. aquifolium* and *I. latifolia* combines the best of both plants. Stems are purplish as with *I. aquifolium* and has similar shape, but smaller size, than *I. latifolia.* This is a handsome plant which is adaptable to many uses in the landscape, provided sufficient space is available.

# *Ilex* x 'Lydia Morris'

**Lydia Morris Holly**

**ZONES:**
6, 7, 8, 9

**HEIGHT:**
8′ to 12′

**WIDTH:**
6′ to 8′

**FRUIT:**
1/4″ to 1/3″ red drupes in fall.

**TEXTURE:**
Medium

**GROWTH RATE:**
Slow to moderate.

**HABIT:**
Rounded; taller than broad.

**FAMILY:**
Aquifoliaceae

**LEAF COLOR:** Extremely dark, lustrous green in all seasons.

**LEAF DESCRIPTION:** SIMPLE, 1″ to 2″ long and wide, almost square (rhombic) with a downward-pointed spine and 2 to 3 lateral pairs. ALTERNATE arrangement.

**FLOWER DESCRIPTION:** Dioecious; NOT ORNAMENTAL.

**EXPOSURE/CULTURE:** Sun or shade. Prefers well-drained, acidic soil and is reasonably drought-tolerant. Pruning is minimal to maintain shape.

**PEST PROBLEMS:** No serious pests.

**RELATED CULTIVARS:** 'John Morris' - The male pollinator form.

**SELECTED CULTIVARS:** None

**LANDSCAPE NOTES:** This cross between *I. cornuta* 'Burfordii' and *I. pernyi* is a handsome, dense shrub that makes a nice foundation, screening, or specimen plant. Very deep green foliage provides an interesting contrast with the lighter foliage of most other plants.

# *Ilex x meserveae* 'Blue Maid'

**Meserve Holly**

**ZONES:**
5, 6, 7

**HEIGHT:**
8′ to 12′

**WIDTH:**
6′ to 8′

**FRUIT:**
1/4″ red berries (drupes).

**TEXTURE:**
Medium

**GROWTH RATE:**
Moderate

**HABIT:**
Dense; broad pyramid or oval.

**FAMILY:**
Aquifoliaceae

**LEAF COLOR:** Lustrous dark green with faint bluish tint.

**LEAF DESCRIPTION:** SIMPLE, 3/4″ to 2″ long and half as wide, elliptic shape with spinose margins. ALTERNATE arrangement.

**FLOWER DESCRIPTION:** Dioecious; NOT ORNAMENTAL.

**EXPOSURE/CULTURE:** Sun or shade. Does best in well-drained, organic soil. Adaptable to clay. Prune to maintain shape.

**PEST PROBLEMS:** No serious pests.

**SELECTED CULTIVARS:** None. This is a cultivar of *I.* x *meserveae,* a cross between *I. rugosa* and *I. aquifolium.*

**RELATED CULTIVARS:** 'Blue Boy' - Male form that is a good pollinator. 'Blue Girl' - The first female form, having excellent fruiting. 'Blue Stallion' - Male form that is a good pollinator. 'Blue Princess' - Has more abundant fruit and darker bluish-green foliage.

**LANDSCAPE NOTES:** Meserve Holly represents a species of Holly that is more hardy than other popular species. The plants have excellent foliage and beautiful berries (female), and can be used as foundation plants, borders, and hedges.

## *Ilex* x 'Nellie R. Stevens'

**Nellie Stevens Holly**

**ZONES:**
6, 7, 8, 9

**HEIGHT:**
15' to 20'

**WIDTH:**
10' to 15'

**FRUIT:**
1/4" to 1/3" bright red berries (drupes).

**TEXTURE:**
Medium

**GROWTH RATE:**
Moderate to rapid.

**HABIT:**
Pyramidal; dense.

**FAMILY:**
Aquifoliaceae

**LEAF COLOR:** Lustrous Dark Green.

**LEAF DESCRIPTION:** SIMPLE, 2 1/2" to 3 1/2" long and 1" to 2" wide, elliptic to somewhat rectangular shape with spinose margins. ALTERNATE arrangement.

**FLOWER DESCRIPTION:** Dioecious; yellowish; NOT ORNAMENTAL.

**EXPOSURE/CULTURE:** Sun or part shade. Prefers rich, well-drained soil, but is adaptable. It is drought-resistant, once established. Prune to shape or control size.

**PEST PROBLEMS:** No serious pests.

**SELECTED CULTIVARS:** None

**RELATED CULTIVARS:** 'Edward J. Stevens' - The male form that is useful as a pollinator.

**LANDSCAPE NOTES:** Nellie Stevens Holly is one of the finest Hollies for taller foundations. It is a multi-purpose plant that makes an outstanding tree-form specimen. Absolutely one of the best!

# *Illicium anisatum*

**Japanese Anisetree**

**ZONES:**
7, 8, 9

**HEIGHT:**
10′ to 12′

**WIDTH:**
6′ to 8′

**FRUIT:**
1″ brown aggregate (follicle); NOT ORNAMENTAL.

**TEXTURE:**
Coarse

**GROWTH RATE:**
Moderate

**HABIT:**
Upright and open.

**FAMILY:**
Illiciaceae

**LEAF COLOR:** Medium green.

**LEAF DESCRIPTION:** SIMPLE, 3″ to 4″ long and one-third as wide, thick and aromatic. Narrow elliptic shape with entire margins. ALTERNATE arrangement. Upright leaves.

**FLOWER DESCRIPTION:** White to yellowish-green. 1″ with 15 to 25 petals. Fragrant. Flowers in early spring.

**EXPOSURE/CULTURE:** Sun or shade. Prefers moist, organic, well-drained soil, but is adaptable to most soils except dry, hot soils. Does well in sandy soils if moist. Prune lightly to maintain natural habit.

**PEST PROBLEMS:** No serious pests.

**SELECTED CULTIVARS:** None

**RELATED SPECIES:** *I. floridanum* - Florida Anisetree. Has broader leaves and maroon to purplish-red flowers. 'Album' has white flowers.

**LANDSCAPE NOTES:** Japanese Anisetree is an interesting plant that is useful as a foundation shrub, natural (unclipped) hedge, or border plant. This is a good plant for naturalizing.

## *Juniperus chinensis 'Spartan'*      Spartan Juniper

**ZONES:**
5, 6, 7, 8, 9

**HEIGHT:**
15′ to 20′

**WIDTH:**
5′ to 6′

**FRUIT:**
1/4″ to 1/2″ smooth brown cone.

**TEXTURE:**
Fine

**GROWTH RATE:**
Moderate

**HABIT:**
Narrow pyramid; dense.

**FAMILY:**
Cupressaceae

**LEAF COLOR:** Rich green.

**LEAF DESCRIPTION:** SCALE-LIKE, juvenile leaves awl-shaped, 1/16″ to 1/4″, 4-ranked in OPPOSITE pairs.

**FLOWER DESCRIPTION:** Yellowish; NOT NOTICEABLE.

**EXPOSURE/CULTURE:** Sun. Will grow in almost any well-drained soil. Very drought tolerant. Pruning is generally not needed.

**PEST PROBLEMS:** Twig blight.

**SELECTED CULTIVARS:** None. This is a cultivar of *J. chinensis.*

**LANDSCAPE NOTES:** Spartan Juniper has rich bright green foliage, and assumes a dense pyramidal habit with little or no shearing. It eventually reaches small tree size. Avoid placing against one-story structures.

## *Juniperus chinensis 'Kaizuka'*

**Hollywood Juniper**

**ZONES:**
5, 6, 7, 8, 9

**HEIGHT:**
8' to 12'

**WIDTH:**
5' to 7'

**FRUIT:**
1/4" to 1/2"; violet, waxy.

**TEXTURE:**
Fine

**GROWTH RATE:**
Moderate

**HABIT:**
Irregular with twisted, cord-like branchlets.

**FAMILY:**
Cupressaceae

**LEAF COLOR:** Rich green.

**LEAF DESCRIPTION:** SCALE-LIKE, 1/16", 4-ranked in OPPOSITE pairs.

**FLOWER DESCRIPTION:** Yellowish; NOT NOTICEABLE.

**EXPOSURE/CULTURE:** Sun. Grows well in any well-drained soil. It does especially well in sandy soils and is often used in coastal plantings. Looks best when NOT pruned. Prune only to control size.

**PEST PROBLEMS:** Bagworms, twig blight, spider mites.

**SELECTED CULTIVARS:** None. This is a cultivar of *J. chinensis.*

**RELATED CULTIVARS:** 'Variegated Kaizuka' - Ends of some branchlets are variegated with creamy yellow.

**LANDSCAPE NOTES:** Hollywood Juniper is a bold accent plant with a somewhat artistic, Japanese effect. Individual plants take on varied characters. Combines well with rock and stone structures. Use in moderation.

## *Juniperus scopulorum* 'Gray Gleam' — Rocky Mountain Juniper

**ZONES:**
4, 5, 6, 7

**HEIGHT:**
10′ to 15′+

**WIDTH:**
3′ to 6′+

**FRUIT:**
1/4″ dark blue, berry-like cone.

**TEXTURE:**
Fine

**GROWTH RATE:**
Slow

**HABIT:**
Upright and narrowly pyramidal; dense.

**FAMILY:**
Cupressaceae

**LEAF COLOR:** Silvery gray-blue, more intense in winter.

**LEAF DESCRIPTION:** SCALE-LIKE, tightly appressed, tips slightly pointed to non-pointed; waxy bloom intensifies silver-gray effect. Branchlets form flattened plates.

**FLOWER DESCRIPTION:** Monoecious; NOT ORNAMENTAL.

**EXPOSURE/CULTURE:** Full sun. Does best in light, well-drained soil. Grows in acid or alkaline soils. This plant is drought-tolerant and does not like humid conditions. Grows dense, but can be sheared to a dense, smooth cone.

**PEST PROBLEMS:** Juniper blight, bagworms.

**BARK/STEMS:** Brown to gray in narrow stripes on older bark.

**SIMILAR CULTIVARS:** 'Blue Heaven' - A conical selection with blue-green foliage. Heavy crop of fruit all season. 'Moonglow' - Broad pyramid with silver-blue foliage. 'Pathfinder' - Has broader pyramidal form and blue-gray foliage. 'Wichita Blue' - Has more vivid blue foliage.

**SELECTED CULTIVARS:** None. This is a cultivar.

**LANDSCAPE NOTES:** 'Gray Gleam' Rocky Mountain Juniper is a beautiful plant for foliage effect during all seasons. Makes a nice screen, foundation plant, or accent plant to dull areas of the garden. The plant is somewhat formal and has limited use for naturalizing. A bright spot in a genus of green.

# *Leucothoe populifolia*

**Florida Leucothoe**

**ZONES:**
7, 8, 9

**HEIGHT:**
8′ to 10′

**WIDTH:**
4′ to 6′

**FRUIT:**
5-valved, brown capsule; NOT ORNAMENTAL.

**TEXTURE:**
Medium

**GROWTH RATE:**
Rapid

**HABIT:**
Multi-stemmed drooping plant.

**FAMILY:**
Ericaceae

**LEAF COLOR:** Lustrous medium green; new leaves reddish.

**LEAF DESCRIPTION:** SIMPLE, 2″ to 3″ long and one-third as wide, lanceolate to ovate-lanceolate shape with serrated or entire margins. ALTERNATE arrangement.

**FLOWER DESCRIPTION:** Light yellow, tiny, in racemes. ATTRACTIVE. Flowers in May.

**EXPOSURE/CULTURE:** Shade or part shade. This plant prefers moist, organic soils. Does well near streams and creeks. Easy to grow as an understory plant. Prune as desired, but looks best natural.

**PEST PROBLEMS:** No serious pests.

**SELECTED CULTIVARS:** None

**LANDSCAPE NOTES:** Leucothoe is an excellent plant for use in natural areas on shaded properties or along streams. It can be sheared to control size and thicken. Looks especially good in combination with native plants such as Rhododendrons. Should be more widely used.

## *Ligustrum japonicum*

**Japanese Privet, Japanese Ligustrum**

**ZONES:**
7, 8, 9, 10

**HEIGHT:**
8' to 12'

**WIDTH:**
5' to 7'

**FRUIT:**
1/4" black berries (drupes); Showy.

**TEXTURE:**
Medium

**GROWTH RATE:**
Rapid

**HABIT:**
Dense; upright.

**FAMILY:**
Oleaceae

**LEAF COLOR:** Lustrous dark green.

**LEAF DESCRIPTION:** SIMPLE, 2" to 3 1/2" long and half as wide, ovate shape with entire margins, VEINS RAISED ON UNDERSIDE (separates it from *L. lucidum*). OPPOSITE arrangement.

**FLOWER DESCRIPTION:** White, tiny, in 5" to 6" panicles. Flowers in spring. ATTRACTIVE and noticeable.

**EXPOSURE/CULTURE:** Sun or shade. Grows well in any soil except wet soil. Easy to grow but not low-maintenance. Usually requires heavy pruning due to rapid growth.

**PEST PROBLEMS:** No serious pests.

**SELECTED CULTIVARS:** 'Howard' - Very bold! New leaves bright yellow. Older leaves bright green. (Featured on next page.) 'Recurvifolium' - Has smaller, noticeably twisted leaves. Usually incorrectly listed as a *L. lucidum* cultivar. 'Rotundifolium' - (Featured in Chapter 6.) 'Variegatum' - Green leaves have creamy-white margins.

**LANDSCAPE NOTES:** Japanese Ligustrum is a thick, vigorous plant that is a proven and reliable performer. A trend in recent years has been to tree-form it as a specimen plant or to use it as an espaliered or semi-espaliered specimen. The plant makes an excellent privacy screen or foundation plant.

## *Ligustrum japonicum* 'Howard'   Golden Japanese Ligustrum

**ZONES:**
7, 8, 9, 10

**HEIGHT:**
8' to 12'

**WIDTH:**
5' to 7'

**FRUIT:**
1/4" black berries (drupes).

**TEXTURE:**
Medium

**GROWTH RATE:**
Rapid

**HABIT:**
Dense and upright; somewhat oval.

**FAMILY:**
Oleaceae

**LEAF COLOR:** New leaves golden yellow; older leaves green.

**LEAF DESCRIPTION:** SIMPLE, 2" to 3" long and half as wide, ovate shape with entire margins. OPPOSITE arrangement.

**FLOWER DESCRIPTION:** Tiny, white, in 5" panicles. Flowers in spring and is noticeable.

**EXPOSURE/CULTURE:** Sun or shade. Grows well in any soil except wet soils. Pruning can be heavy due to rapid growth. Easy to grow, but not maintenance-free.

**PEST PROBLEMS:** No serious pests.

**SELECTED CULTIVARS:** None. This is a cultivar.

**LANDSCAPE NOTES:** This is an interesting variation of the common Japanese Ligustrum. It makes a bold accent plant and is brightest during the warm season. Select the location very carefully, and use the plant in moderation.

# *Ligustrum lucidum*

**Waxleaf Privet, Waxleaf Ligustrum**

**ZONES:**
7, 8, 9, 10

**HEIGHT:**
15′ to 20′

**WIDTH:**
8′ to 10′

**FRUIT:**
1/3″ bluish-black berries (drupes); noticeable.

**TEXTURE:**
Medium

**GROWTH RATE:**
Rapid

**HABIT:**
Upright and open; oval to pyramidal.

**FAMILY:**
Oleaceae

**LEAF COLOR:** Dark green.

**LEAF DESCRIPTION:** SIMPLE, 3″ to 4″ long and 1″ to 2″ wide, ovate to ovate-lanceolate shape with entire margins. Veins are sunken on underside (opposite of *L. japonicum*). OPPOSITE arrangement.

**FLOWER DESCRIPTION:** White, tiny, in 6″ to 8″ panicles. Flowers in early summer. NOTICEABLE.

**EXPOSURE/CULTURE:** Sun or shade. Grows well in most soils except wet soils. Occasional pruning can be helpful to thicken the plant. Considered easy to grow, and is low-maintenance if ultimate height is not important.

**PEST PROBLEMS:** No serious pests.

**SELECTED CULTIVARS:** 'Variegatum' - Has creamy white to white leaf margins.

**LANDSCAPE NOTES:** Waxleaf Privet is often confused with Japanese Privet, and both have been used for similar purposes. However, they are not interchangeable, since Waxleaf grows much larger over time. It is probably best used for taller, unclipped hedges or screens. Anyone can grow this one.

# *Loropetalum chinense*

**Chinese Fringe, Loropetalum**

**ZONES:**
7, 8, 9

**HEIGHT:**
6′ to 8′

**WIDTH:**
6′ to 8′

**FRUIT:**
Brown capsule; NOT ORNA-MENTAL.

**TEXTURE:**
Fine to medium.

**GROWTH RATE:**
Rapid

**HABIT:**
Rounded and broad; some-what irregular.

**FAMILY:**
Hamamelidaceae

**LEAF COLOR:** Dark green and pubescent (hairy).

**LEAF DESCRIPTION:** SIMPLE, 1″ to 1 1/2″ long and half as wide, ovate to elliptic shape with entire margins. Pubescent on both surfaces. ALTERNATE arrangement.

**FLOWER DESCRIPTION:** White or cream colored, 1″ wide in axillary clusters of up to 6 flowers, petals 1″ long, very narrow, long and stringy. Flowers in early spring. VERY ORNAMENTAL.

**EXPOSURE/CULTURE:** Sun or part shade. Does best in well-drained, organic soils. Does not like extremes of either very dry or wet conditions. Can be pruned to almost any habit.

**PEST PROBLEMS:** No serious pests.

**SELECTED CULTIVARS:** 'Roseum' - Has rose-colored flowers.

**LANDSCAPE NOTES:** Chinese Fringe is the common name given because of the beautiful fringe-like flowers in spring. This plant is one of the best in landscaping for espalier or semi-espalier. It can be grown as a large, round shrub or in tree-form. It is best used as a specimen plant for bare wall space.

## *Myrica cerifera*

**Southern Wax Myrtle**

**ZONES:**
7, 8, 9

**HEIGHT:**
8′ to 12′

**WIDTH:**
8′ to 12′

**FRUIT:**
Tiny, waxy-gray berries; in clusters. Attractive.

**TEXTURE:**
Medium

**GROWTH RATE:**
Rapid

**HABIT:**
Upright; irregular and open.

**FAMILY:**
Myricaceae

**LEAF COLOR:** Yellowish-green.

**LEAF DESCRIPTION:** SIMPLE, 2″ to 3″ long and one-fourth as wide, oblong-lanceolate shape with acute tip and serrated margins toward the tip. ALTERNATE arrangement.

**EXPOSURE/CULTURE:** Sun or part shade. The plant is native to sandy wetlands and swamps, but can be grown under a variety of conditions and soil types. Best appearance is evident when not pruned. Easy to grow.

**PEST PROBLEMS:** No serious pests.

**SELECTED CULTIVARS:** 'Nana' - A smaller, medium size shrub. (Featured in Chapter 7.)

**RELATED SPECIES:** *M. pennsylvanica* - Northern Bayberry. A dense, deciduous form that grows in Zones 2 to 6.

**LANDSCAPE NOTES:** Southern Wax Myrtle is an excellent background plant for dwarf plants, expecially Junipers. It has an open, airy habit that gives great contrast in the garden. Provides a semi-private hedge when left natural. Can be sheared and grown as a foundation shrub, or it may be tree-formed to serve as an attractive, small evergreen tree.

## *Nerium oleander*

**Oleander**

**ZONES:**
8, 9, 10

**HEIGHT:**
8' to 10'

**WIDTH:**
6' to 8'

**FRUIT:**
6" to 8" follicles (pairs); NOT ORNAMENTAL.

**TEXTURE:**
Medium to coarse.

**GROWTH RATE:**
Rapid

**HABIT:**
Upright, rounded, and open.

**FAMILY:**
Apocynaceae

**LEAF COLOR:** Grayish-green

**LEAF DESCRIPTION:** SIMPLE, 4" to 6" long and one-fourth as wide, lanceolate shape with entire margins. Usually WHORLED (3 or 4), but sometimes OPPOSITE.

**FLOWER DESCRIPTION:** White, pink, or red, depending on cultivar. 1", 5-petaled flowers, appearing in clusters (cymes) in June and July.

**EXPOSURE/CULTURE:** Sun or part shade. Grows in almost any sandy soils from very dry to slightly wet. The plant is suitable for beach plantings, and is tolerant of urban conditions. Often used in street plantings. Looks best if not pruned.

**PEST PROBLEMS:** Scale, mealybug.

**SELECTED CULTIVARS:** 'Algiers' - Single, deep red flowers. 'Atropurpureum' - Single, purple flowers. 'Calypso' - Single, cherry-red flowers. 'Casablanco' - Single, pure white flowers. 'Hardy Pink' - Single, salmon-pink flowers. 'Hardy Red' - Single, bright red flowers. Prolific. 'Isle of Capri' - Single, light yellow flowers. 'Mrs. Roeding' - Double, salmon-pink. 'Ruby Lace' - Single, ruby-red flowers to 3". Fringed petals. Outstanding. A Monrovia Nurseries introduction. 'Tangier' - Single, soft pink flowers.

**LANDSCAPE NOTES:** Oleander is a beautiful plant that performs well in the South, especially in coastal areas. Foliage, flowers, and habit are all notable. An excellent foundation or border plant. ALL PARTS OF THIS PLANT ARE POISONOUS IF EATEN.

## *Osmanthus x fortunei*    Fortune Tea Olive

**ZONES:**
7, 8, 9

**HEIGHT:**
8' to 12'

**WIDTH:**
5' to 8'

**FRUIT:**
Small drupe; RARELY PRESENT.

**TEXTURE:**
Medium

**GROWTH RATE:**
Moderate

**HABIT:**
Upright, stiff, and oval.

**FAMILY:**
Oleaceae

**LEAF COLOR:** Dark green.

**LEAF DESCRIPTION:** SIMPLE, 2″ to 3″ long and half as wide, oval to elliptic shape with spinose margins (often mistaken for holly). Very stiff and having prominent veins. OPPOSITE arrangement. (Hollies have alternate arrangement.)

**FLOWER DESCRIPTION:** White, tiny, in clusters (cymes). Flowers in fall. Not greatly noticeable, but VERY PLEASINGLY FRAGRANT (similar to *Gardenia*).

**EXPOSURE/CULTURE:** Sun or light shade. Tolerant of a wide range of well-drained soils. Reasonably drought-tolerant. Can be sheared to a variety of shapes, but looks best if pruning is minimal.

**PEST PROBLEMS:** No serious pests.

**SELECTED CULTIVARS:** 'Fruitland' - Supposedly more hardy than the species.

**RELATED SPECIES:** *O. fragrans* - Very fragrant with larger leaves and fewer spines. Less cold hardy (Zone 8).

**LANDSCAPE NOTES:** Fortune Tea Olive has Holly-like leaves and white, fragrant flowers. It is a thick plant for foundation plantings or hedges. It is very easy to grow and makes an outstanding tree-form plant. A good plant to semi-espalier.

# *Photinia glabra*

**Red Photinia**

**ZONES:**
7, 8, 9

**HEIGHT:**
8' to 10'

**WIDTH:**
5' to 6'

**FRUIT:**
1/4" red berries (pome); maturing to black.

**TEXTURE:**
Medium

**GROWTH RATE:**
Rapid

**HABIT:**
Upright and somewhat open.

**FAMILY:**
Rosaceae

**LEAF COLOR:** Dark green; red on new growth.

**LEAF DESCRIPTION:** SIMPLE, 2" to 3" long and 3/4" to1 1/4" wide, elliptic to obovate shape, usually with finely serrated margins. ALTERNATE arrangement.

**FLOWER DESCRIPTION:** White, tiny, in 3" to 4" clusters (corymbs). Flowers in spring; SHOWY.

**EXPOSURE/CULTURE:** Sun or light shade. Prefers well-drained, moist, organic soil. Easy to grow but not drought-resistant. Needs annual fertilization for best color. Responds favorably to pruning (after flowering).

**PEST PROBLEMS:** Leaf spot fungus, CAN BE DESTRUCTIVE.

**SELECTED CULTIVARS:** 'Rubens' - Has more colorful, bright red foliage on new growth.

**RELATED SPECIES:** *P. serrulata* - (Featured in this chapter.) *P. x fraseri* - (Featured on next page.)

**LANDSCAPE NOTES:** This is a versatile plant that is useful for foundations, clipped, and unclipped hedges. Very often used as a specimen plant in tree-form.

## *Photinia x fraseri*

**Red-tip Photinia, Fraser Photinia**

**ZONES:**
7, 8, 9

**HEIGHT:**
10' to 20'

**WIDTH:**
5' to 10'

**FRUIT:**
1/4" red berries (pomes); maturing to black.

**TEXTURE:**
Coarse

**GROWTH RATE:**
Rapid

**HABIT:**
Upright; somewhat oval.

**FAMILY:**
Rosaceae

**LEAF COLOR:** Reddish-green; new growth is bright red.

**LEAF DESCRIPTION:** SIMPLE, 4" to 5" long and one-third as wide, elliptic to obovate shape with cuneate base and acute tip. Margins are finely serrated. ALTERNATE arrangement.

**FLOWER DESCRIPTION:** White, tiny, in 4" to 5" clusters (corymbs). Flowers in spring; VERY SHOWY.

**EXPOSURE/CULTURE:** Sun or light shade. Prefers moist, organic, well-drained soil. More cold-hardy than *P. glabra*. Responds well to fertilization and pruning.

**PEST PROBLEMS:** Fungal leaf spots, CAN BE DESTRUCTIVE.

**SELECTED CULTIVARS:** 'Indian Princess' - More dwarf form with coppery-orange new growth. A Monrovia Nurseries introduction.

**LANDSCAPE NOTES:** Red-tip Photinia is a fast-growing, noticeable plant that makes a quick privacy screen. It makes a nice corner plant for taller structures and is widely used in tree-form. Flowers are abundant on mature, unclipped plants. Probably the best known (and used) plant in the South. A cross between *P. glabra* and *P. serrulata*.

## *Photinia serrulata*

**Chinese Photinia**

**ZONES:**
7, 8, 9

**HEIGHT:**
10′ to 15′

**WIDTH:**
8′ to 12′

**FRUIT:**
1/4″ red berries (pomes).

**TEXTURE:**

**GROWTH RATE:**
Rapid

**HABIT:**
Oval; somewhat irregular.

**FAMILY:**
Rosaceae

**LEAF COLOR:** Medium green; young leaves coppery-red.

**LEAF DESCRIPTION:** SIMPLE, 5″ to 7″ long and one-third as wide, elliptic to oblong-lanceolate shape with serrated margins. ALTERNATE arrangement.

**FLOWER DESCRIPTION:** White, tiny, in 5″ to 6″ clusters (corymbs). Flowers in spring; VERY ORNAMENTAL.

**EXPOSURE/CULTURE:** Sun or light shade. Does best in well-drained, moist soil. Will not tolerate excessively dry or excessively wet soils. Easy to grow. Responds favorably to pruning (after flowering).

**PEST PROBLEMS:** Leaf spots, scale, mildew.

**SELECTED CULTIVARS:** 'Aculeata' - Has reddish stems and longer, more noticeable serrated teeth on margins.

**LANDSCAPE NOTES:** Chinese Photinia makes a nice specimen plant or privacy hedge in the recommended zones. Has attractive exfoliating bark, and looks great in tree-form. Probably superior to Red-tip in many respects, except hardiness. Slightly less cold-hardy than Red-tip.

# *Picea abies* 'Pumila'

**Dwarf Norway Spruce**

**ZONES:**
3, 4, 5, 6, 7

**HEIGHT:**
7' to 8' (after 25 years)

**WIDTH:**
4' to 5' (after 25 years)

**FRUIT:**
4" brown, pendulous, cylindrical cones.

**TEXTURE:**
Fine

**GROWTH RATE:**
Very slow.

**HABIT:**
Globular and dense.

**FAMILY:**
Pinaceae

**LEAF COLOR:** Bright green to bluish-green.

**LEAF DESCRIPTION:** NEEDLE-LIKE, thin and flat, 1/4" to 1/3" long, fine tip, 1 to 2 stomatic lines on lower surface; 4-angled and arranged in rows.

**FLOWER DESCRIPTION:** Monoecious; male flowers are axillary and female flowers are terminal; NOT ORNAMENTAL.

**EXPOSURE/CULTURE:** Sun or light shade. Prefers moist, well-drained soil but is adaptable to type. Pruning can be performed on new growth in spring, but is usually not necessary. Low-maintenance.

**PEST PROBLEMS:** Borers, spruce bud worm, two-spotted mites.

**SELECTED CULTIVARS:** None. This is a cultivar of *P. abies,* a large evergreen tree.

**LANDSCAPE NOTES:** Dwarf Norway Spruce is an attractive specimen plant, rock garden plant, or foundation plant. The handsome twigs are a yellowish-brown color. The major limitation is extremely slow growth.

## *Picea abies var. microsperma* — **Compact Norway Spruce**

**ZONES:**
3, 4, 5, 6, 7

**HEIGHT:**
12′ to 15′

**WIDTH:**
12′ to 15′

**FRUIT:**
4″ pendulous and cylindrical cones.

**TEXTURE:**
Fine

**GROWTH RATE:**
Very slow.

**HABIT:**
Broad and conical, with ascending branches.

**FAMILY:**
Pinaceae

**LEAF COLOR:** Bright green and glossy.

**LEAF DESCRIPTION:** NEEDLE-LIKE, S-curved, 1/4″ long, sharp tip, 1 to 3 stomatic lines, 4-angled. Dense and crowded.

**FLOWER DESCRIPTION:** Monoecious; NOT NOTICEABLE.

**EXPOSURE/CULTURE:** Sun or light shade. Prefers moist, well-drained soil. Adaptable to type. Pruning is usually not necessary.

**PEST PROBLEMS:** Borers, spruce bud worm, two-spotted mites.

**SELECTED CULTIVARS:** None. This is a cultivar of *P. abies,* a large evergreen tree.

**LANDSCAPE NOTES:** This is a somewhat formal shrub that can be used as a specimen, foundation plant, or rock garden plant. It is slow-growing but well worth the wait. OUTSTANDING.

## *Picea pungens 'Compacta'*      **Compact Colorado Spruce**

**ZONES:**
2, 3, 4, 5, 6, 7

**HEIGHT:**
8' to 10'

**WIDTH:**
10' to 12'

**FRUIT:**
Blue-green 4" cone.

**TEXTURE:**
Fine to medium.

**GROWTH RATE:**
Slow

**HABIT:**
Globular and dense.

**FAMILY:**
Pinaceae

**LEAF COLOR:** Bluish-green

**LEAF DESCRIPTION:** NEEDLE-LIKE, approximately 1" long, radially arranged, curving slightly toward tip, stiff and sharply pointed, 3 to 4 stomatic lines on each side.

**FLOWER DESCRIPTION:** Monoecious; NOT NOTICEABLE.

**EXPOSURE/CULTURE:** Sun. The plant prefers moist, well-drained soils that are cool. Mulching is recommended for moisture retention and cooling. Pruning is usually not recommended.

**PEST PROBLEMS:** Spruce bud worm, spider mites.

**SELECTED CULTIVARS:** None. This is a cultivar of *P. pungens,* a large evergreen tree.

**LANDSCAPE NOTES:** Compact Colorado Spruce makes a nice specimen or foundation plant. It is especially suited to rock gardens and is maintenance-free, once established.

# *Pinus sylvestris 'Watereri'*

**Compact Scotch Pine**

**ZONES:**
2, 3, 4, 5, 6, 7, 8

**HEIGHT:**
8′ to 12′

**WIDTH:**
6′ to 10′

**FRUIT:**
1 1/2″ to 2″ oblong, pendulous, brown cones.

**TEXTURE:**
Medium

**GROWTH RATE:**
Moderate

**HABIT:**
Broadly conical with ascending branches.

**FAMILY:**
Pinaceae

**LEAF COLOR:** Steel-blue or bluish-green.

**LEAF DESCRIPTION:** NEEDLE-LIKE, 3/4″ to 1 1/4″ long, stiff and twisted, radially arranged. Appearing in bundles (fascicles) of 2. Several stomatic lines on upper surface.

**FLOWER DESCRIPTION:** Monoecious; female not noticeable, male noticeable in spring.

**EXPOSURE/CULTURE:** Sun or light shade. This plant will thrive in a variety of well-drained soil types. Reasonably drought-tolerant. Pruning is usually not necessary or recommended.

**PEST PROBLEMS:** Pine tip moth, borers.

**SELECTED CULTIVARS:** None. This is a cultivar of *P. sylvestris,* a large evergreen tree.

**RELATED CULTIVARS:** 'Fastigiata' - Columnar form to 20′. 'French Blue' - More compact with brighter blue foliage. A Monrovia Nurseries introduction.

**LANDSCAPE NOTES:** Compact Scotch Pine is a specimen plant that looks good when underplanted with either dwarf conifers or dwarf broad-leaf shrubs. Can be used effectively as a foundation plant on corners of larger structures. Often used as Christmas trees.

## *Pittosporum tobira*

**Pittosporum**

**ZONES:**
8, 9

**HEIGHT:**
8' to 12'

**WIDTH:**
10' to 12'

**FRUIT:**
Small brown capsule; NOT ORNAMENTAL.

**TEXTURE:**
Medium

**GROWTH RATE:**
Moderate

**HABIT:**
Spreading and mounded.

**FAMILY:**
Pittosporaceae

**LEAF COLOR:** Lustrous dark green.

**LEAF DESCRIPTION:** SIMPLE, 2" to 3 1/2" long and half as wide, ovate to obovate shape with entire margins. ALTERNATE or sometimes WHORLED.

**FLOWER DESCRIPTION:** Greenish-white, 1/2" to 1" in small clusters. FRAGRANT. Flowers in spring.

**EXPOSURE/CULTURE:** Sun or shade. Thrives in any well-drained soil from sand to clay. Will tolerate dry, hot conditions. Useful in coastal plantings. Has a dense habit of growth, but can be sheared heavily.

**PEST PROBLEMS:** Mealybugs.

**SELECTED CULTIVARS:** (Several described under *P. tobira* 'Wheelers Dwarf' in Chapter 6.)

**LANDSCAPE NOTES:** Pittosporum is a nice plant of limited hardiness that makes a beautiful foundation plant. It survives especially well in coastal planting in the South. Foliage is quite distinct and interesting. The plant is often used as an indoor plant for interior design.

# *Podocarpus macrophyllus var. maki*

**Podocarpus**

**ZONES:**
7, 8, 9, 10

**HEIGHT:**
10' to 15'

**WIDTH:**
5' to 8'

**FRUIT:**
Small, red seed attached to red aril.

**TEXTURE:**
Medium

**GROWTH RATE:**
Slow

**HABIT:**
Upright and somewhat columnar.

**FAMILY:**
Podocarpaceae

**LEAF COLOR:** Dark green.

**LEAF DESCRIPTION:** NEEDLE-LIKE (resembles Yew), 1" to 2 1/2" long and 1/4" wide. Prominent midrib. Linear shape with acute tip and entire margins. ALTERNATE arrangement, but appearing whorled.

**FLOWER DESCRIPTION:** Dioecious; male catkins and female cones; NOT ORNAMENTAL.

**EXPOSURE/CULTURE:** Sun or shade. Prefers well-drained soil and will not tolerate wet conditions. Will grow in sandy locations and is heat-tolerant. A good choice for beach plantings. Can be pruned into any shape or form, and is often used in topiary.

**PEST PROBLEMS:** Scale

**SELECTED CULTIVARS:** None

**LANDSCAPE NOTES:** Podocarpus is often mistaken for Yew. It makes an interesting accent plant to contrast with broadleaf shrubs. Sometimes used to fill bare space in the foundation or as a corner plant.

## Pyracantha coccinea

**Scarlet Firethorn**

▲ 'Lelandei Monrovia'. Courtesy of Monrovia Nurseries.

**ZONES:**
6, 7, 8, 9

**HEIGHT:**
8' to 16'

**WIDTH:**
8' to 16'

**FRUIT:**
1/4" orange-red pomes in clusters; VERY ORNAMENTAL.

**TEXTURE:**
Medium

**GROWTH RATE:**
Moderate to rapid.

**HABIT:**
Irregular shrub with thorny branches; dense.

**FAMILY:**
Rosaceae

**LEAF COLOR:** Dark green and lustrous.

**LEAF DESCRIPTION:** SIMPLE, 1" to 2" long and 1/2" wide, lanceolate shape to narrow oblanceolate shape with serrulate margins. ALTERNATE arrangement.

**FLOWER DESCRIPTION:** White, 1/4" across, borne in corymbs in late spring on previous season's growth. Somewhat fragrant, abundant, and VERY SHOWY.

**EXPOSURE/CULTURE:** Sun or light shade. Prefers moist, well-drained soil. pH-tolerant and reasonably drought-tolerant. Prune with caution, since the stems have sharp, stiff thorns.

**PEST PROBLEMS:** Fire blight, twig blight, lacebugs, spider mites, scale.

**SELECTED CULTIVARS:** 'Aurea' - A yellow-fruited cultivar. 'Kasan' - Has orange-red fruits and is hardier than the species. Widely used. 'Lelandei Monrovia' - This cultivar has orange-red berries in greater abundance than the species. 'Thornless' - Red fruits produced in abundance on thornless stems.

**RELATED SPECIES:** *P. koidzumi* - (Featured on next page.)

**LANDSCAPE NOTES:** Scarlet Firethorn is spectacular in both bloom and fruit. It is a dense-growing shrub that is excellent for screening or as a border specimen. It is commonly used as an espalier for bare wall space. This plant is not low-maintenace, but is worth the effort.

# *Pyracantha koidzumi*

**ZONES:**
7, 8, 9, 10

**HEIGHT:**
10' to 15'

**WIDTH:**
10' to 15'

**FRUIT:**
1/4" orange to scarlet pome; abundant and showy.

**TEXTURE:**
Medium

**GROWTH RATE:**
Rapid

**HABIT:**
Stiff and irregular; somewhat pendulous.

**FAMILY:**
Rosaceae

**LEAF COLOR:** Dark green in all seasons.

**LEAF DESCRIPTION:** SIMPLE, 1 1/2" to 2 1/2" long and one-third as wide, oblanceolate shape with cuneate base, apex rounded or emarginate, entire margins. ALTERNATE arrangement.

**FLOWER DESCRIPTION:** White, 1/4" and pubescent, 5-petaled, appearing in densely-flowered corymbs. Flowers in mid-spring and is VERY SHOWY.

**EXPOSURE/CULTURE:** Full sun or light shade. Prefers well-drained, moist soil, but is reasonably drought-tolerant. Prune carefully after flowering. Thorn-like stems are hazardous. Grown as an espalier or allowed to be shrub-like.

**PEST PROBLEMS:** Fire blight, lacebugs, spider mites, scab.

**BARK/STEMS:** Young stems reddish, maturing to purple-tinged brown, smooth bark. Lateral stems are very stiff and when mature are thorn-like.

**SELECTED CULTIVARS:** 'Low-Dense' - Mounding type, 3' to 5', with smaller leaves. Vigorous foliage growth often hides fruit. Useful on embankments. 'Santa Cruz' - Scab-resistant form that is prostrate to 3' to 4' in height. Large red fruits. 'Victory' - Scab-resistant form with large red fruits. Large shrub with extremely vigorous growth.

**LANDSCAPE NOTES:** Formosa Firethorn is noted for its abundant fruiting habit. Fruits are very showy from fall to spring. It can be used as a large shrub for screening or as a lawn specimen. It is most often espaliered or semi-espaliered. Well-maintained espaliers are often magnificent in fruit. Unfortunately, this is not a low-maintenance plant.

## *Rhododendron catawbiense* — Catawba Rhododendron

**ZONES:**
4, 5, 6, 7, 8

**HEIGHT:**
8' to 10'

**WIDTH:**
6' to 8'

**FRUIT:**
Brown capsule; NOT ORNA-MENTAL.

**TEXTURE:**
Coarse

**GROWTH RATE:**
Slow

**HABIT:**
Dense and irregular with rounded character.

**FAMILY:**
Ericaceae

**LEAF COLOR:** Dark green.

**LEAF DESCRIPTION:** SIMPLE, 4″ to 6″ long and one-third as wide, elliptic to narrow elliptic shape with entire margins. ALTERNATE arrangement.

**FLOWER DESCRIPTION:** Species is Lilac-rose. Many colors, depending on cultivar, Z″ to 2 1/2″ and long 4″ to 6″ racemes (trusses). Flowers in May. Abundent and attractive.

**EXPOSURE/CULTURE:** Light shade to shade. Rhododendrons must be grown in well-drained soils of acid pH. Consistent moisture level (not wet) must be maintained. When planting, dig shallow hole, if any, and mound with mulch. Maintain heavy mulch. Pruning is seldom necessary.

**PEST PROBLEMS:** Rhododendrons are bothered by many pests, including dieback, rootrot, leaf gall, nematodes, beetles, borers, leaf miners, blight, lace bugs, mealybugs, and scale.

**SELECTED CULTIVARS:** 'Album' - (Featured). Has pure white flowers with yellowish throats. Very hardy.

**LANDSCAPE NOTES:** Rhododendrons are among the most beautiful of flowering shrubs. Catawba Rhododendrons are among the hardiest. They are among the best landscape plants for naturalizing. However, they are not considered care-free or low-maintenance.

## *Taxus x media 'Stricta'*

**Anglojap Yew**

**ZONES:**
4, 5, 6, 7

**HEIGHT:**
12' to 20'

**WIDTH:**
6' to 8'

**FRUIT:**
Pinkish to red aril with brown seed.

**TEXTURE:**
Medium

**GROWTH RATE:**
Somewhat slow.

**HABIT:**
Erect and compact.

**FAMILY:**
Taxaceae

**LEAF COLOR:** Medium green.

**LEAF DESCRIPTION:** NEEDLE-LIKE, 1" to 1 1/2" long and 1/8" wide, linear shape with entire margins. 2 yellowish bands beneath; 2-ranked.

**FLOWER DESCRIPTION:** Monoecious; NOT NOTICEABLE.

**EXPOSURE/CULTURE:** Sun or shade. Prefers well-drained, sandy loam soil. Does not tolerate wet or hot locations in the garden. Has dense habit without pruning, but can be sheared to any shape.

**PEST PROBLEMS:** Rootrot, scale; usually not serious.

**SELECTED CULTIVARS:** None. This is a cultivar of *T.* x *media,* a cross between *T. cuspidata* and *T. baccata.*

**RELATED CULTIVARS:** 'Densiformis' - Female. Broader than tall with light green foliage. One of the hardiest. 'Hatfieldii' - Male. Broad pyramid to 16' with dark green foliage. Radially arranged needles. 'Hicksii' - Male or female. Narrow column to 20'. Dark green foliage with raised midrib. 'Kelseyi' - Female. Very dense and upright with abundant fruit.

**LANDSCAPE NOTES:** Anglojap Yews are very versatile plants that make excellent foundation plants for taller corners. They are often used for hedges, both clipped and unclipped, and are good choices for topiary. Not for the South.

# *Ternstroemia gymnanthera*

**Cleyera**

**ZONES:**
7, 8, 9

**HEIGHT:**
8′ to 10′

**WIDTH:**
4′ to 6′

**FRUIT:**
1/2″ green berry; maturing to red; not especially ornamental.

**TEXTURE:**
Medium

**GROWTH RATE:**
Moderate

**HABIT:**
Upright and dense.

**FAMILY:**
Theaceae

**LEAF COLOR:** Deep green; new growth very lustrous.

**LEAF DESCRIPTION:** SIMPLE, 3″ to 4″ long and 1″ to 1 3/4″ wide, elliptic to obovate shape with entire margins. ALTERNATE arrangement, appearing whorled at the tips.

**FLOWER DESCRIPTION:** White, 1/2″, appearing in pendulous axillary groups. Flowers in May.

**EXPOSURE/CULTURE:** Shade or part shade. Grows in any well-drained soil. Heavy fertilizer will cause excessively long internodes. Responds favorably to pruning, but natural shape should be maintained.

**PEST PROBLEMS:** No serious pests.

**SELECTED CULTIVARS:** None

**LANDSCAPE NOTES:** Cleyera is an excellent large shrub having many uses in the landscape. It looks great in shady areas where many plants "thin out." The foliage and dense habit are its outstanding features. One of the best!

# *Thuja occidentalis 'Emerald'*

**Emerald Arborvitae**

**ZONES:**
3, 4, 5, 6, 7

**HEIGHT:**
10' to 12'

**WIDTH:**
3' to 4'

**FRUIT:**
1/2" brown, woody cone.

**TEXTURE:**
Fine

**GROWTH RATE:**
Moderate

**HABIT:**
Compact and conical; sprays (plates) vertical or horizontal.

**FAMILY:**
Cupressaceae

**LEAF COLOR:** Glossy, bright emerald green.

**LEAF DESCRIPTION:** SCALE-LIKE, to 1/10" long; scales on main branches are glandular (oil-secreting); 4-ranked.

**FLOWER DESCRIPTION:** Monoecious; yellowish; NOT ORNAMENTAL.

**EXPOSURE/CULTURE:** Sun. Prefers well-drained, moist (not wet) soils, and is adaptable to sand or clay. Prefers humid conditions, but is heat- and drought-tolerant. Very responsive to shearing.

**PEST PROBLEMS:** Bagworms, spider mites, tip blight.

**SELECTED CULTIVARS:** None. This is a cultivar of *T. occidentalis,* a large evergreen tree.

**RELATED SPECIES:** *T. orientalis* - Similar to *T. occidentalis,* but the flattened sprays are vertical.

**LANDSCAPE NOTES:** This plant has merit as a foundation plant, specimen, or screen. Relatively easy to grow and hardy. Plant in full sun for superior foliage.

# *Thuja occidentalis* 'Holmstrup'

## Holmstrup Eastern Arborvitae

**ZONES:**
3, 4, 5, 6, 7

**HEIGHT:**
8' to 12'

**WIDTH:**
3 1/2' to 5'

**FRUIT:**
1/2" brown, woody cone.

**TEXTURE:**
Fine

**GROWTH RATE:**
Slow

**HABIT:**
Dense and conical; vertical foliage.

**FAMILY:**
Cupressaceae

**LEAF COLOR:** Apple-green

**LEAF DESCRIPTION:** SCALE-LIKE, to 1/10" long; scales on main branches glandular (oil-secreting); 4-ranked.

**FLOWER DESCRIPTION:** Monoecious; yellowish; NOT ORNAMENTAL.

**EXPOSURE/CULTURE:** Sun. Prefers well-drained, moist soil (not wet). It is adaptable to most soils from sand to clay and is reasonably drought- and heat-tolerant. Can be sheared to very dense character.

**PEST PROBLEMS:** Bagworms, spider mites, tip blight.

**SELECTED CULTIVARS:** None. This is a cultivar of *T. occidentalis*.

**LANDSCAPE NOTES:** 'Holmstrup' has especially tight, sturdy branches. It is useful as a specimen, foundation plant, or screen. It is considered one of the best cultivars of Eastern Arborvitae.

## *Tsuga canadensis* 'Pendula' *(var. sargentii)* — Sargent's Weeping Hemlock

**ZONES:**
3, 4, 5, 6, 7

**HEIGHT:**
10' to 12'

**WIDTH:**
20' to 25'

**FRUIT:**
3/4" brown cone; pendulous.

**TEXTURE:**
Fine

**GROWTH RATE:**
Moderate

**HABIT:**
Broad, dense, and weeping (pendulous).

**FAMILY:**
Pinaceae

**LEAF COLOR:** New growth light green; mature growth dark green.

**LEAF DESCRIPTION:** NEEDLE-LIKE, flattened, 1/4" to 1/2" long, linear shape, toothed. 2-ranked. 2 whitish bands on underside.

**FLOWER DESCRIPTION:** Monoecious; NOT ORNAMENTAL.

**EXPOSURE/CULTURE:** Sun or shade. Prefers moist, well-drained, acid soil. Does not like hot or windy conditions. Responds well to pruning, and is often sheared for dense habit.

**PEST PROBLEMS:** Borers, blister rust, leaf blight, mites, scale.

**SELECTED CULTIVARS:** None. This is a cultivar of *T. canadensis,* a large evergreen tree.

**LANDSCAPE NOTES:** Sargent's Weeping Hemlock is one of the most dramatic accent plants. Location should be carefully selected to attract attention to desirable features in the garden.

## *Viburnum japonicum*

**Japanese Viburnum**

**ZONES:**
7, 8, 9

**HEIGHT:**
8′ to 12′

**WIDTH:**
6′ to 8′

**FRUIT:**
1/4″ to 1/3″ red drupe.

**TEXTURE:**
Coarse

**GROWTH RATE:**
Moderate

**HABIT:**
Upright and stiff.

**FAMILY:**
Caprifoliaceae

**LEAF COLOR:** Dark green and very glossy.

**LEAF DESCRIPTION:** SIMPLE, 4″ to 6″ long and 2″ to 3″ wide, ovate to elliptic shape with entire margins (sometimes slightly toothed). OPPOSITE arrangement.

**FLOWER DESCRIPTION:** White, 1/4″ wide in 4″ clusters (cymes), appearing in spring. Fragrant.

**EXPOSURE/CULTURE:** Sun. Prefers moist, well-drained, organic soil. Pruning is favorable to thicken or control shape.

**PEST PROBLEMS:** No serious pests.

**SELECTED CULTIVARS:** None

**RELATED SPECIES:** *V. odoratissimum* - Leaf is more oval in shape, and flowers appear in 4″ panicles. Less cold hardy than *V. japonicum*.

**LANDSCAPE NOTES:** Japanese Viburnum is a handsome foliage plant with large, shiny leaves. It makes a great foundation plant for taller corners, and contrasts well with fine-textured plants. OUTSTANDING.

# *Viburnum rhytidophyllum*

**Leatherleaf Viburnum**

**ZONES:**
5, 6, 7, 8

**HEIGHT:**
8′ to 12′

**WIDTH:**
5′ to 8′

**FRUIT:**
1/3″ red berries (drupes); clustered.

**TEXTURE:**
Coarse

**GROWTH RATE:**
Moderate

**HABIT:**
Upright, irregular, and open.

**FAMILY:**
Caprifoliaceae

**LEAF COLOR:** Dark green.

**LEAF DESCRIPTION:** SIMPLE, appearing wrinkled, 4″ to 7″ long and one-third as wide, narrow ovate to lanceolate shape with entire margins. Tomentose beneath. Minutely hairy above. OPPOSITE arrangement.

**FLOWER DESCRIPTION:** Yellowish-white, tiny, in 5″ to 6″ clusters (cymes). Flowers in May.

**EXPOSURE/CULTURE:** Shade or part shade. Prefers well-drained, organic soils. Will not tolerate heat or windy locations. Prune as desired, after flowering.

**PEST PROBLEMS:** No serious pests.

**SELECTED CULTIVARS:** None

**RELATED VARIETIES:** var. *roseum* - Buds are pink before opening.

**LANDSCAPE NOTES:** Leatherleaf Viburnum is popular for its wrinkled, leatherlike leaves and abundant red berries that attract birds to the garden. It is best used as a filler plant for bare wall space on taller foundations, or as a border plant for naturalizing.

## *Viburnum tinus*                                    **Laurustinus**

▲ 'Compactum.' Courtesy of Monrovia Nurseries.

**ZONES:**
7, 8, 9, 10

**HEIGHT:**
6′ to 10′

**WIDTH:**
6′ to 10′

**FRUIT:**
Small blue drupe; maturing to black.

**TEXTURE:**
Medium

**GROWTH RATE:**
Moderate

**HABIT:**
Upright, open, and rounded.

**FAMILY:**
Caprifoliaceae

**LEAF COLOR:** Dark green and lustrous.

**LEAF DESCRIPTION:** SIMPLE, 2″ to 3″ long and 1″ to 1 1/2″ wide, oblong-ovate to oblong with entire margins. OPPOSITE arrangement.

**FLOWER DESCRIPTION:** White to pink (pink in bud), appearing in 3″ cymes in late winter to early spring. Fragrant and showy.

**EXPOSURE/CULTURE:** Sun or light shade. Prefers moist, organic, well-drained soil. pH-adaptable. Not drought-tolerant. Mulch for best performance. Prune, as needed, after flowering, or shear as a hedge.

**PEST PROBLEMS:** No serious pests.

**SELECTED CULTIVARS:** 'Compactum' - A dwarf form to about one-half the size of the species. Has smaller leaves. 'Robustum' - Roundleaf Viburnum. This cultivar grows larger and has larger, more rounded leaves.

**LANDSCAPE NOTES:** Laurustinus is a fine landscape plant, but is questionably hardy. Above Zone 9, it probably should be grown in a microclimate. It can be used in foundation plantings, garden borders, or as screening material. Makes a nice clipped hedge.

# *Yucca aloifolia*

**Spanish Bayonet**

▲ 'Variegata'

**ZONES:**
7, 8, 9, 10

**HEIGHT:**
8' to 12'

**WIDTH:**
5' to 6'

**FRUIT:**
Black capsule; NOT ATTRACTIVE.

**TEXTURE:**
Coarse

**GROWTH RATE:**
Moderate

**HABIT:**
Palm-like; stiff trunk and leaves.

**FAMILY:**
Agavaceae

**LEAF COLOR:** Medium green.

**LEAF DESCRIPTION:** SIMPLE, 2' to 3' long and 2" to 2 1/2" wide, narrow linear shape and minutely toothed, sharp margins. TIPS SHARPLY POINTED. Alternate in WHORLED pattern.

**FLOWER DESCRIPTION:** White, 3" on 1' to 2' spikes, arising from crown of plant. Attractive. Summer.

**EXPOSURE/CULTURE:** Sun or light shade. Grows in almost any soil and is especially adapted to hot, dry, sandy conditions. Pruning is not recommended, except to remove seed stalk or sprouts.

**PEST PROBLEMS:** None

**SELECTED CULTIVARS:** 'Variegata' - has yellow leaf margins.

**LANDSCAPE NOTES:** Yuccas make a bold accent plant in the garden. Spanish Bayonet is a tall-growing Yucca that sprouts from the lower trunk to form upright branches. Flower spikes are attractive. Plant well back in bed areas to prevent injury from spines. Very easy to grow and low-maintenance. Great for xeriscaping.

## *Azalea pericylmenoides (Rhododendron periclymenoides)* *

**ZONES:**
4, 5, 6, 7, 8

**HEIGHT:**
5' to 10'

**WIDTH:**
4' to 8'

**FRUIT:**
Brown capsule; NOT ORNA-MENTAL.

**TEXTURE:**
Medium

**GROWTH RATE:**
Slow

**HABIT:**
Spreading and open.

**FAMILY:**
Ericaceae

**LEAF COLOR:** Green in summer; brownish-yellow in fall.

**LEAF DESCRIPTION:** SIMPLE, 2" to 3" long and 3/4" to 1 1/2" wide, elliptic to oblong shape with entire margins. Midrib hairy. ALTERNATE arrangement.

**FLOWER DESCRIPTION:** White, pink, or violet, 1" to 2" long, funnel form, appearing in 6- to 10-flowered clusters. Flowers in spring (April). Fragrant.

**EXPOSURE/CULTURE:** Shade. Prefers organic, moist, well-drained soil, but is adaptable to stony, dry soils. Pruning is minimal to maintain natural shape.

**PEST PROBLEMS:** No serious pests.

**SELECTED CULTIVARS:** None

**LANDSCAPE NOTES:** Pinxterbloom is a great plant for naturalizing in wooded locations, since this is its native habitat. Often used along nature trails and streams. Best effect is attained in the home garden by planting in mass. This is a good, hardy, and reliable plant.

**\*COMMON NAMES:** Pixterbloom Azalea

# *Buddleia davidii*

**Butterfly Bush, Summer Lilac**

▲ 'Alba'

**ZONES:**
5, 6, 7, 8, 9

**HEIGHT:**
8' to 12'

**WIDTH:**
10' to 12'

**FRUIT:**
Tiny brown capsule; NOT ORNAMENTAL.

**TEXTURE:**
Medium to coarse.

**GROWTH RATE:**
Rapid

**HABIT:**
Open and rounded with arching branches.

**FAMILY:**
Loganiaceae

**LEAF COLOR:** Dark green to gray-green. No fall color.

**LEAF DESCRIPTION:** SIMPLE, 5″ to 8″ long and one-fourth as wide, lanceolate shape with finely serrated margins, white tomentose (hairs) beneath. OPPOSITE arrangement.

**FLOWER DESCRIPTION:** Lilac with orange "eye," appearing tightly in spikes to 10″ long. Flowers in late summer through fall.

**EXPOSURE/CULTURE:** Full sun. Prefers well-drained, moist, organic soils, but is durable and adaptable. Prune heavily in early spring, since flowers form on current season's growth. Easy to grow.

**PEST PROBLEMS:** No serious pests.

**SELECTED CULTIVARS:** 'Black Knight' - Very dark, violet-purple flower panicles. 'Charming Summer' - Soft, lavender-pink flowers. Very prolific. 'Dubonnet' - Large panicles of dark purple flowers. Upright growth. 'Empire Blue' - Blue flowers and silvery-green foliage. Vigorous and upright. 'Nanho Alba' - White flower panicles on a compact, spreading plant. Medium size. 'Pink Delight' - Bright pink flowers on spikes to 15″. Especially prolific. 'White Bouquet' - Sparkling white flowers with orange throats. var. *nanhoensis* - Smaller than the species (to 5') with much smaller leaves (4″).

**RELATED SPECIES:** *B. alternifolia* - Has alternate leaves and grows larger and more open than *B. davidii*. It has a pendulous, weeping habit with lilac-purple blooms that appear earlier than *B. davidii*.

**LANDSCAPE NOTES:** Butterfly Bush has a long bloom period and attracts many butterflies to the garden. This is an outstanding later summer specimen for garden borders or perennial plantings, and is especially useful for naturalizing.

## *Calycanthus floridus* — Sweetshrub, Carolina Allspice

**ZONES:**
5, 6, 7, 8, 9

**HEIGHT:**
6' to 10'

**WIDTH:**
6' to 10'

**FRUIT:**
Capsule-like with achenes;
NOT ORNAMENTAL.

**TEXTURE:**
Medium

**GROWTH RATE:**
Moderate

**HABIT:**
Somewhat rounded and
bushy.

**FAMILY:**
Calycanthaceae

**LEAF COLOR:** Gray-green in summer; yellowish to brown in fall.

**LEAF DESCRIPTION:** SIMPLE, 2 1/2" to 5" long and half as wide, ovate or elliptic shape with entire margins. Pale and tomentose on the underside. OPPOSITE arrangement.

**FLOWER DESCRIPTION:** Dark reddish-brown. 2" wide. Solitary. Flowers in spring. Very fragrant.

**EXPOSURE/CULTURE:** Sun or shade. Prefers loamy, moist soils, but is adaptable to all but wet soils. Very pH-adaptable. Prune after flowering to control or shape.

**PEST PROBLEMS:** None

**SELECTED CULTIVARS:** 'Purpureus' - Similar to the species but having purple leaves.

**RELATED SPECIES:** *C. fertilis* - Has glabrous leaves and less fragrance. *C. occidentalis* - Has larger leaves and flowers. Hardy only to Zone 8.

**LANDSCAPE NOTES:** Sweetshrub is an "old timey" plant that has been popular since Colonial days. This is a trouble-free plant that is great in sunny or shaded gardens. A good plant for garden borders or perennial gardens. Stems have a camphor-like smell when crushed.

## *Caragana arborescens*

**Siberian Peashrub**

**ZONES:**
2, 3, 4, 5, 6, 7, 8

**HEIGHT:**
10′ to 15′

**WIDTH:**
10′ to 15′

**FRUIT:**
Brown pod; NOT ORNAMEN-TAL.

**TEXTURE:**
Fine to medium.

**GROWTH RATE:**
Rapid

**HABIT:**
Upright and somewhat rounded.

**FAMILY:**
Fabaceae

**LEAF COLOR:** Light to medium green in summer; yellowish in fall.

**LEAF DESCRIPTION:** EVEN PINNATELY COMPOUND, 6 to 12 leaflets, leaflets 3/4″ to 1″ long and half as wide, obovate to elliptic shape with entire margins. ALTERNATE arrangement.

**FLOWER DESCRIPTION:** Yellow and pea-like, 3/4″ to 1″ long, 1 to 4 in clusters at terminal ends of branches. Flowers in spring.

**EXPOSURE/CULTURE:** Sun or light shade. Adapts to a wide variety of soil types, except very wet soils. Flourishes on poor soil due to nitrogen fixation (legume). Should be pruned after flowering to maintain desired shape.

**PEST PROBLEMS:** No serious pests.

**SELECTED CULTIVARS:** 'Lorbergii' - Extremely narrow linear leaflets with fern-like fine texture. 'Nana' - Dwarf form with contorted branchlets. 'Pendula' - Graceful, weeping form when grafted onto standards. Great for planters.

**LANDSCAPE NOTES:** Peashrub is a nice plant for borders, as a screen, or as a background plant. It can be used as a border specimen when care is given to pruning and shaping. Its greatest asset is its hardy, rugged nature.

## *Cercis chinensis*    **Chinese Redbud**

**ZONES:**
6, 7, 8, 9

**HEIGHT:**
10′ to 15′

**WIDTH:**
6′ to 8′

**FRUIT:**
3″ to 4″ brown pod, bean-like;
NOT ORNAMENTAL.

**TEXTURE:**
Medium to coarse.

**GROWTH RATE:**
Moderate

**HABIT:**
Multi-stemmed, upright, and stiff.

**FAMILY:**
Fabaceae

**LEAF COLOR:** Dark green in summer; yellow in fall.

**LEAF DESCRIPTION:** SIMPLE, 3″ to 4″ long and wide, cordate shape with entire margins, petiole broadened at attachment with leaf blade. ALTERNATE arrangement.

**FLOWER DESCRIPTION:** Rose-purple, 1/2″ to 1″ long, often bunched. Flowers in early spring.

**EXPOSURE/CULTURE:** Sun or light shade. Prefers moist, organic, well-drained soils. Pruning is minimal and is recommended only for shaping.

**PEST PROBLEMS:** Stem canker, borers.

**BARK/STEMS:** Reddish-brown and smooth on young stems; older stems scaly.

**SELECTED CULTIVARS:** 'Nana' - Lower-growing version of the above, to about half as large.

**LANDSCAPE NOTES:** Chinese Redbud is an early-flowering deciduous shrub that can be used in borders for early color. Good specimens can be quite profuse in bloom. Easy to grow.

# *Chionanthus virginicus*

## Grancy Gray-beard, Old-man's-beard

**ZONES:**
5, 6, 7, 8, 9

**HEIGHT:**
8' to 12'

**WIDTH:**
6' to 10'

**FRUIT:**
1/2" dark blue drupe; plum-like.

**TEXTURE:**
Coarse

**GROWTH RATE:**
Slow

**HABIT:**
Spreading and open.

**FAMILY:**
Oleaceae

**LEAF COLOR:** Medium green in summer; yellowish in fall.

**LEAF DESCRIPTION:** SIMPLE, 4" to 7" long and one-third as wide, narrow-elliptic shape with entire margins. OPPOSITE arrangement.

**FLOWER DESCRIPTION:** White, 4 strap-like petals per flower, petals 1" long, flowers appearing in dense 6" panicles. Flowers in May.

**EXPOSURE/CULTURE:** Sun or light shade. Prefers moist, organic soil but is adaptable. Does best with mulching for cooler roots. Prune after flowering. Can be pruned to tree-form with interesting results.

**PEST PROBLEMS:** No serious pests.

**BARK/STEMS:** Young stems green or brown; some pubescent. Older stems gray and smooth to slightly ridged.

**SELECTED CULTIVARS:** None

**RELATED SPECIES:** *C. retusis* - A small to medium size tree. (Featured in Medium Deciduous Trees.)

**LANDSCAPE NOTES:** Gray-beard makes an excellent large shrub or small tree for garden borders. It is often used as a spring focal point since flowers are abundant and very attractive. A proven plant that is very useful in modern landscapes. Often tree-formed.

## *Cotinus coggygria*

**Smoketree, Smokebush**

**ZONES:**
5, 6, 7, 8, 9

**HEIGHT:**
10′ to 12′

**WIDTH:**
8′ to 12′

**FRUIT:**
1/4″ pinkish drupe; NOT ORNAMENTAL.

**TEXTURE:**
Medium

**GROWTH RATE:**
Moderate

**HABIT:**
Rounded and irregular.

**FAMILY:**
Anacardiaceae

**LEAF COLOR:** Gray-green in summer; yellow, orange, or purple in fall.

**LEAF DESCRIPTION:** SIMPLE, 1″ to 3″ long and 5/8″ to 2″ wide, oval shape with obtuse tip and entire margins. ALTERNATE arrangement.

**FLOWER DESCRIPTION:** Pinkish-gray to purplish, tiny, in 8″ many-branched panicles, hairy and smoke-like. Flowers in May and June.

**EXPOSURE/CULTURE:** Sun. Grows in a wide range of soil types and pH levels. Very drought-resistant. Prune after flowering to maintain shape or control size.

**PEST PROBLEMS:** No serious pests.

**SELECTED CULTIVARS:** 'Nordine' - Very hardy form with purplish-red leaves that keep their color well into fall. 'Pendulus' - Has drooping branches. 'Purpureus' - Has purple leaves and darker flowers. 'Royal Purple' - (Featured on next page.)

**LANDSCAPE NOTES:** Smoketree is properly named because of the unusual flowers that resemble little puffs of smoke throughout the shrub. It is a plant to feature and should be used with moderation. This plant has been overshadowed by the purple cultivars, but the species is still useful in landscaping. Great for xeriscaping.

## *Cotinus coggygria 'Royal Purple'*

**Purple Smoketree**

**ZONES:**
5, 6, 7, 8, 9

**HEIGHT:**
10' to 12'

**WIDTH:**
8' to 12'

**FRUIT:**
A compressed 1/4" drupe; NOT ORNAMENTAL.

**TEXTURE:**
Medium to coarse.

**GROWTH RATE:**
Moderate

**HABIT:**
Upright and irregularly rounded.

**FAMILY:**
Anacardiaceae

**LEAF COLOR:** New foliage red, maturing to deep (blackish) purple; holds color through fall.

**LEAF DESCRIPTION:** SIMPLE, 2" to 4" long and 1 1/4" to 2 1/2" wide, elliptic to oval shape with entire margins. ALTERNATE arrangement.

**FLOWER DESCRIPTION:** Purplish-red, tiny, in 8" to 10" multi-branched panicles, appearing like puffs of smoke. Flowers in May and June.

**EXPOSURE/CULTURE:** Sun for best color and bloom. The plant grows in a wide range of soil types and pH levels, and is drought-resistent. Pruning should be accomplished after flowering. Maintain natural shape.

**PEST PROBLEMS:** No serious pests.

**SELECTED CULTIVARS:** None. This is a cultivar of *C. coggygria*.

**LANDSCAPE NOTES:** Purple Smoketree is a bold accent plant to feature in the garden border or accent beds. Care should be taken in choosing a location. One should especially consider the color of adjacent structures or plants. This is an outstanding selection for xeriscaping.

# *Cytisus scoparius*

**Scotch Broom**

**ZONES:**
6, 7, 8

**HEIGHT:**
6′ to 8′

**WIDTH:**
6′ to 8′

**FRUIT:**
2″ brown pod; NOT ORNA-MENTAL.

**TEXTURE:**
Fine

**GROWTH RATE:**
Rapid

**HABIT:**
Rounded and irregular with arching branches.

**FAMILY:**
Fabaceae

**LEAF COLOR:** Medium green in summer; yellowish or brown in fall.

**LEAF DESCRIPTION:** COMPOUND (3-petaled), leaflets 1/2″ long and half as wide, obovate to oblanceolate shape with entire margins. ALTERNATE arrangement.

**FLOWER DESCRIPTION:** Bright yellow, 1″ long, solitary or in pairs, arising from the axils of older wood. Flowers in May. Very profuse and noticeable.

**EXPOSURE/CULTURE:** Sun or light shade. Prefers well-drained, organic soil, but is adaptable. Will thrive in dry, sandy soil. Prune heavily after flowering, if desired, to control size.

**PEST PROBLEMS:** Leaf spot.

**BARK/STEMS:** Stems are glabrous and bright green, providing additional interest in winter.

**SELECTED CULTIVARS:** 'Dorothy Walpole' - Has rose-pink flowers. 'Moonlight' - Has pale yellow flowers. 'Red Favorite' - Has true red flowers. Interesting.

**LANDSCAPE NOTES:** Scotch Broom is an easy-to-grow, dependable plant that can be used to cover difficult areas. Yellow flowers are striking during spring, and bright green winter twigs are interesting and noticeable. A proven performer that still has a place in landscaping.

# Deutzia x magnifica

**Showy Deutzia**

**ZONES:**
6, 7, 8

**HEIGHT:**
6' to 10'

**WIDTH:**
6' to 8'

**FRUIT:**
Brown capsule; NOT ORNA-MENTAL.

**TEXTURE:**
Medium

**GROWTH RATE:**
Moderate

**HABIT:**
Upright and multi-stemmed; arching branches.

**FAMILY:**
Saxifragaceae

**LEAF COLOR:** Dull green with grayish-green tomentose; fading to brown in fall.

**LEAF DESCRIPTION:** SIMPLE, 1" to 3" long and 1/2" to 1 1/4" wide, ovate-oblong shape with serrated margins. OPPOSITE arrangement.

**FLOWER DESCRIPTION:** White, 3/4" in short panicles. DOUBLE. Flowers in late spring. Very prolific.

**EXPOSURE/CULTURE:** Full sun. Grows well in any soil with reasonable moisture and fertility. Mulching will improve flowering. Prune after flowering to control size and shape.

**PEST PROBLEMS:** No serious pests.

**SELECTED CULTIVARS:** 'Eburnea' - Has bell-shaped flowers borne in loose panicles. 'Erecta' - Flowers borne in upright panicles.

**RELATED SPECIES:** *D. scabra* - This species has 6" flower panicles. Has brown, peeling bark. *D. x lemoinei* - This species is a medium-grower that is rounded and more compact.

**LANDSCAPE NOTES:** Showy Deutzia is a reliable shrub that blooms very profusely in late spring. It should be used as a warm season specimen in the garden border. It also makes a fine background plant for perennial plantings. Reliable and easy-to-grow.

## *Elaeagnus multiflora* 'Crispa' — Silver Elaeagnus

**ZONES:**
5, 6, 7, 8

**HEIGHT:**
8' to 10'

**WIDTH:**
8' to 10'

**FRUIT:**
1/2" red achene; drupe-like.

**TEXTURE:**
Medium

**GROWTH RATE:**
Rapid

**HABIT:**
Loose and wide-spreading.

**FAMILY:**
Elaeagnaceae

**LEAF COLOR:** Silver-green with brown scale beneath in summer; silver-brown in fall.

**LEAF DESCRIPTION:** SIMPLE, 1 1/2" to 2" long and 3/4" to 1 1/4" wide, elliptic or ovate shape with entire to slightly undulate margins. ALTERNATE arrangement.

**FLOWER DESCRIPTION:** Pale yellow, 1/2", solitary or in pairs, arising from leaf axils. Flowers in spring. ABUNDANT and very FRAGRANT.

**EXPOSURE/CULTURE:** Sun or light shade. The plant is adaptable as to soil type, and is used on sandy, droughty soils. Prune after flowering as desired to control size or maintain shape.

**PEST PROBLEMS:** Aphids, scale.

**SELECTED CULTIVARS:** None. This is a cultivar of *E. multiflora*.

**RELATED SPECIES:** *E. angustifolia* - Russian Olive. This species is characterized by thorny spines on stems and yellowish fruits. Often found in the wild. Disease-prone. *E. macrophylla* - Silverberry. This species has much larger, green leaves (to 6") and does not have thorns. Compact form. *E. pungens* - (See Large Evergreen Shrubs.)

**LANDSCAPE NOTES:** Silver Elaeagnus is a large, broad shrub that is probably best suited for naturalizing along borders of the garden. The tiny yellow flowers are very pleasingly fragrant. The red fruits are edible, and they attract a variety of birds. This is a worthy plant that should be more widely planted.

## *Exochorda racemosa*
**Pearlbush**

**ZONES:**
5, 6, 7, 8, 9

**HEIGHT:**
9′ to 12′

**WIDTH:**
10′ to 15′

**FRUIT:**
1/4″ 5-valved capsule; NOT ORNAMENTAL.

**TEXTURE:**
Medium

**GROWTH RATE:**
Moderate

**HABIT:**
Globular and irregular.

**FAMILY:**
Rosaceae

**LEAF COLOR:** Gray-green to medium green in summer; brown before dropping in fall.

**LEAF DESCRIPTION:** SIMPLE, 1″ to 2 1/2″ long and half as wide, elliptic to oblong-obovate shape with mostly entire margins, often serrated toward the apex. Whitish beneath. ALTERNATE arrangement.

**FLOWER DESCRIPTION:** White, 1 1/2″ to 2″ across, 5-petaled, appearing in racemes of 5 or more flowers in spring. Buds are pearl-colored before opening. Very abundant and attractive.

**EXPOSURE/CULTURE:** Full sun or light shade. Prefers well-drained, organic soil, but is adaptable to all but very wet soils. Prune after flowering to shape or control.

**PEST PROBLEMS:** No serious pests.

**SELECTED CULTIVARS:** None

**RELATED SPECIES:** *E.* x *macrantha* - More upright form, having greater vigor and denser panicles of flowers.

**LANDSCAPE NOTES:** Pearlbush is an "old timey" plant that has been used extensively in home gardens. It is best suited to borders as a background plant. Not especially noticeable except when flowering.

## *Ficus carica*         Common Fig

**ZONES:**
7, 8, 9, 10

**HEIGHT:**
12′ to 15′

**WIDTH:**
10′ to 15′

**FRUIT:**
Green; pinkish when ripe; 1″ to 2″ pear-shaped receptacle; EDIBLE AND DELICIOUS.

**TEXTURE:**
Coarse

**GROWTH RATE:**
Rapid

**HABIT:**
Spreading and irregular.

**FAMILY:**
Moraceae

**LEAF COLOR:** Dark green in summer; brown to black in fall.

**LEAF DESCRIPTION:** SIMPLE, 5″ to 9″ long and broad, palmately lobed shape with smooth margins, 3 to 5 deeply cut lobes, pubescent beneath. Thick and leathery. ALTERNATE arrangement.

**FLOWER DESCRIPTION:** Flowers are minute and produced inside a green fleshy receptacle; NOT ORNAMENTAL.

**EXPOSURE/CULTURE:** Full sun to part shade. Prefers well-drained, loamy, organic soil, but is adaptable to all but wet soils. Prune in early spring, as desired.

**PEST PROBLEMS:** No serious pests.

**SELECTED CULTIVARS:** 'Brown Turkey' - A popular cultivar having abundant, purplish fruits.

**LANDSCAPE NOTES:** Common Fig is actually a fruit tree that produces abundant fruits for preserves, jellies, or fresh fruit. The tree can be quite attractive in the landscape, and provides a textural change. Locate where dropped fruit will not be a problem. Unfortunately, it is not hardy above Zone 7.

# Forsythia x intermedia

**Showy Forsythia, Yellow Bells**

▼ 'Lynwood Gold'

**ZONES:**
5, 6, 7, 8, 9

**HEIGHT:**
6' to 10'

**WIDTH:**
8' to 12'

**FRUIT:**
Brown capsule with winged seed; NOT ORNAMENTAL.

**TEXTURE:**
Medium

**GROWTH RATE:**
Rapid

**HABIT:**
Broad-spreading and open; arching branches.

**FAMILY:**
Oleaceae

**LEAF COLOR:** Medium green in summer; yellowish to red to burgundy in fall.

**LEAF DESCRIPTION:** SIMPLE, 2" to 4" long and one-third as wide, ovate-lance-olate shape with coarsely serrated margins. OPPOSITE arrangement.

**FLOWER DESCRIPTION:** Bright yellow, 1" long, 4-parted corolla tube, appearing in groups along the stems. Flowers in very early spring. No fragrance.

**EXPOSURE/CULTURE:** Sun for best flowering. Prefers well-drained, loamy soil, but is adaptable to all but the extremes of wet or very dry. Prune heavily after flowering if desired, then let plant attain its natural, gracefully arching habit.

**PEST PROBLEMS:** None

**SELECTED CULTIVARS:** 'Beatrix Farrand' - Larger yellow flowers on upright plant. 'Lynwood Gold' - Heavy bloomer with flower corollas that are more open, giving appearance of larger flowers. Upright habit. 'Nana' - Much smaller form to medium size. 'Spectabilis' - The standard by which all others are judged. Hardiest. Very dependable. 'Spring Glory' - Brilliant yellow flowers. Blooms fully before any leaves appear.

**RELATED SPECIES:** *F. ovata* - The earliest of all Forsythias. This medium size shrub has a slight green tinge to its bright yellow flowers.

**LANDSCAPE NOTES:** Forsythia is one of the first shrubs to flower in spring, and really brightens the landscape. It is best used in borders for accent or screening, and should not be used in foundations. It looks best when allowed to develop its natural shape. This is a very easy to grow shrub that is overplanted, but is very refreshing at a time when most of the garden is still dull. Simply stated, absolutely outstanding!

## *Hamamelis vernalis*

**Vernal Witchhazel**

**ZONES:**
4, 5, 6, 7, 8, 9

**HEIGHT:**
8′ to 12′

**WIDTH:**
8′ to 10′

**FRUIT:**
2-valved, brown capsule; NOT ORNAMENTAL.

**TEXTURE:**
Medium to coarse.

**GROWTH RATE:**
Moderate

**HABIT:**
Irregular and rounded.

**FAMILY:**
Hamamelidaceae

**LEAF COLOR:** Dark green in summer; yellow in fall.

**LEAF DESCRIPTION:** SIMPLE, 3″ to 4″ long and half as wide, obovate to elliptic shape with crenate margins. Downy on veins on undersides; sometimes on upper surface veins. ALTERNATE arrangement.

**FLOWER DESCRIPTION:** Yellow, sometimes reddish, 4-petaled, 1/2″ long and strap-like, appearing in axillary cymes. Flowers in January to March.

**EXPOSURE/CULTURE:** Sun to part shade. Prefers moist, organic soil, but is adaptable. Does not like drought. Prune after flowering to shape. Can be tree-formed for interesting effect.

**PEST PROBLEMS:** No serious pests.

**SELECTED CULTIVARS:** 'Rubra' - Petals are reddish near base.

**RELATED SPECIES:** *H. virginiana* - Common Witchhazel. This is a native species that attains much greater height. It flowers in fall or early winter. *H.* x *intermedia* - This is a hybrid between *H. japonica* and *H. mollis*. This is the species being marketed most, and there are numerous cultivars, many with red flowers. 'Arnold Promise' belongs here.

**LANDSCAPE NOTES:** Vernal Witchhazel blooms during the "drab of winter," making it a welcome site for early color. Fall foliage is excellent, and the plant is best used for naturalizing.

# *Hibiscus syriacus*

**Althea, Rose Of Sharon**

**ZONES:**
5, 6, 7, 8, 9

**HEIGHT:**
8' to 10'

**WIDTH:**
5' to 6'

**FRUIT:**
5-celled, brown capsule; NOT ORNAMENTAL.

**TEXTURE:**
Medium

**GROWTH RATE:**
Rapid

**HABIT:**
Upright and open.

**FAMILY:**
Malvaceae

**LEAF COLOR:** Medium green in summer; dull yellow in fall.

**LEAF DESCRIPTION:** SIMPLE, 3" to 4" long and 2 1/2" to 3" wide, triangular to rhombic-ovate shape with 3-lobed margins (palmate) having coarse teeth.

**FLOWER DESCRIPTION:** White, pink, red, purple, or blue, depending on cultivar. 2" to 3" wide and 5-petaled, single or double. Flowers in August or September and continues into fall.

**EXPOSURE/CULTURE:** Sun or light shade. Prefers moist, organic soil, but is adaptable. Avoid extremely wet or extremely dry soils. Prune heavily, if desired, in early spring.

**PEST PROBLEMS:** Beetles, aphids, spider mites, leaf spots, and powdery mildew.

**SELECTED CULTIVARS:** 'Aphrodite' - Single. Deep rose-pink with red eye. Sterile triploid. USDA introduction. 'Blue Bird' - Single. Blue; dense habit. 'Blushing Bride' - Double. Rich pink flowers. Dense habit. 'Collie Mullens' - Double. Lavender blooms and upright, compact habit. 'Diana' - (Featured on next page.) 'Helene' - Single. White flowers with reddish-purple eyes. Triploid. USDA introduction. 'Minerva' - Single. Lavender-pink with reddish-purple eyes. Triploid. USDA introduction. 'Red Heart' - Single. White with scarlet-red eyes.

**LANDSCAPE NOTES:** Althea is a late-blooming plant that has a long bloom period. It should be used in combination with evergreens in the border or as a late-summer specimen. This is an easy to grow, proven performer.

## *Hibiscus syriacus* 'Diana'

**Diana Rose Of Sharon**

**ZONES:**
5, 6, 7, 8, 9

**HEIGHT:**
7' to 8'

**WIDTH:**
7' to 10'

**FRUIT:**
5-celled, brown capsule; NOT ORNAMENTAL.

**TEXTURE:**
Medium to coarse.

**GROWTH RATE:**
Moderate to rapid.

**HABIT:**
Upright and compact; BROADER SPREADING THAN THE SPECIES.

**FAMILY:**
Malvaceae

**LEAF COLOR:** Dark green in summer; brown in fall.

**LEAF DESCRIPTION:** SIMPLE, 2″ to 4″ long and 1 1/2″ to 3″ wide, THICKER THAN THE SPECIES, triangular shape with coarse-toothed, sometimes lobed, margins. ALTERNATE arrangement.

**FLOWER DESCRIPTION:** White, to 6″ across and STAYING OPEN AT NIGHT. Single. Flowers in late summer and continues until the first freeze.

**EXPOSURE/CULTURE:** Full sun to light shade. Adaptable to most soils except too wet or dry. Will withstand heavy pruning, but this should be accomplished in very early spring.

**PEST PROBLEMS:** Beetles, aphids, spider mites, leaf spots, powdery mildew.

**SELECTED CULTIVARS:** None. This is a cultivar.

**RELATED SPECIES:** *H. rosa-sinensis* - This species is noted for large foliage and huge flowers. Unfortunately, it is hardy only to Zone 10, but can be grown as an annual in other zones.

**LANDSCAPE NOTES:** 'Diana' is one of several outstanding triploids introduced by the U.S. National Arboretum. For those familiar with the "old timey" selections, Diana is certainly in a class of its own. Can be used as a screen or specimen in the garden border. OUTSTANDING.

# *Hydrangea paniculata*

**Panicle Hydrangea**

**ZONES:**
4, 5, 6, 7, 8, 9

**HEIGHT:**
8′ to 12′

**WIDTH:**
8′ to 15′

**FRUIT:**
Dehiscent capsule; NOT ORNAMENTAL.

**TEXTURE:**
Coarse

**GROWTH RATE:**
Rapid

**HABIT:**
Rounded and open.

**FAMILY:**
Saxifragaceae

**LEAF COLOR:** Dark green in summer; tinged yellowish or purplish in fall.

**LEAF DESCRIPTION:** SIMPLE, 4″ to 6″ long and half as wide, elliptic or oval shape with serrated margins, downy underneath. OPPOSITE arrangement.

**FLOWER DESCRIPTION:** Yellowish-white, becoming pinkish, tiny, borne in panicles to 10″ long. Flowers July into fall.

**EXPOSURE/CULTURE:** Sun or light shade. Prefers moist, well-drained, organic soil, but is reasonably adaptable. Will take severe pruning if accomplished in very early spring. Maintain natural shape throughout the warm season.

**PEST PROBLEMS:** Leaf spots, mildew.

**SELECTED CULTIVARS:** 'Grandiflora' - (Featured on next page.) 'Praecox' - Similar, but earlier in flowering. 'Tardiva' - Flowers later than the species.

**LANDSCAPE NOTES:** Panicle Hydrangea is a much-used plant of the past, but still has merit in modern landscaping. The plant is hardy and easy to grow, and responds well to a little attention. Choose the location carefully.

## *Hydrangea paniculata 'Grandiflora'*     Peegee Hydrangea

**ZONES:**
3, 4, 5, 6, 7, 8

**HEIGHT:**
8' to 15'

**WIDTH:**
8' to 10'

**FRUIT:**
Dehiscent capsule; NOT ORNAMENTAL.

**TEXTURE:**
Coarse

**GROWTH RATE:**
Rapid

**HABIT:**
Rounded and open; arching when in bloom.

**FAMILY:**
Saxifragaceae

**LEAF COLOR:** Medium green in summer; brown in fall.

**LEAF DESCRIPTION:** SIMPLE, 3" to 4" long and half as wide, elliptic to oval shape with serrated margins. OPPOSITE arrangement.

**FLOWER DESCRIPTION:** White, becoming pink, tiny flowers appearing in 6" to 10" clusters. Flowers in July or August.

**EXPOSURE/CULTURE:** Sun or light shade. Prefers moist, organic, well-drained soil. Plant should be mulched to maintain moisture level. Prune severely, if desired, during winter or very early spring.

**PEST PROBLEMS:** Leaf spots, mildew.

**SELECTED CULTIVARS:** None. This is a cultivar.

**LANDSCAPE NOTES:** PeeGee Hydrangea is a large-flowered shrub that produces abundant flower clusters in late season. Flower color provides interest as it changes from white to pink. Flowers cling for a long period, making this a nice flower panicle for dried arrangements in the home.

# *Ilex verticillata*

**Winterberry**

**ZONES:**
4, 5, 6, 7, 8, 9

**HEIGHT:**
7′ to 12′

**WIDTH:**
8′ to 15′

**FRUIT:**
1/4″ red drupe in late summer, persisting after leaf drop.

**TEXTURE:**
Medium

**GROWTH RATE:**
Slow to moderate.

**HABIT:**
Rounded and spreading; irregular and open.

**FAMILY:**
Aquifoliaceae

**LEAF COLOR:** Dark green in summer, fading to yellowish in fall.

**LEAF DESCRIPTION:** SIMPLE, 2″ to 4″ long and half as wide, elliptic shape with cuneate base and acuminate apex, serrated margins. ALTERNATE arrangement.

**FLOWER DESCRIPTION:** Dioecious; male in cymes, female in axillary clusters; not showy.

**EXPOSURE/CULTURE:** Sun or part shade. Prefers moist, acid soils since it is native to swampy areas. Will not tolerate alkaline soils or droughty conditions. Prune in early spring to thicken, control, or encourage heavy fruiting.

**PEST PROBLEMS:** Leaf spots and mildews.

**BARK/STEMS:** Young stems are green, maturing to grayish-brown.

**SELECTED CULTIVARS:** f. *chrysocarpa* - This form is a yellow-fruited native plant, having fewer berries than the red types. 'Nana' - A dwarf cultivar, but having larger fruits. 'Winter Red' - This most popular cultivar has larger, abundant fruits that hold later into winter.

**RELATED VARIETIES:** *I. decidua* - Possumhaw. Large shrub to small tree size. Fruits are orange to red. Better adapted to alkaline soils. Has noticeable gray bark similar to *I. vomitoria*. *I. serrata* - Japanese Winterberry. This species has slightly smaller leaves and fruit, and is smaller in overall size. Has been crossed with *I. verticillata* to produce hybrids of merit.

**LANDSCAPE NOTES:** Winterberry is probably best utilized in the border as a winter specimen. It is especially attractive with snow-covered branches. The plant blends nicely with evergreens and is great for naturalizing.

## *Kolkwitzia amabilis* 'Pink Cloud'

**Pink Beautybush**

**ZONES:**
5, 6, 7, 8

**HEIGHT:**
8′ to 12′

**WIDTH:**
5′ to 7′

**FRUIT:**
1/4″ brown capsule; NOT ORNAMENTAL.

**TEXTURE:**
Medium

**GROWTH RATE:**
Moderate to rapid.

**HABIT:**
Upright, vase-shaped, and multi-stemmed.

**FAMILY:**
Caprifoliaceae

**LEAF COLOR:** Dark green in summer; brown in fall.

**LEAF DESCRIPTION:** SIMPLE, 1 1/2″ to 3″ long and 1″ to 2 1/4″ wide, ovate shape with acuminate tip and sparsely serrated margins. New leaves downy on both surfaces. OPPOSITE arrangement.

**FLOWER DESCRIPTION:** Pink, 1/2″ long and wide, appearing in clusters (corymbs) in late spring; NOT FRAGRANT.

**EXPOSURE/CULTURE:** Full sun. Prefers organic, loamy soil, but is adaptable to most well-drained soils. Thin out older stems after flowering.

**PEST PROBLEMS:** No serious pests.

**BARK/STEMS:** Has an interesting brown bark that peels on older stems.

**SELECTED CULTIVARS:** None. This is a cultivar of *K. amabilis*.

**LANDSCAPE NOTES:** Beautybush is a plant that is spectacular in bloom, yet blends into the landscape border when not in bloom. Such a plant has merit in adding variety and interest to the garden.

# *Lespedeza bicolor*

**Bicolor Lespedeza, Bush Clover**

**ZONES:**
5, 6, 7, 8

**HEIGHT:**
8' to 10'

**WIDTH:**
8' to 10'

**FRUIT:**
Small, one-seeded pod; NOT ORNAMENTAL.

**TEXTURE:**
Fine to medium.

**GROWTH RATE:**
Rapid

**HABIT:**
Upright, open, and arching.

**FAMILY:**
Fabaceae

**LEAF COLOR:** Medium to dark green in summer; yellowish-brown in fall.

**LEAF DESCRIPTION:** COMPOUND, trifoliate (3 leaflets), leaflets 1" to 1 1/2" long and half as wide, elliptic shape with entire margins. ALTERNATE arrangement.

**FLOWER DESCRIPTION:** Purple, 1/2", appearing in erect 4" panicles in late summer. Attractive and quite showy.

**EXPOSURE/CULTURE:** Full sun or light shade. The plant is adaptable to most well-drained soils. Should be pruned severely in early spring to encourage lush, new growth.

**PEST PROBLEMS:** None

**SELECTED CULTIVARS:** None important.

**LANDSCAPE NOTES:** Bicolor Lespedeza is appropriately used to add interest and color to garden borders. Often used as a conservation plant to stabilize soil, but especially to attract numerous species of birds and other wildlife. This is a plant for naturalizing.

## *Lonicera fragrantissima* — Winter Honeysuckle

**ZONES:**
5, 6, 7, 8, 9

**HEIGHT:**
6' to 9'

**WIDTH:**
6' to 8'

**FRUIT:**
1/4" red berry.

**TEXTURE:**
Fine to medium.

**GROWTH RATE:**
Moderate to rapid.

**HABIT:**
Rounded and somewhat arching.

**FAMILY:**
Caprifoliaceae

**LEAF COLOR:** Deep green in summer; brown in fall.

**LEAF DESCRIPTION:** SIMPLE, 1 1/2" to 3" long and half as wide, elliptic to oval shape with entire margins. Bluish-green beneath. OPPOSITE arrangement.

**FLOWER DESCRIPTION:** Creamy-white, 1/2" long, appearing in pairs before the leaves. Very fragrant. Blooms in late winter.

**EXPOSURE/CULTURE:** Full sun or part shade. Adapts to a wide range of well-drained soils. Somewhat drought-tolerant. Prune severely, if needed, after flowering.

**PEST PROBLEMS:** No serious pests.

**SELECTED CULTIVARS:** None

**LANDSCAPE NOTES:** Winter Honeysuckle is valuable for early color and fragrance in the garden. Often used as a hedge or screen, it makes a good background plant for smaller species in borders. Reliable and easy to grow.

# *Lonicera tatarica*

**Tatarian Honeysuckle**

**ZONES:**
3, 4, 5, 6, 7, 8

**HEIGHT:**
8′ to 12′

**WIDTH:**
8′ to 10′

**FRUIT:**
1/4″ red berry.

**TEXTURE:**
Medium

**GROWTH RATE:**
Moderate

**HABIT:**
Upright and arching.

**FAMILY:**
Caprifoliaceae

**LEAF COLOR:** Dark green (tinged blue) in summer; brown in fall.

**LEAF DESCRIPTION:** SIMPLE, 2″ to 2 1/2″ long and half as wide, ovate or ovate-lanceolate shape with entire margins. OPPOSITE arrangement.

**FLOWER DESCRIPTION:** Pink or white, 1″ long in axillary pairs, appearing with the leaves in mid-spring; FRAGRANT.

**EXPOSURE/CULTURE:** Full sun. Prefers moist, organic, well-drained soil. Prune after flowering, as desired.

**PEST PROBLEMS:** No serious pests.

**SELECTED CULTIVARS:** 'Alba' - Has white flowers. 'Arnold Red' - Very deep red flowers. 'Grandiflora' - Especially large, white flowers. 'Lutea' - Has pink flowers, followed by yellow fruits. 'Nana' - Dwarf form (2′ to 3′) with pink flowers. 'Rosea' - Flowers rose-colored with pink inside. 'Virginalis' - Has large, white flowers.

**LANDSCAPE NOTES:** Tatarian Honeysuckle is best used as a specimen in the garden border. This is a hardy and reliable plant.

## *Philadelphus* x 'Natchez'

**Natchez Mock Orange**

**ZONES:**
5, 6, 7, 8, 9

**HEIGHT:**
8' to 10'

**WIDTH:**
8' to 10'

**FRUIT:**
Brown capsule; NOT ORNA-MENTAL.

**TEXTURE:**
Medium

**GROWTH RATE:**
Rapid

**HABIT:**
Broad-spreading and arching.

**FAMILY:**
Saxifragaceae

**LEAF COLOR:** Medium green in summer; brownish in fall.

**LEAF DESCRIPTION:** SIMPLE, 2" to 3 1/2" long and half as wide, ovate to oval shape with sparsely serrated margins. Veins downy beneath. OPPOSITE arrangement.

**FLOWER DESCRIPTION:** White, 4-petaled, 2" across, solitary or in small racemes. Flowers in May or June; FRAGRANT.

**EXPOSURE/CULTURE:** Sun or part shade. Does best in well-drained, organic soils. Responds well to pruning, but do not prune in late summer or fall.

**PEST PROBLEMS:** Aphids, mildew, leaf spots.

**SELECTED CULTIVARS:** None. This is a cultivar of questionable parentage.

**RELATED SPECIES:** *P. coronarius* - One of the older species having fragrant flowers, but less spectacular than recent forms. *P.* x *lemoinei* - One of the better hybrids with abundant fragrant flowers in late spring. Compact. *P.* x *virginalis* - Another hybrid of unknown parentage, having double or semi-double, white flowers.

**LANDSCAPE NOTES:** Natchez Mock Orange is an excellent plant to add color and fragrance to dull areas of the garden. It is especially handsome in flower, but is best used in groupings with other plants in the garden border.

## *Poncirus trifoliata* — Hardy Orange

**ZONES:**
6, 7, 8, 9

**HEIGHT:**
10′ to 15′

**WIDTH:**
8′ to 12′

**FRUIT:**
Small, yellowish-orange; edible, but sour.

**TEXTURE:**
Medium

**GROWTH RATE:**
Slow

**HABIT:**
Upright and irregular.

**FAMILY:**
Rutaceae

**LEAF COLOR:** Dark green in summmer; yellowish in fall.

**LEAF DESCRIPTION:** COMPOUND (3 leaflets), leaflets 1 1/2″ to 2″ long and half as wide, elliptic to obovate shape with crenate margins. ALTERNATE arrangement.

**FLOWER DESCRIPTION:** White, 2″ across, appearing in axils of thorns. Flowers in mid-spring. Slightly fragrant.

**EXPOSURE/CULTURE:** Full sun. Adaptable to most soils except wet soils. Somewhat drought-tolerant. Selectively prune with CAUTION after flowering.

**PEST PROBLEMS:** Sometimes attacked by mites.

**BARK/STEMS:** Shiny green with 1″ or longer sharp spines. Older stems have brown bark.

**SELECTED CULTIVARS:** None important.

**LANDSCAPE NOTES:** Hardy Orange is an accent or "conversation piece" in the garden. It's best use is probably as an impenetrable hedge to control traffic. Should not be used where children frequent an area.

## *Spiraea prunifolia* 'Plena'

**Bridal Wreath Spirea**

**ZONES:**
4, 5, 6, 7, 8, 9

**HEIGHT:**
6′ to 8′

**WIDTH:**
8′ to 10′

**FRUIT:**
Dehiscent follicle; NOT
ORNAMENTAL.

**TEXTURE:**
Fine

**GROWTH RATE:**
Rapid

**HABIT:**
Open and spreading; arched
branches.

**FAMILY:**
Rosaceae

**LEAF COLOR:** Lustrous green in summer; reddish-orange in fall.

**LEAF DESCRIPTION:** SIMPLE, 1″ to 1 1/2″ long and half as wide, ovate to elliptic shape with coarsely serrated margins, downy underneath. ALTERNATE arrangement.

**FLOWER DESCRIPTION:** White, double, 1/4″ to 1/2″ across, tightly bunched, appearing in early spring.

**EXPOSURE/CULTURE:** Full sun. This is a rugged plant that will grow almost anywhere. Prune heavily and thin stems to ground level after flowering.

**PEST PROBLEMS:** No serious pests.

**SELECTED CULTIVARS:** None

**RELATED SPECIES:** *S. prunifolia* f. *simpliciflora* - The single-flowered version.

**LANDSCAPE NOTES:** Considered by many to be outdated, this plant certainly has a place in modern design. Very few plants are as reliable or bloom as heavily as Bridal Wreath. Can be massed or grown as an early spring specimen in borders.

## *Spiraea x vanhouttei*

**Vanhoutte Spirea**

**ZONES:**
4, 5, 6, 7, 8

**HEIGHT:**
6′ to 10′

**WIDTH:**
8′ to 12′

**FRUIT:**
Dehiscent follicle; NOT ORNAMENTAL.

**TEXTURE:**
Fine

**GROWTH RATE:**
Rapid

**HABIT:**
Spreading; arched branches.

**FAMILY:**
Rosaceae

**LEAF COLOR:** Blue-green in summer; brown in fall.

**LEAF DESCRIPTION:** SIMPLE, 1″ to 1 1/2″ long and 2/3″ to 1″ wide, rhombic to obovate shape with coarsely serrated margins, sometimes shallowly lobed. ALTERNATE arrangement.

**FLOWER DESCRIPTION:** White, 1/2″ in 3″ to 4″ domed clusters; prolific. Flowers in spring.

**EXPOSURE/CULTURE:** Sun. Thrives under a wide range of soils and conditions. Severe pruning or shearing can be accomplished after flowering as desired.

**PEST PROBLEMS:** None

**SELECTED CULTIVARS:** None

**LANDSCAPE NOTES:** Vanhoutte Spirea makes a nice specimen plant or border plant for a massed effect. It is an early bloomer and adds interest to the garden during a dull part of the season. This species is one of the most common. It should be pruned to its natural shape.

## *Syringa vulgaris*

**Common Lilac**

▲ 'Znayma Lenyna'

**ZONES:**
3, 4, 5, 6, 7

**HEIGHT:**
6′ to 12′

**WIDTH:**
6′ to 9′

**FRUIT:**
Dehiscent capsule; NOT ORNAMENTAL.

**TEXTURE:**
Medium to coarse.

**GROWTH RATE:**
Moderate

**HABIT:**
Upright and open; sometimes leggy.

**FAMILY:**
Oleaceae

**LEAF COLOR:** Dark green in summer; no fall color.

**LEAF DESCRIPTION:** SIMPLE, 2 1/2″ to 5″ long and 1 3/4″ to 4″ wide, ovate shape with cordate base and entire margins. OPPOSITE arrangement.

**FLOWER DESCRIPTION:** Lilac color (species), cultivars variable, tiny, in lateral panicles to 10″ long. VERY FRAGRANT. Flowers in April to May.

**EXPOSURE/CULTURE:** Full sun. Prefers organic soil that is neutral or alkaline in reaction. Tolerant of all but wet conditions. Prune selectively after flowering.

**PEST PROBLEMS:** Bacterial blight, leaf spots, mildew, lilac borer, lilac scale. Many of these can be destructive.

**SELECTED CULTIVARS:** Note: Hundreds exist, but some of the best are described here. 'Angel White' - Clusters of pure white flowers. Great for warmer zones. 'Belle de Nancy' - DOUBLE. Pink flowers. 'Blue Skies' - Excellent, light lavender-blue panicles. Rapid grower. Great for warmer zones. A Monrovia Nurseries introduction. 'Charles Joly' - Deep, wine-red flowers. 'Lavender Lady' - Lavender flowers. Requires little chill. A Monrovia Nurseries introduction. 'President Lincoln' - Pure blue. OUTSTANDING. 'Sensation' - Florets purplish-red, edged with white.

**RELATED SPECIES:** *S. persica* - Persian Lilac. More compact species having abundant but smaller blooms. Many cultivars exist.

**LANDSCAPE NOTES:** Lilacs have been popular for their outstanding blooms and fragrance for many years. The current emphasis is on cultivars for the southernmost zones. This is definitely a plant to feature in the garden.

# *Tamarix ramosissima*

**Salt Cedar**

**ZONES:**
3, 4, 5, 6, 7, 8

**HEIGHT:**
10' to 12'

**WIDTH:**
8' to 10'

**FRUIT:**
Brown capsule; NOT ORNA-MENTAL.

**TEXTURE:**
Fine

**GROWTH RATE:**
Rapid

**HABIT:**
Open and airy; irregular and upright.

**FAMILY:**
Tamaricaceae

**LEAF COLOR:** Light to medium green in summer; brownish in fall.

**LEAF DESCRIPTION:** SIMPLE, tiny and scale-like with salt-secreting glands, Juniper-like. ALTERNATE arrangement.

**FLOWER DESCRIPTION:** Pink, 5-petaled, tiny, in slender 2″ terminal racemes that form panicles. Flowers in summer.

**EXPOSURE/CULTURE:** Full sun. Prefers well-drained, sandy soils. Thrives very well in humid or arid conditions. Prune to keep natural, open habit.

**PEST PROBLEMS:** Mildew, rootrot, scale.

**BARK/STEMS:** Reddish-brown and noticeable due to open habit of growth.

**SELECTED CULTIVARS:** 'Rosea' - Rosey-pink flowers. Late flowering.

**LANDSCAPE NOTES:** Salt Cedar is an excellent plant for naturalizing in garden borders or raised beds. Does well in beach plantings or desert plantings. Great for XERISCAPING.

## *Viburnum dilatatum*

**Linden Viburnum**

**ZONES:**
6, 7, 8

**HEIGHT:**
7′ to 8′

**WIDTH:**
5′ to 6′

**FRUIT:**
Clustered, bright red berries (drupes).

**TEXTURE:**
Coarse

**GROWTH RATE:**
Moderate

**HABIT:**
Upright and dense.

**FAMILY:**
Caprifoliaceae

**LEAF COLOR:** Medium green in summer; reddish in fall.

**LEAF DESCRIPTION:** SIMPLE, 3″ to 4″ long and half as wide, oval to obovate shape with coarsely serrated margins. Hairy (downy) on both surfaces. OPPOSITE arrangement.

**FLOWER DESCRIPTION:** White, tiny, in 4″ to 5″ clusters (cymes). Flowers in May and June.

**EXPOSURE/CULTURE:** Sun or light shade. Prefers moist, organic, well-drained soils. Pruning is minimal to maintain shape.

**PEST PROBLEMS:** None

**SELECTED CULTIVARS:** 'Catskill' - A more compact selection with better fall color. 'Xanthocarpum' - Has yellow fruit in the fall.

**LANDSCAPE NOTES:** Linden Viburnum is a plant to feature in the garden border as an accent plant or in massed plantings. It is desirable for its attractive flower clusters in early summer and for its bright red berries in fall. The coarse texture provides additional contrast. This is a low-maintenance plant.

# *Viburnum lantana*

**Wayfaring Tree**

**ZONES:**
3, 4, 5, 6, 7, 8

**HEIGHT:**
8' to 12'

**WIDTH:**
8' to 12'

**FRUIT:**
Clustered red drupes; maturing to black.

**TEXTURE:**
Somewhat coarse.

**GROWTH RATE:**
Moderate.

**HABIT:**
Upright and rounded.

**FAMILY:**
Caprifoliaceae

**LEAF COLOR:** Dark green in summer; purplish in fall.

**LEAF DESCRIPTION:** SIMPLE, 3″ to 5″ long and 2″ to 4″ wide, ovate shape with dentate to serrated margins, pubescent on both surfaces. OPPOSITE arrangement.

**FLOWER DESCRIPTION:** White, tiny, appearing in 4″ cymes in spring.

**EXPOSURE/CULTURE:** Sun or light shade. Prefers well-drained, organic soil and is pH-tolerant. Pruning is minimal in order to maintain natural shape.

**PEST PROBLEMS:** None

**SELECTED CULTIVARS:** 'Rugosum' - Has larger leaves and larger flower clusters.

**LANDSCAPE NOTES:** Wayfaring Tree is valuable for its flower clusters and fruit, which attracts native birds. It should be used in the border as a specimen or in mass as a screen or background plant. Very hardy!

## *Viburnum macrocephalum*　　　**Chinese Snowball**

**ZONES:**
6, 7, 8, 9

**HEIGHT:**
8′ to 12′

**WIDTH:**
6′ to 10′

**FRUIT:**
Non-fruiting

**TEXTURE:**
Medium to coarse.

**GROWTH RATE:**
Moderate

**HABIT:**
Upright and irregularly
rounded.

**FAMILY:**
Caprifoliaceae

**LEAF COLOR:** Dark green in summer; brownish in fall.

**LEAF DESCRIPTION:** SIMPLE, 3″ to 4″ long and half as wide, elliptic shape with entire margins. OPPOSITE arrangement.

**FLOWER DESCRIPTION:** White, 1″ florets forming a round 6″ to 10″ snowball-like cyme. Flowers in May.

**EXPOSURE/CULTURE:** Sun. Adapts to most well-drained soils. Prune after flowering to remove weak branches or to shape.

**PEST PROBLEMS:** No serious pests.

**SELECTED CULTIVARS:** None

**LANDSCAPE NOTES:** Chinese Snowball is a descriptive name for this attention-getting specimen plant. Probably best grown as a specimen in garden borders, or as a lawn specimen as a substitute for small trees. Spectacular in bloom.

# *Viburnum opulus 'Sterile'*

**Eastern Snowball, Snowball Bush**

**ZONES:**
4, 5, 6, 7, 8

**HEIGHT:**
9' to 12'

**WIDTH:**
8' to 15'

**FRUIT:**
Non-fruiting

**TEXTURE:**
Coarse

**GROWTH RATE:**
Moderate

**HABIT:**
Upright and rounded; somewhat arching.

**FAMILY:**
Caprifoliaceae

**LEAF COLOR:** Dark green in summer; purplish-red in fall.

**LEAF DESCRIPTION:** SIMPLE, 3" to 4" long and broad, Maple-like, 3 to 5 lobes, pubescent beneath. OPPOSITE arrangement.

**FLOWER DESCRIPTION:** White, florets forming 3" to 5" snowball-like cymes. Flowers in May.

**EXPOSURE/CULTURE:** Sun. Adaptable to almost any soil type or pH level. Prune after flowering to shape. Very easy to grow.

**PEST PROBLEMS:** Aphids

**SELECTED CULTIVARS:** None. This is a cultivar of *V. opulus,* European Cranberry Viburnum, having 3" flat-topped cymes. Not as showy as 'Sterile'.

**RELATED CULTIVARS:** 'Nanum' - Dwarf form of the species to 4' or less. Has flat-topped blooms like the species.

**LANDSCAPE NOTES:** Eastern Snowball has blooms similar to Chinese Snowball, but they are less numerous and smaller in size. This makes the plant more useful in the average garden because it is less dominating. Very choice plant.

## *Viburnum plicatum var. tomentosum* — **Doublefile Viburnum**

**ZONES:**
5, 6, 7, 8

**HEIGHT:**
9' to 10'

**WIDTH:**
10' to 12'

**FRUIT:**
1/4" red drupes, maturing to black.

**TEXTURE:**
Medium

**GROWTH RATE:**
Moderate

**HABIT:**
Broad-spreading; horizontal branching.

**FAMILY:**
Caprifoliaceae

**LEAF COLOR:** Dark green in summer; brownish in fall.

**LEAF DESCRIPTION:** SIMPLE, 2 1/2" to 4" long and half as wide, ovate to ovate shape with coarsely serrated margins. Pubescent beneath. OPPOSITE arrangement.

**FLOWER DESCRIPTION:** White, 1" in 3" to 4" fat cymes, outer flowers showy, infertile inner flowers not showy, rising above the foliage giving a layered effect. Flowers in April or May.

**EXPOSURE/CULTURE:** Sun or part shade. Prefers well-drained, moist, organic soil. Very sensitive to overwatering. Prune carefully after flowering to maintain horizontal branching.

**PEST PROBLEMS:** None

**SELECTED CULTIVARS:** 'Mariesii' - Flowers larger and standing taller above the foliage. 'Shasta' - Lower-growing (6') and very dense. Flowers are 1 1/2 times as large. Great for smaller gardens.

**LANDSCAPE NOTES:** Doublefile Viburnum offers a beautiful flower display, followed by an abundant berry crop. However, it is especially interesting for its horizontal, layered effect. It should be given a prominent place in the landscape.

## *Viburnum setigerum*

**Tea Viburnum**

**ZONES:**
4, 5, 6, 7, 8

**HEIGHT:**
10' to 12'

**WIDTH:**
6' to 9'

**FRUIT:**
1/4" bright red drupes; OUT-STANDING.

**TEXTURE:**
Medium to coarse.

**GROWTH RATE:**
Moderate

**HABIT:**
Upright and open.

**FAMILY:**
Caprifoliaceae

**LEAF COLOR:** Bluish-red in spring, green in summer, and orange in fall.

**LEAF DESCRIPTION:** SIMPLE, 3" to 5" long and one-third as wide, ovate-oblong shape with sparsely serrated margins. Veins downy underneath. OPPOSITE arrangement.

**FLOWER DESCRIPTION:** White, tiny, appearing in 2" diameter cymes. Flowers in May.

**EXPOSURE/CULTURE:** Sun or light shade. Requires well-drained soil, preferably loamy. Prune after flowering to maintain natural shape and to prevent legginess.

**PEST PROBLEMS:** None

**SELECTED CULTIVARS:** 'Aurantiacum' - Has orange-yellow fruits.

**LANDSCAPE NOTES:** Tea Viburnum was once used in China to make tea. Today, it certainly has a place in home gardens. It is an interesting plant that produces abundant fruit. Attracts many species of birds.

## *Viburnum x burkwoodii 'Mohawk'*    **Mohawk Burkwood Viburnum**

**ZONES:**
4, 5, 6, 7, 8, 9

**HEIGHT:**
6' to 7'

**WIDTH:**
6' to 7'

**FRUIT:**
1/4" to 1/3" bright red drupes.

**TEXTURE:**
Medium to coarse.

**GROWTH RATE:**
Moderate

**HABIT:**
Upright and irregular.

**FAMILY:**
Caprifoliaceae

**LEAF COLOR:** Dark green in summer; orange-red in fall.

**LEAF DESCRIPTION:** SIMPLE, 2" to 4" long and half as wide, ovate to oblong-ovate shape with sparsely serrated margins, tomentose (hairy) beneath. OPPOSITE arrangement.

**FLOWER DESCRIPTION:** White (buds red before opening), tiny, in 3" to 4" cymes. Flowers open in spring. VERY FRAGRANT.

**EXPOSURE/CULTURE:** Sun to light shade. Prefers well-drained, moist, organic soil of any pH. Will not tolerate wet soils. Prune carefully to maintain natural appearance. Can be sheared if desired.

**PEST PROBLEMS:** Nematodes

**SELECTED CULTIVARS:** None. This is a cultivar of *V. x burkwoodii,* which has pink buds and less fragrance. In addition, it grows 1/3 larger than 'Mohawk'.

**RELATED CULTIVARS:** 'Chenault' - Flowers have a slight rose tint, fading to white. Foliage is bronze in fall.

**LANDSCAPE NOTES:** Mohawk Viburnum is probably the best of the Burkwood Viburnums. The red buds are slow in opening, giving this specimen plant a long period of interest in the natural garden border.

# Vitex agnus-castus

**Vitex, Chaste Tree**

▲ 'Alba'

**ZONES:**
6, 7, 8, 9

**HEIGHT:**
8' to 12'

**WIDTH:**
8' to 12'

**FRUIT:**
Tiny drupe; NOT ORNAMEN-TAL.

**TEXTURE:**
Medium

**GROWTH RATE:**
Moderate to rapid.

**HABIT:**
Multi-stemmed; open and irregular.

**FAMILY:**
Verbenaceae

**LEAF COLOR:** Dark green to gray-green in summer; no fall color.

**LEAF DESCRIPTION:** COMPOUND (palmate with 5 to 7 leaflets; usually 5), leaflets oblong-elliptic to lanceolate shape with occasional teeth (serrated) toward the tip. Grayish tomentose beneath. OPPOSITE arrangement.

**FLOWER DESCRIPTION:** Lilac to lavender color, small, in panicles to 12" long, appearing summer through early fall. Showy but subdued. Fragrant.

**EXPOSURE/CULTURE:** Full sun. Prefers well-drained loamy soil, but is adaptable to dry, sandy exposures. Prune to control size, but do not destroy natural, open habit.

**PEST PROBLEMS:** No serious pests.

**SELECTED CULTIVARS:** 'Alba' - Has white flower panicles. 'Latiflolia' - Compound leaves are shorter and broader. 'Rosea' - Has pink flower panicles.

**RELATED SPECIES:** *V. negundo* - This species attains greater size (to 20') and has leaflets of three rather than five.

**LANDSCAPE NOTES:** Chaste Tree is a late-blooming plant that blends into the border nicely without dominating. It is great for beach plantings, and has possibilities for XERISCAPING. Should be more widely used.

## *Weigela florida*

**Weigela**

▲ 'Java Red'                                                                  ▲ 'Variegated Nana'

**ZONES:**
4, 5, 6, 7, 8

**HEIGHT:**
6' to 10'

**WIDTH:**
6' to 10'

**FRUIT:**
Brown capsule; NOT ORNA-MENTAL.

**TEXTURE:**
Medium

**GROWTH RATE:**
Moderate

**HABIT:**
Erect with arching branches.

**FAMILY:**
Caprifoliaceae

**LEAF COLOR:** Medium green in summer; brownish in fall.

**LEAF DESCRIPTION:** SIMPLE, 2 1/2″ to 4″ long and half as wide, obovate to elliptic shape with finely serrated margins, sometimes undulating. Veins pubescent underneath. OPPOSITE arrangement.

**FLOWER DESCRIPTION:** Rose-pink (cultivars vary), 1″ in small clusters. Flowers in April to May. Very abundant and showy.

**EXPOSURE/CULTURE:** Sun. The plant is adaptable to most well-drained soils. Easy to grow. Prune to remove dead branches or to control.

**PEST PROBLEMS:** None

**SELECTED CULTIVARS:** 'Alba' - Has white flowers. 'Bristol Beauty' - Ruby-red flowers with a long bloom period. 'Eva Supreme' - Medium size (to 5') and having deep crimson flowers. 'Java Red' - Buds carmine-red; flowers deep pink. Dwarf form (4'). 'Minuet' - Very dwarf (2' to 3') with rose-pink flowers and dark green foliage. Foliage is purple-tinged. 'Red Prince' - Medium size (6') with rich red flowers. 'Variegated Nana' - Very dwarf (2' to 3'). Leaves edged in yellow. Deep rose flowers.

**LANDSCAPE NOTES:** Weigela is valued for its use as a specimen plant or border plant. It blooms profusely during spring and is spectacular. A low-maintenance plant that should not be used as a foundation plant. Variegation is bland compared to many variegated plants.

# Chapter 9

# SMALL TREES

**S**mall trees are those trees that mature at approximately 20 feet or less in height. As with any attempt at grouping, there will be some plants that are "borderline" with other size groups. The plants in this chapter include those that are small under average landscape conditions. For instance, Flowering Dogwood can attain a height of 30 feet, but is usually much smaller under average landscape conditions.

The popularity of smaller trees has been influenced by the trend toward smaller residential properties in suburban America. This chapter includes some of the more interesting plants in landscape horticulture. Some possible uses in modern landscaping are as follows:

▼ Shade. Many are useful for primary shade in smaller gardens or near patios and porches.
▼ Variety. Just as we need variety in height of shrubs, small trees provide added interest.
▼ Groupings. The scale of small trees allows massing of interesting specimens.
▼ Raised planters and berms. Such features are often too small to accomodate larger trees.
▼ Foundation plantings. Small trees are usually more appropriate in foundation bed areas (relative to scale), and they are less likely to damage foundations.
▼ Screening. The lower branching habit of many small trees allows some screening without the use of larger shrubs or man-made materials. Often, a well-placed small tree can provide just the right amount of screening for an area.
▼ Color. The small deciduous trees include some of the more spectacular flowering trees. Many have additional interest in fall with colorful leaves or fruit.

## *Cedrus atlantica* 'Glauca Pendula'　　　Weeping Blue Atlas Cedar

**ZONES:**
6, 7, 8, 9

**HEIGHT:**
10'+

**WIDTH:**
10'+

**FRUIT:**
2 1/2" to 3" brown cone.

**TEXTURE:**
Fine

**GROWTH RATE:**
Slow

**HABIT:**
Irregular, spreading, and weeping.

**FAMILY:**
Pinaceae

**LEAF COLOR:** Ice blue to blue-gray.

**LEAF DESCRIPTION:** NEEDLE-LIKE, 1/2" to 3/4" long, pointed at the apex, singly or spirally arranged on stems.

**FLOWER DESCRIPTION:** Monoecious; male cones 3" long and yellowish-green; female cones purplish, maturing to brown.

**EXPOSURE/CULTURE:** Full sun. Requires well-drained soil, but is adaptable to sand or clay. Pruning is usually not necessary, but pruning might be desirable to control shape. Usually requires staking in youth.

**PEST PROBLEMS:** Rootrot

**SELECTED CULTIVARS:** None. This is a cultivar of *Cedrus atlantica,* a large evergreen tree.

**RELATED CULTIVARS:** 'Pendula' - Green-needled version, having erect habit in youth, then weeping.

**LANDSCAPE NOTES:** Weeping Blue Atlas Cedar is a dramatic accent plant with each plant developing its own unique character. Use one plant anywhere in the garden where accent is needed or desired. Cannot go unnoticed.

# *Chamaecyparis pisifera 'Filifera'*

**ZONES:**
4, 5, 6, 7, 8

**HEIGHT:**
15′ to 25′

**WIDTH:**
15′ to 20′

**FRUIT:**
3/8″ orange-brown cone; seldom present.

**TEXTURE:**
Fine

**GROWTH RATE:**
Moderate

**HABIT:**
Pyramidal and dense; branches drooping.

**FAMILY:**
Cupressaceae

**LEAF COLOR:** Dark green.

**LEAF DESCRIPTION:** SCALE-LIKE (juvenile leaves may be awl-like), 2-ranked (opposite pairs), tip sharply acuminate, branchlets filamentous or cord-like.

**FLOWER DESCRIPTION:** Monoecious; NOT CONSPICUOUS.

**EXPOSURE/CULTURE:** Full sun. Prefers well-drained, moist, organic soil of acidic reaction. NOT FOR ARID CLIMATES. Pruning is usually not necessary or desirable.

**PEST PROBLEMS:** No serious pests.

**BARK/STEMS:** Reddish-brown and smooth; exfoliating in thin strips.

**SELECTED CULTIVARS:** None. This is a cultivar of *C. pisifera*, a large, non-pendulous evergreen tree.

**RELATED CULTIVARS:** 'Filifera Aurea' - Similar to above, but having bright yellow foliage. Very noticeable.

**LANDSCAPE NOTES:** Threadleaf Falsecypress is a reliable evergreen tree that maintains its shape with little or no shearing. It is probably best used as a specimen plant to feature in a well-selected site. Drooping foliage is quite interesting and attractive. Easy to grow.

## *Eriobotrya japonica*                                   Loquat

**ZONES:**
8, 9, 10

**HEIGHT:**
15' to 20'

**WIDTH:**
12' to 16'

**FRUIT:**
1" to 2" yellow fruits in spring; edible.

**TEXTURE:**
Coarse

**GROWTH RATE:**
Rapid

**HABIT:**
Rounded and spreading.

**FAMILY:**
Rosaceae

**LEAF COLOR:** Dark green.

**LEAF DESCRIPTION:** SIMPLE, 6" to 10" long and one-third as wide, oval-oblong shape with coarsely serrated margins, veins recessed, downy. ALTERNATE arrangement.

**FLOWER DESCRIPTION:** White, tiny, in 5" panicles, appearing in November and December. Showy, but not spectacular.

**EXPOSURE/CULTURE:** Sun or light shade. Prospers in moist, well-drained, loamy to sandy soils. Can be pruned or sheared as desired.

**PEST PROBLEMS:** Fire blight.

**BARK/STEMS:** Young stems green and downy; older bark brownish-gray and flaking.

**SELECTED CULTIVARS:** 'Gold Nugget' - Has pear-shaped, yellow-orange fruit in summer.

**LANDSCAPE NOTES:** Loquat is used as a specimen plant and has tropical-like foliage. It is one of the best trees for espalier or semi-espalier, but is usually grown in lawn plantings. Edible fruits can be used for jams and jellies.

# Pinus densiflora 'Umbraculifera'

**Tanyosho Pine,
Japanese Umbrella Pine**

**ZONES:**
5, 6, 7

**HEIGHT:**
6′ to 12′

**WIDTH:**
10′ to 15′

**FRUIT:**
2″ brown, oblong cone; pendulous; solitary or bunched.

**TEXTURE:**
Medium

**GROWTH RATE:**
Slow

**HABIT:**
Upright and spreading; flat, umbrella-like head.

**FAMILY:**
Pinaceae

**LEAF COLOR:** Bright green.

**LEAF DESCRIPTION:** NEEDLE-LIKE, 3″ to 4″ long, finely serrated margins, needles in fascicles of 2, bunched and brush-like at stem tips.

**FLOWER DESCRIPTION:** Monoecious; NOT ORNAMENTAL.

**EXPOSURE/CULTURE:** Full sun. Tolerates a wide range of well-drained soils. Can prune new "candle" growth in spring, if desired, to thicken. Best left natural.

**PEST PROBLEMS:** Insects: pine moths, weevils, borers, scales. Diseases: rusts, blights, and nematodes. (Check with local Extension Service regarding pests of *Pinus* in your area.)

**SELECTED CULTIVARS:** None. This is a cultivar of *P. densiflora*, Japanese Red Pine, a very large evergreen tree.

**LANDSCAPE NOTES:** Tanyosho Pine is a plant with very interesting form. It is best used where a Japanese garden effect is desirable, or anywhere accent is desired in the garden. This is an outstanding small tree and rivals the best of the Japanese Pines.

## *Prunus caroliniana*

**Cherry-laurel**

**ZONES:**
7, 8, 9, 10

**HEIGHT:**
15' to 25'

**WIDTH:**
12' to 20'

**FRUIT:**
1/4" to 1/2" black berries (drupes).

**TEXTURE:**
Medium

**GROWTH RATE:**
Rapid

**HABIT:**
Oval shape; irregular.

**FAMILY:**
Rosaceae

**LEAF COLOR:** Dark green.

**LEAF DESCRIPTION:** SIMPLE, 2" to 3" long and half as wide, oblong-elliptic to lanceolate shape with entire margins. ALTERNATE arrangement.

**FLOWER DESCRIPTION:** White, 5-petaled, tiny, in 3" to 4" racemes. Flowers in early spring. Fragrant.

**EXPOSURE/CULTURE:** Sun or part shade. Prefers well-drained, moist soils. Can be pruned or sheared to dense habit. Responds favorably to annual fertilization.

**PEST PROBLEMS:** No serious pests.

**SELECTED CULTIVARS:** 'Bright 'n Tight' - Compact habit and well-branched structure without shearing. A Monrovia Nursery introduction.

**LANDSCAPE NOTES:** Cherry Laurel grows naturally in shrub-form, but the lower branches are often removed for true tree-form effect. It is a versatile plant, having many uses from specimen plant to unclipped hedge. Considered easy to grow, but requires some maintenance.

# *Acer barbatum*

**Florida Maple, Southern Sugar Maple**

**ZONES:**
7, 8, 9

**HEIGHT:**
25' to 30'

**WIDTH:**
15' to 20'

**FRUIT:**
1" to 1 1/2" samara (winged) in spring after flowers.

**TEXTURE:**
Medium

**GROWTH RATE:**
Moderate

**HABIT:**
Upright; spreading.

**FAMILY:**
Aceraceae

**LEAF COLOR:** Medium green in summer; yellow in fall.

**LEAF DESCRIPTION:** SIMPLE, 2" to 3" long and 2" to 4 1/2" wide, 3 to 5 lobes (palmately lobed), lobules rounded. OPPOSITE arrangement.

**FLOWER DESCRIPTION:** Greenish-yellow; NOT ORNAMENTAL.

**EXPOSURE/CULTURE:** Sun or shade. Prefers moist, organic, well-drained soil. Root system should not be confined. Not for parking lots. Pruning is usually not needed.

**PEST PROBLEMS:** No serious pests.

**BARK/STEMS:** Young stems smooth and gray; darker and ridged with age.

**SELECTED CULTIVARS:** None

**LANDSCAPE NOTES:** Florida Maple is a small-growing tree that is limited to the southern states. It is a native tree that can be used in smaller gardens where Maple is desired. Has good fall color, as with most Maples.

## *Acer buergeranum* — Trident Maple

**ZONES:**
5, 6, 7, 8, 9

**HEIGHT:**
20′ to 25′

**WIDTH:**
15′ to 20′

**FRUIT:**
1″ samara (winged) in fall.

**TEXTURE:**
Medium

**GROWTH RATE:**
Moderate

**HABIT:**
Oval or rounded.

**FAMILY:**
Aceraceae

**LEAF COLOR:** Green in summer; yellow, orange, or red in fall.

**LEAF DESCRIPTION:** SIMPLE, 2″ to 4″ long and 2″ to 3″ wide, palmately lobed (3 lobes), lobes pointing forward. OPPOSITE arrangement.

**FLOWER DESCRIPTION:** Yellow-green, appearing with leaves in spring; NOT NOTICEABLE.

**EXPOSURE/CULTURE:** Full sun. Prefers well-drained, organic soil, but is more drought-tolerant than most Maple species. Prune weak or dead branches.

**PEST PROBLEMS:** No serious pests.

**BARK/STEMS:** Gray-brown; peeling to expose orange-brown areas.

**SELECTED CULTIVARS:** None important.

**LANDSCAPE NOTES:** Trident Maple is an attractive small tree for lawn or border areas. It has excellent fall color and stays small enough for small gardens or patio areas. It works well in raised planters or berms, and is more drought-tolerant than other Maples.

# *Acer palmatum*

## Dwarf Green Japanese Maple

▲ 'Roseo Marginata'

**ZONES:**
5, 6, 7, 8

**HEIGHT:**
15′ to 20′ (after many years)

**WIDTH:**
15′ to 20′

**FRUIT:**
1/2″ to 1″ samara in late summer or fall.

**TEXTURE:**
Medium

**GROWTH RATE:**
Very slow.

**HABIT:**
Broad-spreading; open.

**FAMILY:**
Aceraceae

**LEAF COLOR:** Medium green in summer; yellow, red, or orange in fall.

**LEAF DESCRIPTION:** SIMPLE, 3″ to 5″ long and wide, palmately lobed (5 to 7; usually 5), lobes doubly serrated. OPPOSITE arrangement.

**FLOWER DESCRIPTION:** Reddish-purple, tiny, appearing in spring; NOT USUALLY NOTICEABLE.

**EXPOSURE/CULTURE:** Sun or shade. Best in light shade. Prefers well-drained, organic, moist soil. Not drought-tolerant. Provide mulch for best growth. Pruning is usually not necessary.

**PEST PROBLEMS:** Chewing insects; not frequent.

**BARK/STEMS:** Young stems reddish; older bark is smooth and gray.

**SELECTED CULTIVARS:** 'Roseo-Marginata' - Variegated form with pink leaf margins. 'Sangokaku' - Green leaves with red margins. Young bark is coral in color. (Note: Red selections on the next page.)

**LANDSCAPE NOTES:** Dwarf Japanese Maple is the ultimate small tree. It has tree-like qualities even when very young. Since it is slow-growing, it can be used in small gardens or cramped areas. It is great as a specimen in the foundation, borders, or accent beds. Not as popular as the red forms, but just as beautiful.

# *Acer palmatum var. atropurpureum* — Dwarf Red Japanese Maple

▲ 'Bloodgood'

**ZONES:**
5, 6, 7, 8

**HEIGHT:**
15' to 20'

**WIDTH:**
15' to 20'

**FRUIT:**
1/2" to 1" samara in late summer to fall.

**TEXTURE:**
Medium

**GROWTH RATE:**
Very slow.

**HABIT:**
Broad-spreading; open.

**FAMILY:**
Aceraceae

**LEAF COLOR:** Red through most of season, sometimes fading to green; red in fall.

**LEAF DESCRIPTION:** SIMPLE, 3" to 5" long and wide, palmately lobed (5 to 7); usually 5 (lobes doubly serrated or finely serrated. OPPOSITE arrangement.)

**FLOWER DESCRIPTION:** Reddish-purple, tiny, appearing in spring; NOT USUALLY NOTICEABLE.

**EXPOSURE/CULTURE:** Sun or shade. Prefers moist roots on a well-drained site. Provide mulch. Pruning is usually not necessary.

**PEST PROBLEMS:** Chewing insects; not frequent.

**BARK/STEMS:** Young stems reddish; older bark is smooth and gray in color.

**SELECTED CULTIVARS:** 'Bloodgood' - Generally considered the best for holding red color in summer. 'Burgundy Lace' - Delicate, narrow lobes that are lace-like. 'Oshio-beni' - Bright red leaves; finely serrated. (Note: Dissected types featured on next page.)

**LANDSCAPE NOTES:** Red Japanese Maple is one of the most prized small trees in landscaping. Its red foliage makes it a noticeable specimen plant that stays compact for many years. It is often selected for various habits of growth such as crooked trunks or branches. EXPENSIVE.

## *Acer palmatum* var. *dissectum* 'Atropurpureum'*

▲ 'Burgundy Lace'

**ZONES:**
5, 6, 7, 8

**HEIGHT:**
6' to 10'

**WIDTH:**
6' to 10'

**FRUIT:**
1/2" to 1" samara in summer and fall.

**TEXTURE:**
Medium

**GROWTH RATE:**
Slow

**HABIT:**
Round and arching; dense.

**FAMILY:**
Accraceae

**LEAF COLOR:** Red, fading to green in late summer; red in fall.

**LEAF DESCRIPTION:** SIMPLE, 4" to 6" long and wide, palmately lobed (5 to 7, usually), lobes cut to petiole, fern-like and delicate.

**FLOWER DESCRIPTION:** Reddish; NOT NOTICEABLE.

**EXPOSURE/CULTURE:** Sun or shade. Best in part shade. Prefers moist, organic, well-drained soils. Not drought-tolerant. Pruning is minimal to maintain natural shape.

**PEST PROBLEMS:** None

**BARK/STEMS:** Smooth gray on older stems; reddish and glossy on new growth.

**SIMILAR CULTIVARS:** 'Crimson Queen' - Very fine-cut foliage of bright crimson-red. 'Dissectum Flavescens' - Dwarf form (to 6') with yellow-green foliage. Orange in fall. 'Filiferum Purpureum' - Very dark red foliage, changing to bronze-green. 'Garnet' - Garnet colored leaves all season. Very popular. 'Viride' - Has finely cut green leaves.

**LANDSCAPE NOTES:** Cutleaf Japanese Maple is the most refined of the Japanese Maples. It forms a dense mound of beautiful foliage and should be given a prominent place, especially near an entry. It is expensive and found in the finest landscapes.

*****COMMON NAMES:** Threadleaf Japanese Maple, Cutleaf Japanese Maple

# *Albizia julibrissin*

**Mimosa Tree, Silk Tree**

**ZONES:**
6, 7, 8, 9

**HEIGHT:**
20′ to 30′

**WIDTH:**
20′ to 30′

**FRUIT:**
6″ brown pod; bean-like.

**TEXTURE:**
Medium

**GROWTH RATE:**
Rapid

**HABIT:**
Flat-topped and broad-spreading.

**FAMILY:**
Fabaceae

**LEAF COLOR:** Dark green in summmer; brown in fall.

**LEAF DESCRIPTION:** BIPINNATELY COMPOUND, leaflets 1/2″ long, leaflets oblong shape with entire margins, folding at night. ALTERNATE arrangement of compound leaves.

**FLOWER DESCRIPTION:** Rose-pink, 1″ to 2 1/2″, standing above foliage, brush-like with numerous hair-size stamens. Flowers in summer.

**EXPOSURE/CULTURE:** Sun. Very adaptable to soil type and will thrive on poor, neglected sites. Often appears on idle land. Prune to remove broken limbs. Susceptible to breakage due to brittle wood.

**PEST PROBLEMS:** Mimosa Wilt (destructive), webworms.

**BARK/STEMS:** Smooth, medium gray with many lenticels; almost cork-like.

**SELECTED CULTIVARS:** 'Charlotte' - Reported to be wilt-resistant. 'Tryon' - Reported to be wilt-resistant. 'Rosea' - Has deeper rose-colored blooms.

**LANDSCAPE NOTES:** Mimosa is a beautiful tree, especially in bloom. Unfortunately, it was almost eradicated by Mimosa Wilt, but appears to be making a comeback. Wilt-resistant cultivars have been reported in recent years. Definitely a specimen shade tree. ATTRACTS HUMMINGBIRDS!

# *Amelanchier x grandiflora*

## Apple Serviceberry

**ZONES:**
4, 5, 6, 7, 8, 9

**HEIGHT:**
20' to 25'

**WIDTH:**
15' to 20'

**FRUIT:**
1/4" to 1/3" black pome; edible.

**TEXTURE:**
Medium

**GROWTH RATE:**
Moderate

**HABIT:**
Upright and rounded.

**FAMILY:**
Rosaceae

**LEAF COLOR:** Purplish in spring, maturing to green; yellow or orange in fall.

**LEAF DESCRIPTION:** SIMPLE, 2" to 3" long and half as wide, broad elliptic shape with rounded or slightly cordate base, serrated margins, downy underneath, sparsely downy above. ALTERNATE arrangement.

**FLOWER DESCRIPTION:** White, pinkish in bud, 1 1/2" on racemes in spring, 5-petaled. Effective for about a week.

**EXPOSURE/CULTURE:** Full sun or part shade. Prefers well-drained, fertile soil, but will survive under a wide range of conditions. Will withstand dry conditions.

**PEST PROBLEMS:** Leaf spots, fire blight, and chewing insects.

**BARK/STEMS:** Green in youth, maturing brown, then gray with fissures.

**SELECTED CULTIVARS:** 'Autumn Brilliance' - A hardy cultivar with red fall foliage that holds longer than the species. 'Cole' - A new cultivar noted for excellent red fall color. 'Princess Diana' - A very hardy selection with excellent red-orange in fall. 'Robin Hill' - Has true pink buds that fade to white when opening.

**RELATED SPECIES:** *A. arborea* - Downy Serviceberry. This species has gray-green, downy new leaves and white flowers. Has smaller leaves and shorter racemes than *A. grandiflora*. *A. canadensis* - Shadblow Serviceberry. This is a smaller, more shrub-like species with smaller flowers. It is a multi-stemmed plant that spreads by suckers. *A. laevis* - Allegheny Serviceberry. This species is similar to *A. arborea* except that young leaves are purplish-bronze and glabrous. Has orange to red fall color.

**LANDSCAPE NOTES:** Apple Serviceberry is a cross between *A. arborea* and *A. laevis*. It has larger leaves and flowers than either parent. It makes a nice specimen for lawns, garden borders, accent beds, and groupings. Attracts birds.

## *Cercidiphyllum japonicum* 'Pendula'　　Weeping Katsura Tree

**ZONES:**
5, 6, 7, 8

**HEIGHT:**
15' to 20'

**WIDTH:**
20' to 25'

**FRUIT:**
3/4" brown follicles; NOT ORNAMENTAL.

**TEXTURE:**
Medium

**GROWTH RATE:**
Moderate

**HABIT:**
Rounded and weeping.

**FAMILY:**
Cercidiphyllaceae

**LEAF COLOR:** Bluish-green in summer; yellowish in fall.

**LEAF DESCRIPTION:** SIMPLE, 2" to 3" long and wide, broad oval shape with cordate base and crenate margins. (Almost reniform in shape.) OPPOSITE arrangement.

**FLOWER DESCRIPTION:** Dioecious; NOT ORNAMENTAL.

**EXPOSURE/CULTURE:** Sun. The plant is adaptable to soil types, but does not tolerate drought. Mulch and provide water during hot, dry periods. Difficult to transplant. Pruning is usually not necessary.

**PEST PROBLEMS:** No serious pests.

**BARK/STEMS:** Brown to grayish; long, shallow, and vertical furrows.

**SELECTED CULTIVARS:** None. This is a cultivar of *C. japonicum,* a large tree.

**LANDSCAPE NOTES:** Weeping Katsura is a dramatic and interesting specimen plant. Given adequate space, it can constitute a focal point by itself. Not for mass planting. Use as a lawn specimen or in a broad border.

# *Cercis canadensis*

**Eastern Redbud**

▲ 'Alba'

**ZONES:**
4, 5, 6, 7, 8, 9

**HEIGHT:**
20' to 25'

**WIDTH:**
20' to 25'

**FRUIT:**
3" to 5" bean-like, brown pod.

**TEXTURE:**
Medium

**GROWTH RATE:**
Moderate

**HABIT:**
Rounded; multi-stemmed.

**FAMILY:**
Fabaceae

**LEAF COLOR:** Medium green in summmer; yellow in fall.

**LEAF DESCRIPTION:** SIMPLE, 3 1/2" to 5" long and wide, broad cordate shape with entire margins. Petiole enlarged at base of leaf. ALTERNATE arrangement.

**FLOWER DESCRIPTION:** Lavender-pink, eventually losing purple tinge, 1/2" and pea-like, borne solitary or in small bunches. Flowers in early spring. Attractive.

**EXPOSURE/CULTURE:** Sun or shade. Prefers well-drained, moist soils but is tolerant of all but wet soils. Prune to remove dead or weak branches. Allow to develop natural, multi-stem habit.

**PEST PROBLEMS:** Stem canker.

**BARK/STEMS:** Mature bark is reddish-brown to almost black; narrow, shallow ridges.

**SELECTED CULTIVARS:** 'Alba' - Has white flowers. 'Forest Pansy' - Pink flowers with scarlet-purple to maroon leaves. (Featured on next page.)

**RELATED SPECIES:** *C. reniformis* - This species is noted for its lustrous, almost waxy green leaves. Cultivar 'Oklahoma' has dark purple blooms and is possibly more drought-tolerant.

**LANDSCAPE NOTES:** Redbud is one of the first trees to bloom in late winter or early spring. Its perfect heart-shaped leaves add interest during summer. It is a good substitute for Dogwood since the stem structure and plant size are similar. One of the best!

## *Cercis canadensis* 'Forest Pansy'     Forest Pansy Eastern Redbud

**ZONES:**
4, 5, 6, 7, 8, 9

**HEIGHT:**
20′ to 25′

**WIDTH:**
20′ to 25′

**FRUIT:**
4″ bean-like pod.

**TEXTURE:**
Medium

**GROWTH RATE:**
Moderate

**HABIT:**
Rounded head and spreading; often multi-stemmed.

**FAMILY:**
Fabaceae

**LEAF COLOR:** Scarlet-purple, maturing to maroon.

**LEAF DESCRIPTION:** SIMPLE, 3″ to 5″ long and wide, cordate shape with entire margins. Petiole enlarged at base of leaf. ALTERNATE arrangement.

**FLOWER DESCRIPTION:** Pink, 1/2″, solitary or in small groups. Flowers in early spring. Attractive.

**EXPOSURE/CULTURE:** Sun or light shade. Colors best in full sun. Adaptable to most well-drained soils. Pruning is usually not necessary. Looks best if allowed to develop as multi-stemmed tree.

**PEST PROBLEMS:** No serious pests.

**BARK/STEMS:** Young stems are dark red; becoming reddish-brown to reddish-gray with age.

**SELECTED CULTIVARS:** None. This is a cultivar.

**LANDSCAPE NOTES:** Forest Pansy is a bold specimen plant that should be carefully planned for location in the garden. Summer foliage is outstanding and can be utilized to brighten dull areas of the garden. This is a newer selection that will be widely used.

# *Chilopsis linearis*

## Desert Willow

'Burgundy' Courtesy of Monrovia Nursery Co.

**ZONES:**
7, 8, 9, 10

**HEIGHT:**
to 20'+

**WIDTH:**
to 20'+

**FRUIT:**
6" to 8" cylindrical pod (capsule); NOT ORNAMENTAL.

**TEXTURE:**
Fine

**GROWTH RATE:**
Moderate

**HABIT:**
Irregularly rounded and open.

**FAMILY:**
Bignoniaceae

**LEAF COLOR:** Medium green in summer; brownish in fall.

**LEAF DESCRIPTION:** SIMPLE, 4" to 8" long and 1/4" to 3/8" wide, linear-lanceolate shape with entire margins, often curving. Thicker than leaves of *Salix* species. ALTERNATE arrangement.

**FLOWER DESCRIPTION:** Variable color (white, pink, lilac, lavender, or burgundy) depending on cultivar. 2" to 2 1/2" long, funnel-form with 5 lobes. Flowers in late spring and repeats throughout the season.

**EXPOSURE/CULTURE:** Full sun. Prefers light, moist, well-drained soil. Does not perform in heavy clay. pH-adaptable and drought-tolerant. Thrives in the Southwest. Pruning is minimal and selective.

**PEST PROBLEMS:** No serious pests.

**BARK/STEMS:** Young stems green, maturing to red-brown; older bark is gray-brown and irregularly furrowed.

**SELECTED CULTIVARS:** 'Alba' - Has white flowers. 'Barronco' - Has lavender flowers. 'Burgundy' - Has burgundy colored flowers.

**LANDSCAPE NOTES:** Desert Willow is a nice tree for the South or Southwest where droughty conditions exist. It is a versatile tree that can be used as a lawn specimen, in garden borders, accent beds, patios, and other areas. It has possibilities as a street tree for urban conditions, and is great for xeriscaping.

## *Cornus alternifolia* — Pagoda Dogwood

**ZONES:**
3, 4, 5, 6, 7

**HEIGHT:**
20′ to 25′

**WIDTH:**
15′ to 30′

**FRUIT:**
1/4″ bluish-black drupes in late summer.

**TEXTURE:**
Medium

**GROWTH RATE:**
Moderate

**HABIT:**
Horizontal, spreading; branches forming interesting tiers.

**FAMILY:**
Cornaceae

**LEAF COLOR:** Medium to dark green in summer; yellowish to red-purple in fall.

**LEAF DESCRIPTION:** SIMPLE, 2 1/2″ to 5″ long and half as wide, ovate to elliptic shape with entire margins, margins often undulate (wavy), 5 to 6 vein pairs. ALTERNATE arrangement, bunched at stem tip.

**FLOWER DESCRIPTION:** Yellowish-white, tiny, in 2″ to 2 1/2″ flat-topped clusters (cymes), appearing for 1 to 2 weeks in May or June. Fragrant.

**EXPOSURE/CULTURE:** Does best in partial shade but is sun-tolerant. The plant prefers moist, well-drained soil of acidic reaction. Does not tolerate "dry feet." Pruning is usually not necessary.

**PEST PROBLEMS:** Leaf spot, twig blight, cankers, borers. Healthy plants are not usually bothered by cankers or borers.

**BARK/STEMS:** Young stems vary from brown to purplish; older bark is gray with shallow ridges.

**SELECTED CULTIVARS:** 'Argentea' - Leaves variegated with white markings. Sometimes listed as 'Variegata'. Not common.

**LANDSCAPE NOTES:** Pagoda Dogwood is an interesting tree that is often overlooked in landscape planning. The horizontal branching habit is useful in breaking strong vertical lines, such as corners of structures. This plant is ideal for naturalizing in woodland properties or in shaded borders. The plant often flowers profusely in ideal locations, and the berries attract birds to the garden in late summer.

## *Cornus florida*　　　　White Flowering Dogwood

◄ 'Cherokee Princess'

**ZONES:**
5, 6, 7, 8, 9

**HEIGHT:**
20' to 30'

**WIDTH:**
20' to 25'

**FRUIT:**
1/2" red drupes; clustered. VERY ATTRACTIVE.

**TEXTURE:**
Medium

**GROWTH RATE:**
Moderate

**HABIT:**
Rounded and spreading; often multi-stemmed.

**FAMILY:**
Cornaceae

**LEAF COLOR:** Medium green in season; red in fall.

**LEAF DESCRIPTION:** SIMPLE, 3" to 5" long and 2" to 3" wide, ovate to oval shape with entire margins or slightly undulate, veins curving to parallel leaf margins. OPPOSITE arrangement.

**FLOWER DESCRIPTION:** White, 2" to 4"+. The "flower" is actually 4 bracts, with the tiny true flowers being yellow-green and clustered in the center of the bracts. Flowers in April. OUTSTANDING.

**EXPOSURE/CULTURE:** Sun or shade. Best in part shade. Requires well-drained, moist, organic soil. Mulching is necessary for best performance. Shallow-rooted.

**PEST PROBLEMS:** Borers, anthracnose. Dogwood anthracnose can be deadly.

**BARK/STEMS:** Young stems reddish; older bark is dark brown to gray and sectioned into small, uniform segments. Attractive.

**SELECTED CULTIVARS:** 'Cloud Nine' - More compact cultivar that flowers profusely when young. Slower growing. 'Cherokee Chief' - Red Flowers. (See next page.) 'Cherokee Princess' - Larger white flowers than the species. 'Fastigiata' - Has distinct, upright branching habit. White flowers. 'First Lady' - Green foliage with bright yellow variegation. Bold. 'Gigantea' - Has very large flowers to 6" or more. 'Plena' - Double white form, having several large and several small bracts. 'Purple Glory' - A purple-leaved cultivar with dark red flowers. 'Welchii' - Leaves green, cream, and pink. Very noticeable. 'Xanthocarpa' - Yellow-fruited form.

**LANDSCAPE NOTES:** Dogwood is a popular native tree that is interesting in all seasons. Flowers hold longer than many flowering trees, and fall foliage can be spectacular. Very popular as a specimen tree in Azalea or ground cover beds.

## *Cornus florida* 'Cherokee Chief'     Cherokee Chief Red Dogwood

**ZONES:**
5, 6, 7, 8, 9

**HEIGHT:**
20' to 30'

**WIDTH:**
20' to 25'

**FRUIT:**
1/2" red drupes; clustered; very attractive.

**TEXTURE:**
Medium

**GROWTH RATE:**
Moderate

**HABIT:**
Rounded and spreading; sometimes multi-stemmed.

**FAMILY:**
Cornaceae

**LEAF COLOR:** Medium to dark green in season; red in fall.

**LEAF DESCRIPTION:** SIMPLE, 2 1/2" to 5" long and 1 3/4" to 3" wide, ovate to oval shape with entire margins that are slightly undulate, veins curving from midrib to almost parallel with leaf margins. OPPOSITE arrangement.

**FLOWER DESCRIPTION:** Rosey-red, 2" to 3" wide (bracts). True flowers clustered in center where bracts are attached. Flowers in April. Very attractive.

**EXPOSURE/CULTURE:** Sun or shade. Best in part shade. Requires well-drained, moist, organic soil. Mulching is necessary for best performance, especially in full sun. The plant is shallow-rooted and not very drought-tolerant, especially in youth. Prune selectively, if at all.

**PEST PROBLEMS:** Borers, anthracnose. Anthracnose can be destructive. (Check with the Extension Service in your area regarding prevention and treatment.)

**BARK/STEMS:** New stems reddish, maturing to green; older bark brown or gray and sectioned into small blocks.

**SELECTED CULTIVARS:** None. This is a cultivar of *C. florida,* the species.

**LANDSCAPE NOTES:** Cherokee Chief Dogwood is one of the original red-flowered cultivars, and is considered by many to be the best. The rosey-red flowers contrast with the ever-popular white forms. This is a true specimen in both spring and fall. It is useful as a lawn specimen, solitary or grouped, and in planting beds. This plant is especially attractive with an under-planting of white azaleas.

## *Cornus florida var. pringlei* — **Pringle Dogwood**

**ZONES:**
7, 8, 9

**HEIGHT:**
20′ to 25′

**WIDTH:**
10′ to 20′

**FRUIT:**
1/4″ to 1/3″ red drupes in fall.

**TEXTURE:**
Medium

**GROWTH RATE:**
Moderate

**HABIT:**
Spreading to somewhat upright; often multi-stemmed.

**FAMILY:**
Cornaceae

**LEAF COLOR:** Medium to dark green; yellowish or reddish tinged in fall.

**LEAF DESCRIPTION:** SIMPLE, 3″ to 6″ long and half as wide, ovate shape with entire margins that may be slightly undulate, veins curving from midrib toward tip. OPPOSITE arrangement.

**FLOWER DESCRIPTION:** White, 1″ to 1 1/2″ wide, four bracts curving from base and joined at tips to resemble an oriental lantern. True flowers "nested" inside at base of bracts. Flowers in spring with the leaves. Not as abundant as *C. florida.*

**EXPOSURE/CULTURE:** Sun or shade. The plant prefers well-drained soil, dry, alkaline soils but will grow in moist, acid soils. Grows well in the Southwest and the more humid Southeast. Pruning should be minimal and selective.

**PEST PROBLEMS:** Borers, anthracnose.

**BARK/STEMS:** Young stems reddish to green; older bark is brown-gray to almost black with small, uniform blocks.

**SELECTED CULTIVARS:** None

**LANDSCAPE NOTES:** Pringle Dogwood is probably more drought-tolerant than *C. florida,* and is therefore more appropriate for the lower Southwest. The plant is characterized by its unusual flowers. The plant can be used as a lawn specimen, in groups, or in planting beds. This is a great plant for naturalizing.

## *Cornus florida var. rubra*     Pink Flowering Dogwood

**ZONES:**
5, 6, 7, 8, 9

**HEIGHT:**
20′ to 30′

**WIDTH:**
20′ to 25′

**FRUIT:**
1/3″ to 1/2″ red drupes in fall; clustered and attractive.

**TEXTURE:**
Medium

**GROWTH RATE:**
Moderate

**HABIT:**
Spreading and somewhat rounded.

**FAMILY:**
Cornaceae

**LEAF COLOR:** Medium to dark green in summer; red in fall.

**LEAF DESCRIPTION:** SIMPLE, 3″ to 5″ long and half as wide, ovate to oval shape with entire margins, sometimes slightly undulate, veins curving from midrib toward tip. OPPOSITE arrangement.

**FLOWER DESCRIPTION:** Pink, 2″ to 3″ wide (bracts), true flowers clustered in the center where the bracts are joined. Flowers in spring. Very abundant and attractive.

**EXPOSURE/CULTURE:** Sun or shade. Prefers well-drained, moist, organic soils. Requires more attention when grown in sun. Prune only to maintain natural shape.

**PEST PROBLEMS:** Borers, anthracnose. (Consult the local Extension Service regarding anthracnose in your area.)

**BARK/STEMS:** Young stems reddish, maturing to green; older bark is dark gray to almost black and divided into small blocks. Ridges shallow.

**SELECTED CULTIVARS:** None

**LANDSCAPE NOTES:** Pink Dogwood has all the outstanding features of *C. florida*, but adds variety and interest with its pink flowers. The plants are greatly variable from seed, and one should select grafted plants where the shade of pink can be described. True pink is available.

# *Cornus kousa*

**Kousa Dogwood**

**ZONES:**
5, 6, 7, 8

**HEIGHT:**
15' to 25'

**WIDTH:**
15' to 25'

**FRUIT:**
1/2" pinkish drupe (raspberry-like).

**TEXTURE:**
Medium

**GROWTH RATE:**
Moderate to slow.

**HABIT:**
Vase-shaped in youth; spreading and horizontal with age.

**FAMILY:**
Cornaceae

**LEAF COLOR:** Dark green with waxy bloom underneath in summer; scarlet or reddish-purple in fall.

**LEAF DESCRIPTION:** SIMPLE, 2 1/2" to 4" long and half as wide, ovate to elliptic shape with acuminate tip, margins entire to undulate, 4 to 6 vein pairs. Hairy beneath. OPPOSITE arrangement.

**FLOWER DESCRIPTION:** Light green, maturing to white (4 bracts). True flowers are tiny and yellowish, being clustered in center where bracts are joined. Flowers later in spring with the leaves. Flowers on longer pedicels, rising above the foliage.

**EXPOSURE/CULTURE:** Full sun or light shade. Prefers moist, well-drained, organic soil. Will not tolerate wet or very dry conditions. Needs mulch to maintain moisture and cool environment for the roots. Best in acidic soil. Requires little, if any, pruning.

**PEST PROBLEMS:** None serious. Seldom bothered by boring insects.

**BARK/STEMS:** Mature bark grayish with brown due to irregular peeling (exfoliating) nature. Very attractive.

**SELECTED CULTIVARS:** 'Elizabeth Lustgarten' - Dwarf form with weeping habit on upper branches. Slow growing. 'Lustgarten Weeping' - Superior weeping form to 4'. (Featured on next page.) 'Milky Way' - Smaller than the species, but superior in bloom. Flowers may reach 4" to 5" wide. 'Rosabella' - Similar to species but having rose-pink flowers. var. *chinensis* - Superior to the species, having much larger flowers. The best of the lot.

**LANDSCAPE NOTES:** Kousa Dogwood is a great specimen for foundation or border planting. Blooms later than *C. florida* with the foliage.

## *Cornus florida* 'Lustgarten Weeping'     Weeping Kousa Dogwood

**ZONES:**
5, 6, 7, 8, 9

**HEIGHT:**
4' to 5'

**WIDTH:**
4' to 5'

**FRUIT:**
1/3" pinkish drupe (raspberry-like).

**TEXTURE:**
Medium

**GROWTH RATE:**
Slow

**FAMILY:**
Cornaceae

**LEAF COLOR:** Medium green in summer; reddish in fall.

**LEAF DESCRIPTION:** SIMPLE, 2" to 3" long and half as wide, ovate to elliptic shape with acuminate tip, margins entire or slightly undulate, hairy underneath. OPPOSITE arrangement.

**FLOWER DESCRIPTION:** Light green, maturing to white (4 bracts), 1 1/2" to 2 1/2" wide, true flowers clustered in center. Flowers in spring with the leaves.

**EXPOSURE/CULTURE:** Full sun or light shade. Prefers a moist, well-drained, organic soil of acidic reaction. Will not tolerate the extremes of wet or very dry soil. Any pruning should be minimal and highly selective to maintain weeping habit.

**PEST PROBLEMS:** No serious pests.

**BARK/STEMS:** Mature bark gray, exfoliating to expose patches of brown.

**SELECTED CULTIVARS:** None. This is a cultivar of *C. kousa.*

**LANDSCAPE NOTES:** Weeping Kousa Dogwood is a true accent plant that merits a carefully selected location in the garden. Can be used in the foundation or border plantings, shrub or flower beds, and berms. This is a nice plant to accent entries or entrance walks.

# *Crataegus viridis*

**Green Hawthorn**

▲ 'Winter King'

**ZONES:**
4, 5, 6, 7

**HEIGHT:**
20' to 30'

**WIDTH:**
20' to 25'

**FRUIT:**
1/4" to 1/3" bright red pome in fall and winter.

**TEXTURE:**
Medium

**GROWTH RATE:**
Moderate

**HABIT:**
Upright and rounded.

**FAMILY:**
Rosaceae

**LEAF COLOR:** Medium green in summer; red or purple in fall.

**LEAF DESCRIPTION:** SIMPLE, 2" to 3 1/2" long and 1" to 2 1/2" wide, mostly ovate to elliptic shape with coarsely serrated margins, often shallowly lobed. ALTERNATE arrangement.

**FLOWER DESCRIPTION:** White, 1/2" to 3/4" wide, 5-petaled with approximately 20 stamens, appearing in small corymbs in May. Slightly fragrant.

**EXPOSURE/CULTURE:** Sun or light shade. Tolerant of most well-drained soils and pH values. Pruning is minimal to thin or remove undesirable branches.

**PEST PROBLEMS:** Blights, cedar-apple rust, mildews, and both sucking and chewing insects. (Consult the Extension Service for problems in your area.)

**BARK/STEMS:** Stems brown with 2" sharp thorns. Older bark is dark grayish-brown with shallow fissures and small plates.

**SELECTED CULTIVARS:** 'Winter King' - Has gray-green, glaucous stems.

**RELATED SPECIES:** Note: Hortus Third lists over 50 species. Some important species are: *C. crusgalli* - Cockspur Hawthorn. This is a rounded form with horizontal branching. Leaves obovate and very thick. *C. laevigata* - English Hawthorn. A rounded form with 3" leaves (3 to 5 lobes), zig-zag upright branches, and little fall color. Cultivars single or double flowers and white, pink, or red. *C. phaenopyrum* - Washington Hawthorn. This popular species is noted for its abundant red fruits all winter. *C. nitida* - Glossy Hawthorn. This species has bright glossy leaves that turn orange to red in fall.

**LANDSCAPE NOTES:** Green Hawthorn is one of the best Hawthorns. It can be used as a specimen for borders, lawn areas, groupings, or screening. Does well under city conditions, but caution must be exercised due to thorns.

## *Franklinia alatamaha*

**Franklin Tree, Ben Franklin Tree**

▲ Courtesy of Monrovia Nursery Co.

▶
Courtesy of Monrovia Nursery Co.

**ZONES:**
6, 7, 8, 9

**HEIGHT:**
15′ to 20′

**WIDTH:**
8′ to 15′

**FRUIT:**
1″ brown capsule; NOT ORNA-MENTAL.

**TEXTURE:**
Coarse

**GROWTH RATE:**
Moderate

**HABIT:**
Somewhat pyramidal; open.

**FAMILY:**
Theaceae

**LEAF COLOR:** Dark glossy green in summer; orange to red in fall.

**LEAF DESCRIPTION:** SIMPLE, 5″ to 8″ long and 2″ to 3″ wide, oblanceolate to obovate shape with finely toothed serrulate margins. ALTERNATE arrangement.

**FLOWER DESCRIPTION:** White with yellow stamens, 5-petaled, 3″ to 4″ wide, frilly and camellia-like. Flowers late summer through fall. Attractive and showy.

**EXPOSURE/CULTURE:** Sun. Prefers well-drained, organic soil with constant moisture. Should be mulched. Water during periods of drought. Pruning is usually not necessary.

**PEST PROBLEMS:** No serious pests.

**BARK/STEMS:** Grayish and smooth with a few shallow furrows on older bark.

**SELECTED CULTIVARS:** None

**LANDSCAPE NOTES:** Franklin Tree is valued for its large white blooms during fall. In addition, the foliage begins to turn while still in bloom. It makes a nice plant to feature or a border plant for naturalizing. Unusual tree wtih an interesting history.

## *Laburnum* x *watereri*

**ZONES:**
5, 6, 7

**HEIGHT:**
10′ to 15′

**WIDTH:**
8′ to 10′

**FRUIT:**
12″ brown, hanging pod.

**TEXTURE:**
Medium

**GROWTH RATE:**
Slow

**HABIT:**
Upright; open.

**FAMILY:**
Fabaceae

**LEAF COLOR:** Green in summer; brownish in fall.

**LEAF DESCRIPTION:** COMPOUND, trifoliate (3 leaflets), leaflets 1 1/2″ to 3″ long and half as wide, elliptic-ovate to elliptic-oblong shape with entire margins. ALTERNATE leaf arrangement.

**FLOWER DESCRIPTION:** Yellow, 1/2″ to 1″ long in 12″ hanging clusters. Flowers in May.

**EXPOSURE/CULTURE:** Sun or part shade. Prefers well-drained, moist, organic soil, but does not tolerate wet or hot, sunny conditions. Pruning is minimal.

**PEST PROBLEMS:** Twig blight.

**BARK/STEMS:** Young stems bright green; grayish and slightly fissured with age.

**SELECTED CULTIVARS:** 'Vossii' - Extra long flower clusters to 24″.

**LANDSCAPE NOTES:** Goldenchain can be used to brighten dull corners of the yard. It is especially attractive when the long chains of yellow flowers appear. It will blend with other plantings when not in flower. Good accent plant, but, unfortunately, it is shorter-lived than most small trees.

## *Lagerstroemia indica*　　　　　　　　　　　**Crape Myrtle**

▲ 'Natchez'

▲ 'Natchez'

▲ 'Regal Red'

**ZONES:**
7, 8, 9, 10

**HEIGHT:**
10′ to 20′

**WIDTH:**
6′ to 12′

**FRUIT:**
1/2″ brown capsule; NOT ORNAMENTAL.

**TEXTURE:**
Medium

**GROWTH RATE:**
Moderate to rapid.

**HABIT:**
Upright, irregular, and open.

**FAMILY:**
Lythraceae

**LEAF COLOR:** Dark green in summer; yellow to red in fall.

**LEAF DESCRIPTION:** SIMPLE, 1″ to 2 1/2″ long and half as wide, elliptic to oval shape with entire margins, or slightly undulate. OPPOSITE arrangement.

**FLOWER DESCRIPTION:** White, pink, rose, red, lavender, or purple, depending on cultivar. 1″ flowers with frilly petals in 6″ to 12″ upright, often drooping, panicles. Flowers summer through fall. Very showy.

**EXPOSURE/CULTURE:** Full sun. Prefers moist, well-drained soil, but is reasonably drought-tolerant. Blooms on current season's growth, so pruning should be accomplished in late winter. Pruning will incease flower production.

**PEST PROBLEMS:** Powdery mildew, aphids.

**BARK/STEMS:** Young stems medium green; older bark is gray but exfoliating to expose tan, brown, or red inner bark. OUTSTANDING EFFECT.

**SELECTED CULTIVARS:** 'Catawba' - Dark purple flowers and orange-red fall foliage. Mildew-resistant. 'Cherokee' - Rich red blooms. Mildew-resistant. 'Muskogee' - Light lavender flowers. 'Natchez' - White flowers. Cinnamon-red bark. Best of the white cultivars. 'Near East' - Soft pink, crinkly flowers. 'Peppermint Lace' - Deep rose-pink blooms edged with white. Upright habit. 'Potomac' - Medium pink flowers. 'Seminole' - Medium pink flowers. Mildew-resistant. 'Tuscarora' - Coral-pink blooms; light brown bark. Mildew-resistant. 'Watermelon Red' - Watermelon-red frilly flowers. Very popular selection.

**LANDSCAPE NOTES:** Crape Myrtle should be "limbed" to create a multi-stemmed small tree. It is a heavy-flowering specimen plant that works well in Juniper or ground cover beds. Flowering period is quite long, and the "naked bark" is both unusual and handsome. Easy to grow.

# *Magnolia liliiflora*

**Lily Magnolia**

▼ 'O'Neill'

▲ 'O'Neill'

**ZONES:**
5, 6, 7, 8

**HEIGHT:**
10' to 12'

**WIDTH:**
10' to 12'

**FRUIT:**
Brown pod (aggregate); NOT ORNAMENTAL.

**TEXTURE:**
Medium to coarse.

**GROWTH RATE:**
Moderate

**HABIT:**
Upright and open; usually multi-stemmed.

**FAMILY:**
Magnoliaceae

**LEAF COLOR:** Dark green in summer; yellowish in fall.

**LEAF DESCRIPTION:** SIMPLE, 4″ to 6″ long and half as wide, obovate to elliptic shape with entire margins. ALTERNATE arrangement.

**FLOWER DESCRIPTION:** Purplish outside to white inside, 3″ to 5″ wide, 6-petaled, appearing in spring with the leaves. Solitary. Very showy.

**EXPOSURE/CULTURE:** Sun or light shade. Prefers moist, organic, well-drained soils. Best in acidic soil. Pruning is minimal and should be performed immediately after flowering.

**PEST PROBLEMS:** Leaf blight, leaf spots, scale.

**BARK/STEMS:** Young stems brownish; older bark is gray and mostly smooth.

**SELECTED CULTIVARS:** 'Nigra' - Flowers are deep purple-red outside and pink inside. 'O'Neill' - Flowers are mostly pink.

**LANDSCAPE NOTES:** Lily Magnolia is a nice small tree or large shrub that fits nicely into foundation plantings, borders, lawn areas or accent beds. The plant is ideal for today's smaller gardens.

# *Magnolia* x *soulangiana*

**Saucer Magnolia**

▲ 'Alexandrina'

**ZONES:**
5, 6, 7, 8, 9

**HEIGHT:**
10' to 20'

**WIDTH:**
10' to 20'

**FRUIT:**
Brown, aggregate of follicles; NOT ORNAMENTAL.

**TEXTURE:**
Coarse

**GROWTH RATE:**
Moderate to slow.

**HABIT:**
Upright and open.

**FAMILY:**
Magnoliaceae

**LEAF COLOR:** Medium green in summer; brown in fall.

**LEAF DESCRIPTION:** SIMPLE, 4" to 6" long and half as wide, obovate to elliptic shape with entire margins. ALTERNATE arrangement.

**FLOWER DESCRIPTION:** Purplish on outside, white on inside (cultivars vary), 5" to 7" across. Flowers in very early spring. Very showy, but sometimes injured by late frosts.

**EXPOSURE/CULTURE:** Sun or light shade. Prefers well-drained, moist, organic soil. Not tolerant of very wet or dry conditions. Prefers acidic sites. Prune after flowering if needed.

**PEST PROBLEMS:** Scale, mildew.

**BARK/STEMS:** Young stems glossy brown and downy; older bark is silver-gray and mostly smooth.

**SELECTED CULTIVARS:** 'Alexandrina' - Tulip-like flowers. Purplish on outside, white inside. Late blooming. 'Brozzonii' - Flowers white, rose-purple at base. Late blooming. 'Lilliputian' - Pink flowers on a smaller plant. 'Rustic Rubra' - Rosey-red flowers. 'Spectabilis' - Abundant, white flowers.

**RELATED SPECIES:** *M.* x *loebneri* - This is a vigorous hybrid with larger leaves and larger, 12-petaled, strap-like flowers. Blooms late. 'Leonard Messel' has pink flowers. 'Merrill' has white, slightly fragrant flowers.

**LANDSCAPE NOTES:** Saucer Magnolia is an early-blooming tree that is spectacular, especially on older plants. The blooms are abundant and large, making this a plant to feature for spring color. The trend is in development of later-blooming forms to escape frosts and freezing.

# *Magnolia stellata*

**Star Magnolia**

▲ 'Super Star'

**ZONES:**
5, 6, 7, 8, 9

**HEIGHT:**
10' to 15'

**WIDTH:**
7' to 10'

**FRUIT:**
Brown, aggregate of follicles;
NOT ORNAMENTAL.

**TEXTURE:**
Coarse

**GROWTH RATE:**
Slow

**HABIT:**
Upright and open.

**FAMILY:**
Magnoliaceae

**LEAF COLOR:** Medium green in summer; yellow to bronze in fall.

**LEAF DESCRIPTION:** SIMPLE, 3" to 4" long and half as wide, obovate or elliptic shape with entire margins. ALTERNATE arrangement.

**FLOWER DESCRIPTION:** White, 3" to 4" across, 12 to 18 strap-like petals. Flowers in early spring. Very showy, but sometimes ruined by late frosts.

**EXPOSURE/CULTURE:** Sun. Prefers moist, well-drained, acidic soil. Responds better to average and poor conditions than credited. Requires little, if any, pruning after flowering.

**PEST PROBLEMS:** None

**BARK/STEMS:** Brownish to gray and mostly smooth.

**SELECTED CULTIVARS:** 'Super Star' - A larger flowering form on a larger-growing plant. Developed by Ray Bracken Nursery, Easley, SC. 'Royal Star' - Blooms later than the species with large, fragrant flowers. 'Rubra' - Flowers purple-rose, fading to pink. Compact.

**LANDSCAPE NOTES:** Star Magnolia has beautiful star-shaped blooms in early spring. It will grow shrub-like, but is commonly used in tree-form. Later-flowering cultivars are being developed to escape late frost or freeze. Can be quite spectacular in bloom.

## *Mespilus germanica*

**Showy Mespilus**

**ZONES:**
6, 7, 8, 9

**HEIGHT:**
15′ to 20′

**WIDTH:**
10′ to 15′

**FRUIT:**
1″ to 2″ apple-shaped pome;
edible.

**TEXTURE:**
Medium

**GROWTH RATE:**
Moderate

**HABIT:**
Upright and rounded.

**FAMILY:**
Rosaceae

**LEAF COLOR:** Dark green in summer; yellowish in fall.

**LEAF DESCRIPTION:** SIMPLE, 3″ to 5″ long and half as wide, elliptic shape with finely serrated margins. Pubescent on both surfaces. ALTERNATE arrangement.

**FLOWER DESCRIPTION:** White, 1″ to 2″ across, 5-petaled, 30 to 40 stamens, solitary, sepals longer than the petals. Flowers in late spring.

**EXPOSURE/CULTURE:** Full sun. Does well in any well-drained soil. Prune after flowering if needed to shape. Easy to grow.

**PEST PROBLEMS:** No serious pests.

**BARK/STEMS:** Grayish to brown; sometimes thorny.

**SELECTED CULTIVARS:** None

**LANDSCAPE NOTES:** Mespilus is an attractive shrub-like tree that is well-suited to the recommended zones. It is not as commonly used as many, but it certainly has a place in residential gardens. Can be used effectively as a lawn specimen or background material in the garden border.

# *Morus alba 'Pendula'*

**Weeping White Mulberry**

**ZONES:**
4, 5, 6, 7, 8, 9

**HEIGHT:**
20' to 25'

**WIDTH:**
20' to 25'

**FRUIT:**
1" purple drupe (multiple); blackberry-like.

**TEXTURE:**
Coarse

**GROWTH RATE:**
Rapid

**HABIT:**
Global and weeping.

**FAMILY:**
Moraceae

**LEAF COLOR:** Dark green in summer; yellow or brown in fall.

**LEAF DESCRIPTION:** SIMPLE, 3" to 6" long and almost as wide, broadly ovate shape with crenate to dentate-serrulate margins, often lobed (deeply cut). ALTERNATE arrrangement.

**FLOWER DESCRIPTION:** Drooping catkins in spring; NOT ORNAMENTAL.

**EXPOSURE/CULTURE:** Sun or partial shade. Prefers well-drained, moist soil, but is adaptable to a wide range of soils and conditions. Easy to grow. Selective pruning is usually all that is recommended or needed.

**PEST PROBLEMS:** Mildew, mites, scale.

**BARK/STEMS:** Orange-red on younger stems; older bark is brown.

**SELECTED CULTIVARS:** None. This is a cultivar of *M. alba*.

**LANDSCAPE NOTES:** Weeping White Mulberry is a plant to feature in larger gardens. Its greatest attributes are that it is easy to grow and to maintain. Branches weep to ground, so avoid planting lawn grasses underneath. Probably best used as a specimen in shrub borders.

## Prunus cerasifera 'Newport'
### Purple-leaf Plum

▲ 'Thundercloud'

**ZONES:**
4, 5, 6, 7, 8, 9

**HEIGHT:**
20' to 25'

**WIDTH:**
15' to 20'

**FRUIT:**
1/2" to 1" purple drupe in summer; edible.

**TEXTURE:**
Medium

**GROWTH RATE:**
Rapid

**HABIT:**
Broad and rounded.

**FAMILY:**
Rosaceae

**LEAF COLOR:** Reddish-purple in summer and fall. Emerging leaves more intense.

**LEAF DESCRIPTION:** SIMPLE, 1 1/2" to 3" long and half as wide, ovate to obovate shape with finely serrated margins. ALTERNATE arrangement.

**FLOWER DESCRIPTION:** Pink, 1/2" to 1" across, solitary, 5-petaled with many stamens. Flowers in early to mid-spring. Very attractive and fragrant.

**EXPOSURE/CULTURE:** Full sun. Will grow in any well-drained soil. Prune after flowering, if needed. Considered easy to grow and dependable.

**PEST PROBLEMS:** Borers, scale.

**BARK/STEMS:** Young stems purplish with large lenticels; dark gray with shallow fissures on older trunks.

**SELECTED CULTIVARS:** None. This is a cultivar.

**RELATED CULTIVARS:** 'Atropurpurea' - Dense, upright form. New leaves are red. 'Krauter's Vesuvius' - Has deep purple leaves throughout the warm season. Great color! 'Thundercloud' - White flowers and deep purple foliage.

**LANDSCAPE NOTES:** Newport Plum is a bold accent plant that is attractive, but should be used in moderation due to foliage color. Consider the color of nearby structures when using. Looks great against a white wall or background. Can be used as a lawn specimen, border plant, or in groupings.

## *Prunus mume*

**Japanese Apricot**

**ZONES:**
6, 7, 8, 9

**HEIGHT:**
15' to 20'

**WIDTH:**
10' to 20'

**FRUIT:**
1" yellow to green drupe; sour.

**TEXTURE:**
Medium

**GROWTH RATE:**
Moderate

**HABIT:**
Rounded and upright.

**FAMILY:**
Rosaceae

**LEAF COLOR:** Dark green in summer; yellowish in fall.

**LEAF DESCRIPTION:** SIMPLE, 2" to 3" long and half as wide, ovate to elliptic shape with long-pointed apex and serrulate margins. Pubescent underneath. ALTERNATE arrangement.

**FLOWER DESCRIPTION:** Rose-pink, 3/4" to 1" with yellowish stamens, cup-shaped. Flowers in January or February. Very showy.

**EXPOSURE/CULTURE:** Full sun or light shade. Prefers well-drained, organic soil, but is adaptable. Pruning is minimal, but will increase flowering. Prune after flowering, as the plant blooms on previous season's growth.

**PEST PROBLEMS:** This genus is subject to many diseases, especially borers. (Check with the Extension Service for problems in your area.)

**BARK/STEMS:** Young stems are green, becoming gray and slightly fissured with age.

**SELECTED CULTIVARS:** 'Alba Plena' - Has double, white flowers.

**LANDSCAPE NOTES:** Japanese Apricot is valued for its winter flowers, which provide accent during the dull season. During the warmer season it blends nicely with the rest of the landscape and is not a specimen. Can be used as a lawn specimen, shade tree, or border plant.

## *Prunus serrulata* 'Kwanzan'

**Kwanzan Cherry**

**ZONES:**
6, 7, 8, 9

**HEIGHT:**
20′ to 25′

**WIDTH:**
15′ to 20′

**FRUIT:**
Non-fruiting

**TEXTURE:**
Medium

**GROWTH RATE:**
Rapid

**HABIT:**
Vase-shaped when young; more rounded with age.

**FAMILY:**
Rosaceae

**LEAF COLOR:** Dark green in summer; yellowish in fall.

**LEAF DESCRIPTION:** SIMPLE, 2 1/2″ to 4″ long and half as wide, narrow elliptic to oval shape with serrated margins and acuminate to cuspidate tip. ALTERNATE arrangement.

**FLOWER DESCRIPTION:** Deep pink, double, 2″ to 2 1/2″ across, solitary or in small clusters. Flowers in spring. Very attractive.

**EXPOSURE/CULTURE:** Full sun. Adaptable to a wide range of soil types. Prune to shape after flowering, if needed. Very easy to grow.

**PEST PROBLEMS:** Borers, stem canker, scale, webworms.

**BARK/STEMS:** Reddish-brown bark with huge, prominent lenticels.

**SELECTED CULTIVARS:** None. This is a cultivar of *P. serrulata,* a rounded tree with single or double pink to white flowers.

**LANDSCAPE NOTES:** Kwanzan Cherry is a much-used cultivar that is noted for its beautiful, double blooms in spring. This is a specimen tree in bloom. Can be used as a lawn specimen or accent plant for garden borders, rock gardens, and foundations.

# *Prunus serrulata 'Shogetsu'*

**Dwarf Japanese Cherry**

**ZONES:**
5, 6, 7, 8, 9

**HEIGHT:**
10′ to 18′

**WIDTH:**
15′ to 20′

**FRUIT:**
Non-fruiting

**TEXTURE:**
Medium

**GROWTH RATE:**
Moderate

**HABIT:**
Very broad-spreading and somewhat rounded.

**FAMILY:**
Rosaceae

**LEAF COLOR:** Dark green in summer; yellowish in fall.

**LEAF DESCRIPTION:** SIMPLE, 2″ to 3″ long and half as wide, narrow elliptic shape with serrated margins. ALTERNATE arrangement.

**FLOWER DESCRIPTION:** Blush-pink, fading to white. 2″ double, 30-petaled blooms, appearing in corymbs. Extra-heavy flowering in spring. Outstanding.

**EXPOSURE/CULTURE:** Full sun. Grows in any well-drained soil. Prune for strong branching, but maintain natural shape. Easy to grow.

**PEST PROBLEMS:** Borers, stem canker, scale, webworms, Japanese Beetles.

**BARK/STEMS:** Reddish to grayish-brown with large lenticels.

**SELECTED CULTIVARS:** None. This is a cultivar of *P. serrulata*.

**LANDSCAPE NOTES:** This is an extra heavy bloomer that is well-suited to smaller gardens as an accent plant or in borders. One of the showiest small trees in bloom.

## *Prunus subhirtella* 'Pendula' — Weeping Higan Cherry

▲ 'Pendula Plena Rosea'

**ZONES:**
5, 6, 7, 8

**HEIGHT:**
10' to 20'

**WIDTH:**
10' to 20'

**FRUIT:**
1/4" to 1/2" ovoid drupe; NOT ORNAMENTAL.

**TEXTURE:**
Medium

**GROWTH RATE:**
Rapid

**HABIT:**
Upright; weeping branches

**FAMILY:**
Rosaceae

**LEAF COLOR:** Dark green in summer; yellowish to brown in fall.

**LEAF DESCRIPTION:** SIMPLE, 2" to 4" long and half as wide, ovate shape with double-serrate margins. ALTERNATE arrangement.

**FLOWER DESCRIPTION:** Pink, 3/4" wide, appearing in clusters of 2 to 5. Petals are notched. Flowers in early spring and is very showy.

**EXPOSURE/CULTURE:** Full sun. Adaptable to a wide range of well-drained soil types. Prune after flowering, if needed, but maintain natural shape.

**PEST PROBLEMS:** Borers, scale, stem canker, webworms.

**BARK/STEMS:** Reddish-brown with large lenticels. Very attractive.

**SELECTED CULTIVARS:** None. This is a cultivar of *P. subhirtella,* the upright form with light pink flowers.

**RELATED CULTIVARS:** 'Autumnalis' - Slightly pendulous branches with semi-double, pink flowers. 'Rosea' - Erect form with rose-pink flowers.

**LANDSCAPE NOTES:** Weeping Cherry is a dramatic specimen plant in bloom. Careful attention should be given to site selection. Most are "top-grafted," but "bottom-grafted" plants are available and offer an interesting variation. Can be used anywhere in the landscape where accent or focalization is desired. OUTSTANDING.

# *Prunus x blireiana*

**Blireiana Plum**

**ZONES:**
5, 6, 7, 8, 9

**HEIGHT:**
15′ to 20′

**WIDTH:**
10′ to 15′

**FRUIT:**
Small, purplish drupe; sweet and edible.

**TEXTURE:**
Medium

**GROWTH RATE:**
Moderate

**HABIT:**
Upright in youth; rounded and open with age.

**FAMILY:**
Rosaceae

**LEAF COLOR:** Purple-bronze in summer, becoming greenish by fall.

**LEAF DESCRIPTION:** SIMPLE, 1″ to 2″ long and half as wide, ovate shape with serrated margins. ALTERNATE arrangement.

**FLOWER DESCRIPTION:** Pink, 1″ to 1 1/4″ across, double to semi-double, solitary. Flowers in early spring. Very showy and attractive. (Often mistaken for a double-flowering cherry.)

**EXPOSURE/CULTURE:** Full sun. The plant is adaptable to most well-drained soils. Reasonably drought-tolerant. Does best if mulched. Selective pruning may be accomplished after flowering.

**PEST PROBLEMS:** Borers, scale, webworms.

**BARK/STEMS:** Young stems purplish; dark gray on older plants.

**SELECTED CULTIVARS:** 'Moseri' - Has smaller flowers, but more intense, red-purple foliage.

**LANDSCAPE NOTES:** Blireiana Plum is a double-flowering hybrid that is superior to other purple-leaf plums in flower. It blooms earlier than other plums, but later than Japanese Apricot. It can be used anywhere in the garden where accent or focalization is desired. Easy to grow and very hardy. Note: This is a cross between *P. cerasifera* 'Atropurpurea', Purple Cherry Plum, and *P. mume*, Japanese Apricot.

## *Prunus* x *incamp* 'Okame'

**Okame Flowering Cherry**

**ZONES:**
6, 7, 8, 9

**HEIGHT:**
20' to 25'

**WIDTH:**
15' to 20'

**FRUIT:**
Small, reddish drupe.

**TEXTURE:**
Medium

**GROWTH RATE:**
Moderate

**HABIT:**
Upright in youth; rounded and open with age.

**FAMILY:**
Rosaceae

**LEAF COLOR:** Dark green in summer; orange-red in fall.

**LEAF DESCRIPTION:** SIMPLE, 1 1/2″ to 2 1/2″ long and half as wide, ovate shape with doubly serrated margins. ALTERNATE arrangement.

**FLOWER DESCRIPTION:** Carmine-pink, 1″ to 1 1/2″, 5-petaled, solitary or in small clusters, buds rose-pink. Flowers in early spring. Very showy and attractive.

**EXPOSURE/CULTURE:** Full sun. Grows in almost any well-drained soil. Prune after flowering to maintain natural shape or to select strong branching. Easy to grow.

**PEST PROBLEMS:** Borers, stem canker, scale, webworm, Japanese Beetles.

**BARK/STEMS:** Young stems greenish; older bark reddish to grayish-brown with lenticels.

**SELECTED CULTIVARS:** None. This is a cultivar of the cross between *P. incisa* and *P. campanulata*.

**LANDSCAPE NOTES:** Okame Flowering Cherry is a nice small specimen tree for lawns, garden borders, raised beds, and other areas where spring and fall color is desirable. This is a durable plant like most in *Prunus*.

# Stewartia koreana

**Korean Stewartia**

**ZONES:**
5, 6, 7, 8

**HEIGHT:**
20' to 25'

**WIDTH:**
15' to 18'

**FRUIT:**
Brown capsule; NOT ORNA-MENTAL.

**TEXTURE:**
Medium

**GROWTH RATE:**
Moderate

**HABIT:**
Upright and open.

**FAMILY:**
Theaceae

**LEAF COLOR:** Dark green in summer; scarlet and reddish-purple in fall.

**LEAF DESCRIPTION:** SIMPLE, 2" to 4" long and around half as wide, elliptic shape with serrulate margins. Pubescent underneath. ALTERNATE arrangement.

**FLOWER DESCRIPTION:** White with yellow stamens, 2" to 3" wide, stalked. Flowers in summer. Showy.

**EXPOSURE/CULTURE:** Sun to light shade. Prefers well-drained, moist soil of acidic reaction. Pruning is minimal and selective.

**PEST PROBLEMS:** None

**BARK/STEMS:** Exfoliating; reddish-brown or orange-brown inner bark, sometimes mottled silver.

**SELECTED CULTIVARS:** None

**RELATED SPECIES:** *S. ovata* - Mountain Camellia. This species has white flowers with orange anthers. Large shrub size with less noticeable bark. *S. malacodendron* - Silky Stewartia. A large shrub with white 4" flowers having bluish anthers.

**LANDSCAPE NOTES:** Korean Stewartia is a specimen plant for garden usage. The flowers are attractive and the bark is both beautiful and noticeable. Should be used with moderation, preferably in the garden border or as a lawn specimen.

# Chapter 10

## MEDIUM TREES

**F**or the purposes of this text, Medium Trees are defined as those plants that attain an average height of 20′ to 40′ or slightly larger in a landscape setting. Medium trees, like large trees, require more space, and one must carefully consider their ultimate spread and habit of growth in landscape planning.

As with other categories, the medium size trees include some very handsome and interesting trees. Trees like Yoshino Cherry, Bradford Pear, Heritage Birch, and others rival the best in any size grouping.

Medium trees can be used for shade, focalization, screening, windbreaks, variety, accent color, and other uses. In addition, many make nice street trees and are utilized extensively for that purpose.

## *Cunninghamia lanceolata*

**Chinese Fir**

**ZONES:**
7, 8, 9

**HEIGHT:**
20' to 40'

**WIDTH:**
8' to 30'

**FRUIT:**
1" to 1 1/2" round cone; bunched on shoots.

**TEXTURE:**
Medium

**GROWTH RATE:**
Slow

**HABIT:**
Pyramidal and dense.

**FAMILY:**
Taxodiaceae

**LEAF COLOR:** Shiny medium to dark green; bronze-green in fall.

**LEAF DESCRIPTION:** NEEDLE-LIKE, 1" to 2" long and 1/8" to 1/4" wide, linear-lanceolate shape with finely serrated margins, tip sharply acuminate, 2 whitish bands of stomata underneath. ALTERNATE and 2-ranked; spirally arranged.

**FLOWER DESCRIPTION:** Monoecious; male flowers terminal on young shoots, axillary on older shoots; female terminal; NOT ORNAMENTAL.

**EXPOSURE/CULTURE:** Sun or shade. Does best in part shade. Grows best in well-drained, acid soil. Pruning is usually not necessary. Allow the plant to maintain a single-trunk, pyramidal habit.

**PEST PROBLEMS:** Rust

**BARK/STEMS:** Young twigs green; older bark brownish, exfoliating to expose reddish-brown inner bark.

**SELECTED CULTIVARS:** 'Compacta' - Dwarf form (1 1/2' to 2'). Shrub-like with no central leader. 'Glauca' - This cultivar has blue-green foliage. Reputed to be more cold-hardy.

**LANDSCAPE NOTES:** Chinese Fir is an excellent tree that should be more widely used in modern landscaping. It is very different from most conifers, but is slow-growing, so that size is easily controlled. It makes a nice lawn specimen, corner plant for taller structures, or screening material.

# *Cupressus arizonica*

**Arizona Cypress**

**ZONES:**
6, 7, 8, 9

**HEIGHT:**
25' to 40'

**WIDTH:**
20' to 30'

**FRUIT:**
1" round cone, having 6 to 8 thorny scales.

**TEXTURE:**
Fine

**GROWTH RATE:**
Moderate

**HABIT:**
Pyramidal and dense.

**FAMILY:**
Cupressaceae

**LEAF COLOR:** Gray-green to blue-green.

**LEAF DESCRIPTION:** SCALE-LIKE, 1/16" to 1/8" long, densely arranged on flattened branchlets, acuminate tips.

**FLOWER DESCRIPTION:** Monoecious; male cones oblong, female cones globose; NOT ORNAMENTAL.

**EXPOSURE/CULTURE:** Full sun. The plant prefers well-drained soil and arid conditions. Does best in the Southwest. Healthy plants require no pruning or shearing.

**PEST PROBLEMS:** No serious pests.

**BARK/STEMS:** Young stems green; older bark is reddish-brown and exfoliating.

**SELECTED CULTIVARS:** 'Glauca' - Juvenile foliage is an intense silver-gray. var. *glabra* - Similar to the species, but having smooth, red to mahogany-brown bark, exfoliating in thin plates.

**LANDSCAPE NOTES:** Arizona Cypress makes a nice lawn specimen or screen. Sometimes used as a windbreak in the Southwest. This is a drought-tolerant plant that is easy to grow and maintain.

## *Gordonia lasianthus*                                    **Loblolly Bay**

**ZONES:**
8, 9

**HEIGHT:**
30' to 40'

**WIDTH:**
15' to 20'

**FRUIT:**
3/4" brown capsule; NOT ORNAMENTAL.

**TEXTURE:**
Medium

**GROWTH RATE:**
Moderate

**HABIT:**
Upright and open; mostly oval.

**FAMILY:**
Theaceae

**LEAF COLOR:** Dark green and lustrous.

**LEAF DESCRIPTION:** SIMPLE, 3" to 6" long and one-third as wide, elliptic shape, margins entire but sometimes serrated near the tip. ALTERNATE arrangement.

**FLOWER DESCRIPTION:** White, 2" to 2 1/2" across, 5-petaled, mostly solitary, appearing in axils. Flowers in late spring to summer. Not abundant, but very showy.

**EXPOSURE/CULTURE:** Sun to shade. Prefers moist, organic, acid soil. Native to southern swamps. Prune selectively to maintain natural shape.

**PEST PROBLEMS:** No serious pests.

**BARK/STEMS:** Young stems green; older bark gray with shallow furrows.

**SELECTED CULTIVARS:** None

**LANDSCAPE NOTES:** Gordonia is an attractive native plant that can be used as a specimen plant in borders, raised planters, berms, or lawn areas. This is a great plant for naturalizing, but, unfortunately, it is limited to the Southeast.

# *Ilex opaca*

**American Holly**

▲ 'Goldie'

**ZONES:**
6, 7, 8, 9

**HEIGHT:**
20' to 40'

**WIDTH:**
10' to 20'

**FRUIT:**
1/4" dull red drupes (female plants).

**TEXTURE:**
Medium

**GROWTH RATE:**
Slow

**HABIT:**
Pyramidal and upright.

**FAMILY:**
Aquifoliaceae

**LEAF COLOR:** Dark green above, light yellow-green underneath; dull dark green in fall.

**LEAF DESCRIPTION:** SIMPLE, 2" to 3" long and half as wide, elliptic shape with spinose margins, spinose tip. ALTERNATE arrangement.

**FLOWER DESCRIPTION:** Dioecious; male in axillary cymes, female solitary; NOT ORNAMENTAL.

**EXPOSURE/CULTURE:** Sun or part shade. Grows best in moist, organic, well-drained soils of acid reaction. Can be pruned or sheared as desired. Does not grow as thickly as the cultivars.

**PEST PROBLEMS:** Leaf spots and others; none serious.

**BARK/STEMS:** Young stems green; older bark is smooth and light to medium gray. Often with lichens.

**SELECTED CULTIVARS:** 'Goldie' - Yellow berries on female plants. Note: See Large Evergreen Shrubs for other cultivars.

**LANDSCAPE NOTES:** American Holly is a native plant that forms a handsome tree with age. Due to its slow growth, it is sometimes used as a foundation plant. It looks great in natural landscapes, and has many uses, including hedges and border plants. Young plants are usually grown in shrub-form, and then tree-formed when more mature.

## *Juniperus virginiana* — **Eastern Red Cedar**

**ZONES:**
3, 4, 5, 6, 7, 8, 9

**HEIGHT:**
30′ to 50′

**WIDTH:**
10′ to 25′

**FRUIT:**
1/4″ blue to purplish, glaucous cone (berry-like).

**TEXTURE:**
Fine

**GROWTH RATE:**
Moderate

**HABIT:**
Oval in youth; more irregular and open with age.

**FAMILY:**
Cupressaceae

**LEAF COLOR:** Medium to dark green (darker in winter).

**LEAF DESCRIPTION:** SCALE-LIKE, 1/16″ long (needle-like to 1/2″ on older stems), scale leaves tightly overlapping in 4 rows, oval to lanceolate shape and sharply acuminate. OPPOSITE arrangement.

**FLOWER DESCRIPTION:** Dioecious; male yellowish, female green; NOT ORNAMENTAL.

**EXPOSURE/CULTURE:** Full sun; not tolerant of shade. Will grow in any well-drained soil, and is drought-tolerant. Can be sheared to dense thickness if desired. An easy to grow native plant that has possibilites for xeriscaping.

**PEST PROBLEMS:** Juniper blight, bagworms, cedar-apple rust. Note: This is a host for the apple rust fungus. Avoid planting near apple crops.

**BARK/STEMS:** Bark is gray to reddish-brown; older bark exfoliates in vertical strips.

**SELECTED CULTIVARS:** 'Canaertii' - Pyramidal with ascending, cord-like branches. Interesting habit. 'Cupressifolia' - Broad pyramid with dark green foliage and dense habit. 'Idyllwild' - Broad pyramid with irregular, upright habit. 'Manhattan Blue' - Dark, blue-green foliage, forming a tight, compact pyramid.

**LANDSCAPE NOTES:** Eastern Red Cedar can be used for screening, clipped hedges, or windbreaks in sunny locations. The plant develops interesting character with age, displaying a Japanese garden effect. Younger plants are used extensively as Christmas trees.

# *Pinus bungeana*

**ZONES:**
5, 6, 7, 8

**HEIGHT:**
25′ to 40′

**WIDTH:**
15′ to 30′

**FRUIT:**
2″ to 3″ light brown cone.

**TEXTURE:**
Medium

**GROWTH RATE:**
Slow

**HABIT:**
Rounded to oval in youth; open and spreading with age; usually multi-stemmed.

**FAMILY:**
Pinaceae

**LEAF COLOR:** Light green to dark green.

**LEAF DESCRIPTION:** NEEDLE-LIKE, 2 1/2″ to 4″ long, sharply acuminate tip, finely serrated margins, stomatic lines on all sides, appearing in BUNDLES OF 3. Midrib prominent.

**FLOWER DESCRIPTION:** Monoecious; male cones catkin-like, female cones cylindrical to rounded.

**EXPOSURE/CULTURE:** Full sun to light shade. The plant is adaptable to a wide range of well-drained soils. Pruning is not recommended, except to remove broken branches. Easy to grow.

**PEST PROBLEMS:** Beetles, moths, weevils, scales, rusts, blights. (Check with the Extension Service for specific problems in your area.)

**BARK/STEMS:** Young stems glabrous and gray-green; older bark has white to red-brown patches that exfoliate annually. OUTSTANDING.

**SELECTED CULTIVARS:** None

**LANDSCAPE NOTES:** Lacebark Pine is a true specimen plant that should be carefully located in the landscape. It is especially attractive when under-planted with ground covers or dwarf shrubs. The plant is great for borders, foundations, raised beds, and rock gardens. A must for Japanese gardens.

## *Pinus sylvestris*

**Scotch Pine**

**ZONES:**
2, 3, 4, 5, 6, 7

**HEIGHT:**
30′ to 40′

**WIDTH:**
20′ to 30′

**FRUIT:**
2″ to 3″ gray or brown cone.

**TEXTURE:**
Medium

**GROWTH RATE:**
Slow

**HABIT:**
Pyramidal or rounded.

**FAMILY:**
Pinaceae

**LEAF COLOR:** Blue-green to gray-green.

**LEAF DESCRIPTION:** NEEDLE-LIKE, 1″ to 3″ long with acute tip and finely serrated margins, appearing in BUNDLES OF 2, stomatic lines on upper surface. WHORLED IN ALTERNATE PAIRS.

**FLOWER DESCRIPTION:** Monoecious; NOT ORNAMENTAL.

**EXPOSURE/CULTURE:** Sun. The plant is adaptable to most well-drained soil types. Can be sheared into a dense pyramid.

**PEST PROBLEMS:** Beetles, moths, weevils, scales, rusts, blights. (Check with the Extension Service for specific problems in your area.)

**BARK/STEMS:** New stems greenish; older bark grayish-brown and exfoliating in sections to reveal rusty-red inner bark.

**SELECTED CULTIVARS:** 'Albyns' - (See Dwarf Evergreen Shrubs.) f. *argentea* - Tall-growing form with silver cast to leaves. 'Fastigiata' - Narrow, columnar form that has twisted, blue-green foliage. 'French Blue' - Very dense-growing cultivar with bluer foliage than other cultivars. Retains color in winter. 'Watereri' - (See Large Evergreen Shrubs.)

**LANDSCAPE NOTES:** Scotch Pine is a tree used as a lawn specimen, screen, or foundation plant. More formal in appearance than most trees. Often used as Christmas trees.

# *Pinus thunbergiana*

**Japanese Black Pine**

**ZONES:**
5, 6, 7, 8, 9

**HEIGHT:**
30′ to 40′

**WIDTH:**
10′ to 25′

**FRUIT:**
1 1/2″ to 3″ brown, ovate cone.

**TEXTURE:**
Medium

**GROWTH RATE:**
Moderate

**HABIT:**
Mostly pyramidal; often curving or crooked; variable.

**FAMILY:**
Pinaceae

**LEAF COLOR:** Dark green in all seasons.

**LEAF DESCRIPTION:** NEEDLE-LIKE, 3″ to 6″ long, tips sharply acuminate with finely serrated margins. Twisted. Stomatic lines above and underneath. Arranged in ALTERNATE BUNDLES OF 2.

**FLOWER DESCRIPTION:** Monoecious; NOT ORNAMENTAL.

**EXPOSURE/CULTURE:** Sun. Responds favorably to well-drained, fertile, loamy soil, but is adaptable. Drought-tolerant. Often used in beach plantings. Pruning is not recommended, since individual trees develop their own character. Easy to grow.

**PEST PROBLEMS:** Beetle, borers, moths, weevils, scales, rusts, blights. (Check with the Extension Service for specific problems in your area.)

**BARK/STEMS:** Young shoots are orange-yellow, maturing to gray; older bark gray-black and furrowed into long plates.

**SELECTED CULTIVARS:** 'Majestic Beauty' - Has lustrous, dark green foliage. Developed by Monrovia for smog tolerance.

**LANDSCAPE NOTES:** Japanese Black Pines vary in character, but all are usually dense in growth habit. Curving (crooked) ones are often selected for a Japanese effect. The plant is best used as a wind or soundbreak, screen, or specimen tree. Absolutely one of the best! Great for xeriscaping.

383

## *Pinus virginiana*

**Virginia Pine**

**ZONES:**
5, 6, 7, 8

**HEIGHT:**
25′ to 40′

**WIDTH:**
15′ to 25′

**FRUIT:**
2″ to 3″ brown cones; short stalked and abundant.

**TEXTURE:**
Medium

**GROWTH RATE:**
Moderate

**HABIT:**
Rounded and dense.

**FAMILY:**
Pinaceae

**LEAF COLOR:** Medium green to dark green.

**LEAF DESCRIPTION:** NEEDLE-LIKE, tips acuminate with fine points, margins finely serrated. Twisted. Arranged in ALTERNATE BUNDLES OF 2.

**FLOWER DESCRIPTION:** Monoecious; NOT ORNAMENTAL.

**EXPOSURE/CULTURE:** Sun. The plant prefers loamy, acid soil, but will grow on poor, idle land. Shearing terminal "candle" growth in spring will result in extreme compactness for a "Christmas tree" effect.

**PEST PROBLEMS:** Subject to pine pests (see previous plant), but much less susceptible than most pines.

**BARK/STEMS:** Young stems reddish with blue-white pruinose; older bark thin and fissured into small plates.

**SELECTED CULTIVARS:** None

**LANDSCAPE NOTES:** Virginia Pine is considered a "weed" in the wild, and has many nicknames (some inappropriate for this text); however, nursery-grown trees from superior seed are available and are more compact. It holds its lower branches better than other pines and makes an excellent screen. Great for xeriscaping. This plant can be very handsome, and should be given more credibility.

# Quercus glauca

**Japanese Evergreen Oak**

**ZONES:**
7, 8, 9

**HEIGHT:**
30′ to 40′

**WIDTH:**
15′ to 20′

**FRUIT:**
1/2″ brown acorn; 1/3 enclosed by cup.

**TEXTURE:**
Medium

**GROWTH RATE:**
Moderately slow.

**HABIT:**
Upright and rounded; dense.

**FAMILY:**
Fagaceae

**LEAF COLOR:** Green or bronze-green.

**LEAF DESCRIPTION:** SIMPLE, 3″ to 6″ long and 1 1/4″ to 2 1/2″ wide, basal half is entire, sharply serrated from middle to apex, acuminate tip, pubescent underneath. ALTERNATE arrangement.

**FLOWER DESCRIPTION:** Monoecious; male as greenish catkins, female greenish in spikes; NOT ORNAMENTAL.

**EXPOSURE/CULTURE:** Sun or light shade. Prefers moist, well-drained, loamy soil but is adaptable. Cleanup pruning is sometimes necessary. Grows thickly without shearing.

**PEST PROBLEMS:** No serious pests.

**BARK/STEMS:** Young stems green, maturing to brown; prominent lenticels; older bark is smooth and gray.

**SELECTED CULTIVARS:** None

**RELATED SPECIES:** *Q. myrsinifolia* - Chinese Evergreen Oak. This species is similar to *Q. glauca,* but has serrated leaf margins and is more cold-hardy.

**LANDSCAPE NOTES:** Japanese Evergreen Oak is a beautiful, dense evergreen tree that should be more widely used in the recommended zones. The plant makes uniform growth and is definitely a plant to feature. It can be used as a lawn specimen, shade tree, or screening plant. It has a more formal character than deciduous oaks.

## *Acer campestre* 'Queen Elizabeth'    Queen Elizabeth Hedge Maple

**ZONES:**
4, 5, 6, 7

**HEIGHT:**
25' to 35'

**WIDTH:**
20' to 25'

**FRUIT:**
Brown samaras; joined horizontally.

**TEXTURE:**
Medium

**GROWTH RATE:**
Moderate

**HABIT:**
Rounded or oval; dense foliage.

**FAMILY:**
Aceraceae

**LEAF COLOR:** Dark green in summer; yellowish in fall.

**LEAF DESCRIPTION:** SIMPLE, 2 1/4″ to 4″ long and broad, 3 to 5 lobes, deeply cut, smooth edges. OPPOSITE arrangement.

**FLOWER DESCRIPTION:** Greenish in corymbs; NOT ORNAMENTAL.

**EXPOSURE/CULTURE:** Sun. Prefers a well-drained, moist, acid soil, but is adaptable. Reasonably drought-tolerant. Sometimes sheared as a hedge due to low, dense branching. Can be used in the Southwest.

**PEST PROBLEMS:** No serious pests.

**BARK/STEMS:** Young stems brown, maturing to gray; older bark is dark gray with shallow furrows.

**SELECTED CULTIVARS:** None. This is a superior cultivar of *A. campestre*.

**RELATED CULTIVARS:** 'Compactum' - Shrub form to 6'. Great for hedges, but less hardy. 'Schwerinii' - Leaves purple in early spring, maturing to green.

**LANDSCAPE NOTES:** Hedge Maple is an excellent lawn specimen with dense foliage that holds late into fall. Great shade tree. Can be used in shrub borders, but should be underplanted with very shade-tolerant plants. One of the best!

# *Acer griseum*

**Paperbark Maple**

**ZONES:**
5, 6, 7, 8, 9

**HEIGHT:**
20′ to 40′

**WIDTH:**
20′ to 25′

**FRUIT:**
1 1/4″ winged samaras; joined at angles.

**TEXTURE:**
Medium

**GROWTH RATE:**
Somewhat slow.

**HABIT:**
Somewhat oval; upright and open.

**FAMILY:**
Aceraceae

**LEAF COLOR:** Dark green above, silvery underneath; red to orange in fall.

**LEAF DESCRIPTION:** COMPOUND (3 leaflets), leaflets 1 1/2″ to 3″ long and half as wide, elliptic shape with coarsely serrated margins and 3 to 5 pairs of teeth per leaflet. Petioles downy. OPPOSITE arrangement.

**FLOWER DESCRIPTION:** Greenish in pendulous cymes; NOT ORNAMENTAL.

**EXPOSURE/CULTURE:** Sun or part shade. Grows best in a well-drained, moist loam, but will thrive in clay or sandy soils. The plant should receive some shade in areas of extreme summer heat. Prune to shape, but shearing will alter its natural, open habit.

**PEST PROBLEMS:** No serious pests.

**BARK/STEMS:** New twigs are reddish-brown; older bark is cinnamon brown, thin, and exfoliating.

**SELECTED CULTIVARS:** None

**RELATED SPECIES:** *A. mandshuricum* - Manchurian Maple. This trifoliate species is somewhat upright and spreading. Unlike Paperbark Maple, it has smooth bark, but it colors in early fall to a brilliant red.

**LANDSCAPE NOTES:** Paperbark Maple is a true specimen plant due to outstanding bark characteristics. It can be used as a lawn specimen, and looks great in borders, especially when used for naturalizing.

# *Acer miyabei*

**Myabei Maple**

**ZONES:**
5, 6, 7, 8, 9

**HEIGHT:**
30′ to 40′

**WIDTH:**
20′ to 25′

**FRUIT:**
1″ to 2″ winged samaras; horizontally joined.

**TEXTURE:**
Medium

**GROWTH RATE:**
Moderate

**HABIT:**
Upright and rounded; dense.

**FAMILY:**
Aceraceae

**LEAF COLOR:** Medium to dark green in summer; yellowish in fall.

**LEAF DESCRIPTION:** SIMPLE, 3 1/2″ to 6″ long and equally broad, 5-lobed with sparsely dentate lobes, pubescent on lower surface. OPPOSITE arrangement.

**FLOWER DESCRIPTION:** Yellow-green in peduncled corymbs in spring; NOT ORNAMENTAL.

**EXPOSURE/CULTURE:** Sun or light shade. The plant prefers a well-drained, moist, loamy soil. The plant is tolerant of some excess moisture, hence it grows well on banks of streams. Pruning is selective, but usually not necessary.

**PEST PROBLEMS:** No serious pests.

**BARK/STEMS:** Young stems green and downy; older bark gray-brown with shallow furrows.

**SELECTED CULTIVARS:** None

**LANDSCAPE NOTES:** Miyabei Maple makes a fine lawn specimen or shade tree. It has many features similar to *A. campestre,* and if under-planted, should accommodate shade-tolerant groundcovers. Mature plants are quite dense and lovely.

## *Acer negundo*

'Flamingo'
Courtesy of
Monrovia
Nursery Co.

▲ Species

◄ 'Flamingo'
Courtesy of
Monrovia
Nursery Co.

**ZONES:**
3, 4, 5, 6, 7, 8, 9

**HEIGHT:**
30' to 40'+

**WIDTH:**
30' to 40'+

**FRUIT:**
1" to 1 1/2" 2-winged samara in summer.

**TEXTURE:**
Medium

**GROWTH RATE:**
Rapid

**HABIT:**
Rounded and open; sometimes multi-stemmed.

**FAMILY:**
Aceraceae

**LEAF COLOR:** Pale to light green in summer; yellowish in fall.

**LEAF DESCRIPTION:** ODD PINNATELY COMPOUND, 3 to 5 leaflets, leaflets 2 1/2" to 4 1/2" long and half as wide, ovate to ovate-oblong shape with coarsely serrated to slightly lobed margins. Sometimes silvery beneath. OPPOSITE arrangement.

**FLOWER DESCRIPTION:** Dioecious, yellowish; male in corymbs, female in racemes; NOT ORNAMENTAL.

**EXPOSURE/CULTURE:** Full sun to light shade. Prefers moist, organic, well-drained soil, but is adaptable. pH-tolerant and drought-tolerant. Pruning is minimal and selective. Shorter-lived than most *Acer* species, but is suitable for the Southwest.

**PEST PROBLEMS:** Boxelder bugs, borers, anthracnose, leaf spots, cankers.

**BARK/STEMS:** Young stems green and glaucous; older bark is gray-brown and sparsely furrowed.

**SELECTED CULTIVARS:** 'Aureo-marginatum' - Leaflets are green with yellow margins. 'Flamingo' - New leaflets unfold with strong pink, maturing to green with a white margin. 'Variegatum' - Leaflets are green with irregular whitish margins.

**LANDSCAPE NOTES:** Boxelder is a nice deciduous tree that is considered a weed by many gardeners. Its greatest merit is that it grows almost anywhere and is drought-tolerant. It can be used in the lawn area, borders, and backgrounds. The cultivars are quite handsome. Great for xeriscaping.

## *Betula nigra*

**River Birch, Red Birch**

**ZONES:**
3, 4, 5, 6, 7, 8, 9

**HEIGHT:**
25′ to 45′

**WIDTH:**
15′ to 25′

**FRUIT:**
1″ strobile with winged nutlets; NOT ORNAMENTAL.

**TEXTURE:**
Medium

**GROWTH RATE:**
Rapid

**HABIT:**
Upright and open; arching.

**FAMILY:**
Betulaceae

**LEAF COLOR:** Medium green in summer; yellowish in fall.

**LEAF DESCRIPTION:** SIMPLE, 1″ to 3″ long and half as wide, ovate shape with doubly serrated margins. Prominent veins are hairy and raised on lower surface. Leaves drop early in fall.

**FLOWER DESCRIPTION:** Monoecious; male catkins to 2″, female catkins 1/2″ or less; NOT ORNAMENTAL.

**EXPOSURE/CULTURE:** Sun or part shade. Prefers moist, organic, acid soil. Native to moist banks of streams. Defoliates under dry, hot conditions, unless supplemental water is provided. Will not tolerate alkaline soils. Pruning is not recommended.

**PEST PROBLEMS:** Fungal leaf spots.

**BARK/STEMS:** Young stems reddish-brown; older bark is darker reddish-brown, peeling in thin plates to expose light brown inner bark.

**SELECTED CULTIVARS:** 'Heritage' - (Featured on next page.)

**LANDSCAPE NOTES:** River Birch is a beautiful, graceful tree with an open character that allows structures or other background material to show. Probably best used as a lawn or border specimen. Multi-stem plants having three or more trunks are in most demand. The "shaggy" bark with lighter inner bark is extremely noticeable and interesting.

## *Betula nigra 'Heritage'* **Heritage River Birch**

**ZONES:**
4, 5, 6, 7, 8, 9

**HEIGHT:**
25' to 45'

**WIDTH:**
15' to 25'

**FRUIT:**
1" strobile with winged nutlets; NOT ORNAMENTAL.

**TEXTURE:**
Medium

**GROWTH RATE:**
Rapid

**HABIT:**
Upright and open; somewhat arching.

**FAMILY:**
Betulaceae

**LEAF COLOR:** Dark green in summer; yellowish in fall.

**LEAF DESCRIPTION:** SIMPLE, 1" to 3" long and half as wide, ovate shape with doubly-serrated margins. Prominent veins are hairy and raised on the lower surface. ALTERNATE arrangement.

**FLOWER DESCRIPTION:** Monoecious; male catkins to 2", female catkins 1/2" or less; NOT ORNAMENTAL.

**EXPOSURE/CULTURE:** Sun or part shade. Prefers moist, organic, acid soil. Water should be provided during dry, hot conditions to prevent premature defoliation. Will not tolerate high pH soils. Pruning is not recommended.

**PEST PROBLEMS:** Leaf spots.

**BARK/STEMS:** Young stems reddish-brown; older bark is brown, exfoliating to expose a whitish inner bark.

**SELECTED CULTIVARS:** None. This is a cultivar of *B. nigra.*

**LANDSCAPE NOTES:** Heritage Birch has lighter colored inner bark than the species, and is the closest to pure white that is suitable for the Southeast. As with River Birch, specimen plants having three or more trunks are more desirable. The plant should be featured in the lawn or garden border. A nice plant where light shade is desirable, such as near a deck or patio. This is an outstanding cultivar of recent years.

# *Betula pendula*

**European White Birch**

▲ 'Dalecarlica'

**ZONES:**
2, 3, 4, 5, 6, 7

**HEIGHT:**
30′ to 40′

**WIDTH:**
20′ to 30′

**FRUIT:**
1″ strobile with winged nutlet; NOT ORNAMENTAL.

**TEXTURE:**
Medium

**GROWTH RATE:**
Rapid

**FAMILY:**
Betulaceae

**LEAF COLOR:** Dark green in summer; yellowish in fall.

**LEAF DESCRIPTION:** SIMPLE, 1 1/2″ to 3 1/2″ long and half as wide. Broad ovate shape with doubly serrated margins and acuminate tip. ALTERNATE arrangement.

**FLOWER DESCRIPTION:** Monoecious; male catkins 2″ to 3″ long, usually in pairs; female catkins 1/2″ or less; NOT ORNAMENTAL.

**EXPOSURE/CULTURE:** Sun or light shade. Prefers moist, organic, well-drained soils, but is adaptable to a wide range of soils. Will grow at higher pH levels than River Birch. This is not a tree for the Southeast or Southwest. Will not take high heat or dry winds. Pruning is not recommended.

**PEST PROBLEMS:** Bronze Birch Borer. This insect can be destructive, and routine spraying is recommended.

**BARK/STEMS:** Young stems tan; older bark is smooth and white with numerous lenticels and small dark, almost black, patches where branches attach.

**SELECTED CULTIVARS:** 'Dalecarlica' - Similar to the species, but the foliage has deeply cut, coarsely serrated lobes. Quite elegant!

**LANDSCAPE NOTES:** European white birch has beautiful white bark with accents of black. It makes a bold specimen plant in a well-chosen location. Not for the Southeast.

## *Bumelia lycioides*

**Buckthorn Bumelia**

**ZONES:**
6, 7, 8, 9

**HEIGHT:**
25′ to 40′

**WIDTH:**
30′ to 40′

**FRUIT:**
1/4″ to 1/2″ black drupe; NOT ORNAMENTAL.

**TEXTURE:**
Fine

**GROWTH RATE:**
Somewhat slow.

**HABIT:**
Rounded and spreading.

**FAMILY:**
Sapotaceae

**LEAF COLOR:** Dark green in summer; no coloration to brown coloration in fall.

**LEAF DESCRIPTION:** SIMPLE, 2″ to 6″ long and 1″ to 1 1/4″ wide, elliptic to narrow-obovate shape and entire margins. ALTERNATE arrangement, but sometimes whorled on short spurs.

**FLOWER DESCRIPTION:** Whitish, tiny, appearing in somewhat dense, axillary clusters. Flowers in June to July. Can be showy.

**EXPOSURE/CULTURE:** Sun or light shade. The plant prefers moist, organic, well-drained soil, but is somewhat adaptable. Pruning is not necessary.

**PEST PROBLEMS:** None

**BARK/STEMS:** Young stems smooth and gray with very stiff thorns; older bark is gray-brown with shallow furrows and narrow ridges.

**SELECTED CULTIVARS:** None

**LANDSCAPE NOTES:** Buckthorn Bumelia is a native tree that has possibilities as a lawn or shade tree. Older plants have great shape, and the plant is pest-free and reliable.

## *Carpinus betulus 'Fastigiata'*    European Hornbeam

**ZONES:**
4, 5, 6, 7, 8

**HEIGHT:**
25′ to 40′

**WIDTH:**
15′ to 30′

**FRUIT:**
Brown nutlet with 3-lobed wing; joined in pairs.

**TEXTURE:**
Medium

**GROWTH RATE:**
Slow in youth; moderate with age.

**HABIT:**
Conical and upright; densely branched.

**FAMILY:**
Betulaceae

**LEAF COLOR:** Dark green in summer; yellowish in fall.

**LEAF DESCRIPTION:** SIMPLE, 3″ to 4″ long and 1 1/4″ to 2″ wide, ovate to elliptic shape with doubly serrated margins. ALTERNATE arrangement.

**FLOWER DESCRIPTION:** Monoecious; male catkin 1″ to 2″ long, female to 3″ with pairs of 3-lobed bracts; NOT ORNAMENTAL.

**EXPOSURE/CULTURE:** Sun or light shade. The plant prefers well-drained loam, but is adaptable to most any soil except excessively wet soil. Can be pruned, but usually assumes a dense, oval shape without pruning or shearing. Somewhat drought-tolerant. Easy to grow.

**PEST PROBLEMS:** No serious pests.

**BARK/STEMS:** Young stems brown-green and smooth; older bark is smooth and medium gray with rounded ridges.

**SELECTED CULTIVARS:** None. This is a cultivar of *C. betulus.*

**SIMILAR CULTIVARS:** 'Columnaris' - Similar to 'Fastigiata' but having a more slender, pyramidal habit.

**LANDSCAPE NOTES:** This is a plant of handsome foliage and habit. It is often used as a lawn specimen, but makes an excellent hedge or screen. The symmetrical habit gives the plant a more formal appearance. Looks best in a well-manicured setting.

# *Carpinus caroliniana*

## Ironwood, American Hornbeam

**ZONES:**
3, 4, 5, 6, 7, 8

**HEIGHT:**
20′ to 25′

**WIDTH:**
15′ to 20′

**FRUIT:**
Small winged nutlet; NOT ORNAMENTAL.

**TEXTURE:**
Medium

**GROWTH RATE:**
Slow

**HABIT:**
Upright and irregular.

**FAMILY:**
Betulaceae

**LEAF COLOR:** Medium green in summer; yellow to red in fall.

**LEAF DESCRIPTION:** SIMPLE, 1″ to 4″ long and half as wide, ovate to oblong-ovate shape with doubly serrated margins, hairy underneath where veins join midrib. ALTERNATE arangement.

**FLOWER DESCRIPTION:** Monoecious; male catkins, female is lobed; NOT ORNAMENTAL.

**EXPOSURE/CULTURE:** Sun or shade. Prefers moist, organic soils, but adapts to a wide range of conditions. Often found along streams, shaded by larger trees. Pruning is not usually needed.

**PEST PROBLEMS:** Disease-free.

**BARK/STEMS:** Young stems smooth and gray; older bark light to dark gray; very old bark often having ridges.

**SELECTED CULTIVARS:** None

**LANDSCAPE NOTES:** Ironwood has smooth gray bark that sometimes reminds one of iron. It makes an excellent general-purpose tree in the landscape, and is a good selection for naturalizing since it tolerates shade. The leaves are similar to Beech.

## *Catalpa bignoniodes*                Southern Catalpa

**ZONES:**
5, 6, 7, 8, 9

**HEIGHT:**
30' to 40'+

**WIDTH:**
25' to 30'+

**FRUIT:**
Long, greenish capsule, maturing to brown; bean-like, containing many winged seeds.

**TEXTURE:**
Coarse

**GROWTH RATE:**
Rapid

**HABIT:**
Upright, rounded, and open.

**FAMILY:**
Bignoniaceae

**LEAF COLOR:** Medium-dull green in summer; yellowish in fall.

**LEAF DESCRIPTION:** SIMPLE, 5″ to 8″ long and 3″ to 6″ wide, long cordate shape with entire margins and acuminate tip, pubescent veins on underside. Long petioles to 6″. OPPOSITE or sometimes WHORLED.

**FLOWER DESCRIPTION:** White, with 2 yellow stripes and many purple to brown spots in the 2-lipped corolla. 2″ long in terminal panicles to 12″. Very showy. Flowers in spring.

**EXPOSURE/CULTURE:** Sun or light shade. The plant prefers a rich loam but will thrive in most soils or conditions. Very drought-tolerant. Selective pruning is all that is needed to remove dead or broken limbs. Easy to grow.

**PEST PROBLEMS:** Leaf spots, mildews, caterpillars.

**BARK/STEMS:** Young stems greenish, maturing to gray-brown; older bark is reddish-brown and furrowed into small scaly plates.

**SELECTED CULTIVARS:** 'Aurea' - Has bright yellow leaves throughout the season, turning paler yellow in fall.

**RELATED SPECIES:** *C. speciosa* - Western Catalpa. This species forms a large pyramidal tree with larger leaves than *C. bignonioides*. About one zone more cold-hardy.

**LANDSCAPE NOTES:** Southern Catalpa can be used as a lawn specimen or shade tree. It is a native tree and is especially attractive for naturalizing. Its strongest merit is its reliability and adaptive nature. Older trees can be quite picturesque.

# *Chionanthus retusus*

**Chinese Fringetree**

**ZONES:**
6, 7, 8, 9

**HEIGHT:**
25' to 35'

**WIDTH:**
25' to 35'

**FRUIT:**
1/2" dark blue, oval drupe.

**TEXTURE:**
Medium

**GROWTH RATE:**
Slow to moderate.

**HABIT:**
Rounded and spreading.

**FAMILY:**
Oleaceae

**LEAF COLOR:** Lustrous dark green; brownish in fall.

**LEAF DESCRIPTION:** SIMPLE, 3" to 5" long and 2 1/2" to 3" wide. Very thick. Rounded to obovate to elliptic shape with entire margins. Mostly OPPOSITE arrangement.

**FLOWER DESCRIPTION:** White, 3/4" strap-like petals, appearing in dense, terminal panicles 4" wide or more on new growth. Flowers in late spring. Very showy.

**EXPOSURE/CULTURE:** Sun or part shade. Prefers a well-drained, moist, loamy soil, but is somewhat adaptable. Heat-tolerant, but not drought-tolerant. Pruning is not usually necessary, but can be performed after flowering.

**PEST PROBLEMS:** None

**BARK/STEMS:** Young stems are grayish and smooth, having noticeable lenticels; older bark is gray and smooth.

**SELECTED CULTIVARS:** var. *serrulatus* - Similar to the species, but leaves have distinctly serrated margins.

**LANDSCAPE NOTES:** Chinese Fringetree is a true specimen that is spectacular in flower and handsome in foliage. The tree can be used as a lawn specimen or shade tree, and it fits well into both natural or more formal landscapes. Should be more widely used.

# *Firmiana simplex*

**Chinese Parasol Tree**

**ZONES:**
7, 8, 9

**HEIGHT:**
25′ to 35′

**WIDTH:**
20′ to 25′

**FRUIT:**
Brown, leaf-like follicles in panicles; NOT ORNAMENTAL.

**TEXTURE:**
Coarse

**GROWTH RATE:**
Rapid

**HABIT:**
Upright with rounded crown.

**FAMILY:**
Sterculiaceae

**LEAF COLOR:** Green in summer; yellow in fall.

**LEAF DESCRIPTION:** SIMPLE, 5″ to 8″ long and broad, can be larger, 3 to 5 deeply cut lobes with smooth margins and tapering, pointed tips. Cordate base. Palmately veined. ALTERNATE arrangement.

**FLOWER DESCRIPTION:** Lemon-yellow, 1/2″ in 12″ to 20″ panicles, appearing in June.

**EXPOSURE/CULTURE:** Sun or part shade. Prefers well-drained, deep soils. Pruning is usually not necessary, except for selective cleanup. Easy to grow.

**PEST PROBLEMS:** None

**BARK/STEMS:** Bark is gray-green with a cork-like smoothness.

**SELECTED CULTIVARS:** None

**LANDSCAPE NOTES:** Chinese Parasol Tree adds a tropical flavor to the landscape with its large, dense foliage. Its greatest use is the addition of textural contrast in the garden. Yellow-green flower panicles add additional interest. Best used as a focal plant in the lawn or garden borders.

# *Gleditsia triacanthos* var. *inermis* 'Moraine'

**Thornless Honeylocust**

**ZONES:**
4, 5, 6, 7, 8

**HEIGHT:**
30' to 50'

**WIDTH:**
20' to 30'

**FRUIT:**
Fruitless. (Species has 12" bean-like pods.)

**TEXTURE:**
Fine

**GROWTH RATE:**
Moderate to rapid.

**HABIT:**
Upright, spreading, and very open.

**FAMILY:**
Fabaceae

**LEAF COLOR:** Medium to dark green in summer; yellowish in fall.

**LEAF DESCRIPTION:** COMPOUND, 6" to 12" long, pinnate or bipinnate on same plant; leaflets 1" to 1 1/4" long, elliptic to oblong-lanceolate shape with sparsely serrulate margins. ALTERNATE arrangement.

**FLOWER DESCRIPTION:** Greenish racemes; NOT ORNAMENTAL.

**EXPOSURE/CULTURE:** Sun. Plant prefers moist, loamy soils, but is tolerant of a wide range of soil types and pH levels. Salt- and drought-tolerant. Pruning is usually not necessary.

**PEST PROBLEMS:** Honeylocust borer, webworms.

**BARK/STEMS:** Young stems are smooth and greenish; older bark is gray-brown with deep, narrow furrows.

**RELATED CULTIVARS:** 'Shademaster' - Thornless, ascending branches on fruitless plants. 'Sunburst' - (Featured on next page.)

**LANDSCAPE NOTES:** Honeylocust is an open, thin-growing tree that is useful where it is desirable for the background to be seen through the foliage mass. Looks especially attractive near water. A good substitute for dense-growing trees.

## *Gleditsia triacanthos var. inermis 'Sunburst'* Sunburst Thornless Honeylocust

**ZONES:**
4, 5, 6, 7, 8

**HEIGHT:**
30′ to 40′

**WIDTH:**
25′ to 30′

**FRUIT:**
Fruitless

**TEXTURE:**
Fine

**GROWTH RATE:**
Rapid

**HABIT:**
Upright, spreading, and somewhat open.

**FAMILY:**
Fabaceae

**LEAF COLOR:** Leaves on new growth are bright yellow, maturing to green; yellowish in fall.

**LEAF DESCRIPTION:** COMPOUND, 6″ to 10″ long, pinnate or bipinnate on the same plant; leaflets, 1″ to 1 1/2″ long, elliptic to oblong-lanceolate shape with sparsely serrulate margins. ALTERNATE arrangement.

**FLOWER DESCRIPTION:** Greenish racemes; NOT ORNAMENTAL.

**EXPOSURE/CULTURE:** Sun. The plant prefers moist, loamy, well-drained soil, but is adaptable to a wide range of soils and pH levels. Salt- and drought-tolerant. Pruning is usually not necessary.

**PEST PROBLEMS:** Honeylocust borer, webworms.

**BARK/STEMS:** Young stems are smooth and greenish; older bark is gray-brown with narrow furrows.

**SELECTED CULTIVARS:** None. This is a cultivar.

**LANDSCAPE NOTES:** Sunburst Honeylocust is a noticeable specimen tree in spring and summer. It casts light shade, making it a good tree for underplanting with a variety of lower-growing plants. Can be used effectively near decks and patios. A great focal plant. Easy to grow and maintain.

# *Halesia carolina*

**Carolina Silverbell**

**ZONES:**
5, 6, 7, 8, 9

**HEIGHT:**
30' to 40'

**WIDTH:**
20' to 30'

**FRUIT:**
1" to 1 1/2" oblong, brown, dry fruit; 4-winged.

**TEXTURE:**
Medium

**GROWTH RATE:**
Slow

**HABIT:**
Low-branched tree with variable crown; often spreading, but sometimes upright.

**FAMILY:**
Styracaceae

**LEAF COLOR:** Dark green in summer; yellowish in fall.

**LEAF DESCRIPTION:** SIMPLE, 2" to 4" long and half as wide, ovate to elliptic shape with finely serrate to serrulate margins. Pubescent on undersides. ALTERNATE arrangement.

**FLOWER DESCRIPTION:** White, 1/2" to 3/4" long, corolla with 4 shallow lobes, bell-shaped, drooping in axillary clusters on previous season's growth. Flowers in spring. Very showy.

**EXPOSURE/CULTURE:** Sun or light shade. Does best in moist, organic, acid soils. Not tolerant of dry soil or dry, sunny locations. This is a native tree that looks best not pruned.

**PEST PROBLEMS:** No serious pests.

**BARK/STEMS:** Young stems are hairy, becoming "stringy" in nature; older bark is gray-brown to deep charcoal with deep, narrow furrows.

**SELECTED CULTIVARS:** None

**RELATED SPECIES:** *H. monticola* - Mountain Silverbell. This is very similar to *H. carolina,* but is larger in size with larger flowers.

**LANDSCAPE NOTES:** Carolina Silverbell makes a fine specimen or lawn tree. It is especially good for naturalizing, and performs well in garden borders with suitable underplantings of groundcovers or native perennials.

## *Koelreuteria bipinnata*

**Chinese Flame Tree**

**ZONES:**
7, 8, 9, 10

**HEIGHT:**
30′ to 40′

**WIDTH:**
15′ to 25′

**FRUIT:**
Bright rose, 3-valved capsules in panicles. Very bright and showy, almost flame-like.

**TEXTURE:**
Medium

**GROWTH RATE:**
Moderate

**HABIT:**
Upright and spreading (variable); open.

**FAMILY:**
Sapindaceae

**LEAF COLOR:** Medium green in summer; yellowish in fall.

**LEAF DESCRIPTION:** COMPOUND, bipinnate (twice-divided), 18″ to 24″ long; leaflets 2″ to 3″ long and half as wide, ovate to ovate-oblong shape with entire or finely serrated margins. ALTERNATE arrangement.

**FLOWER DESCRIPTION:** Yellow, 1/2″ long in huge panicles, 1 1/2′ to 2′ long and two-thirds as wide. Flowers in late summer to fall. Flowers later than *K. paniculata*. Very showy.

**EXPOSURE/CULTURE:** Full sun. The plant will grow in a wide range of soil types and conditions. Drought-tolerant. pH-tolerant. Pruning is usually not necessary.

**PEST PROBLEMS:** No serious pests.

**BARK/STEMS:** Young stems bright brown to greenish with numerous lenticels; older bark is light gray-brown with shallow furrows.

**SELECTED CULTIVARS:** None

**RELATED SPECIES:** *K. paniculata* (See next page.)

**LANDSCAPE NOTES:** Chinese Flame Tree provides interest in late summer with bright yellow flower panicles. The impact is even more dramatic in fall when the bright rose colored fruits peak. This plant will attain specimen status anywhere in the landscape. Great for massing on larger properties.

# Koelreuteria paniculata

**Goldenrain Tree**

**ZONES:**
5, 6, 7, 8, 9

**HEIGHT:**
20' to 30'

**WIDTH:**
20' to 25'

**FRUIT:**
1" to 1 1/2" thin, 3-valved capsules; yellowish at first, maturing to brown.

**TEXTURE:**
Medium

**GROWTH RATE:**
Moderate

**HABIT:**
Rounded and irregular.

**FAMILY:**
Sapindaceae

**LEAF COLOR:** Dark green in summer; yellowish in fall.

**LEAF DESCRIPTION:** PINNATELY COMPOUND, sometimes bipinnate, to 18", 11 to 17 leaflets; leaflets 2" to 3" long, leaflets ovate to oblong shape, margins shallowly lobed or coarsely serrated. ALTERNATE arrangement.

**FLOWER DESCRIPTION:** Yellow, 1/2" in 12" upright panicles. Flowers in late summer. Very showy.

**EXPOSURE/CULTURE:** Sun or light shade. This plant is adapted to a wide range of well-drained soils. Drought-tolerant. Pruning is usually not necessary.

**PEST PROBLEMS:** No serious pests.

**BARK/STEMS:** Light beige-brown to gray-brown; older bark is shallowly furrowed.

**SELECTED CULTIVARS:** 'Fastigiata' - Narrow, columnar habit. 'September' - Begins bloom later than the species.

**RELATED SPECIES:** *K. bipinnata* - (See previous plant.)

**LANDSCAPE NOTES:** Goldenrain Tree is a definite focal point in the landscape. Both the flowers and fruits add outstanding ornamental value. The plant does well in lawns, raised planters, berms, and borders. It casts light shade and makes a nice patio tree.

## *Magnolia macrophylla*

**Bigleaf Magnolia**

**ZONES:**
6, 7, 8, 9

**HEIGHT:**
30′ to 35′

**WIDTH:**
15′ to 20′

**FRUIT:**
3″ aggregate of follicles; rose-red.

**TEXTURE:**
VERY COARSE!

**GROWTH RATE:**
Moderate

**HABIT:**
Upright and somewhat open; rounded crown.

**FAMILY:**
Magnoliaceae

**LEAF COLOR:** Dark green in summer; no fall color change before dropping.

**LEAF DESCRIPTION:** SIMPLE, 24″ to 30″ long and 10″ to 12″ wide, oblong-obovate shape with subcordate base and smooth, undulate margins. Whitish and pubescent underneath. ALTERNATE arrangement.

**FLOWER DESCRIPTION:** White, 10″ to 12″ across, 6-petaled, inner 3 petals having a purplish blotch at basal end. Fragrant and very showy. Not abundant.

**EXPOSURE/CULTURE:** Sun or part shade. The plant prefers well-drained, moist, organic soil. Not tolerant of wet conditions or dry, arid conditions. Pruning is usually not required.

**PEST PROBLEMS:** No serious pests.

**BARK/STEMS:** Young stems yellow-green and hairy; older bark is light gray and mostly smooth or remotely scaly.

**SELECTED CULTIVARS:** None

**LANDSCAPE NOTES:** The Bigleaf Magnolia is an interesting and unusual tree having huge leaves and flowers. The plant is reputed to have limited use; however, the tree certainly has merit as a specimen tree for larger gardens and properties. It offers a refreshing change from all of the fine-textured plants used in landscaping and allows great textural contrast.

# *Magnolia virginiana*

## Sweetbay Magnolia, Sweetbay

**ZONES:**
5, 6, 7, 8, 9

**HEIGHT:**
20' to 40'

**WIDTH:**
10' to 20'

**FRUIT:**
2" to 3" dark red aggregate of follicles (pod).

**TEXTURE:**
Medium to coarse.

**GROWTH RATE:**
Moderate

**HABIT:**
Upright and open; multi-stemmed.

**FAMILY:**
Magnoliaceae

**LEAF COLOR:** Green with white undersides; brownish-green in fall.

**LEAF DESCRIPTION:** SIMPLE, 3" to 6" long and one-third as wide, elliptic shape with entire margins. ALTERNATE arrangement.

**FLOWER DESCRIPTION:** White, 2 1/2" to 3 1/2" wide. Fragrant. Flowers in May to July. Showy, but not abundant.

**EXPOSURE/CULTURE:** Sun or shade. The plant prefers moist, organic, acid soils similar to its native habitat. Will tolerate wet conditions, but performs poorly in dry, hot locations. Pruning is minimal.

**PEST PROBLEMS:** Leaf spots can be destructive.

**BARK/STEMS:** Young stems are green and smooth; older bark is smooth and gray to gray-brown.

**SELECTED CULTIVARS:** None important.

**LANDSCAPE NOTES:** Sweetbay is a native plant that has many possibilities in the landscape. Its use as a specimen is enhanced when tree-formed and selected for three or more stems. Probably best used in natural borders and under-planted. Evergreen in the southernmost zones, but is deciduous in the northernmost recommended zones.

## *Malus hybrida* — Hybrid Flowering Crabapple

▲ 'Indian Magic'

▲ 'Calloway'

**ZONES:**
4, 5, 6, 7, 8, depending on cultivar.

**HEIGHT:**
20′ to 25′

**WIDTH:**
20′ to 25′

**FRUIT:**
1″ to 2″ red, yellow, or green pome; edible.

**TEXTURE:**
Medium

**GROWTH RATE:**
Moderate to rapid.

**HABIT:**
Usually spreading and rounded; cultivars may be upright or pendulous.

**FAMILY:**
Rosaceae

**LEAF COLOR:** Green to red to purple in summer, depending on cultivar; variable in fall.

**LEAF DESCRIPTION:** SIMPLE, 2″ to 3″ long and half as wide, oval to elliptic shape with serrated margins. ALTERNATE arrangement.

**FLOWER DESCRIPTION:** White, pink, red, or purple, depending on cultivar. 1″ to 2 1/2″ wide. Flowers in spring; some opening before the leaves, others after the leaves. Single or double. Abundant and very attractive.

**EXPOSURE/CULTURE:** Sun. Prefers well-drained, moist soils. Reasonably drought-tolerant. Prune for strong structural branches. Remove crossing or diseased branches.

**PEST PROBLEMS:** Borers, fire blight, cedar apple rust, apple scab.

**BARK/STEMS:** Young stems green to reddish-brown to purplish; older bark shiny gray-brown with lenticels; oldest bark may be scaly.

**SELECTED CULTIVARS:** Note: There are hundreds of cultivars. One should select for disease resistance. Some outstanding cultivars are: 'Calloway' - Single, white flowers. Large red fruits that hold late, after the leaves. 'Dolgo' - Single, white flowers with bright red fruits. Great for jellies. 'Indian Summer' - Double, rosey-red flowers. Bright red fruits. 'Katherine' - Double, pink flowers. Yellow fruits with a red blush. 'Sparkler' - Single, rosey-red flowers. Dark red fruits.

**LANDSCAPE NOTES:** Crabapple is available in many variations of flower, fruit, size, and habit. The plants provide a breathtaking display for around two weeks in spring. Heavy rains sometimes ruin the display. Fruits may be a nuisance near walks or patios. Probably best used as a specimen on lawn areas or borders. Check with the local Extension Service for varieties recommended in your area.

# *Malus floribunda*

**Japanese Crabapple**

**ZONES:**
5, 6, 7, 8, 9

**HEIGHT:**
20' to 25'

**WIDTH:**
20' to 30'

**FRUIT:**
1/2" yellow and red pome.

**TEXTURE:**
Medium

**GROWTH RATE:**
Moderate

**HABIT:**
Rounded and broad-spreading; dense.

**FAMILY:**
Rosaceae

**LEAF COLOR:** Green in summer; yellowish in fall.

**LEAF DESCRIPTION:** SIMPLE, 2" to 3" long and half as wide, ovate to elliptic shape with sharply serrated margins. ALTERNATE arrangement.

**FLOWER DESCRIPTION:** White or pinkish flowers from deep pink buds, single, 1" across. Flowers in early spring. Abundant and showy.

**EXPOSURE/CULTURE:** Sun. Prefers a good, deep loam but is adaptable to most well-drained soils. Reasonably drought-tolerant. Prune selectively for strong branching or to remove diseased or crossing branches. Fruit can be messy in fall.

**PEST PROBLEMS:** Fire blight, apple scab.

**BARK/STEMS:** Young stems green to reddish; older bark is gray-brown, sometimes scaly.

**SELECTED CULTIVARS:** None

**RELATED SPECIES:** *M. sargentii* - This is a white-flowering species with dark red fruits. It is characterized by its very broad habit that may be double its height. One of the best.

**LANDSCAPE NOTES:** Japanese Crabapple is generally regarded as one of the most reliable of the flowering crabapples, having moderate disease resistance. This is a symmetrical tree that has specimen status in spring, but becomes a nice lawn specimen in summer. Avoid planting near walks, patios, and drives due to fruit drop in fall.

## *Oxydendrum arboreum*

**Sourwood, Sorrell Tree**

**ZONES:**
5, 6, 7, 8, 9

**HEIGHT:**
20′ to 40′

**WIDTH:**
15′ to 25′

**FRUIT:**
Gray-brown, 5-valved capsule; persisting and ornamental.

**TEXTURE:**
Medium to coarse.

**GROWTH RATE:**
Slow

**HABIT:**
Upright; somewhat pyramidal.

**FAMILY:**
Ericaceae

**LEAF COLOR:** Dark green in summer; brilliant red to purple in fall.

**LEAF DESCRIPTION:** SIMPLE, 4″ to 8″ long and one-third as wide, oblong elliptic shape with serrulate margins. ALTERNATE arrangement.

**FLOWER DESCRIPTION:** White, tiny, in 6″ to 12″ pendulous racemes. Flowers in summer. Very showy.

**EXPOSURE/CULTURE:** Sun or part shade. The plant prefers a moist, organic, well-drained soil. Develops better shape in sun, but might require supplemental watering. Pruning is usually not necessary.

**PEST PROBLEMS:** Leaf spots, webworms.

**BARK/STEMS:** Young stems are smooth and green; older bark is gray with deep furrows and narrow ridges.

**SELECTED CULTIVARS:** None

**LANDSCAPE NOTES:** Sourwood is a native tree that produces a magnificent display of flowers that resemble Lily-of-the-Valley. Brilliant red leaves in fall contrast with the gray-brown racemes of fruit. This is an outstanding selection as a lawn specimen or border tree. It deserves more consideration in landscaping, as cultivated trees can be outstanding.

## *Parrotia persica*

**Persian Parrotia**

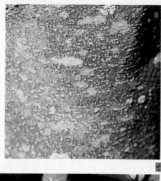

**ZONES:**
5, 6, 7, 8

**HEIGHT:**
20′ to 30′

**WIDTH:**
10′ to 20′

**FRUIT:**
2-valved, brown capsule; NOT ORNAMENTAL.

**TEXTURE:**
Medium

**GROWTH RATE:**
Moderate

**HABIT:**
Oval, upright, and dense; shrub-like.

**FAMILY:**
Hamamelidaceae

**LEAF COLOR:** Dark green in summer; yellow to orange-red in fall.

**LEAF DESCRIPTION:** SIMPLE, 3″ to 4″ long and half as wide, ovate to obovate shape with coarsely dentate margins on apex end, basal half is usually entire. ALTERNATE arrangement.

**FLOWER DESCRIPTION:** Red stamens (apetalous), late winter to early spring; NOT ABUNDANT.

**EXPOSURE/CULTURE:** Sun or light shade. Prefers well-drained, loamy soil and is reasonably drought-tolerant. Plant will respond to shearing, if desired. Shrub-like in habit. Easy to grow.

**PEST PROBLEMS:** Chewing insects.

**BARK/STEMS:** Young stems brown-green; older bark gray, often mottled and variable in color.

**SELECTED CULTIVARS:** None

**LANDSCAPE NOTES:** Persian Parrotia can be used as an accent or lawn specimen. It has possibilities for warm-season screening due to its dense, shrub-like character. The plant becomes more beautiful with age, especially the bark. Very handsome tree.

## *Paulownia tomentosa*

**Royal Paulownia**

**ZONES:**
6, 7, 8, 9

**HEIGHT:**
30′ to 40′

**WIDTH:**
20′ to 30′

**FRUIT:**
1 1/4″ brown, 2-valved capsule containing many-winged seed.

**TEXTURE:**
Coarse

**GROWTH RATE:**
Rapid

**HABIT:**
Upright, rounded, and open.

**FAMILY:**
Bignoniaceae

**LEAF COLOR:** Medium green in summer; green or brown in fall.

**LEAF DESCRIPTION:** SIMPLE, 5″ to 12″ long and two-thirds as wide, broad ovate shape with cordate base and acuminate tip (almost heart-shaped), entire margins, sometimes 3-lobed. Pubescent upper surface; densely pubescent underneath. OPPOSITE arrangement.

**FLOWER DESCRIPTION:** Pale violet, 2″ long or longer, darker spots inside corolla. Fragrant. Flowers in spring before the leaves. Showy.

**EXPOSURE/CULTURE:** Full sun or part shade. Will grow in almost any soil or condition. Wild seedlings germinate almost anywhere - often against foundations or other unwanted locations. Pruning is usually not necessary. Very easy to grow.

**PEST PROBLEMS:** Chewing insects.

**BARK/STEMS:** Young stems green with large lenticels; older bark is gray with shallow fissures. Wood is brittle.

**SELECTED CULTIVARS:** None

**LANDSCAPE NOTES:** Royal Paulownia is often considered a weed. However, given a good site, the plant has possibilities, especially to provide rapid shade on sites lacking trees. Probably best used as a temporary tree. Flowers are quite attractive, although the brown fruits persist throughout winter.

## *Phellodendron amurense*

**Amur Corktree**

**ZONES:**
4, 5, 6, 7, 8

**HEIGHT:**
30′ to 40′

**WIDTH:**
30′ to 40′

**FRUIT:**
1/2″ black drupe; NOT ORNA-MENTAL.

**TEXTURE:**
Medium

**GROWTH RATE:**
Slow to moderate.

**HABIT:**
Rounded and spreading; open.

**FAMILY:**
Rutaceae

**LEAF COLOR:** Dark green in summer; yellowish in fall.

**LEAF DESCRIPTION:** COMPOUND, to 12″, 5 to 13 leaflets; leaflets to 4″ with ovate to elliptic shape and acuminate tips. Margins entire. OPPOSITE arrangement.

**FLOWER DESCRIPTION:** Dioecious; greenish in panicles; NOT ORNAMENTAL.

**EXPOSURE/CULTURE:** Sun. Prefers well-drained, organic soil, but is adaptable to almost any soil or pH level. Does not grow as well during periods of intense heat. Pruning is usually not necessary.

**PEST PROBLEMS:** None

**BARK/STEMS:** Young stems orange-yellow with distinct lenticels; older bark has a cork-like pattern of furrows and ridges.

**SELECTED CULTIVARS:** None

**RELATED SPECIES:** *P. chinensis* - This species is one-third smaller in size, but has larger, more attractive foliage.

**LANDSCAPE NOTES:** Amur Corktree is useful as a shade tree or lawn specimen. It is noted most for its attractive, cork-like bark. In addition, it "cleans" itself quickly in early fall.

## *Pistacia chinensis*

**Chinese Pistache**

▲ Fall Color. Courtesy of Monrovia Nursery Co.

**ZONES:**
6, 7, 8, 9

**HEIGHT:**
30′ to 40′

**WIDTH:**
20′ to 30′

**FRUIT:**
1/4″ to 1/2″ reddish-brown drupe; NOT ORNAMENTAL.

**TEXTURE:**
Medium

**GROWTH RATE:**
Moderate

**HABIT:**
Upright and rounded; somewhat open.

**FAMILY:**
Anacardiaceae

**LEAF COLOR:** Dark green in summer; orange to red in fall.

**LEAF DESCRIPTION:** PINNATELY COMPOUND (12 to 20 leaflets), leaflets 3″ to 4″ long and one-third as wide, narrow elliptic to lanceolate shape with acuminate tips and entire margins. ALTERNATE arrangement.

**FLOWER DESCRIPTION:** Dioecious, greenish; male in racemes, female in panicles; NOT ORNAMENTAL.

**EXPOSURE/CULTURE:** Sun. The plant prefers a well-drained, loamy soil but is very adaptable to a wide range of soils. Drought-resistant. Can be pruned for shaping or to increase density of crown.

**PEST PROBLEMS:** None

**BARK/STEMS:** Young stems beige to tan with lenticels; older bark is gray with shallow furrows, often flaking to expose orange-tinged inner bark.

**SELECTED CULTIVARS:** None

**LANDSCAPE NOTES:** Chinese Pistache is a handsome tree for the lawn. Generally considered a specimen tree, it has many merits, including nice foliage and bark. Fall color can be spectacular in mature, densely-crowned trees. Very easy to grow. Great for xeriscaping.

# *Prunus x yedoensis*

### Yoshino Flowering Cherry

▲ 'Afterglow'

**ZONES:**
6, 7, 8

**HEIGHT:**
25′ to 35′

**WIDTH:**
25′ to 35′+

**FRUIT:**
1/4″ to 1/2″ black drupes; NOT ORNAMENTAL.

**TEXTURE:**
Medium

**GROWTH RATE:**
Rapid

**HABIT:**
Broad-spreading and rounded.

**FAMILY:**
Rosaceae

**LEAF COLOR:** Medium green in summer; brown or yellowish in fall.

**LEAF DESCRIPTION:** SIMPLE, 2″ to 4 1/2″ long and around half as wide, ovate to elliptic to obovate shape with acuminate tips and doubly serrated margins. ALTERNATE arrangement.

**FLOWER DESCRIPTION:** White or pink, single, 1″ in racemes of 4 to 6 flowers. Flowers in early spring before the leaves. Abundant and extremely showy.

**EXPOSURE/CULTURE:** Sun. The plant prefers a well-drained, moist, organic soil. Not especially drought-tolerant in arid climates. Requires little, if any, pruning.

**PEST PROBLEMS:** Borers.

**BARK/STEMS:** Young stems greenish; older bark reddish-brown with huge lenticels.

**SELECTED CULTIVARS:** 'Afterglow' - Similar to the species, but having pink flowers. One of the best! 'Akebono' - Pink form with double flowers.

**LANDSCAPE NOTES:** Yoshino Cherry is an awesome specimen tree that produces a brilliant white display in early spring. It is even more spectacular when used in groupings on larger properties. During winter, the handsome bark provides additional interest. This is the tree used around the tidal basin in Washington, D.C.

## *Pyrus calleryana 'Bradford'*

**Bradford Pear**

▲ Fall Color

**ZONES:**
4, 5, 6, 7, 8, 9

**HEIGHT:**
20' to 35'

**WIDTH:**
15' to 20'

**FRUIT:**
1/4" to 1/2" green-brown pomes; not abundant and NOT ORNAMENTAL.

**TEXTURE:**
Medium

**GROWTH RATE:**
Rapid

**HABIT:**
Broad pyramid; dense.

**FAMILY:**
Rosaceae

**LEAF COLOR:** Dark green in summer; red to purple in fall.

**LEAF DESCRIPTION:** SIMPLE, 1 1/2" to 3 1/2" long and 1" to 2" wide, broad ovate shape with serrated margins, sometimes slightly undulate. ALTERNATE arrangement.

**FLOWER DESCRIPTION:** White, 1/2" in small corymbs. 5-petaled with showy stamens. Abundant and showy.

**EXPOSURE/CULTURE:** Sun. Prefers a deep, well-drained soil, but is adaptable to a wide range of conditions. Drought-tolerant. Pruning is not necessary.

**PEST PROBLEMS:** None. Fire blight-resistant compared to the competing cultivars.

**BARK/STEMS:** Young stems brown and hairy; older bark is gray-brown with narrow and shallow furrows.

**RELATED CULTIVARS:** 'Aristocrat' - Reportedly has stronger branching. Flowers later in less abundance. Fireblight-susceptible. 'Capital' - More narrow form for tight areas. Fireblight-susceptible. 'Redspire' - More open in habit. Yellowish in fall. Fireblight-susceptible.

**LANDSCAPE NOTES:** Bradford Pear is one of the most commonly used trees of modern times. It has beautiful flowers and fall color. In addition, it has a neat, somewhat formal, symmetrical habit. It can be used as a specimen, border, or street tree. It is low-maintenance and easy to grow. May be somewhat overplanted.

# Salix babylonica

**Weeping Willow**

**ZONES:**
4, 5, 6, 7, 8, 9

**HEIGHT:**
20′ to 35′

**WIDTH:**
15′ to 30′

**FRUIT:**
Small, brown capsule; NOT ORNAMENTAL.

**TEXTURE:**
Medium to fine.

**GROWTH RATE:**
Rapid

**HABIT:**
Rounded and weeping.

**FAMILY:**
Salicaceae

**LEAF COLOR:** Light to medium green in summer; yellowish or brownish in fall.

**LEAF DESCRIPTION:** SIMPLE, 4″ to 6″ long and to 1/2″ wide, narrow lanceolate shape with long acuminate tip and serrulate margins. ALTERNATE arrangement.

**FLOWER DESCRIPTION:** Dioecious; NOT ORNAMENTAL.

**EXPOSURE/CULTURE:** Sun or light shade. Prefers well-drained, moist soil. Commonly found near streams. Root system aggressive; clogs sewer drainage lines and competes with lawn grasses. Pruning is not necessary.

**PEST PROBLEMS:** Canker, leaf spots.

**BARK/STEMS:** Young stems yellowish to brown; older bark is gray-brown with shallow furrows.

**SELECTED CULTIVARS:** None

**RELATED SPECIES:** *S. nigra* - Black Willow. This is a native willow of the U.S., and is slightly larger than *S. babylonica*. The tree is irregular, open, and rounded. Easily recognized by the blackish bark.

**LANDSCAPE NOTES:** Weeping Willow is a very graceful specimen plant that makes a nice lawn tree, but is especially attractive when planted near water. It should be carefully located due to the aggressive, fibrous root system.

## *Salix matsudana 'Tortuosa'* — Corkscrew Willow

**ZONES:**
4, 5, 6, 7, 8, 9

**HEIGHT:**
20' to 40'

**WIDTH:**
15' to 20'

**FRUIT:**
Brown capsule; NOT ORNA-MENTAL.

**TEXTURE:**
Medium

**GROWTH RATE:**
Moderate

**HABIT:**
Upright and open; somewhat spreading.

**FAMILY:**
Salicaceae

**LEAF COLOR:** Medium green in summer; yellowish to brown in fall.

**LEAF DESCRIPTION:** SIMPLE, 3" to 5" long and 1/2" wide, narrow lanceolate shape with long acuminate tip and sharply serrated margins. Leaves twisted and distorted. ALTERNATE arrangement.

**FLOWER DESCRIPTION:** Female; NOT ORNAMENTAL.

**EXPOSURE/CULTURE:** Sun or light shade. The plant prefers moist, organic, well-drained soil. Pruning is usually not necessary.

**PEST PROBLEMS:** None

**BARK/STEMS:** Young stems yellowish and hairy; twisted; older bark is gray-brown with narrow furrows.

**SELECTED CULTIVARS:** None. This is a cultivar.

**LANDSCAPE NOTES:** Corkscrew Willow is a specimen tree that should be used in moderation. Its twisted stems and leaves give an interesting, bold effect. One plant is enough to accent an area in most gardens.

## *Salix pentandra*

**Laurel Willow**

**ZONES:**
3, 4, 5

**HEIGHT:**
25′ to 35′

**WIDTH:**
20′ to 25′

**FRUIT:**
Brown capsule; NOT ORNA-MENTAL.

**TEXTURE:**
Medium

**GROWTH RATE:**
Moderate

**HABIT:**
Oval to rounded; dense.

**FAMILY:**
Salicaceae

**LEAF COLOR:** Lustrous dark green in summer; yellowish to brown in fall.

**LEAF DESCRIPTION:** SIMPLE, 3″ to 5″ long and 1 1/2″ to 3″ wide, ovate to elliptic shape with finely serrated margins. ALTERNATE arrangement.

**FLOWER DESCRIPTION:** Dioecious; NOT NOTICEABLE.

**EXPOSURE/CULTURE:** Sun or light shade. The plant prefers moist, deep, organic soil, but is reasonably adaptable. Pruning is not necessary.

**PEST PROBLEMS:** Leaf spots.

**BARK/STEMS:** Young stems greenish and shiny; older bark is gray-brown with shallow furrows.

**SELECTED CULTIVARS:** None

**LANDSCAPE NOTES:** Laurel Willow is a beautiful tree of dense habit and beautiful foliage. It can be used as a shade tree for lawns or in garden borders. This is a fine landscape tree of great beauty.

## *Sassafras albidum*

**Common Sassafras**

**ZONES:**
5, 6, 7, 8, 9

**HEIGHT:**
30′ to 40′

**WIDTH:**
25′ to 30′

**FRUIT:**
Small blue drupe with red stalk.

**TEXTURE:**
Medium

**GROWTH RATE:**
Moderate

**HABIT:**
Irregular with an oval crown.

**FAMILY:**
Lauraceae

**LEAF COLOR:** Bright green in summer; yellow to orange to purplish in fall.

**LEAF DESCRIPTION:** SIMPLE, 4″ to 6″ long and two-thirds as wide, ovate shape with no lobes or having 2 to 3 lobes, deeply cut. Entire margins. Characteristic sassafras scent when crushed. ALTERNATE arrangement.

**FLOWER DESCRIPTION:** Dioecious; greenish-yellow; NOT ORNAMENTAL.

**EXPOSURE/CULTURE:** Sun or part shade. The plant prefers a well-drained, organic, moist soil, but is adaptable to poor sites. Usually not available in the nursery trade. Tends to sucker from roots and forms dense "groves." Prune to remove suckers for single-tree effect.

**PEST PROBLEMS:** Chewing insects, mostly Japanese Beetles.

**BARK/STEMS:** Young stems yellowish-green and smooth; older bark is reddish-brown with deep, narrow furrows.

**SELECTED CULTIVARS:** None

**LANDSCAPE NOTES:** Common Sassafras is easily identified by the characteristic spicy, sassafras odor of crushed leaves, stems, or roots. It is a native tree that can be grown as a single specimen tree or as a thicket. Its chief merit is to provide spectacular fall color. Can be used for warm weather screening when grown as a thicket.

# *Styrax japonicus*

**Japanese Snowbell**

**ZONES:**
5, 6, 7, 8, 9

**HEIGHT:**
25' to 35'

**WIDTH:**
25' to 35'

**FRUIT:**
1/2" grayish-brown drupe.

**TEXTURE:**
Medium

**GROWTH RATE:**
Moderate

**HABIT:**
Broad-spreading and rounded.

**FAMILY:**
Styracaceae

**LEAF COLOR:** Dark green in summer; yellow to reddish in fall.

**LEAF DESCRIPTION:** SIMPLE, 2" to 3" long and half as wide, elliptic shape with entire or sparsely serrated margins. ALTERNATE arrangement.

**FLOWER DESCRIPTION:** White with yellow stamens, 1/2" to 1" long, appearing in 3 to 6 flowered pendulous racemes and having pedicels of 1" long or longer. Flowers in spring. Abundant and showy.

**EXPOSURE/CULTURE:** Sun or part shade. Requires a well-drained, moist soil of acid reaction. Does best in rich, organic soil. Pruning is usually not necessary. Can be grown as a single-trunk or multi-stemmed tree.

**PEST PROBLEMS:** None

**BARK/STEMS:** Young stems green and zigzag; older bark gray-brown to orange-brown with interlacing fissures.

**SELECTED CULTIVARS:** 'Rosea' - Has pink flowers.

**RELATED SPECIES:** *S. obassia* - Fragrant Snowbell. This species has larger leaves to 10" long and fragrant flower racemes to 8". Slightly smaller than *S. japonicus*.

**LANDSCAPE NOTES:** Japanese Snowbell is an attractive tree that can be used as a lawn specimen, shade, or border tree. Can be quite handsome in bloom. Unfortunately, the plant is not recommended for xeriscaping.

# *Syringa reticulata*

**Japanese Tree Lilac**

**ZONES:**
4, 5, 6, 7

**HEIGHT:**
20' to 30'

**WIDTH:**
15' to 20'+

**FRUIT:**
1/2" brown, dehiscent capsule.

**TEXTURE:**
Medium to coarse.

**GROWTH RATE:**
Moderate

**HABIT:**
Upright and open; oval.

**FAMILY:**
Oleaceae

**LEAF COLOR:** Dark green in summer; brown in fall.

**LEAF DESCRIPTION:** SIMPLE, 3" to 5" long and half as wide, broad ovate to ovate-oblong shape with entire margins and acuminate tip. Sometimes slightly undulate. OPPOSITE arrangement.

**FLOWER DESCRIPTION:** Yellowish-white, appearing in panicles 10" to 12" long. Flowers in late spring or early summer. Very showy for around two weeks.

**EXPOSURE/CULTURE:** Sun or light shade. Prefers a well-drained, loamy soil of slightly acid to alkaline pH. Does not perform in the South. Prune selectively after flowering.

**PEST PROBLEMS:** Bacterial blight, leaf spots, mildews, lilac borer, lilac scale.

**BARK/STEMS:** Young stems brown with large lenticels; older bark red-brown with lenticels.

**SELECTED CULTIVARS:** 'Ivory Silk' - Improved flowering with more attractive foliage.

**LANDSCAPE NOTES:** Japanese Tree Lilac is a handsome tree with attractive flowers and bark. It is probably less demanding than *S. vulgaris,* but it still requires some care. It makes a nice lawn specimen or border plant.

# *Ulmus alata*

**Winged Elm**

**ZONES:**
6, 7, 8, 9

**HEIGHT:**
30′ to 40′

**WIDTH:**
15′ to 20′

**FRUIT:**
1/4″ one-seeded samara; hairy with wings surrounding the nutlet.

**TEXTURE:**
Medium

**GROWTH RATE:**
Moderate

**HABIT:**
Somewhat oval and spreading.

**FAMILY:**
Ulmaceae

**LEAF COLOR:** Dark green in summer; yellow to brownish in fall.

**LEAF DESCRIPTION:** SIMPLE, 2″ to 3″ long and 1″ to 1 1/2″ wide, ovate-oblong or elliptic shape with doubly serrated margins. Slightly pubescent underneath. ALTERNATE arrangement.

**FLOWER DESCRIPTION:** Bisexual in racemes; NOT ORNAMENTAL.

**EXPOSURE/CULTURE:** Sun or part shade. The plant prefers a moist, well-drained, loamy soil, but is adaptable. Apparently the plant is pollution-tolerant. Tolerant of wet conditions. Pruning is usually not necessary.

**PEST PROBLEMS:** Mildew. (Not susceptible to Dutch Elm Disease.)

**BARK/STEMS:** Young stems gray-brown with 2 corky wings; older bark gray-brown with shallow furrows.

**SELECTED CULTIVARS:** None

**LANDSCAPE NOTES:** Upon close inspection, Winged Elm is a handsome plant with attractive foliage and very interesting branches. It can be used as a lawn specimen, shade for patios and decks, or in garden borders. This is a fine plant for naturalizing.

# Chapter 11

# LARGE TREES

The large trees featured in this text include plants that mature at a height greater than 40 feet. There are borderline plants, and consideration is given to shape, width, and other features in deciding the size group.

Large trees have an enormous impact on the natural environment. We are reminded often of the role trees play in utilizing excess carbon dioxide and other pollutants, preventing erosion and flooding, and sheltering wildlife. In the man-made landscape, uses of trees include:

▼ **Shade.** Trees cool the garden, providing more pleasure, especially during summer. In addition, the aesthetic effects of shadows should be considered.

▼ **Focalization.** A well-chosen tree, carefully located, can have a dramatic impact on the total landscape.

▼ **Screening.** Trees provide varying degrees of privacy, as well as screening undesirable views.

▼ **Slowing wind speed.** (Windbreaks). Plants help abate cold, uncomfortable drafts. In addition, they help create microclimates, allowing utilization of a wider selection of plant material.

▼ **Pollution control.** In addition to removing gases and particulates, trees absorb nearby sounds (noise pollution). This is especially important for gardens in urban areas or near highways.

▼ **Framing.** Trees are great for framing distant views, but, in addition, background trees and border trees help to frame a structure, creating harmony between the structure and its landscape.

▼ **Energy conservation.** Carefully planned deciduous trees can reduce summer energy needs, while losing their foliage in winter to warm the structure and reduce heating costs.

## *Abies bornmuelleriana*                     Bornmuelleriana Fir

**ZONES:**
4, 5, 6, 7

**HEIGHT:**
50' to 70'+

**WIDTH:**
15' to 25'+

**FRUIT:**
6" cylindrical cone.

**TEXTURE:**
Medium

**GROWTH RATE:**
Slow

**HABIT:**
Tall pyramidal outline.

**FAMILY:**
Pinaceae

**LEAF COLOR:** Dark green; whitish bands underneath.

**LEAF DESCRIPTION:** NEEDLE-LIKE, 1" to 1 1/2" long and 1/12" to 1/10" wide, tips rounded or emarginate, 2 white stomatic bands on undersides, needles encircling branchlets, pointing toward stem apex.

**FLOWER DESCRIPTION:** Monoecious; male flowers pendulous, female flowers erect; NOT ORNAMENTAL.

**EXPOSURE/CULTURE:** Sun or light shade. The plant prefers moist, well-drained sites and cool climates. Not for dry, hot summer conditions. Pruning is not necessary.

**PEST PROBLEMS:** Usually no pests; twig blight is listed.

**BARK/STEMS:** Young stems smooth and green; older bark brown, eventually grooved.

**SELECTED CULTIVARS:** None

**SIMILAR SPECIES:** *A. nordmanniana* - Nordman Fir. This species has yellow-green young branches and deep green needles.

**LANDSCAPE NOTES:** Bornmuelleriana Fir is a fine plant for screening or as a windbreak. The plant would make a nice lawn specimen, especially in youth. It is a handsome plant native to the coast of the Black Sea, and should be more widely considered in this country.

## *Abies grandis*

**Lowland Fir, Giant Fir**

**ZONES:**
5, 6

**HEIGHT:**
90′ to 200′+

**WIDTH:**
30′ to 50′+

**FRUIT:**
2″ to 4″ cylindrical cones; erect.

**TEXTURE:**
Medium

**GROWTH RATE:**
Slow

**HABIT:**
Somewhat conical; horizontal branching with ascending tips.

**FAMILY:**
Pinaceae

**LEAF COLOR:** Dark green; whitish bands underneath.

**LEAF DESCRIPTION:** NEEDLE-LIKE, 1″ to 1 1/2″ long and 1/12″ to 1/10″ wide, tips rounded or emarginate, furrowed above, 2 whitish stomatic bands underneath. PECTINATE arrangement (comb-like).

**FLOWER DESCRIPTION:** Monoecious; male cones pendulous, female erect. NOT ORNAMENTAL.

**EXPOSURE/CULTURE:** Sun or part shade. Prefers moist, well-drained soils. Survives in poor soils so long as moisture is moderate or higher. Restricted to mountains of the Pacific Coast and Montana. Not for the Southwest or Southeast. Pruning is not necessary.

**PEST PROBLEMS:** No pests, usually; twig blight is listed.

**BARK/STEMS:** Young stems olive-green, pubescent and resinous; older bark dark brown and furrowed.

**SELECTED CULTIVARS:** 'Aurea' - Has golden-yellow needles. 'Compacta' - Much smaller, dense plant with needles 1/2″ to 3/4″ long. Better selection for home gardens. 'Pendula' - Has pendulous, weeping habit.

**LANDSCAPE NOTES:** Giant Fir is a timber tree that has limited use in residential landscaping. It has possibilities as a tree for parks, golf courses, or large estates with large acreages of natural land.

## *Abies holophylla* Manchurian Fir

**ZONES:**
5, 6, 7

**HEIGHT:**
50′ to 90′

**WIDTH:**
15′ to 25′

**FRUIT:**
4 1/2″ to 6″ cylindrical, resinous cone.

**TEXTURE:**
Medium

**GROWTH RATE:**
Slow

**HABIT:**
Pyramidal; becoming more open with age.

**FAMILY:**
Pinaceae

**LEAF COLOR:** Bright green above; dull green bands underneath.

**LEAF DESCRIPTION:** NEEDLE-LIKE, 1 1/4″ to 1 3/4″ long and 1/12″ to 1/10″ wide, V-shaped furrow on upper surface, acute tip, having 2 dull green stomatic bands on undersides. PECTINATE arrangement.

**FLOWER DESCRIPTION:** Monoecious; male cones pendulous, female erect; NOT ORNAMENTAL.

**EXPOSURE/CULTURE:** Sun or light shade. Prefers well-drained, moist soils. Pruning is usually not necessary nor recommended.

**PEST PROBLEMS:** No serious pests.

**BARK/STEMS:** Young stems light yellow; older bark is brown and furrowed.

**SELECTED CULTIVARS:** None

**LANDSCAPE NOTES:** Manchurian Fir is a large tree with bright green, noticeable foliage. It has possibilities for specimen status on larger estates or as materials for screens and windbreaks.

# *Abies lasiocarpa*

**ZONES:**
5, 6

**HEIGHT:**
90′ to 120′

**WIDTH:**
20′ to 35′

**FRUIT:**
2 1/2″ to 4″ cylindrical cone; dark purple; grouped.

**TEXTURE:**
Medium

**GROWTH RATE:**
Slow

**HABIT:**
Pyramidal

**FAMILY:**
Pinaceae

**LEAF COLOR:** Pale blue-green above; silvery bands underneath.

**LEAF DESCRIPTION:** NEEDLE-LIKE, 3/4″ to 1 1/4″ long and 1/16″ wide, furrowed on upper surface, acute or round tip, 2 silver-gray stomatic bands underneath. Brush-like, SPIRAL arrangement.

**FLOWER DESCRIPTION:** Monoecious; male cones pendulous, female erect.

**EXPOSURE/CULTURE:** Sun or light shade. Must have a cool, moist climate and well-drained soil. Found only in high mountain areas from Alaska to New Mexico. Pruning is not recommended. Holds up under heavy snow.

**PEST PROBLEMS:** No serious pests at altitude.

**BARK/STEMS:** Young stems silver-gray; older bark is grayish-brown and furrowed.

**SELECTED CULTIVARS:** 'Compacta' - Dwarf cultivar forming a broad cone. Silver-blue foliage. 'Conica' - Very slow-growing dwarf form with dense foliage and conical shape. 'Pendula' - Similar to species, but having a distinct weeping habit. var. *arizonica* - Cork Fir. This is a high-altitude species, small to medium tree, with more intense silvery-blue foliage. Bark is cork-like and yellowish-white.

**LANDSCAPE NOTES:** Rocky Mountain Fir is a timber tree, but the several cultivars and varieties make it a nice tree for commercial/residential landscaping in high-altitude western landscapes. Some cultivars merit specimen status, and all are well-adapted for screens or windbreaks.

# *Cedrus atlantica*

**Atlas Cedar**

**ZONES:**
7, 8, 9

**HEIGHT:**
50′ to 70′+

**WIDTH:**
35′ to 45′

**FRUIT:**
2″ to 2 1/2″ light brown cone.

**TEXTURE:**
Medium

**GROWTH RATE:**
Slow to moderate.

**HABIT:**
Pyramidal to oval; ascending branches.

**FAMILY:**
Pinaceae

**LEAF COLOR:** Green to bluish-green.

**LEAF DESCRIPTION:** NEEDLE-LIKE, 1″ long and 1/16″ wide, triangular in cross-section, acuminate tip, stiff, sometimes singly, but more often spirally arranged on branchlets or small spurs.

**FLOWER DESCRIPTION:** Monoecious; male cones erect to 2″, female erect to 3/4″ long.

**EXPOSURE/CULTURE:** Sun or light shade. The plant prefers fertile, deep, well-drained soils, but is adaptable to all but wet soils. pH-tolerant and drought-tolerant. Will grow more densely in better soils. Pruning is not recommended.

**PEST PROBLEMS:** Blight, rootrot (wet soils).

**BARK/STEMS:** Young stems smooth and gray; older bark is dark gray-brown and furrowed.

**SELECTED CULTIVARS:** 'Aurea' - New needles golden yellow; becoming green in the second year. Branches horizontal. 'Columnaris' - Green-needle form with narrow pyramidal habit. 'Glauca' - (Featured on next page.) 'Pendula' - Weeping form of narrow columnar habit. Needles green.

**RELATED SPECIES:** *C. libani* - Cedar of Lebanon. Very similar to *C. atlantica,* but developing a flat crown and leaning trunk with age.

**LANDSCAPE NOTES:** Atlas Cedar is a fine specimen plant or screening material. This outstanding conifer, unlike many in *Abies* or *Picea,* is very suitable for the heat of the Southeast and Southwest. Should be more widely used!

## *Cedrus atlantica 'Glauca'*     **Blue Atlas Cedar**

**ZONES:**
6, 7, 8, 9

**HEIGHT:**
50′ to 55′

**WIDTH:**
35′ to 40′

**FRUIT:**
2″ to 3″ green-brown cone;
NOT COMMON.

**TEXTURE:**
Medium

**GROWTH RATE:**
Slow

**HABIT:**
Pyramidal; somewhat open.

**FAMILY:**
Pinaceae

**LEAF COLOR:** Silver-blue to gray-blue.

**LEAF DESCRIPTION:** NEEDLE-LIKE, 1″ long and 1/16″ wide, acuminate tip, stiff, more often spirally arranged on branchlets, triangular in cross-section.

**FLOWER DESCRIPTION:** Monoecious; male cones erect to 2″, female erect to 3/4″.

**EXPOSURE/CULTURE:** Sun. Prefers deep, moist, well-drained soil, but is adaptable to any except wet soil. Drought-tolerant. Pruning is not recommended.

**PEST PROBLEMS:** Blight, rootrot (wet soils).

**BARK/STEMS:** Young stems smooth and gray; older bark brown and fissured.

**RELATED CULTIVARS:** 'Glauca Pendula' - (See Small Evergreen Trees.)

**LANDSCAPE NOTES:** Blue Atlas Cedar is a bold accent plant for the residential or commercial landscape. It is so noticeable that careful consideration should be given to site selection. Since growth is slow, it can be used in foundation plantings, planters, rock gardens, and other small areas.

## *Cedrus deodara*

**Deodar Cedar**

**ZONES:**
7, 8, 9

**HEIGHT:**
30' to 50'

**WIDTH:**
25' to 35'

**FRUIT:**
2" to 4" bluish-green to brown cone; barrel-shaped.

**TEXTURE:**
Medium

**GROWTH RATE:**
Moderate

**HABIT:**
Pyramidal with arching branches.

**FAMILY:**
Pinaceae

**LEAF COLOR:** Bluish-green

**LEAF DESCRIPTION:** NEEDLE-LIKE, 1 1/2" to 2" long, sharp-pointed, spirally arranged around the stem in bundles (bunches) to 30 needles.

**FLOWER DESCRIPTION:** Monoecious; male and female cones.

**EXPOSURE/CULTURE:** Sun or light shade. The plant prefers a well-drained, loamy soil. Reasonably drought-tolerant. Pruning is not recommended.

**PEST PROBLEMS:** No serious pests. Cold injury to the top is common.

**BARK/STEMS:** Young stems gray and pubescent; older bark is brown and fissured.

**SELECTED CULTIVARS:** 'Aurea' - Golden Deodar Cedar. Foliage has golden-yellow color all year. Slower growing than the species.

**LANDSCAPE NOTES:** Deodar Cedar is a graceful tree having true Christmas tree shape. The blue-green foliage and light colored cones are very eye-catching. It makes a nice lawn specimen for gardens or parks. Not for smaller properties. Nice conifer for the southern zones.

# *Cryptomeria japonica*

**Cryptomeria**

▲ 'Cristata'

**ZONES:**
6, 7, 8, 9

**HEIGHT:**
50′ to 100′

**WIDTH:**
20′ to 45′

**FRUIT:**
1/2″ to 1 1/4″ brown, globose cone.

**TEXTURE:**
Fine to medium.

**GROWTH RATE:**
Moderate

**HABIT:**
Conical and dense; open with age.

**FAMILY:**
Taxodiaceae

**LEAF COLOR:** Dark green in summer; has bronze tinge in winter.

**LEAF DESCRIPTION:** SCALE-LIKE and awl-shaped, 1/4″ to 1/2″ long, curving inward, stomata on both surfaces, spirally arranged on stems.

**FLOWER DESCRIPTION:** Monoecious; male spike-like, female round.

**EXPOSURE/CULTURE:** Sun or part shade. The plant prefers a deep, moist, loamy soil. pH adaptable. Not drought- or heat-resistant. Should be mulched to maintain consistent moisture. Pruning is not necessary.

**PEST PROBLEMS:** No serious pests.

**BARK/STEMS:** Young stems green; older bark reddish-brown and exfoliating in strips.

**SELECTED CULTIVARS:** 'Aurescens' - Dense form with yellow-green foliage. 'Compacta' - Extra dense form with blue-green foliage. 'Cristata' - Narrow cone to 24′; twigs are broad cocks-comb shape. Outstanding! 'Globosa Nana' - (See Large Evergreen Shrubs.) 'Lobbii' - Branches are more upright; longer, deep green needles. var. *radicans* - Narrow pyramidal shape with a dense crown. More vigorous and faster growing than the species.

**LANDSCAPE NOTES:** Cryptomeria is an elegant, handsome plant for the warmer regions. It can be grown as a lawn specimen or as a natural screen. When grown under favorable conditions, this conifer rivals any in beauty. It makes a good substitute for x *Cupressocyparis leylandii*, and should be more widely used.

## *Magnolia grandiflora*
### Southern Magnolia

**ZONES:**
7, 8, 9

**HEIGHT:**
40' to 50'

**WIDTH:**
25' to 35'

**FRUIT:**
4" to 6" cone-like pod (aggregate of follicles; seeds bright red.

**TEXTURE:**
Coarse

**GROWTH RATE:**
Moderate

**HABIT:**
Pyramidal and dense.

**FAMILY:**
Magnoliaceae

**LEAF COLOR:** Deep lustrous green.

**LEAF DESCRIPTION:** SIMPLE, 6" to 8" long and 2 1/2" to 3" wide, elliptic shape with cuneate base and entire margins, usually pubescent underneath. ALTERNATE arrangement.

**FLOWER DESCRIPTION:** White, 6" to 9" across, having 6 or more petals. Flowers in May to July. Fragrant and very showy.

**EXPOSURE/CULTURE:** Sun or part shade. Prefers deep, organic, moderately moist soils. Not for poor, stony terrain. Pruning is usually not necessary, but shearing will result in a very dense plant.

**PEST PROBLEMS:** No serious pests.

**BARK/STEMS:** Young stems are smooth and green; older bark is mostly smooth and gray.

**SELECTED CULTIVARS:** 'Bracken Brown Beauty' - This plant has very dense, brown-backed foliage. Develops more lateral branches, and is full to the ground. Blooms throughout summer. Developed by Ray Bracken Nursery Co. 'Little Gem' - Dwarf Southern Magnolia. Slow-growing form, maturing to a large shrub or small tree. Foliage is rusty bronze on undersides. Blooms early and again in late season. Introduced by Monrovia Nurseries. 'Majestic Beauty' - Forms a dense pyramid with large, glossy leaves. Large, cup-shaped, fragrant flowers. Outstanding! A Monrovia Nurseries patented plant. 'St. Mary' - A compact and dense small evergreen tree. Leaves are bronzy underneath. Flowers at an early age.

**LANDSCAPE NOTES:** Southern Magnolia is a beautiful flowering tree that is stately in appearance. It is symbolic of the deep South and southern mansions. It looks best on larger properties and is dramatic in combination with brick.

# *Picea glauca*

**White Spruce**

**ZONES:**
2, 3, 4, 5, 6, 7

**HEIGHT:**
30' to 50'

**WIDTH:**
15' to 25'

**FRUIT:**
1" to 2" brown cone.

**TEXTURE:**
Fine

**GROWTH RATE:**
Moderate

**HABIT:**
Pyramidal and dense.

**FAMILY:**
Pinaceae

**LEAF COLOR:** Glaucous green.

**LEAF DESCRIPTION:** NEEDLE-LIKE, 1/2" to 1" long, 2 or 3 stomatic lines above, 3 or 4 lines underneath, 4-sided, acute tip, covered with a whitish bloom. Bunched.

**FLOWER DESCRIPTION:** Monoecious; male catkins, female woody and pendulous.

**EXPOSURE/CULTURE:** Sun or light shade. Prefers rich, moist soil, but is adaptable. Tolerant of severe conditions and often used as a windbreak. Pruning is usually not necessary.

**PEST PROBLEMS:** Stem rot, spider mites.

**BARK/STEMS:** Young stems orange-brown to yellow-brown; older bark is ash brown to gray and thin and scaly.

**SELECTED CULTIVARS:** 'Aurea' - (Featured on next page.) 'Conica' - Very dense and narrow. Conical shape to about 12'. Can be used as a large shrub. 'Densata' - Black Hills Spruce. A more dense form, maturing slowly to medium tree size. 'Pendula' - (Featured in this chapter.) var. *albertiana* - Tall-growing (150') variety with longer needles and narrow crown. This is the White Spruce of the Northwestern U.S. and Alberta, Canada.

**LANDSCAPE NOTES:** White Spruce is a densely layered pyramid that develops beautiful shape when not crowded. It is a specimen tree deserving of a beautiful, lush lawn. Needles have a thin covering of white material similar to grapes. Outstanding tree!

## *Picea glauca 'Aurea'*

**Golden White-Spruce**

**ZONES:**
2, 3, 4, 5, 6, 7

**HEIGHT:**
30′ to 50′

**WIDTH:**
20′ to 25′

**FRUIT:**
1″ to 2″ brown cone.

**TEXTURE:**
Fine

**GROWTH RATE:**
Moderate

**HABIT:**
Pyramidal and very dense.

**FAMILY:**
Pinaceae

**LEAF COLOR:** New needles golden-yellow, maturing to green.

**LEAF DESCRIPTION:** NEEDLE-LIKE, 1/2″ to 1 1/4″ long, 2 or 3 stomatic bands on upper surface, 3 or 4 lines below, 4-sided in cross-section, covered with a thin whitish bloom. Bunched along branchlets.

**FLOWER DESCRIPTION:** Monoecious; male catkin-like, female woody and pendulous.

**EXPOSURE/CULTURE:** Sun or light shade. Prefers rich, organic, moist soil, but is adaptable to all but very wet soils. Tolerant of severe conditions, and is often used as a windbreak. Pruning is not necessary.

**PEST PROBLEMS:** Stem rot, spider mites; neither serious.

**BARK/STEMS:** Young stems yellow-brown; older bark is gray-brown to gray, thin and scaly.

**SELECTED CULTIVARS:** None. This is a cultivar.

**LANDSCAPE NOTES:** Golden White-Spruce has yellow-tipped branches for a short period during the growing season, then matures to a rich, beautiful green for the rest of the year. Overall, it is at least as attractive in the garden as White Spruce. It can be used as a lawn specimen, privacy screen, or windbreak.

## *Picea glauca 'Pendula'*

**Weeping White Spruce**

**ZONES:**
2, 3, 4, 5, 6, 7

**HEIGHT:**
40′ to 50′

**WIDTH:**
8′ to 10′

**FRUIT:**
1″ to 2″ brown cone.

**TEXTURE:**
Fine

**GROWTH RATE:**
Moderate

**HABIT:**
Very narrow, columnar habit; branches tight and appearing layered.

**FAMILY:**
Pinaceae

**LEAF COLOR:** Rich green.

**LEAF DESCRIPTION:** NEEDLE-LIKE, 1/2″ to 3/4″ long, 4-sided, acute tip, 2 or 3 stomatic bands on the upper surface and 3 or 4 bands beneath, lightly covered with a whitish bloom. Bunched tightly on tight branchlets.

**FLOWER DESCRIPTION:** Monoecious; male catkin-like, female woody and pendulous.

**EXPOSURE/CULTURE:** Sun or light shade. Prefers rich, moist soil, but is adaptable to a wide range of conditions. Tolerant of harsh conditions. Pruning is not recommended. Allow plant to develop unique habit.

**PEST PROBLEMS:** Stem rot, spider mites; none serious.

**BARK/STEMS:** Young stems yellow-brown; older bark is gray or gray-brown, eventually developing thin, scaly plates.

**SELECTED CULTIVARS:** None. This is a cultivar.

**LANDSCAPE NOTES:** Weeping White Spruce is a definite specimen plant, having unusual, yet interesting habit. This plant would be hard to hide in the landscape, and the real task would be in locating the plant for maximum effect. Probably best suited for larger estates with a variety of plant material.

# *Picea glehnii*

**Sachalin Spruce**

**ZONES:**
4, 5, 6, 7

**HEIGHT:**
90′ to 100′+

**WIDTH:**
20′ to 30′+

**FRUIT:**
2 1/2″ to 3 1/4″ brown, cylindrical-oblong cone.

**TEXTURE:**
Fine

**GROWTH RATE:**
Slow

**HABIT:**
Conical, narrow crown; ascending branches.

**FAMILY:**
Pinaceae

**LEAF COLOR:** Bright glaucous green.

**LEAF DESCRIPTION:** NEEDLE-LIKE, 1/2″ long, one stomatic line above and 2 to 5 lines beneath, acute or obtuse tip, tightly appressed, curved toward stem tip.

**FLOWER DESCRIPTION:** Monoecious; male catkins, female pendulous.

**EXPOSURE/CULTURE:** Sun or part shade. Prefers cool, moist, organic soil, but is adaptable. pH-tolerant. Mulch to keep roots moist and cool. Pruning is not necessary.

**PEST PROBLEMS:** No serious pests.

**BARK/STEMS:** Young stems reddish and densely villous; older bark is chocolate-brown and exfoliating.

**SELECTED CULTIVARS:** None

**LANDSCAPE NOTES:** Native to Japan, Sachalin Spruce is a handsome tree that is hardy and reliable. It can be used as a lawn specimen, screen, or windbreak. Should be more widely used. Chocolate-brown bark differs from all other *Picea*.

# *Picea omorika*

**Serbian Spruce**

**ZONES:**
5, 6, 7

**HEIGHT:**
50′ to 75′

**WIDTH:**
20′ to 30′

**FRUIT:**
1 1/2″ to 2 1/2″ ovate-oblong cone; purple, maturing to brown.

**TEXTURE:**
Fine to medium.

**GROWTH RATE:**
Slow

**HABIT:**
Pyramidal; some branches ascending, others drooping gracefully.

**FAMILY:**
Pinaceae

**LEAF COLOR:** Dark green and lustrous.

**LEAF DESCRIPTION:** NEEDLE-LIKE, 1/2″ to 3/4″ long, 2 broad white bands underneath, each having 5 to 6 stomatic lines, no stomatic lines above, 2-sided. Alternately arranged and bunched.

**FLOWER DESCRIPTION:** Monoecious; NOT NOTICEABLE.

**EXPOSURE/CULTURE:** Sun or part shade. Prefers a well-drained, moist, deep, organic soil. Very pH-adaptable. Not as adaptable to strong winds as some *Picea* species. Should not be sheared; maintain natural shape.

**PEST PROBLEMS:** Borers

**BARK/STEMS:** Young stems light brown and pubescent; older bark is brown, thin, and scaly.

**SELECTED CULTIVARS:** 'Expansa' - Super dwarf to 2′ and spreading to 12′. Has no main trunk. 'Nana' - Broad cone shape to 12′ in height. Very short needles, 1/4″ to 1/2″ long.

**LANDSCAPE NOTES:** Serbian Spruce is a spruce of interesting habit, being more relaxed or less formal than many of the others. It has merit as a lawn specimen, and could make a nice natural screen for larger gardens. Not suitable as a windbreak for the Midwest. Of the many spruces, this is certainly one of the best for landscaping.

# *Picea orientalis*

**Oriental Spruce**

**ZONES:**
5, 6, 7

**HEIGHT:**
60′ to 80′+

**WIDTH:**
20′ to 30′

**FRUIT:**
2″ to 3″ cylindrical-ovate cone; violet, maturing to brown.

**TEXTURE:**
Fine

**GROWTH RATE:**
Slow

**HABIT:**
Pyramidal; branches ascending or pendulous.

**FAMILY:**
Pinaceae

**LEAF COLOR:** Dark green and glossy.

**LEAF DESCRIPTION:** NEEDLE-LIKE, 3/8″ long, 4-sided, 1 to 4 stomatic lines on all surfaces, obtuse tip, densely arranged, stiff.

**FLOWER DESCRIPTION:** Monoecious; male is red, female violet.

**EXPOSURE/CULTURE:** Sun or part shade. Prefers rich, organic, moist soils, but is adaptable to shallow, mountain soils. Do not prune. Allow plant to develop natural, graceful habit.

**PEST PROBLEMS:** No serious pests.

**BARK/STEMS:** Young stems light brown to yellow and pubescent; older bark is brown and exfoliating in thin plates.

**SELECTED CULTIVARS:** 'Compacta' - Dwarf form having broad conical habit. Height equal to width. 'Gracilis' - Dwarf, oval form to 18′. Dense branching habit and bright green foliage.

**LANDSCAPE NOTES:** Oriental Spruce is a popular tree in the landscape industry. Its habit makes it appropriate for a wide range of landscape themes. It is very similar in habit to Serbian Spruce, and can be used as a lawn specimen or for natural screening. In addition, it is an appropriate plant for public parks and recreational areas. One of the best.

# *Picea pungens*

**Colorado Spruce**

**ZONES:**
3, 4, 5, 6, 7

**HEIGHT:**
70′ to 100′

**WIDTH:**
20′ to 25′

**FRUIT:**
2″ to 3″ beige cones.

**TEXTURE:**
Fine

**GROWTH RATE:**
Slow

**HABIT:**
Narrow, upright pyramid.

**FAMILY:**
Pinaceae

**LEAF COLOR:** Green to blue-green.

**LEAF DESCRIPTION:** NEEDLE-LIKE, 1″ long, 4-sided, 4 to 5 stomatic lines on all sides, acuminate tip. Radially arranged on branchlets.

**FLOWER DESCRIPTION:** Monoecious; NOT ORNAMENTAL.

**EXPOSURE/CULTURE:** Sun or light shade. Prefers cool, moist, organic soil, but is reasonably drought-tolerant. Protect from strong winds. Pruning is not necessary.

**PEST PROBLEMS:** Spider mites.

**BARK/STEMS:** Young stems yellowish-brown to orange; older bark is gray-brown and furrowed.

**SELECTED CULTIVARS:** (See next page, *Picea pungens* f. *glauca.*)

**LANDSCAPE NOTES:** Colorado Spruce is a specimen tree that is noticeable in the landscape. The species has been overshadowed by the large number of new cultivars. However, the species is quite handsome and blends well with the rest of the landscape.

## *Picea pungens f. glauca*

**Colorado Blue Spruce**

'Iseli Foxtail' ▶

**ZONES:**
3, 4, 5, 6, 7

**HEIGHT:**
70′ to 100′

**WIDTH:**
20′ to 25′

**FRUIT:**
2″ to 3″ brown cones.

**TEXTURE:**
Fine to medium.

**GROWTH RATE:**
Slow

**HABIT:**
Narrow, upright pyramid.

**FAMILY:**
Pinaceae

**LEAF COLOR:** Blue to silvery-blue (more blue than *P. pungens*).

**LEAF DESCRIPTION:** NEEDLE-LIKE, 1″ long, 4-sided, acuminate tip, 4 or 5 stomatic lines on all sides, radially arranged and dense. Curving toward branch tips.

**FLOWER DESCRIPTION:** Monoecious; NOT ORNAMENTAL.

**EXPOSURE/CULTURE:** Sun or light shade. Prefers cool, moist, organic soil, but is reasonably drought-tolerant. Protect from strong winds. Not for use as windbreaks in the Midwest. Pruning is usually not necessary.

**PEST PROBLEMS:** Spider mites.

**BARK/STEMS:** Young stems yellow-brown to orange; older bark is gray-brown with shallow furrows.

**SELECTED CULTIVARS:** 'Bakeri' - Dwarf form, 10′ to 12′, with intense blue foliage. Outstanding large shrub. 'Fat Albert' - Smaller, more compact tree. Has upright branching with intense blue foliage. Introduced by Iseli Nursery. 'Glauca Globosa' - (See Dwarf Evergreen Shrubs.) 'Hoopsii' - Dense, upright form with blue-white foliage. Very striking, outstanding selection that grows faster than most *Picea* selections. 'Iseli Foxtail' - Forms a medium size tree with intense blue and twisted foliage. An Iseli Nursery introduction. 'Koster' - This is the best known of the blue forms. Silver-blue foliage and conical habit.

**LANDSCAPE NOTES:** Colorado Blue Spruce is a true specimen plant that is best used in moderation in lawn areas and garden borders. This is the popular form so much in demand, and from which many cultivars have been developed. Many of the newer cultivars have much smaller mature size, which allows use in foundation plantings, rock gardens, raised planters, and many other areas.

# *Picea wilsonii*

**Wilson's Spruce**

**ZONES:**
6, 7

**HEIGHT:**
60' to 75'

**WIDTH:**
20' to 30'

**FRUIT:**
1 3/4" to 2 1/2" light brown, cylindrical cone.

**TEXTURE:**
Fine to medium.

**GROWTH RATE:**
Slow

**HABIT:**
Conical, upright, and dense; drooping tips.

**FAMILY:**
Pinaceae

**LEAF COLOR:** Dark green; medium green on new growth.

**LEAF DESCRIPTION:** NEEDLE-LIKE, 1/2" to 3/4" long, 4-sided, 1 to 2 stomatic lines on upper surfaces, 3 to 4 lines on lower surfaces, acute tip, needles more dense on upper side of branches.

**FLOWER DESCRIPTION:** Monoecious; NOT NOTICEABLE.

**EXPOSURE/CULTURE:** Sun or light shade. Prefers a deep, moist, organic soil, but is adaptable. Mulch to maintain moisture and to keep roots cool. Pruning is not necessary.

**PEST PROBLEMS:** No serious pests.

**BARK/STEMS:** Young stems light gray; older bark is gray brown and often fissured.

**SELECTED CULTIVARS:** None

**LANDSCAPE NOTES:** Wilson's Spruce is a dense-growing tree that may be superior to many of the well-known types of Spruce in both habit and foliage. The plant can be used as a lawn specimen or privacy screen. Due to slow growth, it has possibilities for use in the foundation planting.

## *Pinus heldreichii var. leucodermis*     **Bosnian Pine**

**ZONES:**
6, 7

**HEIGHT:**
60′ to 90′

**WIDTH:**
20′ to 40′

**FRUIT:**
2″ to 3″ black cone, maturing to brown.

**TEXTURE:**
Medium

**GROWTH RATE:**
Slow to moderate.

**HABIT:**
Upright and open; obtuse crown.

**FAMILY:**
Pinaceae

**LEAF COLOR:** Medium to dark green.

**LEAF DESCRIPTION:** NEEDLE-LIKE, 2 1/2″ to 3 1/2″ long, rigid, sharply acuminate, stomatic lines on both surfaces, appearing "brush-like" at branch tips, arranged in FASCICLES (BUNDLES) OF 2.

**FLOWER DESCRIPTION:** Monoecious; male clustered, female solitary; NOT ORNAMENTAL.

**EXPOSURE/CULTURE:** Sun or light shade. Native European habitat is dry, alkaline soil. Reasonably wind-tolerant. Branched to ground in youth. Prune to remove broken or dead branches.

**PEST PROBLEMS:** The *Pinus* genus is subject to many pests. The pests include aphids, bark beetles, blights, littleleaf, moths, rusts, sawflies, scales, webworms, weevils, and others. (Check with the Extension Service for problems in your area.)

**BARK/STEMS:** Young shoots whitish-gray; older bark gray and exfoliating to expose yellowish patches.

**SELECTED CULTIVARS:** 'Aureospicata' - A broadly pyramidal to conical cultivar, having needles with yellow tips. German cultivar.

**LANDSCAPE NOTES:** Bosnian Pine has possibilities for naturalizing in the landscape. In addition, it can be used as screening material or as a windbreak. Unfortunately, it is limited in range.

## *Pinus nigra*

**Austrian Pine**

**ZONES:**
5, 6, 7

**HEIGHT:**
60′ to 100′

**WIDTH:**
25′ to 35′

**FRUIT:**
2″ to 3 1/2″ yellow-brown cone.

**TEXTURE:**
Medium

**GROWTH RATE:**
Moderate

**HABIT:**
Broadly pyramidal in youth; umbrella-like with age.

**FAMILY:**
Pinaceae

**LEAF COLOR:** Dark green.

**LEAF DESCRIPTION:** NEEDLE-LIKE, 3″ to 6″ long, stiff, 12 to 14 stomatic lines, straight or slightly incurved, margins finely serrated. Appearing in FASCICLES OF 2.

**FLOWER DESCRIPTION:** Monoecious; NOT ORNAMENTAL.

**EXPOSURE/CULTURE:** Sun. Prefers moist, well-drained soil but is tolerant of dry, sandy soils. pH-tolerant. Wind-tolerant. Thrives in the Midwest. Pruning is not necessary in youth.

**PEST PROBLEMS:** Pine twig blight. There are many others listed. (See *P. heldreichii* var. *leucodermis.)*

**BARK/STEMS:** Young stems orange-brown; older bark dark gray to brown and deeply furrowed.

**SELECTED CULTIVARS:** 'Nana' - A shrub-like form to about 10′. Broad pyramid that is slow-growing. 'Pendula' - A vigorous-growing form with horizontal to nodding branches. 'Pyramidalis' - Conical, narrow shape with bluish-green foliage. Height is similar to the species.

**LANDSCAPE NOTES:** Austrian Pine makes a nice lawn specimen or border specimen for naturalizing. It has attractive form and foliage and is more of an ornamental plant than most pines. In addition, it is useful for windbreaks and screening and as a sound barrier.

## *Pinus rigida*

**Pitch Pine**

**ZONES:**
5, 6, 7

**HEIGHT:**
40′ to 50′

**WIDTH:**
25′ to 35′

**FRUIT:**
3″ to 4″ brown cone; solitary or grouped.

**TEXTURE:**
Medium

**GROWTH RATE:**
Moderate

**HABIT:**
Irregular and open; somewhat oval.

**FAMILY:**
Pinaceae

**LEAF COLOR:** Yellow-green to dark green.

**LEAF DESCRIPTION:** NEEDLE-LIKE, 3″ to 6″ long, numerous stomata on all surfaces, acuminate tip and finely serrated margins, gently curved and twisted. Appearing in FASCICLES OF 3.

**FLOWER DESCRIPTION:** Monoecious; NOT ORNAMENTAL.

**EXPOSURE/CULTURE:** Sun or light shade. Prefers moist, well-drained soil, but is adaptable. Survives on dry, stony ridges, barren land, or swamps. Frequently used in coastal plantings. Prune to remove broken or damaged branches.

**PEST PROBLEMS:** Usually not bothered, but the possibilities are numerous. (See *P. heldreichii* var. *leucodermis.*)

**BARK/STEMS:** Young stems green to brown and furrowed; older bark is deep gray-brown and furrowed into flat plates.

**SELECTED CULTIVARS:** None

**LANDSCAPE NOTES:** Pitch Pine is a nice plant for naturalizing in the lawn area or garden border. In addition, it is a fine plant for massing as a screen, windbreak, or sound barrier.

# *Pinus strobus*

**ZONES:**
3, 4, 5, 6, 7

**HEIGHT:**
60' to 80'+

**WIDTH:**
25' to 45'

**FRUIT:**
4" to 8" brown, curving cones; often used in decorations.

**TEXTURE:**
Medium

**GROWTH RATE:**
Rapid

**HABIT:**
Somewhat pyramidal; branches whorled at nodes.

**FAMILY:**
Pinaceae

**LEAF COLOR:** Bluish-green

**LEAF DESCRIPTION:** NEEDLE-LIKE, 3 1/2" to 4 1/2" long, obtuse tip, margins finely serrated, 3-sided, stomatic lines on the two ventral surfaces. Appearing in FASCICLES OF 5.

**FLOWER DESCRIPTION:** Monoecious; male catkins yellowish and noticeable.

**EXPOSURE/CULTURE:** Sun or part shade. Will grow in a wide range of soils. Survives in dry or moderately wet soils. Does poorly in the deep South or Southwestern states due to heat stress. Pruning is not necessary, but it can be sheared to extreme density. Often sheared for Christmas trees.

**PEST PROBLEMS:** White Pine Blister Rust, weevils. (For additional pests of *Pinus*, see *Pinus heldreichii* var. *leucodermis*.)

**BARK/STEMS:** Young stems smooth and green-brown; very resinous; older bark is grayish and smooth, maturing to gray-brown with furrows.

**SELECTED CULTIVARS:** 'Fastigiata' - Narrow, columnar form with upright branching. 'Nana' - (See Medium Evergreen Shrubs.) var. *glauca* - The needles of this variety are more intense blue-green.

**LANDSCAPE NOTES:** White Pine has very refined blue-green needles and is very ornamental. The tree has beautiful form, but becomes less attractive with age. It can be used as a lawn specimen, border plant for massing, clipped hedges, or unclipped screens. One of the most ornamental of the *Pinus* genus.

## *Pinus taeda*          **Loblolly Pine**

**ZONES:**
6, 7, 8, 9

**HEIGHT:**
60' to 80'

**WIDTH:**
20' to 30'

**FRUIT:**
2" to 4" ovate dark brown cone.

**TEXTURE:**
Medium

**GROWTH RATE:**
Rapid

**HABIT:**
Upright with irregular crown.

**FAMILY:**
Pinaceae

**LEAF COLOR:** Dark green.

**LEAF DESCRIPTION:** NEEDLE-LIKE, 5" to 8" long, acuminate tip, finely serrated margins, stomatic lines on all surfaces. Appearing in alternate FASCICLES OF 3.

**FLOWER DESCRIPTION:** Monoecious; NOT ORNAMENTAL.

**EXPOSURE/CULTURE:** Sun or part shade. The plant prefers moist, organic soil, but is adaptable to wet soils or dry soils. A southern pine that does well in the Southwest. Prune to remove dead or broken branches.

**PEST PROBLEMS:** (See *Pinus heldreichii* var. *leucodermis.*)

**BARK/STEMS:** Young stems yellowish-brown; older bark is gray-brown with deep furrows and irregular plates.

**SELECTED CULTIVARS:** None

**LANDSCAPE NOTES:** Loblolly Pine is an informal timber tree that is great for naturalizing or as a partial screen. It can be used to "tie" the landscape to the surroundings when wooded areas are adjacent. It blends with many shrubs and trees, and holds lower branches when given plenty of space in full sun.

# *Pseudotsuga menziesii*

**Douglas Fir**

**ZONES:**
4, 5, 6, 7

**HEIGHT:**
50′ to 100′

**WIDTH:**
10′ to 25′

**FRUIT:**
3″ to 4″ light brown cone; pendulous.

**TEXTURE:**
Fine to medium.

**GROWTH RATE:**
Slow to moderate.

**HABIT:**
Pyramidal and dense in youth; opening with age.

**FAMILY:**
Pinaceae

**LEAF COLOR:** Blue-green to dark green, depending on source.

**LEAF DESCRIPTION:** NEEDLE-LIKE, 3/4″ to 1 1/4″ long, 2 stomatic bands beneath having 5 or 6 gray lines, acute or obtuse tip. V-shaped furrow running the length of the top surface. Spirally arranged.

**FLOWER DESCRIPTION:** Monoecious; male flowers axillary, female flowers terminal; NOT ORNAMENTAL.

**EXPOSURE/CULTURE:** Sun or light shade. Prefers moist, well-drained soils, but is moderately drought-tolerant. Shallow, rocky soils produce slower, less quality growth. Should be mulched where moisture is scarce. Pruning is not necessary.

**PEST PROBLEMS:** (See *Pinus heldreichii* var. *leucodermis.*)

**BARK/STEMS:** Young stems yellow-green to gray-brown; older bark is red-brown and deeply furrowed.

**SELECTED CULTIVARS:** 'Fastigiata' - Conical with ascending, upright shoots. More narrow than the species. 'Glauca Pendula' - Has blue-green needles and gracefully drooping branches. var. *glauca* - Slower growing variety with shorter, blue-green needles. Very dense and compact.

**LANDSCAPE NOTES:** Douglas Fir is an important timber tree that has possibilities as an ornamental tree, especially when young. It can be used as a specimen or as a screen. Especially attractive when younger trees are massed on larger estates.

# *Quercus laurifolia*

**Laurel Oak, Darlington Oak**

**ZONES:**
6, 7, 8, 9

**HEIGHT:**
40' to 60'

**WIDTH:**
40' to 60'

**FRUIT:**
1/2" brownish-black acorn; enclosed 1/3 by brown cup.

**TEXTURE:**
Medium

**GROWTH RATE:**
Moderate

**HABIT:**
Spreading with a rounded crown.

**FAMILY:**
Fagaceae

**LEAF COLOR:** Dark green.

**LEAF DESCRIPTION:** SIMPLE, 2" to 4" long and half as wide, elliptic to oblong-obovate shape with entire margins, midrib yellowish, ALTERNATE arrangement.

**FLOWER DESCRIPTION:** Monoecious; male catkins in clusters, female in 1 to many-flowered spikes; NOT ORNAMENTAL OR NOTICEABLE.

**EXPOSURE/CULTURE:** Sun for symmetrical crown development. Prefers deep, moist, organic soil but is adaptable to heavy soils. Somewhat drought-tolerant. Grows more rapidly where moisture is adequate. Pruning is minimal.

**PEST PROBLEMS:** Cankers, gall, rot, caterpillars, mistletoe, leaf miner.

**BARK/STEMS:** Young stems smooth and dark red; older bark is dark brown, eventually having deep furrows and flat ridges.

**SELECTED CULTIVARS:** None

**RELATED SPECIES:** *Q. nigra* - (See Large Deciduous Trees.)

**LANDSCAPE NOTES:** Laurel Oak is a fine lawn specimen or shade tree. Needs plenty of space due to spreading habit that is sometimes greater than the height. The plant is evergreen in the southern zones to semi-deciduous to deciduous in the northernmost zones.

# *Quercus virginiana*

**ZONES:**
7, 8, 9, 10

**HEIGHT:**
40′ to 60′

**WIDTH:**
40′ to 60′

**FRUIT:**
1/2″ to 1″ dark brown acorn; longer than broad, enclosed 1/3 by cup.

**TEXTURE:**
Medium

**GROWTH RATE:**
Slow

**HABIT:**
Broad-spreading and dense; opening with age.

**FAMILY:**
Fagaceae

**LEAF COLOR:** Dark green.

**LEAF DESCRIPTION:** SIMPLE, 2″ to 3″ long and 1/2″ to 1 1/4″ wide, elliptic to oblong-obovate shape with entire margins, sometimes, but rarely toothed, pubescent underneath, thick and leathery. ALTERNATE arrangement.

**FLOWER DESCRIPTION:** Monoecious; NOT ORNAMENTAL OR NOTICEABLE.

**EXPOSURE/CULTURE:** Sun or shade. Native to sandy and wet soils, but it is adaptable to almost any soil. Drought-tolerant. Very young plants can be pruned for structural development; older trees are often sheared to a very dense crown. Graceful when left natural.

**PEST PROBLEMS:** Cankers, galls, rot, caterpillars, mistletoe, leaf miner. NONE SERIOUS.

**BARK/STEMS:** Young stems smooth or pubescent and gray; older bark is dark brownish-black, furrowed and scaly.

**SELECTED CULTIVARS:** None

**LANDSCAPE NOTES:** Live Oak is a tree of the South. It is native to coastal areas from Virginia to Florida, but grows inland to southern Texas. It can be used for shade or as a lawn specimen. It makes a nice street tree and looks great when draped with Spanish Moss.

## *Tsuga canadensis*

**Canadian Hemlock**

**ZONES:**
3, 4, 5, 6, 7

**HEIGHT:**
40′ to 60′

**WIDTH:**
20′ to 30′

**FRUIT:**
1/2″ to 1″ light-brown to brown cone.

**TEXTURE:**
Fine

**GROWTH RATE:**
Moderate

**HABIT:**
Pyramidal with pendulous branches.

**FAMILY:**
Pinaceae

**LEAF COLOR:** Medium green to dark green and glossy.

**LEAF DESCRIPTION:** NEEDLE-LIKE, 1/2″ long, margins finely serrated, rounded tip, tapering from base to tip, furrowed above, 2 white stomatic bands underneath. OPPOSITE and 2-ranked.

**FLOWER DESCRIPTION:** Monoecious; male axillary, female terminal.

**EXPOSURE/CULTURE:** Sun or shade. Prefers cool, moist, well-drained soils. pH-tolerant. Not tolerant of winds or intense sunlight. Grows best when shaded by structures or other trees. Mulch heavily, especially in southernmost zones. Pruning is not usually necessary.

**PEST PROBLEMS:** Blister rust, stem rot.

**BARK/STEMS:** Young stems yellow-brown to gray-brown and pubescent; older bark is reddish-brown to brown with deep, narrow furrows.

**SELECTED CULTIVARS:** 'Albospica' - White tips on young branches. 'Fastigiata' - Narrow, columnar habit. 'Gracilis' - Branchlets drooping at ends; needles smaller than the species. 'Pendula' (var. *sargentii*) - (See Large Evergreen Shrubs.) 'Microphylla' - Has needles less than 1/4″ in length. 'Jeddeloh' - (See Dwarf Evergreen Shrubs.) Note: Many other cultivars exist, especially in Europe.

**LANDSCAPE NOTES:** Canadian Hemlock is most useful as evergreen screening material in the landscape border of larger gardens. It is one of the best conifers for shearing into hedge form. In addition, it makes a nice lawn specimen, but works best when shaded part of the day.

# *Tsuga caroliniana*

**Carolina Hemlock**

**ZONES:**
5, 6, 7

**HEIGHT:**
40' to 60'+

**WIDTH:**
20' to 30'

**FRUIT:**
1" to 1 1/2" brown, cylindrical cone.

**TEXTURE:**
Fine to medium.

**GROWTH RATE:**
Moderate

**HABIT:**
Pyramidal with drooping branches.

**FAMILY:**
Pinaceae

**LEAF COLOR:** Medium to dark green and glossy.

**LEAF DESCRIPTION:** NEEDLE-LIKE, 3/4" to 1" long, margins finely serrated, rounded tip, tapering from base to tip, furrowed above, 2 white stomatic bands beneath. Spiralled around the stem.

**FLOWER DESCRIPTION:** Monoecious; male axillary, female terminal; NOT ORNAMENTAL.

**EXPOSURE/CULTURE:** Sun or shade. Prefers cool, moist, well-drained soil. pH-tolerant. Not tolerant of winds or intense sunlight. Grows best when shaded by structures or other trees. Mulch to keep roots moist and cool. Pruning is not usually necessary.

**PEST PROBLEMS:** Blister rust, stem rot.

**BARK/STEMS:** Young stems yellow-brown to gray and pubescent; older bark reddish-brown with shallow, narrow, fissures.

**SELECTED CULTIVARS:** 'Arnold Pyramid' - Conical form, growing 25' to 30'. Very dense.

**LANDSCAPE NOTES:** Carolina Hemlock can be used as a substitute for Canadian Hemlock, but is 2 zones less hardy and has longer needles.

# x *Cupressocyparis leylandii* Leyland Cypress

**ZONES:**
6, 7, 8, 9

**HEIGHT:**
50′ to 60′

**WIDTH:**
12′ to 15′

**FRUIT:**
3/8″ to 3/4″ brown cones; 8 scales.

**TEXTURE:**
Fine

**GROWTH RATE:**
Moderate

**HABIT:**
Conical to pyramidal; branchlets flattened.

**FAMILY:**
Cupressaceae

**LEAF COLOR:** Dark green.

**LEAF DESCRIPTION:** SCALE-LIKE, 1/8″ to 1/4″ long, acute tip, usually no glands, no whitish markings beneath, tightly appressed.

**FLOWER DESCRIPTION:** Monoecious; NOT ORNAMENTAL OR NOTICEABLE.

**EXPOSURE/CULTURE:** Sun. Prefers deep, moist, well-drained soils, but is adaptable to all but wet soils. pH-adaptable. Can be sheared to control size or to develop a very dense screen. Easy to grow.

**PEST PROBLEMS:** Bagworms

**BARK/STEMS:** Young stems green; older bark is dark reddish-brown, with scales or plates.

**SELECTED CULTIVARS:** 'Castlewellan Gold' - This is a dense, upright-growing form with bright, golden-yellow new growth. 'Green Spire' - Narrow, columnar habit. Branchlets irregularly spaced with varying stem angles. Interesting habit. 'Naylor's Blue' - Has soft, gray-blue foliage. Rapid growth.

**LANDSCAPE NOTES:** Leyland Cypress makes a beautiful lawn specimen, and deserves a well-chosen site. It is often sheared as a hedge and rivals Canadian Hemlock as the best conifer for hedges. Purchase plants grown in containers for best results. The plant is an intergeneric cross between *Cupressus macrocarpa* and *Chamaecyparis nootkatensis*.

# *Acer platanoides*

**Norway Maple**

▲ 'Crimson King'

**ZONES:**
3, 4, 5, 6, 7

**HEIGHT:**
40' to 60'

**WIDTH:**
25' to 40'

**FRUIT:**
2" to 3" winged samara; ripening (brown) in early fall.

**TEXTURE:**
Coarse

**GROWTH RATE:**
Moderate

**HABIT:**
Rounded and dense.

**FAMILY:**
Aceraceae

**LEAF COLOR:** Dark green in summer; yellowish in fall.

**LEAF DESCRIPTION:** SIMPLE, 4" to 6" long and often slightly broader, 5 shallow lobes, lobes acuminate, margins of lobes sparsely dentate. Palmately veined. OPPOSITE arrangement.

**FLOWER DESCRIPTION:** Yellow to greenish-yellow, 1/2", appearing in small corymbs, mostly monoecious and perfect, appearing in early spring before the leaves. NOTICEABLE AND ATTRACTIVE.

**EXPOSURE/CULTURE:** Sun. Prefers moist, well-drained soil, but is adaptable. Marketed in the Southeast, but NOT for the Southeast or Southwest. Heat severely retards growth. Prune for strong branching.

**PEST PROBLEMS:** Stem canker, verticillium wilt.

**BARK/STEMS:** Young stems olive with lenticels; older bark is gray-brown with narrow furrows.

**SELECTED CULTIVARS:** 'Crimson King' - Has red to red-purple leaves throughout the season. Very noticeable. 'Crimson Sentry' - Columnar form with dark purple foliage. 'Drummondii' - Has silvery-white edges to the lighter green leaves. 'Emerald Queen' - Has glossy and leathery, dark green leaves. 'Jade Glen' - This is a more rapid-growing form with dark green leaves. Golden-yellow in fall. 'Royal Red' - Has rich, dark red leaves throughout the season. Similar to 'Crimson King'. 'Schwedleri' - Foliage is purplish-red in spring, maturing to bronzy-green. 'Summer Shade' - Upright; rapid growth. Supposedly more heat-tolerant.

**LANDSCAPE NOTES:** Norway Maple is one of the most commonly used large trees for shade or street plantings. It produces dense shade and is easy to grow in the recommended zones. It is a time-proven plant with many recent cultivars.

# *Acer rubrum*

**Red Maple**

▲ var. *tridens*

**ZONES:**
3, 4, 5, 6, 7, 8, 9

**HEIGHT:**
50' to 60'

**WIDTH:**
30' to 40'

**FRUIT:**
3/4" to 1" winged samara; red maturing to brown in summer.

**TEXTURE:**
Medium

**GROWTH RATE:**
Rapid

**HABIT:**
Oval to rounded and dense.

**FAMILY:**
Aceraceae

**LEAF COLOR:** Dark green and gray to whitish underneath; yellow to orange to red in fall.

**LEAF DESCRIPTION:** SIMPLE, 2" to 5" long and broad, 3 to 5 lobes (See Note), lobes irregularly crenate-serrate, distinctly grayish beneath, palmately veined, red petioles. OPPOSITE arrangement.

**FLOWER DESCRIPTION:** Red, 1/2" to 1" across, mostly monoecious, rarely dioecious, appearing in early spring before the leaves; NOT GREATLY NOTICEABLE.

**EXPOSURE/CULTURE:** Sun or shade. Native to wet, swampy soils, tolerant of a wide range of soils. Not for the Southwest. Moderately drought-tolerant. Mulching recommended. Prune for strong branching.

**PEST PROBLEMS:** No serious pests.

**BARK/STEMS:** Young stems green to reddish with lenticels; older bark is light gray and smooth, becoming darker and furrowed on lower trunk.

**SELECTED CULTIVARS:** 'Autumn Flame' - Has smaller, 3-lobed leaves that color early to a brilliant red. 'Columnare' - 3-lobed form having narrow, columnar habit. Orange to red in fall. 'Drummondii' - Has leathery, deep-cut foliage (5-lobed) with pubescent undersides. Scarlet fruits. 'October Glory' - (Featured on next page.) 'Red Sunset' - (Featured in this section.) NOTE: In the natural environment, Red Maples occur in two forms. *A. rubrum* has five lobes, whereas *A. rubrum* var. *tridens* has 3 lobes and smaller overall leaf size. (See Hortus Third). Many of the best cultivars are var. *tridens* selections.

**LANDSCAPE NOTES:** Red Maple is a native tree that is abundant throughout the U.S., growing in moist wooded areas. It is a fast-growing tree that makes a superb lawn specimen or shade tree. The smooth, gray bark is especially attractive.

# *Acer rubrum* 'October Glory'    October Glory Red Maple

**ZONES:**
3, 4, 5, 6, 7, 8, 9

**HEIGHT:**
40' to 50'

**WIDTH:**
25' to 30'

**FRUIT:**
3/4" to 1" winged samara; reddish, maturing to brown.

**TEXTURE:**
Medium

**GROWTH RATE:**
Rapid

**HABIT:**
Oval and upright.

**FAMILY:**
Aceraceae

**LEAF COLOR:** Dark green and grayish beneath; fall color is brilliant red to red-orange.

**LEAF DESCRIPTION:** SIMPLE, 2" to 4" long and broad, 3 to 5 lobes, lobes irregularly crenate-serrate, palmately veined, red petioles. OPPOSITE arrangement.

**FLOWER DESCRIPTION:** Red, 1/2" to 1", appearing in April before the leaves; NOT GREATLY NOTICEABLE.

**EXPOSURE/CULTURE:** Sun or shade. The plant prefers moist, organic, well-drained soils, but is tolerant of a wide range of soils. Moderately drought-resistant. Mulch for best growth. Prune for strong branching.

**PEST PROBLEMS:** No serious pests.

**BARK/STEMS:** Young stems green to reddish with lenticels; older bark is light to medium gray and smooth, becoming darker and furrowed at the base.

**SELECTED CULTIVARS:** None. This is a cultivar.

**LANDSCAPE NOTES:** October Glory Red Maple is one of the more outstanding cultivars for growth habit and fall color. It makes a fine lawn specimen for shade or fall accent. Fall color is more intense and holds later than 'Red Sunset' (featured on next page.)

## *Acer rubrum* 'Red Sunset'                    Red Sunset Maple

**ZONES:**
3, 4, 5, 6, 7, 8, 9

**HEIGHT:**
40′ to 50′

**WIDTH:**
25′ to 30′

**FRUIT:**
3/4″ to 1″ winged samara; reddish maturing to brown.

**TEXTURE:**
Medium

**GROWTH RATE:**
Rapid

**HABIT:**
Oval or rounded; upright.

**FAMILY:**
Aceraceae

**LEAF COLOR:** Dark green and grayish beneath; red fall color.

**LEAF DESCRIPTION:** SIMPLE, 2″ to 4″ long, almost as wide, 5-lobed, terminal lobe being the longest and largest, lobes irregularly crenate-serrate, palmately veined. OPPOSITE arrangement.

**FLOWER DESCRIPTION:** Red, 1/2″ to 1″ long, appearing in spring before the leaves; NOT GREATLY NOTICEABLE.

**EXPOSURE/CULTURE:** Sun or shade. Best in sun. The plant prefers moist, organic, well-drained soil, but is adaptable to a wide range of soils. Reasonably drought-tolerant. Mulching is recommended for best growth. Prune, if desired, for strong branching.

**PEST PROBLEMS:** No serious pests.

**BARK/STEMS:** Young stems reddish with lenticels; older bark is light to medium gray and smooth, becoming darker and furrowed at the base.

**SELECTED CULTIVARS:** None. This is a cultivar.

**LANDSCAPE NOTES:** Red Sunset Maple is one of the most popular Red Maple cultivars. Fall color can be spectacular under ideal conditions. Does not hold its leaves as long as 'October Glory', but might be somewhat more vigorous. Blends well in the lawn area in summer, but will be noticed in fall!

# *Acer saccharinum*

**Silver Maple**

**ZONES:**
4, 5, 6, 7, 8, 9

**HEIGHT:**
60' to 70'

**WIDTH:**
40' to 50'

**FRUIT:**
2" winged samara in summer; green maturing to brown.

**TEXTURE:**
Medium to coarse.

**GROWTH RATE:**
Rapid

**HABIT:**
Upright; rounded and irregular.

**FAMILY:**
Aceraceae

**LEAF COLOR:** Green, silver underneath; fall color greenish-yellow.

**LEAF DESCRIPTION:** SIMPLE, 4" to 7" long, almost as broad, 5-lobed, terminal lobe being the longest and largest, lobes acuminate with doubly serrated margins, deeply cut, terminal lobe more narrow at the base, pubescent or glabrous beneath. OPPOSITE arrangement.

**FLOWER DESCRIPTION:** Pinkish, 1/2" to 1", appearing in early spring before the leaves; NOT GREATLY NOTICEABLE.

**EXPOSURE/CULTURE:** Sun. The plant prefers moist, deep soils for best growth, but is adaptable. Reasonably drought-tolerant. pH-tolerant. Prune carefully for good structure since the wood is brittle compared to most maples.

**PEST PROBLEMS:** No serious pests. However, there are numerous pests reported including anthracnose, leaf spots, mildews, wilt, cankers, caterpillars, leafhoppers, borers, cottony maple scale, and other scales.

**BARK/STEMS:** Young stems reddish, becoming gray with lenticels; older bark is gray-brown and deeply furrowed, often with scaly plates.

**SELECTED CULTIVARS:** 'Blairii' - This plant is a rapid-growing selection with stronger branching habit. Handles snow and ice better. 'Laciniatum' - A cutleaf form with leaves dissected almost to the midrib. 'Pyramidal' - Has a pyramidal to cone-shaped habit with a central trunk.

**LANDSCAPE NOTES:** Silver Maple is one of the fastest growing large trees. Although many fine Silver Maples exist, most authorities regard it as a temporary tree for quick shade. This is due to susceptibility to breakage by ice or high winds. In spite of this, it certainly is ornamental, and fall color is often very good.

# *Acer saccharum*

**Sugar Maple**

**ZONES:**
3, 4, 5, 6, 7, 8

**HEIGHT:**
55′ to 80′

**WIDTH:**
35′ to 50′

**FRUIT:**
1″ to 2″ winged samara; green becoming brown in fall.

**TEXTURE:**
Coarse

**GROWTH RATE:**
Moderate

**HABIT:**
Rounded and dense.

**FAMILY:**
Aceraceae

**LEAF COLOR:** Medium green in summer; yellow, orange, or orange-red in fall, more often orange.

**LEAF DESCRIPTION:** SIMPLE, 4″ to 7″ long and wide, 3 to 5 lobed (usually 5), sparsely sinused, sinuses U-shaped at base, palmately veined. OPPOSITE arrangement.

**FLOWER DESCRIPTION:** Greenish-yellow, 1/2″ in small, pendulous corymbs, appearing in spring before the leaves; NOT GREATLY NOTICEABLE.

**EXPOSURE/CULTURE:** Sun or part shade. Prefers moist, organic, cool soil, and is often found as an understory tree in moist woodlands. pH-tolerant. Not tolerant of dry, hot, windy locations, especially in the southernmost zones. Mulch for cool, moist roots. Prune for good structural branching.

**PEST PROBLEMS:** Leaf scorch. (See *A. saccharinum* for additional pests.)

**BARK/STEMS:** Young stems brown with lenticels; older bark is smooth and gray-brown; very old trees with furrowed bark.

**SELECTED CULTIVARS:** 'Commemoration' - Oval to rounded form; faster-growing and dense. Fall color yellowish-orange to red. Outstanding cultivar. 'Columnare' - Narrow, upright column for limited spaces. Yellow to orange in fall. 'Green Mountain' - A more heat-resistant form with an oval crown and dark green foliage. Deep orange to red in fall. 'Legacy' - Superior cultivar (Featured on next page). MANY OTHER CULTIVARS EXIST.

**LANDSCAPE NOTES:** Sugar Maple is one of the more brilliant trees for fall color, usually assuming a bright orange. It is one of the thickest shade trees, which limits the survival of lawn grasses beneath. It makes a nice lawn specimen that becomes a focal point in fall. One cannot picture fall without Sugar Maples.

# Acer saccharum 'Legacy'

**Legacy Sugar Maple**

**ZONES:**
3, 4, 5, 6, 7, 8

**HEIGHT:**
55' to 70'

**WIDTH:**
35' to 40'

**FRUIT:**
1" to 2" winged samaras; green, becoming brown in fall.

**TEXTURE:**
Medium to coarse.

**GROWTH RATE:**
Moderate

**HABIT:**
Upright oval in youth; spreading more with age. Very dense.

**FAMILY:**
Aceraceae

**LEAF COLOR:** Dark green in summer; deep orange to red in fall.

**LEAF DESCRIPTION:** SIMPLE, 4" to 7" long and wide, 3 to 5 lobes (usually 5), sparsely sinused, sinuses U-shaped at base, palmately veined. OPPOSITE arrangement.

**FLOWER DESCRIPTION:** Yellowish-green, 1/2" in small corymbs, appearing in spring before the leaves; NOT GREATLY NOTICEABLE.

**EXPOSURE/CULTURE:** Sun or shade. Prefers moist, organic, cool soils. pH-tolerant. Avoid hot, dry locations, even though it is more tolerant that *A. saccharum*. Mulch for best growth. Pruning is minimal for structure.

**PEST PROBLEMS:** (See *A. saccharinum.*)

**BARK/STEMS:** Young stems brownish with lenticels; older bark is smooth and gray, becoming furrowed with age.

**SELECTED CULTIVARS:** None. This is a cultivar.

**LANDSCAPE NOTES:** Legacy Sugar Maple makes a fine specimen for the lawn or garden border. Provides very dense shade where shade is desired. Select the site carefully, because it will become a focal point in fall. This is the finest new cultivar for drought resistance and reliability. Can be grown further south and further west.

## *Aesculus glabra*

**Ohio Buckeye**

**ZONES:**
4, 5, 6, 7

**HEIGHT:**
30' to 50'

**WIDTH:**
30' to 50'

**FRUIT:**
1" round, dehiscent capsule; spiny, containing mahogany seed (Buckeye).

**TEXTURE:**
Coarse

**GROWTH RATE:**
Moderate

**HABIT:**
Rounded, spreading, and dense.

**FAMILY:**
Hippocastanaceae

**LEAF COLOR:** Dark green in summer; yellow to orange in fall.

**LEAF DESCRIPTION:** PALMATELY COMPOUND, usually 5 leaflets, leaflets 3" to 6 1/2" long and one-third as broad, obovate to elliptic-obovate shape with acuminate tip, serrated margins, petiole to 6" long. OPPOSITE arrangement.

**FLOWER DESCRIPTION:** Pale yellow or yellow-green, tiny, 4-petalous, appearing in terminal panicles in early spring with the leaves. Somewhat showy.

**EXPOSURE/CULTURE:** Sun. Prefers a moist, well-drained soil. Somewhat tolerant of alkaline soils. Moderately drought-resistant. Develops leaf scorch in the hot, dry climates of the Southwest. Fairs better in northern zones. Pruning is selective and minimal.

**PEST PROBLEMS:** Anthracnose, fungal leaf spots, chewing insects.

**BARK/STEMS:** Young stems brown and pubescent; older bark is medium to dark gray with narrow, shallow, fissures.

**SELECTED CULTIVARS:** None

**RELATED SPECIES:** *A. arguta* - Texas Buckeye. This is a small tree to 20' that does well in shaded, moist areas of the Southwest. The leaves have 7 to 11 leaflets of elliptic shape. A plant for naturalizing. *A. pavia* - Red Buckeye. This is a small tree of less than 20' that has similar foliage to *A. glabra*. Flowers are red to yellow and attractive.

**LANDSCAPE NOTES:** Ohio Buckeye makes a nice lawn specimen with graceful, pendulous lower branches. It is best underplanted with ground cover due to dense shading. Should not be used in borders or near walks and patios due to the prickly, hard fruit. This is a native tree with adequate fall color and overall ornamental value.

# *Aesculus* x *carnea* 'Rosea'

**Red Horsechestnut**

**ZONES:**
4, 5, 6, 7

**HEIGHT:**
30' to 50'

**WIDTH:**
30' to 50'

**FRUIT:**
Prickly 1" round dehiscent capsule; usually 2 brown seeds.

**TEXTURE:**
Coarse

**GROWTH RATE:**
Moderate

**HABIT:**
Rounded, spreading, and dense.

**FAMILY:**
Hippocastanaceae

**LEAF COLOR:** Dark green in summer; yellowish to orange in fall.

**LEAF DESCRIPTION:** PALMATELY COMPOUND, usually 5 leaflets, leaflets 4" to 6" long and one-third as wide, leaflets ovate-lanceolate to elliptic-oblong shape with serrated margins. OPPOSITE arrangement.

**FLOWER DESCRIPTION:** Rose-pink, tiny, appearing in 6" to 8" terminal, upright panicles in early spring with the leaves; SHOWY.

**EXPOSURE/CULTURE:** Sun or part shade. Prefers a moist, well-drained soil, and is pH-adaptable. Should be mulched, especially in areas of hot, dry conditions. Does better in the northern zones. Pruning is minimal and selective.

**PEST PROBLEMS:** No serious pests. (See *A. glabra*.)

**BARK/STEMS:** Young stems brown and pubescent; older bark is gray with shallow, narrow fissures.

**SELECTED CULTIVARS:** None. This is a cultivar.

**RELATED CULTIVARS:** 'Briotii' - Has scarlet-red flowers. 'O'Neill' - Has deep red flowers.

**LANDSCAPE NOTES:** Red Horsechestnut is a cross between *A. pavia* and *A. hippocastanum* (Horsechestnut). It is a commonly used plant in Europe and Britain that should be more widely used in the U.S. The flowers are attractive and fall color is excellent. Should be used as a lawn specimen away from drive and walks.

## *Betula papyrifera*

**Paper Birch, Canoe Birch**

**ZONES:**
2, 3, 4, 5, 6, 7

**HEIGHT:**
60′ to 80′

**WIDTH:**
20′ to 40′

**FRUIT:**
1″ strobile with winged nut-lets.

**TEXTURE:**
Medium

**GROWTH RATE:**
Moderate

**HABIT:**
Upright and irregularly rounded; single or multi-stemmed trunk.

**FAMILY:**
Betulaceae

**LEAF COLOR:** Dark green in summer; usually bright yellow in fall.

**LEAF DESCRIPTION:** SIMPLE, 3″ to 4″ long and 2″ to 2 1/2″ wide, ovate shape with doubly serrated margins and acuminate tip, pubescent beneath. ALTERNATE arrangement.

**FLOWER DESCRIPTION:** Monoecious; male catkins 2″ to 3″ long and pendulous, female catkins 1″ to 1 1/2″ and erect.

**EXPOSURE/CULTURE:** Sun. Prefers moist, organic, well-drained soils. pH-adaptable. Grows naturally on stream and river banks and in nearby woodlands. Can be grown in the Midwest. Pruning is usually not necessary.

**PEST PROBLEMS:** Bronze birch borer.

**BARK/STEMS:** Young stems red-brown to orange-brown; older bark white, flaking to expose orange inner bark, having black areas, especially at nodes.

**SELECTED CULTIVARS:** None

**LANDSCAPE NOTES:** Paper Birch is a durable, hardy native tree with attractive, noticeable bark. It can be used as a lawn specimen or an accent plant for garden borders. It is a great plant for naturalizing, and looks especially nice in combination with garden pools or streams.

# *Betula platyphylla var. japonica*

**Japanese White Birch**

**ZONES:**
4, 5, 6, 7

**HEIGHT:**
40′ to 60′

**WIDTH:**
15′ to 25′

**FRUIT:**
1″ strobile with winged nutlets.

**TEXTURE:**
Medium

**GROWTH RATE:**
Moderate

**HABIT:**
Upright, rounded, and open.

**FAMILY:**
Betulaceae

**LEAF COLOR:** Dark green in summer; yellow in fall.

**LEAF DESCRIPTION:** SIMPLE, 1 1/2″ to 2 1/2″ long and 3/4″ to 1 1/2″ wide, ovate to triangular shape with truncate to broad-cuneate base and long, acuminate tip. Margins doubly serrated. ALTERNATE arrangement.

**FLOWER DESCRIPTION:** Monoecious; pendulous male catkins, erect female catkins.

**EXPOSURE/CULTURE:** Sun. Prefers moist, organic, well-drained soils. pH-adaptable. Can be grown in the Midwest and survives better than *B. papyrifera* in the heat of the Southwest. Pruning is usually not necessary.

**PEST PROBLEMS:** Bronze birch borer.

**BARK/STEMS:** Young stems reddish-brown and pubescent; older bark is creamy-white and exfoliating to expose an orange inner bark, having black patches, especially at the nodes.

**SELECTED CULTIVARS:** 'Whitespire' - Reportedly resistant to the bronze birch borer.

**LANDSCAPE NOTES:** Japanese White Birch is one of the whitest of all birches, having very noticeable and attractive bark. It is a true specimen in all seasons. This is a great tree for areas in need of light shade, but not dense shade. Makes a great tree for shading patios, casting pleasant shade while allowing air movement. Can be underplanted with a wider range of plants.

# *Carya glabra*

**Pignut Hickory**

**ZONES:**
5, 6, 7, 8, 9

**HEIGHT:**
40′ to 50′

**WIDTH:**
25′ to 30′

**FRUIT:**
4-valved green, dehiscent husk; hard nut inside; edible.

**TEXTURE:**
Medium

**GROWTH RATE:**
Slow

**HABIT:**
Oblong to oval crown; drooping lower branches.

**FAMILY:**
Juglandaceae

**LEAF COLOR:** Dark green in summer; yellow in fall.

**LEAF DESCRIPTION:** ODD PINNATELY COMPOUND, 5 to 7 leaflets (usually 5), leaflets 4″ to 6″ long and one-third as wide, obovate to oblanceolate shape with acuminate tip and serrated margins. ALTERNATE arrangement.

**FLOWER DESCRIPTION:** Monoecious; male 3-branched catkins, females in terminal spike-like clusters; NOT ORNAMENTAL.

**EXPOSURE/CULTURE:** Sun. The plant prefers moist, organic, acid soil, but is somewhat adaptable. Reasonably drought-tolerant. Difficult to transplant. Usually found in landscapes where it established naturally. Pruning is not necessary.

**PEST PROBLEMS:** Tent caterpillars.

**BARK/STEMS:** Young stems red-brown to gray-brown and smooth; older bark is gray with shallow fissures forming a "diamond" pattern.

**SELECTED CULTIVARS:** None

**RELATED SPECIES:** *C. ovata* - Shagbark Hickory. This species grows to 100′ and has noticeable, attractive "shaggy" bark, which is more beautiful with age. *C. tomentosa* - Mockernut Hickory. This species has 5 to 9 leaflets (usually 7) which are pubescent beneath. Petiole and rachis are densely pubescent. *C. cordiformis* - Bitternut Hickory. This species has 5 to 9 leaflets with a pubescent rachis. Easily identified by yellow buds during all seasons. Nuts are too bitter for man or beast.

**LANDSCAPE NOTES:** Pignut Hickory is a fine native tree that has very dense wood (great for firewood) and good form when grown under landscape conditions. Fall color is adequate, though not spectacular. Once established, it is a durable, long-lived tree requiring very little care. Not for use near patios or drives because of fruit.

# *Carya illinoinensis*

**ZONES:**
5, 6, 7, 8, 9

**HEIGHT:**
80' to 100'

**WIDTH:**
40' to 80'

**FRUIT:**
1" to 2" dehiscent husk; nuts reddish-brown with dark spots; edible and delicious.

**TEXTURE:**
Medium

**GROWTH RATE:**
Moderate

**HABIT:**
Oval to broad-spreading with rounded crown.

**FAMILY:**
Juglandaceae

**LEAF COLOR:** Dark yellow-green in summer; more yellowish in fall.

**LEAF DESCRIPTION:** ODD PINNATELY COMPOUND, 10" to 18" long, 11 to 17 leaflets, leaflets to 7" long and to 2 1/2" wide, oblong-lanceolate shape with acuminate tips and doubly serrated margins. Pubescent in spring. ALTERNATE arrangement.

**EXPOSURE/CULTURE:** Sun. Prefers moist, organic soil, but is adaptable. pH-tolerant and drought-tolerant. Found naturally in bottom lands near rivers or streams. Prune for structural development. Regular spraying is essential for fruit crops.

**PEST PROBLEMS:** Tent caterpillars, scab, weevils, and many others. (Check with the Extension Service for pests in your area.)

**BARK/STEMS:** Young stems reddish-brown and pubescent, with lenticels; older bark is grayish-brown and scaly with narrow fissures.

**SELECTED CULTIVARS:** Note: There are hundreds of cultivars. Most were developed for a particular geographic location. Check with the Extension Service for cultivars suitable for your area.

**LANDSCAPE NOTES:** Pecan is an important fruit crop in the U.S. Consequently, it is a very popular lawn tree for home gardens, space permitting. In the home garden it serves as a shade tree, while providing fall fruit for the family. As an ornamental tree, it is very attractive in foliage and has good fall color. Avoid planting nears walks, drives, and patios. Not low-maintenance, but worth the effort. Note: Many authorities use the species spelling of *illinoensis*. I have used *illinoinensis,* which, according to Hortus Third, is the correct spelling.

## *Cercidiphyllum japonicum*

**Katsura Tree**

**ZONES:**
5, 6, 7, 8

**HEIGHT:**
50′ to 60′

**WIDTH:**
30′ to 40′

**FRUIT:**
3/4″ brown follicle; NOT ORNAMENTAL.

**TEXTURE:**
Medium

**GROWTH RATE:**
Moderate

**HABIT:**
Pyramidal to rounded; dense.

**FAMILY:**
Cercidiphyllaceae

**LEAF COLOR:** Bluish-green in summer; yellowish in fall.

**LEAF DESCRIPTION:** SIMPLE, 2″ to 3″ long and wide, broad oval shape with cordate base and crenate margins. Almost reniform in shape. OPPOSITE arrangement.

**FLOWER DESCRIPTION:** Dioecious; staminate and pistillate on separate trees; NOT ORNAMENTAL.

**EXPOSURE/CULTURE:** Sun. The plant is adaptable as to soil types, but does not tolerate drought. Mulch and provide water during hot, dry periods. Difficult to transplant. Prune for structural development, if needed. Not a tree for the Southwest.

**PEST PROBLEMS:** No serious pests.

**BARK/STEMS:** Young stems are smooth and brown with swollen nodes; older bark is light brown to grayish-brown with shallow furrows, somewhat shaggy.

**SELECTED CULTIVARS:** 'Pendula' - (See Small Deciduous Trees.)

**LANDSCAPE NOTES:** Katsura Tree can be used as a lawn specimen or shade tree anywhere in the landscape where sufficient space is available. It should be given a prominent place and plenty of sunlight where it will develop into a gorgeous, symmetrical tree. Although fall color is not spectacular, a healthy specimen is as attractive as any tree. OUTSTANDING TREE.

## *Cladrastis kentuckea*

**ZONES:**
3, 4, 5, 6, 7, 8

**HEIGHT:**
40′ to 50′

**WIDTH:**
20′ to 50′

**FRUIT:**
3″ to 5″ brown pod.

**TEXTURE:**
Medium to coarse.

**GROWTH RATE:**
Moderate

**HABIT:**
Rounded, irregular, and spreading.

**FAMILY:**
Fabaceae

**LEAF COLOR:** Light to medium green.

**LEAF DESCRIPTION:** ODD PINNATELY COMPOUND, 8″ to 10″ long, 7 to 11 leaflets, leaflets 2″ to 4″ long and half as wide, ovate or elliptic shape with entire margins. ALTERNATE arrangement.

**FLOWER DESCRIPTION:** White, 1″ long, appearing in pendulous, terminal panicles to 12″ long. Flowers in late spring. Very ornamental.

**EXPOSURE/CULTURE:** Sun. The plant prefers organic, well-drained soils, but is adaptable to all but wet soils. pH-tolerant. Pruning is selective and structural. Prune in summer after the flowers.

**PEST PROBLEMS:** No serious pests.

**BARK/STEMS:** Young stems are brown and smooth; white pith and yellow wood; older bark is brownish or dark gray and smooth.

**SELECTED CULTIVARS:** 'Rosea' - Similar to species, but having pink flowers.

**LANDSCAPE NOTES:** American Yellowwood is gaining in popularity as an accent or street tree. Its flowers, excellent foliage, and gray bark combine to form a tree of excellent potential for greater use in the landscape industry.

# *Eucommia ulmoides*

**Hardy Rubber Tree**

**ZONES:**
5, 6, 7, 8

**HEIGHT:**
35′ to 55′

**WIDTH:**
25′ to 40′

**FRUIT:**
1″ to 1 1/2″ one-seeded winged fruit; similar to Elm, but much larger.

**TEXTURE:**
Medium

**GROWTH RATE:**
Moderate

**HABIT:**
Oval in youth; rounded with age.

**FAMILY:**
Eucommiaceae

**LEAF COLOR:** Dark green in summer; yellowish-green in fall.

**LEAF DESCRIPTION:** SIMPLE, 4″ to 5″ long and half as wide, elliptic or ovate shape with acuminate tips and serrated margins. ALTERNATE arrangement.

**FLOWER DESCRIPTION:** Dioecious; NOT ORNAMENTAL AND NOT NOTICE-ABLE.

**EXPOSURE/CULTURE:** Sun. The plant adapts to a wide range of well-drained soils. pH-tolerant. Reasonably drought-tolerant. Prune as desired.

**PEST PROBLEMS:** No serious pests.

**BARK/STEMS:** Young stems green-brown; older bark is gray-brown with shallow furrows.

**SELECTED CULTIVARS:** None

**LANDSCAPE NOTES:** Hardy Rubber Tree is a nice lawn specimen or shade tree that offers nice foliage and is essentially pest-free. Not as popular as trees having noticeable flowers or spectacular fall color, but is a worthy tree that deserves consideration. Blends into almost any landscape theme.

# *Fagus grandifolia*

**American Beech**

**ZONES:**
3, 4, 5, 6, 7, 8

**HEIGHT:**
50′ to 80′

**WIDTH:**
40′ to 70′

**FRUIT:**
Prickly, dehiscent husk; 1/2″ triangular, edible nut.

**TEXTURE:**
Medium

**GROWTH RATE:**
Slow

**HABIT:**
Rounded or oval crown; dense.

**FAMILY:**
Fagaceae

**LEAF COLOR:** Dark green in summer; golden brown to bronze in fall.

**LEAF DESCRIPTION:** SIMPLE, 2″ to 4″ long and 1″ to 2″ wide, ovate-oblong to elliptic shape with serrated margins and acuminate tips, veins distinctly sunken on upper surface. ALTERNATE arrangement.

**FLOWER DESCRIPTION:** Monoecious; male in drooping heads, female in small spikes; NOT ORNAMENTAL.

**EXPOSURE/CULTURE:** Sun or shade. Prefers light, well-drained, moist, organic soils. Will grow in heavy soil where the permeability is good. Not for the Southwest. Prune selectively, if needed.

**PEST PROBLEMS:** No serious pests.

**BARK/STEMS:** Young stems lustrous brown with zigzag pattern; older bark is smooth and gray with darker mottles.

**SELECTED CULTIVARS:** None

**LANDSCAPE NOTES:** American Beech forms a huge, rounded tree with beautiful smooth gray bark. The fall color is not spectacular, but is attractive. The small "beechnuts" are edible but sometimes messy. This is not a tree for small gardens, but makes a nice lawn specimen or very dense shade tree.

# *Fagus sylvatica*

**European Beech**

**ZONES:**
3, 4, 5, 6, 7

**HEIGHT:**
50′ to 80′

**WIDTH:**
40′ to 70′

**FRUIT:**
Prickly, dehiscent husk with small, triangular nut.

**TEXTURE:**
Medium

**GROWTH RATE:**
Moderate

**HABIT:**
Oval to rounded; dense and symmetrical.

**FAMILY:**
Fagaceae

**LEAF COLOR:** Dark, lustrous green in summmer; reddish-brown in fall.

**LEAF DESCRIPTION:** SIMPLE, 3″ to 4″ long and half as wide, ovate or elliptic shape with entire margins, usually undulate, 5 to 9 vein pairs (usually 7, which is less than *F. grandifolia*). ALTERNATE arrangement.

**FLOWER DESCRIPTION:** Monoecious; male in drooping head, female in small spikes; NOT ORNAMENTAL.

**EXPOSURE/CULTURE:** Sun or part shade. Prefers moist, light, well-drained, organic soil. Not for the Southwest. Prune for structural development or to remove lower branches.

**PEST PROBLEMS:** No serious pests.

**BARK/STEMS:** Young stems green-brown with zigzag pattern; older bark is gray and smooth with darker mottles.

**SELECTED CULTIVARS:** 'Atropunicea' - Purple leaves (Featured on next page.) 'Aurea-variegata' - Variegated form with yellow leaf margins. 'Fastigiata' - Columnar form. 'Laciniata' - Cutleaf form having lobed or deeply toothed margins. 'Pendula' - Has horizontal main branches that weep at the ends. 'Rotundifolia' - Leaves are smaller (1″) and almost round.

**LANDSCAPE NOTES:** European Beech and its many cultivars is one of the most beautiful of all lawn specimens. The plant requires plenty of space and branches naturally to the ground. The lower branches are often removed to provide dense shade. Unfortunately, it performs poorly in the lower Southeast and Southwest. Not for smaller gardens. Makes a nice plant for parks and other public areas.

# *Fagus sylvatica* 'Atropunicea' ('Cuprea', 'Purpurea') Copper Beech, Purple Beech

**ZONES:**
4, 5, 6, 7

**HEIGHT:**
40' to 60'

**WIDTH:**
30' to 40'

**FRUIT:**
Prickly, dehiscent husk, with 1/2" triangular nut.

**TEXTURE:**
Medium

**GROWTH RATE:**
Moderate

**HABIT:**
Oval to rounded; very dense.

**FAMILY:**
Fagaceae

**LEAF COLOR:** Purplish-green in summer; more copper colored in fall.

**LEAF DESCRIPTION:** SIMPLE, 2 1/2" to 3 1/2" long and half as wide, ovate to elliptic shape with entire margins, usually undulate, usually 7 vein pairs (less than *F. grandifolia*). ALTERNATE arrangement.

**FLOWER DESCRIPTION:** Monoecious; male in drooping heads, female in small spikes; NOT ORNAMENTAL.

**EXPOSURE/CULTURE:** Sun or part shade. Prefers moist, light, well-drained, organic soil. Not for the lower Southeast or Southwest. Pruning is minimal.

**PEST PROBLEMS:** No serious pests.

**BARK/STEMS:** Young stems green-brown with zigzag pattern; older bark is gray and smooth with darker mottles.

**SELECTED CULTIVARS:** None. This is a cultivar.

**LANDSCAPE NOTES:** Copper Beech is a bold accent or specimen plant for the lawn area of larger gardens. The bold foliage holds its color throughout the season, and, consequently, its location should be carefully planned. One must exercise restraint, since this plant is not a plant for massing. As with all Beeches, this plant is great for parks, golf courses, and other public areas.

## *Fraxinus americana* — White Ash

**ZONES:**
3, 4, 5, 6, 7, 8, 9

**HEIGHT:**
60' to 80'

**WIDTH:**
40' to 60'

**FRUIT:**
1" to 2" long single-seeded, winged samara; spring.

**TEXTURE:**
Medium to coarse.

**GROWTH RATE:**
Moderate

**HABIT:**
Oval and upright; somewhat open, becoming more rounded with age.

**FAMILY:**
Oleaceae

**LEAF COLOR:** Dark green in summer; yellowish to orange in fall.

**LEAF DESCRIPTION:** ODD PINNATELY COMPOUND, 8" to 12" long, 5 to 9 leaflets (usually 7), leaflets 3" to 5" long and 1" to 2 1/2" wide, narrow elliptic to ovate-lanceolate shape with acuminate tip and finely serrated margins. OPPOSITE arrangement.

**FLOWER DESCRIPTION:** Dioecious; male and female in panicles; NOT ORNAMENTAL OR NOTICEABLE.

**EXPOSURE/CULTURE:** Sun. The plant prefers moist, organic, deep, well-drained soil, but is adaptable to all but excessively wet or excessively dry soils. Very easy to grow. Prune selectively for structural development.

**PEST PROBLEMS:** Ash borers and other borers, webworms.

**BARK/STEMS:** Young stems gray-green to gray-brown with lenticels; older bark is ash-gray with narrow diamond-shaped furrows and flat ridges.

**SELECTED CULTIVARS:** 'Autumn Applause' - Has deep maroon fall color. 'Autumn Purple' - Has purple foliage in fall. 'Rosehill' - Seedless cultivar with bronze fall color. 'Skyline' - Seedless form with orange to red fall color.

**LANDSCAPE NOTES:** White Ash can be used as a lawn specimen or shade tree. It has nice form and is not as dense as many popular large trees. In open lawn areas it can accomodate grass or many ground cover species as underplantings. This is a nice native tree, but it requires space. Seedless forms are recommended near walks, drives, and patios. Great for parks, golf courses, commercial landscapes.

# *Fraxinus pennsylvanica*

**Green Ash**

**ZONES:**
3, 4, 5, 6, 7, 8, 9

**HEIGHT:**
40′ to 60′

**WIDTH:**
30′ to 40′

**FRUIT:**
1″ to 2″ single-seed, single-winged samara in spring.

**TEXTURE:**
Medium to coarse.

**GROWTH RATE:**
Moderate

**HABIT:**
Oval to rounded and somewhat open.

**FAMILY:**
Oleaceae

**LEAF COLOR:** Dark green in summer; yellowish in fall.

**LEAF DESCRIPTION:** ODD PINNATELY COMPOUND, 8″ to 12″ long, 5 to 9 leaflets (usually 7), leaflets 3″ to 6″ long and 1 1/4″ to 2″ wide, ovate to lanceolate shape with long, acuminate tips and entire to sharply serrated margins. OPPOSITE arrangement.

**FLOWER DESCRIPTION:** Dioecious; male and female appearing in panicles in spring.

**EXPOSURE/CULTURE:** Sun. Prefers moist, deep, well-drained soils, but is adaptable to many well-drained soils and pH levels. More drought-tolerant than *F. americana*. Will grow in the Southwest. Prune for structure or shaping.

**PEST PROBLEMS:** Ash borer and other borers, webworms.

**BARK/STEMS:** Young stems are green, maturing to gray-brown; older bark is ash-gray with diamond-shaped furrows and flat ridges.

**SELECTED CULTIVARS:** 'Cimmaron' - Male form that has bright red fall foliage. 'Marshall's Seedless' - Male form that grows more rapidly than the species. 'Summit' - Female selection with refined appearance. Bright red foliage, turning golden-yellow in fall.

**RELATED SPECIES:** *F. udhei* - Evergreen Ash. A fast-growing, rounded, evergreen tree for Zones 9 and 10. Great street tree for Southern California, Southern Texas, and Florida.

**LANDSCAPE NOTES:** Green Ash is a popular lawn or shade tree over a wide range of the U.S. It is more hardy and drought-tolerant than White Ash, but has similar appearance. Most of the popular cultivars are seedless forms, which allows greater versatility in use. One of the best trees for American gardens.

## *Ginkgo biloba*

**Ginkgo, Maidenhair Tree**

**ZONES:**
4, 5, 6, 7, 8

**HEIGHT:**
40′ to 60′

**WIDTH:**
30′ to 50′

**FRUIT:**
1″ orange, berry-like seed with fleshy covering (female); foul-smelling and objectionable.

**TEXTURE:**
Medium

**GROWTH RATE:**
Slow

**HABIT:**
Upright and irregular.

**FAMILY:**
Ginkgoaceae

**LEAF COLOR:** Green in summer; bright yellow in fall.

**LEAF DESCRIPTION:** SIMPLE, 2″ to 3″ long and broad, petiole to 3″ long, fan-shaped with wavy or incised margin, dichotomously veined. ALTERNATE arrrangement.

**FLOWER DESCRIPTION:** Dioecious; appearing on spurs; male catkin-like, female appearing on long peduncles.

**EXPOSURE/CULTURE:** Sun. The plant prefers moist, well-drained, light soils, but is adaptable to all but wet soils. pH-tolerant and drought-tolerant. Good hardy tree for urban conditions. Pruning is minimal and structural.

**PEST PROBLEMS:** No serious pests.

**BARK/STEMS:** Young stems yellow to gray-brown, exfoliating thread-like "strings"; older bark is ash-gray and furrowed, with furrows lighter in color.

**SELECTED CULTIVARS:** 'Autumn Gold' - The best male form, with symmetrical, radiating branches. 'Fastigiata' - Narrow, columnar habit. 'Princeton Sentry' - Male form with a narrow pyramidal habit. 'Pendula' - Branches somewhat weeping in character. 'Variegata' - Summer foliage has yellow streaks on the green foliage.

**LANDSCAPE NOTES:** Ginkgo is the brightest of the yellow colored trees in fall, which accounts for its popularity. The leaves are a definite fan-shape and distinctively different. One should always select male trees that do not have fruits. The tree can be used in lawn areas or garden borders, but its location should be well-planned, as it will become a focal point of interest in fall.

## *Gymnocladus dioicus*

**ZONES:**
4, 5, 6, 7, 8

**HEIGHT:**
60′+

**WIDTH:**
30′+

**FRUIT:**
4″ to 8″ green pod, maturing to blackish-brown. Note: Pods and seeds are POISONOUS.

**TEXTURE:**
Medium

**GROWTH RATE:**
Moderate

**HABIT:**
Spreading and irregular crown; somewhat open.

**FAMILY:**
Fabaceae

**LEAF COLOR:** Gray-green in summer; yellow in fall.

**LEAF DESCRIPTION:** BIPINNATELY COMPOUND, 18″ to 36″ overall length, 3 to 7 pairs of pinnae along the rachis, pinnae having 3 to 7 pairs of leaflets (pinnules), leaflets 1″ to 2 1/2″ long and half as wide, ovate shape with entire margins. ALTERNATE arrangement.

**FLOWER DESCRIPTION:** Greenish-white, 1″ long in panicles; dioecious or polygamous; male panicles to 4″ long, female to 12″; NOT ORNAMENTAL.

**EXPOSURE/CULTURE:** Prefers moist, organic soils, but is adaptable to a wide range of soils. pH-tolerant and drought-tolerant. Will thrive on poorly drained sites. Pruning is minimal and selective for structural development. Suitable for the Southwest.

**PEST PROBLEMS:** None

**BARK/STEMS:** Young stems green and downy, becoming gray-brown with salmon or pinkish pith; older bark is steel-gray to gray-brown with shallow furrows and recurved ridges.

**SELECTED CULTIVARS:** None

**LANDSCAPE NOTES:** Kentucky Coffee Tree was used by the early settlers as a coffee substitute. Apparently, roasting the beans destroyed the toxins. The tree is hardy and rugged, and will grow almost anywhere. It can be used in lawn areas, street plantings, parks, and golf courses. Plant male trees to avoid the seed pods. This tree should be more widely used, especially on poor sites.

# *Larix laricinia*

American Larch, Tamarack

**ZONES:**
2, 3, 4, 5, 6

**HEIGHT:**
50′ to 80′

**WIDTH:**
20′ to 30′

**FRUIT:**
1/2″ to 3/4″ yellow-brown cone.

**TEXTURE:**
Fine

**GROWTH RATE:**
Moderate

**HABIT:**
Narrow cone in youth; more horizontal with age.

**FAMILY:**
Pinaceae

**LEAF COLOR:** Bright, pale blue-green in summer; yellow in fall.

**LEAF DESCRIPTION:** NEEDLE-LIKE, 1″ to 1 1/2″ long, keeled underneath with 2 stomatic bands, appearing in clusters of 15 to 30 needles, usually on short spurs.

**FLOWER DESCRIPTION:** Monoecious; male globose on axillary shoots, female globose and terminal; NOT ORNAMENTAL.

**EXPOSURE/CULTURE:** Sun. Plant prefers moist, well-drained soils of acid reaction. Reasonably drought-tolerant, but should be mulched heavily for best growth. Pruning is minimal and selective.

**PEST PROBLEMS:** Insects may be numerous. (Check with the Extension Service.)

**BARK/STEMS:** Young stems are smooth and orange-brown; older bark is reddish-brown with thin scales.

**SELECTED CULTIVARS:** 'Glauca' - Developed in Sweden. Has steel-blue foliage.

**RELATED SPECIES:** *L. decidua* - European Larch. This species is less columnar than *L. laricinia*. Many authorities feel this species is superior for landscapes. This might be debatable.

**LANDSCAPE NOTES:** American Larch is one of a handful of deciduous conifers. The plant is not spectacular, but has possibilities for naturalizing in the landscape. Although it is not considered a specimen plant for focalization, older plants can be quite picturesque.

# *Liquidambar styraciflua*

**Sweetgum**

▲ 'Rotundiloba'

**ZONES:**
4, 5, 6, 7, 8, 9

**HEIGHT:**
60' to 90'

**WIDTH:**
40' to 60'

**FRUIT:**
1" round aggregate with spiny burrs; NOT ORNAMENTAL - considered a nuisance.

**TEXTURE:**
Coarse

**GROWTH RATE:**
Moderate

**HABIT:**
Pyramidal and upright.

**FAMILY:**
Hamamelidaceae

**LEAF COLOR:** Dark green in summer; yellow to orange-red to purple in fall.

**LEAF DESCRIPTION:** SIMPLE, 4" to 6" long and wide, distinctly star-shaped (palmately lobed) with 5 lobes, serrated margins and acuminate tips. (No marginal lobes as with Maple.) ALTERNATE arrangement.

**FLOWER DESCRIPTION:** Monoecious; male in terminal racemes, female globose on slender peduncles; NOT ORNAMENTAL.

**EXPOSURE/CULTURE:** Sun. Prefers moist, acid, deep soil for best growth, but is drought-tolerant in the Southeast. Not for the Southwest. Pruning is minimal.

**PEST PROBLEMS:** Scale insects, chewing insects, webworm.

**BARK/STEMS:** Young stems yellowish to reddish-brown, developing corky ridges in second year; older bark is gray-brown with narrow furrows and scaly ridges.

**SELECTED CULTIVARS:** 'Burgundy' - Fall foliage is dark red to purple, holding late into the season. 'Festival' - A narrow, upright form of variable fall color. 'Palo Alto' - A pyramidal form for the South. Uniform growth with orange to red leaves in fall. 'Rotundiloba' - A more narrow-growing form with rounded leaf lobes. Somewhat of a novelty.

**RELATED SPECIES:** *L. formosana* - Formosan Sweetgum. This tree has 3-lobed leaves that turn yellow in fall. Stems do not have corky ridges. Fruits have long, limber spines that are less hazardous than *L. styraciflua*.

**LANDSCAPE NOTES:** Sweetgum is very popular for its brilliant foliage in fall. It is often confused with Maple by the novice gardener because of the star-shaped leaves. The corky ridges add additional interest to the plant. It makes a nice lawn specimen, but should be planted where the burrs will not be a problem. One of the most beautiful trees for fall color.

# *Liriodendron tulipifera*

**Yellow Poplar, Tuliptree**

**ZONES:**
4, 5, 6, 7, 8, 9

**HEIGHT:**
60′ to 100′

**WIDTH:**
25′ to 40′

**FRUIT:**
3″ to 4″ brown, cone-like pod (aggregate of samaras).

**TEXTURE:**
Coarse

**GROWTH RATE:**
Rapid

**HABIT:**
Columnar to rounded.

**FAMILY:**
Magnoliaceae

**LEAF COLOR:** Green in summer; yellow in fall.

**LEAF DESCRIPTION:** SIMPLE, 4″ to 6″ long and wide, leaves resembling profile of a tulip flower, square shape with 2 to 3 lobes on each side of the midrib. Margins entire. Petioles to 6″ long. ALTERNATE arrangement.

**FLOWER DESCRIPTION:** Greenish-yellow, 3″ to 4″ wide, cup-shaped with brush-like stamens, appearing in April to June; ATTRACTIVE, but not abundant.

**EXPOSURE/CULTURE:** Sun or part shade. Native to moist, deep soils along streams and bottomlands. Will grow on higher ground where moisture is adequate. Develops leaf scorch in the Southwest. Pruning is usually not necessary, except to remove broken branches.

**PEST PROBLEMS:** Aphids, gray mold.

**BARK/STEMS:** Young stems are smooth and greenish-brown to reddish-brown; older bark is ash-gray with interlocking furrows and narrow ridges.

**SELECTED CULTIVARS:** 'Arnold' - A narrow, fastigiate form with butter-yellow fall color. Introduced by Monrovia Nurseries. 'Aureo-marginatum' - Similar to the species, except green leaves are edged bright yellow. Very attractive. Marketed by Monrovia Nurseries as 'Majestic Beauty'.

**LANDSCAPE NOTES:** Yellow Poplar is often called Tuliptree because the greenish-yellow flowers have a Tulip shape. It is a good single-trunk tree that can be used as a specimen or lawn tree, usually with great success. Avoid planting near buildings because it is subject to breakage.

# *Metasequoia glyptostroboides*  **Dawn Redwood**

**ZONES:**
5, 6, 7, 8, 9

**HEIGHT:**
60′ to 90′

**WIDTH:**
15′ to 25′

**FRUIT:**
1″ brown cone; long-stalked and pendulous.

**TEXTURE:**
Fine

**GROWTH RATE:**
Moderate

**HABIT:**
Upright and pyramidal, with ascending branches.

**FAMILY:**
Taxodiaceae

**LEAF COLOR:** Dark green in summer; brown in fall.

**LEAF DESCRIPTION:** NEEDLE-LIKE, 1/2″ needles, 2-ranked and opposite on deciduous branchlets (appearance of compound leaves), needles with 2 stomatic bands underneath, upper surface with grooved midvein.

**FLOWER DESCRIPTION:** Monoecious; male axillary or terminal in racemes or panicles, female solitary with numerous seed scales; NOT ORNAMENTAL.

**EXPOSURE/CULTURE:** Sun. The plant is adaptable to most well-drained soils with moderate moisture levels. Performs better in the Southeast than in the Southwest. Pruning is usually not necessary.

**PEST PROBLEMS:** No serious pests.

**BARK/STEMS:** Young stems smooth and red-brown; older bark is dark gray, furrowed, and exfoliating in narrow strips.

**SELECTED CULTIVARS:** 'National' - Narrow conical to pyramidal form. Developed by the U.S. National Arboretum.

**LANDSCAPE NOTES:** Dawn Redwood is a deciduous conifer that is a true fossil dating to the age of dinosaurs. It has good trunk and branching characteristics that look great in winter when the leaves are gone. It is a plant to feature in the landscape. Not for small gardens.

## *Nyssa sylvatica*
### Black Gum, Black Tupelo

**ZONES:**
4, 5, 6, 7, 8, 9

**HEIGHT:**
40′ to 50′

**WIDTH:**
20′ to 25′

**FRUIT:**
1/4″ blue-black berries (drupes); SHOWY.

**TEXTURE:**
Medium

**GROWTH RATE:**
Moderate to slow.

**HABIT:**
Upright and somewhat irregular.

**FAMILY:**
Nyssaceae

**LEAF COLOR:** Dark green in summer; brilliant red or orange in fall.

**LEAF DESCRIPTION:** SIMPLE, 3″ to 5″ long and half as wide, elliptic to obovate shape, entire margins (slightly undulate). ALTERNATE arrangement.

**FLOWER DESCRIPTION:** Usually dioecious, sometimes monoecious; male and female both in clusters; NOT ORNAMENTAL.

**EXPOSURE/CULTURE:** Sun or shade. Prefers moist, organic, acid soils, but will grow in almost any soil, except alkaline, where moisture is adequate. Needs supplemental water in the Southwest. Prune to single trunk.

**PEST PROBLEMS:** No serious pests.

**BARK/STEMS:** Young twigs smooth and ash-gray to red-brown; older bark is dark gray and fissured with blocky ridges.

**SELECTED CULTIVARS:** None. Since the species varies greatly, some standardization of characteristics by nurserymen would be in order.

**LANDSCAPE NOTES:** Black Gum is a native tree that has good form and brilliant fall color. It is an excellent tree to feature in the landscape and is easy to grow. It should be more widely available in the nursery trade.

## *Platanus occidentalis*

**Sycamore, American Planetree**

**ZONES:**
3, 4, 5, 6, 7, 8, 9

**HEIGHT:**
60′ to 90′

**WIDTH:**
50′ to 60′

**FRUIT:**
1″ to 1 1/2″ brown fuzzy ball; (aggregate of achenes); borne singly.

**TEXTURE:**
Coarse

**GROWTH RATE:**
Rapid

**HABIT:**
Oval to somewhat rounded; dense.

**FAMILY:**
Platanaceae

**LEAF COLOR:** Medium green in summer; brown in fall.

**LEAF DESCRIPTION:** SIMPLE, 5″ to 8″ long and wide, 3 to 5 lobes, pointed at the tips, each lobe with shallow U-shaped sinuses, petiole to 3″ long. Palmately veined. ALTERNATE arrangement.

**FLOWER DESCRIPTION:** Monoecious; male and female both are globular on long peduncles; NOT ORNAMENTAL.

**EXPOSURE/CULTURE:** Sun. Native to bottomlands and river banks. Prefers deep, moist, organic soils, but will grow almost anywhere if ample moisture is provided. Tolerant of dry, hot winds of the Southwest.

**PEST PROBLEMS:** Anthracnose

**BARK/STEMS:** Young stems smooth and yellow-brown to gray; zigzag habit; older bark smooth and gray-brown, exfoliating in large irregular plates to expose the whitish or green inner bark.

**SELECTED CULTIVARS:** None

**LANDSCAPE NOTES:** Sycamore is valued for its rapid growth and grayish, peeling bark and colorful inner bark. It should not be used in mass plantings due to fruit droppage and "different" bark. However, it is a plant to feature as a lawn specimen or as a shade tree.

## *Platanus x acerifolia*

**London Planetree**

**ZONES:**
4, 5, 6, 7, 8, 9

**HEIGHT:**
60' to 90'

**WIDTH:**
55' to 70'

**FRUIT:**
1" to 1 1/2" brown, fuzzy ball (aggregate of achenes); Borne in pairs.

**TEXTURE:**
Coarse

**GROWTH RATE:**
Moderate to rapid.

**HABIT:**
Oval to pyramidal in youth; open and rounded with age.

**FAMILY:**
Platanaceae

**LEAF COLOR:** Medium green in summer; yellowish in fall.

**LEAF DESCRIPTION:** SIMPLE, 5" to 7" long and equal or greater in width, 3 to 5 lobes, pointed at the tips, each lobe with a few U-shaped sinuses, petiole to 3" long, palmately veined. ALTERNATE arrangement.

**FLOWER DESCRIPTION:** Monoecious; male and female both globular in separate peduncles; NOT ORNAMENTAL.

**EXPOSURE/CULTURE:** Sun. Prefers deep, organic, moist, well-drained soils of acid or alkaline pH, but will tolerate a wide range of soils. Tolerant of urban conditions. Prune for good structural branching.

**PEST PROBLEMS:** Anthracnose, mildew, cankers, borers.

**BARK/STEMS:** Young stems smooth and yellow-bronze to gray; older bark light brown, exfoliating to reveal whitish inner bark. Very ornamental.

**SELECTED CULTIVARS:** 'Bloodgood' - Has dark green foliage and is more resistant to anthracnose. 'Yarwood' - A superior cultivar that is reportedly mildew-resistant.

**LANDSCAPE NOTES:** London Planetree is a handsome tree, but it requires much space, and it is often too large for many residential gardens. It can be used as a lawn specimen for larger gardens, golf courses, parks, and other areas where space is not limited. In addition, it does well under urban conditions, and makes a nice street tree.

# *Quercus acutissima*

**Sawtooth Oak**

**ZONES:**
4, 5, 6, 7, 8, 9

**HEIGHT:**
40′ to 50′

**WIDTH:**
30′ to 40′

**FRUIT:**
1″ acorn; covered 2/3 by "mophead" or shaggy cup.

**TEXTURE:**
Medium

**GROWTH RATE:**
Moderate

**HABIT:**
Upright oval to somewhat irregular.

**FAMILY:**
Fagaceae

**LEAF COLOR:** Medium green in summer; yellowish in fall.

**LEAF DESCRIPTION:** SIMPLE, 4″ to 6″ long and 1″ to 2″ wide, oblong with bristle-like, serrated margins and acute or acuminate tip. ALTERNATE arrangement.

**FLOWER DESCRIPTION:** Monoecious; male in drooping catkins, female in spikes; NOT ORNAMENTAL.

**EXPOSURE/CULTURE:** Sun. Adapted to a wide range of well-drained soil types. Tolerant of hot conditions but should be mulched for best growth. Pruning is usually not necessary.

**PEST PROBLEMS:** No serious pests.

**BARK/STEMS:** Young stems brownish and glabrous; older bark is dark gray with narrow furrows and cork-like appearance.

**SELECTED CULTIVARS:** None

**LANDSCAPE NOTES:** Sawtooth Oak makes a nice lawn specimen or shade tree. Its foliage is more like that of a chestnut than that of an oak in appearance and in uniformity of shape among trees in the species. It has possibilities as a parking lot tree, and for parks, golf courses, and other public areas. Native to the Orient, it often grows more rapidly than native American Oaks.

# *Quercus alba*

**White Oak**

**ZONES:**
3, 4, 5, 6, 7, 8, 9

**HEIGHT:**
60′ to 90′

**WIDTH:**
50′ to 70′

**FRUIT:**
1/2″ to 1″ light brown, ovoid acorns; enclosed 1/4 by cup.

**TEXTURE:**
Coarse

**GROWTH RATE:**
Slow

**HABIT:**
Somewhat rounded and upright; dense.

**FAMILY:**
Fagaceae

**LEAF COLOR:** Blue-green in summer; yellowish-brown in fall.

**LEAF DESCRIPTION:** SIMPLE, 5″ to 9″ long and half as wide, obovate shape with cuneate base, 5 to 9 rounded lobes (usually 7), lobes usually deep-cut with U-shaped sinuses, lobes obtuse. Margins entire. ALTERNATE arrangement.

**FLOWER DESCRIPTION:** Monoecious; male in drooping catkins, female in spikes; NOT ORNAMENTAL.

**EXPOSURE/CULTURE:** Sun. Native to moist, deep, well-drained bottomlands. Will grow in almost any well-drained soil where moisture is adequate or supplied. Performs poorly on compacted soil. Pruning is minimal.

**PEST PROBLEMS:** No serious pests. Have observed gall on young trees.

**BARK/STEMS:** Young stems are reddish-green to purplish and smooth; older bark is ash-gray with shallow fissures and often flaky. Great effect!

**SELECTED CULTIVARS:** None

**LANDSCAPE NOTES:** White Oak is one of the best native trees for shade. Foliage has a faint blue cast and is quite attractive. The trees are long-lived and attain great size. The scaly bark is very attractive, especially on older trees. Older trees merit specimen status.

# Quercus coccinea

**Scarlet Oak**

**ZONES:**
5, 6, 7, 8, 9

**HEIGHT:**
50′ to 70′

**WIDTH:**
35′ to 50′

**FRUIT:**
1/2″ to 1″ reddish-brown acorn; cup enclosing 1/2 of the nut.

**TEXTURE:**
Coarse

**GROWTH RATE:**
Rapid

**HABIT:**
Irregularly rounded and upright.

**FAMILY:**
Fagaceae

**LEAF COLOR:** Dark green in summer; scarlet red in fall.

**LEAF DESCRIPTION:** SIMPLE, 5″ to 8″ long and 3″ to 5″ wide, obovate in outline with 5 to 9 lobes (usually 7), lobes longer than broad with bristle tips near apex, sinuses distinctly U-shaped. ALTERNATE arrangement.

**FLOWER DESCRIPTION:** Monoecious; male in catkins, female in spikes; NOT ORNAMENTAL.

**EXPOSURE/CULTURE:** Sun or part shade. Native to "higher ground" on sandy, gravelly, or rocky soils on sloping ridges or mountains. Very tolerant of poor soils, so long as the site is well-drained. Pruning is selective for removal of dead or undesirable branches.

**PEST PROBLEMS:** No serious pests.

**BARK/STEMS:** Young stems red-brown to gray-brown and smooth; older bark is dark gray with broad ridges and deep furrows.

**SELECTED CULTIVARS:** None

**LANDSCAPE NOTES:** Scarlet Oak is one of the best Oaks for fall foliage color, and makes an excellent lawn specimen or shade tree. Its leaves are similar to that of Pin Oak, but the leaves are larger. A very nice native tree.

## *Quercus falcata*

**Southern Red Oak**

**ZONES:**
5, 6, 7, 8, 9

**HEIGHT:**
50′ to 60′

**WIDTH:**
50′ to 60′

**FRUIT:**
1/2″ orange-brown acorn; cup enclosing 1/3 of nut.

**TEXTURE:**
Coarse

**GROWTH RATE:**
Rapid

**HABIT:**
Rounded and somewhat open.

**FAMILY:**
Fagaceae

**LEAF COLOR:** Dark green in summer; brown in fall.

**LEAF DESCRIPTION:** SIMPLE, 5″ to 10″ long and 3″ to 5″ wide, obovate outline with 3 to 7 bristle-tipped lobes, base is rounded to cuneate, lobes deeply cut with terminal lobe longer and more narrow at the base. Grayish color and pubescent underneath. ALTERNATE arrangement.

**FLOWER DESCRIPTION:** Monoecious; male in pendulous catkins, female in spikes; NOT ORNAMENTAL.

**EXPOSURE/CULTURE:** Sun or light shade. The plant is native to sandy soils and gravelly, rocky, upland soils. Will grow in most any well-drained soil, and responds favorably to good soil and fertile conditions. Pruning is minimal and selective.

**PEST PROBLEMS:** No serious pests.

**BARK/STEMS:** Young stems reddish-brown to gray and somewhat downy; older bark is dark gray with deep, narrow furrows.

**SELECTED CULTIVARS:** None

**LANDSCAPE NOTES:** Southern Red Oak is a native tree that has potential as a shade tree. Its main disadvantage is that leaves cling to the branches very late into the season. It is a better, more tolerant landscape tree than critics claim.

## *Quercus macrocarpa*

**Bur Oak, Mossycup Oak**

**ZONES:**
3, 4, 5, 6, 7, 8

**HEIGHT:**
60′ to 70′

**WIDTH:**
70′+

**FRUIT:**
1 1/2″ to 2″ brown acorn (one of the largest); cup enclosing 2/3 or more of the nut.

**TEXTURE:**
Coarse

**GROWTH RATE:**
Slow

**HABIT:**
Broad-spreading and rounded; very graceful.

**FAMILY:**
Fagaceae

**LEAF COLOR:** Dark green in summer; yellowish to brownish in fall.

**LEAF DESCRIPTION:** SIMPLE, 6″ to 10″ long and half as wide, obovate outline, usually 3 pairs of lobes below the middle and deeply cut, broader lobe above the middle with shallow sinuses, all lobes having rounded tips. Cuneate base. ALTER-NATE arrangement.

**FLOWER DESCRIPTION:** Monoecious; male in pendulous catkins, female in spikes; NOT ORNAMENTAL.

**EXPOSURE/CULTURE:** Sun. Native to a wide range of well-drained soils from clay to sand and from acid to alkaline. Will grow under a wide range of conditions and is very tolerant. Pruning is minimal and selective.

**PEST PROBLEMS:** Anthracnose, borers, galls, wood rot and others; None serious.

**BARK/STEMS:** Young stems yellow-brown to grayish, often pubescent; older bark is dark gray-brown with deep furrows and flat ridges.

**SELECTED CULTIVARS:** None

**LANDSCAPE NOTES:** Bur Oak is a beautiful, graceful tree that is too broad-spreading for most residential properties. It is better suited to larger areas, such as estates, playgrounds, parks, and golf courses. This is a very long-lived tree that becomes more graceful with age. The large, shaggy fruits make a great conversation piece.

## *Quercus nigra* — Water Oak

**ZONES:**
6, 7, 8, 9

**HEIGHT:**
40' to 70'

**WIDTH:**
45' to 60'

**FRUIT:**
1/2" blackish acorn; cup enclosing 1/3 of the nut.

**TEXTURE:**
Fine to medium.

**GROWTH RATE:**
Moderate

**HABIT:**
Rounded and dense.

**FAMILY:**
Fagaceae

**LEAF COLOR:** Dark green in summer; brown in fall.

**LEAF DESCRIPTION:** SIMPLE, 2" to 3" long and half as wide, obovate shape, 3-lobed at apex or entire. Usually spatula-shaped, petiole very short. ALTERNATE arrangement.

**FLOWER DESCRIPTION:** Monoecious; male in catkins, female in spikes.

**EXPOSURE/CULTURE:** Sun. Plant is native to lowlands and bottomlands having deep, moist soils; however, the plant is very tolerant and adaptable to a wide range of conditions. Grows more slowly in the Southwest. Pruning is minimal and selective.

**PEST PROBLEMS:** Susceptible to many, but relatively disease-free.

**BARK/STEMS:** Young stems are smooth and red-brown; older bark is gray-brown to almost black with smooth areas or shallowly fissured areas.

**SELECTED CULTIVARS:** None

**LANDSCAPE NOTES:** Water Oak is the most commonly used Oak for shade or street plantings in its growth zones. It develops beautiful shape and limb structure. Small leaves are numerous and quite attractive. Trees are usually uniform in shape, and, hence, they are easily matched.

# *Quercus palustris*

**Pin Oak**

**ZONES:**
4, 5, 6, 7, 8, 9

**HEIGHT:**
40′ to 70′

**WIDTH:**
25′ to 40′

**FRUIT:**
1/2″ light brown acorn; enclosed 1/3 by cup.

**TEXTURE:**
Medium

**GROWTH RATE:**
RAPID, under ideal conditions.

**HABIT:**
Pyramidal; lower branches drooping in youth.

**FAMILY:**
Fagaceae

**LEAF COLOR:** Dark green in summer; brilliant red in fall.

**LEAF DESCRIPTION:** SIMPLE, 3″ to 5″ long and 2″ to 3″ wide, oval or ovate shape in outline, 5 to 7 narrow lobes with 3 to 4 bristle tips per lobe, sinuses deeply cut and U-shaped. Similar to *Q. coccinea,* but smaller in size. ALTERNATE arrangement.

**FLOWER DESCRIPTION:** Monoecious; male in catkins, female in spikes.

**EXPOSURE/CULTURE:** Sun. Native to rich bottomlands of acid reaction. Adaptable to a wide range of conditions, but develops chlorosis in high pH soils and performs poorly.

**PEST PROBLEMS:** Subject to several, but usually disease-free.

**BARK/STEMS:** Young stems red-brown and smooth; older bark is gray-brown with shallow fissures and scaly ridges.

**SELECTED CULTIVARS:** 'Sovereign' - More upright branching. Developed for street and highway plantings.

**LANDSCAPE NOTES:** Pin Oak is one of the most beautiful street or parking lot trees. It is equally appropriate and handsome as a lawn specimen. It has drooping lower branches that gradually blend with the upper branches to form a symmetrical, pyramidal shape. Fall foliage is especially attractive and very noticeable.

## *Quercus phellos* — Willow Oak

**ZONES:**
4, 5, 6, 7, 8, 9

**HEIGHT:**
50' to 70'

**WIDTH:**
35' to 50'

**FRUIT:**
1/2" greenish-brown acorn; enclosed 1/3 by cup.

**TEXTURE:**
Fine

**GROWTH RATE:**
Moderate

**HABIT:**
Pyramidal, becoming rounded.

**FAMILY:**
Fagaceae

**LEAF COLOR:** Green in summer; yellowish in fall.

**LEAF DESCRIPTION:** SIMPLE, 3" to 6" long and 1/2" to 1" wide, narrow elliptic to lanceolate shape with cuneate base and acute tip with a small bristle. Margins entire. ALTERNATE arrangement.

**FLOWER DESCRIPTION:** Monoecious; male in catkins, female in spikes; NOT ORNAMENTAL.

**EXPOSURE/CULTURE:** Sun. Native to bottomlands with deep, moist soils. Adaptable to most well-drained sites except high pH soils. Used extensively as a street tree, and transplants easily. Pruning is minimal.

**PEST PROBLEMS:** Subject to several, but usually disease-free.

**BARK/STEMS:** Young stems brown to red-brown and smooth; older bark is dark gray to gray-brown and relatively smooth, becoming shallowly furrowed.

**SELECTED CULTIVARS:** None

**LANDSCAPE NOTES:** Willow Oak makes an excellent street, lawn, or parking lot tree. It is a good substitute for Water Oak, as it sheds its leaves over a shorter period. Lance-shaped leaves are willow-like and interesting. This is one of the best for the recommended zones.

# *Quercus rubra*

**Northern Red Oak**

**ZONES:**
4, 5, 6, 7, 8

**HEIGHT:**
70′ to 90′

**WIDTH:**
50′ to 60′

**FRUIT:**
1″ chestnut-brown acorns; enclosed 1/3 by cup.

**TEXTURE:**
Coarse

**GROWTH RATE:**
Moderate to rapid.

**HABIT:**
Rounded to oval crown; variable.

**FAMILY:**
Fagaceae

**LEAF COLOR:** Dull dark green in summer; reddish-brown to dull red in fall.

**LEAF DESCRIPTION:** SIMPLE, 6″ to 8″ long and 4″ to 5″ wide, oblong or oval in outline, 7 to 11 lobes with 2 to 5 bristle tips per blade, sinuses shallow (compared to *Q. coccinea*). ALTERNATE arrangement.

**FLOWER DESCRIPTION:** Monoecious; male in catkins, female in spikes; NOT ORNAMENTAL.

**EXPOSURE/CULTURE:** Sun. Native to deep, moist, well-drained, acid soils. Subject to chlorosis in alkaline soils. Reasonably drought-tolerant. Pruning is minimal and selective.

**PEST PROBLEMS:** Subject to several, but mostly disease-free.

**BARK/STEMS:** Young stems green to red-brown and smooth; older bark is dark gray-brown with furrows and ridges.

**SELECTED CULTIVARS:** None

**LANDSCAPE NOTES:** Northern Red Oak is a rugged tree that is reliable and durable. It makes a fine shade tree or lawn specimen. It is also very suited for parks and playgrounds, golf courses, and other public areas. Needs plenty of space for best crown development.

# *Quercus shumardii*

**Shumard Oak**

**ZONES:**
5, 6, 7, 8, 9

**HEIGHT:**
50′ to 70′

**WIDTH:**
40′ to 50′

**FRUIT:**
1″ to 1 1/4″ dull brown acorns; enclosed 1/4 to 1/3 by cup.

**TEXTURE:**
Coarse

**GROWTH RATE:**
Moderate to rapid.

**HABIT:**
Oval to rounded; open and spreading.

**FAMILY:**
Fagaceae

**LEAF COLOR:** Dark green in summer; fall color orange to reddish.

**LEAF DESCRIPTION:** SIMPLE, 4″ to 7″ long and two-thirds as wide, oval to obovate shape in outline, 7 to 9 lobes, each with 2 to 5 bristle tips, sinuses deeply cut and U-shaped, cuneate base. ALTERNATE arrangement.

**FLOWER DESCRIPTION:** Monoecious; male in catkins, female in spikes; NOT ORNAMENTAL.

**EXPOSURE/CULTURE:** Sun. Native to well-drained sites near water. Reasonably drought-tolerant, performing better than most Oaks in the Southwest. Tolerant of urban conditions. Pruning is minimal.

**PEST PROBLEMS:** No serious pests.

**BARK/STEMS:** Young stems brown to red-brown and smooth; older bark is dark gray with sparse, shallow fissures.

**SELECTED CULTIVARS:** None

**LANDSCAPE NOTES:** Shumard Oak makes an excellent lawn or shade tree when given adequate space. It is also very tolerant of urban conditions and is a good selection for street tree use. Other uses include parks, playgrounds and golf courses.

# *Quercus stellata*

**Post Oak**

**ZONES:**
5, 6, 7, 8, 9

**HEIGHT:**
40′ to 60′

**WIDTH:**
40′ to 50′

**FRUIT:**
1/2″ to 1″ brown, ovoid acorn; enclosed 1/3 by cup.

**TEXTURE:**
Coarse

**GROWTH RATE:**
Slow to moderate.

**HABIT:**
Oval crown with a central, main stem.

**FAMILY:**
Fagaceae

**LEAF COLOR:** Dark green in summer; brown in fall.

**LEAF DESCRIPTION:** SIMPLE, 6″ to 8″ long and two-thirds as wide, obovate outline, usually 5-lobed, middle pair and terminal lobe much larger than the basal pair. Larger lobes having "sublobes." ALTERNATE arrangement.

**FLOWER DESCRIPTION:** Monoecious; male in catkins, female in spikes; NOT ORNAMENTAL.

**EXPOSURE/CULTURE:** Sun. The plant is native to poor, sandy, dry, and stony soils where it thrives. Will tolerate many sites and conditions. Will grow more rapidly and to greater size on rich, deep soils. Pruning is minimal.

**PEST PROBLEMS:** Subject to several, but mostly disease-free.

**BARK/STEMS:** Young stems brown to orange-brown and downy; older bark is gray-brown with narrow fissures and scaly ridges.

**SELECTED CULTIVARS:** None

**LANDSCAPE NOTES:** Post Oak is native to poor soils, but in the landscape it develops into a nice lawn or shade tree with symmetrical shape and dense foliage. It is a natural for parks, playgrounds, and other public areas. Unlike most Oaks, it has a central trunk, hence, it is called Post Oak.

## *Robinia pseudoacacia*

**Black Locust**

**ZONES:**
4, 5, 6, 7, 8

**HEIGHT:**
40' to 50'

**WIDTH:**
20' to 30'

**FRUIT:**
3" to 4" brown pods (bean-like).

**TEXTURE:**
Fine to medium.

**GROWTH RATE:**
Moderate to rapid.

**HABIT:**
Upright and open; sprouting freely from roots.

**FAMILY:**
Fabaceae

**LEAF COLOR:** Dark green to bluish-green in summer; yellowish in fall.

**LEAF DESCRIPTION:** ODD PINNATELY COMPOUND, 8" to 12" long, 9 to 19 leaflets, leaflets 1" to 2" long and half as wide, leaflets elliptic shape with entire margins. ALTERNATE arrangement.

**FLOWER DESCRIPTION:** White, 1" across, appearing in pendulous racemes 5" to 10" long in May or June. Fragrant and attractive.

**EXPOSURE/CULTURE:** Sun. Grows in almost any well-drained soil, from clay to sand or stony ridges. Lush under poor conditions due to nitrogen fixation. Should be "limbed up" due to thorny spines on stems.

**PEST PROBLEMS:** Borers, scales, cankers. Mostly disease-free.

**BARK/STEMS:** Young stems are greenish-brown to reddish-brown with 1/2" spines (paired) at the nodes; older bark is red-brown to deep gray with interlocking fissures.

**SELECTED CULTIVARS:** 'Decaisneana' - Pink-flowering cultivar. 'Pyramidalis' - Columnar form with spineless branches. 'Semperflorens' - Flowers in late spring and again in fall.

**LANDSCAPE NOTES:** Many authorities consider Black Locust a "weed" to be removed. However, trees on good sites can be attractive and the flowers can be beautiful. It is a great plant for naturalizing in the landscape, but it probably should be avoided where children are present because of the spines and poisonous bark and seeds.

# *Sophora japonica*

**Japanese Pagoda Tree**

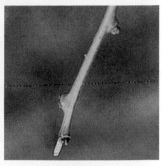

**ZONES:**
4, 5, 6, 7, 8, 9

**HEIGHT:**
40' to 60'

**WIDTH:**
20' to 30'

**FRUIT:**
3" beige pod; numerous seed.

**TEXTURE:**
Fine

**GROWTH RATE:**
Moderate to rapid.

**HABIT:**
Irregularly rounded; loose and open.

**FAMILY:**
Fabaceae

**LEAF COLOR:** Medium green in summer; yellowish in fall.

**LEAF DESCRIPTION:** ODD PINNATELY COMPOUND, 6" to 12" long, 9 to 17 leaflets, leaflets 1 1/2" to 2 1/2" long and half as wide, elliptic shape with entire margins. ALTERNATE arrangement.

**FLOWER DESCRIPTION:** Light yellow, 1/2" in loose panicles to 12" or more, appearing in summer to late summer. Very showy and interesting.

**EXPOSURE/CULTURE:** Sun. Prefers moist, deep, well-drained soil, but is quite adaptable. Drought-tolerant and pH-adaptable. Will thrive in the Southwest. Pruning is selective for structural development.

**PEST PROBLEMS:** Twig blight, cankers, mildew.

**BARK/STEMS:** Young twigs green and smooth; older bark is brown with shallow fissures.

**SELECTED CULTIVARS:** 'Pendula' - This is a smaller-growing form with weeping branches. 'Regent' - Fast-growing cultivar with straight trunk and upright habit.

**LANDSCAPE NOTES:** Japanese Pagoda Tree is noted for its ability to thrive under urban conditions as a street tree with restricted root space. In addition, it makes a nice specimen tree in the landscape, and has interesting, open habit. The flowers appear in late summer and are a welcome sight, being very noticeable on some healthy trees. An outstanding multi-purpose tree.

## *Taxodium distichum* **Bald Cypress**

**ZONES:**
4, 5, 6, 7, 8, 9

**HEIGHT:**
50′ to 60′

**WIDTH:**
20′ to 25′

**FRUIT:**
1″ brown, globose cone.

**TEXTURE:**
Fine

**GROWTH RATE:**
Moderate

**HABIT:**
Usually pyramidal; may be rounded; open and airy.

**FAMILY:**
Taxodiaceae

**LEAF COLOR:** Bright green in summer; bronze to rich brown in fall.

**LEAF DESCRIPTION:** NEEDLE-LIKE, 1/2″ to 3/4″ long, 2-ranked on deciduous branchlets (6″ to 10″ long), needles flat (2-sided) with pointed tips. Branchlets ALTERNATE.

**FLOWER DESCRIPTION:** Monoecious; male catkins clustered and pendulous, female globose.

**EXPOSURE/CULTURE:** Sun or part shade. Native to swampy coastal areas of the Southeast. The plant is adaptable to any soil type of acid reaction, so long as moisture is adequate. Subject to chlorosis on high pH soils. Will shed foliage early in late summer droughts. Pruning is minimal to remove dead branches.

**PEST PROBLEMS:** Blight, spider mites, gall.

**BARK/STEMS:** Young stems reddish-brown; older bark is reddish-brown, often exfoliating in narrow strips.

**SELECTED CULTIVARS:** 'Pendens' - Has drooping branches and larger cones. var. *nutans* - Pond Cypress. This variety has smaller, awl-shaped, appressed foliage that is spirally arranged on branches. Branchlets often pendulous.

**LANDSCAPE NOTES:** Bald Cypress is a deciduous conifer that can be used in the lawn area as a specimen, or in borders or other areas for naturalizing. It looks especially well near streams, ponds, and lakes. In addition, it is a nice plant for massing on larger properties to serve as as warm season screen.

# *Tilia americana*

**American Linden, Basswood**

**ZONES:**
3, 4, 5, 6, 7, 8

**HEIGHT:**
50′ to 75′

**WIDTH:**
25′ to 50′

**FRUIT:**
1/4″ round, gray-green, nut-like structure.

**TEXTURE:**
Medium

**GROWTH RATE:**
Moderate

**HABIT:**
Broad, somewhat pyramidal crown; dense.

**FAMILY:**
Tiliaceae

**LEAF COLOR:** Dark green in summer; yellow in fall.

**LEAF DESCRIPTION:** SIMPLE, 4″ to 6″ long and 3″ to 4″ wide, broad ovate shape with cordate base and acuminate tip, coarsely serrated margins. ALTERNATE arrangement.

**FLOWER DESCRIPTION:** Pale yellow, 1/2″ in 6- to 15-flowered cymes, appearing in late spring. Bract is leaf-like and lanceolate shape to 4″ long, often overlapping leaves. Very interesting effect.

**EXPOSURE/CULTURE:** Sun. Does best in deep, moist, organic loam, but is adaptable to a wide range of well-drained soils. Relatively heat-tolerant, but less drought-tolerant. Prune for good structural branching.

**PEST PROBLEMS:** Borers, cankers, chewing insects. Japanese Beetles love this plant.

**BARK/STEMS:** Young stems gray to greenish-gray; older bark is gray-brown to deepest gray with shallow fissures and flat ridges.

**SELECTED CULTIVARS:** 'Fastigiata' - A narrow, columnar or pyramidal cultivar for smaller properties. 'Redmond' - A dense-growing form of broad pyramidal habit. Reported to be more resistant to leaf scorch.

**LANDSCAPE NOTES:** American Linden makes a nice lawn specimen or dense shade tree for gardens having adequate moisture or supplemental watering. It has nice foliage and flowers that are fragrant in the spring. Not for xeriscaping due to intolerance to drought.

## *Tilia cordata*

**Littleleaf Linden**

**ZONES:**
3, 4, 5, 6, 7, 8

**HEIGHT:**
40′ to 60′

**WIDTH:**
30′ to 40′

**FRUIT:**
Tiny, round, grayish nutlet.

**TEXTURE:**
Medium

**GROWTH RATE:**
Moderate

**HABIT:**
Upright and rounded.

**FAMILY:**
Tiliaceae

**LEAF COLOR:** Dark green in summer; yellowish-green in fall.

**LEAF DESCRIPTION:** SIMPLE, 2″ to 3″ long and broad, cordate shape with acuminate tip and serrated margins. ALTERNATE arrangement.

**FLOWER DESCRIPTION:** Yellowish, 5- to 7-flowered, pendulous, 2″ to 4″ cymes, sometimes erect, bract 3″ to 4″ long and linear shape (leaf-like), appearing in May or June.

**EXPOSURE/CULTURE:** Sun. Prefers moist, deep, well-drained soil of acid or alkaline pH. Reasonably drought-tolerant, but not for the Southwest. Mulch in dry soils. Prune for structure.

**PEST PROBLEMS:** Japanese Beetles and aphids love this plant.

**BARK/STEMS:** Young stems red-brown to brown and smooth; older bark is dark gray-brown with narrow fissures and flat ridges.

**SELECTED CULTIVARS:** 'Greenspire' - The best cultivar. This is a rapid-growing, dense form with oval crown. 'June Bride' - Has more narrow, pyramidal shape and more lustrous foliage. Note: Many others exist.

**LANDSCAPE NOTES:** Littleleaf Linden is an excellent lawn tree for shade or framing. It is a dense tree with excellent foliage, and is easy to grow in the recommended zones.

## *Tilia tomentosa*

**Silver Linden**

**ZONES:**
4, 5, 6, 7, 8

**HEIGHT:**
40′ to 60′

**WIDTH:**
20′ to 30′

**FRUIT:**
1/2″ ovoid nutlet; 5-angled.

**TEXTURE:**
Medium

**GROWTH RATE:**
Moderate

**HABIT:**
Pyramidal to rounded; dense crown.

**FAMILY:**
Tiliaceae

**LEAF COLOR:** Dark green with silvery-white undersides; yellowish in fall.

**LEAF DESCRIPTION:** SIMPLE, 3″ to 5 1/2″ long and wide, cordate shape with unequal base, acuminate tip, serrated margins (sometimes doubly serrated), petiole to 2″ long. ALTERNATE arrangement.

**FLOWER DESCRIPTION:** Pale yellow, borne in several-flowered cymes in late spring to early summer. Bract to 3″ long and leaf-like. Bract more showy than the flowers. Fragrant.

**EXPOSURE/CULTURE:** Sun. Prefers moist, deep, well-drained soil of acid or alkaline pH. Reasonably drought-tolerant, but not for hot, arid regions. Prune for strong structural branching when young.

**PEST PROBLEMS:** Chewing and sucking insects.

**BARK/STEMS:** Young stems green and downy; older bark light gray and mostly smooth, developing ridges and furrows in old age.

**SELECTED CULTIVARS:** 'Green Mountain' - A rapid-growing selection that is supposedly more heat- and drought-tolerant.

**LANDSCAPE NOTES:** Silver Linden is a nice specimen tree for open lawn areas for home gardens, parks, street plantings, and other areas. It is especially attractive on breezy days when the silver leaf undersides are noticeable.

## *Ulmus americana*

American Elm

**ZONES:**
3, 4, 5, 6, 7, 8, 9

**HEIGHT:**
75′ to 100′

**WIDTH:**
40′ to 50′

**FRUIT:**
1/2″ single-seeded, hairy, circular samara; notched on one end; spring.

**TEXTURE:**
Fine to medium.

**GROWTH RATE:**
Rapid

**HABIT:**
Vase-shaped to broad-spreading; open; usually pendulous.

**FAMILY:**
Ulmaceae

**LEAF COLOR:** Dark green in summer; yellowish in fall.

**LEAF DESCRIPTION:** SIMPLE, 3″ to 5″ long and half as wide, oval to elliptic shape with acuminate tip, base often uneven on each side of midrib, doubly serrated margins, pubescent underneath. ALTERNATE arrangement.

**FLOWER DESCRIPTION:** Greenish, tiny, appearing in many-flowered, long-stalked clusters in early spring; NOT SHOWY.

**EXPOSURE/CULTURE:** Sun. Plant is native to swamps and woodlands with moist, organic soils. Will grow in almost any soil, pH level, or condition. Very adaptable, hardy tree (except for diseases). Prune for good structural branching.

**PEST PROBLEMS:** Subject to a large list of pests, including the infamous Dutch Elm Disease, which has devastated great numbers of trees. Phloem necrosis and elm leaf beetles are severe problems.

**BARK/STEMS:** Young stems reddish-brown and usually smooth; older bark is dark gray with narrow, irregular furrows and scaly ridges.

**SELECTED CULTIVARS:** 'Liberty' - Supposedly resistant to Dutch Elm Disease. 'Washington' - Again, supposedly resistant to Dutch Elm Disease.

**LANDSCAPE NOTES:** American Elm was once used in great abundance because of its ability to prosper under harsh conditions. It was used extensively as a street tree. Unfortunately, Dutch Elm Disease has reduced it to a temporary tree, at best. Where elms are desired, one should probably use other species that have proven resistance, or select trees from another genus.

# *Ulmus carpinifolia 'Pioneer'*

**Pioneer Smoothleaf Elm**

**ZONES:**
5, 6, 7, 8

**HEIGHT:**
50′ to 70′

**WIDTH:**
25′ to 50′

**FRUIT:**
1/2″ obovate, winged samara; notched.

**TEXTURE:**
Fine to medium.

**GROWTH RATE:**
Rapid to moderate.

**HABIT:**
Pyramidal to oval; irregular and open.

**FAMILY:**
Ulmaceae

**LEAF COLOR:** Dark green in summer; yellow in fall.

**LEAF DESCRIPTION:** SIMPLE, 2″ to 4″ long and half as wide, ovate to elliptic shape with doubly serrated margins (base usually uneven on each side of midrib), smooth upper surface, pubescent underneath. ALTERNATE arrangement.

**FLOWER DESCRIPTION:** Greenish, tiny in many-flowered, pendulous racemes in early spring; NOT ORNAMENTAL.

**EXPOSURE/CULTURE:** Sun. Grows in a wide range of soil types and climatic conditions. Not as hardy north as *U. americana,* but is more disease-resistant.

**PEST PROBLEMS:** Many; but resistant to Dutch Elm Disease, and phloem necrosis.

**BARK/STEMS:** Young stems brown to gray; older bark is gray and mostly smooth, becoming fissured in old age.

**RELATED CULTIVARS:** 'Homestead' - Actually a hybrid. A rapid-growing form that is resistant to Dutch Elm and phloem necrosis. 'Sapporo Autumn Gold' - Similar to *U. americana,* but resistant to Dutch Elm. Another hybrid.

**LANDSCAPE NOTES:** Pioneer Smoothleaf Elm makes a fine replacement for American Elm. It is resistant to the major diseases afflicting other Elms, and it is a handsome tree for lawn areas or garden borders. This is probably the best of the Smoothleaf Elm cultivars.

# *Ulmus parvifolia*

**Chinese Elm**

**ZONES:**
5, 6, 7, 8, 9

**HEIGHT:**
30′ to 50′

**WIDTH:**
30′ to 40′

**FRUIT:**
1/4″ egg-shaped, hairy, one-seeded samaras; notched; abundant.

**TEXTURE:**
Fine

**GROWTH RATE:**
Rapid

**HABIT:**
Rounded to oval; usually pendulous.

**FAMILY:**
Ulmaceae

**LEAF COLOR:** Medium to dark green and shiny in summer; yellowish in fall.

**LEAF DESCRIPTION:** SIMPLE, 1″ to 2 1/4″ long and half as wide, elliptic to obovate shape with serrated margins, petiole 1/4″ or less. ALTERNATE arrangement.

**FLOWER DESCRIPTION:** Greenish, appearing in many-flowered, pendulous clusters in fall; NOT SHOWY, but abundant.

**EXPOSURE/CULTURE:** Sun. The plant is adaptable to a wide range of soil types and conditions. Will thrive on poor soils in difficult conditions. Very hardy and reliable in Zones 5-9. Pruning is minimal and structural.

**PEST PROBLEMS:** Many, but resistant to Dutch Elm, phloem necrosis, and elm leaf beetles.

**BARK/STEMS:** Young stems red-brown to grayish; older bark is gray-brown and flaky with multi-colored mottles.

**SELECTED CULTIVARS:** ‘Drake’ - Dark green foliage on spreading plant that grows more upright than the species. Rounded crown. ‘Emerald Isle’ - Tree has dense, rounded and spreading form and deep, black-green foliage. Selected by Dir and Richards at the University of Georgia. ‘Sempervirens’ - Evergreen Elm. The tree has broadly-arching branches and a rounded crown. Semi-evergreen to evergreen. Zones 7-10. ‘True Green’ - The truest evergreen of the species. Great for California and Florida. Zones 7-10.

**RELATED SPECIES:** *U. pumila* - Siberian Elm. This is a rugged tree that will grow anywhere, but is usually short-lived. Branches are very brittle.

**LANDSCAPE NOTES:** Chinese Elm is probably the best of the Elms for residential and small commercial properties. It has all the qualities desirable in Elms, while resisting most of the major afflictions of the genus. Outstanding tree.

# *Zelkova serrata*

**Zelkova**

'Green Vase' ▶

**ZONES:**
4, 5, 6, 7, 8

**HEIGHT:**
45' to 70'

**WIDTH:**
45' to 50'

**FRUIT:**
Tiny drupe; NOT NOTICE-ABLE.

**TEXTURE:**
Medium

**GROWTH RATE:**
Rapid

**HABIT:**
Rounded crown with variable spread; usually vase-shaped.

**FAMILY:**
Ulmaceae

**LEAF COLOR:** Green in summer; yellow, orange, or red in fall.

**LEAF DESCRIPTION:** SIMPLE, 2″ to 3″ long and half as wide, ovate to elliptic shape with acuminate tip and coarsely serrated margins. ALTERNATE arrangement.

**FLOWER DESCRIPTION:** Monoecious; male clusters in axils, female clusters more terminal.

**EXPOSURE/CULTURE:** Sun. Prefers deep, moist, well-drained soils, but is adaptable to all but wet soils. pH-tolerant. Will thrive under windy conditions of the Midwest. Pruning is selective and structural.

**PEST PROBLEMS:** Susceptible to many of the same diseases of *Ulmus* (Elm). The tree is listed as being resistant to Dutch Elm Disease. Reports regarding elm leaf beetle are variable.

**BARK/STEMS:** Young stems are reddish-brown to brown; older bark is brown to reddish-brown with numerous large lenticels.

**SELECTED CULTIVARS:** 'Autumn Glow' - Purple foliage color in fall. 'Green Vase' - Much more vigorous than the species with bronze-red fall color. 'Village Green' - Fast-growing cultivar with red fall color. More resistant to Elm diseases and pests.

**LANDSCAPE NOTES:** Zelkova is a fine specimen tree for home gardens, and is a rapid-growing tree with nice foliage. It is tolerant of urban conditions and makes a nice street tree or parking lot tree. Other uses include parks and golf courses.

## Chapter 12

# GRASSES, PALMS, AND BAMBOO

The plants in this chapter are not grouped according to size. They are considered by this author to be "speciality plants," and range from ground cover types to tree size. Palms and bananas are greatly limited in range, and bamboo and grasses are somewhat limited.

The grasses are especially important in modern horticulture, and have increased dramatically in popularity in recent years. Part of the success of grasses is due to the emphasis on xeriscaping. Many are quite drought-tolerant, while displaying interesting habit, colorful foliage, or handsome spikes.

Landscape usages will not be discussed here due to the great variations. See Landscape Notes for individual plants.

## *Beaucarnea recurvata*                    **Ponytail Palm**

**ZONES:**
9b, 10

**HEIGHT:**
to 30′

**WIDTH:**
5′ to 10′

**FRUIT:**
Tiny, 3-valved capsule; NOT
ORNAMENTAL

**TEXTURE:**
Medium

**GROWTH RATE:**
Slow

**HABIT:**
Uright trunk, often curved;
trunk swollen at base; foliage
weeping.

**FAMILY:**
Agavaceae

**LEAF COLOR:** Green during all seasons.

**LEAF DESCRIPTION:** SIMPLE, 3′ to 6′ long and 3/4″ to 1″ wide, recurving, entire margins, parallel venation. WHORLED at stem apex.

**FLOWER DESCRIPTION:** Whitish, tiny, appearing in panicles on mature trees. NOT NOTICEABLE OR ORNAMENTAL. Tiny, 3-winged capsule; NOT ORNAMENTAL.

**EXPOSURE/CULTURE:** Sun or part shade. Prefers moist, organic, well-drained soil. Mulching will improve performance. Pruning is minimal to remove dead foliage.

**PEST PROBLEMS:** No serious pests.

**BARK/STEMS:** Light brown and mostly smooth; large and swollen at ground level.

**SELECTED CULTIVARS:** None

**LANDSCAPE NOTES:** Ponytail Palm is an accent or specimen plant for lawn areas, rock gardens, and foundations in the recommended zone(s). Further north, it can be used as a container plant for patios, decks, and entries, but it must be overwintered indoors, preferably in a humid greenhouse. The plant makes a nice specimen for interior plantscaping where sufficient light and humidity are maintained.

# *Butia capitata*

**ZONES:**
8b, 9, 10

**HEIGHT:**
10′ to 20′

**WIDTH:**
10′ to 15′

**FRUIT:**
1″ long yellowish-orange drupe; edible.

**TEXTURE:**
Coarse

**GROWTH RATE:**
Slow

**HABIT:**
Upright and arching; symmetrical.

**FAMILY:**
Palmae

**LEAF COLOR:** Gray-green to bluish silver-green.

**LEAF DESCRIPTION:** PINNATELY COMPOUND, 5′ to 10′ long, 25 to 50 leaflet pairs, leaflets 12″ to 15″ long and 1″ wide, angled upward and forward. Petiole with marginal spines. WHORLED arrangement.

**FLOWER DESCRIPTION:** Yellow to red, tiny, borne on a stalk rising among the leaves; NOT SHOWY.

**EXPOSURE/CULTURE:** Full sun. The plant prefers moist, sandy soils, but will grow in almost any soil. Thrives in arid or humid climates. Has been grown outdoors in Zone 7, with protection. Prune to remove dead branches.

**PEST PROBLEMS:** No serious pests.

**BARK/STEMS:** Brownish; scaly on older plants where lower branches have been removed.

**SELECTED CULTIVARS:** None

**LANDSCAPE NOTES:** Jelly Palm is one of the hardiest palms. It is a handsome plant that can be used as a specimen for lawns, foundations, rock gardens, and sunny borders. It is a low-maintenance, easy to grow plant that can be used indoors as a container plant, given sufficient light and humidity. It is sometimes sold as Australian Coco Palm, since it was once classified botanically as *Cocos australis*.

## *Carex morrowii* 'Aurea-variegata'

**Variegated Japanese Sedge Grass**

**ZONES:**
5, 6, 7, 8, 9

**HEIGHT:**
10" to 12"

**WIDTH:**
12" to 18"

**FRUIT:**
1/8" 3-angled achene; surrounded by a papery sheath (perigynium); NOT ORNAMENTAL.

**TEXTURE:**
Medium

**GROWTH RATE:**
Slow to moderate.

**HABIT:**
Mounded and arching; spreading by rhizomes.

**FAMILY:**
Cyperaceae

**LEAF COLOR:** Lustrous green leaf margin with creamy-white center stripe.

**LEAF DESCRIPTION:** SIMPLE, arising from basal clump, 12" to 18" long and 3/16" to 3/8" wide, linear shape with parallel venation, thick and stiff. WHORLED from basal clump.

**FLOWER DESCRIPTION:** Tiny, appearing in spikes and having long peduncles, 4 to 6 spikes per plant; NOT SHOWY.

**EXPOSURE/CULTURE:** Sun or shade. Prefers moist, organic soil, but is tolerant of a wide range of conditions, even dry, sandy or clayey soils. Cut back in early spring.

**PEST PROBLEMS:** No serious pests.

**RELATED SPECIES:** *C. buchananii* - Fox Red Curly Sedge. Foliage is reddish-bronze and erect with curled tips. Grows to 2'. *C. elata* 'Bowle's Golden' - Foliage is 18" tall and bright gold with a thin, green margin. *C. glauca* - Blue Sedge. Has silvery-blue foliage to only 6". Best in part shade and moist conditions.

**LANDSCAPE NOTES:** Variegated Japanese Sedge Grass makes a nice ground cover for massing, bordering, or in rock gardens. It is one of the hardiest ornamental grasses, and is much more drought-tolerant than credited. The plant makes a nice substitute for Lilyturf and Mondo Grass for difficult soils and conditions.

## *Chamaerops humilis*

### Mediterranean Fan Palm

**ZONES:**
8, 9, 10

**HEIGHT:**
5' to 10'

**WIDTH:**
5' to 8'

**FRUIT:**
Fleshy, with hard seed; NOT COMMON.

**TEXTURE:**
Coarse

**GROWTH RATE:**
Slow

**HABIT:**
Mounded to round; single or multi-stemmed.

**FAMILY:**
Palmae

**LEAF COLOR:** Medium to dark green (sometimes glaucous-blue); whitish flecks beneath.

**LEAF DESCRIPTION:** PALMATELY COMPOUND, 2' to 3' wide, up to 30 or more leaflets, petioles to 3' or longer with sharp spines pointing toward blade. SPIRALLY arranged around stem.

**FLOWER DESCRIPTION:** Dioecious or polygamodioecious, appearing among leaves; NOT ABUNDANT AND NOT SHOWY.

**EXPOSURE/CULTURE:** Sun or part shade. The plant prefers moist, sandy loam, but is adaptable to a wide range of soil types. Grows under arid or humid conditions. Prune to remove dead leaves.

**PEST PROBLEMS:** No serious pests.

**BARK/STEMS:** Brownish; scaly and having coarse, brown, matted hairs.

**SELECTED CULTIVARS:** None

**LANDSCAPE NOTES:** Mediterranean Fan Palm makes a nice specimen plant for a tropical effect in foundations, lawns, and borders. It is often used in northern zones as a potted or container plant and moved indoors in winter. Makes a nice plant for interior plantscaping where sufficient light is provided.

## *Cortaderia selloana*

**Pampas Grass**

**ZONES:**
7, 8, 9, 10

**HEIGHT:**
8′ to 10′

**WIDTH:**
6′ to 8′

**FRUIT:**
Tiny seed, enclosed in a papery husk; NOT NOTICE-ABLE AND NOT ORNAMEN-TAL.

**TEXTURE:**
Fine to medium.

**GROWTH RATE:**
Moderate to rapid.

**HABIT:**
Rounded and weeping.

**FAMILY:**
Gramineae

**LEAF COLOR:** Gray-green

**LEAF DESCRIPTION:** SIMPLE, 5′ to 8′ long and 1/2″ to 3/4″ wide, elongated linear shape with sharply serrated margins toward the base. WHORLED from basal clump.

**FLOWER DESCRIPTION:** Silver-gray and silk-like, 12″ to 18″ long and 4″ to 6″ wide (plumes), rising above the foliage. Flowers August to November; not fragrant, but VERY SHOWY.

**EXPOSURE/CULTURE:** Sun. Prefers moist, well-drained soil, but is adaptable to all but wet soils. Performs poorly in shade. Shear to within 12″ to 18″ of ground level in very early spring. Easy to grow.

**PEST PROBLEMS:** No serious pests.

**SELECTED CULTIVARS:** 'Pumila' - A dwarf form to 3 feet. 'Rosea' - Similar to the species but having pink flowers. 'Sun Stripe' - Dwarf form to 4′. Each leaf blade having yellow stripes. Patented by Monrovia Nurseries.

**LANDSCAPE NOTES:** Pampas Grass forms a graceful, arching mound that is very noticeable in the landscape, especially in late summer when the plumes begin to show. It is a nice specimen plant for garden borders, rock gardens, and screens. This plant will thrive under harsh conditions, and is a great choice for xeriscaping.

## *Cycas revoluta*

**Sago Palm**

**ZONES:**
9, 10

**HEIGHT:**
6′ to 10′

**WIDTH:**
6′ to 10′

**FRUIT:**
1 1/2″ flattened "naked seed"; red; VERY RARE.

**TEXTURE:**
Coarse

**GROWTH RATE:**
Slow

**HABIT:**
Rounded in outline and open, having arching branches; short trunk.

**FAMILY:**
Cycadaceae

**LEAF COLOR:** Dark green.

**LEAF DESCRIPTION:** PINNATELY COMPOUND, leaflets numerous, 3″ to 6″ long with pointed tips and revolute margins (rolled under), leaflets pectinate, curving slightly toward apex. Petioles WHORLED around upper stem.

**FLOWER DESCRIPTION:** Dioecious; male and female plants producing cone-like inflorescences, female larger; NOT SHOWY AND RARE.

**EXPOSURE/CULTURE:** Part shade. The plant prefers moist, well-drained soil. pH-adaptable. Should be mulched to maintain moisture level. Prune to remove any dead or undesirable leaf branches.

**PEST PROBLEMS:** No serious pests.

**BARK/STEMS:** Brown and very stout.

**SELECTED CULTIVARS:** None

**LANDSCAPE NOTES:** Sago Palm is an excellent foliage plant that is a true specimen. It looks great in the foundation planting as well as for accent in the garden border. The plant can be used in interior plantscaping where soil moisture is maintained and light is sufficient. It is often used further north as a container plant for decks, patios, and entries, then overwintered in a greenhouse or solarium. Note: Sago Palm is actually a tropical gymnosperm.

## *Erianthus ravennae*                    Plume Grass

**ZONES:**
5, 6, 7, 8, 9, 10

**HEIGHT:**
8′ to 10′

**WIDTH:**
4′ to 6′

**FRUIT:**
Tiny seed enclosed in a husk.

**TEXTURE:**
Medium

**GROWTH RATE:**
Moderate

**HABIT:**
Upright, open, and pendulous.

**FAMILY:**
Gramineae

**LEAF COLOR:** Medium green with white center stripe in summer; brownish in winter.

**LEAF DESCRIPTION:** Linear shape, 3′ or longer and 1/2″ to 1″ wide, parallel venation, entire margins. ALTERNATING along stems.

**FLOWER DESCRIPTION:** Silvery plumes (panicles), maturing to gray, sometimes orange or purple tinged in fall, rising above the foliage, plumes 12″ to 18″ long, appearing in late summer and persisting; VERY ORNAMENTAL.

**EXPOSURE/CULTURE:** Full sun. Prefers light, moist, well-drained soils. The plant will not tolerate heavy, wet soils. Shear to within 12″ to 18″ of ground in early spring. Easy to grow.

**PEST PROBLEMS:** No serious pests.

**SELECTED CULTIVARS:** None

**LANDSCAPE NOTES:** Plume Grass is a lovely, graceful accent plant that is hardier than Pampas Grass by two zones. It can be used in foundation plantings, garden borders, rock gardens, and accent beds. It is often grown in mass as screening material. It is not as showy as Pampas Grass, but serves as a great substitute in the northern zones. Great for xeriscaping.

# *Festuca ovina var. glauca*

**Blue Fescue**

**ZONES:**
4, 5, 6, 7, 8, 9

**HEIGHT:**
8″ to 12″

**WIDTH:**
12″ to 18″

**FRUIT:**
4″ light brown seed heads, rising on 12″+ stalks above the foliage; ATTRACTIVE.

**TEXTURE:**
Fine

**GROWTH RATE:**
Rapid

**HABIT:**
Mounded and pendulous clumps; NOT RHIZOMATOUS.

**FAMILY:**
Gramineae

**LEAF COLOR:** Silvery blue-gray.

**LEAF DESCRIPTION:** Linear, 8″ to 12″ long, being narrow with pointed apex and serrulate margins. WHORLED from basal clump.

**FLOWER DESCRIPTION:** Tiny, borne on spike-like panicles throughout the season; NOT ORNAMENTAL.

**EXPOSURE/CULTURE:** Sun or part shade. Will grow on almost any well-drained soil. Does best at a pH of 6.0 to 7.0. Responds well to annual fertilization. Regular pruning will encourage new growth for best color. Shearing of seed heads is optional; some people find them attractive, while others do not.

**PEST PROBLEMS:** No serious pests.

**SELECTED CULTIVARS:** None of merit.

**LANDSCAPE NOTES:** Blue Fescue is an eye-catching ornamental grass that can be used as an edging plant for planting beds or as a massed plant for a ground cover effect. In addition, it can be utilized effectively in perennial flower gardens.

## *Miscanthus sinensis 'Gracillimus'*     **Maiden Grass**

**ZONES:**
4, 5, 6, 7, 8, 9

**HEIGHT:**
4′ to 6′

**WIDTH:**
3′ to 5′

**FRUIT:**
Tiny seed enclosed in a husk;
NOT ORNAMENTAL.

**TEXTURE:**
Medium

**GROWTH RATE:**
Moderate to rapid.

**HABIT:**
Rounded, upright, and arching.

**FAMILY:**
Gramineae

**LEAF COLOR:** Silver-green

**LEAF DESCRIPTION:** Linear, 4′ to 6′ long and to 1/4″ wide with sharply serrated margins and slender acuminate tip. Parallel venation. WHORLED from basal clump.

**FLOWER DESCRIPTION:** Silver-white, 6″ racemes, fan-shaped and plume-like, rising above the foliage in late summer and continuing into late fall. Not as large or showy as *Cortaderia selloana.*

**EXPOSURE/CULTURE:** Sun. Prefers moist, well-drained soil, but is adaptable to all but wet soils. Performs poorly in shade. Shear to 1′ in early spring.

**PEST PROBLEMS:** No serious pests.

**RELATED CULTIVARS:** 'Yakushima' - Dwarf Maiden Grass. This is a free-flowering form, 3′ to 4′ in height. Hardy to Zone 6. (See following pages for others.)

**LANDSCAPE NOTES:** Maiden Grass is a great plant for Japanese gardens, and blends well with water features. It makes a nice plant for naturalizing in borders, and is attractive in mass. The plant is not as showy as *Cortaderia selloana,* but is much more hardy. This is a very versatile plant.

## *Miscanthus sinensis* 'Variegatus'  Variegated Japanese Silver Grass

**ZONES:**
4, 5, 6, 7, 8, 9

**HEIGHT:**
4' to 6'

**WIDTH:**
3' to 5'

**FRUIT:**
Tiny seed enclosed in a husk; NOT ORNAMENTAL.

**TEXTURE:**
Medium

**GROWTH RATE:**
Moderate to rapid.

**HABIT:**
Rounded, upright, and arching.

**FAMILY:**
Gramineae

**LEAF COLOR:** Green with creamy-white stripes.

**LEAF DESCRIPTION:** Linear, 4' to 6' long and 1/2" wide (wider than 'Gracillimus'), sharply serrated margins and acuminate tip, parallel venation. WHORLED from clumps.

**FLOWER DESCRIPTION:** Silver-white, 6" racemes, fan-shaped and plume-like, rising above the foliage. Flowers in later summer through late fall.

**EXPOSURE/CULTURE:** Sun. Prefers moist, well-drained soil, but is adaptable to all but wet soils. Performs poorly in shade. Shear to 1' in early spring.

**PEST PROBLEMS:** No serious pests.

**SELECTED CULTIVARS:** None. This is a cultivar.

**LANDSCAPE NOTES:** Variegated Japanese Silver Grass is a true specimen plant with its variegated foliage and nice plumes. It has similar uses as 'Gracillimus', but is more noticeable; therefore, greater care must be exercised in site selection.

## *Miscanthus sinensis* 'Zebrinus' — Zebra Grass

**ZONES:**
4, 5, 6, 7, 8, 9

**HEIGHT:**
4' to 6'

**WIDTH:**
3' to 5'

**FRUIT:**
Tiny seed enclosed in a husk; NOT ORNAMENTAL.

**TEXTURE:**
Medium

**GROWTH RATE:**
Moderate to rapid.

**HABIT:**
Rounded, upright, and arching.

**FAMILY:**
Gramineae

**LEAF COLOR:** Green with horizontal bands of yellow stripes.

**LEAF DESCRIPTION:** Linear, 4' to 8' long and 1/4" to 1/2" wide with sharply serrated margins and slender acuminate tips. Parallel venation. WHORLED from basal clump.

**FLOWER DESCRIPTION:** Silver-white, 6" racemes, fan-shaped and plume-like, rising above the foliage in late fall and continuing into late fall. Not as large or showy as *Cortaderia selloana*.

**EXPOSURE/CULTURE:** Sun or very light shade. Prefers moist, well-drained soil, but is adaptable to all but wet soils. Performs poorly in shade. Shear to 1' of ground level in very early spring.

**PEST PROBLEMS:** No serious pests.

**SELECTED CULTIVARS:** None. This is a cultivar.

**LANDSCAPE NOTES:** Zebra Grass is a unique variegated grass because the yellow variegation runs in horizontal bands. This unusual plant should be treated as a specimen in borders of the garden, rock gardens, berms, and foundation plantings. It should be used in moderation, but certainly is worthy of consideration. More hardy than *Cortaderia selloana*.

## *Musa acuminata*
**Banana**

**ZONES:**
10

**HEIGHT:**
20'+

**WIDTH:**
10'+

**FRUIT:**
5" to 6" bananas, flecked black; edible.

**TEXTURE:**
Very coarse.

**GROWTH RATE:**
Rapid

**HABIT:**
Upright and open; multiplying by rhizomes.

**FAMILY:**
Musaceae

**LEAF COLOR:** Bright green; green to purplish beneath.

**LEAF DESCRIPTION:** SIMPLE, 6' to 8' long and 1' to 2' wide, pinnately veined, long oblong shape with undulating, smooth margins, often frayed or split along secondary veins, drooping on each side of midrib. Spirally arranged.

**FLOWER DESCRIPTION:** Inflorescence yellow, enclosed by purple petals (bracts), rising on long peduncles from axils of upper foliage; horizontal, but becoming pendulous; male flowers apical, female, basal, opening slowly from apex to base.

**EXPOSURE/CULTURE:** Sun. The plant prefers moist, well-drained, highly organic soil. Protect from wind. Fruit matures 14 weeks after flowers appear. Pseudostem dies after fruiting, so fruiting stems should be cut to ground to encourage rapid development of new pseudostems.

**PEST PROBLEMS:** Spider mites, scale.

**SELECTED CULTIVARS:** 'Dwarf Cavendish' - Dwarf form to about 8' in height and having large flower clusters. 'Enano Gigante' - Dwarf Giant Edible Banana. Dwarf form to 8' with large, dark green leaves, mottled red.

**RELATED GENUS:** *Ensete* - This genus contains 7 species of tropical, palm-like bananas, used primarily as ornamentals, but eaten in some parts of the world. Fruit pulp is minimal with large seeds to 1" long.

**LANDSCAPE NOTES:** Banana is a fruit tree that has ornamental value due to coarse, bold foliage. The coarse foliage contrasts well and serves as a specimen plant or focal point. In the Southeast, the plant is often grown as a herbaceous perennial, which dies to ground level, but recovers in spring. It is often used outdoors as a container plant for a tropical effect around pools, decks, and patios, then overwintered indoors in a cool (not cold) location.

## *Pennisetum alopecuroides* 'Hameln'  **Dwarf Fountain Grass**

**ZONES:**
5, 6, 7, 8, 9, 10

**HEIGHT:**
1 1/2' to 3'

**WIDTH:**
3' to 5'

**FRUIT:**
Brown seeds (palea enclosed by lemma).

**TEXTURE:**
Medium

**GROWTH RATE:**
Moderate to rapid.

**HABIT:**
Compact and spreading; arched branches and blooms.

**FAMILY:**
Gramineae

**LEAF COLOR:** Medium to dark green in summer; brown in winter.

**LEAF DESCRIPTION:** SIMPLE, arising from basal clumps, 1 1/2' to 2 1/2' long and 1/4" to 3/4" wide, parallel venation, linear shape with finely serrated margins. WHORLED from dense clump.

**FLOWER DESCRIPTION:** Buff-colored spike-like blooms (panicles) formed from numerous spikelets, 3" to 6" long on stalks rising above the foliage. Flowers in late summer through fall. Persisting.

**EXPOSURE/CULTURE:** Full sun to light shade. The plant prefers well-drained, moist soils of light texture. Will not tolerate wet soils, but will thrive in dry or sandy conditions. Trim to 1' in early spring to remove dead growth and encourage abundant new growth.

**PEST PROBLEMS:** No serious pests.

**SELECTED CULTIVARS:** None. This is a cultivar of *P. alopecuroides,* a larger form, growing to 4' tall with a much broader spread.

**LANDSCAPE NOTES:** Dwarf Fountain Grass is an excellent plant for massing or as a specimen plant in sunny borders, accent beds, and rock gardens. The plants are considered low-maintenance and easy to grow. Larger clumps may be divided into several new plants. This is one of the most popular ornamental grasses and is especially great for xeriscaping.

## *Pennisetum setaceum 'Rubrum'*　　Purple Fountain Grass

**ZONES:**
7, 8, 9, 10

**HEIGHT:**
3 1/2' to 4'

**WIDTH:**
4' to 5'

**FRUIT:**
Brown seeds; NOT ORNA-
MENTAL.

**TEXTURE:**
Medium

**GROWTH RATE:**
Moderate to rapid.

**HABIT:**
Compact and spreading;
arched branches and blooms.

**FAMILY:**
Gramineae

**LEAF COLOR:** Central leaves green; outer leaves reddish-brown.

**LEAF DESCRIPTION:** SIMPLE, arising from basal clump, 4' to 5' long and 1/2" wide, parallel venation, linear shape with finely serrated margins. WHORLED from clumps.

**FLOWER DESCRIPTION:** Rose-red spike-like blooms (panicles), 12" to 15" long on stalks rising above the foliage, pendulous. Flowers in late summer through fall. Persisting.

**EXPOSURE/CULTURE:** Full sun. The plant prefers well-drained, moist soils of light texture, but is adaptable to all but wet soils. Does well in sunny, dry locations. Prune to 1' in early spring.

**PEST PROBLEMS:** No serious pests.

**SELECTED CULTIVARS:** None. This is a cultivar.

**LANDSCAPE NOTES:** Purple Fountain Grass is similar to *P. alopecuroides*, except for color of foliage and inflorescence. In addition, it is not as cold-hardy. Careful selection of site is important due to color. The plant is drought-tolerant and makes a good selection for xeriscaping. This is a beautiful specimen plant for borders, accent beds, rock gardens, and foundations.

## *Phalaris arundinacea var. picta*  **Ribbon Grass**

▶

Courtesy of
Monrovia Nursery Co.

**ZONES:**
5, 6, 7, 8, 9

**HEIGHT:**
1 1/2′ to 2 1/2′

**WIDTH:**
Indeterminate

**FRUIT:**
Tiny seed enclosed in a husk.

**TEXTURE:**
Medium

**GROWTH RATE:**
Rapid!

**HABIT:**
Upright, irregular, and dense;
spreads by rhizomes.

**FAMILY:**
Gramineae

**LEAF COLOR:** Green and white (alternating stripes).

**LEAF DESCRIPTION:** Linear shape, 8″ to 12″ long and 1/2″ to 3/4″ wide, parallel venation, entire margins. ALTERNATING along stems.

**FLOWER DESCRIPTION:** White to pinkish, tiny, appearing in panicles to 7″ long. Flowers in early summer; NOT ORNAMENTAL.

**EXPOSURE/CULTURE:** Sun or part shade. Grows best in moist, organic soils. The plant is very adaptable, growing on dry sites or wet, boggy areas. Thin (divide) in early spring to rejuvenate. Control spread with a 12″ deep steel or concrete edging, or by planting in containers.

**PEST PROBLEMS:** No serious pests.

**SELECTED CULTIVARS:** None

**LANDSCAPE NOTES:** Ribbon Grass is an attractive variation of *P. arundinacea*, the green form. It is a nice ground cover for larger areas of the garden, and it will thrive in areas too wet for other plantings. Makes a nice plant for dull areas. Containment is necessary, but worth the effort.

## *Phyllostachys aureosulcata*

**ZONES:**
5, 6, 7, 8, 9

**HEIGHT:**
to 30′

**WIDTH:**
Indeterminate

**FRUIT:**
Brown seed; VERY RARE.

**TEXTURE:**
Medium

**GROWTH RATE:**
Rapid, once established.

**HABIT:**
Upright and slender; forming dense groves by spreading rhizomes.

**FAMILY:**
Gramineae

**LEAF COLOR:** Soft green.

**LEAF DESCRIPTION:** 2″ to 6″ long, appearing on branchlets, each branchlet having 3 to 5 leaves, lanceolate shape with entire margins, parallel venation.

**FLOWER DESCRIPTION:** Occuring on spikelets ONLY after many years, often to over 100 years. (Grove dies after flowering, but recovers in 4 to 5 years.)

**EXPOSURE/CULTURE:** Sun to part shade. The plant prefers very moist, organic soil, but will grow in almost any soil where moisture is adequate. Dig or cut unwanted culms. Requires moderate maintenance to control, once established. Not for xeriscaping.

**PEST PROBLEMS:** None

**STEMS:** To 1 1/2″ thick, dull green and scabrous, having alternating yellow grooves on internodes. Branchlets develop at internodes (2 or 3).

**SELECTED CULTIVARS:** None

**RELATED VARIETIES:** *P. aurea* - Golden Bamboo. This species grows to 20′ and has brilliant yellow, lustrous stems. *P. nigra* - Black Bamboo. (See next page.)

**LANDSCAPE NOTES:** Bamboo is one of the best screening materials in the world of plants. In addition, it lends a tropical flavor to the landscape, being native to tropical regions of the world. Yellow Groove Bamboo has wide appeal, because it is one of the hardiest. The big problem with Bamboo is containment of the vigorous rhizomes. Steel edgings or concrete footings 12″ to 18″ deep have proven successful in most cases. Be absolutely sure you want it before planting.

## *Phyllostachys nigra*

**Black Bamboo**

**ZONES:**
7, 8, 9

**HEIGHT:**
to 25′+

**WIDTH:**
Indeterminate

**FRUIT:**
Brown seed; RARE.

**TEXTURE:**
Medium

**GROWTH RATE:**
Rapid, once established.

**HABIT:**
Upright and open; forming dense groves; rhizomatous.

**FAMILY:**
Gramineae

**LEAF COLOR:** Medium green.

**LEAF DESCRIPTION:** 3 1/2″ to 5″ long and 1/2″ wide, appearing on branchlets, each branchlet containing numerous leaves, leaves lanceolate shape with sparsely denticulate margins, glaucous beneath, parallel venation.

**FLOWER DESCRIPTION:** Tiny, appearing on spikelets after many years.

**EXPOSURE/CULTURE:** Sun to part shade. The plant prefers very moist, organic soils, but will grow in almost any soil where moisture is adequate. Dig or cut unwanted culms. Requires moderate maintenance to control, once established.

**PEST PROBLEMS:** None

**STEMS:** Green when young, maturing to brownish black or purple-black; 1 1/4″ in diameter.

**SELECTED CULTIVARS:** 'Henon' - Much larger (50′) than the species with stems to 3″ in diameter. Stems green, maturing to yellowish.

**RELATED GENUS:** *Arundinaria pygmaea* - Dwarf Bamboo. This is a rapid-growing ground cover type to about 1′. Spreads rapidly by rhizomes to a dense mass.

**LANDSCAPE NOTES:** Black Bamboo is another of the many species used for screening or special effects. Long cultivated in Japan, it is used for many purposes, and is often seen around temples and other structures. It is the Bamboo of preference for establishing Japanese gardens and is widely used for that purpose in the U.S.

# *Sabal minor*

**Dwarf Palmetto Palm**

**ZONES:**
8, 9, 10

**HEIGHT:**
3′ to 5′

**WIDTH:**
3′ to 5′

**FRUIT:**
1/2″ black, one-seeded fruits; berry-like.

**TEXTURE:**
Coarse

**GROWTH RATE:**
Slow to moderate.

**HABIT:**
Rounded in outline; very short trunk.

**FAMILY:**
Palmae

**LEAF COLOR:** Bluish-green

**LEAF DESCRIPTION:** COSTAPALMATELY COMPOUND (petiole continuing with the leaflets, giving appearance of a midrib), 2′ to 3′ wide, 30 to 40 leaflets, margins often having thread-like fibers. WHORLED around base.

**FLOWER DESCRIPTION:** Inflorescence whitish, 1/8″ long, appearing in clusters and usually rising above the foliage; NOT SHOWY.

**EXPOSURE/CULTURE:** Sun. The plant prefers light, moist soils, but is adaptable to moist soils and relatively dry conditions. Pruning is minimal to remove dead leaves.

**PEST PROBLEMS:** None

**SELECTED CULTIVARS:** None

**LANDSCAPE NOTES:** Dwarf Palmetto Palm is a nice dwarf palm for coarse foliage texture in the landscape. It is a nice plant to feature as a single specimen, or as a plant for massing in borders. Foliage color is nice and provides additional contrast. This is a much nicer landscape plant than credited by some authors.

# *Sabal palmetto*

**Palmetto Palm**

**ZONES:**
8, 9, 10

**HEIGHT:**
20′ to 25′

**WIDTH:**
12′ to 15′

**FRUIT:**
1/2″ black, one-seeded fruits; berry-like.

**TEXTURE:**
Coarse

**GROWTH RATE:**
Moderate

**HABIT:**
Single trunk; rounded, open crown.

**FAMILY:**
Palmae

**LEAF COLOR:** Medium green.

**LEAF DESCRIPTION:** COSTAPALMATELY COMPOUND, 3′ to 4′ wide, having thread-like fibers, petiole and leaf to 6′ long, fan-like, having 30 to 40 leaflets per leaf. WHORLED around crown of plant.

**FLOWER DESCRIPTION:** Whitish, 3/16″, appearing in 2′ clusters in May through June, appearing among the leaves.

**EXPOSURE/CULTURE:** Sun or part shade. The plant prefers light, moist soils, but is somewhat adaptable. Prune to remove dead leaves.

**PEST PROBLEMS:** None

**BARK/STEMS:** Brownish and smooth to slightly rough. Sheaths of previous leaves forming interesting basketweave pattern.

**SELECTED CULTIVARS:** None

**LANDSCAPE NOTES:** Palmetto Palm is an excellent tree for accent or street use. The trunk is just as interesting as the fan-shaped foliage. It is native to coastal areas and should be used in beach plantings. One of the most beautiful and commonly used palms in the Southeast.

## *Trachycarpus fortunei* — Windmill Palm

**ZONES:**
8, 9, 10

**HEIGHT:**
15′ to 20′

**WIDTH:**
8′ to 12′

**FRUIT:**
1/2″ bluish seed, in panicles; NOT ORNAMENTAL.

**TEXTURE:**
Coarse

**GROWTH RATE:**
Moderate to slow.

**HABIT:**
Upright and open; single trunk.

**FAMILY:**
Palmae

**LEAF COLOR:** Rich green.

**LEAF DESCRIPTION:** PALMATELY COMPOUND, 2 1/2′ to 3′ wide, fan-shaped, leaflets lanceolate shape with flexible tips, petioles toothed near base. WHORLED around stem.

**FLOWER DESCRIPTION:** Yellow, tiny, in 1′ to 2′ panicles, appearing in May through June. Showy.

**EXPOSURE/CULTURE:** Sun or light shade. Prefers moist, organic, well-drained soil. Protect from wind. Prune to remove dead leaves.

**PEST PROBLEMS:** No serious pests.

**BARK/STEMS:** Brownish; covered with black, hairy fibers.

**SELECTED CULTIVARS:** None

**LANDSCAPE NOTES:** Windmill Palm is an attractive plant to feature in the landscape. It is loose and airy and does not dominate the landscape. It can be grown as a specimen in the landscape, garden border, rock garden, or foundation plantings for larger structures. A very nice plant.

# BIBLIOGRAPHY

Bailey, Liberty Hyde. 1949. *Manual of Cultivated Plants.* The Macmillan Co. New York.

Bailey Hortorium of Cornell University. 1976. *Hortus Third.* The Macmillan Co. New York.

Batson, Wade T. 1984. *Landscape Plants for the Southeast.* University of South Carolina Press. Columbia, SC.

Dirr, Michael A. 1990. *Manual of Woody Landscape Plants.* Stipes Publishing Company. Champaign, Illinois.

Glimn-Lacy, Janice, and Peter B. Kaufman. 1984. *Botany Illustrated.* Van Nostrand Reinhold Co., Inc. New York.

Grimm, William Carey. 1962. *The Book of Trees.* The Stackpole Company. Harrisburg, Pennsylvania.

Halfacre, R. Gordon, and Anne R. Shawcroft. 1989. *Landscape Plants of the Southeast.* Sparks Press. Raleigh, NC.

Hannebaum, Leroy. 1981. *Landscape Design.* Reston Publishing Company. Reston, Virginia.

Hume, H. Harold. 1953. *Hollies.* The Macmillan Company. New York.

Keith, Rebecca McIntosh, and F. A. Giles. 1980. *Dwarf Shrubs for the Midwest.* 1980. College of Agriculture Special Publication 60. University of Illinois at Urbana-Champaign.

Krussmann, Gerd. 1985. *Manual of Cultivated Conifers.* Timber Press. Portland, Oregon.

Sargent, Charles Sprague. 1965. *Manual of the Trees of North America.* Volumes I and II. Dover Publications, Inc. New York.

Symonds, George W. D. 1958. *The Tree Identification Book.* William Morrow Co., Inc. New York.

Thode, Frederick W. 1974. *Woody Plant Material for Landscape Use.* Clemson University. Clemson, SC.

Voigt, T. B., Betty R. Hamilton, and F. A. Giles. 1983. *Ground Covers for the Midwest.* University of Illinois Printing Division. Champaign, Illinois.

Walker, Mary C., and F. A. Giles. 1985. *Flowering Trees for the Midwest.* University of Illinois Printing Division. Champaign, Illinois.

Whitcomb, Carl E. 1985. *Know It and Grow It II.* Lacebark Publications. Stillwater, Oklahoma.

Wyman, Donald. 1965. *Trees for American Gardens.* The Macmillan Company. New York.

Wyman, Donald. 1969. *Shrubs and Vines for American Gardens.* The Macmillan Company. New York.

Wyman, Donald. 1971. *Wyman's Gardening Encyclopedia.* The Macmillan Company. New York.

# APPENDIX A

## TREES WORTH CONSIDERING FOR STREET USE OR URBAN CONDITIONS

*Acer buergeranum*
*Acer campestre*
*Acer platanoides*
*Acer rubrum*
*Acer saccharum*
*Acer barbatum*
*Aesculus* x *carnea*
*Betula nigra*
*Betula platyphylla* var. *japonica*
   'Whitespire'
*Carpinus betulus*
*Carpinus caroliniana*
*Cercidiphyllum japonicum*
*Cercis canadensis*
*Cladrastis kentuckea*
*Crataegus* spp.
*Eucommia ulmoides*
*Fraxinus americana*
*Fraxinus pennsylvanica*
*Ginkgo biloba*
*Gleditsia triacanthos* var. *inermis*
*Koelreuteria bipinnata*
*Koelreuteria paniculata*
*Lagerstroemia indica*
*Liquidambar styraciflua*

*Malus* spp.
*Metasequoia glyptostroboides*
*Nyssa sylvatica*
*Pistacia chinensis*
*Platanus occidentalis*
*Platanus* x *acerifolia*
*Pyrus calleryana*
*Quercus acutissima*
*Quercus laurifolia*
*Quercus myrsinifolia*
*Quercus nigra*
*Quercus palustris*
*Quercus phellos*
*Quercus shumardii*
*Quercus rubra*
*Quercus virginiana*
*Sophora japonica*
*Syringa reticulata*
*Taxodium distichum*
*Tilia cordata*
*Tilia tomentosa*
*Ulmus parvifolia*
*Ulmus* x 'Pioneer'
*Zelkova serrata*

# APPENDIX B

## PLANTS WORTH CONSIDERING FOR XERISCAPES

The word xeriscape (pronounced zee-ruh'-scape) evolved in 1981 in Colorado. Severe drought had greatly limited water usage, so the idea of xeriscaping as a new approach to total design emerged.

The goal of xeriscaping is to reduce water requirement in the landscape by 50% or more, while maintaining usefulness, quality, and attractiveness. This can be achieved through appropriate design, especially in creating shaded areas; use of mulches and more efficient irrigation (if any); reduced lawn areas; and through selection of plants with reduced water needs.

## GROUND COVERS

*Arctostaphylos uva-ursi*
*Euonymus fortunei* var. *coloratus*
*Hedera canariensis*
*Hedera colchica*
*Hypericum calycinum*
*Juniperus chinensis* cvs.
*Juniperus conferta*
*Juniperus horizontalis*
*Juniperus procumbens*
*Juniperus squamata*
*Liriope muscari*
*Ophiopogon japonicus*
*Phlox subulata*
*Rosa pimpinellifolia* 'Petite Pink'
*Santolina chamaecyparissus*
*Santolina virens*

## VINES

*Akebia quinata*
*Campsis grandiflora*
*Gelsemium sempervirens*
*Lonicera* x *hecktrottii*
*Lonicera sempervirens*
*Parthenocissus quinquefolia*
*Parthenocissus tricuspidata*
*Rosa banksiae*
*Trachelospermum asiaticum*
*Trachelospermum jasminoides*
*Wisteria floribunda*
*Wisteria sinensis*

## SHRUBS

*Abelia grandiflora*
*Berberis thunbergii*
*Buddleia davidii*
*Calycanthus floridus*
*Caragana arborescens*
*Cercis chinensis*
*Chaenomeles japonica*
*Chaenomeles speciosa*
*Cotinus coggygria*
*Elaeagnus pungens*
*Euonymus alatus*
*Forsythia intermedia*
*Hibiscus syriacus*
*Ilex cornuta*
*Ilex latifolia*
*Ilex vomitoria*
*Ilex* x *attenuata*
*Ilex* x 'Emily Brunner'
*Ilex* x 'Nellie R. Stevens'
*Jasminum floridum*
*Jasminum nudiflorum*
*Juniperus chinensis*
*Juniperus davurica*
*Juniperus sabina*
*Juniperus scopulorum* cvs.
*Juniperus virginiana* cvs.
*Kerria japonica*
*Kolkwitzia amabilis*
*Lagerstroemia indica* cvs.
*Ligustrum japonicum*
*Ligustrum lucidum*
*Ligustrum sinense*
*Lonicera fragrantissima*
*Lonicera tatarica*
*Lonicera xylosteoides*
*Myrica cerifera*
*Nandina domestica*
*Nerium oleander*
*Osmanthus* x *fortunei*
*Photinia* x *fraseri*
*Photinia* x *glabra*
*Photinia serrulata*
*Pinus mugo*
*Spiraea thungbergii*

*Spiraea* x *bumalda*
*Spiraea* x *vanhouttei*
*Syringa vulgaris*
*Thuja occidentalis*
*Thuja orientalis*
*Viburnum lantana*
*Viburnum opulus*
*Viburnum plicatum* var. *tomentosum*
*Vitex agnus-castus*
*Yucca aloifolia*
*Yucca filamentosa*
*Yucca flaccida*
*Yucca gloriosa*

## TREES

*Abies* spp.
*Acer barbatum*
*Acer buergerianum*
*Acer miyabei*
*Acer negundo*
*Catalpa bignonioides*
*Cedrus atlantica*
*Cedrus deodara*
*Chilopsis linearis*
*Crataegus* spp.
X *Cupressocyparis leylandii*
*Cupressus arizonica*
*Eucommia ulmoides*
*Fraxinus americana*
*Fraxinus pennsylvanica*
*Ginkgo biloba*
*Gleditsia triacanthos* var. *inermis*
*Juniperus virginiana*
*Koelreuteria bipinnata*
*Koelreuteria paniculata*
*Lagerstroemia indica*
*Liriodendron tulipifera*
*Liquidambar styraciflua*
*Magnolia liliiflora*
*Magnolia stellata*
*Magnolia* x *soulangiana*
*Myrica cerifera*

*Oxydendron arboreum*
*Paulownia tomentosa*
*Picea* spp.
*Pinus bungeana*
*Pinus heldreichii* var. *leucodermis*
*Pinus nigra*
*Pinus rigida*
*Pinus sylvestris*
*Pinus taeda*
*Pinus thunbergiana*
*Pinus virginiana*
*Platanus* x *acerifolia*
*Platanus occidentalis*
*Pseudotsuga menziesii*
*Pyrus calleryana*
*Quercus acutissima*
*Quercus falcata*
*Quercus macrocarpa*
*Quercus myrsinifolia*
*Quercus shumardii*
*Robinia pseudoacacia*
*Sophora japonica*
*Syringa reticulata*
*Taxodium distichum*
*Ulmus alata*
*Ulmus americana* 'Pioneer'
*Ulmus parvifolia*
*Zelkova serrata*

## GRASSES AND PALMS

*Butia capitata*
*Carex morrowii* 'Aurea-variegata'
*Chamaerops humilis*
*Cortaderia selloana*
*Miscanthus sinensis* and cvs.
*Phalaris arundinacea* var. *picta*
*Pennisetum alopecuroides*
*Pennisetum setaceum*
*Sabal minor*
*Sabal palmetto*
*Trachycarpus fortunei*

# GLOSSARY

**A**   **Accent plant** - A showy plant, having noticeable foliage, flowers, fruit, bark, or shape; used to draw attention to itself or to an area.

**Achene** - A type of fruit that is one-seeded, dry, indehiscent, and usually small.

**Acorn** - The fruit of Oak trees (*Quercus*).

**Acuminate** - Referring to the apex; the tip being triangular to slightly concave and tapering to a point. (See Chapter 1.)

**Acute** - Referring to the apex, where the sides taper in a broad, convex manner to form a point. (See Chapter 1.)

**Adventitious** - Not ordinary; occurring in a location that is unusual. Example: aerial roots.

**Aggregate Fruit** - A fruit comprised of several ripened ovaries from one flower. Example: Blackberry. (See Chapter 1.)

**Alternate** - Referring to leaves or stems, appearing at different locations on the opposite side.

**Ament** - Same as catkin.

**Annual** - A plant that completes its life cycle in one season. It grows from a seed, matures, reproduces, and dies in a single season.

**Anther** - The pollen-bearing "head" of the male flower part (see stamen).

**Apetalous** - Without flower petals.

**Apex** - The terminal tip.

**Appressed** - Pressed closely or flatly, as with scale-like foliage.

**Aril** - A fleshy appendage that covers all or part of a seed.

**Ascending** - Curving or arising upward, to some degree, above the horizontal.

**Asexual** - Without sex; as in propagation without seed.

**Asymmetrical** - Not symmetrical; where one side is not equal to the other in size or form.

**Awl-shaped** - Slender and tapering to a rigid point.

**Axil** - Usually referring to the area where a petiole or peduncle joins a stem, forming an angle.

**Axillary** - Located in the axil, such as an axillary bud.

**B**   **Basal** - Near the base or area of support.

**Base** - The bottom or support; opposite of apex.

**Berry** - A fleshy or pulpy, indehiscent fruit from a single ovary and containing one or more seeds. Example: Grapes.

**Bi** - A prefix meaning two or twice.

**Biennial** - A plant that completes its life cycle in two seasons. The plant produces vegetative growth in the first year and reproductive growth in the second year, before dying. Example: Cabbage.

**Bipinnate** - Twice-pinnate or twice-divided; the main rachis being divided into two or more subdivisions that contain leaflets. Example: Compound leaf of Mimosa.

**Bisexual** - Having both sexes, stamens and pistils, in the same flower.

**Biternate** - A structure having two or more subdivisions of three.

**Blade** - The expanded portion of a leaf; usually flat, but may be needle-like, awl-like, or scale-like.

**Bloom** - 1. A flower. 2. A powdery, somewhat waxy coating of an appendage, usually gray, white, or bluish. Example: The bloom of a grape.

**Bract** - A modified leaf, usually occurring at the base of a single flower or cluster.

**C**

**Calyx** - Collective name for all the sepals of a flower; the outer set of modified leaves, usually green in color. (See Chapter 1.)

**Campanulate** - Being shaped like a bell.

**Capsule** - A dry, dehiscent fruit composed of two or more carpels from a compound pistil, splitting when dry to release the seed. (See Chapter 1.)

**Catkin** - A spike of flowers, usually pendulous, composed of scaly bracts. Example: Male flowers of *Betula*.

**Composite** - Compound; made of two or more distinct parts.

**Compound leaf** - A leaf composed of two or more leaflets attached to a rachis. (See Chapter 1.)

**Cone** - The fruit of conifers; having several scales that bear one or more seeds; each scale attached to a central axis.

**Conical** - Having a geometric cone shape (as with an upside-down ice cream cone).

**Coniferous** - Referring to a plant that is almost always of cone-bearing parentage. Example: Spruces.

**Cordate** - Heart-shaped. (See Chapter 1.)

**Corolla** - The inner whorl of a floral envelope; the parts may be separately attached at the base, or the corolla may be singular at the base, but splitting into lobes at the apex.

**Corymb** - A flat-topped to rounded inflorescence with pedicels attached at alternating points to the peduncle; outer flowers opening first. (See Chapter 1.)

**Crenate** - Having large rounded teeth on the margins. Example: *Ilex crenata*. (See Chapter 1.)

**Crown** - 1. The part of a tree containing foliage and branches. 2. The portion of stem at soil level where stems and roots join.

**Culm** - The stem of grasses and bamboo; most often referring to bamboo culms.

**Cultivar** - Literally, "cultivated variety." Cultivars are variations within a species that are usually propagated asexually.

**Cuneate** - Having a triangular base; coming to a point at the petiole. (See Chapter 1.)

**Cuspidate** - Having an elongated point at the apex; usually concave toward the apex. (See Chapter 1.)

**Cylindrical** - As with a geometric cylinder, being elongated with a rounded cross-sectional shape.

**Cyme** - A mostly flat-topped inflorescence; the central flowers opening first. (See Chapter 1.)

**D** **Deciduous** - Opposite of evergreen; losing all leaves or foliage during fall or early winter. Example: Sugar Maple.

**Defoliate** - To drop (lose) the leaves or foliage.

**Dehiscent** - An organ or appendage that splits along a definite seam; usually referring to fruits that split to release the seeds. Example: Pecan. (See Chapter 1.)

**Deltoid** - Forming an equilateral triangle; usually referring to leaves that are somewhat triangular. Example: *Populus deltoides.*

**Dentate** - Having saw-like teeth that point outward, instead of forward toward the apex; usually referring to leaf margins. (See Chapter 1.)

**Di** - Prefix meaning two.

**Dioecious** - A plant or species having unisexual flowers; staminate and pistillate flowers on separate plants.

**Divided** - Having separated divisions or lobes near the base.

**Dorsal** - Referring to the backside or outer surface of an organ.

**Double Flower** - A flower having more than the usual number of petals; often having several rows.

**Downy** - Having short, fine hairs; usually associated with the soft hairs of a stem or leaf.

**Drupe** - An indehiscent fruit having a fleshy pulp and a stony endocarp enclosing the seed; a stone fruit. Example: Peach (See Chapter 1.)

**E** **Elliptic** - Having the geometric shape of an ellipse, being broader in the middle and tapering toward the apex and base. (See Chapter 1.)

**Elongated** - Longer than broad; usually narrow.

**Emarginate** - Having an apex that is notched or indented; associated with leaf tips. (See Chapter 1.)

**Entire** - Having a smooth margin; not interrupted by teeth or other indentations. (See Chapter 1.)

**Espalier** - A plant that has been trained (pruned) to grow in a flat plane against a structure; usually attached with wire or cord.

**Even-pinnate** - Refers to a compound leaf that has the same number of leaflets on each side of the rachis and lacks a central terminal leaflet.

**Evergreen** - A plant that retains most of its foliage throughout the year. Such plants do drop some leaves periodically to allow for new leaves. Example: Pines.

**Exfoliate** - Referring to the bark of trees, where the bark sheds or peels (exfoliates) in long, narrow strips.

**F** **Fascicle** - A closely or tightly arranged cluster of leaves or other organs. Example: Fascicled needles of Pines.

**Fastigiate** - Has upright, usually closely arranged, branching habit; often narrow upright.

**Fissured** - Usually referring to vertical cracks or furrows in bark; often used synonymously with furrowed.

**Floret** - A tiny or smaller flower; usually referring to one flower of a compound or composite inflorescence.

**Focal Point** - An area or feature of a landscape that attracts attention; may be living or non-living.

**Follicle** - A dry and dehiscent fruit, containing one or more seeds, and opening along one seam or suture.

**Forma** (f.) - A subdivision of a plant species, usually with a trivial difference in one organ; most often propagated asexually.

**Frond** - Referring to foliage of a fern or palm.

**Fruit** - The ripened ovary of a flower, containing the seed.

**Funnelform** - Referring to a corolla that is funnel-shaped or trumpet-shaped; a fused corolla that broadens from base to apex. Example: Flowers of *Campsis grandiflora*.

**Furrowed** - Having vertical cracks or grooves; as with furrowed bark.

**G** **Genus** - A group of plant species with well-defined basic traits or characteristics, having some differences in lesser characteristics.

**Glabrous** - Absent of hairs or pubescence; usually, but not always, having a smooth surface.

**Gland** - An oil-secreting appendage or structure.

**Glaucous** - Covered with a waxy or powdery bloom, usually whitish, gray, or bluish. Example: Grapes.

**Globose** - Circular or globular in shape.

**H** **Hastate** - A leaf having two pointed lobes at the base that project outward.

**Head** - A composite of miniature florets that appear to be one flower. Example: Chrysanthemum. (See Chapter 1.)

**Herbaceous** - Referring to plants lacking a woody stem; usually dying in winter, but sometimes recovering in spring, as with herbaceous perennials.

**Husk** - The outer covering of some fruits.

**Hybrid** - The offspring of a cross between two genetically different plants; usually of different species. Designated by an "X" in written notation.

**I** **Incised** - Referring to leaves that have cuts or indentations; each cut having a depth that is greater than toothed, but more shallow than lobed.

**Indehiscent** - A type of covering that does not split along seams; no defined seams present.

**Inflorescence** - The flowers of a plant; usually referring to grouped or clustered flowers.

**Internode** - The area between two nodes on a stem. (See Chapter 1.)

**Involucre** - One or more spirals of leaves or bracts, appearing tightly beneath a flower or inflorescence.

**J**  **Juvenile** - Young vegetative growth; usually referring to the first season's growth.

**L**  **Lanceolate** - An organ or appendage, usually a leaf, that is much longer than wide; being broad at the base and tapering to a point at the apex; spear-shaped. (See Chapter 1.)
**Lateral** - Referring to an organ or appendage borne on the side; as in lateral buds or lateral roots.
**Lenticel** - A small "corky" area on a stem that allows gas exchange; may be vertical or horizontal to the apex. (See Chapter 1.)
**Linear** - Long, narrow shape as with the leaves of grasses; veins running parallel to the leaf edges.
**Lobe** - A division of an organ, as with the lobes of a leaf.

**M**  **Margin** - The edge of a leaf.
**Midrib** - The mid-vein or primary vein of a leaf or leaflet; the central vein of a pinnately-veined leaf or the central vein of a lobe in a palmately-veined leaf.
**Monoecious** - A plant having unisexual flowers (staminate and pistillate) on the same plant.
**Mucronate** - A leaf apex similar to obtuse, but having a pointed tip. (See Chapter 1.)
**Multiple fruit** - A fruit that is formed by a cluster of several flowers, as with *Morus*.
**Mutation** - A sudden change in the genetic makeup of a plant or plant parts.

**N**  **Node** - The area of a twig or stem where a leaf is attached; sometimes accompanied by a ring. (See Chapter 1.)
**Nut** - A hard and dry indehiscent fruit, being one-sectioned and one-seeded. Example: Acorn.
**Nutlet** - A small nut resembling an achene, but usually having a harder covering.

**O**  **Oblanceolate** - Referring to leaves with an inverse lanceolate shape, being narrow at the base and broader at the apex. (See Chapter 1.)
**Oblong** - Longer than broad. (See Leaf Shapes, Chapter 1.)
**Obovate** - The inverse of ovate; being narrow at the base and broader at the apex. (See Chapter 1.)
**Obtuse** - Narrowly rounded at the apex. (See Chapter 1.)
**Odd-pinnate** - A compound leaf having opposite leaflet pairs and a single, terminal leaflet.
**Opposite** - Joined at the same point (node) on opposing sides, as with opposite leaves.
**Ovary** - The swollen, usually basal, portion of a flower that contains the ovules.
**Ovate** - Somewhat egg-shaped with the basal portion being the broadest. (See Chapter 1.)

**Ovule** - The embryonic seed of a flower ovary, containing the egg.

**P**  **Palmate** - Fan-like structure, radiating from a common origin. Example: Leaf of *Aesculus glabra*.

**Panicle** - An inflorescence with multi-flowered pedicels attached to the peduncle.

**Parallel venation** - Having veins that run parallel to the margins, as with grasses.

**Pectinate** - Having very closely spaced divisions, like the teeth of a comb.

**Pedicel** - The stalk of an individual flower or fruit.

**Peduncle** - The stalk of a flower cluster, to which pedicels attach, or the stalk of a solitary flower.

**Pendulous** - Hanging or drooping.

**Perennial** - A plant that lives more than two seasons (years).

**Perigynium** - A papery sheath surrounding an ovary.

**Petal** - A leaf-like section of the inner floral envelope; often fragrant or showy to attract insects.

**Petiole** - The stalk of a leaf.

**Petiolule** - The stalk of a leaflet in a compound leaf; attaches to the rachis.

**Pinnate** - Having equal segments along each side of a central axis; as with pinnately compound leaves or pinnately veined leaves.

**Pistil** - The female flower part, containing the stigma, style, and ovary.

**Pistillate** - Female; usually referring to flowers with no functional stamen(s).

**Pith** - The central tissue of a stem, which is softer and usually inactive.

**Pod** - A general usage term applicable to dry, dehiscent fruits.

**Polygamodioecious** - Referring to plants having staminate and pistillate flowers on separate plants, but having some bisexual flowers on both or either plant.

**Polygamomonoecious** - Referring to plants having staminate and pistillate flowers on the same plant, but having some bisexual flowers.

**Pome** - A fleshy fruit having a central core and containing seed from a compound ovary. Example: Apple (See Chapter 1.)

**Pruinose** - Having a dust-like or powdery, waxy bloom. (See bloom.)

**Pubescent** - Having short and soft hairs. (See downy.)

**R**  **Raceme** - A clustered inflorescence, usually drooping, with petioles attached to a common peduncle. (See Chapter 1.)

**Rachis** - The primary axis of an inflorescence, or the axis in a compound leaf where leaflets attach.

**Radial** - Developing and spreading from a central axis.

**Reniform** - Broadly heart-shaped, with the width being greater than the length. (See Chapter 1.)

**Resinous** - Producing and secreting resin.

**Rhizome** - An underground stem having nodes and buds that root and send up new shoots or plants. Example: Bamboo.

**Rhombic** - Somewhat diamond-shaped with two acute angles and two obtuse angles; usually referring to a leaf shape.

## S

**Sagittate** - A leaf base having two lobes, one on each side of the axis, which point downward. (See Leaf Shapes, Chapter 1.)

**Samara** - An indehiscent dry fruit having a transparent membrane (wing) attached to a single seed. Example: Ash.

**Scale** - 1. A small appressed leaf, as in *Juniperus*. 2. A leaf-like segment of a cone, bearing one or more seeds.

**Secondary** - The second level of a division, i.e., the lateral roots of a root system.

**Semi-espalier** - To train and grow a plant near or against a structure without attachment.

**Semi-evergreen** - A plant that loses a noticeable portion of its foliage during winter, but retaining some green leaves.

**Sepal** - An individual leaf-like structure at the base of a flower; a division of the calyx.

**Serrate** - Having a sawtooth margin, with the teeth pointed toward the apex.

**Serrulate** - Having very finely serrated margins.

**Sheath** - A tubular structure that surrounds an organ or organs. Example: The sheath surrounding the base of a cluster of pine needles.

**Simple** - A leaf having one blade per petiole, or an inflorescence that is not sub-divided.

**Sinus** - An open space or cavity between two divisions; as in lobed leaves.

**Solitary** - Appearing alone; as with a single flower.

**Spatulate** - Spatula-shaped, with the apex being broader than the base and somewhat rounded. (See Chapter 1.)

**Specimen plant** - A plant having uncommon foliage, flowers, stems, bark, or growth habit; most often used for accent.

**Spike** - An inflorescence having several florets, usually stalkless, attached to a central rachis.

**Spinose** - Having margins with sharp-pointed spines; as in American Holly.

**Stamen** - The male flower part, composed of the filament and anther; the pollen-bearing part of the flower.

**Staminate** - A male flower, having no pistil or female parts.

**Sterile** - Not able to produce viable seed; often not producing fruit.

**Stolon** - An aboveground shoot or stem that roots at its apex to form a new plant. Example: *Vinca minor.*

**Stomate** - A pore in the leaf epidermis, more often on the underside, which allows gas exchange.

**Strobile** - A cone-like fruit consisting of tightly layered sporophylls on a central axis.

**Subspecies** (subsp.) - A subdivision within a species, having minor variations from the species, but not constituting a variety.

**Sucker** - A stem originating below ground from the roots and forming a new shoot of the main plant.

**Symmetrical** - Referring to the structure of an organ or appendage that is divisible into very similar halves, i.e., the shape of a plant or plant parts, such as flowers.

**T**  **Tendril** - A thread-like projection of a stem that twines around objects in climbing; a climbing method of some vines.

**Ternate** - Occurring in threes.

**Tomentose** - A dense mat of fine hairs; appearing woolly.

**Tri** - A prefix meaning three.

**Trifoliate** - Having three leaves.

**Trifoliolate** - Having three leaflets per leaf.

**Truncate** - Having a flat base that forms a 90-degree angle to the midrib. (See Chapter 1.)

**Twice-divided** - Same as bipinnate.

**Twig** - The terminal growth of a branch in one season.

**U**  **Umbel** - An inflorescence that is convex to flat-topped with the pedicels attached to the peduncle at a common point.

**Undulate** - Being wavy; as with an undulating leaf margin.

**V**  **Venation** - The pattern or arrangement of veins in a leaf.

**Ventral** - Opposite of dorsal; the front or inner surface of an organ or appendage.

**Villous** - Having long hairs, but not matted, as with tomentose.

**W**  **Whorl** - A circular arrangement of three or more, i.e., whorled leaf arrangement.

# INDEX OF BOTANICAL NAMES

# INDEX OF COMMON NAMES

# TASSAJARA COOKBOOK

"When you cook,
you are not just working on food,
you are working on yourself,
you are working on others."

—SHUNRYU SUZUKI ROSHI

# TASSAJARA COOKBOOK

lunches, picnics & appetizers

Karla Oliveira, M.S., R.D.

*Photographs by*

Patrick Tregenza and Renshin Judy Bunce

Gibbs Smith, Publisher
TO ENRICH AND INSPIRE HUMANKIND
Salt Lake City | Charleston | Santa Fe | Santa Barbara

First Edition
11 10 09 08 07   5 4 3 2 1

Text © 2007 Karla Oliveira, M.S., R.D.
Photographs © 2007 Patrick Tregenza and Renshin Judy Bunce

Published by
Gibbs Smith, Publisher
P.O. Box 667
Layton, Utah 84041

Orders: 1.800.835.4993
www.gibbs-smith.com

Designed by Black Eye Design
Printed and bound in China

Library of Congress Cataloging-in-Publication Dat
Oliveira, Karla.
Tassajara cookbook : lunches, picnics & appetizers / Karla Oliveira ; photographs by Patrick Tregenza and Renshin Judy Bunce. — 1st ed.
    p. cm.
 ISBN-13: 978-1-4236-0097-8
 ISBN-10: 1-4236-0097-5
 1. Vegetarian cookery.  I. Title.

 TX837.O45 2007
 641.5'636—dc22
                           2007012378

*This book is dedicated*
*to my sons, Colin and Jackson,*
*for just being.*

# contents

# acknowledgments

I would like to thank David Zimmerman at Tassajara for his encouragement, valuable input, and being there to help with this book whenever needed.

To Sonja Gardenswartz for seeing her live her practice as Tenzo with patience and openness and for her faith in me to do this book.

To the Guest Cooks and Bag Lunch Crew past, present and future for their creativity over the years for making the Bag Lunch what it is today, and for bringing their kitchen practice into our lives. I would specifically like to acknowledge David, Anke, Mako, Kathy, Linda, Jana, Darcy, Raiwin, and the others who gave me input or left valuable notes on the Bag Lunch.

To Edward Espe Brown for his teachings, humor and generous spirit.

To my editor, Melissa Barlow, for her patience, insight and kindness. To Richard Raymond for his kind support over the years. And to my sons, Colin and Jackson, for their help in the kitchen and input with the recipes. And finally, to the San Francisco Zen Center for this wonderful opportunity.

I would also like to acknowledge some of the many cookbooks and sources used as the creative backbone for these recipes by the Guest Cooks. There are certainly more than I can list so please be assured, the Guest Cooks thank you. Some of the books are: *The Tassajara Recipe Book, Garden Feasts, Moosewood, The Tempeh Cookbook, Vegetarian Cooking for Everyone, The Unplugged Cookbook, Chez Panisse Desserts, World of the East, Vegetarian Appetizers,* and *The Garden of Vegan.*

# foreword

What's for lunch? We all need to eat. And we have lunch in various ways: bag lunch, cafeteria, diner, burger place, deli or restaurant.

What's the occasion? Perhaps it's everyday on-the-go fueling up. Maybe it's just food, something to get done and out of the way, or maybe it's time for a break—a real respite and time for nourishment and sustenance.

During the Tassajara guest season, the Zen meditation community opens its gates to visitors, and since there's no radio, no TV, no movies, a few newspapers perhaps a day or two old, there is not much to do except eat.

Many of our visitors appreciate the chance to take a vacation and enjoy time being idle: napping, reading a book, having a cup of tea. Relaxing with a set menu, family-style breakfast and dinner, Tassajara guests are presented with a choice for lunch: "Would you care to eat in the dining room or make a bag lunch?"

Of course, if you haven't been to "Bag Lunch," you haven't a clue to the incredible extravagance—the luscious display of breads, cheeses, spreads, sauces, salsas, fruits, home-baked cookies, chips, guacamole, tomato slices, lettuces, nut butters, jams and jellies.

It's a far cry from the first bag lunches made forty years ago when the kitchen made them all the same: cheese sandwich, an apple or orange, some carrot or celery sticks, and a cookie. But this turned out to be down right frustrating for would-be flavor connoisseurs.

The solution was simple. Put out a display of ingredients and let people activate their innate capacity to make choices and improvise lunch. Now no two are the same!

We can give thanks to all those caring for and producing foods. And we can appreciate the hard work and generosity of time and spirit that Karla Oliveira has put into this collection.

We make choices with our eating habits. We don't have to do what we've always done. You can use this cookbook and begin to savor your opportunities to eat. Bon Appetite.

—Edward Espe Brown

*Bag Lunch Spread*

# introduction

The Tassajara Zen Mountain Center, founded in the 1960s, is a year-round Buddhist monastery deep in the Ventana Wilderness near Carmel Valley, California. Tassajara is owned by the San Francisco Zen Center, which also started Green's Restaurant, a very popular vegetarian restaurant (and cookbook) in the San Francisco area. In order to support itself, Tassajara hosts guests and retreats from April to September, offering beautiful and peaceful surroundings complete with hot springs, creek, Japanese bath houses and wonderful food—often the primary reason people visit. And for the Tassajara residents, the guest season abounds with Zen practice opportunities.

In addition to offering three delicious vegetarian meals a day, there is an option to take the Tassajara Bag Lunch. The Bag Lunch allows guests the freedom to hike, go to the swimming pool, creek, or to just relax in the garden. The Bag Lunch offers a gastronomical picnic feast along with a very beautiful visual experience. Each day the Bag Lunch provides as many as twenty different colorful spreads, several roasted vegetables, salads, marinated tofu, cheeses, fresh baked bread, olives, pickles, chutneys and delicious desserts to name just a few.

This book has been created in response to Tassajara guests who have requested the Bag Lunch recipes over the years. These recipes have been adapted from other cookbooks by the Guest Cooks and Bag Lunch Crew at Tassajara. The Guest Cooks and Bag Lunch Crew are Zen residents and students who usually have no formal cooking experience or training, but work in the kitchen as a very important part of their Zen practice. The recipes are quite simple but they have been prepared with great attention and care. This is what makes the food special. The Zen students bring their *zazen* practice (meditation) into their work, taking the leap out of the conditioned small mind, into the freedom and generosity of the mind that is accepting, fresh, and full of possibility. It is the unfettered mind of a beginner, otherwise known as "Beginner's Mind." Cooking as a Zen student is a way to practice generosity, patience, concentration, and thoughtful effort but in Zen, not worrying about the outcome. Here is the paradox—the students have to be concerned with the outcome of the food while not being concerned.

So it being said that if the Zen students cook with a Beginner's Mind, then we all can. And as with any cookbook, the recipes are meant as guidelines. One needs to taste for his or her own and decide as to whether or not a recipe needs more of this or less of that or if it needs an ingredient at all. This is "owning our own reality," as Edward Brown says—cooking for what we want it to be, taking that leap of faith in ourselves.

The Bag Lunch is also a highly creative endeavor, and the Guest Cooks and Bag Lunch Crew are given full creative license to use leftover beans and vegetables—anything left from making the guest meals—to create unique, spur of the moment delicacies, as Edward Brown calls it "The Tassajara Creative Catering Company." This is important given the remoteness of Tassajara, as well as a desire not to waste food. Cooking for the Bag Lunch is also limited, as the ovens and stoves are often in use preparing the guest meals—so little cooking is needed in these recipes.

The food at Tassajara has remained relatively unchanged in many ways since first opening, though it now reflects some of the current eating trends such as more international offerings and exotic food combinations. Since the beginning, Tassajara's cuisine has been built using the same fundamentals

as those at the San Francisco Zen Center's celebrated restaurant, Green's. Tassajara also uses fresh, local organic fruits, vegetables, and herbs whenever possible, high-quality oils and other staples, fresh-ground herbs and spices, and homemade bread.

The ingredients are an important and fundamental part to fine food. Keep this in mind when preparing the recipes in this book. Given the availability of modern conveniences such as canned organic beans, pitted olives, and soup stock pastes, quality doesn't have to be sacrificed to simplify preparation. But more importantly, as Edward Brown says, "the best cooking does not depend on anything more special than the willingness to do the work of putting yourself on the line, on the table. You get to know the ingredients within and without, and how changeable they are, and put them together for everyone to see and, even more revealing, to taste."

This book is a valuable resource for picnics, snacks, appetizers, and "little plates." You'll find an array of finger foods that are easy to put together when there is little time to cook a meal. Many of these recipes can be made in advance as well. It is also a good resource for recipes to use when camping or when traveling. It also provides many ideas for alternatives to those suffering from

allergies, be it dairy, wheat, or soy, and for those desiring to eat fewer carbohydrates or animal products.

As a nutritionist writing this book, there needs to be a word about nutrition. The *Tassajara Cookbook* does include recipes that use high-fat ingredients such as butter and cheeses. And there is always the possibility of substituting some of the lower fat alternatives now available in stores. But keep in mind that variety and moderation are the keys to a healthy diet, a well-known

fact when looking at the diets of other cultures such as those in Italy or Asia. Also, the vast majority of the book contains very healthful recipes full of fiber found in the whole grains; essential fatty acids found in the nuts, seeds, and olive oil, and vitamins and minerals found in the fresh organic fruits and vegetables.

I think Julia Child's Diet Plan says it all: "Eat modestly, widely, don't take seconds, and enjoy yourself."

# dairy spreads

Orange-Pecan Cream Cheese  19

Olive-Herb Cream Cheese  19

Leek Cream Cheese  20

Feta-Ricotta Herb Spread  20

Trois Fromage (Elanor's Cheese Ball)  23

Artichoke-Walnut Spread  25

Sweet Veggie Tapenade  26

Gorgonzola Spread  28

Fennel Mustard Butter  28

Artichoke Frittata  29

Orange-Pecan Cream Cheese

# Orange-Pecan Cream Cheese

*Orange zest and orange juice add just a touch of sweetness to this delicious spread. Try it on toasted bagels for breakfast.*

½ cup pecans
8 ounces cream cheese, softened
juice of 1 large orange
1½ tablespoons grated orange peel

Toast and chop the pecans. Blend remaining ingredients with a food processor or by hand; stir in pecans. Cover and chill until ready to serve.

MAKES 1½ CUPS

VARIATION: *This recipe can also be whipped until it's light and frothy and served as a dip with fresh fruit.*

# Olive-Herb Cream Cheese

*Olives and fresh herbs make a wonderful, earthy spread. Use it with roasted vegetables or crisp crackers.*

8 ounces cream cheese, softened
2 tablespoons fresh herbs, chopped
¼ teaspoon salt
½ cup olives, niçoise or other black olive, pitted

Blend cream cheese, herbs, salt, and olives with a food processor or by hand; cover and chill until ready to serve.

MAKES 1½ CUPS

# Leek Cream Cheese

*This makes a very simple, yet elegant spread. Try filling baked mini puff pastry shells for a gourmet treat.*

1 bunch leeks, chopped (white parts only)
1 tablespoon butter
1 tablespoon minced garlic
½ cup white wine

½ teaspoon each fresh tarragon, thyme, and oregano
salt and pepper
8 ounces cream cheese, softened

Cut leeks, discarding the tough upper green parts and then wash thoroughly. Saute in butter; when beginning to soften, add garlic, wine, and seasonings. Allow the mixture to cool, and then stir into the cream cheese.

MAKES 2 CUPS

# Feta-Ricotta Herb Spread

*This makes a fine spread to serve with crackers or bread along with olives, some fresh-grilled vegetables or roasted peppers. Or, serve it along side Sun-Dried Tomato Hummus (see page 59), Baba Ghanoush (see page 33), fresh mint and pita bread to create a Mediterranean feast.*

1 cup ricotta cheese
1 cup crumbled feta cheese
2 teaspoons olive oil

¼ cup chopped parsley
2 teaspoons fresh chives or scallions
½ teaspoon dill

Mix all ingredients thoroughly by hand or in a food processor; cover and chill until ready to serve.

MAKES 2 CUPS

VARIATION: *This recipe can also be mixed with any or all of the following ingredients, mixed with a little water, and shaped into a log: sun-dried tomatoes, olives, fresh herbs (great with dill), or fresh mint.*

"When you wash the rice, wash the rice; when you cut the carrots, cut the carrots; when you stir the soup, stir the soup."

—SHUNRYU SUZUKI ROSHI'S ADVICE TO EDWARD BROWN

# Trois Fromage
# (Elanor's Cheese Ball)

*This traditional cheese ball recipe is anything but traditional—serve it as a cheese log covered with toasted nuts or blend it and use it as a spread in a small attractive bowl. Serve with crackers, crudités, or crostini.*

6 ounces cream cheese, softened
⅓ cup crumbled blue cheese
1 teaspoon horseradish, or to taste
1 clove garlic, crushed
½ cup grated cheddar cheese
chopped parsley
chopped nuts

Blend one-third of the cream cheese and all of the blue cheese in a food processor. Form this mixture into a log shape on a plate or platter. Next, combine another third of the cream cheese with the horseradish and garlic. Spread this mixture over the first layer. Blend the remaining cream cheese with the grated cheddar cheese. Spread this mixture over the second layer. Garnish or decorate with chopped parsley or nuts. Instead of layering, you can roll the cheese mixture into 2-inch balls and coat with black pepper, minced nuts or fresh herbs. This is best if made a day ahead.

Alternatively, all the ingredients can be combined and blended in a food processor or by hand to make a creamy spread.

MAKES 1 CUP

# Artichoke-Walnut Spread

*This recipe is one of the most popular spreads offered at the Tassajara Bag Lunch. Its rich, decadent flavor makes an excellent appetizer served with crostini.*

½ cup toasted walnuts
½ cup firm silken tofu (or ricotta cheese)
12 artichoke hearts canned in water, drained
¼ cup olive oil
½ cup grated Parmesan, asiago, or a mixture of asiago and provolone cheese
2 tablespoons minced fresh oregano, or other fresh herb
2 cloves garlic, minced
⅓ cup fresh lemon juice, or to taste
salt and pepper

Grind the walnuts in a food processor until fine. If using silken tofu, wrap in a towel and press with a heavy weight for 30 minutes before using. Add the rest of ingredients and blend in the food processor or by hand until chunky but a uniform mixture; cover and chill until ready to serve.

MAKES 2 CUPS

# Sweet Veggie Tapenade

*This is a wonderful medley of leeks, a colorful trio of bell peppers, and Parmesan cheese. The flavors deepen as it sits.*

4 medium leeks, finely chopped (tender white parts only)
1 red bell pepper, finely chopped
1 yellow bell pepper, finely chopped
1 green bell pepper, finely chopped
1 medium yellow onion, finely chopped
1 small red onion, finely chopped
2 tablespoons olive oil
2 tablespoons chopped parsley
¼ cup grated Parmesan or Asiago cheese (optional)
pinch of chili flakes
salt and pepper

Saute leeks, bell peppers, and onions in olive oil until tender. In a medium bowl, combine hot sauteed vegetables with remaining ingredients while stirring to melt the cheese. Add salt and pepper to taste. Serve warm or cold.

MAKES 4 CUPS

# Gorgonzola Spread

*Blue cheese and juicy red grapes make a stunning combination. Serve this spread with crispy pita triangles, toasted party rye, or crispy garlic-flavored breadsticks for dipping.*

½ cup crumbled Gorgonzola, Roquefort, or blue cheese
4 ounces cream cheese, softened
½ cup ricotta cheese
1 teaspoon dry mustard
½ to 1 cup yogurt (depending on desired consistency)

Blend Gorgonzola, cream cheese, ricotta cheese, and dry mustard by hand or in a food processor. Next, add enough yogurt to create a spreadable consistency. Cover and chill until ready to serve.

MAKES 2 CUPS

# Fennel Mustard Butter

*Serve this delicious, fragrant butter as a spread on sandwiches or roasted fresh vegetables such as asparagus.*

1 tablespoon fennel seeds
1 teaspoon chopped fresh rosemary
½ cup butter, at room temperature
1 tablespoon fresh lemon juice
2 teaspoons Dijon mustard
1 clove garlic, minced
salt and pepper

Stir fennel seeds in a small skillet over medium heat until starting to brown, about 1 minute. Place in spice mill and grind to a coarse powder; transfer to a small bowl. Add remaining ingredients to bowl and stir to blend. Season with salt and pepper; cover and chill. This can be made 2 days ahead.

MAKES ½ CUP

# Artichoke Frittata

*This frittata may be just the recipe for those looking for a high-protein sandwich filling. Just cut into thin slices, top with fresh vegetables, and place on hearty whole-grain bread. This frittata would also be great as a picnic item, with a pile of pickled red onion rings on the side. Using fresh artichokes when in season are delicious but water-packed work just as well.*

3 large artichokes
juice of 1 large lemon
3 to 5 tablespoons virgin olive oil, divided
1 large clove garlic, sliced
salt
15 peppercorns, coarsely ground in a mortar
½ cup finely chopped parsley, divided
6 to 8 eggs, lightly beaten
½ cup coarsely grated Romano cheese

Preheat oven to 350 degrees F. If using fresh artichokes, break off the outer leaves and then cut off the top two-thirds of the greens. Trim the outsides, cut the artichokes into quarters, and immediately put them in a bowl with cold water to cover; add the lemon juice. Keep the artichokes in the lemon water until finished slicing to prevent browning. Remove the choke from each piece with a knife. Thinly slice each artichoke quarter into 3 or 4 pieces and return them to the water. Just before cooking, remove the pieces from the water and blot them dry with a towel. If using water-packed artichokes, simply rinse in a colander and slice into quarters.

Heat 2 tablespoons olive oil in an 8-inch frying pan with garlic. When the garlic colors, remove it and then add the artichoke quarters. Give the pan a shake right away to coat the pieces with oil, season with salt and pepper and then add about 2 tablespoons parsley. Saute until the artichokes are browned and thoroughly cooked.

Beat the eggs, season them lightly with salt, and add the remaining parsley, cheese, and cooked artichokes. Oil an 8 x 8-inch baking pan and then pour in the mixture. Bake for about 20 minutes, or until set and slightly browned. Cool thoroughly then slice and serve.

MAKES 1 (8 X 8-INCH) PAN

# vegan spreads

Baba Ghanoush  33

Quinoa Caviar  35

Curried Eggplant Spread  36

Roasted Eggplant Compote  38

China Moon Eggplant Spread  39

Roasted Red Bell Pepper Spread  40

Fig and Kalamata Olive Tapenade  43

Black Kalamata Olive Spread  43

Persian Olive, Walnut, and Pomegranate Tapenade  44

Cilantro Pesto  46

Garden of Vegan Tapenade  46

Basil, Lime, and Pumpkin Seed Pesto  48

Basil "Cream"  51

Sun-Dried Tomato Pesto with Walnuts or Almonds  52

Olive, Basil, and Walnut Spread with Madeira  54

Basil, Walnut, and Sun-Dried Tomato Spread  55

Anka's Roasted Red Bell Pepper Spread with Chiles and Lime  56

Nut Butter Spread  56

Tarragon Onion Spread  57

Creamy Tempeh with Garlic and Dill  57

Black Bean Spread  58

Sun-Dried Tomato Hummus  59

Garlic, Cilantro and Chipotle Hummus  61

Sonia's Caper-Garlic Hummus  61

Tempeh Spread with Capers and Onions  62

Rosemary Aioli  63

Vegan Spinach Dip  64

Western-Style Shira-ae  65

Roasted Garlic Dip  66

Creamy Tofu Dip  66

Black Olive Spread with Basil  67

"Zen is not some kind of excitement, but concentration
on our usual everyday routine."

—SHUNRYU SUZUKI ROSHI

# Baba Ghanoush

*The roasted eggplant gives this spread its sultry and rich flavor. Serve with lavosh or inside fresh pita bread with a bowl of pungent olives.*

    1 medium eggplant
    2 cloves garlic, minced
    ¼ cup fresh lemon juice
    ¼ cup sesame tahini
    ½ teaspoon salt
    black pepper
    cayenne
    pinch of cardamom (optional)
    1 tablespoon olive oil
    1 tablespoon chopped parsley

Scoop out the eggplant pulp and discard the skin. Place the pulp, garlic, lemon juice, tahini, salt, pepper, cayenne, and cardamom, if using, in a food processor; puree until smooth and then adjust seasonings. To serve, make a trough in the center of the dip and spoon the olive oil into it. Sprinkle with parsley.

MAKES 1½ CUPS

VARIATION:

    1 tablespoon olive oil
    1 cup minced onion
    ½ pound mushrooms, minced
    ½ teaspoon salt
    1 teaspoon dill

Heat olive oil and then add remaining ingredients and saute 10 to 15 minutes, or until tender. Stir into pureed eggplant mixture above.

# Quinoa Caviar

*This caviar is uniquely different and delicious. When cooked, quinoa really does resemble fish eggs, so you may get some puzzled stares or comments from your guests. As a spread, it's an easy way to get some of this super-nutritious quinoa into your diet.*

1 eggplant
2 onions, minced
2 cloves garlic, minced
1 tablespoon olive oil
1 cup quinoa
2 cups water
salt and pepper
¼ cup minced cilantro
¼ cup minced parsley
1½ tablespoons soy sauce
2 tablespoons lemon juice

Roast eggplant as described on page 38.

Saute the onions and garlic in olive oil until soft. Stir in the quinoa and lightly toast for 1 minute. Stir in the water and salt to taste; bring to a boil. Reduce heat, cover the pan, and gently simmer the quinoa for 15 minutes. Remove from heat and let stand for 10 minutes. Uncover the pan and fluff the quinoa with a fork; transfer to a bowl and let cool.

Puree the eggplant with the cilantro, parsley, soy sauce, and lemon juice in a food processor. Stir this mixture into the quinoa. Adjust seasoning, adding soy sauce, pepper, or lemon juice to taste. Garnish with sprigs of cilantro and parsley, if desired.

MAKES 4 CUPS

# Curried Eggplant Spread

*The exotic flavors of curry complement this tasty eggplant salad. Serve it as part of a composed salad plate or with cracker bread or toasted pita. This spread is also good blended with a small amount of yogurt and served as a dip.*

1 large eggplant
1 cup diced red bell pepper
1 medium onion, diced
2 tablespoons minced garlic
1 tablespoon olive oil
1 tablespoon minced parsley
1 tablespoon wine vinegar
½ teaspoon salt
¼ teaspoon pepper
1 tablespoon curry powder
juice of 1 lemon

Roast the eggplant and red bell peppers as described on page 38.

Saute onion and garlic in olive oil. Blend in a food processor with eggplant pulp and all other ingredients. Season to taste.

MAKES 4 CUPS

# Roasted Eggplant Compote

*This is a colorful, light, and easy spread that can be served as part of a composed salad plate, appetizer, or sandwich filling.*

1 large eggplant
3 red bell peppers
1 bunch scallions
½ cup balsamic vinegar
½ teaspoon salt
½ teaspoon pepper

Preheat the oven to 400 degrees F. With a sharp knife, make incisions all over the eggplant and place on a lightly oiled baking sheet. Add the peppers to the pan and bake until both are thoroughly soft and wrinkled all over, about 1 hour.

Put the bell peppers in a covered bowl to steam for 10 minutes or so. When peppers and eggplant are cool enough to handle, scrape off the skins and discard.

Puree in a food processor with remaining ingredients until slightly chunky or smooth; adjust seasonings.

MAKES 4 CUPS

## Eggplant Spreads

If eggplant is in season, there is no reason to salt before roasting. However, if they're out of season, the eggplants might be bitter. To remove the bitterness, salt them lightly after cutting them open and let stand for about 30 minutes. Rinse and dry thoroughly before proceeding. For roasting eggplant: slice eggplant in half and spread lightly with olive oil. Put on an oiled baking sheet and bake at 450 degrees F for at least 45 minutes, or until tender and the skin is slightly blackened and wrinkled; cool. The large globe eggplant is easier to handle than the narrow Italian or Asian varieties.

# China Moon Eggplant Spread

*These Asian flavors combined with eggplant make a delicious spread. The sesame oil and brown sugar add depth and sweetness, while freshly grated ginger and dried chili pepper gives the spread a refreshing spiciness. Try rolling in softened rice paper rolls with shredded vegetables. Best if used within a few days.*

1 large eggplant
1 tablespoon minced garlic
⅓ cup sliced green onions
1 tablespoon minced ginger
2 tablespoons minced cilantro
½ teaspoon dried chili flakes (or hot chili oil)
1 tablespoon soy sauce
1 tablespoon brown sugar
½ tablespoon rice vinegar or mirin
1 tablespoon hot water
1 tablespoon toasted sesame oil

Roast eggplant as described on page 38.

When the eggplant is cool, scrape pulp off skin and puree in a food processor. Stir together the remaining ingredients except sesame oil. Heat a wok with the sesame oil. When the oil is hot, add the sauce and stir a couple of times. Add pureed eggplant and stir to blend.

MAKES 1 CUP

# Roasted Red Bell Pepper Spread

*This spread is perfect for garlic lovers. Keep in mind the garlic is raw when adding, so be sure its not too hot. This spread is immensely popular at the Tassajara Bag Lunch.*

6 red bell peppers, fresh or roasted in jar
light olive oil, for the peppers
4 to 5 cloves garlic
1½ tablespoons oil
2 teaspoons red wine vinegar
salt and pepper

Preheat oven to 400 degrees F. Brush the peppers with the light olive oil. Set them on a baking sheet and bake them until the skins are wrinkled and lightly colored, about 40 minutes. Place in a bowl and cover with a plate until cool. When cool, remove the skins and scrape the seeds and ribs from inside.

Mince the peppers and add remaining ingredients. Let sit about 2 hours before serving.

MAKES 3 CUPS

*Fig and Kalamata Olive Tapenade*

# Fig and Kalamata Olive Tapenade

*A very simple, yet very exotic tapenade. Serve it with Middle Eastern flat bread, fresh feta cheese, and garlicky olives.*

    5 fresh black figs
    1 tablespoon capers, rinsed
    1 tablespoon kalamata olives, pitted
    1 tablespoon olive oil
    2 teaspoons balsamic vinegar

Trim the hard stem end from the figs and then blend everything together in a food processor until smooth; cover and chill. It's best if used that day, but will keep for another day.

MAKES 1 CUP

# Black and Kalamata Olive Spread

*This is a strong and robust spread and a small amount goes a long way. It's also a good complement to plain hummus—serve them marbled or layered together, or separately with crackers or crostini. Also good in deviled eggs or even on pizza.*

    1 cup black olives, pitted
    2 cups kalamata olives, pitted
    ⅓ cup capers, rinsed
    1 tablespoon minced garlic
    1 teaspoon dried basil
    ¼ cup fresh parsley

Blend all ingredients together in a food processor until smooth.

MAKES 2 CUPS

# Persian Olive, Walnut, and Pomegranate Tapenade

*Middle Eastern dishes often use whole pomegranate seeds in their dishes for wonderful color, flavor, and texture. In this recipe, the seeds burst their sweet-tart flavor into the creamy tapenade. For a real treat, serve it Persian style with a plate of fresh herbs (mint, parsley, dill, and scallions), a chunk of feta cheese, cucumber slices, and pita or traditional Middle Eastern flat bread.*

1 cup unseasoned green olives, such as Picholines, pitted
⅔ cup toasted walnuts, finely chopped
½ cup whole pomegranate seeds
¼ cup chopped cilantro
1 clove minced garlic
2 tablespoons extra virgin olive oil
lemon juice
salt
2 pita rounds, cut into triangles

Finely mince the olives. In a bowl, combine the olives, walnuts, pomegranate seeds, cilantro, garlic, and olive oil; stir to mix. Add a few drops of lemon juice and salt if necessary. The mixture may not need salt if the olives are salty.

Preheat the oven to 375 degrees F. Toast the pita triangles on a baking sheet until lightly colored and crisp, about 8 to 10 minutes; let cool. Serve tapenade with the pita toasts.

MAKES 1½ CUPS

# Cilantro Pesto

*This is creamy, rich pesto for cilantro lovers. Its bright green color and fresh flavor will enhance any sandwich. Try making a Mexican pizza or burrito with queso fresco, black beans, fresh chiles, and tomatoes. Or use it with other pestos with pasta or vegetable toppings.*

2 cloves garlic
½ cup raw almonds
1 bunch cilantro
3 tablespoons lemon juice
¾ cup olive oil
½ teaspoon salt

Place all ingredients in a food processor in the order listed above and blend until smooth. If you want it more or less chunky, decrease or increase the proportions of lemon juice and oil, but always kept the ratio of 3 parts oil to 1 part lemon juice.

MAKES 1 CUP

# Garden of Vegan Tapenade

*This very rich tapenade can be topped on slices of crispy potatoes, cucumber slices, or even hard-boiled eggs for a wonderful appetizer. For lunch, try it on rye crisp crackers or whole-grain bread.*

1 cup kalamata olives, pitted
2 cloves garlic, minced
10 to 12 sun-dried tomatoes, rehydrated
¼ cup capers, rinsed
1 cup olive oil
2 tablespoons Bragg's Liquid Aminos or tamari

Blend all ingredients together until coarse in a food processor.

MAKES 1 CUP

Cilantro Pesto

# Basil, Lime, and Pumpkin Seed Pesto

*This is an excellent pesto packed with nutrition and fiber. The freshness of the lime and basil are a great complement to the rich, nutty flavor of pumpkin seeds.*

1 cup raw pumpkin seeds
1 cup basil, packed
4 tablespoons lime juice
3 cloves garlic
2 tablespoons olive oil
salt and pepper

Lightly toast pumpkin seeds and grind until they stick to the walls of the food processor. Add the remaining ingredients. Add more olive oil or lime juice to thin if necessary.

**MAKES 1 CUP**

Basil "Cream"

# Basil "Cream"

*Basil and cashews make a wonderful combination to create a rich, creamy spread. Make this spread at the height of summer when fresh basil is available. Serve in place of mayonnaise or mustard on sandwiches, with grilled vegetables and tofu, or even on pasta!*

1 cup cashews
9 to 10 cups fresh basil
¼ cup lemon juice
1 tablespoon miso
olive oil
pepper
4 to 5 fresh spinach leaves

Grind cashews in a food processor. Add basil, lemon juice, and miso and then blend until smooth. Add olive oil and pepper as needed to make a creamy consistency, and add the fresh spinach leaves to help keep the color vibrant and bright.

MAKES 1 CUP

# Sun-Dried Tomato Pesto with Walnuts or Almonds

*The intense flavor of sun-dried tomatoes and the tartness of lemon juice create a striking balance. Try spreading it over cream cheese or goat cheese on crackers, crostini, or breads. As with other pestos, it can also be served on pasta, grilled vegetables, baked potatoes, or even pizza.*

1 cup sun-dried tomatoes
1 clove garlic
½ cup walnuts or almonds
2 tablespoons fresh lemon juice
½ cup extra virgin olive oil
2 tablespoons each fresh basil, oregano, and dill (or 1 teaspoon each dried)

Steam or simmer the sun-dried tomatoes until soft. In a food processor, add the garlic, sun-dried tomatoes, and nuts. Add remaining ingredients and process until smooth.

MAKES 1 CUP

# Olive, Basil, and Walnut Spread with Madeira

*The sharp flavor of pimiento-stuffed olives is mellowed here by the other ingredients, creating a tantalizing pesto-like spread. It can launch any Greek or Italian menu with real gusto. If you want to serve it with crackers, choose some that are plain and simple so they don't compete with the flavor of the spread.*

1 cup pimiento-stuffed olives, drained
⅔ cup chopped basil leaves
½ cup raw walnuts
¼ cup Madeira or dry sherry
1 tablespoon fresh lemon juice
2 cloves garlic, minced
several grinds of pepper

Puree all the ingredients together in a food processor until thick and fairly homogenous. Prepare the spread well ahead of time, if possible, so the flavors have time to blend. Cover and chill; can be stored in the refrigerator for up to a week, but return to room temperature before serving.

MAKES 1½ CUPS

# Basil, Walnut, and Sun-Dried Tomato Spread

*This is a rich, flavorful spread and a little goes a long way. It's a great complement to grilled vegetables and baked potatoes. Or, simply combine it with yogurt to serve as a dip.*

1 cup sun-dried tomatoes
3 cloves garlic
3 tablespoons lemon juice
1 cup raw walnuts
1 cup fresh basil
1 teaspoon dried oregano
1 teaspoon dried dill
1 cup olive oil

Steam or simmer the sun-dried tomatoes until soft. Place all the ingredients in a food processor and blend until smooth.

MAKES 2½ CUPS

# Anka's Roasted Red Bell Pepper Spread with Chiles and Lime

*This southwest-inspired recipe was created by Anka, the head of the Bag Lunch Crew one summer at Tassajara. It's a delicious low-fat and colorful spread.*

5 red bell peppers, roasted
2 tablespoons lime juice
1½ tablespoons olive oil
1 serrano chile, seeded and minced
½ cup chopped cilantro
salt and pepper

Roast bell peppers as described on page 38 and then dice. Combine the peppers with the remaining ingredients and mix by hand.

MAKES 2 CUPS

VARIATION: *Instead of serrano chiles, use 2 tablespoons rinsed capers and a pinch of cayenne.*

# Nut Butter Spread

*This Bag Lunch favorite has lots of protein, essential fats and minerals—sort of a super nutritious peanut butter! It is hand mixed to keep its chunky texture. Try it spread on celery for "ants on a log" with raisins.*

⅓ cup sunflower seeds, lightly toasted
⅓ cup sesame seeds, lightly toasted
⅓ cup cashews, toasted and chopped
2 cups peanut butter
1 cup tahini
1 teaspoon honey

Mix thoroughly until well combined. Use in place of peanut or other butters on bread and crackers.

MAKES 2 CUPS

# Tarragon Onion Spread

*This mixture of onion, lemon, and fresh tarragon creates a delicious, vibrant spread. It can be used as a dip or spread, especially with marinated tofu and roasted vegetables. To use as a dip, thin with water or lemon juice.*

| | |
|---|---|
| 1 tablespoon olive oil | ¼ cup lemon juice |
| 1 onion, minced | ½ teaspoon salt |
| 5 cloves garlic, minced | black pepper |
| 2 tablespoons fresh tarragon | 1 cup water |
| 2 bay leaves | |

Heat the olive oil in a saute pan and then add onion and garlic; cook until soft, about 5 minutes. Add tarragon and bay leaves and cook 5 minutes more. Add remaining ingredients and cook about 15 minutes, stirring occasionally, until mixture is very thick. Remove bay leaves and blend mixture in a food processor to create a creamy texture.

MAKES ABOUT 1 CUP

# Creamy Tempeh with Garlic and Dill

*Lemon, garlic, and herbs are the perfect complement to tempeh in this delicious spread.*

6 ounces tempeh
¼ cup oil
2 tablespoons lemon juice or apple cider vinegar
½ teaspoon salt
½ cup water
1 clove garlic, minced
¼ teaspoon dill
2 tablespoons parsley

Cut the tempeh into 1 x 1-inch pieces and steam for 20 minutes. Combine all the ingredients except the parsley in a food processor and blend until smooth. Garnish with the parsley and serve chilled.

MAKES 1½ CUPS

# Black Bean Spread

*This spread/dip is very easy to prepare. Try using it on crispy corn tortillas or chips, or serve with Monterey Jack or cheddar cheese, a little sour cream and roasted red bell pepper.*

2 cups cooked black beans
1 small red onion, minced
3 tablespoons minced cilantro
1 clove garlic, minced
1 teaspoon herb mixture*
1 teaspoon cumin
2 teaspoons lime juice
¼ teaspoon salt

Place all ingredients together in a food processor and blend until smooth.

MAKES 2 CUPS

*Herb mixture: Equal amounts of oregano, paprika, and cayenne ground in a spice mill.*

# Sun-Dried Tomato Hummus

*Toasted sesame tahini and sun-dried tomatoes give this traditional Middle Eastern spread an especially rich flavor and bright color. Try it on celery, cucumber slices, or zucchini instead of bread.*

    2 cups chickpeas (garbanzo beans), soaked overnight
    ¼ teaspoon salt
    6 to 8 sun-dried tomatoes, rehydrated
    ¾ cup tahini
    3 cloves garlic, minced
    2 tablespoons lemon juice or apple cider vinegar
    ¼ cup olive oil
    1 tablespoon Bragg's Liquid Aminos or tamari
    1 teaspoon cumin
    ½ teaspoon salt
    ¼ teaspoon cayenne pepper

Drain the chickpeas and then cover them generously with fresh water; bring to a boil. Lower the heat to a slow boil, add ¼ teaspoon salt, and cook until the beans are completely soft, about 1 ½ hours, or more. Other alternatives are to cook the chickpeas in a pressure cooker or to use 1 (12-ounce) can. If using canned, be sure to rinse well before using.

Drain the chickpeas and put in a food processor with the sun-dried tomatoes, tahini, garlic, lemon juice, olive oil, Bragg's, cumin, ½ teaspoon salt, and cayenne pepper; process until smooth. Extra liquid may be necessary to thin; use the cooking liquid from the beans, water, or additional olive oil. Taste and adjust the salt, lemon, and oil to your liking.

MAKES 3 CUPS

"There is nothing more zen than careful observation of the
obvious. If you keep practicing that, you'll figure it out."

—EDWARD ESPE BROWN

# Garlic, Cilantro and Chipotle Hummus

*This is a delicious, spicy hummus. Serve on Middle Eastern flatbread or try with tortilla chips along with guacamole.*

1½ cups cooked chickpeas
3 tablespoons tahini
½ cup fresh-squeezed lemon juice
½ to 1 teaspoon canned chipotle, or to taste
½ cup chopped cilantro
3 cloves garlic, minced
½ teaspoon salt

Combine chickpeas and tahini in a small bowl and cream together or put in a food processor and puree. Add the remaining ingredients and blend until smooth and creamy. Add water to thin if necessary and add salt to taste. Garnish with fresh cilantro and minced chipotle.

MAKES 2 CUPS

# Sonia's Caper-Garlic Hummus

*This hummus shows how versatile hummus can be. It is delicious and attractive given the addition of whole capers. Keep in mind it will be salty with the capers, so be careful when adding more salt.*

1½ cups cooked chickpeas
3 tablespoons tahini
½ cup fresh-squeezed lemon juice
2 tablespoons capers, rinsed
3 cloves garlic, minced
salt

Combine chickpeas, tahini, and lemon juice in a small bowl and cream together or put in a food processor and puree. Add the remaining ingredients by hand and mix well.

MAKES 2 CUPS

# Tempeh Spread
# with Capers and Onions

*The pungent lemon and caper flavors add vibrancy to this creamy spread. Try this spread rolled up in lavosh or on crispy crackers.*

6 ounces tempeh
½ cup water
1 bay leaf
1 tablespoon tamari
2 tablespoons capers, drained
2 green onions, minced
¼ cup chopped celery
¼ cup mayonnaise (regular or vegan)
1 tablespoon fresh lemon juice

In a saute pan, combine tempeh, water, bay leaf, and tamari and simmer for 20 minutes. Cool and drain the tempeh and then grate. Mix tempeh with remaining ingredients. The mixture should be a spreading consistency; cover and chill until ready to serve.

**MAKES 2 CUPS**

# Rosemary Aioli

*The rich and creamy flavor of this non-dairy spread comes from the rosemary-infused oil. Use it in place of butter on grilled vegetables or bread.*

3 sprigs fresh rosemary
¼ cup olive oil
3 teaspoons fresh rosemary, or more to taste
3 cloves garlic
2 tablespoons fresh lemon juice, or more to taste
2 (12-ounce) blocks soft tofu
salt

To make the rosemary-infused oil, place washed sprigs of fresh rosemary in a clean jar and pour in the olive oil. Let sit for a few days in the refrigerator until the flavor is strong enough. Remove and discard the herbs. Keep oil covered in the refrigerator. This will keep for up to several months if not used right away.

To finish the spread, blend the rosemary-infused oil with all the remaining ingredients in a food processor until smooth. Taste and adjust seasonings. The rosemary flavor should be very strong.

**MAKES 2 CUPS**

# Vegan Spinach Dip

*Try serving this dip with pita bread or sliced raw vegetables, or use as a sandwich filling.*

1 pound fresh spinach
8 ounces water chestnuts
1 cup Tofu Mayonnaise (see page 92)
10 ounces silken tofu
2 tablespoons grated onion
2 cloves garlic, minced
1 teaspoon basil
2 teaspoons tarragon
2 teaspoons dill weed
1 tablespoon minced parsley
1 ¼ teaspoons salt, or to taste
½ teaspoon black pepper

Wash and cook spinach until wilted; drain and squeeze dry. Dice water chestnuts and set aside. Combine remaining ingredients in a food processor and process until well combined.

Stir together the spinach, water chestnuts, and tofu mixture. Refrigerate for several hours or overnight.

MAKES 4 CUPS

# Western-Style Shira-ae

*This salad makes an unusual, yet delicious high-protein spread or sandwich filling.*

6 ounces soft tofu, mashed
1 tablespoon tahini
1 tablespoon lemon juice
1½ tablespoons rice vinegar
½ teaspoon salt or 1 tablespoon red miso
1 teaspoon sake or white wine
1 cucumber or small carrot, cut into thin rounds
2 hard-boiled eggs, chopped
¼ cup chopped walnuts
¼ cup raisins
2 tablespoons cucumber pickles, minced (optional)

Combine first six ingredients in a food processor and blend until smooth. Gently stir in the remaining ingredients and serve immediately.

MAKES 2 CUPS

# Roasted Garlic Dip

*Roasting garlic gives it a rich and buttery consistency. And using this roasted garlic dip is delicious and rich in protein.*

¾ cup soft or silken tofu, drained
2 tablespoons apple cider vinegar
1 tablespoon maple syrup
½ teaspoon salt
pinch black pepper
6 cloves roasted garlic
½ onion, diced
1 to 2 teaspoons olive oil

Combine all ingredients in a food processor and blend until smooth and creamy.

MAKES 1 CUP

# Creamy Tofu Dip

*Serve this dip with a platter of celery and carrot sticks, sliced jicama, whole green beans, cucumbers, cherry tomatoes, and Jerusalem artichokes.*

10 ounces soft tofu
½ cup oil
2 tablespoons lemon juice
1½ tablespoons honey
¼ cup chopped parsley
2 tablespoons minced dill pickles
1 tablespoon minced onion
½ teaspoon mustard
½ teaspoon salt

Combine all ingredients together in a food processor and blend until smooth.

MAKES ABOUT 2 CUPS

# Black Olive Spread with Basil

*Delicious olives combined with fresh basil—what could be better?*

1 cup black olives, pitted
1½ tablespoons capers
1 clove garlic
Juice of 1 lemon
4 tablespoons olive oil
Fresh ground pepper, to taste
2 tablespoons minced fresh basil
½ teaspoon sugar (optional)

Combine all ingredients in a food processor and blend until smooth. If too salty, add optional sugar. Taste and adjust seasonings.

**MAKES ABOUT 1 CUP**

# pâtés & loaves

# Almond Pâté

*This recipe is from* The Tassajara Recipe Book *by Edward Brown. This savory, flavorful nut pâté claims the distinction of being possibly the most requested recipe during the guest season. Tassajara uses it as a sandwich spread and as an ingredient in the Nut Loaf (see page 77). Try this pâté as a filling for mushrooms, or as a "nut chutney" for grains or vegetables.*

1 cup minced onion
1 tablespoon butter
½ teaspoon freshly ground cumin
½ teaspoon savory
½ teaspoon fine herbs
1 cup raw almonds, ground fairly fine
½ cup plus 2 tablespoons toasted breadcrumbs
2 tablespoons minced parsley
1 teaspoon tamari
1 small clove garlic, minced
salt and fresh-ground pepper
2 to 4 tablespoons mayonnaise or sour cream
lemon slices

Cook the onion in the butter over low heat with the cumin, savory, and fine herbs until they are soft.

Scrape the onion mixture into a bowl. Using your fingers, work in the almonds, breadcrumbs, parsley, tamari, and garlic. Taste and season with salt and pepper.

Gradually mix in the mayonnaise or sour cream until the mixture holds together. Shape it into a log or press into a serving bowl and garnish with overlapping slices of lemon.

MAKES 2 CUPS

# Mushroom Pâté

*This is a rich, full-flavored pâté that can be served as a snack, appetizer, or for picnics.*

1 red onion, finely chopped
2 cloves garlic, minced
2 cups finely chopped mushrooms
1 cup red wine
1 tablespoon nutritional yeast

1 teaspoon dried herbs (for example,
   sage, thyme, rosemary, nutmeg)
salt and pepper
1 cup toasted walnuts

Saute the onion, garlic, and mushrooms in red wine until all the moisture has evaporated.

Remove from heat and add nutritional yeast, herbs, and salt and pepper to taste. In a food processor, grind the walnuts, then add the cooked mixture and blend until smooth. Cool and spoon into a bowl to serve; garnish with a few toasted walnuts.

MAKES 3 CUPS

# Mushroom-Almond Pâté

*This pâté was a very popular recipe that guests often asked for and, in fact, was given to Tassajara by a guest. It was originally made with breadcrumbs but guest cooks replaced them with almond meal to increase the nutritional value. For a high-fiber pâté, one can substitute oat bran for the almond meal.*

1 to 2 cloves garlic, minced
1 small yellow onion, finely chopped
4 to 5 tablespoons butter
¾ pound mushrooms, finely chopped
¼ cup cooking sherry or Marsala

¾ teaspoon salt
½ teaspoon ground thyme
⅛ teaspoon white pepper
1 cup finely ground almonds

Saute garlic and onion in 4 tablespoons butter until translucent. Add mushrooms and cook until soft. Add more butter if needed (the butter gives the pâté-like texture) and cook off any remaining liquid. Add sherry and cook off the alcohol. Taste and adjust seasoning with salt, thyme, and white pepper; add the almond meal. Cool and then put into bowls, mounding attractively.

MAKES 2 CUPS

*Mushroom Pâté*

# Asian Walnut Pâté

*A great sandwich spread served with alfalfa sprouts, or use as a dip for vegetables or crispy pita wedges.*

1 cup ground walnuts
1 pound firm tofu, drained and crumbled
2 cloves garlic, minced
2 tablespoons toasted sesame oil
2 tablespoons tahini
3 tablespoons yellow white miso
2 teaspoons umeboshi plum paste
3 tablespoons Tofu Mayonnaise (see page 88)
3 tablespoons maple syrup
juice of 2 lemons
⅛ teaspoon cayenne, or to taste
¼ cup minced parsley
¼ cup chopped pimientos

Combine all ingredients together, except parsley and pimientos, in a food processor and process until very smooth. Transfer to a large bowl and then stir in parsley and pimientos.

**MAKES 4 CUPS**

# Savory Sunflower Pâté

*This earthy pâté is rich in flavor and nutrition.*

1 medium onion, coarsely chopped
½ cup virgin olive oil, divided
½ cup warm water
¼ cup tamari
1 to 2 large potatoes, peeled and diced
1 cup raw, shelled sunflower seeds
½ cup whole wheat flour
½ cup nutritional yeast
1 to 2 cloves garlic
1½ teaspoons dried herbs (for example, sage, basil, oregano, marjoram, thyme)

Preheat oven to 350 degrees F. Saute onion in 1 tablespoon olive oil until soft. Add onion and all other ingredients to a food processor and blend until very smooth. The mixture needs to be very thick to hold its shape.

Pour mixture into two greased loaf pans and bake until set, about 1 hour; cool thoroughly. Once cooled, loosen the loaves from the pan with a table knife and then remove carefully. Wrap in plastic wrap and store in the refrigerator for up to 2 weeks, or freeze up to 3 months.

MAKES 2 LOAVES

VARIATION: *Add ½ to 1 cup chopped cilantro or parsley with 1 cup dried breadcrumbs or rolled oats to mixture.*

# Pâté Tempeh

*Serve this hearty spread with seed crackers, crostini, or toasted pita triangles.*

1 cup slivered almonds
1 small onion, minced
1 clove garlic, minced
½ pound mushrooms, sliced
2 tablespoons olive oil
8 ounces tempeh
1 teaspoon tamari
½ teaspoon each thyme and sage
salt

Preheat oven to 350 degrees F. Spread almonds on a baking sheet in one layer and bake until golden, about 10 minutes. Saute the onion, garlic, and mushrooms in oil until soft. Cut the tempeh into ½-inch cubes and add to the mushroom mixture.

Add tamari, thyme, sage, and salt to taste. Cook mixture about 15 minutes, or until most of the liquid has evaporated.

In a food processor or blender, grind the almonds. Add the remaining ingredients and process until the pâté is thick and smooth. Cover and chill; will keep about 1 week.

**MAKES 2 CUPS**

# Parisienne Pâté

*An Asian-inspired French pâté—a delectable dish for guests. Serve with crackers or thin slices of toast.*

> 8 ounces tempeh, cut in half
> 1 cup vegetable stock
> 1 bay leaf
> 2 cups cubed sourdough bread (½-inch cubes)
> 2 tablespoons olive oil
> 1 medium onion, chopped
> 2 tablespoons tamari
> 1 tablespoon mirin
> ½ teaspoon marjoram
> ½ teaspoon thyme
> ½ teaspoon nutmeg

Heat oven to 350 degrees F. In a medium saucepan, simmer the tempeh halves in vegetable stock with bay leaf for 10 minutes. Remove bay leaf and tempeh.

Add more stock to the saucepan, enough to make ¾ cup, and bread cubes and let soak. Heat olive oil and saute onion until soft. After the tempeh has cooled, grate.

In a food processor (or you can mash by hand), combine the grated tempeh, soaked bread, onion, and remaining ingredients; blend until smooth. Pack mixture into a lightly oiled 1-quart ovenproof bowl. Cover bowl with foil and place in a pan of hot water. Bake for 30 minutes, remove cover, and bake another 20 to 30 minutes. Cool, unmold onto a plate, and garnish with fresh herbs.

MAKES 3 CUPS

"When you are practicing, you realize that your mind is like a screen. If the screen is colorful, colorful enough to attract people, then it will not serve its purpose. So to have a screen which is not colorful—to have a pure, plain white screen—is the most important point."

—SHUNRYU SUZUKI ROSHI

# Three Nut Pâté

*This is another favorite of the Tassajara guests. Fresh basil makes a wonderful addition to this pâté. This recipe is best if made ahead and allowed to sit a few hours before serving for the flavor to develop.*

½ cup each almonds, cashews, and walnuts
1 onion, coarsely chopped
½ cup sliced scallions
1 tablespoon minced garlic
¼ teaspoon allspice
½ teaspoon dried thyme
1 bay leaf
2 tablespoons olive oil
¼ cup red wine
2 tablespoons soy sauce
½ cup chopped fresh basil
¼ cup dried breadcrumbs
¾ cup firm tofu, crumbled (optional)*
salt and pepper

Preheat the oven to 350 degrees F. Spread the nuts in one layer on a baking sheet and toast for 10 to 15 minutes until golden brown. Then grind the nuts to a fine powder; set aside.

Saute the onion, scallions, garlic, allspice, thyme, and bay leaf in olive oil until soft. Add red wine and soy sauce and cook until almost dry. Add basil to onion mixture and continue cooking until well combined. Add breadcrumbs, tofu, if desired, and salt and pepper to taste. Blend mixture together in a food processor. Spoon into a serving dish and garnish with fresh basil leaves.

MAKES 2 CUPS

*\*If using tofu, increase breadcrumbs to 1 cup.*

# The Nut Loaf

*This very popular nut loaf requested by guests at Tassajara for the last 25 years was originally published in* The Tassajara Recipe Book *by Edward Brown. It's a good way to use any leftover cheese you may have accumulated. The type of cheese you can use is flexible, but try to include some strongly-flavored cheese such as Brie, Gorgonzola, Gruyère, or Smoked Gouda. When making the Almond Pâté, double the recipe so there is some for this nut loaf. It took some tinkering to produce a loaf that did not crumble to pieces upon removal from the pan, or later upon slicing.*

1½ cups sliced mushrooms

2 cloves garlic, minced

1 green bell pepper, diced

½ teaspoon each thyme, oregano,
    marjoram, tarragon, and basil

½ teaspoon salt

¼ teaspoon pepper

2 tablespoons olive oil or butter

2 cups cooked brown rice or 2 cups
    dried breadcrumbs

4 eggs

1 cup Almond Pâté (see page 67)

½ cup toasted cashews

1 cup ricotta cheese (or cottage cheese
    or yogurt)

1 cup grated mixed cheese (see recipe
    introduction)

2 tablespoons minced parsley

Preheat oven to 350 degrees F. Saute mushrooms, garlic, bell pepper, and seasonings in olive oil or butter until tender. If using breadcrumbs instead of rice, toast 4 slices bread until brown, cool slightly, and then grind in a food processor until fine.

Beat eggs in a large bowl, then stir in all remaining ingredients. Add enough ricotta or cottage cheese so that the mixture binds together firmly. Add more grated cheese and herbs to taste—the mixture should taste strong and savory.

Thoroughly grease two loaf pans. Put nut loaf into pans, smoothing the top with a spatula. Bake for approximately 1 hour. Loaves should be golden brown and firm to the touch. Be sure to not overcook or they will tend to be dry. Let sit for 5 to 10 minutes; then turn out on a wire rack to cool. The loaves freeze well for up to 1 month.

MAKES 2 LOAVES

# Jesse's "Lighter-Less Dairy" Loaf

*This recipe is similar to The Nut Loaf on page 77, but a lighter version adapted by a student.*

2 tablespoons olive oil
1½ cups chopped onions
1 teaspoon dried sage
½ teaspoon dried thyme
2 cups sliced mushrooms
1 cup roasted cashews, chopped
1 cup roasted walnuts, chopped
1 teaspoon tamari
salt and pepper
1 cup cooked brown rice
1 cup grated carrots
½ cup grated cheddar cheese
2 eggs, beaten
1 cup dried breadcrumbs
dried chili pepper flakes (optional)

Heat oven to 350 degrees F. Heat olive oil over medium heat. Saute the onions with herbs until translucent; add the mushrooms, cashews, and walnuts and saute until they start to stick to the bottom of the pan and are nicely browned. Add the tamari and salt and pepper to taste.

In a large bowl, combine the rice, carrots, and onion mixture and combine until well mixed. Add the cheese, eggs, breadcrumbs, and chili flakes, if desired, to taste.

Generously grease two loaf pans and fill with loaf mixture. Bake for 1 hour, or until the tops are slightly golden. Serve with mushroom gravy if desired.

MAKES 2 LOAVES

# Vegetable-Walnut Pâté

*Guests love this pâté and seem to think it tastes like real chopped liver . . .*

1 tablespoon olive oil
½ cup minced onion
½ teaspoon salt
1½ cups chopped green beans
2 hard-boiled eggs (optional)
¼ cup chopped walnuts
1 to 2 tablespoons white wine or 2 teaspoons lemon juice
1 to 2 tablespoons mayonnaise
½ cup chopped parsley
pepper

Heat oil in a small skillet. Add onion and salt and saute over medium heat until onion begins to brown, about 10 minutes. Add the green beans and saute until tender.

Combine all ingredients together in a food processor and blend until a smooth paste forms. Spoon into a serving dish.

MAKES 3 CUPS

# tofu, tempeh & egg salad sandwich fillings

# Herb-Crusted Tofu

*This recipe is from* Vegetarian Cooking for Everyone *by Deborah Madison.*

16 ounces firm tofu
1 cup dried breadcrumbs
½ cup grated Parmesan or asiago cheese
1 tablespoon chopped parsley
1 teaspoon dried basil or marjoram
½ teaspoon dried thyme
½ teaspoon dried savory
1 egg, beaten with 2 tablespoons milk or soy milk
olive oil for frying

Slice the tofu into about ⅓-inch-thick pieces, then across to form triangles. Set the triangles on paper towels to drain. Meanwhile, combine the breadcrumbs, cheese, and herbs in a shallow dish. Dip each tofu triangle into the egg mixture and then the breadcrumb mixture, coating both sides.

Film a skillet with olive oil. When hot, add the tofu and fry on both sides over medium heat until golden and crisp, about 10 to 12 minutes.

MAKES ABOUT 18 TRIANGLES

# Happy Tuna Salad

*This is a very simple and delicious salad spread. Kids will love it. Serve it on bread, lettuce, or use it to stuff vegetables such as celery.*

8 ounces tempeh
1 cup diced celery
¼ cup sliced scallions
¼ cup sweet pickle relish
2 tablespoons minced parsley
½ cup mayonnaise

Steam tempeh for 20 minutes; cool and grate. Put the grated tempeh and remaining ingredients together in a bowl and mix well. Chill several hours before serving.

MAKES 1½ CUPS

# Egg Salad

*This recipe makes great egg salad and was found in* Secrets to Making Egg Salad *by "The Egg Maker" at Tassajara one season.*

To cook eggs, put a few inches of cold water in a saucepan, add a few pinches of salt and bring to a boil. Reduce heat to a simmer, then carefully add eggs making one layer. Cover and cook 20 minutes; cool with cold water. If the water warms up from the eggs, drain and replace with more cold water—this is essential for helping the eggs to peel easier later.

Use an egg slicer to chop the eggs once peeled. Constants in egg salad are chopped celery and a smaller amount of some kind of onion—green, red, or white will work. Shallots are also nice. Other constants are mayonnaise (or nayonnaise), salt, pepper, and Dijon or stone-ground mustard. Tassajara's most common recipe was simply to add sweet pickle relish to the above. Adding yogurt and curry powder is also tasty. Other popular additions are fresh or dried dill, other fresh minced herbs, cumin, chopped olives, sun-dried tomatoes, or chopped almonds.

# Eggless Egg Salad

*This unique salad has lots of texture, nutrition, and rich flavor from the sesame and peanut oils. It can be used the same as any egg salad—in pita, on bread, crackers, or greens.*

12 ounces firm tofu
3 scallions, minced
1 medium carrot, coarsely grated
1 stalk celery, finely minced
⅓ cup toasted sunflower seeds

1 teaspoon grated ginger
Tofu Mayonnaise (see page 92)
salt and fresh-ground pepper
tamari sauce

Cut the tofu into a bowl in ½-inch cubes. Add the scallions, carrot, celery, sunflower seeds, and ginger and then mix gently. Add the Tofu Mayonnaise, season to taste with the salt, pepper, and tamari sauce, and mix once again. Chill until ready to serve.

MAKES 2½ CUPS

# No Egg Salad

*This eggless salad spread is more traditional and has less fat than the Eggless Egg Salad. Try this mixture on pumpernickel bread topped with alfalfa sprouts.*

12 ounces firm tofu, mashed
¼ teaspoon tumeric
1 stalk celery, chopped
¼ cup minced onion
1½ tablespoons mayonnaise

1 tablespoon minced parsley
½ teaspoon dried dill
½ teaspoon salt
¼ teaspoon dry mustard
¼ teaspoon celery seed

Combine all ingredients in a bowl and mix well. Chill for about 1 hour before serving.

MAKES 2 CUPS

# Tofu Salad Sandwich Spread

*From the* Green's Cookbook: *"This salad has been on the Green's Restaurant menu since it opened. The tofu is seasoned with fresh herbs, mustard, capers, scallions, and finely diced vegetables, which also give it texture. This is a light, moist, satisfying sandwich filling, especially good on whole wheat bread."* The version below has had some creative input from Tassajara's guest cooks. I've also made this using wasabi mayonnaises and received rave reviews.

18 ounces firm tofu
5 tablespoons finely diced red bell pepper
5 tablespoons finely diced celery
4 tablespoons finely diced carrot
2 tablespoons minced red onions
2 tablespoons finely chopped fresh herbs: parsley, thyme, marjoram, and savory
½ cup mayonnaise or 5 tablespoons sesame oil
1½ tablespoons Dijon mustard
1 teaspoon red wine vinegar or sherry vinegar
tamari
salt and pepper

Rinse the tofu in cool water. To dry and crumble the tofu, place it in a clean towel, gather the corners together, and twist the towel around it until all the water has been squeezed out. Put the tofu in a bowl with the vegetables, herbs, mayonnaise or sesame oil, Dijon mustard and vinegar. Lightly mix everything together with a fork and then season with tamari, salt, and pepper. Although the taste may be bland at first, the flavors of the vegetables and herbs will strengthen and gradually permeate the salad as it sits. If possible, let it sit at least 30 minutes before using.

MAKES 3 CUPS

# Mexican Tempeh Salad

*This is a delicious variation to other tempeh, or tofu salads and children love it! Try adding some chipotle chiles for extra heat.*

1 cup vegetable stock

½ cup tamari

8 ounces tempeh

½ cup minced yellow onion

2 medium tomatoes, diced and drained well

2 tablespoons minced cilantro

½ cup salsa

⅓ cup mayonnaise

1 tablespoon fresh lemon juice

salt and pepper

Combine the vegetable stock and tamari in a saucepan. Add the tempeh and simmer for 20 minutes; drain. After the tempeh has cooled, grate, and then combine with remaining ingredients; mix well. Chill 1 hour before serving.

MAKES 2½ CUPS

VARIATION: *Try adding chipotle chiles. They are available canned for easy use. But remember, a little goes a long way.*

# Tofu Mayonnaise

*This is a homemade, non-dairy alternative to mayonnaise, otherwise known as Nayonniase.*

6 ounces soft tofu

1½ to 2 tablespoons fresh lemon juice

2 tablespoons oil

½ teaspoon salt or 1 tablespoon red miso

black pepper, to taste

Combine all ingredients in a food processor and blend until smooth.

MAKES ABOUT 1 CUP

*For a variety of mayonnaise flavors try adding some of these variations to the recipe above: Add ¼ cup diced onion; curry powder; 1 teaspoon chipotle chiles; fresh grated gingerroot; dill and garlic; diced celery and onion; 2 tablespoons tahini; miso; ¼ cup chopped leeks; dried herbs, such as oregano, marjoram, sorrel, and caraway.*

*Mexican Tempeh Salad*

# Tempeh Salad

*This is a tempeh version of tuna salad. For a variation, use tempeh made with hijiki and add fresh dill.*

1 cup vegetable stock
½ cup tamari
8 ounces tempeh
¾ cup chopped celery
¼ cup chopped dill pickles
½ cup minced red, yellow, or green onions
⅓ cup mayonnaise
1 tablespoon fresh lemon juice
¼ teaspoon pepper
paprika

Combine the vegetable stock and tamari in a saucepan. Add tempeh and simmer for 20 minutes; drain. After the tempeh has cooled, grate and then combine with remaining ingredients; mix well. Sprinkle with paprika and chill 1 hour before serving.

MAKES 2½ CUPS

# Tofu "Bits"
# in Kosho's Secret Tenzo Sauce

*Tofu Bacon Bits? Looks like this sauce isn't a "secret" anymore! Great with split pea soup or as a salad topping.*

SECRET TENZO SAUCE
 ½ cup tamari
 ⅓ cup mirin
 ¼ cup honey
 2 tablespoons sesame oil
 ½ teaspoon dry mustard

 32 ounces firm tofu

Preheat oven to 300 degrees F.

Combine all the ingredients for the Secret Tenzo Sauce. Crumble the tofu and toss with the sauce. Bake for 2 to 3 hours, stirring now and then. The "bits" are done when they are crunchy and granular.

MAKES 3 CUPS

# chutneys, sauces & salsas

# Pineapple-Papaya Chutney

*Make this fresh chutney in late spring and summer when papayas are in season. Fresh chiles, lime, and fragrant spices make this very lively. This chutney goes well with marinated tofu or grilled vegetables.*

3 cups cubed fresh pineapple (½-inch pieces)
1½ cups white vinegar
1 cup firmly packed brown sugar
1 medium onion, finely chopped
2 jalapeno peppers, finely chopped
2 cloves garlic, minced
½ cup finely chopped preserved ginger
½ cup seedless raisins
½ cup chopped papaya
½ fresh lime, peeled, seeded, and chopped
¼ cup chopped pitted dates
1 teaspoon cardamom
½ teaspoon salt
¼ teaspoon each ground cloves, ground allspice, and cayenne
¼ cup fresh lemon juice

Combine all ingredients except lemon juice in a heavy saucepan and bring to a boil. Reduce heat and simmer 1 hour, stirring frequently. Stir in lemon juice and simmer an additional 5 minutes. Cool completely before serving.

**MAKES 1 QUART**

*Variation: Any fruit such as peaches, apricots, plums, mangos, or apples can be substituted for the pineapple and/or papaya.*

# Apricot Chutney

*Fresh ginger and cayenne add just a hint of heat to this rich chutney. It makes a delicious sandwich with cream cheese.*

1 pound dried apricots
10 cloves garlic
3 to 6 inches ginger
1¼ cups red wine vinegar, divided
2 cups white sugar
¼ teaspoon salt
¼ to ¾ teaspoon cayenne
½ cup currants
¾ cup golden raisins

Soak the apricots in 4 cups of boiling water for 1 hour. Cut into ¼-inch pieces or chop until chunky in a food processor; set aside. Blend garlic, ginger, and ¼ cup vinegar in a food processor. Mix apricots, ginger mixture, remaining vinegar, sugar, salt, and cayenne and bring to a boil. Simmer for 45 minutes to 1 hour; add currants and raisins and simmer gently until thick. Allow the chutney to sit for 1 or 2 hours before serving.

The chutney will keep in the refrigerator for a 1 to 2 weeks if stored in a tightly sealed container.

MAKES 3 CUPS

# Date Chutney

*This chutney is delicious with goat cheese or cream cheese.*

1 cup pitted and chopped dried dates
1 tablespoon finely diced ginger
⅛ to ¼ teaspoon cayenne
½ teaspoon salt
4 tablespoons water
2 tablespoons chopped cilantro
juice of 1 lemon

Put all ingredients, except lemon juice, into a food processor and blend until smooth.Spoon into a bowl and add lemon juice, mixing thoroughly. Serve at room temperature.

MAKES 1 CUP

# Spicy Peanut Sambal

*This spicy, nutty sauce is good served with small salad-like dishes, fried tempeh, or raw vegetables. In Indonesia, this sambal is made in a mortar but you can use a blender or food processor instead, though it won't be the same consistency.*

3 to 4 jalapenos, chopped
4 cloves garlic
¼ cup peanut butter
5 teaspoons soy sauce
4 teaspoons lime juice
4 teaspoons tamarind paste
4 teaspoons brown sugar
2 tablespoons water, or more

Put all ingredients into a blender and blend until smooth. If the sauce seems too thick, add water a teaspoon at a time to reach the desired consistency.

MAKES ½ CUP

# Kamal's Sweet Tomato Chutney

*This spicy-sweet chutney is great with goat cheese and roasted vegetables.*

¼ teaspoon fenugreek
¼ teaspoon fennel
2 bay leaves
¼ teaspoon ground mace
¼ teaspoon garam marsala
3 medium-sized tomatoes (about ¾ pound total), finely chopped
10 cloves garlic, minced
1½ teaspoons grated ginger
¼ cup raisins
¼ teaspoon cayenne
2 cups white vinegar
1¼ teaspoons salt
2 cups sugar

Grind the first 5 ingredients together in a spice mill and set aside. Combine the tomatoes, garlic, ginger, raisins, cayenne, and spice mixture in a heavy skillet. Cook, uncovered, over medium-high heat, stirring occasionally, until most of the liquid is evaporated, about 12 minutes.

Add the vinegar, salt, and sugar and bring to a boil. Reduce the heat, cover, and simmer until thick, about 15 to 20 minutes. Spoon into clean jars and seal or refrigerate.

MAKES 2 CUPS

# Sweet and Fragrant
# Pineapple Chutney

*What do you do with a pineapple that is too tart? Turn it into this delicious chutney.*

1 average-sized, medium-ripe pineapple
1½ teaspoons ground cumin
1½ teaspoons ground fennel
¼ teaspoon cinnamon
¼ to ½ teaspoon cayenne
¼ to ½ teaspoon black pepper
juice of l lemon
1½ teaspoons coarse salt, or to taste
1½ cups sugar

Peel and core the pineapple. Put the pineapple into a food processor and process until coarsely pureed (or chop the pulp finely, using a sharp knife).

Put the pureed pineapple and all the other ingredients in a medium-sized pan over medium heat. Heat the mixture, stirring often, until the sugar completely dissolves and bring to a boil. Cook, uncovered, over low heat until the contents of the pan look thick and glazed like jam, about 30 minutes.

Turn off the heat, pour into sterilized jars, and seal. Although it is ready to serve, the flavor improves with 2 to 3 days of resting at room temperature. It will keep indefinitely until opened, then it needs to be refrigerated.

MAKES 4 CUPS

# Peach Chutney

*Make this chutney during the summer when peaches are sweet and plentiful. Serve over fresh soft cheeses with crackers as an appetizer or with savory spreads to add balance.*

2 tablespoons oil
1 cup finely chopped onion
2 cloves garlic
10 ripe peaches, peeled and sliced
2 to 4 tablespoons cider vinegar
¼ cup honey

¼ teaspoon cinnamon
⅛ teaspoon nutmeg
⅛ teaspoon cardamom
⅛ teaspoon cayenne
1 teaspoon fresh grated ginger

Heat the oil and saute onion and garlic until golden brown. Add the peaches and cider vinegar and cook until the peaches begin to soften. Add the remaining ingredients and simmer until the sauce reaches a chunky consistency, about 30 minutes or so. Spoon into clean jars and seal or refrigerate up to 2 weeks.

MAKES 1 QUART

# Mint Chutney

*Mint, ginger and chiles give a vibrant flavor to sandwiches, or mix with yogurt and serve as a dip.*

4 cups fresh mint leaves, packed
1 medium-sized onion, chopped
1 ounce fresh gingerroot, peeled and chopped
4 fresh green chiles
1 tablespoon fresh lemon juice
1½ tablespoons water
1½ tablespoons oil
sugar, to taste

In a blender, combine the mint leaves and all other ingredients. Blend to a fine paste. Store in covered container in refrigerator up to 1 week.

MAKES 1 CUP

"Empowering yourself to cook means giving yourself permission to try things out, to find things out. You allow your curiosity and enthusiasm some space to cavort, tasting and experimenting with unfamiliar (and familiar) ingredients. Although you may have a tentative plan or agenda, still you leave yourself space to follow your nose or play it by ear."

—EDWARD ESPE BROWN

# Green Coconut Chutney

*This chutney is unlike that of other chutneys in taste and texture. Try it with grilled vegetables, tofu, or curries.*

1 lemon
1 to 2 fresh green chiles, seeded and chopped
½ cup chopped fresh mint or cilantro
2 scallions, chopped
1 teaspoon salt
1 cup shredded coconut
1 teaspoon oil
2 teaspoons black mustard seeds
2 teaspoons cumin seeds

Peel the lemon so the white pith remains, then cut into pieces and remove seeds.

Put into a blender or food processor with the chiles, mint, scallions, and salt and puree. Add coconut and continue blending until it forms a smooth paste, adding water if necessary.

Heat oil in a small pan and fry the mustard seeds until they pop, then add the cumin seeds. Add to the coconut paste and stir. Serve at room temperature. This chutney solidifies if chilled. Keeps refrigerated for 1 week.

**MAKES 2 CUPS**

# Date-Coconut Chutney

*This sweet and savory chutney adds exotic taste and texture to sandwiches.*

4 ounces pitted dates, chopped
3 tablespoons shredded coconut
4 tablespoons fresh lemon juice
2 tablespoons grated ginger
½ teaspoon ground fennel seeds
½ teaspoon coriander
¼ cup chopped fresh parsley
½ teaspoon salt
¼ teaspoon cayenne (optional)

Mix together all ingredients and let sit for flavors to blend. If too thick, add lemon juice or water. Store tightly covered in the refrigerator. Keeps about 2 weeks.

MAKES 1 CUP

# Peanut Chutney

*Mako's words of wisdom: It is important that cilantro always be chopped before using in a food processor or blender to ensure even blending. Use this chutney as a condiment spread on sandwiches, with grilled tofu or vegetables, or with curries.*

2 hot green chiles, seeded, deveined, and chopped
1 cup roasted peanuts
½ cup chopped cilantro
1 teaspoon coriander
1 tablespoon grated fresh ginger
½ cup yogurt
1 teaspoon sugar
½ teaspoon salt

Put ingredients together in a blender and blend until a fine but slightly coarse mixture forms. If necessary, let the mixture sit for an hour so that it softens, then resume blending into a soft paste. Serve at room temperature. Store in covered container in refrigerator up to 1 week.

MAKES 2 CUPS

# Miso Sauce

*This sauce is delicious with deep-fried eggplant and the Wa Fu Dressing (see page 128) for salads. It's a very adaptable sauce.*

kombu or kombu/shiitake stock, rice vinegar, or sesame oil to thin to desired
  consistency
¼ cup mirin
⅓ cup sugar
¾ cup white miso

Heat the stock and whisk in the other ingredients (don't bring to a full boil for the sake of the miso). Can thicken with cornstarch. Store in a covered container in refrigerator.

MAKES ABOUT 1½ CUPS

# Sweet Pepper Sauce

*This roasted pepper and tomato sauce can be used as a compliment to polenta, pasta or roasted vegetables.*

1½ pounds sweet bell peppers
2 tablespoons olive oil
1 cup chopped onion
¼ cup chopped celery with leaves
1 teaspoon minced garlic
1½ cups peeled, seeded, and minced tomatoes
½ teaspoon thyme
salt and pepper, to taste

Preheat oven to 400 degrees F. Place bell peppers on a lightly oiled baking pan and roast for 45 minutes, turning once or twice, until the skin is charred. Cut roasted peppers into ½-inch strips. Heat oil and saute onion and celery until wilted and golden. Add garlic and cook for 30 seconds. Stir in tomatoes, peppers, and thyme. Cover and simmer for 5 minutes. Uncover and simmer for 15 to 30 minutes (or until thickened, which depends on the juiciness of the tomatoes). Puree the mixture in a blender or food processor until smooth. Season with salt and pepper.

# Cappon Magro Sauce

*Try this sauce over hot potatoes, beets, artichokes, hard-boiled eggs, or in pasta salad.*

1 thick slice white bread, crusts
removed
2 tablespoons red wine vinegar
1 clove garlic, minced
2 tablespoons marjoram leaves
3 tablespoons capers, drained

½ cup pine nuts
1 cup finely minced parsley
2 tablespoons pitted green olives
⅓ to ½ cup extra virgin olive oil
salt and pepper, to taste

Soak the bread in vinegar. In a mortar and pestle, combine the garlic, marjoram, capers, pine nuts, parsley, and olives. Pound them until you have a coarse puree. Add the soaked bread and olive oil and grind some more. Season with salt and pepper and add a little more oil and/or vinegar if necessary to thin. The sauce should be thick, almost like a paste. Store in a covered container in refrigerator upto 1 week.

MAKES 2 CUPS

# Romesco Sauce

*There are many versions of this Catalan sauce, but this version is well suited for vegetables and as a topping for sandwiches or crostini. Try it over warm white beans or roasted potatoes.*

⅓ cup blanched almonds, or a mixture
of hazelnuts and almonds
1 roasted red bell pepper, seeded and
diced
3 cloves garlic
1 tablespoon chopped parsley
¼ teaspoon salt

1 teaspoon sweet paprika
½ teaspoon red pepper flakes
¼ cup red wine vinegar or sherry
vinegar
½ cup extra virgin olive oil, preferably
Spanish
salt and pepper, to taste

Toast the almonds until they are lightly browned. Finely chop them in a food processor, then add the remaining ingredients except the vinegar, oil, salt, and pepper and puree. Gradually pour in the vinegar, then the oil. Taste for salt and pepper. Store in a covered container in refrigerator up to 1 week.

MAKES 2 CUPS

# Chermoula
# (Moraccan Green Sauce)

*This Moroccan marinade for fish is also wonderful with vegetables—especially sweet ones like beets, carrots, and winter squash, or the more tender tomatoes and eggplant.*

4 cloves garlic, coarsely chopped

1 teaspoon salt

⅔ cup finely chopped cilantro

⅓ cup finely chopped parsley

1½ teaspoons sweet paprika

½ teaspoon cumin

⅛ teaspoon cayenne

¼ cup extra virgin olive oil

juice of 2 lemons

Pound the garlic with the salt in a mortar until smooth. Add the cilantro and parsley and pound a little more to bruise the leaves and release their flavor. Stir in the spices, olive oil, and lemon juice, to taste. Store in refrigerator up to 1 week.

MAKES 1½ CUPS

# Yogurt Sauce
# with Cayenne and Dill

*Although simple, this sauce is excellent spooned over grains, tossed with raw vegetables, or even stirred into lentils or spinach to make a quick salad. Since it's a condiment, use whole milk yogurt to give it body and texture.*

1 cup whole milk yogurt

½ cup sour cream

1 large clove garlic, minced

½ teaspoon salt

2 teaspoons chopped fresh dill

¼ teaspoon cayenne or hot paprika, or to taste

Whisk the yogurt and sour cream together. Mash the garlic with the salt in a mortar to a paste; measure 1 teaspoon, then add it to the yogurt with the dill and cayenne. Refrigerate for 1 hour to let the flavors to develop.

MAKES 1½ CUPS

# Cha Cha Sauce

*This peanut sauce is an adaptation of a peanut sambal used in Indonesian dishes. Try it with deep-fried strips of tempeh or tofu.*

8 cloves garlic, mashed into a paste
2½ tablespoons grated gingerroot
¼ cup tamarind paste
¼ cup lime juice
¼ cup brown sugar
⅓ cup tamari
½ cup chunky peanut butter
cayenne pepper, to taste
salt and pepper, to taste
dry mustard to taste (optional)

Mix together all ingredients in a bowl. The hotness and blend of flavors depends on your personal preference as always. Leave some chunks of peanuts when blending for a nice texture. Add water to thin if necessary. Store in a covered container in refrigerator up to 2 weeks.

**MAKES 2 CUPS**

# Pine Nut Sauce
# with Lemon and Garlic

*This tartar sauce uses pine nuts, but depending on where in the Middle East it's made, the nuts could be almonds, hazelnuts, or walnuts. It's excellent with cooked greens, grilled vegetables, and warm pita bread.*

1 slice dense white bread, crusts removed
1 clove garlic
¼ teaspoon salt
½ cup pine nuts, toasted
½ to 1 cup water or vegetable stock
2 tablespoons fresh lemon juice
salt
chopped parsley
paprika or cayenne, to taste

Cover the bread with a little water and set aside to soak. In a mortar or food processor, grind the garlic, salt, and nuts. Squeeze the bread to remove the water. Add bread to the mix as well. Add water or stock until the sauce is smooth and thin, then season with lemon juice and taste for salt. The sauce will thicken as it sits so you may need to thin it out again with a little warm water. Pour into a bowl, sprinkle with a little chopped parsley and a dash of paprika or cayenne. Store in a covered container in refrigerator up to 1 week.

MAKES 2 CUPS

# Salsa de Mancha Manteles

*A mole-lover's salsa! Try this with crisp tortilla chips or compose an appetizer plate trio using this salsa, Black Bean Spread (see page 000), Mexican Tempeh Salad (see page 88), and fresh corn tortillas.*

½ cup blanched, roasted almonds
3 tablespoons toasted sesame seeds
½ stick cinnamon
½ cup raisins
1 tablespoon vegetable oil (or sunflower, safflower, or soy)
1 clove garlic
2 cups dried red chiles, boiled and ground
1 ounce dark chocolate, chopped
sugar, to taste
salt, to taste

Place almonds, sesame seeds, cinnamon, and raisins into a food processor and blend to make a paste; set aside.

In a large pan, add oil and cook garlic until browned. Add the ground chiles and the almond mixture and cook until thickened. Add the chocolate and heat through until melted. Add the sugar and salt to taste. If the paste is very thick or spicy, try adding a little tomato paste. Store in refrigerator up to 2 weeks.

**MAKES 2 CUPS**

# Salsa Verde with Walnuts and Tarragon

*Everything in this sauce should be chopped fine—by hand for the best flavor and texture.*

½ cup walnut pieces
2 small cloves garlic
1 cup Italian parsley (about 1 large bunch)
2 tablespoons tarragon
2 tablespoons capers, rinsed
1 cup extra virgin olive oil
1 teaspoon red wine vinegar, or to taste
salt and fresh-ground pepper, to taste

Combine the nuts, garlic, parsley, tarragon, and capers in a small bowl. Stir in the oil and vinegar, then season with salt and pepper to taste. Store in a jar in refrigerator.

MAKES 2 CUPS

# Cilantro Salsa

*Use this as a dip, in sandwiches in place of condiments, or with grilled vegetables.*

1 jalapeno pepper
1 large bunch cilantro, stems removed
½ cup basil leaves
¼ cup mint leaves
2 cloves garlic, minced
juice from 1 or 2 limes
¼ cup water
½ cup plus 2 tablespoons olive oil
½ teaspoon cumin
½ teaspoon coriander
salt, to taste

Chop everything very finely, then stir in water, oil, and seasonings. Taste for salt and adjust the balance of lime juice to oil if needed. Store in a covered container in refrigerator up to 1 week.

MAKES 2 CUPS

# marinades for tofu, tempeh & vegetables

"In the beginner's mind there are many possibilities,
but in the expert's there are few."

—SHUNRYU SUZUKI ROSHI

At Tassajara, the Bag Lunch Crew often uses an experimental approach to marinades. They try using different amounts of soy sauce, mushroom stir-fry sauce, mirin, sake, rice vinegar, and sesame oil in combination with pickled ginger, minced fresh ginger, minced garlic, chili flakes, red onion slices, red pepper slices, scallions, basil, peanut butter (thinned with water), and tahini (thinned with water).

They also went for an Italian approach with olive oil mixed with equal parts of balsamic vinegar and soy sauce in combination with fresh herbs such as rosemary, oregano, basil, thyme, sage, and savory.

For marinating tofu, simply cut each block into ⅓-inch-thick slices or for triangles, cut each slice again diagonally to make a triangle. (A block of tofu could be anywhere from 4 to 6 ounces depending on the brand.) The marinade is then poured over the tofu and baked for 20 to 30 minutes at 350 degrees F.

If pressed tofu is needed, place the tofu on a pie plate and top with a second plate. Weight the plate with a heavy pan and press for at least 30 minutes. If the tofu used was fresh and fairly dry when marinated, the marinade can be boiled, strained, and kept refrigerated for reuse.

Although some recipes call for marinating the tofu for hours or overnight, Deborah Madison (*Green's Cookbook*), says that another effective use of a marinade is to use it as a cooking liquid. Simply pour the marinade over the tofu as it cooks. Try it either way.

The marinades listed for tofu can also be used for vegetables. For vegetables such as zucchini, squash, and eggplant, cut them into ¼- to ⅓-inch-thick slices, dip into bowls of marinade and place on an oiled sheet pan. Leave the portobello and shiitake mushrooms whole so they retain their juices. Bake for 15 to 20 minutes at 375 degrees F. Turn over and bake another 15 to 20 minutes, or until tender but still retaining their texture. For deeper flavors, marinate the vegetables for up to 2 hours, then cook as desired.

Suggested vegetables that lend themselves well to marinating are red and green bell peppers, summer squashes, new potatoes, onions, fennel, mushrooms, southwestern peppers, and eggplant. Try roasting, grilling, or baking after marinating. At Tassajara, the marinated vegetables are baked or roasted when used for the Bag Lunch.

*Sesame Marinade*

# Sesame Marinade

*This recipe is from* Vegetarian Cooking for Everyone *by Deborah Madison. This marinade makes an excellent sauce for grilled eggplant and Chinese noodles as well as tofu.*

2 tablespoons light sesame oil

1 tablespoon dark sesame oil

¼ cup soy sauce

5 teaspoons balsamic or rice wine vinegar

1½ tablespoons sugar, or to taste

½ teaspoon red pepper flakes

2 tablespoons chopped scallions

1½ tablespoons chopped cilantro

Combine all ingredients together in a bowl and stir until the sugar is dissolved. Taste and adjust for sweetness if needed. Depending on the type of soy sauce you've used, you may need to add more sugar for balance.

MAKES 1 CUP

# Orange-Balsamic Marinated Tofu

*This citrus-flavored marinade goes particularly well with fresh basil. Use any leftover marinade to dress a salad made of mixed greens, sliced oranges and slivered almonds.*

12 ounces firm tofu

3 tablespoons fresh lemon juice

3 tablespoons fresh orange juice

⅔ cup balsamic vinegar

4 cloves garlic, minced

1 teaspoon salt

1 cup olive oil

fresh basil, chopped, to taste (optional)

Slice the block of tofu into thirds and then cut each third into slices. Combine all ingredients except tofu in a bowl and mix well; adjust seasonings. Pour marinade over tofu and let sit for at least 2 hours or longer in the refrigerator. Remove tofu from marinade and put on a slanted surface, usually a cutting board or baking tray to drain; drain for 20 minutes. It is now ready to grill, bake, or fry.

MAKES ABOUT 1½ CUPS

# The Tassajara Marinated Tofu

*This marinade is from* The Tassajara Recipe Book *by Edward Espe Brown. This is a strong marinade, very rich in earthy flavors. If using tofu, be sure to cut it into about ½-inch slices in order for it to absorb the marinade. This is the main marinade Tassajara uses to make brochettes—marinated tofu and vegetables on skewers for grilling or on the barbecue.*

2 (12-ounce) blocks firm tofu
½ ounce dried mushrooms
1 cup water
2 teaspoons dried oregano
2 cloves garlic, minced
½ cup fruity olive oil
½ cup sherry wine vinegar or red wine vinegar
½ cup red wine
½ cup soy sauce (tamari if possible)
pinch of ground cloves
½ teaspoon salt
fresh-ground black pepper

Drain and press the tofu (as explained on page 115) to remove excess water.

In a saucepan, simmer the mushrooms in water for 15 minutes. Toast the oregano in a small frying pan over medium heat until it becomes aromatic (without burning).

Combine all ingredients except tofu. Bring to a boil and simmer about 3 to 4 minutes more.

Cut the tofu into 4 slices and place in a baking dish. Pour the hot marinade over the tofu. Marinate in the refrigerator for at least 2 hours, preferably overnight. The tofu can marinate several days. Grill, bake, or broil tofu or vegetables as desired.

MAKES ABOUT 3 CUPS

# Judith's Marinade

*The addition of mirin gives this marinade a subtle sweetness.*

| | |
|---|---|
| 1 cup tamari | ⅓ cup sesame oil |
| ⅔ cup mirin | 2 teaspoons dry mustard |
| 2 cloves garlic, minced | ¾ cup water |

Combine all ingredients in a small bowl. Can use to marinate vegetables or tofu.

MAKES 3 CUPS

# Tofu Teriyaki

*This recipe is also from* The Tassajara Recipe Cookbook *by Edward Espe Brown. This dish is fairly juicy, so it's excellent served over plain rice or noodles.*

| | |
|---|---|
| 2 (12-ounce) blocks firm tofu | 1 tablespoon grated fresh ginger |
| 1 cup soy sauce | 6 cloves garlic, minced |
| ½ cup sake or white wine | ¼ cup sesame oil |
| ½ cup sugar (or part honey) | 1½ teaspoons dry mustard |

Cut the tofu blocks in half and press as described on page 115 if necessary. Cut the tofu in approximately 1 x 1 x 2-inch-thick slices.

Meanwhile, combine the rest of the ingredients in a saucepan and heat to boiling; simmer for 10 minutes. Pour the hot marinade over the tofu and let marinate a few hours or overnight, if desired. Bake tofu, uncovered, at 350 degrees F for about 45 minutes, or until heated through. You can also saute onions, bell peppers and mushrooms for about 2 minutes, layer with tofu, and then bake as directed above.

MAKES ABOUT 3 CUPS

# Tofu Marinated
# with Parsley and Olive Oil

*This tofu is a little unusual, as the tofu is not cooked after marinating. It has a fresh, herb and garlic taste. It can be grilled or, if preferred, it can be baked at 350 degrees F for about 40 minutes.*

2 (12-ounce) blocks firm tofu
3 cloves garlic, minced
1 cup finely chopped parsley
½ teaspoon salt
pinch black pepper
3 tablespoons capers
⅓ cup fresh lemon juice
fresh herbs such as basil, oregano, or thyme (optional)
⅓ cup olive oil

Slice blocks of tofu into thirds and then each third into slices, then into cubes. Mix garlic, parsley, salt, pepper, capers, lemon juice, and fresh herbs, if using, in a small mixing bowl. Let stand for a few minutes, and then pour in the olive oil; stir to combine. Coat each piece of tofu with the mixture and then layer in shallow sheet pan. Let stand overnight and serve on platters with a garnish of fresh herbs. Serve at room temperature.

MAKES ABOUT 3 CUPS

# Honey-Mustard Tofu

*This is the most requested tofu recipe for the Bag Lunch at Tassajara.*

½ cup fresh lemon juice
¼ cup olive or other vegetable oil
2 tablespoons honey
¼ cup Dijon mustard
salt and fresh-ground pepper, to taste
1 (12-ounce) package firm tofu

Preheat oven to 350 degrees F. Whisk the lemon juice, oil, honey, and mustard in a small bowl; add salt and pepper and then set aside.

Drain and press tofu if necessary. Cut block of tofu into thirds and then each third into triangles. Place in a 9 x 13-inch baking pan and pour the marinade over top, making sure to completely cover. Let tofu marinate for at least 2 hours and then bake for 20 to 30 minutes, or until crispy but still moist inside.

MAKES 6 TRIANGLES

# Hoisin Marinade

*This is a classic hoisin marinade, delicious for barbecued tofu.*

¼ cup hoisin sauce
¼ cup mirin
2½ tablespoons soy sauce
1½ tablespoons brown sugar
1½ tablespoons ketchup
3 cloves garlic, minced

Combine all ingredients in a bowl and blend well.

MAKES 1 CUP

"So the secret is to just say 'Yes!' and jump off from here. Then there is no problem. It means to be yourself, always yourself, without sticking to an old self."

—SHUNRYU SUZUKI ROSHI

# salads, dressings, pickles & relishes

# Couscous Salad

*The flavors of Dijon mustard and coriander add zing to this delicious grain salad. A perfect addition to any picnic.*

1⅓ cups water
1 cup couscous
½ teaspoon salt
⅓ cup olive oil
¼ cup lemon juice
2 cloves garlic, minced
1½ teaspoons Dijon mustard
1½ teaspoons ground coriander
fresh-ground black pepper, to taste
1 cup cooked garbanzo beans
½ cup chopped green onions
1 cup chopped tomato
½ cup seeded and chopped cucumber
½ cup minced parsley

In a small saucepan, bring the water to a boil and add the couscous and salt. Remove the pan from the heat, cover, and let sit 5 minutes. Just before using, fluff with a fork.

To make the dressing, whisk together the olive oil, lemon juice, garlic, Dijon, coriander, and pepper in a small bowl.

In a large bowl, combine the couscous, garbanzo beans, green onions, tomato, cucumber and parsley; mix well. Add the dressing and toss to combine. Chill for at least 2 hours before serving to allow the flavors to develop.

MAKES ABOUT 4 CUPS

# Edamame Salad

*This is a delicious way to incorporate fresh, high-protein edamame into your diet. Serve it as a side to Tofu Teriyaki (see page 123).*

¾ ounce dried arame (seaweed)
3 tablespoons rice vinegar
3 tablespoons soy sauce
2 tablespoons sesame oil
1 teaspoon sugar
1 tablespoon sesame seeds
1 red bell pepper, cut into thin slices
1 green bell pepper, cut into thin slices
1 cup fresh edemame, cooked
16 ounces soba noodles, cooked

Soak the seaweed in warm water to cover for 5 minutes. Drain and then squeeze out excess water.

Stir together the rice vinegar, soy sauce, sesame oil, and sugar in a bowl until well dissolved. Combine the sesame seeds, bell peppers, edamame, and noodles and then toss with dressing. Serve cold.

MAKES 1½ QUARTS

VARIATION: *Instead of using soba noodles, increase edamame noodles to 16 ounces and make it a marinated vegetable salad.*

# Cabbage Shanghai Salad

*This is a delicious, light salad. Try using it as a complement to Asian meals.*

2 cups hot water
4 cups shredded nappa cabbage
2 cloves garlic, minced
1 teaspoon ginger
2 tablespoons black sesame seeds
½ cup rice vinegar
2 tablespoons sesame oil
2 tablespoons honey
salt, to taste

Just before serving, pour hot water over cabbage, cover and let sit to wilt, about 10 minutes; drain. Combine remaining ingredients in a separate bowl and then toss with cabbage.

MAKES 1½ QUARTS

# Eggplant and Red Pepper Salad

*This salad makes a wonderful addition to antipasto platters with Tuscan White Bean Salad (see page 137), hard-boiled eggs, and olives.*

1 pound Japanese eggplant, ¼-inch diagonal slices
2 tablespoons olive oil
3 cloves garlic, minced
salt and fresh-ground pepper, to taste
1 red bell pepper, cut into matchsticks
¼ cup thinly sliced shallots
2 tablespoons pine nuts, lightly toasted
balsamic vinegar, to taste

Toss eggplant with olive oil, garlic, salt, and pepper. Bake at 400 degrees F for 15 to 20 minutes, or until just barely done. Combine eggplant, bell pepper, shallots, and pine nuts (reserve a few for the garnish) in a small bowl. Add balsamic vinegar to taste. Garnish with reserved nuts.

MAKES 4 CUPS

# Peperonata

*Try this summer dish when tomatoes and peppers abound. Serve it with bruschetta, pasta, or composed salad plates.*

2 tablespoons olive oil
1 onion, diced
2 cloves garlic, thinly sliced
1 bay leaf
½ teaspoon minced fresh thyme
1 each red, yellow, and green bell pepper, diced or sliced
¼ teaspoon salt
3 ripe tomatoes, peeled, seeded, and diced
pepper, to taste

Heat the olive oil in a wide skillet. Add the onion, garlic, bay leaf, and thyme. Cook over medium-high heat, stirring frequently, until the onions are soft and lightly colored, about 10 minutes. Add the peppers, season with salt, and raise the heat. Cook briskly until the peppers begin to soften, then add the tomatoes and reduce the heat to medium. Simmer, stirring occasionally, until the excess water from the tomato has cooked away, about 15 minutes. Discard bay leaf. Taste for salt and season with pepper.

MAKES 4 CUPS

# Green Rice Salad

*This salad gets its vibrant green color from fresh herbs. Serve at picnics or barbecues with tofu and vegetable brochettes.*

BALSAMIC VINAIGRETTE
  ¼ cup olive oil
  1 tablespoon balsamic vinegar
  2 teaspoons fresh lemon juice
  1½ tablespoons minced green onions
  1 tablespoon minced parsley
  2 to 3 cloves garlic, minced
  ¼ teaspoon sugar
  salt and pepper, to taste

  1 cup cooked long-grain brown rice
  1 cup cooked long-grain white rice
  ½ cup finely chopped green onions
  1 to 1½ cups fresh herbs, minced (parsley, cilantro, oregano, tarragon, or thyme)
  ½ cup grated white cheddar or asiago cheese
  1 cup frozen peas, thawed
  ⅓ cup pine nuts
  shredded lettuce
  sprig of fresh herbs

Combine all the vinaigrette ingredients together. Toss with the warm rice and then let cool. Toss with onions, herbs, cheese, peas, and nuts. Serve on shredded lettuce, and garnish with fresh herbs.

MAKES 1½ QUARTS

# Mango Pepper Salad

*This is a delightful and refreshing salad. Serve it in hollowed-out vegetables as a salad or appetizer, or compose a lunch plate with this and Garlic, Cilantro, and Chipotle Hummus (see page 61).*

3 mangos, cut into ¾-inch cubes
2 green bell peppers, julienned
½ red onion, sliced, then cut slices in half to create moons
2 tablespoons chopped mint
¼ cup wine vinegar
2 tablespoons brown sugar
1 tablespoon olive oil
salt and fresh-ground pepper, to taste
cilantro, for garnish

Combine all ingredients in a bowl and let sit about 30 minutes before serving.

MAKES 1½ QUARTS

# Tuscan White Bean Salad

*This recipe is great with Eggplant and Red Pepper Salad (see page 133), hard-boiled eggs, and olives on antipasto plates. You can also add diced red bell peppers and/or carrots.*

2 whole cloves
2 bay leaves
several sprigs fresh thyme
several fresh sage leaves
few black peppercorns
1½ cups dried small white beans, soaked overnight
2 to 3 cloves garlic, minced
½ teaspoon salt
1½ to 2 teaspoons Dijon mustard
3 tablespoons sherry wine vinegar
⅔ cup olive oil
1 small red onion, diced
½ cup diced celery
1 tablespoon each minced summer savory or fresh oregano and Italian parsley
6 to 8 kalamata olives, finely chopped
salt and fresh-ground black pepper, to taste

Tie the cloves, bay leaves, thyme, sage, and peppercorns into a piece of cheesecloth or put into a tea ball. Simmer the beans with the herbs in 2 quarts water until tender and soft, but still hold their shape, about 1 hour; drain and remove herbs.

Pound the garlic and salt into a paste and combine with the mustard and vinegar. Whisk in the olive oil and taste for seasoning. While the beans are still warm, gently toss with the vinaigrette and remaining ingredients; adjust seasonings. Garnish with olives and herbs. For deeper flavor, allow the salad to marinate before serving.

MAKES 2 QUARTS

# Indonesian Salad
# with Peanut Dressing

*This salad is definitely worth the effort. The rich peanut dressing is the perfect complement to fresh, crunchy vegetables and tofu.*

1 tablespoon peanut oil

16 ounces firm tofu, cut into 1-inch cubes

6 cups mixed baby salad greens

1 cup French green beans or sugar snap peas, lightly blanched

1 carrot, peeled and julienned

2 medium tomatoes, cut into 4 wedges each

1 cup mung bean sprouts

1 small cucumber, peeled, seeded, and sliced into moons

¼ cup cilantro leaves

PEANUT DRESSING

½ cup firm silken tofu

3 tablespoons peanut butter

2 tablespoons soy sauce

5 tablespoons rice vinegar

2 tablespoons maple syrup

1 tablespoon sugar

1 tablespoon grated ginger

¼ teaspoon red chili flakes

4 tablespoons light coconut milk

1 scallion, finely chopped

Heat oil in a small skillet and cook tofu cubes until lightly browned. Drain on paper towels and set aside. On a large platter, arrange salad greens, green beans, carrot, tomatoes, sprouts, and cucumber. Sprinkle with tofu cubes.

For the dressing, combine all ingredients in a blender and blend until smooth and creamy. Pour dressing over salad and serve garnished with cilantro leaves.

MAKES 1½ QUARTS

"Enter into your own body. There you'll find a
solid place to put your feet."

—KABIR

# Cabbage Salad with Miso "Floating Cloud" Dressing

*The Miso Floating Cloud Dressing is very popular at Tassajara and is what sets this cabbage salad apart. It is also good with a salad made of cabbage, tomatoes, and tofu.*

⅔ cup vegetable oil (or safflower, sunflower, or soy)
1 teaspoon sesame oil
¼ cup lemon juice or rice vinegar
¼ cup red miso
1 clove garlic, minced
¼ teaspoon each powdered ginger and dry mustard, or to taste
4 cups shredded green cabbage
1 red bell pepper, julienned
1 red onion, julienned
½ cup toasted walnuts

Whisk together in a bowl the oils, lemon juice or vinegar, miso, garlic, ginger, and mustard.

Toss the cabbage, bell pepper, onion, and nuts in a medium-sized bowl. Pour dressing over top and mix well. Serve.

MAKES 1½ QUARTS

# Japanese Marinated Salad
# with Diced Tofu

*This salad can also be used as a sandwich filling if drained well before using.*

2 tablespoons soy sauce

3 tablespoons sesame oil

1 tablespoon rice vinegar

½ teaspoon sugar

12 ounces extra-firm tofu, pressed and cut into ½-inch cubes

1 cucumber, peeled, seeded, and diced

1 small carrot, diced

1 tomato, chopped fine

10 green beans, blanched and chopped fine

Whisk together the soy sauce, oil, vinegar, and sugar in a small bowl. Then combine the tofu and vegetables in a large bowl. Add dressing, cover bowl, and marinate for 8 to 10 hours in the refrigerator. Drain the vegetables slightly before serving.

MAKES 2 CUPS

# Tabbouli Salad

*This is a traditional Tabbouli salad, but here currants embellish the recipe.*

| | |
|---|---|
| 1 cup bulgur | salt and fresh pepper |
| 2¼ cups boiling water | 3 tablespoons fresh lemon juice |
| 1 cup minced green onions | ½ cup chopped mint |
| 1 cup minced parsley | 4 tablespoons olive oil |
| 1 tomato, chopped | ¼ cup currants (optional) |

Put the bulgur into a medium bowl and cover with boiling water. Cover the bowl with a plate and let sit for 20 minutes; drain with a fine mesh strainer.

Add the green onions, parsley, tomato, salt, and pepper and mix well; add lemon juice and then refrigerate. Just before serving, add mint, olive oil, and currants, if desired, and toss well. Serve in a bowl lined with lettuce leaves.

**MAKES ABOUT 5 CUPS**

# Tassajara Bean Salad

*This is Tassajara's version of the traditional bean salad recipe. The Balsamic Vinaigrette goes particularly well with beans. Canned beans can also be used, but be sure to rinse well before using.*

½ cup dried black beans, cleaned, rinsed, and soaked, or 1 cup canned
½ cup dried white beans, cleaned, rinsed, and soaked, or 1 cup canned
½ cup dried pink beans, cleaned, rinsed, and soaked, or 1 cup canned
1 cup fresh green beans, slice into ½-inch diagonals
¼ cup sliced black olives
1 each red and green bell pepper, diced
½ cup diced celery
½ cup diced water chestnuts
fresh herbs, to taste (oregano, parsley, rosemary, thyme)

BALSAMIC VINAIGRETTE
⅓ cup balsamic vinegar
2½ tablespoons red wine vinegar
2 shallots, minced
salt and pepper, to taste
1¼ cups extra virgin olive oil

Cook the dried beans separately. Drain the beans, cover them with 6 cups fresh water and then bring to a boil. Boil, uncovered, for 10 minutes; skim off any foam. Lower the heat, cover, and simmer until the beans are tender, about 1 hour. If using canned beans, skip this step but rinse the beans well.

To make the vinaigrette, combine vinegars, shallots, and salt and pepper; whisk in the olive oil and taste for balance. While the beans are still warm, gently combine the beans with the vinaigrette; set aside.

Drop green beans into boiling water for 1 minute, remove, drain and rinse in cold water; set aside.

Combine the beans, green beans, and remaining ingredients. Toss with the vinaigrette and serve.

MAKES 1½ QUARTS

"This is the secret of the teaching. It may be so, but it is not always so. Without being caught by words or rules, without many preconceived ideas, we actually do something, and doing something, we apply our teaching."

—SHUNRYU SUZUKI ROSHI

# Wa Fu Dressing

*Try this dressing with a salad of wakame, carrots, daikon, cucumbers, radishes, and cherry tomatoes. Dress generously.*

½ cup tamari
¼ cup sugar
¾ cup rice vinegar
1 tablespoon sesame oil
1 tablespoon toasted sesame seeds

Combine all ingredients in a bowl and mix well. Chill before using.

# Lime Ume Dressing

*This dressing is great with daikon or carrot-based salads. Soak them briefly, then drain well. Garnish with slivered nori.*

½ cup lime juice
1½ tablespoons ume plum paste (umeboshi)
½ cup sugar
salt, to taste (this brings out the crucial flavor of the ume—otherwise it is too sweet/tart)

Combine all ingredients in a small bowl and whisk well to blend. Serve chilled.

# Avocado Dressing

*Serve on cabbage salads with fruit or vegetables. This dressing will keep its clear green color for several days in the refrigerator.*

1 medium-sized ripe avocado, peeled and pitted
1 small onion, chopped
½ cup sour cream
2 tablespoons lemon juice
pinch of black pepper
dash of Tabasco
1 teaspoon salt

In a food processor, combine avocado and onion and blend until smooth. Combine in a small bowl with sour cream, lemon juice, pepper, Tabasco, and salt. Beat until smooth.

# Poppy Seed Dressing

*This dressing is a favorite for salads with fruit and greens.*

½ cup honey
6 tablespoons cider vinegar
5 tablespoons olive oil
2 small shallots, minced
4 teaspoons Dijon mustard
2 teaspoons poppy seeds
salt and fresh-ground pepper, to taste

Whisk all ingredients together in a small bowl.

# North African Lemon Dressing

*This dressing is suggested for salads with tomatoes, sweet onions, cucumbers, green peppers, or fruit salads and cottage cheese. At Tassajara, we use it often with salads of lettuce and grapefruit sections. A delicious variation can be made by using limes in place of lemons.*

zest of 2 lemons
¼ cup lemon juice
1½ teaspoons salt
⅛ teaspoon cayenne or Tabasco sauce
2 cloves garlic, minced
⅔ to ¾ cup olive oil
½ teaspoon coriander
½ teaspoon cumin
½ teaspoon dry mustard
½ teaspoon paprika
1 teaspoon sugar

Combine all ingredients in a bowl; mix well and chill before serving.

# Mustard Vinaigrette

*Serve this vinaigrette with mixed greens or over fresh tomato slices.*

¼ teaspoon tarragon
¼ teaspoon fennel seed, ground
2 tablespoons sherry vinegar
¼ teaspoon salt
2 tablespoons Dijon mustard
3 tablespoons melted butter
½ cup olive oil

Combine tarragon, fennel, vinegar, salt, and mustard in a small bowl. Whisk in butter and olive oil. Taste and adjust seasonings.

# Marinated Mozzarella

*Bocconcini, bite-sized balls of fresh mozzarella, makes a very attractive appetizer with this marinade.*

⅓ cup balsamic vinegar
3 cloves garlic, minced
3 tablespoons Dijon mustard
3 tablespoons minced mixed fresh herbs (parsley, thyme, or marjoram)
2 cups olive oil
1 pound bocconcini

Combine all ingredients in a bowl and mix well. Let stand at least 1 hour garnished with fresh herbs.

MAKES 2 CUPS

VARIATION: *Balsamic vinegar is quite strong and dark. For a lighter version, use sherry wine vinegar or red wine vinegar.*

# Antipasto Agrodolce
# (Sweet and Sour Vegetables)

*Try this Italian appetizer as part of an antipasto dish with fresh mozzarella, olives, and sliced baguettes.*

2 bulbs garlic
2 tablespoons olive oil
2 sprigs fresh rosemary or thyme
2 red or yellow bell peppers, roasted and cut into ½-inch strips
2 red onions, quartered
½ cup plus 2 tablespoons balsamic vinegar
1 tablespoon butter
1 pound Japanese eggplant, cut into ¼-inch diagonals
salt and pepper, to taste

Preheat oven to 350 degrees F. The garlic, peppers, and onions can be roasted in the oven at the same time but note varying cooking times. Cut off the stem ends of the garlic and place cut side down in a small baking dish. Coat with olive oil and top with fresh herbs. Cover and roast until just tender, about 1 hour. When cool, squeeze cloves out of husks; set aside. To roast the peppers, place in a baking dish and roast for 30 to 40 minutes or so. When done, place the peppers in a paper bag and let sit a few minutes. Remove skins and seeds and then cut into ½-inch strips. To roast the onions, place in a baking dish and drizzle with 2 tablespoons balsamic vinegar, butter, and enough water to cover, toss gently. Roast for 30 minutes until tender but firm.

Meanwhile, heat ½ cup balsamic vinegar until it is has a slightly syrupy consistency. After the garlic is roasted, toss the eggplants with half of the garlic, salt, and pepper and brush with the reduced balsamic vinegar. Bake, uncovered, for 15 to 20 minutes, or until just tender. Dress the pepper strips with balsamic vinegar, the remaining half of the roasted garlic, salt, and pepper. Arrange the vegetables on a platter and garnish with roasted garlic if desired.

MAKES 2 QUARTS

# Daikon Ginger Pickles

*These are sweet pickles. Keep in mind if you use brown sugar, the pickles will be somewhat brown. Serve with the Tassajara Marinated Tofu (see page 125) or with sandwiches to add flavor and texture to the meal.*

1 cup water
½ teaspoon salt
½ cup fresh ginger, cut into ¹⁄₁₆-inch slices
½ cup rice vinegar
5 tablespoons brown or white sugar
1¾ cups mirin
3 cups daikon, cut into ¹⁄₁₆-inch slices

Bring water and salt to a boil. Blanch ginger in water for 30 seconds; drain and set aside. In same pan, heat rice vinegar, sugar, and mirin until dissolved.

Slice daikon into slices, if too large, cut in halves or quarters to make bite-sized pieces. Put daikon and liquid mixture into a plastic container and cover; stir once a day. Pickles are ready in 5 days and keep for up to 1 month refrigerated.

MAKES 3 CUPS

# Mama Sawyer's
# Cucumber Relish

*These are sweet cucumber pickles and go well with savory marinated tofu or when a little something sweet is needed to complete a composed salad plate.*

    3 large cucumbers, peeled
    1 large onion, peeled
    ½ teaspoon salt
    1 cup white vinegar
    1 cup sugar
    3 tablespoons flour
    1 teaspoon celery seed
    1 teaspoon yellow mustard seed
    4 teaspoons tumeric

Dice the cucumbers and onion into ½-inch pieces, add salt and let sit overnight; drain.

In a medium saucepan, combine the cucumber mixture with the remaining ingredients and then boil for 5 minutes.

MAKES 4 CUPS

# Pungent Cucumbers

*Serve these pickles alongside Asian-inspired themes such as Tofu Teriyaki, Edamame Salad and Sesame Cookies. Or simply serve inside of sandwiches and rollups.*

4 large cucumbers, peeled, seeded, and sliced into ¼-inch half moons
½ cup bell peppers, cut into ⅛ x 2-inch strips
1 quart boiling water
¼ cup sugar
½ cup red wine vinegar
3 tablespoons grated ginger
2 tablespoons minced serrano chile pepper
2 tablespoons soy sauce
¼ cup sesame oil
2 dried red chiles
¼ cup Szechwan peppercorns

Mix cucumbers with bell peppers and place in a colander. Pour 1 quart boiling water over vegetables and let drain. Mix sugar, vinegar, ginger, serrano chiles, and soy sauce in a small saucepan and heat until the sugar dissolves.

In a separate skillet, heat oil, and add dried chiles and peppercorns. When the chiles have turned dark red, remove from heat and strain the oil into the sugar mixture. Mix with the cucumber mixture and let marinate for 2 to 6 hours. Serve cold.

MAKES 4 CUPS

# Pickled Red Onions

*These onion pickles go particularly well with Southwestern food. They are delicious with marinated black beans or rice salad.*

2 medium red onions, peeled and sliced into ¼-inch-thick rounds
1 quart boiling water
⅔ cup rice wine or champagne vinegar
⅔ cup water
pinch of sugar
pinch of hot pepper flakes
½ teaspoon black peppercorns

Place the onion rounds into a colander inside a bowl. Cover with boiling water and let sit for 3 to 5 minutes, or until the onions begin to soften and lose their sharp taste; drain and cover with vinegar and water. Add a pinch of sugar to cut the acidity and sprinkle with hot pepper flakes and black peppercorns. Cover and refrigerate until cool. These hold well, so make them in advance of serving.

**MAKES 2 CUPS**

# Mushrooms a la Greque

This rich mushroom appetizer is good served with other marinated vegetables such as beets, or part of an antipasto platter.

MARINADE

¼ cup olive oil
½ cup corn oil
¼ cup red wine vinegar
1 bay leaf
1 teaspoon chervil
½ teaspoon oregano
1 tablespoon parsley
1 tablespoon dry mustard
1 teaspoon salt
¼ teaspoon fresh-ground pepper
1 pound mushrooms
¼ cup dry red wine

Bring all the marinade ingredients to a boil in a large pot, boil about 5 minutes. Add mushrooms; stir until they are moistened. Cover and cook another 5 minutes. Let the mushrooms cool; add the red wine. If desired, you can also drain the mushroom mixture before adding the wine.

MAKES 4 CUPS

# dairy cookies

# Chocolate Chews

*Edward Brown says this isn't his recipe but everyone at the Zen Center believes it is. . . . These cookies are probably the most popular cookie ever served at Tassajara.*

½ pound semisweet chocolate
3 ounces unsweetened chocolate
½ cup butter
¾ teaspoon instant coffee
3 eggs
1 cup brown sugar
1 cup unbleached flour
½ teaspoon baking powder
¼ teaspoon salt
2 teaspoons vanilla extract
1½ cups chocolate chips

Preheat oven to 325 degrees F. In a double boiler, melt the semisweet and unsweetened chocolate, butter, and coffee together.

Meanwhile, beat the eggs and brown sugar together until light in color and thick. Sift together the flour, baking powder, and salt.

Let the chocolate mixture cool slightly and then whisk into the eggs and sugar. Stir in the vanilla extract and then gently fold in the dry ingredients. Stir in the chocolate chips.

Drop by tablespoon onto a greased cookie sheet and bake for 12 to 15 minutes. Cool on a wire rack.

**MAKES ABOUT 4 DOZEN COOKIES**

# Sonia's Shortbread Cookies

*These non-traditional, but delicious, shortbread cookies use nuts to replace part of the wheat flour, and confectioners' sugar and oil to make the cookies light and fluffy.*

1 cup butter (or use ½ cup butter and ½ cup vegetable oil)
½ cup confectioners' sugar
2 cups unbleached flour
2 cups ground nuts (almonds, walnuts, and/or pecans)
1 teaspoon baking powder

Preheat oven to 325 degrees F. Cream the butter and sugar together until light and fluffy. In another bowl, combine the flour, nuts, and baking powder; add to the butter mixture.

Drop by tablespoons onto a greased cookie sheet and bake for 12 to 15 minutes. Cool on a wire rack.

MAKES ABOUT 3 DOZEN COOKIES

# Gingersnaps

*This is a traditional gingersnap recipe but uses rich Blackstrap molasses to deepen the flavor of the cookies.*

½ cup butter, at room temperature
¾ cup brown sugar
2 teaspoons Blackstrap molasses
1 egg
1½ tablespoons powdered ginger (double if using fresh)
2 teaspoons cinnamon
¼ teaspoon salt
½ teaspoon baking soda
½ teaspoon baking powder
1½ cups unbleached flour
½ cup white sugar

Preheat oven to 350 degrees F. Cream the butter, brown sugar, and molasses together and beat well. Add egg and beat until smooth.

In another bowl, stir together the ginger, cinnamon, salt, baking soda, baking powder, and flour. Gradually add to the butter mixture, blending thoroughly.

Roll the dough into balls about 1 inch in diameter. Coat each ball by rolling in the sugar. Flatten each ball with the bottom of a glass. Bake cookies on a greased cookie sheet for about 15 minutes, or until nicely browned. Cool on a wire rack.

VARIATIONS: *To bring out the ginger flavor, add some mustard powder and a pinch of cayenne or black pepper. Also, feel free to mix dry and fresh ginger and add diced pieces of candied ginger. Doubling the molasses is also good.*

MAKES ABOUT 1 DOZEN COOKIES

# Pineapple-Coconut Bars

*Transport yourself to the islands with these tropical-tasting cookie bars. They are the next best thing to being on a beach under a palm tree.*

½ cup butter, at room temperature
1 cup firmly packed brown sugar
2 eggs
¼ teaspoon almond extract
¾ cup unbleached flour
¾ teaspoon baking powder
½ teaspoon salt
¾ cup flaked coconut
1 (8-ounce) can crushed pineapple, drained well

In a large bowl, beat butter and sugar together until creamy; beat in eggs and almond extract. In another bowl, stir together flour, baking powder, and salt; gradually add to butter mixture, blending thoroughly. Stir in coconut and pineapple.

Spread mixture evenly in a greased and floured 9-inch-square baking pan. Bake at 350 degrees F for 25 to 30 minutes, or until the top springs back when lightly touched. Let cool in pan on a wire rack, then cut into 1 x 2 ¼-inch bars.

MAKES 3 DOZEN BARS

# Sesame Cookies

*These sesame cookies have a rich and buttery taste and are a favorite of children.*

⅔ cup canola oil or other vegetable oil
1 cup brown sugar
1 egg
1 teaspoon vanilla
1 teaspoon lemon zest
1 cup toasted sesame seeds
1 cup toasted coconut
2 cups unbleached flour
1 teaspoon baking powder
½ teaspoon baking soda
¾ teaspoon salt

Beat the oil, brown sugar, egg, vanilla, and lemon zest together. Stir in the sesame seeds and coconut.

In another bowl, stir together the flour, baking powder, baking soda, and salt; add to the sugar mixture and mix until combined. Do not overwork the dough or the cookies will be hard.

Shape dough into balls that are 1 inch in diameter. Flatten with a fork or spoon. Place on an ungreased cookie sheet and bake at 350 degrees F for 10 to 15 minutes, or until slightly browned on the bottom. Cool on a wire rack.

MAKES ABOUT 2½ DOZEN COOKIES

Krunch Bars

# Krunch Bars

*These bars are super easy and really good. Great for picnics or traveling as they don't crumble or fall apart.*

⅔ cup butter, at room temperature
1 cup brown sugar
4 cups quick-cooking oats
½ cup light corn syrup

1 tablespoon vanilla
¾ cup chocolate chips
⅔ cup peanut butter

Preheat oven to 350 degrees F. Cream the butter and brown sugar together; add the oats, corn syrup, and vanilla. Spread into a greased 9 x 13-inch pan and bake for 15 minutes; let cool.

In top of a double boiler, melt the chocolate chips and peanut butter together; spread mixture evenly over the oatmeal mixture. When set, cut into squares or bars.

MAKES ABOUT 3 DOZEN BARS

# Butterscotch Blondies

*These wonderful bars are really like rich butterscotch brownies.*

1½ cups butter, at room temperature
1½ cups brown sugar
2 eggs
1 tablespoon vanilla
2 cups unbleached flour

1½ teaspoons baking powder
½ teaspoon salt
¾ cup butterscotch morsels
¾ cup nuts (walnuts or pecans)

Preheat oven to 350 degrees F. In a large bowl, beat the butter and sugar together until smooth; beat in eggs and vanilla. In another bowl, combine the flour, baking powder, and salt; add to creamed mixture, blending well. Stir in the butterscotch morsels and nuts.

Spread batter evenly in a greased 9 x 13-inch pan. Bake for 20 to 25 minutes, or until a toothpick inserted in the center comes out clean. Let cool in pan on a wire rack and then cut into bars.

MAKES 12 TO 16 BARS

# Cappuccino Coins

*We blend the flavor of coffee and chocolate in these "little coins of caffeine bliss." These cookies are a favorite of Tassajara guests.*

½ cup butter, at room temperature
½ cup sugar
½ cup dark brown sugar
4 eggs
4 cups unbleached flour
1 tablespoon instant coffee
1 tablespoon unsweetened cocoa powder
1 teaspoon cinnamon
½ teaspoon salt
1 cup semisweet chocolate chips, finely ground

Using an electric mixer, cream the butter and sugars together on medium speed until smooth. Scrape down the sides of the bowl with a rubber spatula and add eggs; mix well. Add the flour, instant coffee, cocoa, cinnamon, salt, and chocolate chips; mix thoroughly for 2 to 3 minutes.

Gather the dough together and turn onto a lightly floured board. Using lightly floured hands, roll the dough into 2 or 3 even 1-inch-thick logs. Wrap the logs separately in plastic wrap. Refrigerate until firm, about 1 hour.

Move oven rack to middle position. Preheat oven to 350 degrees F. Line a large cookie sheet with parchment paper. Slice the chilled logs into ¼-inch-thick coins and then place ½ inch apart on the lined cookie sheets.

Bake until the cookies are lightly golden and firm enough at the edges to slide off the parchment without sticking, about 15 to 17 minutes. Cool on the cookie sheets set on wire racks.

MAKES ABOUT 3½ DOZEN COOKIES

# Orange-Pistachio Cookies

*Orange and pistachio are a delicious flavor combination, and the pistachios add a delightful crunch to these soft cookies.*

1½ cups butter, at room temperature
¾ cup sugar
2 eggs
½ teaspoon vanilla
½ teaspoon orange extract
3 cups unbleached flour
½ teaspoon salt
5 tablespoons orange zest
2 cups chopped pistachios (or toasted and skinned hazelnuts)

Preheat oven to 350 degrees F. Cream butter and sugar together; beat in eggs, vanilla, and orange extract.

In another bowl, combine flour, salt, and orange zest. Stir into butter mixture and then stir in nuts.

Roll dough into balls about 1 inch in diameter then flatten slightly with the back of a spoon. Place on a greased cookie sheet. Bake about 15 minutes, or until slightly brown around the edges. Cool on a wire rack.

MAKES ABOUT 3 DOZEN COOKIES

# Tart Lemon Bars or Lemon Tart

*These are buttery, sweet-tart dreams. The best of all lemon bar recipes combined to make The One. Serve these refreshing lemon bars or lemon tart as a finale for a special meal.*

2⅓ cups unbleached flour, divided
1½ cups sugar, divided
2 teaspoons baking powder, divided
¼ teaspoon baking soda
½ teaspoon salt
1 cup butter, at room temperature
4 eggs
6 tablespoons fresh lemon juice
1½ teaspoons lemon zest

Preheat oven to 350 degrees F. To make the crust, mix together 2 cups flour, ½ cup sugar, 1 teaspoon baking powder, baking soda, and salt. Work in the butter to make a soft dough. Pat into a greased 9 x 13-inch pan and then bake for 20 minutes.

While the crust is baking, make the filling. Mix the remaining flour and baking powder and set aside. In another bowl, mix remaining sugar, eggs, lemon juice, and lemon zest. Stir in the baking powder mixture. Pour over the hot crust (it is important the crust be hot or the filling will not stick to it). Bake for 25 minutes, or until the filling is set.

VARIATIONS: *Pat crust into pie or tart tins and bake as tarts; glaze with sour cream. Roy from Israel doubled the sugar for the crust, and for the filling, he added orange extract and more lemon juice and lemon zest.*

MAKES ABOUT 3 DOZEN BARS

# Mocha Shortbread Cookies

*Use a good-quality chocolate to bring out the best in these rich butter cookies.*

2 ounces bittersweet chocolate
2 cups unbleached flour
½ teaspoon baking powder
¼ teaspoon instant coffee
⅛ teaspoon cinnamon
1 cup butter, at room temperature
½ cup brown sugar
½ cup ground walnuts or almonds
walnuts or almonds, for garnish

Preheat oven to 350 degrees F. In the top of a double boiler, melt chocolate. Combine flour, baking powder, instant coffee, and cinnamon in a bowl and set aside.

In another bowl, cream the butter and sugar together; beat in the melted chocolate and ground nuts. Stir in the flour mixture.

Roll the dough into balls, about the size of a rounded tablespoon; flatten and then press in a walnut half or almond. Place on a greased cookie sheet and bake 10 to 15 minutes, but watch carefully as they are already brown. Cool on a wire rack.

MAKES ABOUT 3 DOZEN

VARIATION: *You can also reduce sugar slightly in recipe, and roll balls into sugar, then flatten and press with nuts.*

# Dried Apricot Macaroons

*These not too sweet gems are perfect for coconut lovers.*

1 cup sugar
4 cups unsweetened flaked coconut, divided
1 cup chopped dried apricots
4 large egg whites
¼ teaspoon salt
1 tablespoon butter, melted
½ teaspoon almond extract
½ teaspoon vanilla

Preheat oven to 350 degrees F. Line cookie sheets with parchment paper. Mix sugar, 3 cups coconut, apricots, egg whites, and salt together with your hands. Add melted butter and extracts; combine well. Refrigerate for at least 1 hour.

Moisten the palms of your hands with cold water. Roll 1 tablespoon of the dough mixture between your palms, squeezing tightly together to form a compact ball. Roll each ball in remaining coconut.

Place on a greased cookie sheet about 1 inch apart. Bake until edges are golden brown, about 15 minutes. Cool on a wire rack.

MAKES 2 DOZEN COOKIES

VARIATION: *After forming dough into a compact ball, place on a clean surface and using a spatula, flatten one side at a time to form a pyramid shape. Bake as above and then let cool completely. Melt 3 ounces semisweet chocolate and 1 teaspoon butter in a bowl set over a pan of simmering water. Stir occasionally until melted. Dip top ½ inch of each pyramid into chocolate mixture.*

# Nut-Chocolate Bars
# "Unsurpassed"

*These are a chewy and surprisingly moist cookie.*

2 cups unbleached flour
1 teaspoon baking powder
¼ teaspoon baking soda
½ teaspoon salt
⅔ cup butter, at room temperature
2 cups brown sugar
2 eggs
2 teaspoons vanilla extract
2 cups chopped nuts
1½ cups chocolate chips

Preheat oven to 350 degrees F. In a medium bowl, combine the flour, baking powder, baking soda, and salt. Cream the butter and then add the sugar. While continuing to beat, add the eggs, vanilla, nuts, chocolate chips, and dry ingredients.

Spread in a greased 9 x 13-inch pan and bake for 30 minutes, or until done. While still warm, cut into squares or bars.

MAKES ABOUT 3 DOZEN BARS

# Chewy Oatmeal Cookies
# with Chocolate Chips and Coconut

*Oatmeal cookies with chocolate chips and coconut—what could be better?*

½ cup butter, at room temperature
½ cup brown sugar
½ cup white sugar
1 egg
½ teaspoon vanilla
¾ cup unbleached flour
½ teaspoon salt
½ teaspoon baking soda

½ teaspoon cinnamon
½ teaspoon cloves
½ teaspoon nutmeg
1½ cups quick-cooking oats
½ cup raisins
½ cup chocolate chips
¼ cup flaked coconut (optional)

Preheat oven to 375 degrees F. In a large bowl, cream butter and sugars together; beat in the egg and vanilla. In another bowl, mix the flour, salt, baking soda, cinnamon, cloves, nutmeg, and oats.

Gradually add the dry ingredients to the butter mixture, blending thoroughly. Stir in the raisins, chocolate chips, and coconut, if desired. Bake on an ungreased cookie sheet for 8 to 10 minutes. Cool on a wire rack.

MAKES ABOUT 2½ DOZEN COOKIES

# Chocolate Truffles

*Chocolate truffles couldn't be any easier. Try rolling the truffles in different coatings and leave some plain for a great visual effect. Chopped pistachios make a nice contrast to the dark chocolate.*

1 pound semisweet chocolate (bittersweet bar or chocolate chips)
¾ cup heavy cream
½ cup unsweetened cocoa powder
chopped nuts and/or shredded coconut (optional)

Break or chop the chocolate into medium-sized pieces. Place it in the top of a small double boiler over hot water on low heat; cover and let stand until melted. Uncover and stir until completely melted and reaches 120 degrees F on a candy thermometer.

Remove the top of the double boiler and heat the cream to a boil; cool to 115 degrees F. Add the melted chocolate to the cream, stirring slowly until well combined. (If the chocolate cooled to lower than 115 degrees F, reheat to at least 115 degrees F.) Cover with plastic wrap and cool.

When the mixture is firm enough to hold a definite shape (like the consistency of peanut butter), place a piece of wax paper in front of you. Using a slightly rounded teaspoon or melon baller, scoop some of the mixture for each truffle. Roll each scoop into a ball and then roll in cocoa powder or chopped nuts and/or shredded coconut.

MAKES ABOUT 3 DOZEN COOKIES

# Butterscotch-Chocolate Chip Brownies

*Very quick brownies!*

1½ cups butterscotch or chocolate chips or ¾ cup of both
½ cup butter, at room temperature
1 cup flour
4 eggs
1½ cups sugar
1 teaspoon vanilla
1 cup chopped cashews

Preheat oven to 350 degrees F. In a saucepan, melt the chocolate and/or butterscotch chips and butter over low heat. Remove from heat and beat in flour, eggs, sugar, and vanilla. Stir in cashews.

Pour into a greased 9-inch-square pan. Bake for 20 to 25 minutes, or until a toothpick inserted in the center comes out clean. Let cool in pan on a wire rack completely before cutting into bars.

MAKES ABOUT 1½ DOZEN BARS

# $250 Neiman Marcus Cookies

*Save these ultra rich cookies for a special occasion.*

½ cup butter, at room temperature
½ cup white sugar
½ cup brown sugar
1 egg
½ teaspoon vanilla
1½ cups oatmeal, ground into a fine powder
¾ cup unbleached flour
¼ teaspoon salt
½ teaspoon baking powder
½ teaspoon baking soda
1½ cups semisweet chocolate chips
4 ounces Hershey's semisweet chocolate bar, grated
¾ cup chopped walnuts

Preheat oven to 375 degrees F. In a large bowl, beat the butter and sugars together until smooth and creamy. Beat in the egg and vanilla.

Combine the oatmeal, flour, salt, baking powder, and baking soda in a separate bowl and then add it to the creamed mixture and blend until smooth. Add the chocolate chips, grated chocolate bar, and walnuts; mix well.

Roll the dough into balls about 1 inch in diameter and place on lightly greased cookie sheet about 2 inches apart. Bake for 10 minutes. Cool on a wire rack.

MAKES ABOUT 2½ DOZEN COOKIES

# vegan cookies & sweets

# Date and Coconut Cookies
## (Auntie Nuke's)

*For the past twenty-five years, these vegan cookies have been requested by Tassajara guests.*

½ cup nuts, roasted
½ cup date pieces
1½ teaspoons nutritional yeast
½ cup shredded coconut
2 cups unbleached flour*
½ teaspoon baking powder
¼ teaspoon salt
¾ cup maple syrup
1½ teaspoons vanilla
½ cup canola oil or other vegetable oil

Preheat oven to 325 degrees F. Put the nuts and date pieces into a food processor and chop together. Put mixture into a medium-sized bowl and then add the yeast, coconut, flour, baking powder, and salt; mix well.

In another small bowl, combine the maple syrup, vanilla, and oil. Mix into the dry mixture and stir together until the dough is firm and holds it shape. Spoon by tablespoon onto a greased baking sheet and bake for 20 to 25 minutes. Cool on a wire rack.

MAKES ABOUT 2½ DOZEN COOKIES

*For a wheat-free alternative, blend baby oats until fine and use in place of flour.*

# Mixed Dream Cookies

*These cookies are full of texture and just slightly sweet. Delicious with a fresh pot of tea.*

½ cup dried apricots
1 cup mixed nuts, roasted (any combination such as walnuts, sunflower seeds, cashews, almonds, pumpkin seeds, peanuts)
½ cup soy margarine
¼ cup confectioners' sugar, sifted
1½ teaspoons vanilla
½ cup honey
1 cup unbleached flour
¼ teaspoon salt

Preheat oven to 325 degrees F. If the apricots seem very dry, soak in hot water and then drain, saving the liquid; chop apricots into small bits.

In a food processor, chop the mixed nuts; set aside. In a large mixing bowl, cream the margarine and then beat in the confectioners' sugar, vanilla, and honey.

In another bowl, combine the flour and salt; fold into the margarine mixture.

Add the nuts and chopped apricots and mix well. If the dough seems stiff, add some of the apricot soaking liquid. Use a small ice cream scoop or melon baller to drop dough onto greased baking sheets. Bake for 20 to 25 minutes, depending on the size of the balls. Cool on a wire rack.

MAKES ABOUT 1½ DOZEN COOKIES

# Spicy Oatmeal Raisin Cookies

*A traditional recipe adapted for vegan eating but with a unique blend of spices. Delicious!*

| | |
|---|---|
| 3 cups rolled oats | pinch of cardamom |
| 1 cup unbleached flour | pinch of cayenne pepper |
| ½ teaspoon salt | 1 banana, mashed |
| 1 teaspoon baking soda | ½ cup dry sweetener* |
| 1 teaspoon cinnamon | 2 tablespoons oil |
| 1 teaspoon nutmeg | 1 cup soy milk |
| 1 teaspoon ground ginger | 1 teaspoon apple cider vinegar |
| 1 teaspoon ground cumin | ¾ cup raisins |
| ½ teaspoon black pepper | ½ cup chocolate chips |

Preheat oven to 375 degrees F. In a large bowl, stir the oats, flour, salt, baking soda, and spices together. Add the banana, sweetener, oil, soy milk, vinegar, raisins, and chocolate chips. Stir gently until just mixed.

Scoop tablespoon-sized portions onto a greased baking sheet and bake for 8 to 10 minutes for soft cookies, or 16 to 20 minutes for more crisp cookies. Cool on a wire rack.

*Try using sucanat, sugar, or other alternatives. Some people choose to limit their intake of refined or simple sugar, here are some other alternatives to use in the cookies.*

| Sweetner | Substitute for each cup refined sugar | Reduced total liquid per cup of sugar |
|---|---|---|
| Barley malt or rice syrup | 1½ cups | Slightly |
| Honey | ¾ cup | ⅛ cup |
| Fruit juice concentrate | ¾ cup | ⅛ cup |
| Maple syrup | ¾ cup | ⅛ cup |
| Molasses | ½ cup | None |

# Lemon Poppy Seed Shortbread Cookies

*These lemony cookies melt in your mouth.*

2 cups unbleached flour
¼ cup poppy seeds
¼ cup arrowroot powder
½ teaspoon nutmeg
¼ teaspoon salt
1 cup margarine
⅔ cup dry sweetener*
3 tablespoons fresh lemon juice
2 tablespoons lemon zest
2 teaspoons vanilla

Preheat oven to 375 degrees F. Stir the flour, poppy seeds, arrowroot powder, nutmeg, and salt together. In another bowl, cream the margarine, sweetener, lemon juice, lemon zest, and vanilla.

Add the margarine mixture to the flour mixture and stir until just mixed. Using a tablespoon, spoon the dough onto a greased baking sheet. Bake for 10 to 12 minutes. Cool on a wire rack.

MAKES ABOUT 2½ DOZEN

VARIATION: *An alternative would be to roll out the dough ¼ inch thick, bake on a baking sheet, and then cut after baking*

*See page 187.

# Lemon Cookies

*Refreshingly light and tart, these lemon cookies are delicious!*

½ cup rice or corn syrup
½ cup maple syrup
zest from 2 lemons
juice from 2 lemons
½ cup canola oil
1 cup unbleached flour
4 tablespoons arrowroot powder
¼ teaspoon salt

Preheat oven to 350 degrees F. Whisk the syrups, lemon zest, lemon juice, and canola oil together. In another bowl, combine flour, arrowroot powder, and salt.

Pour the syrup mixture into the flour mixture and whisk until combined. Spoon ½ tablespoons of dough onto baking sheets about 4 inches apart. Bake for 6 minutes and then rotate baking sheet, turn and bake other side; bake another 7 minutes, or until golden brown along the edges.

MAKES ABOUT 1½ DOZEN

VARIATION: *Press the dough balls flat after putting onto baking sheets.*

# Non-Dairy Cocoa Cookies

*Rich chocolate gems with just enough texture.*

1 cup maple syrup
1 cup canola oil or other vegetable oil
1½ cups whole wheat pastry flour
½ cup rolled oats
½ cup cocoa powder
2 tablespoons arrowroot powder
½ cup chopped walnuts, almonds, or coconut

Preheat oven to 350 degrees F. Mix the syrup with the oil. In another bowl, sift the flour, oats, cocoa powder, and arrowroot. Stir in chopped nuts or coconut.

Pour the syrup mixture over the flour mixture and stir with as few strokes as possible so the dough is not over mixed. Drop by tablespoons onto a greased baking sheet about 1 inch apart. Bake for 15 to 18 minutes. The cookies will be soft and lightly brown at the bottom when done, do not over bake them. They will harden as they cool.  Cool on a wire rack.

MAKES ABOUT 2½ DOZEN COOKIES

# Pat Walton's Oatmeal Cookies

*This recipe originated in the '70s at Tassajara. If carob doesn't appeal to you, you can substitute chocolate chips.*

⅓ cup soy milk
½ teaspoon cider vinegar
½ cup margarine
¼ cup shortening
¾ cup brown sugar
½ cup honey
1½ teaspoons vanilla
¾ cup unbleached flour
½ teaspoon salt
½ teaspoon baking soda

¾ teaspoon cinnamon
½ teaspoon nutmeg
½ teaspoon cloves
¾ cup ground pecans
2 cups quick oats
½ cup raisins, soaked in water
¾ cup carob or chocolate chips
½ cup flaked coconut

Preheat oven to 350 degrees F. Combine the soy milk and cider vinegar and set aside in a warm place. Cream the margarine, shortening, brown sugar, honey, and vanilla together in a large bowl.

In another bowl, mix the flour, salt, baking soda, cinnamon, nutmeg, and cloves. Add to the margarine mixture along with the soy milk mixture; mix well. Stir in the pecans, oats, drained raisins, carob chips, and coconut.

Drop by tablespoon onto a greased baking sheet and bake for 12 minutes, or until done. Cool on a wire rack.

MAKES ABOUT 4 DOZEN (2½-INCH) COOKIES

# Tim's Variation to Pat Walton's Oatmeal Cookies

*Banana adds a creaminess and tropical flavor to these spicy oatmeal cookies.*

½ teaspoon apple cider vinegar*
¼ cup soy milk*
1 banana, mashed
¼ cup canola oil
2 tablespoons molasses
¾ cup honey
¾ teaspoon vanilla
2½ cups baby rolled oats
1½ cups whole wheat flour, sifted

½ teaspoon salt
¾ teaspoon baking soda
1½ teaspoons cinnamon
¼ teaspoon nutmeg
¼ teaspoon cloves
1 cup pecans, chopped
1 cup chocolate chips
½ cup flaked coconut
pecan halves (optional)

Preheat the oven to 375 degrees F. Mix the cider vinegar and soy milk together and then set aside in a warm place until ready to use. Cream together the banana, oil, molasses, honey, vanilla, and oats.

In a separate bowl, combine the flour, salt, baking soda, cinnamon, nutmeg, and cloves. Add to the banana mixture and blend well. Mix in the pecans, chocolate chips, and coconut.

Drop by tablespoon onto a greased baking sheet. Press in a pecan half on top of cookie before baking if you like. Bake for 12 minutes. The cookies won't look done but they will firm up when cooled. Cool on a wire rack.

MAKES ABOUT 4 DOZEN COOKIES

*In place of apple cider vinegar and soy milk, you can use the "egg replacer" recipe below:*

½ teaspoon soy flour
½ teaspoon arrowroot powder
pinch of lecithin
1½ teaspoons warm water

# Thumbprints

*One of the most popular vegan cookies. They are delicious, easy to make, and beautiful cookies. Also a great cookie to make with your children!*

  1 cup unbleached flour*
  2 cups almonds, ground
  4 cups baby rolled oats
  ½ teaspoon salt
  1 cup maple syrup
  1 cup canola oil or vegetable oil
  ½ cup jam, thinned with water

Preheat oven to 350 degrees F. In a medium-sized bowl, combine the flour, almonds, oats, and salt.

In another bowl, mix together the syrup and oil. Add to the dry ingredients using your hands and mix well. Let dough sit 15 minutes before using.

Roll dough into ¾-inch balls. Place close together on baking sheets. Make a little dent in the top of each ball and then fill with ½ teaspoon or less of the jam. Bake for 15 minutes, or until slightly brown. Do not over bake. Cool on a wire rack.

VARIATIONS: *Use honey in place of maple syrup, add ½ cup peanut butter and reduce oil by ¼ cup. Or use ½ cup honey and ½ cup maple syrup in place of 1 cup maple syrup and 1 cup mini chocolate chips.*

MAKES ABOUT 5 DOZEN

*For wheat-free (no wheat flour), use finely blended baby oats.*

# No-Bake Cocoa-Coconut Sweets

*These super easy cookies satisfy even the pickiest chocolate lover.*

2½ tablespoons cocoa powder
¾ cup maple syrup
¼ cup soy milk
½ teaspoon vanilla
¼ cup margarine
1½ cups baby rolled oats
¼ cup peanut butter
1¾ cups flaked coconut, divided

Mix the cocoa and syrup together in a saucepan; add the soy milk, vanilla, and margarine; heat until liquefied and just reaches a boil. Stir the mixture, scraping the sides, being sure not to let it burn; cool mixture.

In a separate bowl, combine oats and peanut butter together using your hands. Next, pour in the cocoa mixture and add 1 cup coconut; blend with your hands until well mixed.

Roll dough into 1-inch balls. If the mixture is too wet, add more oatmeal or roll the balls into remaining coconut. They will be somewhat sticky but will harden as they cool. Put on a tray and store in refrigerator.

**MAKES ABOUT 3 DOZEN COOKIES**

# Chocolate Chip Cookies

*Orange extract brightens the flavor of these traditional chocolate chip cookies.*

2½ cups whole wheat flour
1½ teaspoons baking powder
½ teaspoon salt
½ cup honey
½ cup maple syrup
⅓ cup canola oil or other vegetable oil
1 teaspoon orange extract
1 cup chocolate chips

Preheat oven to 350 degrees F. Sift flour, baking powder, and salt. In another bowl, mix honey and syrup together; stir in the oil. Add orange extract and beat until blended. Add flour mixture and mix well. If too wet, add more sifted flour.

Add chocolate chips and mix well. Drop by teaspoons on a greased baking sheet. Bake for 15 minutes, or until lightly browned. They will harden as they cool, be sure not to over bake. Cool on a wire rack.

MAKES ABOUT 2 DOZEN COOKIES

# Chocolate-Peppermint
# Chocolate Chip Cookies

*Not quite Girl Scout Thin Mints, but a delicious vegan alternative.*

2¾ cups unbleached flour
½ cup cocoa
1½ teaspoons baking powder
½ teaspoon salt
½ cup margarine, softened or canola oil
1 cup maple syrup
1½ teaspoons peppermint extract
1 teaspoon vanilla extract
1½ cups chocolate chips

Preheat oven to 350 degrees F. Combine flour, cocoa, baking powder, and salt. In another bowl, beat the margarine, syrup, and peppermint and vanilla extracts together until smooth.

Add to the dry mixture and then stir in chocolate chips and mix. Drop by teaspoon onto a greased baking sheet; flatten with the back of a spoon. Bake 12 to 16 minutes. Cool on a wire rack.

MAKES ABOUT 2 DOZEN COOKIES

# Siobhan's Granny's
# Matrimonial Cake (Date Bars)

*A traditional date bar but made with margarine rather than butter.*

1½ cups date pieces or pitted dates
½ cup warm water
2 cups flour
2 cups rolled oats
½ teaspoon salt
¾ cup maple syrup
½ cup margarine (or use ¾ cup vegetable oil and add another ½ cup flour)
1½ teaspoons vanilla

Preheat oven to 375 degrees F. Soften dates by soaking in warm water; then blend mixture in food processor until smooth and set aside. For the dough, mix flour, rolled oats, and salt. Combine syrup, margarine, and vanilla together; add to oat mixture. Spread the dough into a greased 9 x 13-inch pan as evenly as possible, reserving one-fourth for the topping. Next spread on reserved date mixture. Crumble reserved dough mixture over the date mixture. Bake for 30 to 35 minutes and then cool and cut into squares.

Note: If you use butter or margarine, cut it into the dry ingredients and then add ½ cup brown sugar. Save one-fourth for topping and reduce amount of maple syrup by ½ cup.

MAKES 12 TO 16 BARS

# Maple-Coated Nuts

*This recipe was first originated by Tassajara "old timer," Iva Jones. This became a bag lunch favorite that the Bag Lunch Crew tried to keep permanently stocked as people looked depressed when they were told them they weren't available that day. In peak season, a gallon of this recipe would only last about a week.*

3 cups walnuts
salt, to taste
½ to ¾ cup maple syrup

Preheat oven to 350 degrees F. Line a baking sheet with wax paper. Fill pan with the walnuts in one layer; don't pile too much or the nuts won't roast well. Bake for 10 to 12 minutes.

Remove, and while still warm, put into a strainer and rub the walnuts against the side to remove the bitter skins. Put back onto pan and salt liberally to taste. Then pour enough maple syrup over the nuts so that they are thoroughly coated but not too gooey. Spread evenly into one layer with a spatula.

Return to oven for 10 to 15 minutes more, or until well-roasted. After removing from oven, stir well to eliminate sticking to the pan later.

MAKES 3 CUPS

# Poached Spiced Figs

*These delicious wine-soaked figs are a Bag Lunch favorite. Use fresh figs when available.*

1½ cups fruity red wine
6 tablespoons sugar
1 x 3-inch-strip orange zest
6 peppercorns
1 whole clove
2 allspice berries
½ pound dried California figs

Bring all the ingredients but the figs to simmer in a non-corroding saucepan. Add the figs and cook them at a very slight simmer until they are tender when pierced with the tip of a knife. This will take anywhere from 30 minutes to 1½ hours, depending entirely on the figs.

Remove the figs to a container with a slotted spoon, raise the heat, bring the syrup to a boil, and reduce by one-third. Pour it over the figs and chill. They will keep for 1 to 2 weeks and will benefit from sitting in their syrup for a few days.

Serve with a little of their syrup and some cream to pour over top, or by themselves as a complement to a picnic, appetizer, or dessert.

MAKES ½ POUND

# Peppered Mixed Nuts
# with Lemon and Capers

*This very popular nut mix served at the Bag Lunch at Tassajara is taken from Deborah Madison's book* Vegetarian Cooking for Everyone. *Of course, it is adapted by whoever made it that day . . .*

1 cup capers
1½ cups canola oil
2 cups assorted roasted, unsalted nuts (about ½ pound)
2 teaspoons fresh lemon juice
½ teaspoon fresh-ground pepper, or to taste
2 teaspoons finely grated lemon zest

Preheat oven to 300 degrees F. Drain and rinse capers and then transfer to a paper towel–lined baking sheet; gently pat with more paper towels. Let dry completely for about 1 hour.

Heat oil in a medium saucepan until it registers 350 degrees F on a deep-fry thermometer. Carefully add ¼ cup capers and fry, stirring constantly, until golden brown, about 3 minutes. Using a long-handled slotted spoon, transfer capers to a paper towel–lined baking sheet. Adjusting the heat as necessary to maintain oil temperature, continue adding capers in ¼ cup increments until all the capers have been fried. Reserve 2 tablespoons of the cooking oil; let cool.

In a bowl, toss nuts with reserved oil, lemon juice, and pepper. Spread mixture evenly on a rimmed sheet pan. Toast nuts in oven, stirring occasionally, until golden brown, about 25 minutes. Remove from oven; let cool, about 20 minutes. Sprinkle with lemon zest and then toss with fried capers. Mixture can be stored in an airtight container at room temperature up to 2 weeks.

**MAKES 2 CUPS**

# Mixed Nut Granola
# with Oat Bran

*Granola used in the Bag Lunch at Tassajara is meant to be a sweet snack. It can be combined with dried fruits and nuts as part of a trail mix or as a topping for yogurt. This recipe can even be eaten by itself as a rich, concentrated source of protein and carbohydrates.*

⅓ cup sunflower, soy, or canola oil

¼ cup maple syrup

3 tablespoons honey

1½ teaspoons vanilla extract

⅛ teaspoon almond extract

¾ teaspoon cinnamon

⅛ teaspoon ground allspice

½ teaspoon salt

½ cup flaked wheat

½ cup oat bran

2½ cups rolled oats

½ cup raw cashews, chopped

½ cup raw almonds, chopped

½ cup raw pecans, chopped

Preheat oven to 350 degrees F. Mix oil, syrup, honey, extracts, cinnamon, allspice, and salt in a bowl.

In a separate large bowl, mix the remaining ingredients together. Toss the oil mixture with the dry ingredients and mix to coat thoroughly. Spread the mixture on two sheet pans and bake until golden brown, about 30 minutes. Stir after 15 minutes so that it browns evenly. Cool completely and then store in a tightly covered jar.

MAKES ABOUT 5 CUPS

# Almond-Sunflower Seed Granola

*This recipe for a more "traditional" granola. It has more oats and less nuts and even less sweetener, so it's a bit lighter than Mixed Nut Granola with Oat Bran (see page 205).*

4 cups rolled oats
⅓ cup raw wheat germ
⅓ cup almonds
⅓ cup sunflower seeds
1½ teaspoons cinnamon
¼ teaspoon nutmeg
¼ teaspoon salt
⅓ cup raisins
¼ cup canola oil
¼ cup maple syrup
1 teaspoon vanilla extract
⅛ teaspoon almond extract

Preheat oven to 350 degrees F. Mix rolled oats, wheat germ, almonds, sunflower seeds, cinnamon, nutmeg, salt, and raisins in a large bowl.

In a separate bowl, combine the oil, syrup, and extracts and then add to dry ingredients. Mix thoroughly until well coated. Spread the mixture on two sheet pans and bake until golden, for about 30 minutes. Stir after 15 minutes so that it browns evenly. Cool completely and then store in a tightly covered jar.

**MAKES ABOUT 5 CUPS**

"Ritual, prayer, your innermost request—please find your own way to bring yourself to your meal, to sitting down at the table and taking the time to eat with gratitude, enjoyment, and gusto."

—EDWARD ESPE BROWN

# Composing Your Moveable Feast

"Take the time to give each task its due—it comes out in the food: a generosity of spirit. Call it rejoicing, tenderness, graciousness, or simple attention to detail, the quality of caring is an ingredient everyone can taste."

—TENZO KYOKUN (INSTRUCTIONS FOR THE TENZO)

*There are many ways to create a sandwich as there are sandwiches. Be adventurous and see for yourself.*

# Making a Sandwich

*"Spreads are used to make sandwiches more interesting." —Edward Brown*

One way to make a sandwich is to put any spread, pâté, or sandwich filling on a slice of bread, add some fresh-sliced or roasted vegetables, and spread mayonnaise, chutney, or aioli on the other slice of bread to finish things off.

Sonja, the Tenzo at Tassajara, says to start with a protein base (cheese or tofu), add some roasted or raw vegetables in the middle, and put a different spread on each slice of bread. She also recommends using rolled up lettuce instead of bread to hold the sandwich fillings. Edward Brown sometimes puts five spreads on both bread slices so that every bite has a different taste.

If you are trying to cut down on bread products or wheat, there are many alternatives to bread included in the following pages. Try using the various suggestions and more.

In terms of condiments, try Rosemary Aioli, Cashew Butter, or even chutneys to make your sandwiches more exciting. Chutneys add a special zest to sandwiches—whether heating them up or cooling them down.

Homemade pickled vegetables, marinated artichokes, green olives, and other tart, pickled things are good served alongside your sandwich.

Nuts accent meals with their rich flavor and texture. Nutritionally they are excellent sources of the "good fats," protein, vitamins and minerals, and a small amount goes a long way. At Tassajara, we offer granola as a sweet treat or as an alternative to cookies or trail mix. It offers the sweetness of cookies and trail mix, but is much lighter.

*Try a whole new taste with these combinations of spreads, pâtés, and chutneys:*
Honey Mustard Tofu with Pineapple Chutney

Roasted Vegetables with Marinated Tofu and Rosemary Aioli

Leek Cream Cheese with Sweet Vegetable Tapenade

Herb-Crusted Tofu with Basil "Cream" and Pickled Red Onions

# Accoutrements

*These are some of the offerings at the Tassajara Bag Lunch. Include as many as you like in your lunch or picnic.*

CONDIMENTS:

Stone-ground mustard
Yellow mustard
Mayonnaise
Nayonnaise
Herb-infused olives
Olive oil
Red wine vinegar
Peanut butter
Jelly

PICKLES/OLIVES:

Green olives
Kalamata olives
Nicoise olives
Pickled cucumbers
Mini pickles
Marinated mushrooms
Capers
Pepperocini
Marinated potatoes

CHEESES/BUTTERS/EGGS:

Swiss cheese
Gouda cheese
Monterey Jack cheese
Vermont cheddar cheese
Plain cream cheese
Feta cheese
Red pepper cream cheese
Chipotle cream cheese
Garlic butter
Chipotle butter
Deviled eggs

Hard-boiled eggs

VEGETABLES:

Lettuce
Sliced tomatoes
Cherry tomatoes
Heirloom tomatoes
Sliced cucumbers
Avocado halves
Carrot sticks
Celery sticks
Radishes
Jicama
Raw cauliflower
Raw broccoli
Raw red, green, and yellow bell peppers
Sliced onions
Alfalfa sprouts
Pea sprouts
Fresh herbs-parsley, tarragon, oregano, dill
Roasted shitake mushrooms
Roasted fennel
Roasted zucchini
Roasted garlic
Roasted mushrooms with fresh herbs
Roasted bell peppers
Roasted eggplant

OTHER:

Fresh fruit
Lemon wedges
Dried fruit
Granola

# Where Do I Put My Spreads?

*Use the items below instead of bread to serve alongside spreads, pâtés, and vegetables for a picnic, or as a base for appetizers.*

### INSTEAD OF BREAD
### (RECIPES BELOW)

Crostini
Crispy tortilla cups
Crunchy flour tortilla triangles
Bruschetta
Stuffed zucchini cups
Wonton wedges
Bagel chips
Croustades
Pita crisps
Filo cups

### OTHER IDEAS:

Crisp potato slices
Cucumber slices
Stuffed hard-boiled eggs
Hollowed-out/stuffed red/green peppers, tomatoes, and other vegetables

Hollowed-out fruits
Toasted party rye
Crispy breadsticks
"On leaves"-Romaine, endive, radicchio…
Lebanese pita bread (thicker pita bread with no pocket)
Lavosh (for pinwheels)
Puff pastry
Pumpernickel bread
Mini toasts
Melba toast
Spring roll wrappers
Rice paper wrappers
Wonton skins
Flour or corn tortillas or "wraps" (for pinwheels)
Crackers: Ak Mak, water, rye krisp, rice
Rice cakes

### CROSTINI

*These are crusty Italian toasts.*

Preheat the oven to 400 degrees F. Cut a baguette into ⅓-inch-thick slices. Lightly brush both sides with olive oil. Arrange the slices in a single layer on a baking sheet and bake for 2 minutes on each side, or until golden brown. They will harden as they cool. Serve at room temperature.

### TOAST POINTS

*Try, wheat, rye, or even pumpernickel bread.*

Trim crusts off sandwich bread, then cut each slice in half on the diagonal. Or use a cookie cutter to cut into other shapes such as hearts, stars, etc. Arrange the bread on a baking sheet in a single layer and bake at 350 degrees F for 5 minutes on each side, or until dry and lightly toasted. The toast points can also be grilled for 3 to 5 minutes.

### CRISPY TORTILLA CUPS

*Try flavored tortillas or wraps to add color and flavor.*

Preheat oven to 350 degrees F. Using a knife or biscuit cutter, cut flour or corn tortillas into 4-inch rounds. Make four equally placed ½-inch cuts around the edge of the tortilla. Wrap the tortillas in foil and heat in the oven for 5 minutes, or until soft. Cover to keep warm. Place the tortillas into lightly oiled muffin cups, overlapping where the cuts meet. Lightly brush with olive oil and bake for 10 to 12 minutes, or until crispy. They will firm up as they cool. Let cool on a wire rack.

### CRUNCHY FLOUR TORTILLA TRIANGLES

*An alternative to corn chips.*

Preheat the broiler. Cut 8-inch tortillas into fourths (or more, if you want smaller pieces); brush both sides lightly with olive oil. Place on a baking sheet and prick the surface in several places with a fork. Broil 4 to 5 inches from the heat for about 1 to 2 minutes on each side, or until lightly browned. Watch carefully as they toast quickly. Put on a plate to cool. They will get crunchier as they cool.

### BRUSCHETTA

*These are small, toasted bread slices.*

Slice fresh or day-old French or Italian bread into ½ to ¾-inch-thick slices. Preheat the broiler, a stovetop grill to 400 degrees F, or a toaster oven. Toast or grill the bread in one layer, until both sides are golden brown and crisp on the outside, yet still chewy on the inside. If using an oven, bake for about 3 minutes on each side. If using a broiler, the time will be less so watch to prevent the bread from burning.

### STUFFED ZUCCHINI CUPS

*These tiny cups are attractive and a nice way to add more vegetables to your diet.*

Using two 8-inch zucchini, trim and discard the ends of both. Cut the zucchini crosswise into ¾-inch-thick slices. Using a melon baller, scoop out the center of each slice, leaving a shell a little less than ¼ inch thick. Steam the cups in a covered steamer until just barely tender, about 4 minutes. Drain the cups upside down on a plate covered with a paper towel.

### WONTON WEDGES

*For added flavor, sprinkle lightly with Parmesan cheese or dried herbs such as oregano, basil, or thyme.*

Preheat oven to 375 degrees F. Lightly brush a baking sheet with butter. Cut a stack of wonton skins in half diagonally. Place the triangles in a single layer on the baking sheet and brush the tops lightly with butter. Bake for 4 to 5 minutes, or until golden brown. Remove from baking sheet and cool on a wire rack.

### BAGEL CHIPS

*Use a variety of bagels for added flavor and color. Day-old bagels work great!*

Preheat oven to 375 degrees F. Cut each bagel into six ¼-inch-thick rounds. Cut in half again for half moon shapes or break the toasted rounds into smaller chips after cooling. Place the slices in a single layer on a baking sheet. Toast the slices in the oven for 6 to 8 minutes, turning once, or until lightly browned on both sides and crisp.

### CROUSTADES

*Try these tasty and tiny toasted bread cups.*

Preheat the oven to 350 degrees F. Cut fresh wheat, white, or other type of bread, into 3-inch rounds. Gently press into mini-muffin cups and bake for about 10 minutes, or until the bread cups are lightly browned. Let cool in the pan on a wire rack.

### PITA CRISPS

*These crisps are best when prepared just before using. For added flavor, sprinkle with Parmesan cheese and dried oregano or basil.*

Split horizontally one 6- or 7-inch white or whole wheat pita round. Preheat the broiler. Arrange the pita halves, rough-side up, on a baking sheet. Lightly brush with olive oil. Using kitchen shears, cut each pita half into 8 triangles. Broil for about 2 minutes, or until the triangles are lightly browned and the cheese is melted, if using. Be careful to watch closely so they don't burn. Serve warm or at room temperature.

### FILO CUPS

*A light and delicate way to present rich fillings.*

Thaw 4 sheets frozen filo dough. Preheat oven to 350 degrees F. Place 1 filo sheet on a cutting board and lightly brush with melted butter. Top with the remaining sheets, stacking one at a time and lightly brushing each layer with butter. Cut the stacked sheets into 12 squares. Mold the squares into muffin cups, allowing the pointed ends to extend above the cups. Bake for 4 to 6 minutes, or until golden brown. Let cool in pans on a wire rack.

# Lunch Bag Ideas

*I've included this section to present environment-friendly ways to pack your lunch or picnic. No need to throw anything into the landfill with these wonderful storage containers. Food also stays fresh and either hot or cold eliminating the need to microwave or refrigerate!*

| LUNCH BAGS | STORE | PRICE $ |
|---|---|---|
| Super Lunch Bag | LL Bean | 15.00 |
| Nylon Lunch Totes and Sacks | The Container Store | 4.99–12.99 |
| Deluxe Lunch Bag with Cooler | PriceHot.com | 6.99 |
| Deluxe Insulated Picnic Cooler | PriceHot.com | 9.99 |

| PLASTIC STORAGE CONTAINERS | | |
|---|---|---|
| Lunch on the Go | Chef's Catalog | 14.99 |
| Lunch N 'Things Container | Tupperware | 11.00 |
| Insulated Containers, snack jars | Home Village Wholesale | 2.99–9.99 |
| Heavy Duty | | |
|    Thermal Lunch Box and Caddy | Home Village Wholesale | 9.99 |
| Laptop Lunch System | American Style Bento Boxes and Lunch Jars | 11.99–19.99 |
| The Lunch Date | Laptop Lunches | 33.99–124.99 |

| STAINLESS STEEL CONTAINERS | | |
|---|---|---|
| Stainless Thermos Lunch Jars | Tiger, Nissan | 11.99–45.99 |
| 3 Tier Chinese Lunch Box | The Wok Shop | 24.95 |
| "Ms. Bento" Stainless Lunch Jar | | |
|    comes with cloth bag | iKitchen.com | 39.99 |
| Nissan Wide Mouth Thermos | | |
|    Lunch Tote TLN 1400x | Zaccardi's | 36.95 |
| Bombay Express "Lunch Box" | Asiana West | 12.95 |
| 555 Stainless Lunch Box | Asiana West | 12.95–14.95 |
| Bento-Hakoya Collection | | |
|    Japanese Lunch Box | Asiana West | 24.95 |
| Executive Mini Vacuum Thermos | | |
|    with strainer and infuser | Asiana West | 29.95–30.95 |
| Japanese Lunch Jars | Zojirushi | 53.99 |
| Wide Stainless Thermos | The Gourmet Kitchen | 36.99 |

# Index

**Metric Conversion Chart**

Liquid and Dry Measures

| U.S. | Canadian | Australian |
| --- | --- | --- |
| 1/4 teaspoon | 1 mL | 1 ml |
| 1/2 teaspoon | 2 mL | 2 ml |
| 1 teaspoon | 5 mL | 5 ml |
| 1 Tablespoon | 15 mL | 20 ml |
| 1/4 cup | 50 mL | 60 ml |
| 1/3 cup | 75 mL | 80 ml |
| 1/2 cup | 125 mL | 125 ml |
| 2/3 cup | 150 mL | 170 ml |
| 3/4 cup | 175 mL | 190 ml |
| 1 cup | 250 mL | 250 ml |
| 1 quart | 1 liter | 1 litre |

**Temperature Conversion Chart**

| Fahrenheit | Celsius |
| --- | --- |
| 250 | 120 |
| 275 | 140 |
| 300 | 150 |
| 325 | 160 |
| 350 | 180 |
| 375 | 190 |
| 400 | 200 |
| 425 | 220 |
| 450 | 230 |
| 475 | 240 |
| 500 | 260 |